Researching World War I

Researching World War I

A Handbook

Edited by Robin Higham
with Dennis E. Showalter

GREENWOOD PRESS
Westport, Connecticut • London

Library of Congress Cataloging-in-Publication Data

Researching World War I : a handbook / edited by Robin Higham with Dennis E. Showalter.
   p. cm.
  Includes bibliographical references and index.
  ISBN 0–313–28850–X (alk. paper)
  1. World War, 1914–1918—Study and teaching—Handbooks, manuals, etc. I. Title:
Researching World War One. II. Higham, Robin D. S. III. Showalter, Dennis E.
D522.4.R47 2003
940.3—dc21   2003045532

British Library Cataloguing in Publication Data is available.

Library of Congress Catalog Card Number: 2003045532
ISBN: 0–313–28850–X

First published in 2003

Greenwood Press, 88 Post Road West, Westport, CT 06881
An imprint of Greenwood Publishing Group, Inc.
www.greenwood.com

Printed in the United States of America

The paper used in this book complies with the
Permanent Paper Standard issued by the National
Information Standards Organization (Z39.48–1984).

10 9 8 7 6 5 4 3 2 1

Contents

Preface

Researching World War I: A Handbook is designed to enable the neophyte, the graduate student, or the professional needing guidance in a tangential field to get his or her bearings in the literature of the 1914–1918 War, or the Great War, as it was called until 1939.

The book follows the pattern set in Loyd Lee's two-volume guide to the Second World War. Because the subject matter is geographically broad and technologically progressive, the *Handbook* deals first with the major European powers, then with the minor powers, the Middle East, the United States, Japan, Africa, and the British Empire. The final chapters cover the war at sea and in the air, and the industrial and technical infrastructure.

Readers and researchers need to be aware that they must peruse the chapters on the Allies and the Central Powers while at the same time bearing in mind that most countries fought on a number of fronts in a complex struggle. Thus, for instance, Austria-Hungary fought against Italy, Serbia, Romania, and Russia. References to Serbia and Romania will be found in the Balkan chapter. Italy had to be reinforced by France and Britain in 1917, and Russia fought Germany and Austria-Hungary, as well as Turkey. Britain and Germany battled not only on the Western Front in France, but also at sea and in the air. And all these opponents had their own industrial struggles in the mobilization for total war.

While the 1914–1918 War is thought of as a European conflict, the Middle East was a significant theater with action at Gallipoli (the Dardanelles) in Turkey in 1915, an Allied expedition to Salonika in 1916–1918, and campaigns from Egypt into the Ottoman Empire in Palestine and Arabia as well as from India up the Mesopotamian river valleys. In all these activities, British and

French Imperial forces were involved while the Imperial Japanese Navy assisted the Allies with Mediterranean convoys.

Readers and researchers will find each chapter laid out to lead from the general to the particular. At the end of each chapter is an alphabetical list by author of works cited or of importance for the topic. A detailed index will provide access to concepts, titles, and authors.

Two concluding features should also be noted. First, the suggestions for further research indicate weaknesses and voids in the field that should prompt additional studies in these areas. Second, the list of contributors identifies the experts in the field of World War I history who have made this book possible.

Robin Higham
Manhattan, Kansas
December 2002

Introduction

Robin Higham

The 1914–1918 War, the Great War, or the First World War as it was variously known, was in its day the greatest cataclysm Europe had known. Some 61 million troops of 16 nations were directly involved and suffered 7.8 million killed outright or died of wounds, 19.6 million wounded, treated and survived, and 7 million missing or prisoners of war. On any day in the war there were one million horses in service, whose feeding, care, and burial were a constant problem. Yet as the war expanded, so did the numbers of railway trains and motor vehicles.

Such was the slaughter that on the Western Front the total of battle casualties actually exceeded those from disease. In part this was due to the emergence of modern medicine from 1880, in part from the military's desperate need for men, and in part from the availability of vaccines to immunize soldiers, sailors, and airmen from tetanus, typhoid, and dysentery through the rigid use of sanitation. Yet typhus and cholera were rampant on the Eastern Front. Another major medical problem that also affected the availability of troops was the plethora of brothels, many especially run by the militaries themselves to control diseased prostitutes.

World War I was an all-out war that mobilized not only the manpower at home, but also that abroad. The French brought their colonial troops from North Africa to the Western Front, and the British tried an Indian Army Corps briefly in the first year of the war on the Western Front, but much more successfully in Mesopotamia and the Near East, as it was then commonly called. The Russians and Austro-Hungarians conscripted and deployed their minorities, and the British even imported Chinese labor on a contract basis. More than this, the struggle saw most countries mobilizing their women as well.

In fact, the management of what become known as the planned economy required that not all skilled men be enlisted, but that many of them be "badged" as being vital to the war economy and thus were not to be pressed to volunteer or to be drafted. But before most countries realized this, they had already lost many of these important workers to the services and a good many already to death before they could be recovered and others stopped from going. Labor had to be directed in the national interest. And women came quickly to be seen by the war managers as vital to the national effort. This posed three problems: women were different from men physically and emotionally and they had different responsibilities at home; for these new laborers to be employed effectively, complex jobs had to be broken down so that any unskilled worker could quickly learn how to do a simple part of them. And unionized workers had to be persuaded that the national interest or patriotism demanded that the workforce be diluted in this manner. The result was that by the end of the war in Britain, the aircraft industry—a new and unprecedented enterprise—was more than half female.

The very life-or-death nature of the 1914–1918 War was such that increasingly the government intervened in everyday life with everything from rationing of food, clothing, shoes, and the like both to conserve shipping space and foreign currency on the one hand and to compel people to eat and live more frugally on the other. Much of this apparatus, which had not generally been seen since medieval famine times, became the model for the Second World War, 1939–1945. Of especial concern was the physical state of the male side of the nation as revealed in military physical examinations. It was so poor in Britain that it led to the creation in 1918 of the Ministry of Health and in 1930 to that of the Royal Army Dental Corps, which also came to serve the Royal Air Force. On the other hand, the military did well in tropical campaigns for they had become from the 1880s one of the world's leaders in tropical medicine. Yet it must be remembered that there were many diseases and health and sanitation problems for which no one then had the solution.

The U.S. Civil War (1861–1865) had provided many examples of wound ballistics, and the medical reports of that war had been inspired by the failure of the medical and nursing services in the Crimean War (1854–1856). Modern high velocity weapons, when used in conjunction with the mud, earth, and dust of shell-torn battlefields, gave nasty wounds. Too often the filthy material with which the soldier's clothes were covered was punched into the wounds and caused them to fester within 24 hours. It was to deal with the imperatives of medical aid that everything from litters and stretcher bearers to field hospitals and surgery were radically reorganized, for the sooner men were got off the battlefield, into surgery, and on to convalescence, the sooner they would be available again to the army. To take care of those who would never again become fit, other forms of social aid were gradually established, but the numbers were overwhelming, especially for those nations that collapsed or disintegrated at the end of the war, such as Austria-Hungary and Russia.

The very evidence of casualties, the new conditions of trench warfare, forecast by the battles around Petersburg in 1865, Plevna in 1877–1878, in the

Russo-Japanese War (1904–1905) and at the Chatalja Lines (1912–1913), and the development of shrapnel, plunging fire, and gas all called for new battlefield protection for the soldier, his NCOs, and his officers.

Thus scientists and technologists were mobilized in most services. For head protection steel helmets appeared slowly in all armies, field dressings with morphine ampules were sewn into the front corners of uniform jackets, and gas masks were introduced. Officers had to be taught to inspect for trench foot. Better offensive and defense weapons had to be developed, from hand grenades and trench mortars to sound-ranging equipment for counter-battery work for the artillery, not to mention tanks. At sea the competition between armor and shells continued, but the war on, under, and above the seas intensified the need for all sorts of new scientific-technological material. There was much concern with the volatility of naval gunnery supplies and magazines, with getting the maximum power out of the engines and improving fuel consumption, with signaling, and with the interception and decoding of enemy messages and the location of his ships. The development of undersea boats, another continuation of nineteenth-century evolutions that was accelerated by the war, led to concern to protect capital ships from torpedoes and mines, to an understanding of the forces of underwater explosions, and to greater attempts to deal with their causes. Thus one line of development was the blister to replace nets hung overside to take the force of underwater explosions; another was the development of the paravane to sweep mines aside, cut their cables, and enable them to be destroyed by rifle fire.

A whole new field was the development of the submarine and the U-boat and counter-measures against them. The submarine especially involved the understanding and development of electrical propulsion and the means to recharge the batteries. This in its turn led to a search for the means of making faster submarines that could keep up with the surface fleet until contact with the enemy was made, at which point they would submerge in ambush hoping that the opponent could be lured back over their trap. On the one beam this led to the development of steam-powered submersibles and on the other to very big gun ones. Not untypically of many wartime developments, these new vessels combined past science and technology in new combinations to try to create a winning weapon.

And if that were true below the surface, so also it was above it, with the use of Zeppelins for long-range reconnaissance with their ability to hover for hours and of long-range flying boats both to provide intelligence and to counter Zeppelins. The recognition of the scouting potential of the air arm saw the development of both small airships for that purpose and for anti-submarine patrol, and also of fighting airplanes. By the end of the war, the British Grand Fleet did not sortie without an aircraft carrier or two and some 150 aircraft launchable from carriers, cruisers, and towed barges.

To make all weapons effective, scientists spent time and money on explosives, propellants, fuses, and sighting devices, and gases, which meant physics, chemistry, and metallurgy.

The war at sea and in the air was tied directly to the battlefield in that both were much involved with the acquisition and allocation of natural, transportation, and industrial resources. Welsh coal went to France, American steel to England, Indian jute and North American wheat to the Allies. The Central Powers were similarly engaged in various exchanges of vital materials. And the classic case of interdependence and grand strategy was, of course, the attempt to break through the Dardanelles and the Bosphorus to open a route to Russia so that her manpower could be armed and used effectively in the Allied cause and her timber in France and Britain.

The massive hunger of the fighting forces and of their supporters challenged nineteenth-century managers at every level. It was true that their customers still had seasonal appetites—shell consumption was computed as being very much less in the winter, for instance, than in the summer. Even so it was immense. Shortages developed for a number of reasons, not the least of which was that managers, the armed forces included, had trouble in forecasting their needs, especially when the imagined short war became ever less likely to come to a conclusion. Not only did the armies and navies expand, but also consumption went up dramatically—in the U.S. Army the consumption of artillery ammunition rose by 2000 percent over peacetime allowances. This meant the adjustment of a very long line from the raw materials source to the battlefield with the necessity of the coordination and synchronization of everything from buttons to bombs. No wonder that at the end of the war governments wanted official histories written so that they would not lose the lessons learned in four tough years.

Getting food and other materials from the ports to distribution points and shipping finished materials and food, clothing, and other supplies to the fronts demanded another nineteenth-century expertise, the ability to run railways. This included schedules, emergency transshipments of troops and weapons and supporting materiel, and coping with accidents, war damage, and wastage. To do this successfully countries had to co-opt railway management, engineers, and other personnel, including skilled tracklayers. Moreover, as wonderful as were all machines, they still had to have daily and routine maintenance and sometimes complete rebuilding, if they could be salvaged at all. Locomotives, rolling stock, and motor vehicles had constantly to be watched, even though they did not consume fuel 24 hours a day as did horses. Aircraft were an extreme case in point in terms of wastage and repair. Fighters on the Western Front were lost at the rate of 66 percent per month of new aircraft manufactured, though many of the machines in use were rebuilds. Bomber losses were less, and in less intensive theaters as low as 20 percent. Many of the losses occurred in training and ferrying. And training was certainly an immense and immensely important activity in all branches of each of the services.

Not only the newly inducted, but even veterans needed to be trained or retrained. The necessary organization had very largely not existed in peacetime owing to the very small size of most services, though the Continental conscript forces had been put through a system to make them mobilizeable for instant action before they went into the reserves. Most services took recruits straight into the regimental barracks and de-civilianized them there. Given the small wastage in peacetime, the regimental system worked. Officers might go to a cadet academy, but when they reported to the regiment or the ship, they were then given the real training they needed to do their job in wartime. But war overwhelmed this system. It took away the officers and NCOs as well as the trained cadre of men and the reserves. And the brutal battles of the 1914–1918 War saw a large percentage killed or wounded in short order. Moreover, the expansion was so rapid and so large that units could not fight and train new recruits at the same time. The stark realities of this were seen most sharply in the air services, where almost no one knew how to fly in 1914. So a training system had to be organized, staffed, and provided with a curriculum by people who had never fought in the air. The result was that combat training and flights on type were neglected. Pilots arrived in France with 15 hours, when they needed much more than that to be able to fly and survive, let alone shoot down an opponent. The result was 50 percent losses, more due to accidents than combat. As war in the air gradually meant formation flying and squadron combat, so training was increased to vitiate losses and to get a viable force in the air. Airmen were among the many who had to learn to manage their resources for combat efficiency.

Naval services, too, found that they had to undertake the training and disciplining of crews for them to be able to do their jobs.

Many accounts of the First World War are misleading in that they give the impression for one reason or another that the memoirist, the participants, the heroes, spent all their time in the front lines in dreadful conditions, a myth perpetuated by the illustrations chosen or mislabeled. In reality in the British Army at least, an infantry man who survived each tour might have spent 90 days in the frontline trench spread out over the 365 days in the year and depending upon the quietness of the line at the time. Another 90 days, or a fourth of the year, were spent in support trenches, and the other six months out of the trenches in logistics duties, rest, on leave, or training. The officers generally got more leave than did the men. The latter, under the care of their senior non-commissioned officers, nearly always drew some fatigue carrying parties to resupply the front lines during the dark of night or to unload trains and wagons, and the like. Early in the war their training while in rest generally consisted of the old routine of square-bashing (drilling on the parade ground), but as the war demanded more precise and complex military actions, including worming from shell-hole to shell-hole shelter and cutting barbed wire as well as night patrols, training had to be made more realistic. But just as in the air real squadron formation flying was not achieved until toward the end of 1917, so the same was true of infantry and all-arms education. The Germans took the lead because they were more acutely aware of the costs of the battlefields. They realized that not only did victory come from well-drilled and prepared troops, but that also defeat could be avoided by the same means as well as by a real understanding of the nature of war. Thus the Germans trained their troops to dig deep, reinforce dugouts, erect pillboxes with no backs (so that they were traps to attackers who occupied them facing to their rear), and hold their front lines lightly letting attackers who broke in struggle forward until they were exhausted. Then the Germans launched their often successful counter-attacks.

Successful education and training depended upon the lessons from combat getting back to training organizations and regimental bases, and being read, understood, and acted upon there and in the higher echelons. Victory depended upon realizing that it was not just frontline bravery that would win.

There has been much written and talked about the influence of the nineteenth-century theorists such as Clausewitz, Jomini, DuPicq, Mahan, Foch, von Moltke, and von Schlieffen upon the manner of fighting the First World War. And it is true that there were both theoretical and practical streams that had their impact. But what was equally important was how the higher echelons of the services and the higher direction of the nations conceived of the war at any time and place and how they projected that conception. This affected tactics, operational art, strategy, and grand strategy. In a twentieth-century war that meant being able to see a future two or three years down the road when the really big battalions, fleets, or wings would be fighting weapons. It meant having a conception of what a war would be like and what it would need if it were to be prosecuted successfully.

Because of the all-pervading nature of a modern industrialized war, it meant seeking and taking advice at all levels. Unfortunately, neither politicians, monarchs, nor the aristocratic officer corps had much grasp of the realities of economic, medical, scientific, technological, or even the social aspects of a worldwide war. And many of the military showed that they had prejudiced and flawed views of the way to conduct campaigns. And many senior officers retained these ideas throughout the conflict the further they were forced away from the battlefields by the lethality of the new long-range weapons. When war deteriorated to trench warfare, few of them had paid attention to the lessons of the U.S. Civil War or of the Russo-Japanese War, in which massed frontal attacks conducted with all the élan in the world had been shown to be so costly as to be, perhaps, beyond Pyrrhic in their successes.

Unlike in earlier wars when a small professional army fought a campaign largely detached from the home front as in the eighteenth century, but more like the Napoleonic Wars, the Great War demanded that the state control news. Ever since the advent in the Crimean War of correspondents, the telegraph, photography, and the illustrated weekly, it had become essential for the government at home to be concerned with morale both on the fighting front and at home. This meant not only censorship and the relation of news and rations, but posters and other means of keeping up morale. On the fighting front this was equally important, as the mutinies in the French army, the Russian Navy, and the Italian forces all made plain in 1917.

Nor was it just a matter of morale at home and at the front; many troops ended up fighting and being granted leave in countries that were neither their own nor the enemy's. Officers and men, nurses, and others found themselves in a foreign country—allied, protected, or occupied. And often they were there with allies, colonials, and even, in Greece, with neutrals. Yet, any way it was seen, the war was dynamic, diverse, deadly, dug in, enduring, diseased, and affected by donkeys and "dames."

The war started in the Balkans with an Austrian attack on Serbia in very mountainous country through which the Serbs were eventually driven to Gorfu and then transferred to Salonika, where they joined the Allied expeditionary force that had been evacuated from the ill-managed attempt to force the Dardanelles and seize the Turkish capital of Constantinople (later Istanbul). That Levantine campaign started as an ambitious amphibious operation for which the commanders had no real plans and the troops little training. At Salonika from 1916 on they gardened or perished from diseases of the Third World. Two other attempts to deal with the eastern end of the Central Powers saw British and colonial troops, including Indians, fighting the Ottoman Turks in the desert reaches of their empire. The confusion in the High Command was seen in the ill-fated attempt to advance on Baghdad. That advance ended at Kut, but it was followed up by a better force, still under the command of the India Office in London, that took Baghdad in 1917.

In the meantime the Turks had made an attempt to sever the lifeline of the British Empire by seizing the Suez Canal. They were held through 1916 and then pushed back through Gaza. Finally, they were thrust right out of Palestine and Syria by a combination of regular forces advancing up the coast after the devastating battle of Megiddo and irregular Arab forces operating up the railway north from Medina also to Syria, the last push being nearly 300 miles.

Much farther south, in Africa, a small German colonial force mostly composed of askaris and bearers gave British and South African forces a merry chase for three years. In both the Dardanelles (Gallipoli) miscarriage and the Palestine campaign, Australian and New Zealand forces, known together as Anzacs, played a major role.

Far to the north of the Middle East, but the original objective of the Dardanelles campaign, lay Russia. This great monarchy had only begun to modernize in 1895, but it had then been hit by the Japanese in 1904–1905 and had been set back. The tsarist government was struggling to adjust to a nascent democracy and to the middle-class industrialist and entrepreneur supported by French capital, the basis of the Dual Alliance, to which Britain had adhered through the *Entente cordiale* with France of 1904 and the rapprochement with Russia in 1908. Unfortunately the Tsar and the aristocrats who ran the government and the army had trouble realizing that the small industrial middle class had some idea of what it would take to train, arm, and supply the massive Russian field armies in their battles with both the German and the Austro-Hungarian Empires, handicapped as they were by distances, lack of railroads, factory capacity, and an efficient general staff. Moreover, because of the space involved, the Eastern Front remained one of maneuver until the collapse of Russia in 1917–1918. But while the Russians and the Germans both had to fight two-front wars, with the Russian being contiguous, the Austro-Hungarians started with a two-front war, expanded it when Italy entered the war in 1915 to three fronts, and ended with a fourth front against the Anglo-French expeditionary force threatening from Salonika, not to mention having to put down Romania in 1916. And while war on the Polish-Russian plain had mobility, much of Austrian fighting was in the

Carpathians, the Alps, or the Balkan mountains. This dispersion caused the old Viennese machinery to creak, as the Austro-Hungarians had never spent more than three days on maneuvers before the war began. The Turks, under German tutelage, were much better prepared for war in 1914.

The Germans had relied on their Schlieffen Plan to give them a quick victory in the west against the French and then to switch from the defensive in the east to the offensive. Their thorough preparation for a short war enabled them to use their railways to defeat the Russians at Tannenberg in 1914. But it did not mean the end of their troubles, for the war bogged down in the west and they found themselves engaged in exactly that long two-front war they had since 1870 aimed to avoid by diplomatic or military means. Nevertheless, thanks in part to the Russian revolutions of 1917, they were able to sift forces from the Eastern to the Western Front, and eventually also to Italy to help the Austrians. But after the disaster of Caporetto on the Izonso, that victory of the Central Powers was countered by Anglo-French forces sent by train from France to northern Italy.

In spite of appearances, the Eastern was probably the more dangerous front for the Germans and Austro-Hungarians just because it was so fluid. It is, moreover, interesting to speculate what might have happened if the Russians had been able to let the middle class manage the war economy successfully and if Turkey had been knocked out of the war so that western rifles and other supplies could have reached the manpower on the steppes.

For western supplies to reach the Russians or any other fighting front, the Entente allies had to win the battle of the Atlantic and of the narrow seas, for the war was not only about confused national ambitions and perceptions, but also about managing resources, especially since strategic and tactical considerations were vitiated by prolonged trench warfare. On the other hand, the very reasons that tactics, strategy, and grand strategy as well as operational art stultified was that the higher direction of the Great War was in the hands of people who had trouble envisaging it.

The world stumbled into the First World War because the political and military leaders did not understand the economic, social, and ideological dynamics of the movements they thought they were directing. And after the war started, they still had confused concepts of what they were fighting for and what the end result was to be. In other words, neither before the war nor during it did the leaders have a sensible idea of what it would take to accomplish their ill-defined goals. The secondary literature and the primary records now available make this clear.

One of the major historiographical debates for decades was over who started the 1914–1918 War. It stemmed from the fact that since Russia and Austria-Hungary disintegrated in the course of the war, by the time the peace came to be signed only Germany remained to be blamed in the infamous Clause 232 of the Treaty of Versailles, the Germans having no one of the cleverness of a Talleyrand to use *legitimacy* as a means of essentially restoring the *status quo ante bellum*. As we now recognize, not only were many people and countries, in a sense, to blame for the outbreak of hostilities and the failure to contain them after Vienna moved to carry out a long-sought "punishment" of Serbia for the death of the Archduke at Sarajevo, but also that history itself is far more complex than the dictators of the Versailles peace wished to heed.

The reasons why the war did break out and spread so rapidly to so many powers was that politicians in general, including certain influential monarchs, did not know the process of mobilization, the signals that it sent to others, nor the immense consequences of engaging in a modern war. Such an act included political, military, diplomatic, economic, scientific and technological, medical, social, and ideological factors.

Nor had the military thought through the ramifications of mobilization and of going to war. The Austrian staff had never carried out maneuvers that lasted more than three days. Moreover, in maneuvers the *enemy* in general did what he was supposed to do. The Germans with their Great General Staff had worked out war to a timetable. So when it did not repeat 1870, they faced far greater tasks than they had envisaged. In fact one of the truisms of military history seems to be that the worst possible case turns out to be one that had never been foreseen by all but ignored visionaries.

The coming of the war was complicated, moreover, by the two alliance systems that were meant to deter war, but that, unlike the NATO–Warsaw Pact systems of the 1947–1990 period, talked too much in terms of Darwinian survival of the fittest and of "Der Tag" (the day) when the opposing forces would meet on the field of battle. And because of the confrontational nature of the Entente and the Central Powers, it can be said that World War I started because of too many armaments, while World War II came about because of too few. And as an *obiter dicta* it may be added that the Cold War did not grow hot because so many people were aware of the lessons of 1914, 1939, and 1941 (the latter in both the USSR and at Pearl Harbor).

Just as the armies took three years to build up to the climax of 1918 because it had taken them that long to mobilize, equip, train and move forward a nation in arms, so it also took both the grand-strategic commanders and the commanders in the fields and fleets that long to realize how the war might and should be won.

Study of the patterns of the war shows that after the first moving confrontations and the exhaustion of supplies, each national force had to regroup, rethink, and make another try in 1915, which also was not decisive. Shortages, casualties, and industrial necessities had then to be considered. But military leaders, brought up in peacetime or colonial wars, kept imagining that they could either make a dramatic breakthrough or that they could wear the opponent down by attrition. It was this that caused the French premier Clemenceau to say "War was too serious to be left to the generals," to which the British army countered that it was something that the frocks (politicians in their frock coats), the civilians, in their ignorance should not be allowed to control. Neither group recognized that a defensive that would force their opponent to agree to a clearly defined return to prewar boundaries, if necessary in the classic manner of compensation extorted from the minor players, was a sound and sensible policy. Instead battles such as the Somme, Passchendaele, Verdun, and the 17 on the Izonso were allowed to inflict endless slaughter; only at Gallipoli in 1915 was a force withdrawn when its cause was seen to be hopeless, and only then, perhaps, because the colonials indicated they were fed up.

The battles of 1864–1865, of 1870–1871, and of 1904–1905 had shown that for safety the commanders had to move farther and farther to the rear. The result was that they not only lost touch, but also increasingly failed to realize the time taken for movements, whether of orders from Headquarters to regimental and other forward commanders or of the speed of advance of infantry in the face of barbed wire, machine guns, shell holes, dust, mud, noise, and the confusion of a modern battlefield. And the same applied to the clashes of major fleets at sea. At the one great confrontation in the North Sea, neither commander-in-chief nor even subordinates could see either end of his line, let alone the enemy in the sea-fog of war. Additionally, no one liked night fighting because of its uncertainties. And the whole affair was complicated by a poor understanding of the necessity on the one hand for wireless (W/T) silence until the obvious moments when both sides were clearly in touch and the C-in-C's needed to know this. Back on land, it was also essential that those who decrypted signals and were familiar with the enemy's *modus vivendi* and *modus operandi* should tell their superiors what raw signals intercepts meant.

In large part the failures in command can be traced back to the rigidity of the Victorian command structures and to the inability to appreciate the necessity for listening to both "hostilities only" civilians with a wider view of the world and to technical experts in armed forces and industrialized societies who had some grasp of the realities of war.

The application of innovation devolved in technical services such as submarines, tanks, and aviation upon the most junior officers. They quickly learned what worked and what did not and how to overcome such difficulties because their lives were in danger. But higher authorities imbued with military protocol and hierarchical social attitudes were unwilling to hear or read their reports.

Unfortunately the unwillingness to listen and learn plagued the victors after 1918, while the vanquished were much more determined to draw lessons and set about ways to avoid ever fighting such a pointless war again. Nearly all parties wrote either staff studies or started official historical accounts of those aspects of the recent war that they considered important. Unfortunately it takes about 25 years to write the story of a major war, and, well before that time was up, more pressing events either diverted the official historians or bent their narratives out of shape. In some cases controversies arose, such as over the Battle of Jutland, so that it was many years after the Second World War before these matters were resolved, at least until the next generation of historians appeared.

What also made history difficult was the destruction of documents at various times and from various causes, as well as the perspective of the archivists charged with preserving these materials, not to mention the money available.

The participants themselves provided memoirs in waves in which the last to write might often win the battle, at least of words. Naturally the higher commanders wrote to state their cases not only in official reports, but also in memoirs. Officers who had had extraordinary careers, been much decorated, or who had a tale publishers considered interesting wrote in the first decade after the war. There then followed a slump until the veterans reached the age of reminiscences and grandchildren as they themselves passed the age of 45 and began in earnest to join veterans' organizations. The 1939–1945 War coincided with many of these writings while then more junior officers found themselves with fresh experience of high command, enabling them to combine their tales in a saleable work. A new wave of autobiographies of the Great War began to appear in the 1960s and have dribbled on ever since, ending probably in the year 2000 when the 18-year-olds of 1918 were centenarians.

In the meantime waves of secondary works and even the publication of documents have followed somewhat similar patterns.

Today the First World War remains in modern memory as an incredible experience of our parents and grandparents. Its battlefields are partially preserved, its equipment and accoutrements exhibited in museums, and its dead commemorated in monuments both at home and in foreign lands, always to be visited with curiosity and amazement, as well as a growing understanding.

The chapters that follow are intended to provide guidance to the immense literature of a global war. They are in no sense a complete guide nor do they list all the works, documentation, and archives available. They do suggest access to the works that will corroborate or challenge the picture of the war presented above.

SUGGESTIONS FOR FURTHER RESEARCH

While the individual authors make suggestions specific to their topics, some more general questions may be posed. Looking at the structure of the management of war, questions remain as to how different countries handled this, whom did they co-opt, and what tools did they have on hand or develop to enable them to do the job. The United States produced studies or reports early on the various aspects of war production and logistics, the British published the 12-volume history of the Ministry of Munitions that is most suggestive—but what happened in other countries? The Russian story is badly in need of revision, the German is obscure, and the French is poorly known in English. Topics connected with factory financing, erection and production, shipping and railway management, and administrative processes and their legacies. Did nationalized administration of railways work better than private? How was manpower controlled and its needs commissioned, how were women and youths poured in to "dilute" the working structure and to weaken unions, if that was part of the grand strategy of cabinets? How was the social fabric affected by the demands for food, shelter, labor and the like? How did medicine, writ large, benefit from the war? How much were all these subjects an acceleration of nineteenth-century legacies and in themselves a boon to the new century after 1918?

BIBLIOGRAPHY

Gleichen, Lord Edward, ed. *Chronology of the Great War, 1914–1918.* London, 1918–1920 (3 vols.); reprinted London: Greenhill Books, 1988 in hardback and 2000 in paperback.

1

Origins

Dennis Showalter

For the sake of brevity and to limit repetitive citations this chapter presents no more than an outline of the major lines of interpretation on the Great War's origins. It pays special attention to diplomatic references—not least because even good monographs on diplomatic subjects are increasingly difficult to publish. The chapter also concentrates on the armed forces of the belligerents, with the intention of providing guidance to a complex military dynamic that ultimately played the decisive role in the war's outbreak.

GENERAL WORKS

Samuel Williamson's essay in the *Oxford Illustrated History of the First World War* [252] offers an excellent article-length overview of the conflict's origins. James Joll, *The Origins of the First World War* [103] remains the best brief monograph, and the analytical contributions by Joachim Remak [185] and Paul Schroeder [200] remain seminal. The first asserts the war's essentially Balkan origins; the second emphasizes the overstressing of Europe's diplomatic system. Two works by British authors, published at the end of the century, offered diametrically opposite interpretations of the war's genesis. John Keegan [106] emphasized German ambitions and aggressiveness; Niall Ferguson [54] argued that Britain overrated the German threat and unnecessarily escalated a continental conflict into a world war. The latter line of argument was further developed by John Charmley [25].

Of the numerous short readers dealing with the war's origins, David Stevenson's contribution [215] is most up to date in its text and bibliography. The second edition of Gordon Martel's volume in Longman's *Seminar Studies in History* [143] is the most comprehensive. Joachim Remak's volume [186] in the earlier Berkshire series remains a useful combination of narrative and references. Holger Herwig's contribution to the Heath Problems series [169] is German-focused but no less useful for that—and for the bibliography, which reflects Herwig's mastery of the published sources.

Four anthologies on the war's origins stand out. The 1966 volume edited by Walter Laqueur and George Mosse [128] was state of the craft when published, and it remains a useful introduction to many of the themes that dominated the rest of the century. The revised edition of Hans Koch's often-overlooked *The Origins of the First World War,* published in 1984 [117], features a first-rate analysis of Gerhard Ritter's strengths and weaknesses by Karl-Heinz Janssen. (Cf. Norman Stone's more critical treatment of Ritter [217] in the 1980 *Historical Journal.*) *The Coming of the First World War,* edited in 1988 by Richard Evans and Hartmut Pogge von Strandmann, took a country-by-country approach and incorporates state-of-the-craft scholarship and first-rate analysis [51]. Keith Wilson's collection [40] was up to date when published and remains solid.

John Langdon [127] briefly and competently surveys the historiography of the war's origins. His work may be complemented by Schlarp's now dated analysis [197] of the Great War in Soviet historiography. And while most of the major primary source collections were published between the world wars, the two-volume *Dokumentation* by Immanual Geiss [67] and its English abridgment certify their editor's scholarly industry and intellectual honesty. Undergraduates and graduate students alike may use these volumes with a confidence usually inapplicable to similar works.

The late 1970s witnessed a spate of comparisons between the then-existing international situation and that of 1914. Much of this literature was done from a political-science perspective; much of it proved ephemeral. Christopher Layne offered the most perceptive criticism of the analogy [130]. Among the best of the specific works incorporating it, Stephen van Evera discussed the failure of the great powers to cooperate in 1914 [239]. Jack Levy focused on the increasingly limited choices perceived by all the powers in the period immediately preceding the conflict [132].

MATRICES

Among works emphasizing particular issues, Arno Mayer's *The Persistence of the Old Regime* [146] focuses on the consequences of an increasingly anachronistic aristocratic ruling class. Immanuel Geiss [68] concentrates on industrial capitalism. Still useful among older works are Dwight Lee's survey [131] of European diplomacy between 1902 and 1914; L. C. F Turner's summary [235] of diplomatic and military interactions during the July Crisis; and Geoffrey Barraclough's analysis of the international breakdown that began at Agadir in 1911 [7]. Klaus Hildebrand [89] and Egmont Zechlin [261] interpret the July Crisis in European contexts, with plenty of blame to go around.

Avner Offer's analysis [165] of the role of global agricultural issues in the war's origins is idiosyncratic but provocative. From an opposite perspective Michael Adams, *The Great Adventure: Male Desire and the Coming of World War I,* interprets the conflict in a context of male sexuality [1]. Daniel Pick's *War Machine* [177] includes an outstanding analytical survey of the late nineteenth century's rationalization of mass killing in the name of a toxic blend of idealism and anxiety. If Paul Crook challenges the familiar notion of Darwinism as essentially warlike [38], Sandi Cooper [35] emphasizes the evolution since Waterloo of public patriotism throughout Europe. The contributions to Kennedy and Nicholls support Cooper by their discussions of the relationships of nationalism and racism in Germany and Britain [111]. Roland Stromberg [221] and Robert Wohl [257] present the contributions of Europe's intellectuals to the coming catastrophe. A. J. Morris shifts from positive to negative in arguing for the self-reinforcing fear of war in *fin de siecle* Britain [160]—a mindset reinforced by the growing number of pulp works on imaginary wars anthologized by I. F. Clarke [29, 30].

ANTI-MILITARISM

The distinguishing characteristics of anti-war movements in pre–Great War Europe were small size and high ambivalence. Sandi Cooper stresses the institutional weakness of French pacifism [34]; Chickering, *Imperial Germany and a World Without War* [27], makes much the same points for Germany. E. N.–R Stargardt [210] shows the anti-militarism of German Social Democrats was as much an instrument to challenge the Empire as a moral principle. Middle-class peace groups emphasizing international cooperation along parliamentary lines achieved nothing outside their own meeting rooms, as demonstrated by Uhlig [236] and Schumann [204]; while the weakness of proletarian international solidarity is the theme of Howorth's well done essay [93]. More successful in limiting the conduct of war were the Hague peace conferences of 1899 and 1907. As Jost Duelffer demonstrates [44], the agreements proceeding from these meetings at least provided some frameworks of accepted conduct once the shooting started.

ARMED FORCES AND SOCIETIES

Geoffrey Best's article on Europe's militarization [15] and V. G. Kiernan's analysis of the impact of universal conscription [114] combine for an excellent introduction to the subject. Paul Kennedy's anthology, *The War Plans of the Great Powers* [113], remains standard. Arguably the best overview, however, is another classic anthology, *Military Strategy and the Origins of the First World War.* This work [153] is based on an issue of *International Security* published in 1984 and has a political-science focus. Among its useful contributions are Scott Sagan's case for offensive doctrine as manifesting perceived weakness rather than perceived strength, and Marc Trachtenberg's demonstration that statesmen willingly abandoned political military solutions during the July Crisis.

Herrmann [84] and Stevenson [214] emphasize the increasing significance of the arms race in the years prior to 1914. Marc Trachtenberg's essay on the meaning of mobilization in 1914 [229] and Avner Offer's critique of the role of honor [196] combine to demonstrate the unlikelihood of withdrawal from the brink in 1914. The relevant contributions in *Knowing One's Enemies,* Ernest May's anthology on intelligence assessments in the era of the world wars [145] establish the fact that the more Europe's armed forces knew about one another, the more conscious they became of their own shortcomings. Their response was an emphasis on offensive operations seeking battles of annihilation [Wallach, 241] even when, as Stig Foerster mordantly argues, the generals knew there was virtually no chance of achieving such victories [153].

BALKANS

The Great War did begin over "some damn fool thing in the Balkans." For the Serbian perspective, see David Mackenzie on that state's self-image as the Balkan Piedmont [149]; Lampl [126] on economic development; Lubibratic on the terrorist Mlada Bosna [139]; and Mackenzie again on "Colonel Apis" [148]. Gale Stokes surveys the still-largely incomplete documentary material [216]. The essays in the Kiraly and Ddjordevic anthology on the Balkan Wars are uneven, but provide local perspectives [116]. Barbara Jelavich [101], Andrew Rossos [195], and E. C. Thaden [228] cover Russia's growing involvement. Gregor Schoellgen [199] surveys Anglo-German relations in the New East; Crampton's *Hollow Detente* [37] focuses on the immediate prewar period. Doerte Loeding [137] stresses growing Austro-German rivalry in the region—a point developed by Simmons in his description of what he calls a German war-risk policy [206]. Sullivan's analysis of German-Turkish diplomacy [222] is more moderate. Wallach [241] stresses the general lack of harmony between the two powers on military questions—poor preparation for aggressive cooperation.

The general changes in Mediterranean naval policies and balances between 1908 and 1914 are admirably presented by Paul Halpern [80]. From the diplomatic perspective, Childs [28] focuses on the Italo-Turkish War; Miller presents the breakdown of the "Concert of Europe" during the First Balkan War [154]; and Batowski [10] continues the tale of entropy with his essay on the failure of the Balkan alliance of 1912.

COUNTRIES

France

Conner's unpublished dissertation [33] is a good overview of the French parliament's role in making foreign policy. Hayne [82] addresses the Foreign Office. Ralston [180] discusses the army as an instrument of policy. Douglas Porch covers its institutional aspects in *The March* to *the Marne* [178]. Jauffret [100] considers the issue of reserves; Gerd Krumeich [119] analyzes the origins of the Three Years' Law. Walser [243] discusses the ups and downs of the Third Republic's naval policy; Theodore Ropp's finally published dissertation on the same subject, though researched and completed in the 1930s [192], has held up very well. Peter Jakobs is a good introduction, in terms of both publication date and content, for the Franco-Russian Alliance [97]. George Kennan's magisterial overview of *The Fateful Alliance* [110] correctly emphasizes that relationship's centrality to the war's outbreak. Perti Luntinnen [140] discusses French knowledge of Russian war plans from 1880 to 1914; James Long's dissertation on the economic aspects of the relationship [138] is broader in scope than its title suggests.

Turning westward, P. J. V. Rolo [191] introduces the Anglo-French Entente; Christopher Andrew [5] presents Delcasse's role in its making; and Samuel Williamson [253] analyzes its military aspects. Horst Lademacher's discussion of the issue of Belgian neutrality acts as a counterpoint—Germany was not the only state finding that circumstance awkward [121]. John Keiger's essay on efforts to improve relations with Germany [109], torpedoed by the Agadir incident of 1911–1912, as described by Oncken [167] and Allain [4], is complemented by his survey of French policy and diplomacy in the immediate prewar years [108].

Russia

William Fuller's overview in *Strategy and Power in Russia, 1600–1914* [64] is an excellent introduction to this subject. It is best complemented by Geyer [69] and by Wilfong's excellent essay on Russia's place in the great powers' pecking order prior to 1914 [248]. For the internal details of prewar policy making, McDonald's survey [147] is balanced by Perrin's essay on the Council for State Defence [173] and Allshouse's still-solid dissertation [3] on Aleksander Isvolskii.

Public opinion played a surprisingly central role in Russian policy. Ferenczi [53] and Judith Head [83] survey critical aspects. Oppel's article [168] shows the increasing discord between Russia and Germany after 1905; Spring evaluates the balance of power in Russia's French connection [209]. In the latter context, Girault's monograph on France's Russian loans and investments remains definitive [71]. It connects to a degree with Goldstein's fine dissertation [72] on the development of Russian defense industries.

For more specific military information, Menning, *Bayonets before Bullets* [151], is the best overview in any language of the development of the Russian army prior to World War I. Ropponen [194] offers a still solid survey of European evaluations of Russia's military power. Steinberg [212] and van Dyke [238] cover the General Staff. Wilfong [248] evaluates the army's reconstruction after 1905; Neilson gives the British perspective on the results [164]. J. J. Williams [249] analyzes the strategic aspects of the Anglo-Russian Entente of 1907.

The best general surveys of Russia before the war are Lincoln, *In War's Dark Shadow* [134], and Lieven, *Russia and the Origins of the First World War* [133]. Linke's monograph [135], though focusing on the war itself, is good for its discussion of the absence of coherent foreign policy goals in 1914.

Britain

Aaron Friedberg's model of *The Weary Titan* [62] tends to shape current discussion of Britain's policies despite Keith Nielson's [163] spirited corrective. Zara Steiner is excellent for the role of the Foreign Office, appropriately stressing the extent to which British diplomacy at this period was independent of public and parliamentary influence [213]—a point overlooked by M. R. Gordon's article [76]. Hinsley's anthology on prewar foreign policy [90] has excellent contributions by R. T. B. Langhorne on Anglo-German relations and by Michael Ekstein on the Triple Entente, as well as Ekstein's piece on Grey and imperial Germany in 1914: while F. R. Bridge establishes the declining importance of Austria in British calculations [20]. Among other institutions of government, d'Ombrian, *War Machinery and High Policy* [43], is a fine survey of the defense administration in the decade prior to the war. Rhodri Williams [250] covers the Conservative Party.

The decisive role of imperial security in determining British policy continues to be stressed by Keith Wilson [254, 255]. Horst Jaeckel. by contrast, establishes the declining status of India as a strategic factor [96]; while Fröhlich [63] and Hatton [81] trace the path "from confrontation to coalition" in Africa. As for Anglo-German relations in general, Robert Massie's popular narrative *Dreadnought* [144] misleads as much as it informs; Paul Kennedy's more perceptive analysis of the Anglo-German relationship is virtually inaccessible to general readers [112]. Sean Lynn-Jones [141] discusses the balance of détente and deterrence in the relationship between 1911 and 1914.

Among material on the war's immediate outbreak, Manfred Rauh [182] stresses the importance to Germany of the British naval agreements with Russia in early 1914. D. C. Watt covers British reactions to Sarajevo [245]. Harry Young [259] highlights the German misunderstanding of British intentions in the July Crisis, nevertheless arguing neutrality was not a practical option.

Prewar militarism in Britain is discussed—and exaggerated—in the general essay by Ann Summers [226]. Getting to the real thing, Lawler's dissertation [129] links Britain's decline to its defense budget. David French, *British Economic and Strategic Planning,* is a far more sophisticated analysis of the relationship of economics to diplomacy and politics [61]. Bastable for Armstrong [9] and Trebilcock for Vickers [232] modify conventional views on these "merchants of death." In the field of war planning, Moon [158] and Summerton [227], both dissertations often cited and never published, combine for an overview of the shift from defense to power projection at the end of the nineteenth century. Chris Bassford presents the growing influence of Clausewitz [8], while John Ferris highlights the increasing role of signals intelligence [55]. Gooch, *The Plans of War* [75], remains solid on the role of Britain's new general staff. Travers's seminal articles focus on institutional change—or its absence—in the army [230, 231]. Philpott's essay [176] has a broader perspective than its title suggests—a fortunate thing in view of French's limited capacities.

Turning to naval matters Padfield, *The Great Naval Race* [170], is the best of the numerous general-reader accounts of the prewar competition. Fairbanks is a perceptive overview of the literature [52], stopping just before Jon Sumida [223, 224, 225] and Nicholas Lambert [122, 123, 124] turned scholarship on the subject inside out with their research on warship design and naval strategy. Gollin [73] and Keaney [106] admirably cover the rise of British air power.

Italy

The least of the great powers and the last of the Central Powers has two general analyses of its politics and diplomacy by Richard Bosworth [18, 19]. Gabriele and Guiliano [65] offer the best overview of the state's naval policies. John Gooch, *Army, State and Society in Italy, 1870–1915* [74], is excellent at policy and planning levels. Of the general works, vol. 2 of Virgili Ilari, *Storia del servizio militaire in Italia, La "nazione armata," (1871–1918)* [95], stands out. Di Ionic's dissertation [42] covers Italy's Balkan policies in the decade before the war. A German translation makes available Finnish scholar Risto Ropponen's solid work on German and Austrian perceptions of Italy's value as an ally [193]; while Michael Palumbo [171] analyzes the German army's disappointment at Italy's behavior in 1914.

Austria

Was it a doomed empire? Joachim Remak's "The Healthy Invalid" [184] challenges the cliché in general terms; Samuel Williamson presents Austria-Hungary as an autonomous actor in 1914 [251]; and F. C. Bridge [21] has the best overview of Habsburg foreign policy. Among specific studies, Peterson's treatment of Austria's turn to Germany for support in early July [174] is well reasoned, well documented, and unfamiliar. William Jannen's survey [98] of the Monarchy's final decision for war demonstrates that it was an independent decision—whose shock effect on Germany is documented by the military attaché's reports [118].

The Austro-German military alliance is best surveyed in Lothar Höbelt's excellent article [91]. Hobelt also describes the initial breakdown of common planning for the Eastern theater [92]. Norman Stone remains standard on the Moltke-Conrad relationship [219]; Herwig [85] gives details of Allied cooperation—or rather its absence—in 1914. The Habsburg army is surveyed in Gunther Rothenberg's general history, *The Army of Francis Joseph* [196]; Istvan Déak [39] covers the officer corps. Scott Lackey does a solid job [120] discussing the army of the Beck years, while Josef Mann's dissertation [142] picks up Blasius Schemua's brief term as Chief of Staff. H. J. Pantenius [172] discusses the plans for war with Italy; Tunstall's dissertation [234] is unsurpassed (and far superior to the publisher-truncated monograph) on Austrian plans for the Eastern Front, and it can be used with Stone [218] to enhance analysis of the mobilization itself. All of the above works may be supplemented by the encyclopedic Volume 5 of *Die Habsburger Monarchie, Die bewaffnete Macht* [244].

Germany

The disproportionate length of this section reflects the dominant influence of the Fischer Thesis on the historiography of World War I during the past four decades [58]. Fritz Fischer produced literally dozens of essays and pamphlets developing aspects of his argument or denouncing his critics [56]. Perhaps the ultimate distillation of his position is *1914: Wir sind nicht hineingeschlittert* [57], published in 1983. John Moses is a solid analysis of the first stage of the historiography of the controversy [162]; Kaiser extends the spectrum of approaches to the war's origins [105]. Pregaglia [179] is up to date on the relevant Italian scholarship. Holger Herwig's *The First World War: Germany and Austria* [86] is, however, the best recent restatement of the Central Powers' systemic contributions to the war's outbreak. It may be supplemented by the essays in Wolfgang Mommsen's *Imperial Germany, 1867–1918* [156].

The Fischer Thesis was consistently reinforced from a German Democratic Republic that interpreted the war as a specific consequence of Germany's particular forms of capitalism and militarism. Gutschke's monograph and the related bibliographic essay [78, 79] are typical of the official East German position—which was of course the only position.

Almost as significant as the Fischer Thesis itself was the controversy that developed around the diaries of Kurt Riezler [187], Chancellor Theobald von Bethmann-Hollweg's confidential secretary during the 1914 crisis. If the published version was genuine, it offered the possibility of modifying Fischer's position that the war was a consequence of planned German aggression. If the diaries could be proved to have been subsequently altered, the Fischer thesis was correspondingly confirmed. In a German academic culture that makes controversy an art form, the sides chosen reflected political as well as intellectual positions [50, 202]. The result was inconclusive in that the diaries changed few minds.

Of the specialized works, Konrad Jarausch's biography of Bethmann [99] admirably integrates issues of foreign and domestic policy. It can be supplemented by Jost Duelffer's edition of Bethmann's own memoirs [16] and by the diaries of Berlin journalist Theodor Wolff [208]. John Röhl [188] stresses the personal factor in decision-making—especially the erratic personality of Kaiser William II.

In broader policy contexts, Wolfgang Petter's analysis of threat perception in the Second Reich [175] complements Gregor Schöllgen's fine anthology on the Reich's foreign policy [198]. Works with specific themes include Peter Winzen on Buelow's *Weltpolitik* [256]; Barbara Vogel [240] and Fritz Epstein [49] on the "Russian threat"; and Heiner Raulff on Germany's French policy in 1904–1905 [183]. Albrecht Moritz [159] argues that preventive war was not seriously considered during the first Morocco crisis. Bernd Schulte stresses German aggressive policies in Turkey and the Balkans [203].

The interpretation of Imperial Germany as an irredeemably militaristic/ authoritarian system with a built-in impulse to aggression has been locked more tightly in place by the pronounced leftward shift of the historians' community in Germany since the 1990 unification. Manfred Rauh [182] poses about the best recent challenge to the prevailing orthodoxy. The essays in Gasser [66] and Duelffer and Holl [45] reaffirm conventional wisdom on the subject. Wernecke [247], on public opinion and foreign policy in 1914, and Berghahn [14] and Deist [41], on the navy as an instrument of national integration, remain standards. Rohkraemer is a recent overview of popular militarist mentalities incorporated in the patriotic societies [190]. Coetzee [32] is solid on the Germany Army League; Geoff Eley's dissertation [47] on its naval counterpart has long been standard. Chickering [26] is a case study of an organization whose effectiveness that seldom matched its rhetoric; vom Bruch [22] offers a similar treatment of educators' political involvement.

The institutionalization of war preparation is the theme of Bucholz's outstanding monograph, *Moltke, Schlieffen, and Prussian War Planning* [23]. Mombauer [155] focuses on the role of Moltke the Younger. Addington [2] is dated, but remains a useful introduction. Hughes [94], Groote [77], and Löbel [136] offer some of the historical and ideological dimensions of the Schlieffen Plan; Zuber's controversial and well-documented *Inventing the Schlieffen Plan* denies it ever existed in any coherent form [262]. Tunstall [234] covers the Eastern theater. Michael Geyer's brief work on German armament policy [70] is particularly useful for the prewar period; Berghan and Diest is a model *Dokumentation* on the general subject [12]. Lothar Burchard [24] offers a counterpoint by demonstrating the limited nature of concrete economic preparation for war.

Turning directly to the armed forces, Showalter [205] discusses the army's inner dynamics. Schulte, *Die deutsche Armee 1900-1914* [201], is more detailed and more critical; Storz [220] places the German army in European contexts. Förster's seminal monograph *Der doppelte Militarismus* [60] asserts the growth of a "dual militarism," directed internally as well as externally. Dukes [46] is solid on the Army law of 1913. Kitchen's *The German Officer Corps 1890–1914* [115] may be supplemented by that of Clemente [31] and Moncure [157] on officer training—the latter superior in its dissertation version to the monograph. Hartmut John [102] is excellent on the reserve officers who were the key to the army's effectiveness in the Great War. John Morrow remains definitive for the prewar rise of air power [161]. Steinberg [211] and Herwig [88] provide overviews of the navy. Weir [246] discusses procurement and construction policies. Epkenhans [48] and Lambi [125] deal with policy and operations. Lambi's work is particularly thorough and correspondingly convincing on the navy's sense of it own limitations.

BIBLIOGRAPHY

1. Adams, Michael C. C. *The Great Adventure: Male Desire and the Coming of World War I*. Bloomington: Indiana University Press, 1990.

2. Addington, Larry H. *The Blitzkrieg Era and the German General Staff 1865–1914*. New Brunswick, NJ: Rutgers University Press, 1971.

3. Allshouse, Robert H. "Aleksander Izvolskii and Russian Foreign Policy, 1910–1914." Ph.D. Dissertation, Case Western Reserve University, 1977.

4. Allain, V. C. *Agadir 1911*. Paris: Universite, 1976.

5. Andrew, Christopher. *Theophile Delcasse and the Making of the Entente Cordiale*. New York: Macmillan, 1968.

6. Avetian, Andrei Sergevich. *Russko-germanskie diplomaticheskie otnosheniia nakunae pervoi mirovoi voiny, 1910–1914* [*Russo-German Diplomatic Relations on the Eve of the First World War*]. Moscow: "Nauka," 1985.

7. Barraclough, Geoffrey. *From Agadir to Armageddon*. New York: Holmes & Meier, 1982.

8. Bassford, Christopher. *Clausewitz in English*. New York: Oxford University Press, 1994.

9. Bastable, Marshall John. "Arms in the State: The History of William G. Armstrong and Company, 1859–1914." Ph.D. Dissertation, University of Toronto, 1990.

10. Batowski, Henryk. "The Failure of the Balkan Alliance of 1912." *Balkan Studies* 7 (1966): 111–122.

11. Behnen, Michael. *Ruestung-Buendnis-Sicherheit. Dreibund und Informeller Imperialismus 1900–1908* [*Armaments-Alliance-Security. Triple Alliance and Informal Imperialism, 1900–1908*]. Tuebingen: Niemeier, 1985.

12. Berghahn, Volker, Wilhelm Deist. *Ruesturg im Zeichen der Wilhelmischen Weltpolitik. Grundlegende Dokumente 1890–1914* [*Armaments in the Context of Wilhelmine Global Policy: Basic Documents 1890–1914*]. Düesseldorf: Droste, 1988.

13. Berghahn, Volker R. *Germany and the Approach of War in 1914*. New York: St. Martin's, 1973.

14. Berghahn, Volker R. *Der Tirpitz-Plan. Genesis und Verfall einer innenpolitischen Krisenstrategie unter Wilhelm II* [*The Tirpitz Plan. Genesis and Collapse of a Domestic Crisis Strategy under William II*]. Düesseldorf: Droste, 1971.

15. Best, Geoffrey. "The Militarization of European Society, 1870–1914." *The Militarization of the Western World*. ed. John Gilles. New Brunswick: Rutgers University Press, 1989, 13–44.

16. Bethmann Hollweg, Theobald von. *Betrachtungen zur Weltkriege* [*Reflections on the World War*]. Ed. Jost Duelffer, 2nd ed. Essen: Hobling, 1989.

17. Blansdorf, Agnes A. "Der Weg der Riezler-Tagebuecher. Zum Kontroverse ueber die Echtheit der Tagebuecher Kurt Riezlers" ["The Course of the Riezler Diaries. On the Controversy over the Genuineness of the Diaries of Kurt Riezler"]. *Geschichte in Wissenschaft und Unterricht* 35 (1984): 651–684.

18. Bosworth, Richard. *Italy, the Least of the Great Powers: Italian Foreign Policy before the First World War*. Cambridge: Cambridge University Press, 1979.

19. Bosworth, Richard. *Italy and the Approach of the First World War*. New York: St. Martin's, 1983.

20. Bridge, F. R. *Great Britain and Austria-Hungary, 1906–1914: A Diplomatic History.* London: Weidenfeld & Nicholson, 1972.

21. Bridge, F. R. *From Sadowa to Sarajevo: The Foreign Policy of Austria-Hungary, 1866–1914.* London: Routledge, 1972.

22. Bruch, Ruediger vom. "Deutschland und England. Heeres-oder Flottenverstarkung?" Politische Publizistik deutschen Hochschullehrer, 1911/12" ["Germany and England: Army or Fleet Buildup? Political Publications of German Professors, 1911/1912"]. *Militaergeschichtliche Mitteilungen* 29 (1981): 7–36.

23. Bucholz, Arden. *Moltke, Schlieffen and Prussian War Planning.* New York: Berg, 1991.

24. Burchard, Lothar. *Friedenswirtschaft und Kriegsvorsorge. Deutschlands wirtschaftliche Bestrebungen vor 1914* [Peace Economics and Provision for War: Germany's Economic Efforts before 1914]. Boppard: Boldt, 1968.

25. Charmley, John. *Splendid Isolation? Britain, the Balance of Power and the Origins of the World War.* London: Hodder and Stoughton, 1999.

26. Chickering, Roger, "Der Deutsche Wehrverein und die Reform der deutschen Armee 1912–1914" [The German Army League and the Reform of the German Army 1912–1914]. *Militaergeschichtliche Mitteilungen* 25 (1979): 7–33.

27. Chickering, Roger. *Imperial Germany and a World Without War.* Princeton: Princeton University Press, 1975.

28. Childs, T. W. "Mediterranean Imbroglio: The Diplomatic Origins of Modern Libya (The Diplomacy of the Belligerents during the Italo-Turkish War, 1911–1912)." Ph.D. Dissertation, Georgetown University, 1982.

29. Clarke, I. F., ed. *The Great War with Germany, 1890–1914: Fictions and Fantasies of the War-to-Come.* Liverpool: Liverpool University Press. 1997.

30. Clarke, I. F. *The Tale of the Next Great War, 1871–1914: Fictions of Future Warfare and Battles Still-to-Come.* Liverpool: University of Liverpool Press, 1995.

31. Clemente, Steven E. *For King and Kaiser! The Making of the Prussian Army Officer, 1860–1914.* Westport, CT.: Greenwood, 1992.

32. Coetzee, Marilyn Shevin. *The German Army League. Popular Nationalism in Wilhemine Germany.* New York: Oxford University Press, 1990.

33. Conner, Thomas H. "Parliament and the Making of Foreign Policy: France under the Third Republic, 1875–1914." Ph.D. Dissertation, University of North Carolina, Chapel Hill, 1983.

34. Cooper, Sandi E. "Pacifism in France, 1889–1914: International Peace as a Human Right." *French Historical Studies* 17 (1991): 359–86.

35. Cooper, Sandi E. *Patriotic Patriotism: Waging War in Europe, 1815–1914.* New York: Oxford University Press, 1991.

36. Cox, Gary. "Of Aphorisms, Lessons, and Paradigms: Comparing the British and German Official Histories of the Russo-Japanese War," *The Journal of Military History* LVI (1992), 389–401.

37. Crampton, R. J. *The Hollow Détente: Anglo-German Relations in the Balkans, 1911–1914.* London: Prior, 1979.

38. Crook, Paul. *Darwinism, War and History: The Debate over the Biology of War from the "Origin of Species" to the First World War.* Cambridge: Cambridge University Press, 1994.

39. Déak, Istvan. *Beyond Nationalism. A Social and Political History of the Habsburg Officer Corps 1848–1918.* New York: Oxford University Press, 1990.

40. *Decisions for War, 1914.* Ed. Keith Wilson. New York: St. Martin's Press, 1995.

41. Deist, Wilhelm. *Flottenpolitik und Flottenpropaganda* [*Naval Policy and Naval Propaganda*]. Stuttgart: Deutsche Verlagsanstalt, 1976.

42. Di Ionic, Anthony. "Italy, Austria, Hungary, and the Balkans, 1904–1914: Italy's Appraisal." Ph.D. Dissertation, University of Illinois, 1980.

43. d'Ombrian, Nicholas. *War Machinery and High Policy. Defense Administration in Peacetime Britain 1902–14.* Oxford: Clarendon Press, 1973.

44. Duelffer, Jost. *Regeln gegen den Krieg? Die Haager Friedenskonferenzen 1899 und 1907 in der internationalen Politik* [*Rules against War? The Hague Peace Conferences of 1899 and 1907 in International Politics*], Berlin: Ullstein, 1981.

45. Duelffer, Jost, and Karl Holl. *Kriegsmentalitaet im Wilhelmischen Deutschland 1890–1914* [*War Mentality in Wilhelmian Germany 1890–1914*]. Göttingen: Vandenhoeck and Ruprecht, 1986.

46. Dukes, Jack. "Militarism and Arms Policy Revisited: The Origins of the German Army Law of 1914." *Another Germany: A Reconsideration of the Imperial Era.* Ed. J. R. Dukes and J. Remak. Boulder, CO: Westview, 1987: 19–39.

47. Eley, Geoff. "The German Navy League in German Politics, 1898–1914." Ph.D. Dissertation, University of Sussex, 1974.

48. Epkenhans, Michael. *Die wilhelminische Flottenrüstung, 1908–1914: Weltmachtstreben, Industrieller Fortschritt, Soziale Integration* [*Wilhelmian Naval Armament, 1908–1914: World Power, Industrial Progress, Social Integration*]. Munich: R. Oldenbourg, 1991.

49. Epstein, Fritz T. "Der Komplex 'Die russische Gefahr' und sein Einfluss auf die deutsch-russischen Beziehungen un 19. Jahrhundert" ["The 'Russian Danger' Complex and Its Influence on German-Russian Relations in the 19th Century in Germany and World Power in the19th and 20th Centuries"] in *Deutschland in der Weltpolitik des 19. und 20. Jahrhunderts.* Ed. I. Geiss and B. J. Wendt. 2nd ed. rev. Düsseldorf: Droste, 1974: 149–152.

50. Erdmann, Karl Dietrich. "Zur Echtheit der Tagebuecher Kurt Riezlers: Eine Antikrilik" ["On the Authenticity of the Kurt Riezler Diaries. A Reply to Critics"]. *Historische Zeitschrift* 236 (1983): 371–402.

51. Evans, R. J. W., and Hartmut Pogge von Strandmann. *The Coming of the First World War.* Oxford: Clarendon, 1988.

52. Fairbanks, Charles H. "The Origins of the *Dreadnought* Revolution: A Historiographical Essay." *International History Review* 13 (1991): 246–72.

53. Ferenczi, Caspar. *Aussenpolitik und Oeffentlichkeit in Russland, 1906–1912* [*Foreign Policy and Public Opinion in Russia, 1906–1912*]. Husum: Mattheisen, 1982.

54. Ferguson, Niall. *The Pity of War.* London: Allen Lane, 1998.

55. Ferris, John. "Before 'Room 40': The British Empire and Signals Intelligence, 1898–1914." *The Journal of Strategic Studies* 12 (1989): 431–457.

56. Fischer, Fritz. *Der Erste Weltkrieg und das deutsche Geschichtsbild. Beiträge zur Bewaeltigung eines historischen Tabus. Aufsaetze uns Vorträge aus drei Jahrzenten* [*The First World War and the German View of History: Contributions to the Mastering of a Historical Taboo. Essays and Lectures from Three Decades*]. Düsseldorf: Droste, 1977.

57. Fischer, Fritz. *Juli 1914: Wir sind nicht hineingeschlittert* [*July 1914. We Did Not Stumble into It*]. Reinbek: Rohwolt, 1983.

58. Fischer, Fritz. *Griff nach der Weltmacht: Die Kriegszielpolitik des kaiserlichen Deutschlands 1914/18.* Düsseldorf: Droste, 1961. [Translated as *Germany's Aims in the First World War.* (London, 1967)]

59. Förster, Stig. "Der Deutsche Generalstab und die Illusion des Kurzen Krieges, 1871–1914. Metakritik eines Mythos" ["The German General Staff and the Short-War Illusion, 1871–1914"]. *Militaergeschichtliche Mitteilungen* 54 (1995), 61–95.

60. Förster, Stig. *Der doppelte Militarismus. Die deutsche Heeresrüsturgspolitik zwischen Status-Quo-Sicherung und Aggression, 1890–1913* [*Dual Militarism. German Armaments Policy between Status Quo Preservation and Aggression, 1890–1913*]. Stuttgart: Steiner, 1983.

61. French, David. *British Economic and Strategic Planning 1905–1915.* London: Unwin, 1982.

62. Friedberg, Aaron L. *The Weary Titan. Great Britain and the Experience of Relative Decline, 1895–1905.* Princeton, NJ: Princeton University Press, 1988.

63. Fröhlich, Michael. *Von Konfrontation zur Koexistenz: Die deutsch-englishen Koloniallbeziehungen in Afrika zwischen 1884 und 1914* [*From Confrontation to Coexistence: German-English Colonial Relations in Africa between 1884 and 1919*]. Bochum: Brochmeyer, 1990.

64. Fuller, William C. *Strategy and Power in Russia, 1600–1914*. New York: Free Press, 1992.

65. Gabriele, Mariano, and Guiliano Friz. *La politica navale italiana dal 1885 al 1915* [*Italian Naval Policy from 1885 to 1915*]. Rome: Ufficio Storico della Marina Militare, 1982.

66. Gasser, Alfred. *Preussischer Militärgeist und Krisentfesselung 1914. Drei Studien zum Ausbruch des Ersten Weltkrieges* [*Prussian Militarism and the Unfettering of Crisis. Three Studies on the Outbreak of the First World War*]. Basel, Frankfurt a.M.: Helbing, 1985.

67. Geiss, Immanuel, ed. *Julikrise und Kreigsausbruch 1914: Eine Dokumentensammlung* [*The July Crisis and the Outbreak of War, 1914. A Document Collection*]. 2 vols. Hannover: 1963–1964.

68. Geiss, Immanuel. *Der lange Weg in die Katastrophe. Die Vorgeschichte des Ersten Weltkrieges 1815–1914* [*The Long Road to Catastrophe. The Prehistory of the First World War, 1815–1914*]. Munich: 1990.

69. Geyer, Dietrich. *Russian Imperialism: The Interaction of Domestic and Foreign Policy, 1860–1914*. Tr. Bruce Little. New Haven: Yale University Press, 1987.

70. Geyer, Michael. *Deutsche Rüstungspolitik 1860–1980* [*German Armament Policy 1860–1980*]. Frankfurt: 1984.

71. Girault, Rene. *Emprunts russes et divestissements francais en Russie, 1887–1914* [*Russian Loans and French Investments in Russia. 1887–1914*]. Paris: Comite pour l'histoire . . . , 1973.

72. Goldstein, Edward R. "Military Aspects of Russian Industrialization: The Defense Industries 1890–1917." Ph.D. Dissertation, Case Western Reserve University, 1977.

73. Gollin, Alfred. *The Impact of Air Power on the British People and Their Government, 1909–1914*. Stanford: Stanford University Press, 1989.

74. Gooch, John. *Army, State, and Society in Italy, 1870–1915*. New York: St. Martins, 1989.

75. Gooch, John. *The Plans of War. The General Staff and British Military Strategy c. 1900–1916*. London: Routledge, 1974.

76. Gordon, M. R. "Domestic Conflict and the Origins of the First World War: The British and the German Cases." *The Journal of Modern History* 46 (1974): 191–266.

77. Groote, Wolfgang von. "Historische Vorbilder des Feldzuges 1914 im Westen" ["Historical Models of the 1914 Campaign in the West"]. *Militaergeschichtliche Mitteilungen* 47 (1990): 33–55.

78. Gutsche, Willibald. "Die Aussenpolitik des Kasserlichen Deutschlands und der Ausbruch des Ersten Weltkreiges in der Geschichtsschreibung der DDR" ["The Foreign Policy of Imperial Germany and the Outbreak of the First World War in the Historical Writing of the German Democratic Republic"]. *Zeitschrift für Geschichtswissenschaft* 37 (1989): 782–95.

79. Gutsche, Willibald. *Der gewollte Krieg: der deutsche Imperialimus und der 1. Weltkrieg* [*The Intentional War: German Imperialism and the First World War*] Koeln: Kiepenhauer & Witsch, 1984.

80. Halpern, Paul C. *The Mediterranean Naval Situation, 1908–1914*. Cambridge: Harvard University Press, 1971.

81. Hatton, P. H. S. "Harcourt and Solf: The Search for an Anglo-German Understanding through Africa, 1912–1914." *European Studies Review 1* (1971).

82. Hayne, M. B. *The French Foreign Office and the Origins of the First World War 1898–1914*. New York: Oxford University Press, 1993.

83. Head, Judith. "Russian Attitudes towards Germany and Austria." Ph.D. Dissertation, North Texas State University, 1981.

84. Herrmann, David. *The Arming of Europe and the Making of the First World War*. Princeton: Princeton University Press, 1997.

85. Herwig, Holger H. "Disjointed Allies: Coalition Warfare in Berlin and Vienna, 1914." *The Journal of Military History* 54 (1990): 265–80.

86. Herwig, Holger H. *The First World War: Germany and Austria-Hungary, 1914–1918*. London: Arnold, 1997.

87. Herwig, Holger H. "The German Reaction to the *Dreadnaught* Revolution." *International History Review* 13 (1991): 273–83.

88. Herwig, Holger H. *"Luxury" Fleet: The Imperial German Navy, 1888–1918.* London, Boston: Allen and Unwin, 1980.

89. Hildebrand, Klaus. "Julikrise 1914: Das europaesche Sicherheitsdilemma. Betrachtungen über den Ausbruch der Ersten Weltkrieges" ["July Crisis 1914: The European Security Dilemma. Observations on the Outbreak of the First World War"]. *Geschichte in Wissenschaft und Unterricht* 36 (1985): 469–502.

90. Hinsley, F. H., ed. *British Foreign Policy under Sir Edward Grey.* Cambridge: Cambridge University Press, 1977.

91. Höbelt, Lothar. "Österreich-Ungarn und das Deutsche Reich als Zweibundpartner" ["Austria Hungary and the German Empire as Alliance Partners"]. *Österreich und die deutsche Frage im 19. und 20. Jahrhundert.* Ed. H. Lutz and H. Rumpler. Munich, 1982: 256–81.

92. Höbelt, Lothar. "Schlieffen, Beck, Potiorek und das Ende der gemeinsamen deutsch-oesterrechischen-ungarischen Aufmarschplaene in Osten" ["Schlieffen, Beck, Potiorek, and the End of Joint German-Austro-Hungarian Deployment Plans in the East"]. *Militaergeschichtliche Mitteilungen* 36 (1984): 7–30.

93. Howorth, Joylon. "French Workers and German Workers: The Impossibility of Internationalism, 1900–1914." *European History Quarterly* 15 (1985): 71–97.

94. Hughes, Daniel. "Schlichting, Schlieffen, and the Prussian Theory of War in 1914." *Journal of Military History* 59 (1995): 257–77.

95. Illari, Virgilio. *Storia del servicio militaire in Italia.* Vol. 2, *La "Nazione Armata" (1871–1918)* [*The History of Military Service in Italy.* Vol. 2, *The "Nation in Arms" (1871–1918)*]. Rome: Rivista Millitaire, 1990.

96. Jaeckel, Horst. *Die Nordwestgrenze in der Verteidigung Indieno 1900–1908 und der Weg En-glands zum russischen-brititschen Abkommen von 1907* [*The Northwest Frontier in the Defense of India, 1900–1908, and England's Way to the Russo-British Alliance of 1907*]. Koln: Westdeutscher Verlag, 1968.

97. Jakobs, Peter. *Das Werden des franzoesisch-russischen Zweibundes, 1890–1894* [*The Origin of the Franco-Russian Alliance, 1890–1894*]. Wiesbaden: Harassowitz, 1968.

98. Jannen, William, Jr. "The Austro-Hungarian Decision for War in July 1914." *Essays on World War I.* Ed. S. R. Williamson and P. Pastor. New York: Brooklyn College, 1983: 55–83.

99. Jarausch, Konrad. *The Enigmatic Chancellor: Bethmann Hollweg and the Hubris of Imperial Germany.* New Haven: Yale University Press, 1973.

100. Jauffret, Jean-Charles. "L'Organisation de la Reserve a l'epoque de la revanche 1871–1914" ["The Organization of the Reserves in the Era of Revenge, 1871–1914"]. *Revue Historique des Armées.* 1989 (1): 27–37.

101. Jelavich, Barbara. *Russia's Balkan Entanglements, 1806–1914.* Cambridge: Cambridge University Press, 1991.

102. John, Hartmut. *Das Reserveoffizierkorps im Deutschen Kaiserreich, 1890–1914. Ein sozialgeschichtlicher Beitrag zur Untersuchung der gesellschaftlichen Militarisierung im Wilhelmischen Deutschlands* [*The Reserve Officer Corps in the German Empire, 1890–1914: A Social-Historical Contribution to the Study of Social Militarization in Willhelmian Germany*]. Frankfurt a.M. and New York: Lang, 1981.

103. Joll, James. *The Origins of the First World War.* London and New York: Longman, 1984.

104. Kahler, Miles. "Rumors of War: The 1914 Analogy." *Foreign Affairs.* 1979/80: 374–96.

105. Kaiser, David E. "Germany and the Origins of the First World War." *Journal of Modern History* 55 (1983): 442–74.

106. Keaney, Thomas A. "Aircraft and Air Doctrinal Development in Great Britain, 1912 to 1914." Ph.D. Dissertation, University of Michigan, 1975.

107. Keegan, John. *The First World War.* New York: Knopf, 1999.

108. Keiger, John. *France and the Origins of the First World War.* New York: St. Martin's, 1983.

109. Keiger, John. "Jules Cambon and Franco-German Detente, 1907–1914." *Historical Journal* 26 (1983): 641–59.

110. Kennan, George. *The Fateful Alliance: France, Russia and the Coming of the First World War.* New York: Pantheon, 1984.

111. Kennedy, Paul, and Anthony Nicholls, eds. *Nationalist and Racialist Movements in Britain and Germany before 1914.* London: Macmillan, 1981.

112. Kennedy, Paul. *The Rise of the Anglo-German Antagonism 1860–1914.* London: Unwin, 1980.

113. Kennedy, Paul, ed. *The War Plans of the Great Powers, 1880–1914.* Boston: Allen and Unwin, 1985.

114. Kiernan, V. G. "Conscription and Society in Europe before the War of 1914–1918." *War and Society: Historical Essays in Honor and Memory of J. R. Western.* Ed. M. R. D. Foot. London: Elek, 1973: 141–58.

115. Kitchen, Martin. *The German Officer Corps, 1890–1914.* Oxford: Clarendon, 1968.

116. Kiraly, Bela K., and Dimitrije Djordevic, eds. *East Central European Society and the Balkan Wars.* Highland Lakes, NJ: Atlantic, 1987.

117. Koch, H. W., ed. *The Origins of the First World War.* 2nd ed. London: Macmillan, 1984.

118. Kronenbitter, Günther. "Die Macht der Illusionen. Julikrise und Kriegsausbruch 1914 aus der Sicht des Deutschen Militärattachés in Wien" ["The Power of Illusions: The July Crisis and the Outbreak of War in 1914 from the Perspective of the German Military Attache in Vienna"]. *Militaergeschichtliche Mitteilungen* 57 (1998), 509–18.

119. Krumeich, Gerd. *Armaments and Politics in France on the Eve of the First World War.* Tr. S. Conn. Dover, NH: Berg, 1984.

120. Lackey, Scott Warren. *The Rebirth of the Habsburg Army: Friedrich Beck and the Rise of the General Staff.* Westport, CT: Greenwood Press, 1995.

121. Lademacher, Horst. *Die belgische Neutraliteat als Problem der Europäische Politik 1830–1914* [*Belgian Neutrality as a Problem of European Diplomacy, 1830–1914*]. Bonn: Rohrscheidt, 1971.

122. Lambert, Nicholas A. "Admiral Sir John Fisher and the Concept of Flotilla Defence, 1904–1909." *Journal of Military History* 59 (1995), 639–60.

123. Lambert, Nicholas A. "British Naval Policy, 1913–1914: Financial Limitation and Strategic Revolution." *Journal of Modern History* 67 (1995), 595–626.

124. Lambert Nicholas A. *Sir John Fisher's Naval Revolution.* Columbia: University of South Carolina Press, 1999.

125. Lambi, Ivo N. *The Navy and German Power Policies, 1862–1914.* Boston: Unwin, 1984.

126. Lampl, John R. "Financial Structure and the Economic Development of Serbia, 1878–1912." Ph.D. Dissertation, University of Wisconsin, 1971.

127. Langdon, John W. *July 1914. The Long Debate, 1918–1990.* New York: Berg, 1991.

128. Laqueur, Walter, and George L. Mosse, eds. *1914: The Coming of the First World War.* New York: Harper, 1966.

129. Lawler, Harold E., Jr. "Defense Spending and the Relative Decline of the British Economy, 1875–1914." Ph.D. Dissertation, University of Connecticut, 1989.

130. Layne, Christopher. "1914 Revisited: A Reply by Miles Kahler." *Orbis* 24 (1981): 719–50.

131. Lee, Dwight E. *Europe's Crucial Years: The Diplomatic Background of World War I, 1902–1914.* Hanover, NH: New England, 1974.

132. Levy, Jack S. "Preferences, Constraints, and Chaos in July 1914." *International Security* 15 (3), 1990–91: 151–86.

133. Lieven, D. C. B. *Russia and the Origins of the First World War.* New York: St. Martin's, 1983.

134. Lincoln, W. Bruce. *In War's Dark Shadow: The Russians before the Great War.* New York: Oxford University Press, 1983.

135. Linke, Horst Günther. *Das zarische Russland und der Erste Weltkrieg. Diplomatie und Kriegsziele 1914–1917* [*Tsarist Russia and the First World War. Diplomacy and War Aims, 1914–1917*]. Munich: Fink, 1982.

136. Löbel, Uwe. "Aspekte der Kriegsbilddiskussion und Schlieffens Aufmarschplanung. Ein Beitrag zur Herausbildurg der Militärdoktrin des deutschen Imperalismus" ["Aspects of War Prediction and Schlieffen's Deployment Planning. A Contribution the Formation of German Imperialism's Military Doctrine"]. *Revue Internationale d Histoire Militaire* 71 (1989): 67–78.

137. Löding, Dörte. *Deutschlands und Oesterreich-Ungarns Balkanpolitik von 1913 bis 1914 unter besonderer Berücksichtigung ihrer Wirtschaftsinteresse* [Germany's and Austria-Hungary's Balkan Policy from 1912 to 1914, with Particular Consideration of their Economic Interests]. Hamburg: 1969.

138. Long, James W. "The Economics of the Franco-Russian Alliance 1904–06." Ph.D. Dissertation, University of Wisconsin, 1968.

139. Lubibratic, Drago. *Mlada Bosna i Sarajevski atentat* ["*Young Bosnia*" *and the Sarajevo Assassination*]. Sarajevo: 1964.

140. Lunttinen, Perti. *French Information on the Russian War Plans, 1880–1914.* Helsinki: SHS, 1984.

141. Lynn-Jones, Sean M. "Detente and Deterrence: Anglo-German Relation, 1911–1914." *International Security* 11 (Fall 1986): 121–50.

142. Mann, Josef. "Feldmarschalleutnant Blasius Schemua. Chef des Generalstabes am Vorabend des Weltkrieges, 1911–1912" ["Lieutenant Field Marshal Blasius Schemua. Chief of the General Staff on the Eve of World War, 1911–1912"]. Ph.D. Dissertation, University of Vienna, 1978.

143. Martel, Gordon. *The Origins of the First World War.* 2nd ed. London and New York: Longman, 1996.

144. Massie, Robert K. *Dreadnaught: Britain, Germany, and the Coming of the Great War.* New York: Random House, 1991.

145. May, Ernest R., ed. *Knowing One's Enemies: Intelligence Assessment before the Two World Wars.* Princeton: Princeton University Press, 1984.

146. Mayer, Arno. *The Persistence of the Old Regime: Europe to the Great War.* New York: Pantheon, 1981.

147. McDonald, D. M. *United Government and Foreign Policy in Russia, 1900–1914.* Cambridge: Harvard University Press, 1992.

148. Mackenzie, David. *Apis: The Congenial Conspirator. The Life of Colonel Dragutin T. Dimietrevic.* New York: Columbia, 1989.

149. Mackenzie, David. "Serbian Nationalist and Military Organization and the Piedmont Idea, 1844–1914." *East European Quarterly* 16 (1982): 323–44.

150. Mackenzie, John, ed. *Popular Imperialism and the Military: 1850–1950.* Manchester: University of Manchester Press, 1992.

151. Menning, Bruce. *Bayonets before Bullets: The Imperial Russian Army, 1861–1914.* Bloomington: Indiana University Press, 1992.

152. Midlarsky, Manus J. *The Onset of World War.* Boston: Unwin, 1988.

153. *Military Strategy and the Origins of the First World War.* Ed. Steven E. Miller, Sean M. Lynn-Jones, and Stephen van Evera. Rev. ed. Princeton: Princeton University Press, 1991.

154. Miller, J. M., Jr. "The Concert of Europe in the First Balkan War, 1912–1913." Ph.D. Dissertation, Clark University, 1961.

155. Mombauer, Anneka. *Helmuth von Moltke and the Origins of the First World War.* New York: Cambridge University Press, 2001.

156. Mommsen, Wolfgang J. *Imperial Germany 1867–1918: Politics, Culture, and Society in an Authoritarian State.* London: Arnold, 1995.

157. Moncure, John. "Forging the King's Sword: Military Education between Tradition and Modernity: The Case of the Royal Prussian Cadet Corps, 1571–1918." Ph.D. Dissertation, Cornell University, 1991.

158. Moon, H. R. "The Invasion of the United Kingdom. Public Controversy and Official Planning, 1888–1918." 2 vols. Ph.D. Dissertation, University of London, 1968.

159. Moritz, Albrecht. *Das Problem des Praeventivkrieges in der deutschen Politik waehrend der ersten Marokkokrise.* Bern: Lang, 1974.

160. Morris, A. J. *The Scaremongers: The Advocacy of War and Rearmament, 1896–1914.* London: Routledge, 1984.

161. Morrow, John H. *Building German Airpower, 1909–1914.* Knoxville: University of Tennessee Press, 1976.

162. Moses, John. *The Politics of Illusion. The Fischer Controversy in German Historiography.* London: Prior, 1975.

163. Neilson, Keith. " 'Greatly Exaggerated': The Myth of the Decline of Great Britain before 1914." *International History Review,* 13 (1991): 695–725.

164. Neilson, Keith. "Watching the 'Steamroller': British Observer and the Russian Army before 1914." *The Journal of Strategic Studies* 8 (1985): 199–217.

165. Offer, Avner. *The First World War. An Agrarian Interpretation.* Oxford: Clarendon Press, 1989.

166. Offer, Avner. "Going to War in 1914: A Matter of Honor?" *Politics and Society* 23 (1995), 213–41.

167. Oncken, Emily. *Panthersprung nach Agadir: Die deutsche Politik während der zweiten Marokkokrise, 1911* [Panther's Leap to Agadir. German Policy during the Second Morocco Crisis, 1911]. Düsseldorf: Droste, 1981.

168. Oppel, Bernard F. "The Waning of a Traditional Alliance. Russia and Germany after the Portsmouth Peace Conference." *Central European History* 5 (1972): 318–29.

169. *The Outbreak of World War I: Causes and Responsibilities.* Ed. Holger H. Herwig. Boston: Houghton Mifflin, 1997.

170. Padfield, Peter. *The Great Naval Race: Anglo-German Naval Rivalry 1900–14.* London: Hart Davis, 1974.

171. Palumbo, Michael. "German-Italian Military Relations on the Eve of World War II." *Central European History* 12 (1979): 343–71.

172. Pantenius, Hans Jürgen. *Der Angriffsgedanke gegen Italian bei Conrad von Hoetzendorff* [*Conrad von Hoetzendorff's Plans for an Offensive against Italy*]. 2 vols. Vienna: 1984.

173. Perrins, M. "The Council for State Defense, 1905–1909: A Study in Russian Bureaucratic Policy." *Slavonic and East European Review* 58 (1980): 376–99.

174. Peterson, M. B. A. "Das oesterreich-urgarische Memorandum an Deutschland von 5. Juli, 1914" ["The Austro-Hungarian Memorandum to Germany of July 5, 1914"]. *Scandia* 30 (1964): 138–90.

175. Petter, Wolfgang. "'Enemies' and 'Reich Enemies.' An Analysis of Threat Properties and Political Strategy in Imperial Germany, 1871–1914." *The German Military in the Age of the Cold War.* ed., W. Deist. Leamington Spa: Berg, 1985: 22–39.

176. Philpott, William. "The Strategic Ideas of Sir John French." *Journal of Strategic Studies* 12 (1989): 458–78.

177. Pick, Daniel. *War Machine. The Rationalization of Slaughter in the Modern Age.* New Haven: Yale University Press, 1993.

178. Porch, Douglas. *The March to the Marne: The French Army, 1871–1914.* Cambridge: Cambridge University Press, 1981.

179. Pregaglia, Patrezia. "A Trent' anni dalla controversia Fischer: 'Assalto al portere mondiale' e la storiografia italiana." *Politico,* 55 (1990): 351–60.

180. Ralston, David B. *The Army of the Republic: The Place of the Military in the Political Evolution of France, 1871–1914.* Cambridge: MIT Press, 1967.

181. Rauh, Manfred. "Die britisch-russische Marinekonvention von 1914 und der Ausbruch des Ersten Weltkriegs" ["The British-Russian Naval Convention of 1914 and the Outbreak of the First World War"]. *Militaergeschichtliche Mitteilungen* 41 (1987): 37–62.

182. Rauh, Manfred. "Die 'deutsche Frage' von 1914: Weltmachtsstreben und Obrigkeitstaat?" ["The 'German Question' of 1914: The Quest for World Power and the Authoritarian State?]

Die Deutsche Frage im 19 und 20. Jahrhundert. Ed. J. Becker and A. Hillgruber. Munich: Vogel, 1983.

183. Raulff, Heiner. *Zwischen Machtpolitik und Imperialimus Die Deutsche Frankreichpolitik 1902–05* [*Between Power Politics and Imperialism: Germany's French Policy, 1902–05*]. Düsseldorf: Droste 1976.

184. Remak, Joachim. "The Healthy Invalid: How Doomed Was the Habsburg Empire?" *Journal of Modern History* 41 (1969): 127–41.

185. Remak. Joachim. "1914 The Third Balkan War: Origins Reconsidered?" *Journal of Modern History* 43 (1971): 353–66.

186. Remak, Joachim. *The Origins of World War I 1871–1914.* New York: Holt, Rinehart, 1967.

187. Riezler, Kurt. *Tagebuecher, Aufsätze, Dokumente* [*Diaries. Essays. Documents*]. Ed. K. D. Erdmann. Goettingen: Vandenhoek, 1972.

188. Röhl, John G. "Der Militärpolitische Entscheidungsprozess in Deutschland am Vorabend des Ersten Weltkrieges" ["The Process of Military-Political Decision-Making in Germany on the Eve of the First World War"]. In *Kaiser, Hof und Staat. Wilhelm II und die deutsche Politik.* Munich: Beck, 1987: 175–202.

189. Röhl, John. "An der Schwelle zum Weltkrieg: Eine Dokumentation über den 'Kriegsrat' von 8 Dezember 1912" ["On the Threshold of World War: A Documentation on the 'War Council' of December 8, 1912"]. *Militaergeschichtliche Mitteilungen* 21 (1977): 77–134.

190. Rohrkraemer, Thomas. *Der Militarismus der "kleinen Leute." Die Kriegervereine im Deutschen Kaiserreich 1871–1914* [*The Militarism of the Little People: The Veterans' Associations in the German Empire, 1871–1914*]. Munich: Oldenbourg, 1990.

191. Rolo, P. J. V. *Entente Cordiale: The Origin and Negotiations of the Anglo-French Agreements of 8 April, 1904.* London: Macmillan, 1969.

192. Ropp, Theodore. *The Development of a Modern Navy: French Naval Policy, 1871–1904.* Annapolis: Naval Institute Press, 1987.

193. Ropponen, Risto. *Italien als Verbuendeter.Die Einstellung der Politischen und Miliarischen Führung Deutschlands und Österreich-Ungarns zu Italien von der Niederlagen von Adua bis zum Ausbruch des Weltkrieges 1914* [*Italy as Ally: Germany's and Austria-Hungary's Political and Military Approaches to Austria from the Defeat of Adua to the Outbreak of the World War of 1914*]. Tr. C. Krotzl. Helsinki: SHS, 1986.

194. Ropponen, Risto. *Die Kraft Russlands. Wie Beurteilte die politische und Militärische Führung der Europaeschen Grossmächte in der Zeit von 1905 bis 1914 die Kraft Russland?* [*Russia's Power: How Did the Political and Military Leadership of Europe's Great Powers Evaluate Russia's Strength in the Period from 1905 to 1914?*] Helsinki: 1968.

195. Rossos, Andrew. *Russia and the Balkans: Inter-Balkan Rivalries and Russian Foreign Policy, 1908–1914.* Toronto: University of Toronto Press, 1981.

196. Rothenberg, Gunther E. *The Army of Francis Joseph.* West Lafayette, IN: Purdue University Press, 1976.

197. Schlarp, K. H. *Ursachen und Entstehung des Ersten Weltkrieges in Lichte der sowjetischen Geschichtsschreibung* [*Causes and Consequences of the First World War in the Light of Soviet Historical Writing*]. Hamburg: Metzner, 1971.

198. Schöllgen, Gregor. *Escape into War? The Foreign Policy of Imperial Germany.* New York: Berg, 1990.

199. Schöllgen, Gregor. *Imperialismus und Gleichgewicht. Deutschland, England und die orientalische Frage, 1871–1914* [*Imperialism and Balance. Germany, England, and the Eastern Question, 1871–1914*]. Munich: Oldenbourg, 1984.

200. Schroeder, Paul W. "World War I and Galloping Gertie: A Reply to Joachim Remark." *Journal of Modern History* 44 (1972): 319–45.

201. Schulte, Bernd F. *Die deutsche Armee 1900–1914. Zwischen beharren und verändern* [*The German Army, 1900–1914. Between Inertia and Change*]. Düsseldorf: Droste, 1977.

202. Schulte, Bernd F. *Die Verfaelschung der Riezler Tagebücher* [*The Falsification of the Riezler Diaries*]. Frankfurt: Lang, 1988.

203. Schulte, Bernd F. *Vor dem Kriegsausbruch 1914. Deutschland, die Türkei und der Balkan* [*Before the Outbreak of War, 1914: Germany, Turkey, and the Balkans*]. Düsseldorf: Droste, 1980.

204. Schumann, Rosemarie. "'Friede durch Recht!' Das Bürgerlich Friedensprogramm von der Jahrhundertwende bis zum Ersten Weltkrieg" ["'Peace through Justice:' The Bourgeois Peace Program from the Turn of the Century to the First World War"]. *Revue Internationale d'Histoire Militaire* 71 (1989): 88–101.

205. Showalter, Dennis E. "Army and Society in Imperial Germany: The Pains of Modernization." *Journal of Contemporary History* 181 (1983): 583–618.

206. Simmons, Robert E. "German Balkan Diplomacy, 1906–1913. The Genesis and Implementation of a War-Risk Policy." Ph.D. Dissertation, Auburn University, 1982.

207. Snyder, Jack. *The Ideology of the Offense. Military Decision-Making and the Disasters of 1914.* Ithaca: Cornell University Press, 1984.

208. Sösemann, B., ed. *Theodor Wolff: Tagebuecher 1914–1919* [*Theodor Wolff: Diaries, 1914–1919*]. 2 vols. Boppard: Boldt, 1984.

209. Spring, D. W. "Russia and the France-Russian Alliance, 1905–14: Dependence or Independence?" *Slavonic and East European Review* 66 (1988): 364–92.

210. Stargardt, E. N. R. "The Practice and Theory of Anti-Militarism in German Social Democracy." Ph.D. Dissertation, Cambridge University, 1989.

211. Steinberg, Jonathan. *Yesterday's Deterrent: Tirpitz and the Birth of the German Battle Fleet.* London: MacDonald, 1965.

212. Steinberg, John Warner. "The Education and Training of the Russian Central Staff: A History of the Imperial Nicholas Military Academy, 1832–1914." Ph.D. Dissertation, Ohio State University, 1990.

213. Steiner, Zara. *The Foreign Office and Foreign Policy, 1898–1914.* Cambridge: Cambridge University Press, 1969.

214. Stevenson, David. *Armaments and the Coming of War: Europe, 1904–1914.* Oxford: Clarendon Press, 1996.

215. Stevenson, David. *The Outbreak of the First World War: 1914 in Perspective.* Houndmills: Macmillan, 1997.

216. Stokes, Gale. "The Serbian Documents from 1914: A Preview." *Journal of Modern History* 48 (Supplement): 1976.

217. Stone, Norman. "Gerhard Ritter and the First World War." *Historical Journal* 13 (1970): 158–71.

218. Stone, Norman. "Die Mobilmachung der oesterriechischen-ungarischen Armee 1914" ["The Mobilization of the Austro-Hungarian Army, 1914"]. *Militärgeschitchliche Mitteilungen* 16 (1974): 64–95.

219. Stone, Norman. "Moltke-Conrad: Relations between the Austro-Hungarian and German General Staffs, 1909–1914." *Historical Journal* 9 (1966): 201–28.

220. Storz, Dieter. *Kriegsbild und Ruestung vor 1914. Europaeische Landstreitkrafe vor dem Ersten Weltkrieg* [*Images of War and Armaments before 1914. Europe's Land Forces before the First World War*]. Herford: Mittler, 1992.

221. Stromberg, Roland. *Redemption by War: The Intellectuals and 1914.* Lawrence: University Press of Kansas, 1982.

222. Sullivan, Charles D. "Stamboul Crossings: German Diplomacy in Turkey, 1908 to 1914." Ph.D. Dissertation, Vanderbilt University, 1977.

223. Sumida, Jon. "British Naval Administration and Policy in the Age of Fisher." *Journal of Military History* 54 (1990): 1–26.

224. Sumida, Jon. *In Defense of Naval Supremacy: Finance, Technology, and British Naval Policy, 1889–1914.* London: Routledge, 1993.

225. Sumida, Jon. "Sir John Fisher and the Dreadnought: The Sources of Naval Mythology." *Journal of Military History* 59 (1995), 619–37.

226. Summers, Ann. "Militarism in Britain before the Great War." *History Workshop Journal* 2 (1976): 104–23.

227. Summerton, N. W. "The Development of British Military Planning for a War against Germany 1904–1914." 2 vols. Ph.D. Dissertation, University of London, 1970.

228. Thaden, E. C. *Russia and the Balkan Alliance of 1912.* University Park: Pennsylvania State University Press, 1965.

229. Trachtenberg, Marc. "The Meaning of Mobilization in 1914." *International Security* 15 (3), 1990–91: 120–30.

230. Travers, T. E. H. "Technology, Tactics, and Morale: Jean de Bloch, the Boer War, and the British Military Theory 1900–1914." *Journal of Modern History* 51 (1979): 264–86.

231. Travers, T. E. H. "The Offensive and the Problem of Innovation in British Military Thought, 1870–1915." *Journal of Contemporary History* 13 (1978): 531–53.

232. Trebilcock, Clive. *The Vickers Brothers. Armaments and Enterprise 1854–1914.* London: Europa, 1977.

233. Trumpener, Ulrich. "War Premeditated? German Intelligence Operations Military 1914." *Central European History* 9 (1976): 58–85.

234. Tunstall, Graydon A. "The Schlieffen Plan: The Diplomacy and Military Strategy of the Central Powers in the East, 1905–1914." Ph.D. Dissertation, Rutgers University, 1975.

235. Turner, L. C. F. *Origins of the First World War.* New York: Norton, 1970.

236. Uhlig, Ralph. *Die Interparlamentarische Union 1889–1914. Friedenssicherungsbemühungen in Zeitalter des Imperialismus* [*The Inter-Parliamentary Union, 1889–1914. Attempts to Secure Peace in the Age of Imperialism*]. Stuttgart: Steiner, 1988.

237. Ullrich, Völker: "Das deutsche Kalkül in der Julikrise 1914 und die Frage der Englischen Neutralität." *Geschichte in Wissenschaft und Unterricht* 34 (1983): 73–97.

238. Van Dyke, Carl. *Russian Imperial Military Doctrine and Education, 1832–1914.* New York: Greenwood Press, 1990.

239. van Evera, Stephen. "Why Cooperation Failed in 1914." *World Politics* 38 (1985): 80–117.

240. Vogel, Barbara. *Deutsche Russlandpolitik. Das Scheitern des deutschen Weltpolitik unter Bülow 1900–1906* [*Germany's Russian Policy. The Failure of German Global Policy under Buelow, 1900–1906*]. Düsseldorf: Droste, 1973.

241. Wallach, Jehuda. *Anatomie einer Militaerhilfe. Die preussisch-deutsche Militaermissionen in der Türkei, 1835–1919* [*Anatomy of Military Assistance: Prussian-German Military Missions to Turkey, 1835–1919*]. Düsseldorf: Droste, 1976.

242. Wallach, Jehuda. *The Dogma of the Battle of Annihilation,* Westport, CT: Greenwood, 1986.

243. Walser, Ray. *France's Search for a Battle Fleet: Naval Policy and Naval Power, 1898–1914.* New York, Garland, 1992.

244. Wandruszka, A., and P. Urbanitsch, ed. *Die Habsburger Monarchie 1848–1918.* Vol. V, *Die Bewaffnete Macht* [*The Habsburg Monarchy, 1848–1918.* Vol. V, *The Armed Forces*]. Vienna: Akad. der Wissenschaft, 1987.

245. Watt, D. C. "The British Reactions to the Assassination at Sarajevo." *European Studies Review* 1 (1971): 233–47.

246. Weir, Gary. *Building the Kaiser's Navy: The Imperial Naval Office and German Industry in the von Tirpitz Era, 1890–1919.* Annapolis: Naval Institute Press, 1992.

247. Wernecke, Klaus. *Der Wille zur Weltgeltung. Aussenpolitik und Öffentlichkeit am Vorabend des Ersten Weltkrieges* [*The Will to International Standing: Foreign Policy and public Opinion on the Eve of the First World War*]. Düsseldorf: Droste, 1969.

248. Wilfong, Walter T. "Rebuilding the Russian Army, 1905–1914: The Question of a Comprehensive Plan for the Natural Defense." Ph.D. Dissertation, Indiana University, 1977.

249. William, J. J. "The Strategic Background to the Anglo-Russian Entente of August, 1907." *Historical Journal* 9 (1966): 360–73.

250. Williams, Rhodri. *Defending the Empire: The Conservative Party and British Defense Policy, 1899–1915.* New Haven: Yale University Press, 1991.

251. Williamson, Samuel R., Jr. *Austria-Hungary and the Origins of the First World War.* New York, St. Martin's, 1991.

252. Williamson, Samuel R., Jr. "The Origins of the War." *The Oxford Illustrated History of the First World War,* ed. H. Strachan. Oxford: Oxford University Press, 1999: 9–25.

253. Williamson, Samuel R., Jr. *The Politics of Grand Strategy: Britain and France Prepare for War 1904–1914.* Cambridge: Harvard University Press, 1969.

254. Wilson, Keith. "Imperial Interests in the British Decision for War: The Defense of India in Central Asia." *Review of International Studies* 9 (1984): 189–203.

255. Wilson, Keith. *The Policy of the Entente: Essays on the Determinants of British Foreign Policy, 1904–1914.* Cambridge: Cambridge University Press, 1985.

256. Winzen, Peter. *Bülows Weltmachtkonzept* [*Buelow's Concept of Global Policy*]. Boppard: Boldt, 1977.

257. Wohl, Robert. *The Generation of 1914.* London: Weideenfeld & Nicholson,1979.

258. Wohlforth, William C. "The Perception of Power: Russia in the Pre-1914 Balance." *World Politics* 39 (1987): 353–81.

259. Young, Harry. "The Misunderstanding of August 1, 1914." *Journal of Modern History* 48 (1976): 644–665.

260. Zechlin, Egmont. "Die Adriakrise und der 'Kriegsrat' von 8. Dezember 1912." *Krieg und Kriegsrisiko* ["The Adriatic Crisis and the 'war Council' of December 8, 1912" *War and the Risk of War*]. Düesseldorf: Droste, 1979: 11–159.

261. Zechlin, Egmont. "Julikrise und Kriegsausbruch 1914." *Politik und Geschichte: Europa 1914: Krieg und Frieden* ["The July Crisis and the Outbreak of War, 1914," *Policy and History. Europe 1914. War and Peace*]. Ed. Landeszentrale für Politische Bildung. Kiel: 1985.

262. Zuber, Terence. *Inventing the Schlieffen Plan.* Oxford: Oxford University Press, 2002.

2

Germany

Daniel Moran

BIBLIOGRAPHIES AND GENERAL HISTORIES

The Great War marked an epoch in the history of Germany, and it has inspired an immense historical literature. Yet, except in military terms, the war years have not (yet) defined a period within German historiography. Roughly the same can be said of all the war's major losers. As in the cases of Austria-Hungary, Russia, and the Ottoman Empire, the literature on the war in Germany has been disproportionately preoccupied either by the fatality of its consequences or by the impulse to interpret it as a great coming-home-to-roost of chicks hatched years before. Until relatively recently, study of the war has been pulled toward the more encompassing problems of Weimar on the one hand and the *Kaiserreich* on the other. This is by no means a wholly bad thing, since it is all too common for wars to be treated as utterly exceptional episodes. Recent work, moreover, has shown greater immunity to this tendency.

The present essay can do no more than outline the mountain of scholarship devoted to the German conduct and experience of the war. The emphasis is on recent work, on books rather than articles, and as far as possible on work focused on the war years as such. Much of value on the war may be found in the literature on Weimar and the Empire, but space precludes the inclusion of such titles here. If English editions of German works are known to the author, they have been cited in preference to the original.

Few works published before 1970 have been included, on the grounds that anyone following the bibliographic trail backward from more recent scholarship will inevitably encounter the foundational works produced during the preceding half-century. This earlier literature is surveyed in Chickering [37], Gunzenhäuser [88], Rohwer [209], the Gebhardt *Handbook* [62], Showalter [235], and Pollard [194]. The annual bibliographies published since 1960 by the *Bibliothek für Zeitgeschichte* [20] and since 1952 by the Berlin Academy of Science [13] routinely include sections on the First World War. The quarterly bibliographical supplements published by the *Vierteljahrshefte für Zeitgeschichte* are also valuable. These are periodically collected and published in book form [122].

Among general histories the most detailed is the three volume set edited by Fritz Klein [135], which, like much East German scholarship on the war, is preoccupied by a search for harbingers of the DDR. Chickering [38] is excellent, especially considering its length. Kielmansegg [131], Herwig [107], Herzfeld [108], and Mai [163] emphasize military events. The essay collections edited by Geiss [82] and especially Michalka [167] are comprehensive.

WAR AIMS

Napoleon said the most telling question one can ask about a war is "What is the war about?" Whether or not this is true—compare "What is Hamlet about?" for instance—the Germans undoubtedly had a hard time working out a consistent answer for themselves during the war. The problem has remained contentious ever since, to the point where it does not go too far to say that the modern historiography of the Great War in Germany has been shaped above all by this issue. The 1950s saw the publication of two important studies in English, by Hans Gatzke [80] and Henry Cord Meyer [166], both of which emphasized the deep ambition of Germany's objectives. The problem really snapped into focus in the early 1960s, however, thanks to the path-breaking work of Fritz Fischer [76], who argued that the war was deliberately begun, and persisted in, for extravagant territorial objectives that were still cherished by the political and military leadership up to a few months before the war ended.

It is a measure of Fischer's achievement that, despite the polemical character of his work, his basic insistence on the far-reaching nature of German goals is now generally accepted. How these were arrived at, and how seriously they influenced the conduct of the war, remain in dispute. Where Fischer finds consistency and conspiracy, Gerhard Ritter [206] emphasizes the conflict between civil and military authorities, the overweening arrogance of the latter, and the natural escalation of objectives that usually accompanies wars of attrition. Karl-Heinz Janssen [127] has called attention to the confounding influence of the German states, which promoted specific interests at each other's expense, and made the formulation of coherent objectives at the center more difficult. A considerable literature has arisen around German policy in Eastern Europe, where German plans came closest to realization. In addition to the scholarship on Brest-Litovsk, discussed below, there are specialized studies of German policy with respect to Poland [83, 153], Finland [24], the Caucasus [22], the Ukraine [28], and the Baltic [104, 272]. There have been a number of efforts to survey all the arguments and strike some sort of balance. Those by Thompson [256], Mommsen [172], and Jäger [123] are among the most successful.

MILITARY HISTORY

However one conceives German objectives in the First World War, it was certainly the armed forces that were expected to achieve them. Their history remains difficult to reconstruct, however, owing to the destruction of the Potsdam archives at the end of World War II. Although some new material may yet come to light as a result of German reunification and the collapse of the Soviet Union, this is an area where official and regimental histories, memoirs, and older works published between the wars retain a fundamental importance that would otherwise have diminished with the passage of time. All such material is enumerated in the bibliographies and general military histories cited above.

Among Germany's senior leadership, Falkenhayn has been best served by biographers, thanks to the fine work by Afflerbach [1]. It is a puzzle that no comparable effort has been expended on Ludendorff. Kitchen [134] provides a critical portrait, plus one of his chief political agents, the staff officer Max von Bauer [133]. The latter discussion may be compared to Vogt [271]. Barnett [8] includes dispassionate chapters on both Ludendorff and Moltke. Hindenburg's military career has attracted less attention from his biographers than one might expect. The most informative are Bütow [33] and Maser [165]. On Germany's supreme commander, William II, see Deist [49] and the recent biographies by Cecil [36] and Gutsche [90].

A good deal of work on the high command has focused on the prevalence of dissention and dispute within it [51, 89, 144]. The failure of military and naval authorities to coordinate their actions has also been closely studied [103, 239, 241]. On the transfer of command from Falkenhayn to Hindenburg and Ludendorff, see Janssen [125]. Gerhard Rakenius' study of Groener [198] covers the last months of the war and its immediate aftermath.

For an overall appraisal of German military performance, one should turn first to Holger Herwig's essay [105]. Horst Rhode considers the logistical difficulties they faced [205]. For more operational detail, there are a number of good campaign and battle histories: Unruh on Langemarck [266]; Showalter on Tannenberg [236]; Werth on Verdun [279]; Haffner and Venohr [91] and Paul [193] on the Marne; Paschall [192] on the war's final year. Still more basic are several studies of German tactics: Wayne [274] analyzes defensive fighting, while Gudmundsson [87] and Samuels [213] focus on the advent of stormtroops and the recovery of the offensive. On the assimilation of new military technology see Linnenkohl [154] and Zabecki [293]. Hebert's book on mountain warfare [99] is more generally valuable than its specialized title suggests.

The German navy has lately come in for close study, on which see Bird [23] and Herwig [106], as well as the excellent general history of the naval war by Halpern [94], which makes much use of German materials. Tarrant's studies of Jutland [252] and the submarine war [253] are enormously informative. Germany's nascent air force is not quite so well served, but see Kilduff [132] and Morrow [179].

A great deal of attention has been paid to the experience, as distinct from the conduct, of the war. The multifaceted nature of this subject doubtless accounts for the fact that it has mainly been address via edited volumes, rather than monographs. The best are those by Wette [280], Knoch [139], Renz [201], and Hirschfeld et al. [110]. Ulrich [264] offers a critical analysis of the military mail, a critical source for much work in this field. The issue of desertion has received careful attention from Lipp [155], Ziemann [295], and Jahr [124]; while those taken prisoner have been studied by Gerald Davis [43]. The wounded, and the provisions for their care, are the subject of a good study by Robert Whalen [283]. And of course all those who survived the war became veterans, for which see the studies by Berghahn [12] and Diehl [53].

INTERNATIONAL RELATIONS

Germany, like its opponents, confronted three basic diplomatic problems during the war: how to maintain cooperative and efficient relations with its allies; how to bring the war to an end on terms that served its interests; and how to forestall any changes in the military balance that might make victory impossible. Although none of the main belligerents succeeded across the board, Germany's failures in all three areas were grave, and they have commanded a good deal of attention from scholars.

The best general study of wartime diplomacy is Stevenson [249], who presents German conduct in a comparative light. L. L. Farrar [66] is brief and incisive. Germany's most important ally was of course Austria-Hungary, on whose behalf Germany had putatively gone to war in the first place. Thereafter relations between the two Central Powers were uniformly rocky, as Silberstein [238] and Shanafelt [233] show. This was so in part because of German impatience with Austria's poor military performance, which undermined strategic coordination between the alliance partners [39, 210], and more generally because it proved difficult to conceive of any outcome to the war that would serve the interests of both parties [129]. This manifested itself in a number of ways, notably in disputes over territorial and political arrangements in Eastern Europe [153]. By the middle of the war Austria was clearly prepared to settle for far less than anything Germany would consider, a divergence of views that it turn made it difficult for the Central Powers to formulate terms of their own—a problem highlighted by Wolfgang Steglich's studies of the inter-allied diplomacy [243, 245, 246].

Whether Italy can be considered a German ally at the outset of the war is a matter of semantics: German and Austrian war plans both took for granted that Italy would abandon the Triple Alliance once the shooting started. That Italy should have become a belligerent on the other side was nevertheless a setback—on which see Montecone [177] and Muhr [186]. In contrast, the Ottoman Empire's entry into the war on the German side, however likely it may seem in retrospect, could not have been counted on in advance. German efforts to culti-vate and manage its relations with Istanbul are detailed by Ulrich Trumpener [260], while Frank Weber shows how even the good fortune of Ottoman support could become a source of friction between Germany and Austria [275].

Why the First World War lasted as long as it did—why, in the face of over-whelming military futility, peace should have proven so elusive—is at least as difficult a question to answer as that of why the war began. Although one might argue that the military facts in 1915 were already entirely conducive to a quick settlement, 1917 appears to have been the year the war truly might have ended, but did not. Wolfgang Steglich's work [242–246] explores the intense interaction of military and diplomatic events, interest-group politics, and so forth in meticu-lous fashion. L. L. Farrar's essays are a compact treatment of the same period [64, 65]. The introduction to Wilhelm Winterhager's study of Danish mediation efforts [288] surveys the overall state of research. A recent monograph on Ger-many's repeated attempts to conclude a separate peace with Japan [98] may serve as a reminder that the First World War was indeed a global conflict.

With no country were Germany's wartime relations of more critical impor-tance than with the United States. The essays edited by Hans-Jürgen Schröder [223] provide an outstanding overview, ranging far beyond the diplomatic, to include cultural and economic relations as well. As was often the case, German policy combined elements of subversion and reasonableness. For the first, see Friedhelm Koopmann [142]; for the second, Torsten Oppelland [191], who demonstrates how large America's attitude loomed among members of the Reichstag. Reinhard Doerries' biography of Germany's ambassador to Wash-ington, Count Bernstorff, is a fine survey of American-German relations to 1917 [54]. Schwabe [226, 228] is good on German-American relations after America entered the war.

On Brest-Litovsk, the culmination of German policy and strategy in the East, the best general study is still John Wheeler-Bennett [285], which can be supple-mented by the documents edited by Hahlweg [93]. Winfried Baumgart has stud-ied the relatively neglected topic of German policy toward Russia after the treaty was signed [11]. His comparative analysis of Brest-Litovsk and Versailles [10] is also important, though not entirely convincing in its effort to portray both treaties as compromises rather than *Diktats*.

Brest-Litovsk was not the only treaty between Germany and its eastern oppo-nents. A separate peace with the Ukraine, concluded a month earlier, has recently been interpreted as something of a bright spot in Ukrainian national history [113]. The settlement with Romania is also the subject of a recent mono-graph [27].

DOMESTIC POLITICS

The history of German domestic politics during the war is dominated by three issues: civil-military relations; the initial, halting steps toward the assertion of parliamentary authority after 1916; and the management of the war economy, discussed in the next section, below. Even had Germany avoided ultimate defeat, there can be little doubt that the net result of four years of war would have been a constitutional crisis of major proportions [116].

The starting point for any investigation of civil-military relations is the collection of documents edited by Wilhelm Deist [44]. The last two volumes of Ritter's *Sword and Scepter* [206] have stood the test of time reasonably well, but their basic sympathy for the German civilian leadership is not universally shared. Karl-Heinz Janssen [126] and Bruno Thoss [257] have been less inclined to portray civilians as well-meaning dupes, while Falkenhayn in particular has recently found a strong advocate in Heinz Kraft [144]. Farrar [67] raises the question of how far military authorities, and the strategic problems they were charged with solving, may have influenced the decision for war. Bernd Stegemann [241] considers the same issue in the context of the submarine campaign in 1917. Civil-military rivalry also extended into the arena of public opinion, on which see Stegmann [247].

Among German political leaders, a good deal of attention has fallen on the figure of the Imperial Chancellor, Theobald von Bethmann Hollweg, of whom Paul von Metternich observed that he exemplified the adage about the road to hell being paved with good intentions. Modern scholarship, surveyed by Klaus Hildebrand [109], has been hard pressed to improve on Metternich's judgment. It is certainly shared by Bethmann's modern biographers [128, 269, 291], and arguably by Bethmann himself, whose memoirs have recently been republished in fine fashion by Jost Dülffer [19].

Reinhard Schiffers [218] and Dieter Grosser [86] treat the uneasy relationship of German parliamentarians to the Kaiser's government on the one hand and to democracy on the other. For a more optimistic appraisal of the wartime parliamentary regime see Rauh [200]. Among political parties, the SPD and the Center Party have received the most attention. On the former, Susanne Miller [168] is outstanding. On political Catholicism, see Rudolf Morsey [180] and Heinrich Lutz [157], both of whom place the main weight on the early years of the Weimar Republic; and Klaus Epstein's splendid if occasionally uncritical biography of Matthias Erzberger [61], the preeminent parliamentary figure of the war. Robert Wheeler [284] is essential on the Independent Socialists. On the origins of the German Communist Party, see Wohlgemuth [290] and the pertinent chapters in Weitz [277]. The dynamics of party politics further to the right are dissected in Hagenlücke [92] and in Scheck [234], and in Dirk Stegmann's account of the feud between Stresemann, leader of the National Liberals, and Alfred Hugenberg, chief director of Krupp and paladin of the anti-democratic right [248].

The best histories of state politics in wartime are Klaus-Peter Müller's study of Badenese particularism [187], Hartwig Thieme's book on the National Liberals in Prussia [255], and two works on Bavaria, by Willy Albrecht [2] and Karl-Ludwig Ay [6], both of whom emphasize the deep alienation of Bavarian opinion from Berlin. Had the war continued, a Bavarian effort to conclude a separate peace was not out of the question.

For politics beyond the confines of parties and institutions, the place to begin is Mommsen's work on public opinion under Bethmann's administration [173, 174]. Gottfried Schramm [222] analyses the integrative effects of the war in Germany and Russia, which, needless to say, were not sufficient in either case to forestall serious disenchantment. Francis Carsten's study of the peace movement in Germany and England [35] offers the advantages of a comparative perspective; Wilfried Eisenbeiss's fine dissertation [59] is incisive on the German side. Ludwig Quidde, whose unflinching pacifism would win him the Nobel Peace Prize in 1927, wrote a memoir of the German anti-war movement that was only discovered in 1979 [196]. Other issues could also bring people into the streets. Richard Evans has written a solid account of civil disturbances in Hamburg, motivated by grievances over suffrage [63]. This is also a rich literature on labor unrest, discussed below.

WAR ECONOMY AND INDUSTRIAL MOBILIZATION

The history of the German war economy revolves around two issues: the impact of the war on relations between labor and capital; and the inflationary consequences of the way the war was financed. The best introduction to both problems is the work of Gerald Feldman [70, 72, 73], who has argued that the exigencies of war production shifted relations between labor and capital toward rapprochement at the expense of the middle classes, who suffered material disadvantages and became more disenchanted, demanding, and "proletarian" in their outlook—an argument elaborated in various ways by Jürgen Kocka [140], Andreas Kunz [149], Peter Lyth [158], and Herman Lebovics [152]. Feldman's work, like that of Carl-Ludwig Holtfrerich [111] and Michael Schneider [220], suggests that the basic economic dynamics of the Weimar Republic are rooted in the inflationary pressures created by wartime borrowing, and more generally in the willingness of business to pay inflated labor costs, a habit acquired in wartime, which would keep wages rising in advance of real productivity throughout the 1920s. It is, in other words, the economic consequences of the war, rather than of the peace, that mattered in the long run.

There is no comprehensive general history of the war economy as such. Konrad Roesler [208] and Hans Ehlert [58] offer broad treatments of financial and administrative matters, while Hopbach [112] and Buschmann [32] consider the outlook of the industrialists. So does Hattke [96], specifically with respect to the economic exploitation of Belgium. Lothar Burchardt [30] and Michael Geyer [85] provide essential background.

For Germany's initial efforts at economic mobilization see the studies of Walther Rathenau by Burchardt [31] and Gerhard Hecker [101]. Rathenau is a figure of enormous consequence for the German war effort. The best biography is by Ernst Schulin [224], whose interpretation oddly resembles that of modern biographers of Bethmann Hollweg: like the "chancellor without qualities," Rathenau, the man with every talent, emerges as a deeply conflicted figure who can never quite master the moral ambiguities imposed by circumstances.

No aspect of the war economy has been investigated more thoroughly than the history of industrial workers. The best overview is provided by Feldman's seminal monograph [70] and the essays edited by Gunther Mai [159]. Zunkel [298], Armeson [5], Ratz [199], Hecker [100], and Tobin [258] focus on the militarization of labor and on the relations among union leaders, capitalists, and military authorities. The labyrinthine administrative arrangements that economic mobilization engendered are covered in Ehlert [58]. On trade union organization see the enormous study by Hans-Joachim Bieber [21] and the collection of documents edited by Klaus Schönhoven [221].

Recent scholarship on the working class in wartime features a great many local studies, not all of which live up to their claims to be of more than local significance. Those that do include Friedhelm Boll on Lower Saxony [26], Volker Ullrich on Hamburg [261], Hermann Schäfer on Baden [215], Merith Niehuss on Augsburg [188], and Klaus-Dieter Schwarz on Nuremberg [230]; Jürgen Reulecke on the Rhineland [202–204]; and Manfred Scheck [216] and Gunther Mai [164] on Württemberg. For foreign workers in Germany, see Friedrich Zunkel [297].

The most important scholarship on women during the war has been done by Ute Daniel [42], whose results challenge the traditional interpretation of the war as, on the whole, a liberating experience for women. Stefan Bajohr [9] presents the experience of the First World War against that of the Second. Ute Stoll [250] and Anneliese Seidel [232] are important local studies, focusing on official policy toward women and workers in general. For the psychosocial impact of the war on gender relations, see Kundrus [148] For what happens when the men come home, see Richard Bessel [16].

Shortly after the war ended, the *Reichsgesundheitsamt* calculated that 763,000 German civilians had died, largely owing to the effects of malnutrition. The management of the war economy in the countryside was therefore a matter of enormous consequence, as Avner Offer has demonstrated [190]. Yaney [292] describes the administrative apparatus. Agricultural mobilization inevitably had political repercussions, on which see the relevant chapters in Flemming [78], Müller's study of Baden [187], and Bernard Sicken's account on conditions in Wesel [237]. The problem of keeping everyone fed stemmed on the one hand from the effects of the Allied blockade [270, 150, 207] and on the other from the draining of rural manpower into war industries and the armed forces [171, 225, 296]. The overall consequences of economic warfare for the health and well-being of the civilian population are summarized by Paul Weindling [276] and Armin Triebel [259].

CULTURE AND SOCIETY

It was recognized long before 1914 that a major war would transform German society. Exactly how it would do so and what direction such a transformation would take were less easy to foresee, and they remain difficult problems to this day. The best routes into this complex of issues are probably via the first chapter of Bessell [18], which provides a compact, basically statistical overview of the war's social consequences, or through Mai's suggestive essay on the *Burgfrieden* [161]. His study of Württemberg includes a valuable review of the literature [164].

There have been a lot of well-done works recently on the theme of "mobilization," including the important comparative volume edited by John Horne [115] and specialized studies by Reinhard Rürup [211], Karl von See [231] Christian Geinitz [81], Theodor Raithel [197], and Jeffrey Verhey [268]. One point of mobilization was, of course, national integration, on which see Kruse [147] and the first part of Fritzsche [79]. The attitude of artists and intellectuals toward the war is well studied in Flasch [77], Denham [52], and Mommsen [175, 176], whose ideas are summarized in English in Horne [115].

The history of daily life among civilians during the war has been investigated chiefly via local case studies, for instance Volker Ullrich on Hamburg [262], Hans-Ulrich Ludewig on Brunswick [156], and Reinhard Oberschelp and Karl-Heinz Grotjahn on Lower Saxony [189], the last a major collection of documents. Winter and Robert [287] is informative on conditions in Berlin. The essays edited by Peter Knoch [139] include some useful reflections on the methodological requirements for this sort of history.

As Obershelp and Grotjahn propose, the experience of the war on the home front often came down to "steel and turnips"—ever-increasing demands for work and "efficiency," and less and less to eat in the bargain. It almost goes without saying that a disproportionate number of those undergoing these experiences were women and children. Ute Daniel's work on female workers has already been mentioned. Ursula von Gersdorff [84] carries the same theme through 1945. Sabine Hering [102] focuses on the ideological impact of war work for the women's movement, while Cornelie Usborne [267] considers the related issue of "pronatalism" as an element of wartime mentality. As to the children for whom working women continued to care, Klaus Saul has studied the day-to-day life of those still in school [214], while Jürgen Reulecke [203] and Gudrun Fiedler [75] consider youth movements within the middle class. One social group of importance to both women and children was doctors, on which see Eckart and Gradmann [57].

The control of public opinion in wartime was a priority for all belligerent governments, and in this area the Germans were neither more determined nor more successful than their opponents. Measures to control the German public mind are surveyed by Koszyk [143] and Creutz [40], and deconstructed in Quandt and Schichtel [195]. Ungern-Sternberg von Pürkel [265] treats an important episode of intellectual complicity in the regulation of ideas. Hans Barkhausen [7] and Klaus Kreimeier [145] examine efforts to adapt the nascent medium of film to official purposes, which also figures in Stark [240].

Whether censorship and propaganda improved Germany's chances to win the war is hard to say. That they helped form the political culture of the postwar era seems beyond dispute. This can be seen clearly in studies of how Germans thought about and remembered two symbolically resonant "episodes" of the war: one that really did occur—the defeat on the Marne [151]—and another, a mythical struggle against partisan warfare in occupied Belgium [286], that did not. Richard Bessel [17] and David Welch [278] consider the whole issue in more general terms.

Teachers and clergymen, two groups with privileged access to the public, have also come in for scholarly investigation. The former have been well studied by Klaus Schwabe [227, 229] and Gunther Mai [160]. The best introduction to the views of the Protestant clergy is a collection of public statements, from Germany and elsewhere, assembled by Gerhard Besier [15]; on the Catholic side, see Heinrich Missalla [170].

However great the integrative effects of total war may have been, they generally stopped short of embracing German Jews, whose experiences are surveyed by Werner Mosse and Arnold Paucker [185] and by Christard Hoffman in Horne [115]. George Mosse has contributed a typically penetrating essay [182]. Egmont Zechlin examines official policy [294]. For one particularly chilling episode, the army's "Jewish Census" of 1916, see the articles by Werner Angress [3, 4].

The emotional and cognitive consequences of organized violence on an unprecedented scale are the subject of a series of stimulating essays by Bernd Hüppauf [117–120] and a book by Klaus Vondung [273]. Modris Eksteins's celebrated *Rites of Spring* [60] is insightful in its treatment of German material, as are the German chapter of Robert Wohl's *The Generation of 1914* [289] and George Mosse's work on how war is experienced, assimilated, and remembered [183, 184]. Manfred Hanisch [95] also takes death and remembrance as his theme. Finally, no one interested in the state of mind of the *Frontkämpfer* should overlook Klaus Theweleit's astonishing *Male Phantasies* [254].

DEFEAT AND REVOLUTION

In the last nine months of 1918 a variety of forces—strategic miscalculation, economic hardship, political disenchantment, and psychological fatigue—all came together with an increasing preponderance of enemy strength to defeat Germany's armed forces and bring down the empire. The best general history of the Revolution, by Kluge [137], emphasizes events after the Armistice. A. J. Ryder [212], David Morgan [178], and John Mishark [169], all focus on ideological and organizational factors on the German left, and are more informative about wartime events leading up to the collapse. So are the regional studies by Jürgen Tampke on the Ruhr [251] and Karl Bosl on Bavaria [29]. Francis Carsten places Germany's experience in a broader context [35].

Klaus Schwabe demonstrates the decisive influence of American policy on German conduct at the end [228], while Leo Haupts presents a strong defense of German efforts to achieve a compromise peace [97].

The military developments that set the revolutionary dynamic in motion are appraised by Eberhard Kessel [130] and Wilhelm Deist [46, 50], the former focusing on the collapse of morale at the highest levels of the army, the latter on the state of mind of common soldiers. Dieter Dreetz examines the efforts of the military leadership to salvage the remnants of a beaten force [55]. Deist has also done pioneering work on the declining state of naval morale [48] and on the "suicide sortie" order that provided the spark for the tinder [47]. There is also a good study of the mutinies in English by Daniel Horn [114].

As in all modern revolutions, the posture of the armed forces was critical to shaping the course of events, and also in limiting the revolution's extent. The best general study is by Kluge [137], who has also written a specialized article on the Württemberg militia [136]. Ernst-Heinrich Schmidt focuses on the "home army"—forces stationed in the interior of Germany [219]—while Dreetz [56] and Wette [281] examine the conduct of demobilized forces returning from the front.

For relations between the armed forces and the working class, normally strained both before and during the war, see Deist [45] and Kruse [146]. Hürten [121] and Kohlhaas [141] argue for the nonrevolutionary character of the Soldiers' Councils, most of which cooperated with the army leadership and Ebert's government. Mai [162] provides a more detailed social analyses of these groups.

Nearly all the histories of the working class in wartime discussed in the section on The War Economy, above, deal with the role of workers in the Revolution. For a general appraisal, see Feldman, Kolb, and Rürup [74]. Finally, there are two articles by Gerald Feldman on the Stinnes-Legien agreement [68, 69], which together with the Ebert-Groener pact constituted the last dregs of the Fortress Peace with which the war began.

FURTHER RESEARCH

The central challenges for historians of Germany in the First World War, as perhaps for students of all the major belligerents, are those of synthesis and comparison. The German literature on the war, outstanding in many ways, is notably more specialized and fragmented than that of, say, Great Britain, a reflection in part of the gaps that exist in the German archives (especially the military ones) and also of diverging national historiographical traditions. Nevertheless, a beginning scholar contemplating work in the field could do worse than consider recent work on British social and cultural history during the war (described elsewhere in this volume) and seek to apply similarly syncretic methods on the German side. A general plea must also be made on behalf of comparative history, the universal solvent for all myths of national exceptionalism—in which German history has always been fertile—and the only way to be sure which elements of a nation's experience are indeed unique.

Among specific problems that could clearly do with additional attention, some goods ones are: all aspects of the conduct of the war on the Eastern Front, far less well served than the war in the West; the reality, or lack of if, of the so-called *Burgfrieden;* the social history of rural groups and the countryside; German relations with the Ottoman Empire; and the problem of sustaining social mobilization once the initial excitement of 1914 had worn off (an issue central to the question of why the war managed to go on so long). If there is a unifying thread linking the best current work on Germany during the war, even in the military sphere, it is a shared concern with cultural issues, a trend that seems likely to continue for a while longer.

BIBLIOGRAPHY

1. Afflerbach, Holger. *Falkenhayn: Politisches Denken und Handeln im Kaiserreich.* Munich: Oldenbourg, 1996.

2. Albrecht, Willy. *Landtag und Regierung in Bayern am Vorabend der Revolution von 1918* [Parliament and Government in Bavaria on the Eve of the Revolution of 1918]. Berlin: Duncker und Humblot, 1968.

3. Angress, Werner T. "Das deutsche Militär und die Juden im Ersten Weltkrieg." *Militärgeschichtliche Mitteilungen* 19 (1976): 77–146.

4. Angress, Werner T. "The German Army's 'Judenzählung' of 1916." *Leo Baeck Institute Yearbook* 23 [1978]: 117–35.

5. Armeson, Robert B. *Total War and Compulsory Labor: A Study of the Military-Industrial Complex in Germany during World War I.* The Hague: M. Nijhoff, 1964.

6. Ay, Karl-Ludwig. *Die Entstehung einer Revolution: Die Volksstimmung in Bayern während des Ersten Weltkrieges* [Origins of a Revolution: Popular Opinion in Bavaria during the First World War]. Berlin: Duncker und Humblot, 1968.

7. Barkhausen, Hans. *Filmpropaganda für Deutschland im Ersten und Zweiten Weltkrieg.* Hildeshiem and New York: Olms Presse, 1982.

8. Barnett, Correlli. *The Swordbearers: Supreme Command in the First World War.* London: Eyre & Spottiswoode, 1963.

9. Bajohr, Stefan. *Die Hälfte der Fabrik: Geschichte der Frauenarbeit in Deutschland 1914 bis 1945* [Half the Factory: The History of Female Labor in Germany, 1914 to 1945]. Marburg: Verlag Arbeiterbewegung und Gesellschaftswissen, 1979.

10. Baumgart, Winfried. "Brest-Litovsk und Versailles: Ein Vergleich zweier Friedensschlüsse." *Historische Zeitschrift* 210 (1970): 583–619.

11. Baumgart, Winfried. *Deutsche Ostpolitik, 1918: Von Brest-Litovsk bis zum Ende des Ersten Weltkrieges.* Munich: Oldenbourg, 1966.

12. Berghahn, Volker R. *Der Stahlhelm: Bund der Frontsoldaten.* Düsseldorf: Drosto, 1966.

13. Berlin-Brandenburgischen Akademie der Wissenschaften. *Jahresberichte für Deutsche Geschichte.* East Berlin: Akademie Verlag, 1952.

14. Bermbach, Udo. *Vorformen parlamentarischer Kabinettsbildung: Der Interfraktionelle Ausschuß 1917/18 und die Parlamentarisierung der Reichsregierung* [Precursors to the Creation of the Parliamentary Cabinet: The Interparty Committee of 1917–18 and the Parliamentarization of the Imperial Government]. Cologne and Opladen: Westdeutscher Verlag, 1967.

15. Besier, Gerhard. *Die protestantischen Kirchen Europas im Ersten Weltkrieg.* Göttingen: Vandenhoeck & Ruprecht, 1984.

16. Bessel, Richard. " 'Eine nicht allzu große Beunruhigung des Arbeitsmarktes': Frauenarbeit und Demobilmachung in Deutschland nach dem Ersten Weltkrieg ['A not-so-great disturbance of the Labor Market': Female Labor and Demobilization in Germany after the First World War]." *Geschichte und Gesellschaft* 9 (1983).

17. Bessel, Richard. "The Great War in German Memory: The Soldiers of the First World War, Demobilization, and Weimar Political Culture." *German History* 6 (1988).

18. Bessel, Richard. *Germany after the First World War.* Oxford and New York: Oxford University Press, 1993.

19. Bethmann Hollweg, Theobald von. *Betrachtungen zum Weltkriege.* 2 vols. Berlin: R. Hobbing, 1919–21; reprinted, 1989, edited by Jost Dülffer.

20. Bibliothek für Zeitgeschichte. *Jahresbibliographie.* Frankfurt, 1960–1989; Coblenz, 1990.

21. Bieber, Hans-Joachim. *Gewerkschaften in Krieg und Revolution: Arbeiterbewegung, Industrie, Staat und Militär in Deutschland, 1914–1920* [Industrial Works in War and Revolution: The Labor Movement, Industry, the State, and the Military in Germany, 1914–1920]. Hamburg: Christians, 1981.

22. Bihl, Wolfdieter. *Die Kaukasus-Politik der Mittelmächte.* Vienna: Boehlau, 1975.

23. Bird, Keith W. *German Naval History: A Guide to the Literature.* New York: Garland, 1985.

24. Böhme, Helmut. "Die deutsche Kriegszielpolitik und Finnland im Jahre 1918 [The Politics of German War Aims and Finland in 1918]." In Imanuel Geiss and Bernd Jürgen Wendt, eds., *Deutschland in der Weltpolitik des 19. und 20. Jahrhunderts.* Düsseldorf: Bertelsmann Universitätsverlag, 1973, 377–96.

25. Boll, Friedhelm. "Spontaneität, der Basis und politische Funktion des Streiks 1914 bis 1918: Das Beispiel Braunschweig [Spontaneity as the Basis and Political Function of Strikes, 1914–1918: The Example of Brunswick]." *Archiv für Sozialgeschichte* 17 (1977): 337–66.

26. Boll, Friedhelm. *Massenbewegungen in Niedersachsen, 1906–1920: Eine sozialgeschichtliche Untersuchung zu den unterschiedlichen Entwicklungstypen Braunschweig und Hannover* [Mass Movements in Lower Saxony, 1906–1920: A Social-Historical Investigation of the Distinctive Modes of Development in Brunswick and Hanover]. Bonn: Verlag Neue Gesellschaft, 1981.

27. Bornemann, Elke. *Der Frieden von Bukarest, 1918.* Frankfurt: Lang, 1978.

28. Borowsky, Peter. *Deutsche Ukrainepolitik 1918: Unter besonderer Berücksichtigung der Wirtschaftsfragen* [German Policy toward Ukraine, 1918: With Particular Reference to Economic Questions]. Lübeck and Hamburg: Matthiesen, 1970.

29. Bosl, Karl, ed. *Bayern im Umbruch* [Bavaria in Upheaval]. Munich and Vienna. R. Oldenbourg, 1969.

30. Burchardt, Lothar. "Die Auswirkungen der Kriegswirtschaft auf die deutsche Zivilbevölkerung im Ersten und im Zweiten Weltkrieg [The Consequences of the War Economy for the German Civil Population in the First and Second World Wars]." *Militärgeschichtliche Mitteilungen* 15 (1974): 65–98.

31. Burchardt, Lothar. "Walther Rathenau und die Anfänge der deutschen Rohstoffbewirtschaftung im Ersten Weltkrieg [Walther Rathenau and the Origins of the German Raw Materials Management in the First World War]." *Tradition* 15 (1970): 169–96.

32. Buschmann, Birgit. *Unternehmenspolitik in der Kriegswirtschaft und in der Inflation: Die Daimler-Motoren-Gesellschaft 1914–1923* [Entrepreneurial Politics in the War Economy and the Inflation: The Daimler Motor Works, 1914–1923]. Stuttgart: F. Steiner, 1998.

33. Bütow, Wolf J. *Hindenburg: Heerführer und Ersatzkaiser* [Hindenburg: Military Leader and Substitute Emperor]. Bergisch Gladbach: Lübbe, 1984.

34. Carsten, Francis L. *Revolution in Central Europe, 1918–1919.* London: M. Temple Smith, 1972.

35. Carsten, Francis L. *War against War: British and German Radical Movements in the First World War.* Berkeley: University of California Press: 1982.

36. Cecil, Lamar. *William II: Emperor and Exile, 1900–1941.* Chapel Hill: University of North Carolina Press, 1996.

37. Chickering, Roger. "Imperial Germany at War," in *Imperial Germany: A Historiographical Companion.* Westport, CT: Greenwood Press, 1996, 489–512.

38. Chickering, Roger. *Imperial Germany and the Great War, 1914–1918.* Cambridge: Cambridge University Press, 1998.

39. Craig, Gordon A. "The World War I Alliance of the Central Powers in Retrospect: The Military Cohesion of the Alliance." *Journal of Modern History* 37 (1965): 336–44.

40. Creutz, M. *Die Pressepolitik des kaiserlichen Regierung während des Ersten Weltkriegs* [The Press Policy of the Imperial Government during the First World War]. Frankfurt a.M., 1996.

41. Cron, Hermann. *Geschichte des Deutschen Heeres im Weltkrieg 1914–1918.* Berlin: K. Siegismund, 1937.

42. Daniel, Ute. *The War From Within: German Working-Class Women in the First World War.* Oxford: Oxford University Press, 1997.

43. Davis, Gerald H. "Deutsche Kriegsgefangene im Ersten Weltkrieg in Russland [German Prisoners of War in the First World War in Russia]." *Militärgeschichtliche Mitteilungen* 31 (1982): 37–49

44. Deist, Wilhelm, ed. *Militär und Innenpolitik im Weltkrieg 1914–1918.* 2 vols. Düsseldorf: Droste, 1970.

45. Deist, Wilhelm. "Armee und Arbeiterschaft, 1905–1918." *Francia* 2 (1974): 458–81.

46. Deist, Wilhelm. "Der militärische Zusammenbruch des Kaiserreiches: Zur Realität der 'Dolchstoßlegende' [The Military Collapse of the Empire: On the Reality of the 'Stab-in-the-Back Legend']." In Ursula Büttner, ed., *Das Unrechtsregime: Internationale Forschung über den Nationalsozialismus,* vol. 1: *Ideologie, Herrschaftssystem, Wirkung in Europa.* Hamburg: Christians, 1986.

47. Deist, Wilhelm. "Die Politik der Seekriegsleitung und die Rebellion der Flotte Ende Oktober 1918 [The Politics of the War at Sea and the Fleet Rebellion of October 1918]." *Vierteljahrshefte für Zeitgeschichte* 14 (1966): 341–68.

48. Deist, Wilhelm. "Die Unruhen in der Marine, 1917–18 [Unrest in the Navy, 1917–1918]." *Marine-Rundschau* 168 (1971): 325–43.

49. Deist, Wilhelm. "Kaiser Wilhelm II als oberster Kriegsherr." In John Röhl, ed., *Der Ort Kaiser Wilhelm II in der deutschen Geschichte.* Munich: R. Oldenbourg, 1991, 25–42.

50. Deist, Wilhelm. "Verdeckter Militärstreik im Kriegsjahr 1918? [The Concealed Military Strike of 1918?]" In Wolfram Wette, ed., *Der Krieg des kleinen Mannes: Eine Militärgeschichte von unten.* Munich: Piper, 1992, 146–68.

51. Deist, Wilhelm. "Zur Institution des Militärbefehlshabers und Obermilitärbefehlshabers im Ersten Weltkrieg [The Institutions of Military Command in the First World War]." *Jahrbuch für die Geschichte Mittel- und Ostdeutschlands* 13/14 (1965): 222–40.

52. Denham, Scott D. *Visions of War: Ideologies and Images of War in German Literature before and after the Great War.* Berne and New York: P. Lang, 1992.

53. Diehl, James M. "The Organization of German Veterans, 1917–1919." *Archiv für Sozialgeschichte* 11 (1971): 141–84.

54. Doerries, Reinhard R. *Imperial Challenge: Ambassador Count Bernstorff and German-American Relations, 1908–17.* Translated by Christa D. Shannon. Chapel Hill and London: University of North Carolina Press, 1989.

55. Dreetz, Dieter. "Bestrebungen der OHL zur Rettung des Kerns der imperialistischen deutschen Armee in der Novemberrevolution [Efforts by the Supreme Command to Save the Core of the Imperial German Army during the November Revolution]." *Zeitschrift für Militärgeschichte* 8 (1969): 50–66.

56. Dreetz, Dieter. "Rückführung des Westheeres und Novemberrevolution [The Retreat of the Army in the West and the November Revolution]." *Zeitschrift für Militärgeschichte* 7 (1968): 578–89.

57. Eckart, Wolfgang U., and Christoph Gradmann, eds. *Die Medizin und der Erste Weltkrieg.* Pfaffenweiler: Centaurus-Verlagsgesellschaft, 1996.

58. Ehlert, Hans Gotthard. *Die wirtschaftliche Zentralbehörde des Deutschen Reiches 1914 bis 1919* [The Central Economic Administration of the German Empire, 1914–1919]. Wiesbaden: F. Steiner, 1982.

59. Eisenbeiss, Wilfried. *Die bürgerliche Friedensbewegung in Deutschland während des Ersten Weltkrieges: Organisation, Selbstverständnis und politische Praxis, 1913/14–1919* [German Peace Movements during the First World War: Organization, Self-Image, and Political Practice, 1913/14–1919]. Frankfurt and Bern: Lang, 1980.

60. Eksteins, Modris. *Rites of Spring: The Great War and the Birth of the Modern Age.* Boston: Houghton Mifflin, 1989.

61. Epstein, Klaus. *Matthias Erzberger and the Dilemma of German Democracy.* Princeton: Princeton University Press, 1959.

62. Erdmann, Karl Dietrich. *Der Erste Weltkrieg.* In Herbert Grundmann, ed., *[Gebhardt] Handbuch der deutschen Geschichte,* vol 4, part 1. Stuttgart: Ernst Klett Verlag, 1973.

63. Evans, Richard J. " 'Red Wednesday' in Hamburg: Social Democrats, Police and Lumpenproletariat in the Suffrage Disturbances of 17 January 1916." *Social History* 4 (1979): 1–31.

64. Farrar, L. L., Jr. "Opening to the West: German Efforts to Conclude a Separate Peace with England, July 1917–March 1918." *Canadian Journal of History* 10 (1975): 73–90.

65. Farrar, L. L., Jr. "Separate Peace—General Peace—Total War. The Crisis in German Policy during the Spring of 1917." *Militärgeschichtliche Mitteilungen* 20 (1976): 51–80.

66. Farrar, L. L., Jr. *Divide and Conquer: German Efforts to Conclude a Separate Peace, 1914–1918.* New York: Columbia University Press, 1978.

67. Farrar, L. L., Jr. *The Short-War Illusion: German Policy, Strategy and Domestic Affairs, August–December, 1914.* Santa Barbara, Calif.: ABC-Clio 1973.

68. Feldman, Gerald D. "German Business between War and Revolution: The Origins of the Stinnes-Legien Agreement," in Gerhard A. Ritter, ed. *Entstehung und Wandel der Modernen Gesellschaft: Festschrift für Hans Rosenberg zum 65. Geburtstag.* Berlin: De Gruyter, 1970, 312–41.

69. Feldman, Gerald D. "The Origins of the Stinnes-Legien Agreement: A Documentation." *Internationale wissenschaftliche Korrespondenz zur Geschichte der deutschen Arbeiterbewegung* 19/20 (1973): 45–103.

70. Feldman, Gerald D. *Army, Industry, and Labor in Germany, 1914–1918.* Princeton: Princeton University Press, 1966.

71. Feldman, Gerald D., ed. *German Imperialism, 1914–1918: The Development of a Historical Debate.* New York: Doubleday, 1972.

72. Feldman, Gerald D. *Iron and Steel in the German Inflation, 1916–1923.* Princeton: Princeton University Press, 1977.

73. Feldman, Gerald D. *The Great Disorder: Politics, Economics, and Society in the German Inflation, 1914–1924.* Oxford: Oxford University Press, 1993.

74. Feldman, Gerald D., Eberhard Kolb, and Reinhard Rürup. "Die Massenbewegungen der Arbeiterschaft in Deutschland am Ende des Ersten Weltkrieges (1917–1920) [Mass Movements among the Workers in Germany at the End of the First World War]." *Politische Vierteljahreschrift* 13 (1972): 84–105.

75. Fiedler, Gudrun. *Jugend im Krieg: Bürgerliche Jugendbewegung, Erster Weltkrieg, und sozialer Wandel, 1914–1925* [Youth in War: Civilian Youth Movements, the First World War, and Social Change, 1914–1925]. Cologne: Verlag Wissenschaft und Politik, 1989.

76. Fischer, Fritz. *Germany's Aims in the First World War.* New York: W. W. Norton, 1967.

77. Flasch, Kurt. *Die geistige Mobilmachung: Die deutschen Intellectuellen und der Erste Weltkrieg* [Intellectual Mobilization: German Intellectuals and the First World War]. Berlin: Fest, 2000.

78. Flemming, Jens. *Landwirtschaftliche Interessen und Demokratie: Ländliche Gesellschaft, Agrarverbände und Staat, 1890–1925* [Agrarian Interests and Democracy: Rural Society, Agrarian Associations, and the State, 1890–1925]. Bonn: Verlag Neue Gesellschaft, 1978.

79. Fritzsche, Peter. *Germans into Nazis.* Cambridge: Harvard University Press, 1998.

80. Gatzke, Hans W. *Germany's Drive to the West: A Study of Western War Aims during the First World War.* Baltimore: Johns Hopkins University Press, 1950.

81. Geinitz, Christian. *Kriegsfurcht und Kampfbereitschaft: Das Augusterlebnis in Freiburg— Eine Studie Zum Kriegsbeginn 1914* [Fear of War and Readiness to Fight: The Experience of August 1914 in Freiburg—A Study of the Onset of War]. Essen: Klartext, 1998.

82. Geiss, Imanuel. *Das Deutsche Reich und der Erste Weltkrieg.* Munich: Carl Hanser Verlag, 1978.

83. Geiss, Imanuel. *Der polnische Grenzstreifen, 1914–1918: Ein Beitrag zur deutschen Kriegszielpolitik im Ersten Weltkrieg* [The Polish Border Strip, 1914–1918: A Contribution to the Politics of German War Aims in the First World War]. Lübeck: Matthiesen, 1960.

84. Gersdorff, Ursula von. *Frauen im Kriegsdienst, 1914–1945* [Women in War Service, 1914–1945]. Stuttgart: Deutsche Verlags-Anstalt, 1969.

85. Geyer, Michael. *Deutsche Rüstungspolitik, 1860–1980* [German Armaments Policy, 1860–1980]. Frankfurt a.M.: Suhrkamp, 1984.

86. Grosser, Dieter. *Von monarchischen Konstitutionalismus zur parlamentarischen Demokratie: Die Verfassunspolitik der deutschen Parteien im letzten Jahrzehnt des Kaiserreiches* [From Constitutional Monarchy to Parliamentary Democracy: The Constitutional Policies of the German Parties in the Last Decade of the Empire]. The Hague: M. Nijhoff, 1970.

87. Gudmundsson, Bruce I. *Stormtroops Tactics: Innovation in the German Army, 1914–1918.* New York: Praeger, 1989.

88. Gunzenhäuser, Max. *Die Bibliographien zur Geschichte des Ersten Weltkriegs: Literaturbericht und Bibliographie.* Frankfurt a.M.: Bernard & Graefe Verlag für Weherwesen, 1964.

89. Guth, Ekkehart P. "Der Gegensatz zwischen dem Oberbefehlshaber Ost und dem Chef des Generalstabes des Feldheeres 1914/15 [The Conflict between Army Command East and the Chief of the General Staff, 1914–1915]." *Militärgeschichtliche Mitteilungen* 35 (1984): 75–111.

90. Gutsche, Willibald. *Wilhelm II: Der letzte Kaiser des Deutschen Reiches.* Berlin: Deutscher Verlag der Wissenschaften, 1991.

91. Haffner, Sebastian, and Wolfgang Venohr. *Das Wunder an der Marne: Rekonstruction des Entscheidungsschlacht des Ersten Weltkrieges* [The Miracle on the Marne: A Reconstruction of the Decisive Battle for the First World War]. Bergisch Gladbach: Lübbe, 1982.

92. Hagenlücke, Heinz. *Deutsche Vaterlandspartei: Die nationale Rechte am Ende des Kaiser-reiches* [The German Fatherland Party: The Nationalist Right at the End of the Empire]. Düsseldorf: Droste, 1997.

93. Hahlweg, Werner, ed. *Der Friede von Brest-Litowsk: Ein unveröffentlichter Band aus dem Werk des Untersuchungsausschusses der Deutschen Verfassungsgebenden Nationalversammlung und des Deutschen Reichstages* [The Peace of Brest-Litovsk: An Unpublished Volume from the Work of the Investigative Committee of the German Constituent Assembly and the Reichstag]. Düsseldorf: Droste, 1971.

94. Halpern, Paul G. *A Naval History of World War I.* Annapolis: Naval Institute Press, 1994.

95. Hanisch, Manfred. *Gefallen für das Vaterland.* Erlangen: Universitätsbund Erlangen-Nürnberg, 1994.

96. Hattke, Brigitte. *Hugo Stinnes und die drei deutsch-belgischen Gesellschaften von 1916* [Hugo Stinnes and the Three German-Belgian Associations of 1916]. Stuttgart: Kohlhammer, 1990.

97. Haupts, Leo. *Deutsche Friedenspolitik, 1918–1919.* Düsseldorf: Droste, 1976.

98. Hayashima, Akira. *Die Illusion des Sonderfriedens: Deutsche Verständigungspolitik mit Japan im ersten Weltkrieg* [The Illusion of a Separate Peace: Germany's Policy of Conciliation with Japan in the First World War]. Munich and Vienna: Oldenbourg, 1982.

99. Hebert, Günther. *Das Alpenkorps.* Boppard am Rhein: H. Boldt, 1988.

100. Hecker, Gerhard. "'Metallum-Aktiengesellschaft': Industrielle und staatliche Interessenidentität im Rahmen des Hindenburg-Programmes." *Militärgeschichtliche Mitteilungen* 35 (1984): 113–39.

101. Hecker, Gerhard. *Walther Rathenau und sein Verhältnis zu Militär und Krieg.* Boppard am Rhein: H. Boldt, 1983.

102. Hering, Sabine. *Die Kriegsgewinnlerinnen: Praxis und Ideologie der deutschen Frauenbewegung im Ersten Weltkrieg* [Women War Profiteers: Practice and Ideology of Female Labor in the First World War]. Pfaffenweiler: Centaurus, 1990.

103. Herwig, Holger H. "Admirals versus Generals: The War Aims of the Imperial German Navy, 1914–1918." *Central European History* 5 (1972): 208–33.

104. Herwig, Holger H. "German Policy in the Eastern Baltic Sea in 1918: Expansion or Anti-Bolshevik Crusade?" *Slavic Review* 32 (1973): 339–57.

105. Herwig, Holger H. "The Dynamics of Necessity: German Military Policy during the First World War." In Allan R. Millett and Williamson Murray, eds., *Military Effectiveness*, vol. 1: *The First World War*. Boston, 1988.

106. Herwig, Holger H. *"Luxury" Fleet: The Imperial German Navy, 1888–1918*. Boston: Allen & Unwin, 1980.

107. Herwig, Holger. *The First World War: Germany and Austria-Hungary, 1914–1918*. London: Arnold, 1997.

108. Herzfeld, Hans. *Der Erste Weltkrieg*. Munich: Deutscher Taschenbuch Verlag, 1968.

109. Hildebrand, Klaus. *Bethmann Hollweg, der Kanzler ohen Eigenschaften?* [Bethmann Hollweg, the Chancellor without Qualities?]. Düsseldorf: Droste, 1970.

110. Hirschfeld, Gerhard, Gerd Kumeich, Dieter Langewiesche, and Hans-Peter Ullmann, eds. *Kriegserfahrungen: Studien zur Sozial- und Mentalitätsgeschichte des Ersten Weltkriegs* [Experiences of War: Studies of Mentality and Society in the First World War]. Essen: Klartext, 1997.

111. Holtfrerich, Carl-Ludwig. *The German Inflation, 1914–1923: Causes and Effects in International Perspective*. Berlin and New York: De Gruyter, 1986.

112. Hopbach, Achim, *Unternehmer im Ersten Weltkrieg : Einstellungen und Verhalten württembergischer Industrieller im "Grossen Krieg"* [Entrepreneurs in the First World War: Attitudes and Conduct of Württemberg Industrialists in the Great War]. Leinfelden-Echterdingen: DRW-Verlag Weinbrenner, 1998.

113. Horak, Stephan M. *The First Treaty of World War I: Ukraine's Treaty with the Central Powers of February 9, 1918*. New York: Columbia University Press, 1988.

114. Horn, Daniel. *The German Naval Mutinies of World War I*. New Brunswick, N.J.: Rutgers University Press, 1969.

115. Horne, John, ed., *State, Society, and Mobilization in Europe during the First World War*. Cambridge: Cambridge University Press, 1997.

116. Huber, Ernst Rudolf. *Deutsche Verfassungsgeschichte seit 1789*, volume 5: *Weltkrieg, Revolution und Reichserneuerung, 1914–1919* [German Constitutional History since 1789, volume 5: World War, Revolution, and the Revival of the State, 1914–1919]. 2nd ed., rev. Stuttgart: Kohlhammer, 1982.

117. Hüppauf, Bernd. " 'Der Tod ist verschlungen in den Sieg': Todesbilder aus dem Ersten Weltkrieg und der Nachkriegszeit ['Death is Devoured in Victory': Images of Death from the First World War and the Postwar Period]." In *Ansichten vom Krieg: Vegleichende Studien zum Ersten Weltkrieg in Literatur und Gesellschaft*. Königstein: Forum Academicum, 1984.

118. Hüppauf, Bernd. "Langemarck, Verdun, and the Myth of a *New Man* in Germany after the First World War." *War and Society* 6 (1988): 70–103.

119. Hüppauf, Bernd. "Über den Kampfgeist: Ein Kapitel aus der Vor- und Nachbereitung eines Weltkrieges [On the Fighting Spirit: A Chapter on the Preparation and After-Effects of a World War]." In Anton-Andreas Guha and Sven Papcke, eds., *Der Feind den wir brauchen, oder: Muss Krieg sein?* Königstein: Forum Academicum, 1985.

120. Hüppauf, Bernd. "War and Death: The Experience of the First World War." In Mira Crouch and Bernd Hüppauf, eds., *Essays on Morality*. Kensington, Australia: University of New South Whales Press, 1985.

121. Hürten, Heinz. "Soldatenräte in der deutschen Novemberrevolution 1918 [Soldiers' Councils in the German Revolution of November 1918]." *Historisches Jahrbuch* 90 (1970): 299–328.

122. Institute für Zeitgeschichte. *Bibliographie zur Zeitgeschichte, 1953–1989*. Munich, 1991.

123. Jäger, Wolfgang. *Historische Forschung und politische Kultur in Deutschland: Die Debatte 1914–1980 über den Ausbruch des Ersten Weltkrieges* [Historical Scholarship and Politi-

cal Culture in Germany: The Debate on the Outbreak of the First World War, 1914–1980]. Göttingen: Vandenhoeck & Ruprecht, 1984.

124. Jahr, Christoph. *Gewöhnliche Soldaten: Desertion und Deserteure im deutschen und britishchen Heer, 1914–1918* [Regular Soldiers: Desertion and Deserters in the German and British Armies, 1914–1918]. Göttingen: Vandenhoeck & Ruprecht, 1998.

125. Janssen, Karl-Heinz. "Der Wechsel in der Obersten Heeresleitung 1916 [The Change in the Supreme Military Command, 1916]." *Vierteljahrshefte für Zeitgeschichte* 7 (1959): 337–71.

126. Janssen, Karl-Heinz. *Der Kanzler und der General: Die Führungskrise um Bethmann Hollweg und Falkenhayn 1914–1916* [The Chancellor and the General: The Leadership Crisis between Bethmann Hollweg and Falkenhayn, 1914–1916]. Göttingen: Musterschmidt, 1967.

127. Janssen, Karl-Heinz. *Macht und Verblendung: Die Kriegszielpolitik der deutschen Bundesstaaten, 1914–1918* [Power and Blindness: The Wars Aims Policies of the German States, 1914–1918]. Göttingen: Musterschmidt, 1963.

128. Jarausch, Konrad. *The Enigmatic Chancellor: Bethmann Hollweg and the Hubris of Imperial Germany.* New Haven: Yale University Press, 1972.

129. Kapp, R. W. "Divided Loyalties: The German Reich and Austria-Hungary in Austro-German Discussions of War Aims, 1914–1916." *Central European History* 17 (1984): 120–39.

130. Kessel, Eberhard. "Ludendorffs Waffenstillstandsforderung vom 29. September 1918 [Ludendorff's Cease-Fire Order of 29 September 1918]." *Militärgeschichtliche Mitteilungen* 4 (1968): 65–86.

131. Kielmansegg, Peter, Graf. *Deutschland und der Erste Weltkrieg.* Frankfurt am Main: Akademische Verlagsgesellschaft Athenaion, 1968.

132. Kilduff, Peter. *Germany's First Air Force, 1914–1918.* London: Arms and Armour, 1991.

133. Kitchen, Martin. "Militarism and the Development of Fascist Ideology: The Political Ideas of Colonel Max Bauer, 1916–1918." *Central European History* 7 (1975), 199–220.

134. Kitchen, Martin. *The Silent Dictatorship: The Politics of the German High Command under Hindenburg and Ludendorff, 1916–1918.* London: Croom Helm, 1976.

135. Klein, Fritz, et al. *Deutschland im Ersten Weltkrieg.* 3 vols. 2nd ed., East Berlin: Akademie-Verlag, 1970.

136. Kluge, Ulrich. "Das 'Württembergische Volksheer' 1918/19: Zum Problem der bewaffneten Macht in der deutschen Revolution [The Württemberg Militia in 1918–19: On the Problem of Armed Force in the German Revolution]." In Günther Döker and Winfried Stefani, eds., *Klassenjustiz und Pluralismus: Festschrift für Ernst Fraenkel zum 75. Geburtstag.* Hamburg: Hoffman und Campe, 1973, 92–130.

137. Kluge, Ulrich. *Die Deutsche Revolution 1918/19: Staat, Politik und Gesellschaft zwischen Weltkrieg und Kapp-Putsch.* Frankfurt am Main: Suhrkamp, 1985.

138. Kluge, Ulrich. *Soldatenräte und Revolution: Studien zur Militärpolitik in Deutschland, 1918–1919* [Soldiers' Councils and Revolution: Studies on Military Politics in Germany, 1918–1919]. Göttingen: Vandenhoeck und Ruprecht, 1975.

139. Knoch, Peter, ed. *Kriegsalltag: Die Rekonstruktion des Kriegsalltags als Aufgabe der historischen Forschung und der Friedenserziehung* [Daily Life in Wartime: The Reconstruction of Daily Life in War as a Task of Historical Scholarship and Peace Education]. Stuttgart: Klett, 1989.

140. Kocka, Jürgen. *Facing Total War: German Society, 1914–1918.* Cambridge: Harvard University Press, 1984.

141. Kohlhaas, Wilhelm. "Macht und Grenzen der Soldatenräte in Württemberg, 1918/19 [The Power and Limits of the Soldiers' Councils in Württemberg, 1918–19]." *Zeitschrift für Württembergische Landesgeschichte* 32 (1973): 537–43.

142. Koopmann, Friedhelm. *Diplomatie und Reichsinteresse: Das Geheimdienstkalkül in der deutschen Amerikapolitik 1914 bis 1917* [Diplomacy and the Imperial Interest: The Secret Service and Germany's America Policy, 1914 to 1917]. Frankfurt am Main: Peter Lang, 1990.

143. Koszyk, Kurt. *Deutsche Pressepolitik im Ersten Weltkrieg.* Düsseldorf: Droste, 1968.

144. Kraft, Heinz. *Staatsräson und Kriegsführung im kaiserlichen Deutschland, 1914–1916: Der Gegensatz zwischen Generalstabschef von Falkenhayn und dem Oberbefehlshaber Ost im Rahmen des Bündniskrieges der Mittelmächte* [Reasons of State and Military Leadership in Germany, 1914–1916: The Conflict between Chief of Staff Falkenhayn and Army Command East in the Context of Coalition War by the Central Powers]. Göttingen: Muster-Schmidt, 1980.

145. Kreimeier, Klaus. *The UFA Story: A History of Germany's Greatest Film Company.* New York: Hill and Wang, 1996.

146. Kruse, Wolfgang. "Krieg und Klassenheer: Zur Revolutionierung der deutschen Armee im Ersten Weltkrieg" [War and the Class Army: On the Radicalization of the German Army in the First World War]. *Geschichte und Gesellschaft* 22 (1996): 530–61.

147. Kruse, Wolfgang. *Krieg und nationale Integration: Eine Neuinterpretation des sozialdemokratischen Burgfriedensschlusses 1914/15* [War and National Integration: A New Interpretation of Social Democratic Participation in the Fortress Peace, 1914–15]. Essen: Klartext Verlag, 1993.

148. Kundrus, Birthe. *Kriegerfrauen: Familie, Politik und Geschlechterverhältnisse im Ersten und Zweiten Weltkrieg* [Warrior's Wives: Family, Politics, and Gender Relations in the First and Second World Wars]. Hamburg: Christians, 1995.

149. Kunz, Andreas. *Civil Servants and the Politics of Inflation in Germany, 1914–1924.* Berlin and New York: De Gruyter, 1986.

150. Kuropka, Joachim. *Image und Intervention: Innere Lage Deutschlands und britische Beeinflussungsstrategien in der Entscheidungsphase des Ersten Weltkrieges* [Image and Intervention: Internal Conditions in Germany and British Strategies to Exert Influence during the Final Phase of the First World War]. Berlin: Duncker und Humblot, 1978.

151. Lange, K. *Marneschlacht und deutsche Öffentlichkeit, 1914–1939: Eine verdrängte Niederlage und ihre Folgen* [The Battle of the Marne and German Public Opinion, 1914–1939: A Repressed Defeat and its Consequences]. Düsseldorf: Droste, 1974.

152. Lebovics, Herman. *Social Conservatism and the Middle Classes in Germany, 1914–1933.* Princeton: Princeton University Press, 1969.

153. Lemke, Heinz. *Allianz und Rivalität: Die Mittelmächte und Polen im Ersten Weltkrieg.* Berlin: Böhlaus, 1977.

154. Linnenkohl, Hans. *Vom Einzelschuss zur Feuerwalze: Der Wettlauf zwischen Technik und Taktik im Ersten Weltkrieg* [From Single Shots to Rolling Fire: The Interaction of Technology and Tactics in the First World War]. Coblenz: Bernard & Graefe, 1990.

155. Lipp, Anne. "Friedenssehnsucht und Durchhaltebereitschaft: Wahrnehmungen und Erfahrungen deutschen soldaten im ersten Weltkrieg" [Longing for Peace and the Will to Endure: The Perceptions and Experience of German Soldiers in the First World War]. *Archiv für Sozialgeschichte* 36 (1996): 279–82.

156. Ludewig, Hans-Ulrich. *Das Herzogtum Braunschweig im Ersten Weltkrieg: Wirtschaf—Gesellschaft—Staat* [The Duchy of Brunswick in the First World War: Economy—Society—State]. Brunswick: Selbstverlag des Geschichtsvereins, 1984.

157. Lutz, Heinrich. *Demokratie im Zwielicht: Der Weg der deutschen Katholiken aus dem Kaiserreich in die Republik, 1914 bis 1925* [Democracy in Twilight: German Political Catholicism from the Empire to the Republic, 1914 to 1925]. Munich: Kösel-Verlag, 1963.

158. Lyth, Peter J. *Inflation and the Merchant Economy: The Hamburg Mittelstand, 1914–1924.* New York: Berg Publishers, 1990.

159. Mai, Gunther, ed. *Arbeiterschaft 1914–1918 in Deutschland.* Düsseldorf: Droste, 1985.

160. Mai, Gunther. "'Aufklärung der Bevölkerung' und 'Vaterländischer Unterricht' in Württemberg, 1914–1918" ['Popular Enlightenment' and 'Patriotic Instruction' in Württemberg, 1914–1918. *Zeitschrift für Württembergische Landesgeschichte* 36 (1977): 199–235.

161. Mai, Gunther. "Burgfrieden und Sozialpolitik in Deutschland in der Anfangsphase des Ersten Weltkrieges (1914/15)" [The Fortress Peace and Social Policy in Germany in the First Phase of the First World War]. *Militärgeschichtliche Mitteilungen* 20 (1976): 21–50.

162. Mai, Gunther. "Die Sozialstruktur der württembergischen Soldatenräte, 1918/19" [The Social Structure of the Württemberg Soldiers' Councils, 1918–19]. *Internationale wissenschaftliche Korrespondence zur Geschichte der Arbeiterbewegung* 14 (1978): 3–28.

163. Mai, Gunther. *Das Ende des Kaiserreichs: Politik und Kriegführung im Ersten Weltkrieg.* Munich: Deutscher Taschenbuch Verlag, 1987.

164. Mai, Gunther. *Kriegswirtschaft und Arbeiterbewegung in Württemberg, 1914–1918* [The War Economy and the Workers Movement in Württemberg, 1914–1918]. Stuttgart: Klett-Cotta, 1983.

165. Maser, Werner. *Hindenburg: Eine politische Biographie.* Rastatt: Moewig, 1989.

166. Meyer, Henry C. *Mitteleuropa in German Thought and Action, 1815–1945.* The Hague: M. Nijhoff, 1955.

167. Michalka, Wolfgang, ed. *Der Erste Weltkrieg: Wirkung, Wahrnehmung, Analyse.* Munich: Piper, 1994.

168. Miller, Susanne. *Burgfrieden und Klassenkampf: Die deutsche Sozialdemokratie im Ersten Weltkrieg* [The Fortress Peace and Class Struggle: German Social Democracy in the First World War]. Düsseldorf: Droste, 1974.

169. Mishark, John W. *The Road to Revolution: German Marxism and World War I, 1914–1919.* Detroit: Moira Books, 1967.

170. Missalla, Heinrich. *"Gott mit uns": Die deutsche katholische Kriegspredigt, 1914–1918* ['God with Us': German Catholic Chaplains, 1914–1918]. Munich: Kösel-Verlag, 1968.

171. Moeller, Robert G. *German Peasants and Agrarian Politics, 1914–1924: The Rhineland and Westphalia.* Chapel Hill and London: University of North Carolina Press, 1986.

172. Mommsen, Wolfgang J. "Die deutsche Kriegszielpolitik, 1914–1918: Zum Stand der Diskussion." In Walter Laqueur and George L. Mosse, eds., *Kriegsausbruch 1914.* Munich: Nymphenburger Verlagshandlung, 1970, 60–100.

173. Mommsen, Wolfgang J. "Die deutsche öffentliche Meinung und der Zusammenbruch des Regierungssystem Bethmann Hollwegs im Juli 1917" [German Public Opinion and the Collapse of Bethmann Hollwegs' Government in July 1917]. *Geschichte in Wissenschaft und Unterricht* 19 (1968).

174. Mommsen, Wolfgang J. "Die Regierung Bethmann Hollweg und die öffentliche Meinung, 1914–1917" [The Government of Bethmann Hollweg and Public Opinion, 1914–1917]. *Vierteljahrshefte für Zeitgeschichte* 17 (1969): 117–59.

175. Mommsen, Wolfgang J., ed. *Kultur und Krieg: Die Rolle der Intellektuellen, Künstler und Schriftsteller im Ersten Weltkrieg* [Culture and War: The Role of Intellectuals, Artists, and Writers in the First World War]. Munich, 1996.

176. Mommsen, Wolfgang, "German Artists, Writers, and Intellectuals and the Meaning of the War, 1914–1918," in John Horne, ed., *State, Society and Mobilization in Europe during the First World War.* Cambridge: Cambridge University Press, 1997, 21–38.

177. Monticone, Alberto. *Deutschland und die Neutralität Italiens, 1914–1915.* Wiesbaden: Steiner, 1982.

178. Morgan, David W. *The Socialist Left and the German Revolution: A History of the German Independent Social Democratic Party, 1917–1922.* Ithaca: Cornell University Press, 1975.

179. Morrow, John H., Jr. *German Air Power in World War I.* Lincoln: University of Nebraska Press, 1982.

180. Morsey, Rudolf. *Die Deutsche Zentrumspartei, 1917–1923.* Düsseldorf: Droste, 1966.

181. Mosse, George L. "National Cemeteries and National Revival: The Cult of the Fallen Soldiers in Germany." *Central European History* 14 (1979): 1–20.

182. Mosse, George L. "The Jews and the German War Experience." In *Masses and Man: Nationalist and Fascist Perceptions of Reality.* New York, 1980, 263–83.

183. Mosse, George L. "War and the Appropriation of Nature." In *Germany in the Age of Total War.* Ed. by Volker Berghahn and Martin Kitchen. London: Oxford University Press, 1981, 102–22.

184. Mosse, George L. *Fallen Soldiers: Reshaping the Memory of the World Wars.* London and New York: Oxford University Press, 1989.

185. Mosse, Werner, and Arnold Paucker, eds. *Deutsches Judentum in Krieg und Revolution, 1914–1923: Ein Sammelband.* Tübingen: J. C. B. Mohr, 1971.

186. Muhr, Josef. *Die deutsch-italienischen Beziehungen in der Ära des Ersten Weltkrieges (1914–1922)* [German-Italian Relations in the Era of the First World War, 1914–1922]. Göttigen: Musterschmidt, 1977.

187. Müller, Klaus-Peter. *Politik und Gesellschaft: Der Legitimitätsverlust des badischen Staates, 1914–1918* [Politics and Society: Loss of Legitimacy of the State of Baden, 1914–1918]. Stuttgart: W. Kohlhammer, 1988.

188. Niehuss, Merith. *Arbeiterschaft in Krieg und Inflation: Soziale Schichtung und Lage der Arbeiter in Augsburg und Linz, 1910 bis 1925* [The Working Classes in War and Inflation: Social Stratification and the Position of Workers in Augsburg and Linz, 1910–1925]. Berlin and New York: De Gruyter, 1985.

189. Oberschelp, Reinhard, and Karl-Heinz Grotjahn. *Stahl und Steckrüben: Beiträge und Quellen zur Geschichte Niedersachsens im Ersten Weltkrieg (1914–1918)* [Steel and Turnips: Contributions and Sources for the History of Lower Saxony in the First World War, 1914–1918]. Hameln: C. W. Niemeyer, 1993.

190. Offer, Avner. *The First World War: An Agrarian Interpretation.* Oxford: Oxford University Press, 1989.

191. Oppelland, Torsten. *Reichstag und Aussenpolitik im Ersten Weltkrieg: Die deutschen Parteien und die Politik der USA, 1914–1918* [The Reichstag and Foreign Policy in the First World War: The German Parties and the Policy of the United States, 1914–1918]. Düsseldorf: Droste, 1995.

192. Paschall, Rod. *The Defeat of Imperial Germany, 1917–1918.* Chapel Hill: University of North Carolina Press, 1989.

193. Paul, Wolfgang. *Entscheidung im September: Das Wunder an der Marne* [Decision in September: The Miracle on the Marne]. Esslingen: Bechtle, 1974.

194. Pollard, A. W., ed. *Subject Index of the Books Relating to the European War, 1914–1918, acquired by the British Museum, 1914–1920.* London: Bibliographical Society, 1922; reprinted 1966.

195. Quandt, Siegfried, and Horst Schichtel, eds. *Der Erste Weltkrieg als Kommunikationsereignis* [The First World War as a Communications Event]. Giessen: Justus-Liebig-Universität, 1993.

196. Quidde, Ludwig. *Der deutsche Pazifismus während des Weltkrieges 1914–1918: Aus dem Nachlass Ludwig Quiddes* [German Pacifism during the First World War, 1914–1918: From the Papers of Ludwig Quidde]. Ed., Karl Holl and Helmut Donat. Boppard am Rhein: H. Boldt, 1979.

197. Raithel, Thomas. *Das "Wunder" der inneren Einheit. Studien zur deutschen und französischen Öffentlichkeit bei Beginn des Ersten Weltkriegs.* Bonn: Bouvier, 1996.

198. Rakenius, Gerhard W. *Wilhelm Groener als erster Generalquartiermeister: Die Politik der Obersten Heeresleitung, 1918/19* [Wilhelm Groener as Quartermaster General: The Politics of the Military High Command, 1918–1919]. Boppard am Rhein: H. Boldt, 1977.

199. Ratz, Ursula. "Sozialdemokratische Arbeiterbewegung, bürgerliche Sozialreformer und Militärbehörden im Ersten Weltkrieg [The Social Democratic Workers Movement, Middle Class Reformers, and Military Officials in the First World War]." *Militärgeschichtliche Mitteilungen* 37 (1985): 9–33.

200. Rauh, Manfred. *Die Parlementarisierung des Deutschen Reiches* [The Parliamentarization of the German Empire]. Düsseldorf: Droste, 1979.

201. Renz, Irina, ed. *Keiner fühlt sich hier mehr als Mensch . . . Erlebnis und Wirkung des Ersten Weltkriegs* [No One Here Felt More than a Man . . . The Experience and Consequences of the First World War]. Essen; Klartext, 1993.

202. Reulecke, Jürgen. "Der Erste Weltkrieg und die Arbeiterbewegung im rheinisch-westfälischen Industriegebiet [The First World War and the Workers Movement in the Rhineland-Westphalia Industrial Region." In *Arbeiterbewegung am Rhein und Ruhr: Beiträge zur Geschichte der Arbeiterbewegung im Rheinland-Westfalen.* Wueppertal: Hammer, 1974.

203. Reulecke, Jürgen. "*Männerbund* versus the Family: Middle-Class Youth Movements and the Family in Germany in the Period of the First World War." In Richard Wall and Jay Winter, eds., *The Upheaval of War: Family, Work, and Welfare in Europe, 1914–1918.* Cambridge: Cambridge University Press, 1988, 439–52.

204. Reulecke, Jürgen. "Städtische Finanzprobleme und Kriegswohlfahrtspflege im Ersten Weltkrieg unter besonderer Berücksichtigung der Stadt Barmen [Financial Problems and the Provision of Social Welfare in the First World War, with Particular Reference to the City of Barmen]." *Zeitschrift für Stadtgeschichte, Stadtsoziologie und Denkmalpflege* 2 (1975): 48–79.

205. Rhode, Horst. "Faktoren der deutschen Logistik im Ersten Weltkrieg" [Aspects of German Logistics in the First World War]. In Gérard Canini, ed., *Les fronts invisibles: nourrir-fournir-soigner: actes du colloque international sur la logistique des armées au combat pendant la première guerre mondiale, organisé à Verdun les 6, 7, 8 juin 1980.* Nancy: Presses Universitaires de Nancy, 1984.

206. Ritter, Gerhard. *The Sword and the Scepter: The Problem of Militarism in Germany,* 4 volumes. Coral Gables, FL: University of Miami Press, 1969–73.

207. Roerkohl, Anne. *Hungerblockade und Heimatfront: Die kommunale lebensmittelversorgung in Westfalen während des Ersten Weltkrieges* [Hunger Blockade and the Home Front: Communal Food Provisioning in Westphalia during the First World War]. Stuttgart: F. Steiner, 1991.

208. Roesler, Konrad. *Die Finanzpolitik des Deutschen Reiches im Ersten Weltkrieg* [The Financial Policies of the German Empire in the First World War]. Berlin: Duncker & Humblot, 1967.

209. Rohwer, Jürgen, ed. *Neue Forschungen zum Ersten Weltkrieg.* Coblenz: Bernard & Graefe, 1985.

210. Roschmann, H. "Deutsch-österreichische Bundnispolitik im Ersten Weltkrieg." *Europäische Wehrkunde* 30 (1981): 455–65.

211. Rürup, Reinhard. "Der 'Geist von 1914' in Deutschland: Kriegsbegeisterung und Ideologisierung des Krieges im Ersten Weltkrieg [The 'Spirit of 1914' in Germany: War Enthusiasm and the Ideologization of War in the First World War]." In Bernd Hüppauf, ed., *Ansichten vom Krieg: Vergleichende Studien zum Ersten Weltkrieg in Literatur und Gesellschaft* [Perspectives on War: Comparative Studies on the First World War in Literature and Society]. Königstein: Forum Academicum, 1984.

212. Ryder, A. J. *The German Revolution of 1918: A Study of German Socialism in War and Revolt.* Cambridge: Cambridge University Press, 1967.

213. Samuels, Martin. *Doctrine and Dogma: German and British Infantry Tactics in the First World War.* New York: Greenwood Press, 1992.

214. Saul, Klaus. "Jugend im Schatten des Krieges: Vormilitärische Ausbildung, Kriegswirtschaftlicher Einsatz, Schulalltag in Deutschland, 1914–1918 [Youth in the Shadow of War: Pre-Military Training, Economic Participation, and Daily Life at School in Germany, 1914–1918." *Militärgeschichtliche Mitteilungen* 34 (1983): 91–184.

215. Schäfer, Hermann P. *Regionale Wirtschaftspolitik in der Kriegswirtschaft: Staat, Industrie und Verbände während des Ersten Weltkrieges in Baden* [Regional Economic Policy and the War Economy: The State, Industry, and Trade Unions during the First World War in Baden]. Stuttgart: W. Kohlhammer, 1983.

216. Scheck, Manfred. *Zwischen Weltkrieg und Revolution: Zur Geschichte der Arbeiterbewegung in Württemberg, 1914–1920* [Between World War and Revolution: On the History of the Workers Movement in Württemberg, 1914–1920]. Cologne and Vienna: Böhlau, 1981.

217. Scherer, André, and Jacques Grünewald, eds. *L'Allemagne et les problèmes de la paix pendant la première guerre mondiale.* 4 vols. Paris: Presses Universitaires de France, 1962–78.

218. Schiffers, Reinhard. *Der Hauptausschuß des Deutschen Reichstags, 1915–1918: Formen und Bereiche der Kooperation zwischen Parlament und Regierung* [The Central Committee of the German Reichstag, 1915–1918: The Form and Extent of Cooperation between Parliament and Government]. Düsseldorf: Droste, 1979.

219. Schmidt, Ernst-Heinrich. *Heimatheer und Revolution 1918: Die militärischen Gewalten im Heimgebiet zwischen Oktoberreform und Novemberrevolution* [The Home Army and Revolution in 1918: Military Power at Home between the Reforms of October and the November Revolution]. Stuttgart: Deutsche Verlags-Anstalt, 1981.

220. Schneider, Michael. "Deutsche Gesellschaft im Krieg und Währungskrise, 1914–1924 [Germany Society in the War and Currency Crisis, 1914–1924]." *Archiv für Sozialgeschichte* 16 (1986): 301–20.

221. Schönhoven, Klaus, ed. *Die Gewerkschaften im Weltkrieg und Revolution, 1914–1919* [The Trade Unions in the World War and the Revolution, 1914–1919]. Cologne: Bund-Verlag, 1985.

222. Schramm, Gottfried. "Militarisierung und Demokratisierung: Typen der Massenintegration im Ersten Weltkrieg [Militarization and Democratization: Forms of Mass Integration in the First World War]." *Francia* 3 (1976): 475–97.

223. Schröder, Hans-Jürgen. *Confrontation and Cooperation: Germany and the United States in the Era of World War I, 1900–1924.* Providence and Oxford: Berg, 1993.

224. Schulin, Ernst. *Walther Rathenau: Repräsentant, Kritiker, und Opfer seiner Zeit.* Göttingen and Frankfurt: Musterschmidt, 1979.

225. Schumacher, Martin. *Land und Politik: Eine Untersuchung über politische Parteien und agrarische Interessen, 1914–1923* [Land and Politics: An Investigation of Political Parties and Agrarian Interests, 1914–1923]. Düsseldorf: Droste, 1978.

226. Schwabe, Klaus. "Die amerikanische und die deutsche Geheimdiplomatie und das Problem eines Verständigungsfriedens im Jahre 1918 [American and German Secret Diplomacy and the Problem of a Compromise Peace in 1918]." *Vierteljahrshefte für Zeitgeschichte* 19 (1971): 1–32.

227. Schwabe, Klaus. "Zur politischen Haltung der deutschen Professoren im Ersten Weltkrieg" [On the Political Conduct of German Professors in the First World War]. *Historische Zeitschrift* 193 (1961): 601–34.

228. Schwabe, Klaus. *Deutsche Revolution und Wilson-Frieden.* Düsseldorf: Droste, 1971.

229. Schwabe, Klaus. *Wissenschaft und Kriegsmoral: Die deutschen Hochschullehrer und die politischen Grundfragen des Ersten Weltkrieges* [Scholarship and the Ethics of War: German Secondary School Teachers and the Basic Political Questions of the First World War]. Göttingen: Musterschmidt-Verlag, 1969.

230. Schwarz, Klaus Dieter. *Weltkrieg und Revolution in Nürnberg.* Stuttgart: E. Klett, 1971.

231. See, Klaus von. *Die Ideen von 1789 und die Ideen von 1914: Völkisches Denken in Deutschland.* Frankfurt: Athenaion, 1975.

232. Seidel, Anneliese. *Frauenarbiet im Ersten Weltkrieg als Problem der staatlichen Sozialpolitik, dargestellt am Beispiel Bayerns* [Womens' Work in the First World War as a Problem of State Social Policy in Bavaria]. Frankfurt am Main: R. G. Fischer, 1979.

233. Shanafelt, Gary W. *The Secret Enemy: Austria-Hungary and the German Alliance, 1914–1918.* New York: Columbia University Press, 1985.

234. Scheck, Raffael. *Alfred von Tirpitz and German Right-Wing Politics, 1914–1930.* Atlantic Highlands, NJ: Humanities Press, 1997.

235. Showalter, Dennis E. *German Military History, 1648–1982: A Critical Bibliography.* New York: Garland, 1984.

236. Showalter, Dennis E. *Tannenberg: Clash of Empires.* Hamden, CT: Archon Books, 1991.

237. Sicken, Bernhard. "Die Festungs- und Garnisonstadt Wesel im Ersten Weltkrieg: Kriegsauswirkungen and Versorgungsprobleme [The Fortress- and Garrison City of Wesel in the First World War: The Effects of War and Problems of Provisioning." In Bernhard Kirchgäsner and Günter Scholz, eds., *Stadt und Krieg*. Sigmaringen: Jan Thorbecke, 1989.

238. Silberstein, Gerard E. *The Troubled Alliance: German-Austrian Relations, 1914 to 1917*. Lexington: University Press of Kentucky, 1970.

239. Stahl, Friedrich-Christian. "Der Grosse Generalstab, seine Beziehung zum Admiralstab und seine Gedanken zu den Operationsplänen der Marine [The Great General Staff, Its Relation to the Admiralty Staff, and Its Ideas about Naval Operational Plans]." *Wehrkunde* 12 (1963).

240. Stark, Gary. "All Quiet on the Home Front: Popular Entertainments, Censorship and Civilian Morale in Germany, 1914–1918," in Frans Coetzee and Marilyn Shevin-Coetzee, eds., *Authority, Identity, and the Social History of the Great War*. Providence, RI, and Oxford: Berg, 1995, 57–80.

241. Stegemann, Bernd. *Die deutsche Marinepolitik, 1916–1918*. Berlin: Duncker & Humblot, 1970.

242. Steglich, Wolfgang, ed. *Der Friedensappel Papst Benedikts XV. vom 1. August 1917 und die Mittelmächte* [The Peace Feeler of Pope Benedict XV of 1 August 1917 and the Central Powers]. Wiesbaden: F. Steiner, 1970.

243. Steglich, Wolfgang, ed. *Die Friedensversuche der kriegführenden Mächte im Sommer und Herbst 1917* [The Search for Peace by the Warring Powers in the Summer and Fall of 1917]. Wiesbaden: F. Steiner, 1984.

244. Steglich, Wolfgang, ed. *Die Verhandlungen des 2. Unterausschusses des parlamentarischen Untersuchungsausschusses über d. päpstliche Friedensaktion von 1917* [Proceedings of the Second Subcommittee of the Parliamentary Exploratory Committee with Respect to the Papal Peace Initiative of 1917]. Wiesbaden: F. Steiner, 1974.

245. Steglich, Wolfgang. *Bündnissicherung oder Verständigungsfrieden: Untersuchungen zu dem Friedensangebot der Mittelmächte vom 12. Dezember 1916* [Alliance Solidarity or Compromise Peace: An Investigation of the Central Powers' Peace Offer of 12 December 1916]. Göttingen: Musterschmidt, 1958.

246. Steglich, Wolfgang. *Die Friedenspolitik der Mittelmächte, 1917–18*. Wiesbaden: F. Steiner, 1964.

247. Stegmann, Dirk. "Die deutsche Inlandspropaganda 1917/18: Zum innenpolitischen Machtkampf zwischen OHL und ziviler Reichsleitung in der Endphase des Kaiserreiches" [German Domestic Propaganda, 1917–1918: On the Political Power Struggle between the Military Command and the Civilian Leadership in the Last Phases of the Empire]. *Militärgeschichtliche Mitteilungen* 12 (1972): 75–116.

248. Stegmann, Dirk. "Hugenberg contra Stresemann: Die Politik der Industrieverbände am Ende des Kaiserreichs [Hugenberg versus Stresemann: The Politics of Industrial Associations at the End of the Empire]." *Vierteljahrshefte für Zeitgeschichte* 24 (1976): 329–78.

249. Stevenson, David. *The First World War and International Politics*. Oxford: Oxford University Press, 1988.

250. Stoll, Uta. *Arbeiterpolitik im Betrieb: Frauen und Männer, Reformisten und Radikale, Fach- und Massenarbeiter bei Bayer, BASF, Bosch und in Solingen (1900–1930)* [Worker Politics in the Factory: Women and Men, Reformers and Radicals, Skilled and Unskilled Labor at Bayer, BASF, and in Solingen, 1900–1930]. Frankfurt am Main: Campus-Verlag, 1980.

251. Tampke, Jürgen. *The Ruhr and Revolution: The Revolutionary Movement in the Rhenish-Westphalian Industrial Region, 1912–1919*. Canberra: Australian National University Press, 1979.

252. Tarrant, V. E. *Jutland, The German Perspective: A New View of the Great Battle, 31 May 1916*. Annapolis: Naval Institute Press, 1995.

253. Tarrant, V. E. *The U-Boat Offensive, 1914–1945*. Annapolis: Naval Institute Press, 1989.

254. Theweleit, Klaus. *Male Phantasies.* 2 vols. Chicago: University of Chicago Press, 1977–78.

255. Thieme, Hartwig. *Nationaler Liberalismus in der Krise: Die nationalliberale Fraktion des preussischen Abgeordnetenhauses, 1914–1918* [National Liberalism in Crisis: The National Liberal Caucus of the Prussian State Assembly, 1914–1918]. Boppard am Rhein: H. Boldt, 1968.

256. Thompson, Wayne C. "The September Program: Reflections on the Evidence." *Central European History* 11 (1978): 348–54.

257. Thoss, Bruno. "Nationale Rechte, militärische Fuhrung und Diktaturfrage in Deutschland, 1913–1923" [The Nationalist Right, Military Leadership, and the Question of Dictatorship in Germany, 1913–1923]. *Militärgeschichtliche Mitteilungen* 42 (1987): 27–76.

258. Tobin, Elizabeth H. "War and the Working Class: The Case of Düsseldorf, 1914–1918." *Central European History* 17 (1985), 257–99.

259. Triebel, Armin. "Variations in Patterns of Consumption in Germany in the Period of the First World War." In Richard Wall and Jay Winter, eds., *The Upheaval of War: Family, Work, and Welfare in Europe, 1914–1918.* Cambridge: Cambridge University Press, 1988, 159–95.

260. Trumpener, Ulrich. *Germany and the Ottoman Empire, 1914–1918.* Princeton: Princeton University Press, 1968.

261. Ullrich, Volker. *Die Hamburger Arbeiterbewegung vom Vorabend des ersten Weltkrieges bis zur Revolution 1918/19* [The Workers' Movement in Hamburg from the Eve of the First World War to the Revolution of 1918–19]. 2 vols. Hamburg: Lüdke, 1976.

262. Ullrich, Volker. *Kriegsalltag: Hamburg im ersten Weltkrieg* [Daily Life in Wartime: Hamburg in the First World War]. Cologne: Prometh, 1982.

263. Ullrich, Volker. *Vom Augusterlebnis zur Novemberrevolution: Beiträge zur Sozialsgeschichte Hamburgs und Norddeutschlands im ersten Weltkrieg, 1914–1918* [From the Experience of August to the Revolution of November: Contributions to the Social History of Hamburg and Northern Germany in the First World War, 1914–1918]. Bremen: Donat, 1999.

264. Ulrich, Robert. "Feldpostbriefe des Ersten Weltkrieges: Möglichkeiten und Grenzen einer all-tagsgeschichtlichen Quelle" [Military Mail in the First World War: Possibilities and Limitations as a Social-Historical Source]. *Militärgeschichtliche Mitteilungen* 53 (1994): 73–84.

265. Ungern-Sternberg von Pürkel, Jürgen, and Wolfgang von Ungern-Sternberg. *Der Aufruf "An de Kulturwelt!": Das Manifest der 93 und die Anfänge der Kriegspropaganda im Ersten Weltkrieg* [The Summons to People of Culture: The Manifesto of the Ninety-Three and the Beginnings of War Propaganda in the First World War]. Stuttgart: Franz Steiner Verlag, 1996.

266. Unruh, Karl. *Langemarck: Legende und Wirklichkeit.* Coblenz: Bernard & Graefe, 1986.

267. Usborne, Cornelie. " 'Pregnancy Is the Woman's Active Service': Pronatalism in Germany during the First World War." In Richard Wall and Jay Winter, eds., *The Upheaval of War: Family, Work, and Welfare in Europe, 1914–1918.* Cambridge: Cambridge University Press, 1988.

268. Verhey, Jeffrey. *The Spirit of 1914.* Cambridge: Cambridge University Press, 2000.

269. Vietsch, Eberhard von. *Bethmann Hollweg: Staatsmann zwischen Macht und Ethos* [Bethmann Hollweg: A Statesman between Power and Ethics]. Boppard am Rhine: H. Boldt, 1969.

270. Vincent, C. Paul. *The Politics of Hunger: The Allied Blockade of Germany, 1915–1919.* Athens, OH, and London: Ohio University Press, 1985.

271. Vogt, Adolf. *Oberst Max Bauer: Generalstabsoffizier im Zwielicht, 1869–1929.* Osnabrück: Biblio Verlag, 1974.

272. Volkmann, Hans Erich. *Die deutsche Baltikumpolitik zwischen Brest-Litowsk und Compiègne: Ein Beitrag zur "Kriegszieldiscussion"* [Germany's Baltic Policy between Brest-Litovsk and Compiègne: A Contribution to the "War Aims Discussion"]. Cologne and Vienna: Böhlau Verlag, 1970.

273. Vondung, Klaus. *The Apocalypse in Germany.* Columbia, MO: University of Missouri Press, 2000.

274. Wayne, Graeme Chamley. *If Germany Attacks: The Battle in Depth in the West.* London: Faber and Faber, 1940.

275. Weber, Frank G. *Eagles on the Crescent: Germany, Austria and the Diplomacy of the Turkish Alliance, 1914–1918.* Ithaca: Cornell University Press, 1970.

276. Weindling, Paul. "The Medical Profession, Social Hygiene and the Birth Rate in Germany, 1914–1918." In Richard Wall and Jay Winter, eds., *The Upheaval of War: Family, Work, and Welfare in Europe, 1914–1918.* Cambridge: Cambridge University Press, 1988, 417–37.

277. Weitz, Eric D. *Creating German Communism, 1890–1990: From Popular Protests to Socialist State.* Princeton: Princeton University Press, 1997.

278. Welch, David. *Germany, Propaganda, and Total War, 1914–1918.* London: Athlone, 2000.

279. Werth, German. *Verdun: Die Schlacht und der Mythos.* Gladbach: Lübbe, 1979.

280. Wette, Wolfram, ed. *Der Krieg des kleinen Mannes: Eine Militärgeschichte von unten.* Munich: Piper, 1992.

281. Wette, Wolfram. "Die militärische Demobilmachung in Deutschland, 1918/19 unter besonderer Berücksichtigung der revolutionären Ostseestadt Kiel" [Military Demobilization in Germany, 1918–19, with Special Reference to the Revolutionary City of Kiel]. *Geschichte und Gesellschaft* 12 (1986): 63–80.

282. Wette, Wolfram. "Reichstag und 'Kriegsgewinnlerei' (1916–1918): Die Anfänge parlamentarischer Rüstungskontrolle in Deutschland" [The Reichstag and 'War Profiteering,' 1916–1918: The Beginnings of Parliamentary Control of Armaments in Germany]. *Militärgeschichtliche Mitteilungen* 36 (1984): 31–56.

283. Whalen, Robert Weldon. *Bitter Wounds: German Victims of the Great War, 1914–1939.* Ithaca and London: Cornell University Press, 1984.

284. Wheeler, Robert. *USPD und Internationale: Sozialistischer Internationalismus in der Zeit der Revolution* [The Independent Socialist Party and the International: Socialist Internationalism at the Time of the Revolution]. Frankfurt: Ullstein, 1975.

285. Wheeler-Bennett, John W. *The Forgotten Peace: Brest-Litovsk, March 1918.* New York: W. Morrow, 1939.

286. Wieland, Lothar. *Belgien 1914: Die Frage des belgischen "Franktireurkrieges" und die deutsche öffentliche Meinung von 1914 bis 1936* [Belgium 1914: The Question of Belgian "Partisan Warfare" and German Public Opinion from 1914 to 1936]. Frankfurt an Main and New York: Peter Lang, 1984.

287. Winter, J. M, and Jean-Louis Robert, eds. *Capital Cities at War: London, Paris, Berlin, 1914–1919.* Cambridge: Cambridge University Press, 1997.

288. Winterhager, Wilhelm Ernst. *Mission für den Frieden: Europäische Mächtepolitik und dänische Friedensvermittlung im Ersten Weltkrieg* [Mission for Peace: European Power Politics and Danish Peace Mediation in the First World War]. Stuttgart: F. Steiner, 1984.

289. Wohl, Robert. *The Generation of 1914.* Cambridge: Harvard University Press, 1979.

290. Wohlgemuth, Heinz. *Die Entstehung der Kommunistischen Partei Deutschlands 1914 bis 1918* [The Origins of the German Communist Party, 1914–1918]. Berlin: Dietz, 1978.

291. Wollstein, Günter. *Theobald von Bethmann Hollweg: Letzter Erbe Bismarcks, Erstes Opfer der Dolchstosslegende* [Theobald von Bethmann Hollweg: Last Heir of Bismarck, First Sacrificed to the Stab-in-the-Back Legend]. Göttingen and Zurich: Muster-Schmidt Verlag, 1995.

292. Yaney, George L. *The World of the Manager: Food Administration in Berlin during World War I.* New York: Peter Lang, 1994.

293. Zabecki, David. *Steel Wind: Colonel Georg Bruchmüller and the Birth of Modern Artillery.* Westport, CT: Praeger, 1994.

294. Zechlin, Egmont. *Die deutsche Politik und die Juden im Ersten Weltkrieg.* Göttingen: Vandenhoeck and Ruprecht, 1969.

295. Ziemann, Benjamin. "Fahnenflucht im deutschen Heer, 1914–1918" [Desertion in the German Army, 1914–1918]. *Militärgeschichtliche Mitteilungen* 55 (1996): 93–130.

296. Ziemann, Benjamin. *Front und Heimat: Ländliche Kriegserfahrungen im südlichen Bay-ern, 1914–1923* [Front and Hometown: The Experience of War in Rural Southern Bavaria, 1914–1923]. Essen: Klartext, 1997.

297. Zunkel, Friedrich. "Die ausländischen Arbeiter in der deutschen Kriegswirtschaftspolitik des 1. Weltkrieges" [Foreign Workers in the German War Economy in the First World War]. In Gerhard A. Ritter, ed., *Entstehung und Wandel der modernen Gesellschaft: Festschrift für Hans Rosenberg zum 65. Geburtstag.* Berlin: De Gruyter, 1970, 280–311.

298. Zunkel, Friedrich. *Industrie und Staatssozialismus: Der Kampf um die Wirtschaftsordnung in Deutschland, 1914–1918* [Industry and State Socialism: The Struggle over Economic Organi-zation in Germany, 1914–1918]. Düsseldorf: Droste, 1974.

3

France

Gary Cox

Two fundamental beliefs inform this chapter: France was both the supreme victor and victim of the Great War, and France's contribution, the "price of glory," has never been adequately understood or acknowledged in the Anglo-Saxon world.

All great wars are won through synergy, and yet some countries, some societies, are called upon to shoulder more of a conflict's burdens. Just as the Soviet Union was the linchpin of the Grand Alliance that destroyed Hitler, so was France the vital heart of an earlier alliance that vanquished Imperial Germany. The effort required for victory, literally in order to stagger across the finish line, would test the country to its very breaking point: "incomprehensible" was the word used to describe the magnitude of the French sacrifice by one of her greatest historians, Jean-Baptiste Duroselle, in his *La grande guerre des français* [133]. Yet English-speaking writers have generally preferred to focus on Britain and her own heroic contribution: even the epic of Verdun has been eclipsed, in Anglo-America, by the horrors and heroism of the Somme and Passchendaele.

The relative neglect of the French experience is easily explainable. In addition to language, there are numerous barriers that separate the French from the English-speaking world. Certainly the cultures' experience after the Great War were vastly different: "D-Day" and the "Few" form a stark contrast to the "the sorrow and the pity" of the Occupation. Perhaps most important however in the failure to acknowledge the French achievement has been the historiography of the Great War itself.

The historical understanding of World War I has developed in three waves. The first was the flood of books that began during the war and continued for about ten years or so after the Armistice. These were essentially victory paeans that celebrated the destruction of Prussian militarism while mourning the cost: one thinks of valedictories like Kipling's *Irish Guards in the Great War* and the inevitable spate of "how I won the war" memoirs by the generals.

With the emergence of the *Kriegsschuldfrage* and the publication of works like S. B. Fay's *Origins of the World War* [144], the historiography of the war entered its second phase. The war was transformed into a vast all-consuming Moloch, worshiped by feckless statesmen and homicidal generals, and at whose altars millions had been pointlessly sacrificed. This image became so powerful that this revisionist history quickly became the "orthodox" view of the war; in Britain, developed by the facile pens of such writers as David Lloyd George and B. H. Liddell Hart, it stressed the uniqueness and immensity of Britain's sacrifice, at times almost implying that a cabal of French politicians and generals had lured an unsuspecting Britannia into a vast continental war. In America this idea was transformed into the "merchants of death" theme: the war had been made to make the world safe for the investments of big business. This view of World War I focused on the blunders of the leaders and on one's own sufferings, and left scarce time or effort to empathize with one's allies. These ideas form the core of the standard interpretation of World War I—in textbooks, on film, in the history community, to this day. John Laffin's 1988 evocatively titled *British Butchers and Bunglers of World War I* suggests the residual power of this viewpoint.

The third wave of historical work on the Great War began in the 1960s with the publication of two books. Barbara Tuchman's enormously popular *Guns of August* [389], while still firmly rooted in the "orthodox" interpretation of the conflict, combined brilliant writing and story-telling with tendentious history to awaken a new generation to the fascination of the Great War. Tuchman prompted a torrent of well-written if narrowly conceived popular works, which perpetrated the "butchers and bunglers" thesis. Fritz Fischer's *Griff nach der Weltmacht* was the second book, and it was enormously important. Fischer's thesis of an aggressive Germany, willing to risk a great-power war for hegemony, ignited a firestorm of debate that still echoes and re-engaged academic historians in the meaning of the Great War. The "Fischer thesis" suggested another way of looking at the war—as a necessary response to the threat of German conquest. D. J. Goodspeed [181], while disagreeing with the Fischer thesis, would suggest in his comparative *German Wars* the essential similarity of World War I and II: a second thirty years' war that saw the hecatombs of France and Flanders transferred to the Soviet Union after the twenty years' truce. He noted that the "butchers and bunglers" thesis consistently underestimated the scale of effort needed to defeat a great power like Germany, and conveniently left the politicians, like Lloyd George, "off the hook" in evading their responsibilities for the war's human carnage by their demands for a "total peace" that could be attained only by a total war.

French scholarship has to some degree mirrored these historiographical "waves," although only a few French historians ever accepted the revisionist interpretation. France may have waged war badly, her expenditure of human life prodigal; but France was hardly ever seen as responsible for the war's outbreak. As to the war itself—in the past three decades there has been an explosion of interest in France about the totality of the experience. One can get a flavor of this interest on the World Wide Web, simply by calling up any of the online services that offer contemporary French books. In the history section those on offer remind one of the titles typically available in the United States on the American Civil War. From the battlefield to the boudoir, from the home front to diplomacy, virtually every aspect of France's effort has been studied. The interest in "ceux de '14'" seems insatiable, and it has spawned an important group of prolific and erudite specialists—Annette Becker, Jean-Jacques Becker, Stéphane Audoin-Rouzeau, Pierre Miquel, Guy Pedroncini, and Alain Denizot to name only a few—who have devoted their professional careers to the exploration of virtually every aspect of the French experience.

GENERAL TEXTS

Two works more than any others might serve as a sound introduction to the Great War and France's role in this conflict. For a general overview of the war, its background, causes, conduct, and interplay with European, indeed with a global society, Pierre Renouvin's *La Crise européene et la Grande Guerre* [355] is an excellent starting place. Volume XIX of the classic "Peuples et civilisations" series, Renouvin's survey provides a balanced account of the entire period from the perspective of one of France's greatest modern historians. Last updated in the 1960s, the book also supplies generous and detailed bibliographical citations, broken down by chapter and topic. For a specific introduction that concentrates solely on France's role in the war, Jean-Baptiste Duroselle [133] is essential. Duroselle focuses on the sheer magnitude of the French effort, moving assuredly from the battlefield to the economy, society and intellectual life. The book's bibliography is an excellent guide for any scholar intent on further study. For a survey of French history from the 1890s through the Great War, Michel Leymarie's *La France contemporaine* [255] stresses the profound transformation the country experienced in this quarter century. Of the numerous French histories of the war, recommended is Marc Ferro's *The Great War* [146], which combines narrative with thematic analysis. Ferro emphasizes the "promiscuity of death" and its impact on society. For military operations General Louis Koeltz's *La guerre de 1914–1918* [232] provides a summary written by a survivor-combatant who later to rose to high command. Raymond and Jean Pierre Cartier's *La Première Guerre Mondiale* [68] emphasizes the experience of the soldier, his daily life, fears, anguish, and miseries. Pierre Miquel, in *La grande guerre* [282], offers a superb, prize-winning interpretative history. Miquel also attempts to paint a portrait of the daily life of France, not only from the perspective of the soldier, but also of French society as a whole in *La Grande Guerre au jour le jour* [283]. Wonderfully eclectic and episodic, Miquel describes such occurrences as the use of the wireless, the movies, even the distribution of the tobacco ration—to evoke the totality of the French experience.

BIBLIOGRAPHIES

While there are several English language bibliographies like Enser's *Subject Bibliography* [137] that serve as a useful starting place, many of these have the obvious limitation of confining themselves to works in the English language. To encompass the mass of French language material, one can research chronologically. A good starting place is Jean Vic [393], whose five-volume bibliography *Littérature de guerre* was completed in 1923. For the period down to World War II, the *Revue d'histoire de la Guerre mondiale* [356], which appeared in seventeen volumes between 1923 and 1939, can be consulted. Each issue reviews new books and articles, and it usually includes a bibliographical essay on a particular topic. The most complete list of materials can be compiled from the national publications, *Répertoire bibliographique de l'histoire de France* [376], and from 1939 (to the present), its replacement, the *Bibliographie annuelle de l'histoire de France* [91]. Both appeared in yearly volumes. Both are comprehensive, endeavoring to cover almost every aspect of French history. In the new series in particular the cross-referencing is generally excellent. Early works on social and economic issues can be found in Bloch's *Bibliographie méthodique* [44].

POLITICAL AND DIPLOMATIC BACKGROUND

A wonderful comparative introduction of the political and diplomatic problems that beset France in two world wars can be found in Anthony Adamthwaite's *Grandeur and Misery* [1]. Of the numerous accounts of the turbulent Third Republic, J. M. Mayeur and M. Réberioux [271] provide a modern overview in *The Third Republic*. Jacques Chastenet *Histoire de la Troisième République* [77] provides an impressive narrative, emphasizing the power of nationalism and its consequences during the war years. For a detailed breakdown of political and legislative activity, Georges Bonnefous' *Histoire politique* [47] provides year-by-year summaries of key domestic issues, legislation, elections, and such hard-to-find details as cabinet composition. To consider French politics and the political "mood" of France, Eugen Weber's assertion of a rising nationalism in *The Nationalist Revival in France* [400], while contentious, is an important starting place. The Dreyfus Affair, with its political, diplomatic, military, and societal implications, requires its own bibliography. Jean Denis Bredin's *The Affair* [51] is a sound and eminently readable summary of this epic of espionage, jurisprudence, and popular opinion. The intersection of military and political issues is treated in Gerd Krumeich *Armament and Politics* [236], whose study of the passage of the "three year law," which in 1913 extended the term of conscription for French draftees and helped close the gap between German and French trained manpower, skillfully links the worlds of diplomacy, military affairs, and domestic politics. For a wonderful study of the manners and mores of the Third Republic on the eve of the war, Edward Berenson's *The Trial of Madame Caillaux* [36] uses the murder trial of the wife of a controversial politician to illuminate French politics and society.

Political affairs during the war itself can be considered in two stages: the period of the so-called *union sacrée* with its rising tensions between the army high command and the government; and the crisis of 1917 and the coming of Clemenceau. Renouvin, in *The Forms of War Government* [352], provides an overview of how the French government actually carried out its tasks during the war, treating the government's relations with public power, civil liberties, public services, and parliament itself. Since most historians now seem to agree that the *union sacrée* was more slogan than solemn commitment, one of the best ways to view the political scene during the war is through the voluminous memoirs and biographies that present French political life from the perspective of its practitioners; virtually all have left an *apologia* for their role in the coming of the war and conduct. For the war's outbreak and its early period Raymond Poincaré's massive eleven-volume memoir, *Au service de la France* [330], is especially important since he was such an activist president; see also Keith Eubank's biography of the pivotal diplomat Paul Cambon [138]. One of the most controversial of all France's politicos of these years was Joseph Caillaux: the sensationalism surrounding his wife's shooting of Gaston Calmette and Caillaux's own murky dealings with anti-government (his enemies claimed pro-German) factions in 1917 have obscured his role as the proponent of some sort of detente or improved *modus vivendi* with Germany. Jean-Claude Allain [5] offers the most nuanced vision of a still controversial life. Caillaux, of course, offers his own defense of his efforts in *Mes mémoires* [55]. For the growing tension between an Olympian high command that resisted political oversight and the French government, Jere Clemens King, *Generals and Politicians* [229], remains the essential starting point. King demonstrates the slow but inevitable shift in power from the high command to the politicos, culminating of course in Clemenceau. David Dutton's article "The Union Sacrée and the French Cabinet Crisis" [135] discusses how this long-term crisis in civil-military relations brought about the end of the *union sacrée*.

The year 1917 was the pivotal year of the war; certainly it shook the French Army to its foundations, strained the home front to its breaking point, and brought the "Tiger" to power. A popular and readable account of this crisis is Richard M. Watt's *Dare Call It Treason* [398]. Although focused on the military mutinies, Watt provides both background and a compelling, popular sketch of the French state under the excruciating strain of this war. The *Revue d'histoire moderne et contemporaine* [11] dedicated an entire issue to 1917, with important articles on public opinion, politics, and civil-military relations. The political impact of the failure of the Nivelle offensive is discussed in Henri Castex's *L'affaire du Chemin des Dames* [70]. The French constitution allowed parliamentary committees to meet in secret to discuss matters of national security; Castex covers the committee work of both the Assembly and the Senate. For the growing anti-war movement in France, Marvin H. Kabakoff's dissertation "The Composition of the Anti-War Movement" [220] shows how the divisions between middle class pacifists and more radical socialists and anarchists fatally split this enterprise. The role of collaboration in the pacifist movement is traced in Nicholas Papayanis "Collaboration and Pacifism in France" [308]. German attempts to organize a peace party in France are detailed in Alfred Kupferman's "Les Débuts de l'offensive morale allemande" [237]. Henry Contamine in "La France devant la Victoire" [92] maintains that despite these anti-war movements, there was never a serious threat to the French government; he then summarizes the major issues that faced France on the eve of victory.

Diplomatic studies conveniently organize themselves around France's role in the outbreak of the war, then about French diplomacy during the war itself.

As a great power, the role of France in the tragedy of 1914 is of course fully analyzed in all the standard works. Of the classic treatments, Sydney B. Fay [144] is most skeptical about the motives and machinations of France and Russia. He is joined in this attitude by the provocative and readable D. J. Goodspeed [181]. The French answer to *Die grosse Politik*—the postwar publication of German diplomatic documents—was the 41-volume *Documents diplomatiques français* [160]. For the formation of the Triple Entente, George F. Kennan's two volumes—*The Decline of Bismarck's European Order* and *The Fateful Alliance* [227, 228] treat both the German decision to jettison the "re-insurance Treaty" and the forging of the Franco-Russian alliance. Kennan is especially severe on military leaders whose narrow professionalism left them ignorant of the scale and scope of modern war. The crucial addition of Great Britain to the anti-German alliance, especially in its military perspectives, is addressed in S. R. Williamson's *Politics of Grand Strategy* [406]. Essential for understanding the French role in the 1914 crisis is John F. V. Keiger's *France and the Origins* [223], which emphasizes the importance of Raymond Poincaré, an activist president in a time of even more than usual cabinet instability, and concludes that France entered the war for essentially a negative reason—not to have done so would compromise national security. M. B. Hayne in *The French Foreign Office* asserts that an independent and powerful Quai d'Orsay played a decisive role in the unfolding of the French response to the July crisis [197].

To scan French diplomacy during the war itself, Albert Pingaud's three-volume study, *Histoire diplomatique,* is a solid starting place [327]. David Stevenson's *French War Aims* [379] treats this important question. Stevenson reminds that the war took its "hideous course" not only because of a military stalemate, but because of a diplomatic one as well. Stevenson believes, nonetheless, that French politicians had fewer choices than their allies or enemies: essentially, the war came down to submission to German demands or continued resistance. Pierre Renouvin describes the evolution of French war aims as eventually encompassing a limited program in "les Buts de guerre" [351]; Roy Prete challenges [338] Renouvin's assertions that France's ultimate war aims were modest in "Since Renouvin: A Reconsideration of French War Aims." Prete's "French Military War Aims" [335] also traces the army's program not only to reclaim Alsace-Lorraine, but also to annex the Saar coal basin and the left bank of the Rhine, and to break up the German Empire itself. An important aspect of diplomacy during the war was its "secret negotiations," which focused on the development of new allies or on trying to make peace. Guy Pedroncini *Les negotiations sécrète* [313] discusses both these efforts, while dealing in detail with the secret diplomacy that led to the armistice.

In addition to her own immediate war aims, France as a great power maintained global diplomatic interests. For Franco-Italian relations, Pierre Guillen, *La France et l'Italie* [188], has edited a series of essays. For the French intervention in Greece, Alexander T. Mitrakos, *France in Greece* [287], examines the objects and conduct of French diplomacy. That French activity in the Balkans was not about military necessity but economic expansion is asserted by D. J. Dutton in *The Politics of Diplomacy* [134]. For Turkey, L. Bruce Fulton in "France and the End of the Ottoman Empire" [165] believes that French policy was reactive to German initiatives, hoped to preserve the Ottoman Empire until 1915, and only then decided to pursue both territorial and economic compensations from the empire's collapse and division. Yves-Henri Nouailhat, in "Français, Anglais et Américains" and *France et États-unis* [299, 301], traces Franco-American relations from the outbreak of war to the peace settlement. French relations with the new Soviet regime are summarized in Anne Hogenhuis-Seliverstoff's *Les Rélations franco-soviétiques* [202].

For the end of the war, Pierre Renouvin provides a balanced diplomatic and political history in *L'armistice de Rethonde* [350] that considers the situation from multiple perspectives. Of the myriad memoirs and biographies available for the latter stages of the war, Clemenceau's are obviously the most important. Besides the "Tiger's" own remembrances, *Grandeur and Misery of Victory* [81], the best portraits of this remarkable man include Duroselle's massive (1,000-page) biography, *Clemenceau* [131], and David S. Newhall's, whose assessment of Clemenceau is underscored by his subtitle, *A Life at War* [297]. Generally accorded the designation "classic" is D. R. Watson's *Georges Clemenceau* [397]. Important is Watson's assertion that Clemenceau was the "necessary man" because of "dark forces" emerging in Germany; only he could have led France to a necessary victory—although at horrific cost. For an intimate account of the workings of the Clemenceau ministry, Jean Jules Mordacq has left a four-volume memoir, *Le ministère Clemenceau* [290].

ECONOMIC AND INDUSTRIAL MATTERS

The most important studies of the French economic effort during the war are dated, but they still provide an excellent starting place for research. Three substantial volumes in the Carnegie series on the *Economic and Social History of the War* (James T. Shotwell, ed.) deal with France. Arthur Fontaine, *French Industry during the War* [154], notes the growth of French industry until 1917, followed by a period of severe shortages and contractions, spawned by a dearth of raw materials, the submarine campaign, the diversion of U.S. shipping, and the congestion of the French railway net. Michel Augé-Laribé and Pierre Pinot, *l'Agriculture pendant la Guerre* [16], describe a *laissez-faire* agricultural and food supply system.

For the cost of the war, and how it was paid for, see Henri Truchy's *The War Finance of France* [387]. Most of the supporting or subsidiary studies of the French economy in this period also date from the 1920s, but there are signs that the historiography is beginning to address this lacuna. For the role of finance and trade in prewar economic and diplomatic affairs, Raymond Poidevin's *Les relations économiques* [329] examines Franco-German enterprise and asserts that economic rivalry, which grew in the years before the war, in no way caused the conflict but did help sour relations and make the rupture much easier. For French investment to Russia, René Girault [177] explores the quarter-century before the outbreak of the war in *Emprunts russes*. For the growth of French industry Jean William Dereymez, "Les usines de Guerre" [112], provides a study of one department. Francis Koerner's "L'Economie du Massif Central" [233] discusses the severe short- and long-term disruptions the economy suffered because of the war. Jon Lawrence et al. in "The Outbreak of War and Urban Economy" [249] provide a comparative investigation of urban economic and social problems that emerged in Berlin, Paris and London during the first months of the conflict. Economic warfare emerged as an important mechanism in waging total war. Marjorie M. Farrar, *Conflict and Compromise* [141], has done groundbreaking work on the French involvement in this aspect of the war's prosecution. Farrar outlines the French role in establishing a diplomatic blockade of Germany. The French efforts included abortive attempts to buy up materials in neutral countries to keep them from German hands, and pressure on the Americans to adhere to a total embargo of Germany. Yves-Henri Nouailhat [300] suggests that France made strong efforts to make permanent the re-orientation of the world's economy developed during the war; in essence, to maintain in place a form of economic warfare against Germany into the postwar period, a view essentially confirmed by Marc Trachtenberg's "A New Economic Order" [386]. One of the few modern monographs on the country's economic system can be found in J. Godfrey *Capitalism at War* [179], whose study of a war-driven economy paints a picture of ongoing struggle between bureaucrats, ministers, the Assembly, and the industrialists.

In addition to the focus on the labor movement in Annie Kriegel's seminal work on the development of the French communist party, *Aux origines du communisme français* [235], French labor's role in the war is treated in John N. Horne's comparative study *Labor at War* [204]; Horne maintains that French workers' support of the war hinged on hopes that victory would bring reforms. Patrick Fridenson's "Impact of the First World War" [163] stresses the far-reaching ramifications of the war on French labor: specifically, the growth of the foreign labor force; the emergence of the communist party; the increased role of the state in economic life; and the bifurcation of the labor movement into a reform and revolutionary component. The role of women in the workforce is discussed by Jean Louis Robert "Women and Work in France" [359]. Robert asserts that the First World War marked the apogee of the trend toward increased participation by women in the French workplace—a trend in motion since the mid–nineteenth century, and which reversed itself, resulting in a steady decline in women's employment after the war.

SOCIAL HISTORY AND MANPOWER

Social history is one of the many new fields of historical inquiry that has blossomed since the days of the Great War. Much of its research is new, therefore, and expansive. Like the word *society* itself, social history can be very broadly defined; thus, inclusion is this section is of necessity arbitrary. Titles discussed in other sections could just as easily fit here. Pierre Paraf, himself a survivor of the war, provides a moving portrait of French society in *La France de 1914* [309]. The best introduction to the study of French society during the war itself is Patrick Fridenson's *1914–1918: L'Autre Front* [162]. This volume both sums up and challenges the traditional historiography of the home front by asserting that there was indeed a second front to the war—French society, and that many of the first conclusions developed about this home front need revision. He insists that in the face of war the divisions in French society and politics simply continued; that the transformations of the economy were not a hiatus, but growth "by unusual means"; and that in the face of such major changes as the expanding role of the state, it proved impossible to turn back the clock once the war was over. The prolific Jean-Jacques Becker offers a study of the "great transformation" produced by the war in *La France en guerre* [32]. Becker's *The Great War and the French People* also studies French attitudes toward the struggle [33]. Complementing Becker's work, P. J. Flood offers a study of one department that considers the question of why the French were able to sustain their will to fight in *France 1914–1918* [150]. Although focused on the foundation of the communist party, Annie Kriegel's *Aux origines* [235] is indispensable for the study of the home front. For a portrait of ordinary life behind the lines, Gabriel Perreux's *La Vie quotidienne* [318] provides the best introduction. Manpower shortages brought large numbers of foreign workers to France; for the problems they engendered in French society, see John Horne's *Labor at War* [204]. Essential for the study of the status of women during the war is Françoise Thébaud's *La Femme au temps de la Guerre* [385]. That the war failed to "deliver the goods" as far as rising expectations regarding women's rights were concerned is the subject of Steven C. Hause in "More Minerva than Mars" [196]. He notes that women did not achieve equality during the war, did not retain jobs in the postwar workforce, and did not receive the right to vote until 1944.

In addition to the combatants, the French societal experience of the Great War must include not only those departments shielded by the French battle line, but those areas of France, all or part of twenty departments, occupied by the enemy. Richard Cobb *French and Germans* [85] compares the experiences of occupation between the First and Second World Wars. An important aspect of the Great War experience was the deprivation felt by both occupiers and the occupied. Helen MacPhail's *The Long Silence* [273] analyzes the mechanisms and responses to the occupation; hunger, more than terror, was the theme of the period. For the problem of forced deportation of civilians, see Jean Claude DeCamps' *Maubeuge 1914–1918* [101]. France's Roman Catholic prelate Yves Cardinal Congar as a ten-year-old schoolboy recorded his experience of the occupation at Sedan in *Journal de la Guerre* [14]. A torrent of memoirs continues to emerge describing "ordinary life" behind the French front. The journal of Paul Hess, *Vie à Reims* [201], who daily faced bombardment in the great cathedral town, is but a recent example.

The rich rubric of social history has produced a plethora of special studies, only a few of which can be mentioned. Annette Becker [27] has produced a stirring volume that describes a "revival" of religion in France that married old practices and new beliefs in *Guerre et la foi*. Religion produced a diptych during the war of "fervor and death," which after the war became a "triptych" of fervor, death, and remembrance. Jacques Fontana in *Les Catholics français* [155] focuses specifically on their role in the war. Charles E. Bailey "The Verdict of French Protestantism" [19] asserts that despite appeals from German Protestants for "solidarity," French Protestants fully supported their country. France operated some seventy "concentration camps" for internees during the war, some of whom included the first Alsatians "liberated." While not in any sense "death camps," they were places of privation that illustrated, according to Jean Claude Farcy, *Les Camps de Concentration français* [140], that war was indeed now total. Maurice Rajsfus [341] takes a jaundiced view of censorship, imposed on the country by the army and frequently maintained by the local police in *La Censure militaire*.

MILITARY PREPARATIONS AND MOBILIZATION

French strategic planning and preparations for war in 1914 were of course themselves the product of the army's prewar experiences and its appreciations of future developments. Gary Cox, *The Halt in the Mud* [97], considers the beginnings of French strategic planning in the early nineteenth century and illustrates the continuity in understanding that informed the making of French strategy. "La Débâcle," as Zola characterized the French defeat in 1870, decisively shaped the ideas of a generation of French generals and politicians about the nature and requirements of a future war. No finer one-volume introduction and summary of this seminal conflict is available than Michael Howard's *Franco-Prussian War* [206]. The epochal defeat of 1870 was by no means the only influence on the prewar French Army. In the swirling cauldron of politics that was the Third Republic, the army was both a "player" in the great game and the subject of much political infighting and intrigue. No single work explains the army's situation better, especially in relation to such important and controversial decisions as Plan XVII, than Douglas Porch's *The March to the Marne* [332]. Walter S. Barge's dissertation, "The Generals of the Republic" [22], has analyzed the dossiers of 488 generals promoted between 1889 and 1914. France's military leaders were increasingly bourgeois republicans, competing in a promotion system that valued colonial experience and was increasingly political in nature. Jan K. Tanenbaum's *General Maurice Sarrail* [383] examines the career of a "left-wing" general. For general surveys of the army, still useful is David Ralston's *The Army of the Republic* [342]. Louis Garros, in *L'Armée du Grand-Papa* [171], emphasizes the period 1871–1914, complaining that hasty French reforms to meet the threat of Bismarck in 1873 resulted in a "mirror-image" problem between the French and German armies that led to the war's enormous losses. Garros also blames Britain for 500,000 French dead in 1914 because London vetoed Joffre's intention to move into Belgium to meet the onrushing Schlieffen Plan.

The development of French strategic and tactical ideas, most importantly the French Plan XVII, and the tactical doctrine, *"offensive à outrance,"* remains controversial. Standard-bearers for the "generals were blockheads" school are Tuchman [389]—very influential (did she ever meet a general she liked?)—Liddell Hart, *Reputations Ten Years After* [258], and such early critics as Percin *1914* [316]. This school generally cites the pernicious influence of such theoretical works as Ardant du Picq *Études sur le combat* [325], with his emphasis on moral forces in war, and Jean Colin's *Transformations de la guerre* [89], as inspirers of the controversial tactical ideas of de Grandmaison, *Deux Conférences* and *Dressage de l'infanterie* [184, 185] and Foch, *De la conduite de la guerre* and *Des principes de la guerre* [151, 152], traditionally blamed with Joffre as the originators for the disastrous French offensives in 1914. While this "butchers and bunglers" interpretation still maintains at least a popular hold on the imagination, the works of Henry Contamine, *La Revanche* [93], and Arthur Conte's biography *Joffre,* [95] have argued for a more nuanced understanding. Contamine is especially important in arguing that lack of understanding at the tactical level, complemented by poor training, produced a distortion of doctrine in 1914. Providing crucial context to this debate is Douglas Porch [332], who has shown how the same republicans who despised the professional military and held it responsible for the failures of 1914 bear more than a little of the responsibility for the "massacre of our infantry" as Percin [317] bluntly put it. Prete's "Preparation of the French Army" [337] with its balanced analysis is perhaps the place to begin any exploration of this still controversial and polemical problem. A. Marchand's *Plans de concentration* provides a useful summary of the evolution of the French plans for war [265]. The most modern assessment of the critical question—what did Joffre know (about the Schlieffen Plan) and when did he know it?—is Jan K. Tanenbaum's "French Estimates of Germany's Operational War Plans" [382].

All accounts of the French mobilization of 1914 now must defer to Jean-Jacques Becker's *1914* [31]. Becker's magisterial analysis decisively labels as myths the two standard interpretations of France in 1914: that the French embraced the war with great enthusiasm, and that the French people were duped by their political leadership. He insists that the *Union sacrée* was a short term measure that in no way implied any person or party relinquishing fundamental positions. Becker has also in *Le Carnet B* [30] reconstructed and explained the

famous potential arrest list of those persons suspected of being willing to inter-
fere with mobilization. While "Carnet B" was not implemented in 1914, Becker
concludes that the concerns that underscored its development were not foolish;
most on the lists were committed anarchists who had "talked a good fight" and
seemed to represent a significant threat to public order.

MILITARY OPERATIONS

The sheer magnitude of the French war-making effort makes the study of the
country's military operations perhaps the most daunting and difficult of the
major subtopics that encompass the overall theme of "France at War." The literature is immense and growing, and French historians, like their American con-
freres who study their own Civil War, show no signs of losing interest in the
"sharp edge of the sword." Perhaps the best way to break down the topic of military operations into at least semi-manageable "chunks" is to consider (however
briefly): 1) the campaign of 1914—the First Battle of the Marne and the "race to
the sea"; 2) Joffre's "grignotage" (nibbling away)—his description of the bloody
attritional offensives of 1915, and which also can be extended to encompass the
German riposte, the French "Iliad" of Verdun; 3) the tumultuous events of 1917:
the Nivelle offensive, the mutinies, and the coming of Pétain; 4) the 1918 crisis
and the emergence of Foch; 5) French operations away from the Western Front;
and finally, 6) the experience of the war, from the generals to the poilu.

The principal documentary source for French military operations is the General Staff's *l'Armée française dans la grande guerre* [160]—thirty-four volumes
that include both a narrative history, devoid, it must be said, of any analysis, as
well as a compendium of orders, memoranda, and other documents that outline
the fighting of the war.

The opening phase of the war included the disastrous failure of Plan XVII—
Joffre's all-out offensive to win the war, the bittersweet victory of the Marne,
and the development and solidifying of the trench line prompted by the "race to
the sea." Besides the books already discussed above that deal with mobilization
(many of which take the story through the battle of the Marne), Prete, in "French
Strategic Planning and the Deployment of the BEF," identifies the delays and
misunderstandings surrounding the movement of the British Expeditionary
Force (BEF) to France as the roots of the uneasy wartime western alliance [336].
Robert B. Asprey's *The First Battle of the Marne* [13] remains a useful, intelligent summary, notable for his sensitivity to the misapplication of tactical doctrine by local French commanders. Impressionistic and evocative is Georges
Blond, *The Marne* [45], who is scathing in his description of the "red trouser
battles" of 1914. He characterizes the French uniform of 1914, which featured
the notorious "pantalon rouge," as the most irrational ever devised! For an excellent analysis of the entire Marne campaign, Henri Isselin's *The Battle of the
Marne* [212] provides a discussion very favorable to French commanders and
emphasizing the role of intelligence in decision-making. Perhaps the best
account of the First Marne from the French perspective is Henri Contamine *La*

Victoire de la Marne [94]. Contamine stresses Joffre's contribution, but he is most evocative in detailing the cost of this victory: Saturday, 23 August, was the bloodiest day—27,000 killed—in French history. In only four and a half months of 1914, Contamine reminds, France lost 265,000 dead. Raymond Recouly provides a breathless, eyewitness account of these bloody events from the perspective of a staff captain in *General Joffre and his Battles* [348]. J. Ratinaud [343] specifically details the "race to the sea" in *La course à la mer.* Prete provides an overarching view of the entire 1914 campaign from the perspective of coalition warfare in his dissertation, "The War of Movement on the Western Front" [339].

There are few separate accounts of the terrible French bloodbaths of 1915, most being subsumed under more general accounts of the experience of war (below). Losir Gurial's "*Je les grignote*" [189] provides an analysis of Joffre's strategy of "nibbling" away at the enemy. For discussion of individual engagements, the *Mémoires du Maréchal Joffre* [215], and individual "trench memoirs" are useful. Arthur Conte's biography is a defense of Joffre [95] claiming that the "grignotage" of 1915 was absolutely essential to keep Russia in the war.

For France, 1916 will forever remain the year of Verdun. This enormous test of endurance—the battle stretched from February to December 1916—produced staggering casualties and unimaginable suffering. It is the "Gettysburg squared" of the historiography of the French in battle. For English-speaking readers, the best introduction remains Alistair Horne's poignant *Price of Glory* [203]. Alain Denizot provides a history of the fortress of Verdun and its environs during the entire war—*Verdun* [111]—that puts the battle into perspective. Modern French accounts all stress the soldiers' battle. Denizot's thesis, "Les Conditions de la bataille" [109], Gerard Canini's *Combattre à Verdun* [60], and Pierre Miquel's *Mourir à Verdun* [285] are excellent sources. Miquel writes of the peculiar horror of this tiny (about 25 square kilometers) "high place," where an entire generation of Europeans was sacrificed. Georges Blond's *Verdun* [46] marries this universe of suffering with the problems of the high command; still, Blond reports laconically that the most intense memory of the summer of 1916 was "putrefaction." Marshal Henri Petain's *La bataille de Verdun* [320] is a useful source to understand his role in the French victory.

The hour of crisis came for France in 1917, when a series of "mutinies" threatened to wreck the army, drive France from the war, and give victory to Germany. Watt [398] provides an immensely readable overview. For the Nivelle offensive, the promised victory that produced only another enormous butcher's bill and the refusal of the poilu to continue such imbecilic attacks, Pierre Miquel's *Les Chemin des Dames* [280] provides a fine narrative account. Jean Ratinaud [344] stresses the crucial changes the mutinies produced, personified in the rise of Petain and Clemenceau, in *1917*. The indispensable work on this entire episode is Guy Pedroncini's *Les Mutineries* [312]. Pedroncini examines the entire question of army discipline (1914–1917), the actual mutinies, the re-establishment of command authority, and the meaning of the crisis. Pedroncini has gone on to produce sterling works examining every aspect of the career of France's military savior, Henri Petain, including a two-volume biography [314,

315]. Petain was of course the crucial figure at Verdun, and even more important, in saving the army in 1917. Leonard V. Smith has written a brilliant study of the "collective indiscipline," as he terms it, of one division in *Between Mutiny and Obedience* [374].

Much of the scholarship on military operations in 1918 naturally focuses on Ludendorff's great offensives and on the great allied counterattack in which American and British forces played a predominant role. Claude Dufresne *Ce jour-là* [127] provides a French perspective on these events; filled with anecdotes, this popular account pays fulsome tribute to the American contribution, while stressing the Franco-American halting of Ludendorff on the Chemin des Dames as the crucial moment of this nine-month battle. Patrick de Gmeline in *Le 11 novembre* [178] examines the last day of the war. For the grand strategy of 1918, the biographies already mentioned, especially Clemenceau's, are the essential starting place. Foch's *Memoirs* [153] provides the military perspective. Foch himself ended the war enshrined briefly as one of the "great captains" of history, but his reputation has never recovered from B. H. Liddell Hart's *Man of Orleans* [257] biography. This portrait of Foch lacks context, but it is a readable and important analysis.

French operations on other fronts have received considerably less attention. The French role in the Gallipoli Campaign is critically examined in George H. Cassar's *The French and the Dardanelles* [69], which notes that the genesis of the "eastern" plan came from France and was vetoed by Joffre, who suffers withering criticism not only for helping ensure the ultimate failure of the campaign, but also for his disinclination to learn from experience and "criminal obstinacy" that destroyed the "flower" of the French Army. Raymond A. Callahan's "What about the Dardanelles?" [56] is useful for examining Cassar's charges and bringing the entire controversy into much-needed perspective. For a French account of the Gallipoli fighting, see Michel Herubel *La bataille de Dardanelles* [200]. For French operations in Greece, Alan Palmer's *Gardeners of Salonika* [307] is a convenient summary. Military operations in Africa are summarized in Yves Jouin's "Les Campagnes d'Afrique" [217, 218]. The contributions of France's African colonies to her war effort are detailed in Marc Michel's *L'Appel à Afrique* [276].

The experience of war is the essential theme of literally countless memoirs, some still appearing as they are discovered on the shelves and in the attics of France. To do them full justice would require a multivolume bibliography and a lifetime of study. Fortunately, Jean Norton Cru [98] has provided an essential analysis of the "first generation" of these accounts, including biographical information on authors, a summary of their work, and an evaluation of each book's contents. Cru, who spent twenty-eight months in the trenches, took upon himself the enormous task of collating dozens of these recollections. He excluded the memoirs of most high-ranking officers, for example, for the simple reason that most never got very close to the front! His work, the famous *Témoins,* was completed in 1929. Similar interests are reflected in a colloquium chaired by

Gerard Canini, *Combattre à Verdun* [60]. Henri Desagneaux's *Journal de guerre* [115] might stand as a classic example of this enormous mass of "trench memoirs." Desagneaux was an infantry captain who survived four years at the front, including fighting at Verdun. Perhaps the best way to sample these memoirs is the brilliant war history of André Ducasse, Jacques Meyer, and Gabriel Perreux *La Guerre racontée par les combattants* [124]. Their account is included here (instead of in the general histories of the war above) because of their emphasis on the lot of the soldiers and their reliance on soldiers' memoirs to document their portrait—indispensable to gaining an understanding of the soldier's war.

The "generals' war" is best covered in their memoirs. Virtually every member of the high command explained and defended himself. Those who failed are catalogued in Paul Allard's *les Dessous de la Guerre* [5]. Conte and Pedroncini provide the best available biographies on Joffre and Petain respectively. Outspoken and early criticism of the generals is the subject of the works of the already-mentioned Alexandre Percin [316; 317].

With virtually every aspect of military life and operations chronicled, special note might be made of Stéphane Audoin-Rouzeau's *Men at War* [15], which uses "trench journalism," the myriad papers created by the denizens of this "troglodyte world," to examine the *mentalité* of the frontline soldier. Gerard Canini in *Les Fronts Invisibles* has edited an important set of colloquium papers organized around the theme of supply and logistics [61]. Julie Wheelwright *The Fatal Lover* [404] actualizes the famous story of Mata Hari and uses it to examine the ambiguous status of women in modern conflict. Richard Speed addresses the important topic of French treatment of prisoners of war in *Prisoners, Diplomats and the Great War* [378].

DEMOBILIZATION

Unfortunately for the French the "war to end all wars" did not end with a "peace to end all peace." There are relatively few treatments of demobilization as a phenomenon precisely because all too soon French attention was galvanized on the worsening economic and political tensions that ushered in the 1930s. Adamthwaite [1] provides an excellent narrative to tie together the two halves of France's "second thirty years war." Much of the history of the aftermath deals with loss. Hugh Clout's *After the Ruins* [84] describes the rebuilding of northern France. The victims of military justice are remembered by Nicolas Offenstadt in *Les Fusillés de la Grande Guerre* [302]. War memorials and their meaning have generated an enormous volume of research. Annette Becker *Les monuments aux morts* [28] examines French monuments to the dead; Jay Winter's *Sites of Memory* [407] puts these structures into a European perspective. Antoine Prost, *Les Anciens Combattants* [340], has provided a substantial study of the role of French veterans in the interwar period. For treatment of the wounded and their place in society, Sophie Delaporte's *Les Gueles cassées* [103] is evocative.

AREAS OF FURTHER RESEARCH

Despite the massive quantity of literature dealing with France and the war, there are some areas that would benefit from additional treatment. The French wartime economy needs additional research, particularly since the bulk of the numerous studies available were all done in the 1920s. For the war itself, the terrible battles of 1915, in which France suffered her greatest losses, would benefit from individual analysis. These studies would hopefully cast more light on Joffre's "grignotage." Of all the generals, Foch seems most in need of a modern consideration to unravel the mixture of mysticism and ability that encompasses his character. The entire phenomenon of demobilization—how France disassembled her army and its supporting mechanisms—is also a neglected subject.

BIBLIOGRAPHY

As already noted, the literature available on France and the Great War is immense— and steadily growing. This bibliography was twice as long in its initial draft, and it claims only to offer a reasonable introduction to what was clearly a defining moment in the long history of France. The above-listed numbers and short titles are fully cited below. One of the many places Frenchmen show their glorious individuality is in capitalization. To attempt to impose an Anglo-Saxon order on such Gallic creativity and self-expression would be churlish. Vive la France!

1. Adamthwaite, Anthony. *Grandeur and Misery: France's bid for power in Europe, 1914–1940.* London: Arnold, 1995.

2. Agathon. *les Jeunes Gens d'aujourd'hui.* Paris: Plon-Nourrit, 1913.

3. Ailleret, Charles. *L'organisation du nation en temps de guerre.* Bourdeaux: J. Bière, 1935.

4. Albrecht-Carrié, René. *France, Europe and the Two World Wars.* New York: Harper, 1961.

5. Allain, Jean Claude. *Joseph Caillaux,* 2 vol. Paris: Imprimerie nationale, 1978–1981.

6. Allard, Paul. *les Dessous de la guerre révélés par les comités secrets.* Paris: Éditions de France, 1932.

7. Amicales des 155e—355e régiments d'infanterie. *La Sainte Biffe: histoire du 155e régiment d'infanterie de Commercy pendant la guerre de 1914–1918, evoquée par les survivants en mémoire des 115 officiers et 3985 sous-officiers, caporaux et soldats tués et disparus.* Nice: École Don Bosco, 1976.

8. Amoureux, Henri. *Pétain avant Vichy: la guerre et l'amour.* Paris: A. Fayard, 1967.

9. Anderson, Benjamin M. *Effects of the War on Money, Credit and Banking in France and the United States.* New York: Oxford University Press, 1919

10. Andrew, Christopher, and Kanya-Forstner, A. *France Overseas. The Great War and the Climax of French Imperial Expansion.* London: Thames & Hudson, 1981.

11. "L'année 1917," in *Revue d'histoire moderne et contemporaine,* (January–March 1968).

12. Artaud, Denise. *la Question des dettes interalliées et la reconstruction de l'Europe (1917–1929),* 2 vol. Lille: Librairie H. Champion, 1978.

13. Asprey, Robert B. *The First Battle of the Marne.* Philadelphia: J. B. Lippincourt, 1962

14. Audoin-Rouzeau, Stéphane, Congar, Dominique, and Congar, Yves. *Journal de la Guerre 1914–1918.* Paris: Cerf, 1997.

15. Audoin-Rouzeau, Stéphane. *Men at War 1914–1918: National Sentiment and Trench Journalism during the First World War.* Providence: Berg, 1992.

16. Augé-Laribé, Michel. *l'Agriculture pendant la guerre.* Paris: Presses universitaires de France (henceforth PUF), 1925.

17. Autin, Jean. *Foch ou, la triomphe de la volonté.* Paris: Perrin, 1987.

18. Azan, P. *Franchet d'Esperey.* Paris: Flammarion, 1949.

19. Bailey, Charles E. "The Verdict of French Protestantism Against Germany in the First World War." *Church History* 58 (1989): 66–82.

20. Baillou, Jean., ed. *les Affaires étrangères et le Corps diplomatique français.* Paris: Éditions du Centre national de la recherché scientifique, 1984.

21. Barbusse, Henri. *le Feu (Journal d'un escouade).* Paris: Flammarion, 1916.

22. Barge, Walter Shepherd, Sr. "The Generals of the Republic: The Corporate Personality of High Military Rank in France, 1889–1914." Ph.D. dissertation, University of North Carolina, 1982.

23. Barnett, Corelli. "Travail, Famille, Patrie: General Philippe Pétain." in *The Swordbearers: Supreme Command in the First World War.* Bloomington: Indiana University Press, 1975.

24. Bayliss, Gwyn. *Bibliographic Guide to the Two World Wars.* London: Bowker, 1977.

25. Barreyre, P. G. *Carnets de route de P. G. Barreyre, poilu girondin 1914–1919.* Bourdeaux: Centre regional de documentation pédagogique, 1990.

26. Beaufre, général André. *La France de la Grande Guerre 1914/1919.* Paris: Cultur, arts, loisirs, 1971.

27. Becker, Annette. *Guerre et la foi à la mort de la mémoire.* Paris: A. Colin, 1994.

28. Becker, Annette. *Les monuments aux morts.* Paris: Éd. Errance, 1989.

29. Becker, Annette. *Oubliés de la grande guerre: humanitaire et culture de guerre 1914–1918, populations occupés, déportés civils, prisonniers de guerre.* Paris: Éd. Noêsis, 1998.

30. Becker, Jean-Jacques. *Le Carnet B: les pouvoirs publics et l'anti-militarisme avant la guerre de 1914.* Paris: Éditions Klincksieck, 1973.

31. Becker, Jean-Jacques. *1914: Comment les Français sont éntrés la guerre: Contribution à l'étude de l'opinion public printemps-été 1914.* Paris: Presses de la Fondation nationale des sciences politiques, 1977.

32. Becker, Jean-Jacques. *La France en guerre, 1914–1918. La grande mutation.* Bruxelles: Éd. Complexe, 1988.

33. Becker, Jean-Jacques. *The Great War and the French People.* New York: Berg, 1990

34. Becker, Jean-Jacques, and Kriegel, A. *Juillet 1914: le mouvement ouvrier français et la guerre.* Paris: A. Colin, 1964.

35. Becker, Jean-Jacques, and Berstein, Serge. *Victoire et Frustrations, 1914–1919.* Paris: Éd. Du Seuil, 1990.

36. Berenson, Edward. *The Trial of Madame Caillaux.* Berkeley: University of California Press, 1992.

37. Bernand, Henri. *An 14 et la campagne des illusions.* Bruxelles: Renaissance du livre, 1983.

38. Bernard, Léon. *la Guerre et la Santé publique.* Paris: Presses universitaires de la France, 1929.

39. Bertrand, Adrien. *Victory of Lorraine, August 24–September 12, 1914.* Paris: T. Nelson, 1919.

40. Bidou, Henry. *Histoire de la Grande Guerre.* Paris: Firmin-Didot, 1934.

41. Blanchard, Raoul. *les Forces hydro-électriques pendant la guerre.* Paris: Presses universitaires de la France, 1925.

42. Blin, Colonel. *Aperçus sur la guerre mondiale.* Paris: Charles Lavauzelle, 1932.

43. Bloc, Marc. *Memoirs of War, 1914–1915.* Ithaca: Cornell University Press, 1980.

44. Bloch, Camille. *Bibliographie méthodique de l'histoire économique et sociale de la France pendant la guerre.* Paris: Presses universitaires de la France, 1925.

45. Blond, Georges. *The Marne.* Harrisburg, PA: Stackpole,1966.

46. Blond, Georges. *Verdun.* New York: Macmillan, 1964.

47. Bonnefous, Georges. *Histoire politique de la Troisième République:* Tome Second, La Grande Guerre (1914–1918). Paris: Presses universitaires de la France, 1957.

48. Bornecque, Henri. *La France et la Guerre—formation de l'opinion publique pendant la guerre.* Paris: Payot, 1921.

49. Boucher, Colonel Arthur. *la France victorieuse dans la guerre de demain, étude stratégique.* Paris: 1912.

50. Bourget, Pierre. *Fantassins de '14 de Pétain au poilu.* Paris: Presses de la Cité, 1964.

51. Bredin, Jean-Denis. *The Affair: The Case of Alfred Dreyfus.* New York: George Braziller, 1986.

52. Buffetaut, Yves. *1917 Spring Offensives: Arras, Vimy, le Chemin des Dames.* Paris: 1997.

53. Cabiati, Aldo. *Grande Guerra alla fronti di Francia.* Bologna: 1940.

54. Cahen-Salvador, Georges. *les Prisonniers de guerre 1914–1918.* Paris: 1929.

55. Caillaux, Joseph. *Mes mémoires.* 3 vol. Paris: Plon, 1942–1947.

56. Callahan, Raymond A. "What About the Dardanelles?" *American Historical Review* 78 (1973): 641–48.

57. Cambon, Henri. *Paul Cambon, ambassadeur de France, 1843–1924.* Paris: 1937.

58. Cambon, Paul. *Correspondence.* 3 vol. Paris: 1940–1946.

59. Campagne, Louis. *Chemin de croix 1914–1918.* Paris: 1930.

60. Canini, Gerard. *Combattre à Verdun: Vie et souffrance quotidienne du soldat 1916–1917.* Nancy: Presses Universitaires de Nancy, 1988.

61. Canini, Gerard. ed. *Les Fronts Invisibles: Nourir, Fournir, Soigner. Actes des colloque international sur la Logistique des Armées au Combat pendant la Première Guerre Mondiale.* Nancy: Presses Universitaires de Nancy, 1984.

62. Canini, Gerard. ed. *Mémoire de la Grande Guerre: Témoins et Témoignages.* Nancy: Presses Universitaires de Nancy, 1989.

63. Carher, Claude, et Pedroncini, Guy [ed.]. *La Bataille de Verdun.* Colloquium of the Institut de conflits contemporains. Paris: 1997.

64. Carher, Claude, and Pedroncini, Guy. *Les troupes coloniales dans la grande guerre.* Paris: 1997.

65. Carpentier, Marcel. *Un cyrard au feu.* Paris: 1964.

66. Carré, Henri. *Les Grandes Heures du Général Pétain: 1917 et la crise moral.* Paris: 1952.

67. Carroll, E. Malcolm. *French Public Opinion and Foreign Affairs, 1870–1914.* New York: 1931.

68. Cartier, Raymond, and Jean Pierre. *La Première Guerre Mondiale.* 2 vol., Paris: Presses de la Cité, 1982.

69. Cassar, George H. *The French and the Dardanelles: A Study of Failure in the Conduct of War.* London: Allen & Unwin, 1971

70. Castex, Henri. *L'affaire du Chemin des Dames: les comités secrets.* Paris: 1998.

71. Castex, Henri. *Verdun, années infernales: la vie du soldat au front d'août 1914 à septembre 1916.* Paris: 1980.

72. Chabert, Roland. *Printemps aux tranchées. Notes de campagne de Josephe Astier, soldat de la grande guerre. 6 mars-1er juillet 1916.* Lyons: Élie Bellier, 1982.

73. Chaline, Nadine-Janette. éd. *Chrétiens pendant la Première Guerre mondiale.* Paris: 1993.

74. Challner, Richard. *The French Theory of the Nation in Arms, 1866–1939.* New York: 1952.

75. Chambure, A. de. *Quelques guides de l'opinion publique en France pendant la Grande Guerre. 1914–1918.* Paris: 1918.

76. Charles-Roux, François. *l'Expédition des Dardanelles au jour le jour.* Paris: 1920.

77. Chastenet, Jacques. *Histoire de la Troisième République, t. IV: Jours Inquiet et Jours Sanglants, 1906–1918.* Paris: Librairie Hachette, 1955.

78. Chastenet, Jacques. *Raymond Poincaré.* Paris: Juillard, 1948.

79. Chatenay, Victor. *Mon journal de 14–18.* Angers: 1968.

80. Christine, René. *La Première Guerre Mondiale. Consequences pathologiques pour les combattants français du front occidental.* Paris: 1997.

81. Clemenceau, Georges. *Grandeur and Misery of Victory.* New York: Harcourt Brace & Co., 1930.

82. Clementel, Étienne. *la Guerre et le Commerce. La France et la Politique économique interalliée.* Paris: 1931.

83. Cloarec, Vincent. *La France et la question de Syrie 1914–1918.* Paris: 1998.

84. Clout, Hugh. *After the Ruins: Restoring the Countryside of Northern France after the Great War.* Exeter: 1996.

85. Cobb, Richard. *French and Germans, Germans and French: A Personal Interpretation of France under Two Occupations, 1914–1918/1940–1944.* Hanover, NH: University Press of New England, 1983.

86. Cochet, Annick. "l'Opinion et le moral des soldats en 1916 d'après les archives du contrôle postal," 2 vol. Thèse. Paris X-Nanterre: 1986.

87. Cochet, François. *Rémois en guerre: l'héroïsation au quotidien.* Nancy: 1993.

88. Colin, général Henry Louis. *La côte 304 et le Mort Homme 1916–1917.* Paris: 1934

89. Colin, commandant Jean. *Les Transformations de la guerre.* Paris: 1911.

90. Collins, Ross. *The Development of Censorship in World War I France.* Columbia, SC.: 1992.

91. Comité français des sciences historiques et Centre national de la recherche scientifique. *Bibliographie annuelle de l'histoire de France.* Paris: from 1953/54.

92. Contamine, Henry. "La France devant la Victoire." *Revue d'histoire moderne et contemporaine.* 16(1969): 131–41.

93. Contamine, Henry. *La Revanche, 1871–1914.* Paris: Berger-Levrault, 1957.

94. Contamine, Henry. *La Victoire de la Marne.* Paris: Éditions Gallimard, 1970.

95. Conte, Arthur. *Joffre.* Paris: Olivier Orban, 1991.

96. Corvisier, André. ed. *Histoire militaire de la France,* t. III. Paris: 1992.

97. Cox, Gary P. *The Halt in the Mud: French Strategic Planning from Waterloo to Sedan.* Boulder, CO: Westview Press, 1994.

98. Cru, Jean Norton. *Témoins: Essai d'analyse et de critique de souvenirs de combattants édités en français de 1915 à 1928.* Paris: 1929.

99. Dahlin, Elba. *French and German Public Opinion on Declared War Aims, 1914–1918.* Stanford: Stanford University Press, 1933.

100. Debeney, général. *La Guerre et les Hommes. Réflexions d'après guerre.* Paris: 1937.

101. DeCamps, Jean Claude. *Maubeuge 1914–1918: La Grande Guerre et les déportations civiles.* Maubeuge: 1998.

102. Dédéyan, Charles. *Une guerre dans le mal des hommes.* Paris: 1971.

103. Delaporte, Sophie. *Les Gueules cassées. Les blessés de la face de la Grande Guerre.* Paris: 1996.

104. Delmas, Jean. *L'État-Major français et le front oriental (Novembre 1917–Novembre 1918).* Paris: 1965.

105. Delvert, Charles. *Carnets d'un fantassin.* Paris: n.d.

106. Delvert, Charles. *Histoire d'une compagnie.* Paris: 1918.

107. *Demain,* nos. 1–30 (1916–1918). [reprint; Geneva: 1970].

108. Demazes, général. *Joffre, la victoire du caractère.* Paris: 1955.

109. Denizot, Alain. "Les Conditions de la bataille de Verdun." Thèse, 3e cycle. Paris: 1983.

110. Denizot, Alain. *Douaumont 1914–1918. Verité et légende.* Paris: 1998.

111. Denizot, Alain. *Verdun 1914–1918.* Paris: 1996.

112. Dereymez, Jean William. "Les usines de Guerre (1914–1918) et le cas de la Saone-et-Loire." *Cahiers d'Histoire* 26 (1981): 151–81.

113. Derfler, Leslie. *Alexandre Millerand: The Socialist Years.* The Hague: 1977.

114. Derou, Jean. *les Relations franco-portugaises (1910–1926).* Paris: 1986.

115. Desagneaux, Henri. *Journal de guerre '14–'18.* Paris: Denoel, 1971.

116. Deygas, capitaine F. J. *l'Armée d'Orient dans la guerre mondiale 1915–1919.* Paris: 1932.

117. D'Esmard, J. *Galliéni.* Paris: 1965.

118. Desmarest, Jacques. *La Grande Guerre (L'évolution de la France contemporaine, vol. 4).* Paris: 1978.

119. Dorgelès, Roland. *les Croix de bois.* Paris: 1919.

120. Drachkovitch, Milorad. *Le socialismes français et allemand et la problème de la guerre, 1870–1914.* Geneva: 1953.

121. Droit, Jean. *Témoin d'outre guerre.* Paris: 1991.

122. Dubail, général Auguste. *Quatre années de commandement, 1914–1918: Journal de campagne.* 3 vol. Paris: 1920–1921.

123. Dubois, général. *Deux ans de commandement sur le front de France, 1914–1916.* Paris: 1921.

124. Ducasse, André. *La Guerre racontée par les combattants.* 2 vol. Paris: 1930.

125. Ducasse, André, Meyer, Jacques, and Perreux, Gabriel. *Vie et Mort des Français, 1914–1918: Simple Histoire de la Grande Guerre.* Paris: Librairie Hachette, 1959.

126. Dufourg, Robert. *Grand désillusion: printemps 1917.* Paris: 1917.

127. Dufresne, Claude. *Ce jour-là: La Victoire 1918.* Paris: Librairie Académique Perrin, 1988.

128. Duhamel, Georges. *Vie des martyrs.* Paris: 1933.

129. Dulles, Eleanor L. *The French Franc 1914–1928: The Facts and Their Interpretation.* New York: 1929.

130. Dupaquier, Jacques. ed. *Histoire de la population française, t. IV: De 1914 à nos jours.* Paris: 1988.

131. Duroselle, Jean-Baptiste. *Clemenceau.* Paris: 1988.

132. Duroselle, Jean Baptiste. *France de la Belle Époque.* Paris: 1992.

133. Duroselle, Jean-Baptiste. *La grande guerre des français, 1914–1918.* Paris: 1998.

134. Dutton, David. *The Politics of Diplomacy: Britain and France in the Balkans in the First World War.* London: 1998.

135. Dutton, David. "The Union Sacrée and the French Cabinet Crisis of October 1915." *European Studies Review* 8 (1978): 411–24.

136. Engerand, Fernand. *la Bataille des frontières (août 1914).* Paris: 1920.

137. Enser, A. G. S. *A Subject Bibliography of the First World War: Books in English 1914–1978.* London: 1979.

138. Eubank, Keith. *Paul Cambon, Master Diplomatist.* Norman, OK: 1960.

139. Falls, Cyril. *Marshal Foch.* London: 1939.

140. Farcy, Jean-Claude. *Les Camps de Concentration français de la première guerre mondiale 1914–1920.* Paris: 1995.

141. Farrar, Majorie Milbank. *Conflict and Compromise: The Strategy, Politics and Diplomacy of the French Blockade, 1914–1918.* The Hague: 1974.

142. Farrar, Marjorie Milbank. *Principled Pragmatist. The Political Career of Alexandre Millerand.* New York: 1991.

143. Favitski de Probobysz, commandant de. *Répertoire bibliographique de la litterature militaire et coloniale française depuis cent ans.* Paris: 1935.

144. Fay, Sidney B. *The Origins of the World War.* New York: 1930.

145. Fayolle, maréchal Marie-Émile. *Cahiers secrets de la Grande Guerre.* Paris: 1964.

146. Ferro, Marc. *The Great War 1914–1918.* London: Routledge & Keegan Paul, 1973.

147. Ferry, Abel. *Carnets secrets (1914–1918).* Paris: 1957.

148. Field, Frank. *Three French Writers and the Great War. Barbusse, Drieu de la Rochelle, Bernanos: Studies in the Rise of Communism and Fascism.* London: 1975.

149. Fischer, Maurice. *la 66e Division à la bataille d'Amiens, mai-août 1918. Visions de guerre intégrale.* Paris: 1931.

150. Flood, P. J., *France 1914–1918: Public Opinion and the War Effort.* New York: St. Martin's Press, 1990.

151. Foch, Ferdinand. *De la conduite de la guerre: la manoeuvre pour la bataille.* Paris: 1903.

152. Foch, Ferdinand. *Des principes de la guerre: conférences faites en 1900 à l'École supérieure de guerre.* Paris: 1903.

153. Foch, Ferdinand. *The Memoirs of Marshal Foch.* Garden City, NY: 1931.

154. Fontaine, Arthur. *French Industry During the War.* New Haven: 1926.

155. Fontana, Jacques. *Les Catholiques français pendant la Grande Guerre.* Paris: 1990.

156. France. Armée. Service historique. *Guide bibliographique sommaire d'histoire militaire et coloniale française.* Paris: Imprimerie Nationale, 1969.

157. France. Armée. Service historique. *Inventaire sommaire de la guerre; Série N: 1872–1919. Ministère d'État chargé de la défense nationale, État-major de l'armée de terrre, Service historique.* 14 v. Troyes: n.d.

158. France. Armée. Service historique. *Répertoire numérique des journaux des marches et opérations 1914–1918,* 2 v. [Jean Nicot, ed.] Paris: Imprimerie Nationale, 1967–68.

159. France. Ministère des affairs étrangères. *Documents diplomatiques français, 1871–1914.* 41 v. Paris: Imprimerie Nationale, 1929–59.

160. France. Ministère de la Guerre. État-major de l'armée. Service historique. *Les Armées Françaises dans la Grande Guerre,* 34 v. Paris: Imprimerie Nationale, 1922–38.

161. Franzius, Enno. *Caillaux: Statesman of Peace.* Stanford: 1976.

162. Fridenson, Patrick. *The French Home Front, 1914–1918.* Providence, RI: Berg, 1992.

163. Fridenson, Patrick. "The Impact of the First World War on French Workers." In Wall, Richard, and Winter, Jay., eds. *The Upheaval of War: Family, Work and Welfare in Europe, 1914–1918.* Cambridge: Cambridge University Press, 1988.

164. Frois, Marcel. *la Santé et le Travail des femmes pendant la guerre.* Paris: 1926.

165. Fulton, L. Bruce. "France and the End of the Ottoman Empire." In Kent, Marian, ed. *The Great Powers and the End of the Ottoman Empire.* London: George Allen & Unwin, 1984.

166. Gaillard, André. *1918: les Chemins de l'Armistice.* Paris: 1998.

167. Galliéni, Josephe Simon. *Mémoires du Général Galliéni: Défense de Paris.* Paris: 1920.

168. Gambiez, Général F., and Suire, Colonel M. *Histoire de la première guerre mondiale 1914–1918.* 2 v. Paris: Fayard, 1968.

169. Gamelin, général Maurice. *Manoeuvre et victoire de la Marne.* Paris: 1954.

170. Gamborotto, Laurent. *Foi et patrie: la predication du protestisme français pendant la Première Guerre mondiale.* Geneva: 1996.

171. Garros, Louis. *L'Armée du Grand-Papa: De Gallifet à Gamelin, 1871–1939.* Paris: Librairie Hachette, 1939.

172. Gay, Georges. *la Bataille de Charleroi, août 1914.* Paris: 1937.

173. Genevoix, Maurice. *Ceux de "14."* 4 v. Paris: 1949.

174. Gérard, Jo. *'14–'18 insolite: Rien que des aventures extraordinaires.* Paris: Éditions Meddens, 1966.

175. Gide, Charles, et Oualid, William. *la Guerre et la Vie sociale. Le Bilan de la guerre pour la France.* Paris: 1931.

176. Giono, Jean. *To the Slaughterhouse.* London: 1969.

177. Girault, René. *Emprunts russes et investissements français en Russie, 1887–1918.* Paris: 1973.

178. Gmeline, Patrick de. *Le 11 Novembre 1918. La 11e heure du 11e jour du 11e mois.* Paris: 1998.

179. Godfrey, J. *Capitalism at War: Industrial Policy and Bureaucracy in France 1914–1918.* New York: Berg, 1987.

180. Goldberg, Harvey. *The Life of Jean Jaurès.* Madison, WI: 1962.

181. Goodspeed, D. J. *The German Wars. 1914–1945.* Boston: 1977.

182. Gorce, Paul Marie de la. *La République et son armée.* Paris: 1963.

183. Goutard, A. *La Marne Victoire inexploitée.* Paris: 1968.

184. Grandmaison, Colonel François Loyzeau de. *Deux Conférences.* Paris: 1911.

185. Grandmaison, Colonel François Loyzeau de. *Dressage de l'infanterie en vue du combat offensif.* Paris: 1908.

186. Griset, Pascal, and Beltran, Alain. *L'Economie française 1914–1945.* Paris: 1994.

187. Grouard, Auguste. *La Conduite de la guerre jusqu'à la Bataille de la Marne.* Paris: 1968.

188. Guillen, Pierre, ed. *la France et l'Italie pendant la Première Guerre mondiale.* Grenoble: 1976.

189. Gurial, Losir. *"Je les grignote . . ." Champagne 1914–1915.* Paris: 1965.

190. Gunzenhäuser, Max. *Die Bibliographien zur Geschichte des Ersten Weltkrieges.* Frankfurt: 1964.

191. Hager, Philip. *The Novels of World War I: An Annotated Bibliography.* New York: 1981.

192. Halpern, Paul G. *The Mediterranean Naval Situation, 1908–1914.* Cambridge: 1971.

193. Hanna, Martha. *Mobilization of the Intellect: French Scholars and Writers during the Great War.* Cambridge: 1996.

194. Hanotaux, Gabriel. *Histoire Illustrée de la Guerre de 1914.* 19 v. Paris: 1915–24.

195. Hartesfeldt, Fred R. van., ed. *The Dardanelles Campaign, 1915: Historiography and Annotated Bibliography.* Westport, CT: 1997.

196. Hause, Steven C. "More Minerva than Mars: The French Women's Rights Campaign and the First World War." In Higonnet, Margaret Randolph, Jenson, Jane, Michel, Sonya, Wertz, Margaret. *Behind the Lines: Gender and the Two World Wars.* New Haven: Yale University Press, 1987.

197. Hayne, M. B. *The French Foreign Office and the Origins of the First World War.* Oxford: Clarendon Press, 1993.

198. Hellot, F. E. A. *Les commandement des généraux Nivelle et Pétain.* Paris: 1936.

199. Henry, Marliène Patten. *Monumental accusations: The Monuments aux morts as expressions of popular unrest.* New York: 1996.

200. Herubel, Michel. *La bataille des Dardenelles 1914–1916, ou la tragédie announcée.* Paris: 1998.

201. Hess, Paul. *Vie à Reims pendant la guerre de 1914–1918: Notes et impressions de bombardé.* Paris: 1998.

202. Hogenhuis-Seliverstoff, Anne. *les Relations franco-soviétiques. 1917–1924.* Paris: 1981.

203. Horne, Alistair. *The Price of Glory: Verdun 1916.* New York: Harper Colophin Books, 1962.

204. Horne, John. *Labor at War: France and Britain, 1914–1918.* New York: Oxford University Press, 1991.

205. Hovi, Kalvero. *Cordon sanitaire, barrière de l'Est? The Emergence of a New French Eastern European Alliance Policy, 1917–1919.* Turku: 1979.

206. Howard, Michael. *The Franco-Prussian War: The German Invasion of France 1870–71.* n.p.: 1961.

207. Howard, Michael. "Men against Fire: Expectations of War in 1914." In Miller, Steven E., Lynn-Jones, Sean M., and Van Evera, Stephen, eds. *Military Strategy and the Origins of the First World War.* Princeton: 1991.

208. Huber, Georg. *Die französische Propaganda im Weltkrieg gegen Deutschland 1914 bis 1918.* Munich: 1928.

209. Huber, Marcel. *la Population de la France pendant la guerre.* Paris: 1931.

210. Huguet, Général A. *Britain and the War: A French Indictment.* London: 1928.

211. Huss, Marie-Monique. "Protonatalism and the Popular Ideology of the Child in Wartime France: The Evidence of the Picture Postcard," in Wall, R., and Winter, J., eds. *The Upheaval of War.* Cambridge: 1988.

212. Isselin, Henri. *The Battle of the Marne.* Garden City, NY: Doubleday & Co., 1966.

213. Jackson, J. Hampden. *Clemenceau and the Third Republic.* New York: Colliers, 1962.

214. Janin, général. *Ma mission en Sibérie, 1918–1920.* Paris: 1933.

215. Joffre, Marshal Joseph J. C. *Mémoires du Maréchal Joffre, 1910–1917.* 2 v. Paris: Plon, 1932.

216. Johnson, Hubert C. *Breakthrough: Tactics, Technology and the Search for Victory on the Western Front in World War I.* Novato, CA: 1994.

217. Jouin, Y. "Les Campagnes d'Afrique, 1914–1915." *Revue historique de l'armée* 20 (1964): 143–55.

218. Jouin, Y. "Les Campaigns d'Afrique 1914–1918." *Revue historique de l'armée* 21 (1965): 75–90.

219. Jubert, Raymond. *Verdun.* Nancy: Presses Universitaires de Nancy, 1989.

220. Kabakoff, Marvin Howard. "The Composition of the Anti-War Movement in France in World War I." Ph.D. diss., Washington University (St. Louis), 1975.

221. Kahn, André. Journal de guerre d'un juif patriote: 1914–1918. Paris: 1978.

222. Kaspi, André. *le temps des Américains.* Paris: 1976.

223. Keiger, John F. V. *France and the Origins of the First World War.* New York: St. Martin's Press, 1983.

224. Keiger, John F. V. *Raymond Poincare.* New York: 1997.

225. Kemp, Tom. *The French Economy, 1913–1939.* London: 1972.

226. Kennedy, Paul. *The War Plans of the Great Powers, 1880–1914.* London: 1979.

227. Kennan, George F. *The Decline of Bismarck's European Order.* Princeton: Princeton University Press, 1979

228. Kennan, George F. *The Fateful Alliance: France, Russia, and the Coming of the First World War.* New York: Pantheon Books, 1984.

229. King, Jere Clemens. *Generals and Politicians: Conflict Between France's High Command, Parliament, and Government, 1914–1918.* Westport CT: Greenwood Press, 1951.

230. Kirchner, Klaus. *Flügblatter aus Frankreich, 1914–1918.* Erlangen: 1992.

231. Kluck, Colonel-Général Alexander von. *la Marche sur Paris.* Paris: 1922.

232. Koeltz, Général Louis. *La Guerre de 1914–1918: Les opérations militaires.* Paris: Éditions Sirey, 1966.

233. Koerner, Francis. "L'Economie du Massif Central durant la première guerre mondiale." *Revue historique* 277 (1987): 67–81.

234. Kosyk, Wolodymyr. *la Politique de la France à l'égard de l'Ukraine, mars 1917–février 1918.* Paris: Publications de la Sorbonne, 1981.

235. Kriegel, Annie. *Aux origines du communisme français, 1914–1920, contribution à l'histoire du mouvement ouvrier français.* Paris: Mouton, 1964.

236. Krumeich, Gerd. *Armaments and Politics in France on the Eve of the First World War.* Dover, NH: Berg Publishers, 1984.

237. Kupferman, Alfred. "Les Débuts de l'offensive morale allemande contre la France (Décembre 1914-Décembre 1915)." *Revue historique* 249 (1973): 91–114.

238. Labayle Couhat, Jean. *French Warships of World War I.* London: 1974.

239. Lachaux, Gérard. *1917, la bataille du Chemin des Dames.* Laon: 1997.

240. Lacouture, Jean. *DeGaulle: The Rebel, 1890–1944.* New York: Norton, 1990.

241. Laffargue, général André. *Foch et la Bataille de 1918.* Paris: 1967.

242. Langle de Cary, Fernand. *Souvenirs de commandement, 1914–1916.* Paris: 1935.

243. Lanrezac, Charles L. M. *La Plan de Campagne Français et le premier mois de la guerre.* Paris: 1929.

244. Larcher, commandant M. *la Grande Guerre dans les Balkans.* Paris: 1930.

245. Larcher, commandant M. *la Guerre turque dans la guerre mondiale.* Paris: 1923.

246. Lastours, Sophie de. *1914–1918: La France gagne la guerre des codes secrets.* Paris: 1998.

247. Laure, général. *Pétain.* Paris: 1941.

248. Laurent, André. *La Bataille de la Marne (1914).* Paris: Éditions Horvath, 1982.

249. Lawrence, Jon, Dean, Martin, and Robert, Jean-Louis. "The Outbreak of War and the Urban Economy: Paris, Berlin and London, 1914." *Economic History Review* 45 (1992): 564–93.

250. Le Bon, Gustave. *Enseignements psychologiques de la guerre européene.* Paris: 1915.

251. Le Bon, Gustave. *Premières Conséquences de la guerre. Transformation mentale des peuples.* Paris: 1916.

252. Lefebvre, J. H. *L'Enfer de Verdun evoqué par les témoins et commenté par J. H. Lefebvre.* Paris: 1983.

253. Lemaire, Françoise. *Les films militaires français de la Première Guerre mondiale; catalogue des films muets d'actualité realisés par le Service cinématographique de l'Armée.* Ivry: 1997.

254. Lepick, Oliver. *La grande guerre chimique, 1914–1918.* Paris: 1998.

255. Leymarie, Michel. *La France contemporaine. De la Belle Époque à la Grande Guerre, le triomphe de la République.* Paris: 1999.

256. L'Hôpital, commandant. *Foch, l'Armistice, et la Paix,* 2 v. Paris: 1931.

257. Liddell Hart, B. H. *Foch: The Man of Orléans*. London: 1931.

258. Liddell Hart, B. H. *Reputations Ten Years After*. London: 1928.

259. Lowry, Bullitt. *Armistice 1918*. Kent, OH: 1996.

260. Luzzato, Sergio. *L'Împot du sang: la gauche française à l'épreuve de la guerre mondiale (1900–1945)*. Lyon: 1996.

261. Malvy, Louis Jean. *Mon crime*. Paris: 1921.

262. Mangin, Charles. *Lettres de guerre, 1914–1918*. Paris: 1950.

263. Mangin, Louis-Eugène. *Le Général Mangin*. Paris: 1990.

264. March, Lucien. *Mouvement des prix et des salaires pendant la guerre, 1914–1920*. Paris: 1925.

265. Marchand, A. *Plans de concentration de 1871 à 1914*. Paris: Berger-Levrault, 1926.

266. Mare, André. *Carnets de guerre*. Paris: 1996.

267. Marshall-Cornwall, Sir James H. *Foch as Military Commander*. New York: 1972.

268. Martin, Benjamin F. *France and the Après-Guerre: Illusions and Disillusionment*. Baton Rouge: 1999.

269. Marty, A. *La Poste militaire en France (campagnes 1914–1919)*. Paris: 1922.

270. Mayeur, Jean-Marie. *La vie politique sous la Troisième République (1870–1940)*. Paris: 1984.

271. Mayeur, Jean-Marie and Réberioux, M. *The Third Republic from Its Origins to the Great War, 1871–1914*. Cambridge: 1984.

272. McDougall, Walter A. *France's Rhineland Diplomacy, 1914–1929*. Princeton: 1978.

273. McPhail, Helen. *The Long Silence: Civilian Life under the German Occupation of Northern France, 1914–1918*. London: 1999.

274. Meyer, Jacques. *le 11 Novembre*. Paris: 1964.

275. Meyer, Jacques. *La vie quotidienne des soldats pendant la Grande Guerre*. Paris: Hachette, 1967.

276. Michel, Marc. *L'Appel à Afrique: Contributions et Réactions à l'Effort de Guerre en A.O.F (1914–1919)*. Paris: Publications de la Sorbonne, 1982.

277. Michel, Marc. *Galliéni*. Paris: 1989.

278. Michon, Georges. *La préparation à la guerre: la loi de trois ans*. Paris: 1935.

279. Millerand, Alexandre. *Pour la défense nationale. Une année au ministère de la Guerre (14 Janvier 1912–12 Janvier 1913)*. Paris: 1913.

280. Miquel, Pierre. *Le Chemin des Dames*. Paris: 1997.

281. Miquel, Pierre. *14–18: Mille Images Inédites*. Paris: 1998.

282. Miguel, Pierre. *La Grande Guerre*. Paris: Librairie Arthème Fayard, 1983.

283. Miquel, Pierre. *La Grande Guerre au jour le jour*. Paris: Librairie Arthème Fayard, 1988.

284. Miquel, Pierre. *Les Hommes de la Grande Guerre, Histoires vraies*. Saint Amand: 1988.

285. Miquel, Pierre. *Mourir à Verdun*. Paris: 1995.

286. Miquel, Pierre. *Les poilus d'Orient*. Paris: 1923.

287. Mitrakos, Alexander T. *France in Greece during World War I: A Study in the Politics of Power*. Boulder, CO: East European Monographs, 1982.

288. Monier, Frédéric. *La France Contemporaine: les années vingt*. Paris: 1999.

289. Montherlant, Henri de. *Chant funèbre pour les morts de Verdun*. Paris: 1924.

290. Mordacq, Jean Jules. *Le ministère Clemenceau*, 4 v. Paris: Plon, 1930–31.

291. Moulton, Harold; Lewis, Cleona. *la Dette française*. Paris: 1926.

292. Mourelos, Yannis G. *l'Intervention de la Grèce dans la Grande Guerre (1916–1917)*. Athènes: 1989.

293. Muller, Commandant. *Joffre et la Marne*. Paris: 1931.

294. Négrier, Général François de. *Lessons from the Russo-Japanese War*. London: 1905.

295. Neillands, Robin. *The Great War Generals on the Western Front, 1914–1918*. London: 1998.

296. Neré, J. *The Foreign Policy of France from 1914 to 1945*. London: 1975.

297. Newhall, David. *Clemenceau: A Life at War*. Lewiston, NY: Edward Mellen Press, 1991.

298. Nobécourt, R. G. *Les Fantassins du Chemin des Dames*. Paris: 1967.

299. Nouailhat, Yves-Henri. *les Américains à Nantes et à Saint-Nazaire, 1917–1919.* Paris: 1972.

300. Nouailhat, Yves-Henri. "Français, Anglais, et Américains face au problème de la réorganisation du commerce international (1914–1918)." *Relations internationales* 10 (1977): 95–114.

301. Nouailhat, Yves-Henri. *France et États-unis, Août 1914–Avril 1917.* Paris: 1979.

302. Offenstadt, Nicholas. *Les Fusillés de la grande guerre et la mémoire collective (1914–1999).* Paris: 1999.

303. Ormesson, N. B. Wladimir d'. *Auprès de Lyautey.* Paris: 1963.

304. Painlevé, Paul. *Comment j'ai nommé Foch et Pétain.* Paris: 1923.

305. Palat, Général Pierre Lehautcourt. *La Grande Guerre sur le Front Occidental,* 14 v. Paris: 1917–1930.

306. Paléologue, M. *Three Critical Years, 1904–1906.* London: 1935.

307. Palmer, Alan. *The Gardeners of Salonika.* London: Andre Deutsch, 1965.

308. Papayanis, Nicholas. "Collaboration and Pacifism in France during World War I." *Francia* 5 (1977): 425–52.

309. Paraf, Pierre. *La France de 1914.* Paris: Éditions de Sorbier, 1981.

310. Pastre, J-L. Gaston. *Trois ans de front: Belgique, Aisne et Champagne, Verdun, Argonne, Lorraine: notes et impressions d'un artilleur.* Nancy: 1990.

311. Pedroncini, Guy et al. *Histoire militaire de la France, v. 3: De 1871 à 1940.* Paris: 1994.

312. Pedroncini, Guy. *Les Mutineries de l'armée française, 1917.* Paris: Presses universitaires de France, 1968.

313. Pedroncini, Guy. *Les négotiations secrète pendant la grande guerre.* Paris: Flammarion, 1969.

314. Pedrocini, Guy. *Pétain général-en-chef, 1917–1918.* Paris: Presses universitaires de la France, 1974.

315. Pedrocini, Guy. *Pétain: le soldat et la gloire, t. I.* Paris: 1989.

316. Percin, Général Alexandre. *1914: Les erreurs du Haut Commandement.* Paris: A. Michel, 1922.

317. Percin, Général Alexandre. *Le Massacre de notre infanterie. 1914–1918.* Paris: A. Michel, 1921.

318. Perreux, Gabriel. *La vie quotidienne des civils en France pendant la Grande Guerre.* Paris: 1966.

319. Peschaud, Marcel. *Politique et Fonctionnement des transports par chemin de fer pendant la guerre.* Paris: 1926.

320. Pétain, Maréchal H. P. *La Bataille de Verdun.* Paris: Plon, 1934.

321. Petit, Lucien. *Histoire des finances extérieures de la France pendant la guerre de 1914–1919.* Paris: 1929.

322. Petit, Pierre. *Souvenirs de guerre, 1 Août 1914–15 Octobre 1915,* 3 v. Paris: Académie européene du livre, 1990.

323. Phillips, Jill M. *Darkling Plain: The Great War in History, Biography, Diary, Poetry, Literature and Film—a Bibliography.* New York: 1980.

324. Picard, Roger. *le Mouvement syndical pendant la guerre.* Paris: 1927.

325. Picq, Charles Ardant du. *Études sur le Combat: Combat antique et moderne.* Paris: 1942.

326. Pierrefeu, Jean de. *Plutarch a menti.* Paris: 1933.

327. Pingaud, Albert. *Histoire diplomatique de la France pendant la Grande Guerre.* 3 v. Paris: 1938–1941.

328. Pinot, Pierre. *le Contrôle du ravitaillement de la population civile.* Paris: 1920.

329. Poidevin, Raymond. *Les relations économiques et financières entre France et l'Allemagne de 1898 à 1914.* Paris: 1969.

330. Poincaré, Raymond. *Au service de la France.* 11 v. Paris: Plon, 1926–1974.

331. Porch, Douglas. "The French Army in the First World War" in Millet, Alan R., and Murray, Williamson. eds. *Military Effectiveness, v.1: The First World War.* Boston: Unwin Hyman, 1989.

332. Porch, Douglas. *The March to the Marne: The French Army 1871–1914.* Cambridge: Cambridge University Press, 1981.

333. Porter, Charles W. *The Career of Théophile Delcassé.* Philadelphia: 1936.

334. Pourcher, Yves. *les Jours de guerre. La Vie des Français au jour le jour entre 1914 et 1918.* Paris: 1994.

335. Prete, Roy A. "French Military War Aims, 1914–1916." *The Historical Journal* 28 (1985): 887–99.

336. Prete, Roy A. "French Strategic Planning and the Deployment of the BEF in France in 1914." *Canadian Journal of History* 24 (1989): 42–62.

337. Prete, Roy A. "The Preparation of the French Army prior to World War I: An Historiographical Reappraisal." *Canadian Journal of History* 26 (1991): 241–66.

338. Prete, Roy A. "Since Renouvin: A Reconsideration of French War Aims." *Proceedings of the American Meeting of the Western Society for French History* 10 (1982): 461–71.

339. Prete, Roy. "The War of Movement on the Western Front, August-November 1914: A Study in Coalition Warfare." Ph.D. dissertation, University of Alberta: 1979.

340. Prost, Antoine. *Les Anciens Combattants et la société française 1914–1939.* 3 v. Paris: Firmin Didot, 1977

341. Rajsfus, Maurice. *La Censure militaire et policière, 1914–1918.* Paris: 1999.

342. Ralston, David. *The Army of the Republic: The Place of the Military in the Political Evolution of France.* Cambridge: Harvard University Press, 1967.

343. Ratinaud, Jean. *La Course à la mer: De la Somme aux Flandres (Septembre 14–Novembre 17, 1914).* Paris: Fayard, 1967.

344. Ratinaud, Jean. *1917 ou la révolte des poilus.* Paris: Fayard, 1960.

345. Rearick, Charles. *The French in Love and War: Popular Culture in the Era of the Two World Wars.* New Haven: 1997.

346. Rebérioux, Madeleine. *The Third Republic from Its Origins to the Great War.* Cambridge: 1982.

347. Reboul, Lieutenant-Colonel. *Mobilisation industrielle, t. 1: Des fabrications de guerre en France de 1914 à 1918.* Paris: 1925.

348. Recouly, Raymond. *General Joffre and his Battles.* New York: 1917.

349. Recouly, Raymond. *le Mémorial de Foch. Mes entretiens avec le maréchal.* Paris: 1929.

350. Renouvin, Pierre. *L'armistice de Rethonde.* Paris: Éditions Gallimard, 1968.

351. Renouvin, Pierre. "Les Buts de Guerre du Gouvernement Français 1914–1918," *Revue historique* 235 (1966): 1–38.

352. Renouvin, Pierre. *The Forms of War Government in France.* New Haven: Yale University Press, 1927.

353. Renouvin, Pierre. *Histoire des relations internationales, t. VI: De 1871 à 1914: l'apogée de l'Europe.* Paris: 1955.

354. Renouvin, Pierre. *The Immediate Origins of the War.* New Haven, CT: 1928.

355. Renouvin, Pierre. *Peuples et Civilisations v. XIX: La Crise européenne et la Grande Guerre (1904–1918).* Paris: Presses Universitaires de France, 1962.

356. *Revue d'histoire de la guerre mondiale,* 17v. Paris: 1923–39.

357. Rials, Stéphan. *Administration et organisation: de l'organisation de la bataille à la bataille de l'organisation dans l'administration française.* Paris: 1977.

358. Ribot, Alexandre. *Journal d'Alexandre Ribot et correspondances inédites, 1914–1922.* Paris: 1936.

359. Robert, Jean-Louis. "Women and Work in France during the First World War." In Wall, Richard, and Winter, Jay. eds, *The Upheaval of War Family Work and Welfare in Europe, 1914–1918.* Cambridge: Cambridge University Press, 1988.

360. Rocolle, P. *L'hécatombe des généraux.* Paris: Lavauzelle, 1980.

361. Romaine, Jules. *Verdun.* New York: 1939.

362. Ronarc'h, Pierre. *Souvenirs de la Guerre,* v 1. Paris: 1921.

363. Rousseau, Frédéric. *La guerre censurée. Une histoire des combattants européens de 14–18.* Paris: 1999.

364. Rouvier, Frédéric. *En ligne. L'Église de France pendant la Grande Guerre (1914–1918).* Paris: 1919.

365. Rowe, Barbara Jean. "Testimony to War: Literature by French Soldiers in the Great War, 1914–1918." Ph.D. dissertation, University of Massachusetts: 1979.

366. Rowher, Jürgen. *Neue Forschungen zum Ersten Weltkrieg: Literaturberichte und Bibliographien von 30 Mitgliedstaaten der "Commission internationale d'histoire militaire comparée."* Koblenz: 1985.

367. Sarrail, Général Maurice. *Mon commandement en Orient.* Paris: E. Flammarion, 1920.

368. Schor, Ralph. *La France dans la première guerre mondiale.* Paris: 1997.

369. Sherman, Daniel J. *The Construction of Memory in Inter-War France.* New York: 1999.

370. Siebert, Ferdinand. *Aristide Briand: Ein Staatsmann zwischen Frankreich und Europa.* Zurich and Stuttgart: 1973.

371. Simonet, Benjamin. *Franchise militaire: De la bataille des frontières aux Combats de Champagne, 1914–1918.* Paris: 1986.

372. Sivais, Bertrand. *Le Service postal militaire français pendant la guerre de 1914–1918.* Paris: 1975.

373. Slater, Catherine. *Defeatists and Their Enemies: Political Invective in France, 1914–1918.* New York: Oxford University Press, 1981.

374. Smith, Leonard V. *Between Mutiny and Obedience: The Case of the French Fifth Infantry Division during World War I.* Princeton: Princeton University Press, 1994.

375. Snyder, Jack K. *The Ideology of the Offensive: Military Decision Making and the Disasters of 1914.* Ithaca: Cornell University Press, 1984.

376. Société française de Bibliographie. *Répertoire bibliographique de l'histoire de France.* Paris: 1920–1939.

377. Spears, Brigadier General E. L. *Liaison 1914.* London: 1932.

378. Speed, Richard B., III. *Prisoners, Diplomats and the Great War: A Study in the Diplomacy of Captivity.* New York: Greenwood Press, 1990

379. Stevenson, D. *French War Aims Against Germany, 1914–1919.* Oxford: The Clarendon Press, 1982.

380. Stone: Judith. *The Search for Social Peace. Reform Legislation in France, 1890–1914.* Albany, NY: 1985.

381. Suarez, Georges. *Briand, sa vie, son oeuvre,* 6 v. Paris: 1938–1952.

382. Tanenbaum, Jan K. "French Estimates of Germany's Operational War Plans," in May, Ernest R. [ed]. *Knowing One's Enemies: Intelligence Assessments before the Two World Wars.* [Ernest R. May, ed.] Princeton: Princeton University Press, 1984.

383. Tanenbaum, Jan Karl. *General Maurice Sarrail, 1856–1929: The French Army and Left Wing Politics.* Chapel Hill: University of North Carolina Press, 1974.

384. Tardieu, André. *le Mystère d'Agadir.* Paris: 1914.

385. Thébaud, Françoise. *La Femme au temps de la Guerre de 14.* Paris: Stock, 1986.

386. Trachtenberg, Marc. "'A New Economic Order': Étienne Clementel and French Economic Diplomacy during the First World War." *French Historical Studies* 10 (1977): 315–41.

387. Truchy, Henri. *The War Finance of France.* New Haven: 1927.

388. Tuberque, Jean-Pierre. *Les Journaux des Tranchées.* Paris: 1999.

389. Tuchman, Barbara. *The Guns of August.* New York: Macmillan, 1962.

390. Tyng, Sewell. *The Campaign of the Marne.* New York: 1935.

391. Valluy, Général Jean-Étienne. *La Première Guerre Mondiale (1914–1918).* 2 v. Paris: Larousse, 1968.

392. Varillon, Pierre. *Joffre.* Paris: 1956.

393. Vic, Jean. *Littérature de guerre, manuel méthodique et critique des publications de langue française.* 5 v. Paris: 1918–1923.

394. Villatte, captaine Robert. *Les conditions géographiques de la guerre. Étude de géographie militaire sur le front français, 1914–1918.* Paris: 1925.

395. Voivenal, Paul. *Avec la 67e Division de Réserve.* 4 v. Toulouse: 1933–1938.

396. Wallach, Jehuda. *Uneasy Coalition: The Entente Experience in World War I.* Westport, CT: 1993.

397. Watson, David Robin. *Georges Clemenceau.* London: Eyre Methuen, 1974.

398. Watt, Richard M. *Dare Call It Treason.* New York: 1963.

399. Weber, Eugen. *France Fin de Siècle.* Cambridge, MA: 1986.

400. Weber, Eugen. *The Nationalist Revival in France.* Berkeley: University of California Press, 1959.

401. Weltkriegbücherei Institut für Weltpolitik. *Systematische Bibliographien mit Verfasserregister des deutschen und aüslandischen Schriftums zur Geschichte und Vorgeschichte des Weltkrieges mit seinen Folgen und zur historisch-politschen Auslandskunde.* Individual volumes include: *Bibliographie zur militäischen Geschichte Franksreich im Weltkrieg.* Berlin 1937; *Bibliographie zur Wirtschafts, Sozial -und Geistesgeschichte Franksreich im Weltkrieg.* Berlin: 1937; *Bibliographie zur politischen Geschichte Franksreich in der Vorkriegszeit und im Weltkrieg.* Berlin: 1937.

402. Weygand, Général Maxime. *Foch.* Paris: 1947.

403. Weygand, Général Maxime. *Le 11 Novembre.* Paris: 1932.

404. Wheelwright, Julie. *The Fatal Lover: Mata Hari and the Myth of Women in Espionage.* London: Collins & Brown, 1992.

405. Williams, John. *Mutiny, 1917.* London: 1962.

406. Williamson, S. R. *The Politics of Grand Strategy: Britain and France Prepare for War, 1904–1914.* Cambridge: Harvard University Press, 1969.

407. Winter, Jay. *Sites of Memory, Sites of Mourning: The Great War in European Cultural History.* Cambridge: 1995.

408. Wormser, Georges. *la République de Clemenceau.* Paris: 1961.

409. Wright, Gordon. *Raymond Poincaré and the French Presidency.* Stanford: 1942.

4

Great Britain

Ian F. W. Beckett

From being a relatively neglected period in British historiography, interest in the First World War has continued to grow over the past two decades. In many respects, it has been arguably a product of successive anniversaries.

A BBC Television series, *The Great War* from 1964, is fondly remembered although its unavailability outside the confines of the Imperial War Museum until its release on video in late 2001 has safeguarded it from the rigorous historical revisionism that would have otherwise exposed it long ago as deeply flawed. Indeed, something of the background of the series and of the somewhat traditional parameters of those episodes dealing with the British Army's conduct of the war are explored in Bond's invaluable guide to the development of British military historiography of the war from its earliest contemporary historians to the present, *The First World War and British Military History* [15].

While the focus is primarily military, the various essays in Bond also reflect the wider historiographical debate that has taken place and suggest that key texts from the 1920s and 1930s such as the war memoirs of Churchill, Lloyd George, and Robertson were still essentially setting the historical agenda as late as the l960s. A contributing factor, of course, was that it was by no means clear initially that Cabinet papers would be released into the public domain under the 50-Year Rule, introduced by the Public Records Act of 1958. While some papers were made available under an informal 30-Year Rule prior to its introduction under the Public Records Act of 1967, most official archives relating to the war were not open to historians until the mid-1960s. Only then could necessary correctives be applied to the formative memoirs. Further stimulus to scholarly research was also provided by the sixtieth and seventieth anniversaries, even if popular writing continued to focus on the seemingly perennial obsession with the Somme, Passchendaele, and similar disasters for British arms.

Wolff's *In Flanders Fields* [242] and Clark's *The Donkeys* [42] had revived the images of blood and mud for a new readership in the 1960s much as *Oh What a Lovely War* did for the theatre and, later, cinema goers [172, 175, 199]. Similarly, by-now familiar themes pervaded the oral testimony presented by authors in the 1970s and 1980s and were also manifested to some extent in the founding of the Western Front Association in 1980.

Nonetheless, historiography has advanced spectacularly on many fronts since the 1960s and there are now a number of sophisticated modern general accounts of Britain during the Great War to supplement Woodward's *Great Britain and the War of 1914–1918* [247]. Turner's *Britain in the First World War* [215] provides a useful introduction aimed at the sixth-former and first-year undergraduate to the results of modern research on the political, social, economic, demographic, imperial, strategic, military, and naval aspects of British involvement. Such themes are not integrated altogether successfully in the chronological narrative of Wilson, *The Myriad Faces of War* [233] and, while light on social aspects, Bourne's more structured thematic account, *Britain and the Great War* [20], is probably the better overall introductory study. Harvey's *Collision of Empires* [113] makes some useful comparisons between Britain's conduct of both world wars and the French Revolutionary and Napoleonic Wars although often drifting into detail on minutiae.

Perhaps the best modern survey, however, is to be found in the essays edited by Constantine, Kirby, and Rose, *The First World War in British History* [44], which provide an up-to-date summary of the most recent research on political, social, economic, diplomatic, military, demographic, and cultural aspects. What is particularly evident from this collection is the shift between the 1970s and the 1990s from interpreting the postwar period as representing discontinuity with prewar Britain to emphasizing the continuities between the prewar and postwar periods. In many respects, the former trend toward emphasizing discontinuity and, therefore, the greater impact of the war upon Britain, was associated with Marwick, whose pioneering work on the Great War, *The Deluge,* first appeared in 1965 [152]. Now in a second edition with an extended introductory essay taking into account further research, Marwick has modified his conclusions to some extent. His four-tier "model" of "total war" as an agent of social change was a development of his later writings, but his themes remain relevant to the wider consideration of the war's impact. Alongside the revisionism of the contributors to Constantine, Kirby, and Rose, however, should be seen that of De Groot's *Blighty* [52], which provides a sustained critique of the assumption that the war resulted in any profound social change.

How Britain came to enter the war at all was one of the first fruits of the opening of the archives, yet it remains a matter of some historical controversy. Steiner's contribution to the Macmillan series on the origins of the war, *Britain and the Origins of the First World War,* is the standard account [203], although it is also one of the earliest volumes in the series. The military entanglement with

France and that attempted with Belgium is the subject of Philpott's *Anglo-French Relations and Strategy on the Western Front* [179], Williamson's *The Politics of Grand Strategy* [227], and of a number of Keith Wilson's essays [228, 229], while the Coogans [45] reveal precisely who knew of the "moral commitment" prior to 1914. The decision-making process in the crucial days of August 1914 is illuminated by Valone [217], Brock [25], and Keith Wilson [230]. Essentially, the current debate is whether long-term British interests would or would not have been better served by remaining neutral. The case for neutrality has been put most forcibly by Ferguson [70, 71], whose flights into the realm of counter-factual or "virtual" history is less than convincing. Indeed, Ferguson's episodic study of Britain at war, *The Pity of War,* though interesting on war finance, is not only highly idiosyncratic but, on military aspects, highly misleading. The case against neutrality has been best, and persuasively, articulated by Trevor Wilson in an article [232] and *The Myriad Faces of War.*

The domestic context in which Britain approached war has been increasingly examined although generally such pressures are still not regarded as the determining factor in the decisions of 1914. French [81] is a useful discussion of the "Edwardian crisis." Much attention in the past has been given to any evidence of the manifestation of militarism in pre-war Britain, but it would appear that militarism only existed in diluted form. Equally, there was a pacifist movement although its influence in August 1914 was as slight in Britain as elsewhere. Carsten [35] and Robbins [189] chart the anti-war movement thereafter and it might be said that there has been a similar tendency to exhaustive examination of conscientious objection by Kennedy and Rae [130, 183] when only 16,500 claims for exemption from military service were made on such grounds: almost 780,000 men were exempted for other reasons. Perhaps a more significant factor to be considered is the impact of Irish Home Rule, which was very much in evidence at the moment that Britain entered the war. Hennessey [116] and Lawlor [135] cover developments during the wartime years, while Hartley examines Ireland's continued relevance for British foreign relations, not least with the United States [112].

Britain was ill prepared to meet the challenge of modern total war, as is clear from Kennedy's measured overview in *Military Effectiveness* [129]. For one thing, while Kitchener, who was appointed Secretary of State for War in August 1914, anticipated a long rather than a short war, he overturned Haldane's prewar plans to use the Territorial Force as a means of wartime expansion. Cassar [36], Neilson [161] and Simkins [202] all examine Kitchener's motivations, while French [80] establishes the wider prewar expectations of a strategy of "business as usual." Neilson further draws attention to the crucial role of Russia in Kitchener's strategic calculations [162], while the continuing strategic problems of partnership with France are covered by Philpott's *Anglo-French Relations and Strategy* as well as Rhodri Williams [226], who concentrates on the gestation of the battle of Loos in September 1915, and by Greenhalgh [100] and Strachan [204], who consider the origins of the Somme offensive of July 1916.

Britain's wartime strategy as a whole, together with the aims it was designed to achieve, was another aspect to which historians devoted themselves at an early stage once the official records were opened. The pioneer was Guinn in *British Strategy and Politics* [107] with Rothwell's *British War Aims and Peace Diplomacy* [192] building in the consideration of war aims. The wider political significance of war aims has since been explored by Goldstein [94] with specific areas of British diplomatic concerns addressed by Calder [31], Egerton [62], Fest [73], Jaffe [124], Louis [142], and Nelson [163]. Gooch [95] further contributed to the military participation in the debate on war aims while, following his study of the prewar period, French has now completed his detailed study of strategy and war aims with two monographs, *British Strategy and War Aims* taking the story to 1916 [83] and *The Strategy of the Lloyd George Coalition* from 1916 to 1918 [87], supplemented by some important individual articles [85, 86]. The search for alternatives to the Western Front is an important aspect of the strategic debate. The fertile mind of Churchill permeated this debate, and two volumes of Gilbert's massive biography cover the war years [93]. French, of course, has largely redrawn the old interpretation of "westerners" versus "easterners" by postulating a division over means rather than ends and seeing the real contest between those like McKenna and Runciman advocating limited liability and an essentially maritime strategy on the one hand and those, like both Robertson and Lloyd George, grasping the nettle of a Continental strategy. Nevertheless, the struggle between politicians and soldiers for the control of theatre if not general strategy remains a central consideration. Dutton [60], Woodward [245, 246], and French himself [88] map the familiar signposts along the far from smooth path of civil-military relations such as the Calais Conference, the Nivelle affair, the creation of the Supreme War Council and the Maurice debate.

As already indicated, the wartime army intended to achieve the strategic objectives was essentially Kitchener's creation, for the existing Regulars and Territorials were to be greatly outnumbered by the "New Armies" of volunteers, to which Simkins' *Kitchener's Army* [202] is the invaluable guide, while the slow evolution of a more coherent manpower policy is chronicled in detail by Grieves [102]. The highly complicated pattern of recruiting and the myth of the "rush to the colours" has been the subject of some detailed regional studies such as Osborne [170] as well as more general but highly suggestive treatments by Dewey [56] and Winter [237]. The particular case of recruiting in Ireland has been receiving increasing attention [22, 32, 33, 53, 54, 74, 169] as has that of Wales [120, 121, 176, 178]. A very welcome recent addition to the literature has been the collection of essays on the Scottish experience of the war by Macdonald and McFarland [145], which ranges well beyond the purely military. Beckett [9] provides an introductory essay on conscripts, while the beginning of conscription itself in 1916 is covered by Adams and Poirier [2]. Other aspects of military participation such as the Volunteer Training Corps [8, 171] and the participation of Jews [180] and blacks [132] have also been touched upon.

The essays by Beckett and by Simpson in Liddle's *Home Fires and Foreign Fields* [139], Beckett in Turner's *Britain in the First World War,* and all in the collection edited by Beckett and Simpson, *A Nation in Arms* [7], provide a general guide to the social consequences for the army of massive wartime expansion.

Beckett and Simpson also provide a context for some of the more detailed individual unit studies that have emerged in recent years, since it is increasingly obvious that no one unit was the same and that the individual's experience thus varied enormously. It must be said that intellectuals like Sheffield [197] or the soldier poets who form the basis for Fussell's influential but highly flawed work, *The Great War and Modern Memory* [91], were wholly unrepresentative of the mass of wartime servicemen. Indeed, Fuller [90] has argued persuasively that the "export" of British mass popular culture to the rear areas in France and Flanders was the essential element in the maintenance of British morale when that of most other armies effectively cracked. As in other areas, interest has tended to be concentrated on relatively minor matters—in this case, wartime executions [167] and mutinous disorders, the majority of which occurred only after the war as a result of the pressure for rapid demobilization [49, 191].

In turn, however, the attention on executions has generated scholarly investigations into matters of morale. Thus, building upon older works such as Keegan's *The Face of Battle* [128], later studies by Englander [63–65, 67], Mackenzie [146], Schweitzer [196], Schneider [195], and Bourne and Sheffield in their contributions to the weighty collection of essays edited by Cecil and Liddle, *Facing Armageddon* [41], have provided an increasingly sophisticated view of morale and discipline. Shell shock and other medical responses to the war have also been examined by Bogacz [14], Bourke [19], Koven [134], and Leese [136], while medical aspects of the war are also probed in *Facing Armageddon* and in the essays edited by Cooter, Harrison, and Sturdy [47].

Space precludes dealing with the many studies of individual campaigns, which have continued to generate interest. A refreshing development, however, has been recent attempts to escape the near obsession with the Western Front on the part of popular authors and to deal in a scholarly fashion with other theatres such as Mesopotamia [50] and Italy [39]. Equally, the fascination with generalship has retained its grip on many popular authors and it is still the case that some of those served by the older biographies have yet to be revisited by modern historians. A modern biography of Henry Wilson is still awaited, though Robertson has now been well served by Woodward [246] and Allenby, at least in the Middle East, by Hughes [122]. Cassar [37] and Holmes [117] reach very similar conclusions with regard to Sir John French. The much-maligned staff would also be worth further investigation, while work is now belatedly under way on both corps and divisional commanders [21].

Not unexpectedly, there is no lack of modern interest in the case of Douglas Haig, although a new updated edition of his papers would be well worthwhile. On the one hand, Haig can still generate extreme hostility and, on the other, the continuing reverence of his perennial defender, Terraine, who first stated the case in *Douglas Haig: The Educated Soldier* [207]. The continued division of opinion is evident in the essays edited by Liddle on Passchendaele [140], a campaign also covered in great detail by Prior and Wilson's *Passchendaele: The Untold Story* [234]. Somewhere in the middle, although not necessarily definitive, is De Groot's *Douglas Haig* [51], whose work on Haig's prewar career is arguably more impressive than his coverage of the war years. A further, balanced appraisal also emerges from the essays edited by Bond and Cave, *Haig* [16]. Haig's real but undeclared role in the postwar "battle of the memoirs" is covered in the essays in Bond's *The First World War and British Military History,* but also by French [82] and Beckett [10], while various aspects of the work of Edmonds, the Official Historian, can be found additionally in another article by French [84] and those by Travers [209] and Williams [225].

Mention of Travers introduces the increasing work now being devoted to the operational and tactical level of the war on the Western Front. Essentially, Travers in articles and books such as *The Killing Ground* and *How the War Was Won* [209, 210, 212, 213] has tended to seek an explanation for the difficulties of the British army in coming to terms with the new conditions of warfare in what might be termed the managerial problems. In this respect, therefore, Haig merely personified much that was wrong with the military establishment as a whole although proving wholly inconsistent in his approach to operational planning. Graham [12, 97, 98] and Prior and Wilson [181, 234] have concentrated more on the technical problems of achieving "break-in" and converting this to "break-through." Though often illuminating, neither party's contributions to the ongoing debate have been altogether convincing in the varying explanations advanced for eventual British success in 1918. In particular, there is some fundamental disagreement on the capabilities of the tank, its particular contribution to victory debated by, among others, Travers [211] and Harris [108]. Arguably, however, there is an emerging consensus that British successes in 1918 owed most to German failures. Nonetheless, as evident from essays in Cecil and Liddle's *Facing Armageddon,* those by Lee and Simkins in the collection edited by Bond, *Look to Your Front* [17], and the work of Griffith [105] and his collaborators [104], there is another emerging consensus that the army's tactical performance was much improved by late 1917. Increasingly, too, emphasis is turning to the army's underrated victory in the field in the "last Hundred Days" [55, 109]. The question remains how far the perceived improvement in British performance was directed from above or simply emerged from below as a result of evolving experience on the part of lower formations.

Richter [187] deals with the British approach to gas warfare and Pattison with that of science generally [177]. One specialized aspect of the military conduct of the war, namely intelligence, has seen much attention. Occleshaw [164] offers a not always convincing overview, while the essays edited by Dockrill and French address the interconnection of intelligence with strategy [59]. Ferris [72] provides exhaustive detail of signals intelligence based on surviving documents but this is hard going for the nonenthusiast. Sheffy uses many of the same documents to cover in detail intelligence in the Palestine campaign [200].

There has been rather less work on the Royal Navy and the Royal Air Force. There are useful introductory essays on the Navy in Liddle's *Home Fires and Foreign Fields* and Turner's *Britain in the First World War,* while a number of essays in Cecil and Liddle's *Facing Armageddon* address both services. The definitive account of the naval war is to be found in the five volumes of Marder's

From the Dreadnought to Scapa Flow [151], while Gordon [96] has contributed a detailed study of those command traits that contributed to the defects evident at Jutland. Beesley [11] adds to the evidence on intelligence by addressing the role of the Admiralty's Room 40. Cooper [46] provides an overview of the emergence of the RAF from the Royal Flying Corps, while Paris [174] highlights the fear and fascination engendered in Britain by the aeroplane.

Another feature of modern total war affecting the conduct of operations was the enormously inflated demand for munitions and the work of both Fraser [78] and French [79] on the shells scandal, which hastened the collapse of the Asquith government, is an appropriate point at which to turn to the political and socioeconomic consequences of the war. Hazelhurst's *Politicians at War* [114] provided an early overview of the politics of the first phase of the war up to the creation of the first coalition in the wake of the shells scandal. Turner's *British Politics and the Great War* [216] covers the remainder of the war and Morgan [158] also concentrates on the Lloyd George coalition. The creation of the Asquith and Lloyd George coalitions has been a particular interest of historians, Fraser [77] focusing on the creation of the former and Fry [89] and McEwen [148] on its demise, while Murphy studies Lloyd George [160]. Stubbs has contributed an essay on the Unionists [205]. The best account of the Labour Party is McKibbin [150], while Winter illuminates a number of aspects of the socialist response to war [235].

One particular controversy has been McKibbin's claim, also addressed by Tanner [206], that the extension of the franchise in 1918 rather than participation in the direction of the war was primarily responsible for Labour's advance. Franchise reform itself is covered by Pugh [182].

A number of historians have been concerned with the Liberals and their leadership, Wilson [231] seeking to explain how the party was destroyed by the war. Cassar [38] is the most recent study of Asquith's war leadership, while the late John Grigg [106] reached only 1916 in his biography of Lloyd George. Other politicians than Churchill are less well served, although there is Grieves on Eric Geddes [103].

The introduction of businessmen like Geddes into government, like much else heralded as a consequence of the Lloyd George coalition, was not quite as unique as was proclaimed at the time. Indeed, the machinery of government had begun to change long before December 1916. The essays edited by Burk, *War and the State* [27], are an essential starting point with case studies of Cabinet, Treasury, and the Ministries of Food, Labour, Munitions and Reconstruction. They can be supplemented by Adams on the Ministry of Munitions [3] and by Rose on the Central Control Board [190]. The struggle to create a war economy, the growth of state intervention generally, and the emergence of other new ministries is a theme of the general studies such as the essays in Constantine, Kirby and Rose's *The First World War in British History* as well as Bourne's *Britain and the Great War,* De Groot's *Blighty* and Wilson's *The Myriad Faces of War.* Its effects, together with other factors on the economy, can be followed in Balderston [5], Ferguson [70], McDermott [147], Milward [156], and those essays edited by Winter [236] dealing with the relationship between the Ministry of

Munitions and the optical industry and the "dope scandal" of 1915 surrounding the production of cellulose. British dependence upon the United States for the financial means of fighting the war is clear from Burk's monograph [28], while other aspects of often uneasy Anglo-American relations generally can be traced in Fowler [76] and Kernek [131]. Businessmen themselves are subjected to scrutiny by Boswell and Johns [18] and the effect of the war on industrial competitiveness by Greasley and Oxley [99].

The relationship of both politicians and soldiers with the press has drawn a number of scholars, Lovelace [143] concentrating upon the issue of control and censorship with McEwen [148, 149] touching on both censorship and ownership. The press was naturally an instrument for propaganda, the latter subject as a whole being examined by Messinger [155] and Sanders and Taylor [194]. The impact of theatre [43], photography [34], the infant cinema and, especially, the pioneering wartime film, *The Battle of the Somme,* has been the subject of detailed analysis [4, 186]. The effect of propaganda on the treatment of one particular group within Britain, namely Germans, has also been considered [173, 220]. The role of the Church of England in national morale is covered by Wilkinson [224], while contributing to war charities [75] and even visiting museums [127] could contribute to the war effort.

How opinion or attitudes were influenced leads perhaps naturally to the wider consideration of the impact of war upon society. As indicated earlier, Marwick's question in *The Deluge* as to whether war led to genuine social change or merely accelerated long-term structural trends has been superseded in some respects by De Groot's question in *Blighty* as to whether there was any degree of change at all. Winter's work on demography, originally set out in a pioneering series of essays but now usefully summarized in his monograph, *The Great War and the British People* [237], is of vital importance in assessing the degree of social change within the context of the dysgenic effects of war losses and of paradoxically healthier standards of living and higher life expectancy. The collections of essays Winter has edited with Wall [219] sets change in a European context, with essays on pronatalism and eugenics, family life, women and the working class. Dwork contributes in particular to the effect of the war on children's health [61], while Waites [218] sees the war as increasing rather than lessening class divisions. Indeed, Reid [184, 185] sees the working class being essentially strengthened by the war, although much of the detailed evidence for the experience of labor thus far has rested on engineering. Industrial relations generally are covered by Wrigley [248–250], with Horne providing a comparison with France [119]. Other studies [111, 154, 159, 193, 222, 223] have concentrated on particular aspects of the trade union movement, which undoubtedly advanced its bargaining position during the war irrespective of how far those gains were sustained after 1918. Bush provides a valuable study of one particular industrial locality and indicates how valuable more such local studies would be [29]. Agriculture has been well covered by Barnett [6] and Dewey [57], while Offer's highly original work, *The First World War: An Agrarian Interpretation* [165], has pointed to the importance of agricultural production generally in relation to the British and German war efforts.

One area of debate that has been extremely well served is the question of the impact of the war on the position of women. Of course, there has been a lively debate on whether or not the war was primarily responsible for the extension of female suffrage in 1918, but there is also the wider matter of the overall benefit or otherwise of wartime participation. A starting point is Marwick's illustrated history, *Women at War* [153], but more recent general studies are Thom's *Nice Girls and Rude Girls* [208] and Woollacott's *On Her Their Lives Depend* [244], both concentrating on munitions workers, which can be used to extend the original overview by Braybon, *Women Workers in the First World War* [24]. Buckley [26], Harrison [110], Levine [138], and Woollacott [243] deal with what might be termed a traditional role with respect to the relationship of women with the military, embracing the wartime debate on sexual morality.

Crosthwait [48] explores the increasing use of women in auxiliary military roles, which went beyond the previous restriction to nursing, and Robert [188] examines paramilitary pretensions. Holt [118] has an additional and contrasting input into those works on the 1918 extension of the franchise discussed earlier. In many respects, there is an even wider debate among feminist historians as to the relationship between war and gender, aspects of which are touched upon by Braybon in her contribution to Constantine, Kirby, and Rose's *The First World War in British History* and by De Groot, who takes a rigorously conservative view of the feminist agenda in *Blighty.*

The return of women to a primarily domestic role following the war leads, in turn, to the matter of the degree to which any wartime expectations of substantial postwar change were realized. A pioneering essay by Abrams [1] sets a scene of frustrated hopes of reconstruction, while Johnson [126] and Lowe [144] point the finger at politicians. Housing has seemingly attracted more interest than some other areas since Johnson can be supplemented with Orbach [168]. Education and health has also attracted some interest as indicated in the essays in Burk's *War and the State* [27] and Constantine, Kirby, and Rose's *The First World War in British History.* As Ward [221] shows, demobilization was achieved without the subsequent growth of radical ex-servicemen's movements in Britain as opposed to Continental states. As previously mentioned, there were some disorders among British troops in both France and also in Britain, but the revolutionary potential was small indeed [64–66]. One attempted solution to potential social problems was the encouragement of settlement by veterans on the land in Britain and the empire, Fedorowich [68] being one contribution to this emerging field of research interest.

Dockrill and Goold [58], Goldstein [94], and Lentin [137] provide surveys of Britain's diplomacy and achievements in the various peace settlements of 1919, while the wider context is suggested in the essays edited by Boemeke, Feldman, and Glaser, *The Treaty of Versailles,* a number of which deal with Britain [13]. Jeffery's [125] study of the postwar difficulties of the army in coping with the implications of the settlements is an indication that the victory that had been achieved was partly illusory. The belief that the sacrifice had been in vain was to increase through the 1920s and 1930s and a distinct "myth" of the war emerged

[198–89], but it is important not to exaggerate, as does Fussell's *The Great War and Modern Memory,* the extent of the supposed revulsion against the war. Recent studies of wartime and postwar literature [23, 40, 166] make it clear that the public's taste was for "middle-brow" fiction and poetry rather than the products of "modernism" usually associated with the war's cultural legacy [123]. Much the same was true of film [175], as well as art and music [69, 201], while wartime popular culture [43, 240] was dominated by patriotic themes. Commemoration, too, illustrates the persistence of the traditional rather than modernist forms as suggested by the work of Winter in *Sites of Memory, Sites of Mourning,* and the collection edited with Sivan, *War and Remembrance* [238, 241]. Winter's lead has been followed by an increasing interest in the varying forms of commemoration in Britain [30, 92, 101, 115, 133], including postwar battlefield pilgrimage [141].

Indeed, as suggested by Moorhouse's illuminating study of the impact of the Gallipoli landings on the Lancashire town of Bury, *Hell's Foundations* [157], six of whose sons won the Victoria Cross "before breakfast" on 25 April 1915, the perception of the war in the interwar period was very different from that supposed when the image of the war was re-invented in the 1960s. As suggested at the beginning of this chapter, it is the strength of that perceived myth of the war in Britain that remains the greatest obstacle to historical understanding.

BIBLIOGRAPHY

1. Abrams, P. "The Failure of Social Reform, 1918–20." *Past and Present* 24 (1963): 43–63.

2. Adams, R. J. Q., and Poirier, P. F. *The Conscription Controversy in Great Britain, 1900–1918.* London: Macmillan, 1987.

3. Adams, R. J. Q. *Arms and the Wizard: Lloyd George and the Ministry of Munitions, 1915–16.* London: Cassell, 1978.

4. Badsey, Stephen. "The Battle of the Somme: British War Propaganda." *Historical Journal of Film, Radio and Television* 3 (1983): 99–115.

5. Balderston, Theo. "War, Finance and Inflation in Britain and Germany, 1914–18." *Economic History Review* 42 (1989): 222–44.

6. Barnett, L. Margaret. *British Food Policy during the First World War.* London: Collins, 1985.

7. Beckett, Ian. F. W., and Simpson, Keith. R. (eds). *A Nation in Arms: A Social Study of the British Army in the First World War.* Manchester: Manchester University Press, 1985.

8. Beckett, Ian. F. W. "Aspects of a Nation in Arms: Britain's Volunteer Training Corps in the Great War." *Revue Internationale d'Histoire Militaire* 63 (1985): 27–39.

9. Beckett, Ian. F. W. "The Real Unknown Army: British Conscripts, 1916–19." In Becker, J-J., and Audoin-Rouzeau, S. (eds). *Les sociétés européennes et la guerre de 1914–18.* Paris: Université de Paris X-Nanterre, 1990: 339–56.

10. Beckett, Ian. F. W. *The Judgement of History: Sir Horace Smith-Dorrien, Lord French and 1914.* London: Tom Donovan, 1993.

11. Beesley, Patrick. *Room 40: British Naval Intelligence, 1914–18.* Oxford: Oxford University Press, 1984.

12. Bidwell, Shelford, and Graham, Dominick. *Firepower. British Army Weapons and Theories of War, 1904–45.* London: Allen & Unwin, 1982.

13. Boemeke, Manfred, Feldman, Gerald, and Glaser, Elizabeth (eds). *The Treaty of Versailles: A Reassessment after 75 Years.* Cambridge: Cambridge University Press, 1998.

14. Bogacz. Ted. "War Neurosis and Cultural Change in England, 1914–22: The Work of the War Office Committee of Enquiry into Shell-shock." *Journal of Contemporary History* 24 (1989): 227–56.

15. Bond, Brian, ed. *The First World War and British Military History.* Oxford: Oxford University Press, 1991.

16. Bond, Brian, and Cave, Nigel, eds. *Haig: A Reappraisal 70 Years On.* Barnsley: Pen & Sword, 1999.

17. Bond, Brian, ed. *Look to Your Front: Studies in the First World War.* Staplehurst: Spellmount, 1999.

18. Boswell, Jonathan, and Johns, Bruce. "Patriots or Profiteers? British Businessmen and the First World War." *Journal of European Economic History* 11 (1982): 423–45.

19. Bourke, Joanna. *Dismembering the Male: Men's Bodies, Britain and the Great War.* London: Reaktion Books, 1996.

20. Bourne, J. M. *Britain and the Great War, 1914–18.* London: Edward Arnold, 1989.

21. Bourne, J. M. "British Generals in the First World War." In Sheffield, Gary, ed., *Leadership and Command: The Anglo-American Experience since 1861.* London: Brasseys, 1997: 93–116.

22. Bowman, Tim. "The Irish Recruiting and Anti-recruiting Campaigns, 1914–18," in Taithe, Bertrand, and Thornton, Tim, eds., *Propaganda: Political Rhetoric and Identity, 1300–2000.* Stroud: Sutton Publishing, 1999: 223–38.

23. Braco, Rosa Maria. *Merchants of Hope: British Middlebrow Writers and the First World War.* Providence, RI: Berg, 1993.

24. Braybon, Gail. *Women Workers in the First World War.* London: Croom Helm, 1981.

25. Brock, Michael. "Britain Enters the War." In Evans, R. J. W., and Von Strandmann, Hartmut Pogge, eds., *The Coming of the First World War.* Oxford: Oxford University Press, 1988: 145–78.

26. Buckley, Suzanne. "The Failure to Resolve the Problem of Venereal Disease among the Troops in Britain during World War One" in Bond, Brian, and Roy, Ian (eds.), *War and Society: A Yearbook of Military History.* London: Croom Helm, 1977: 65–85.

27. Burk, Kathleen, ed. *War and the State: The Transformation of British Government.* London: Allen & Unwin, 1982.

28. Burk, Kathleen. *Britain, America and the Sinews of War, 1914–18.* London: Collins, 1985.

29. Bush, Julia. *Behind the Lines: East London Labour, 1914–19.* London: Merlin, 1984.

30. Bushaway, Bob. "Name upon Name: The Great War and Remembrance." In Porter, Roy, ed., *Myths of the English.* Cambridge: Cambridge University Press, 1992: 136–67.

31. Calder, Kenneth. *Great Britain and the Origins of the New Europe, 1914–18.* Cambridge: Cambridge University Press, 1976.

32. Callan, Patrick. "British Recruitment in Ireland, 1914–16." *Revue Internationale d'Histoire Militaire* 63 (1985): 41–50.

33. Callan, Patrick. "Recruiting for the British Army in Ireland during the First World War." *Irish Sword* 17 (1987): 42–56.

34. Carmichael, Jane. *First World War Photographers.* London: Routledge, 1989.

35. Carsten, F. L. *War Against War: British and German Radical Movements in the First World War.* London: Batsford, 1982.

36. Cassar, G. H. *Kitchener: Architect of Victory.* London: William Kimber, 1977.

37. Cassar, G. H. *The Tragedy of Sir John French.* Newark: University of Delaware Press, 1985.

38. Cassar, G. H. *Asquith as War Leader.* London: Hambledon, 1994.

39. Cassar, G. H. *The Forgotten Front: The British Campaign in Italy, 1917–18.* London: Hambledon, 1998.

40. Cecil, Hugh. *The Flower of Battle: British Fiction Writers of the First World War.* London: Secker & Warburg, 1995.

41. Cecil, Hugh, and Liddle, Peter, eds. *Facing Armageddon: The First World War Experienced.* London: Leo Cooper, 1996.

42. Clark, Alan. *The Donkeys.* London: Hutchinson, 1961.

43. Collins, L. J. *Theatre at War, 1914–18.* London: Macmillan, 1998.

44. Constantine, Stephen, Kirby, Maurice, and Rose, Mary, eds. *The First World War in British History.* London: Edward Arnold, 1995.

45. Coogan, John W., and Coogan, Peter F. "The British Cabinet and the Anglo-French Staff Talks, 1905–14: Who Knew What and When Did He Know?" *Journal of British Studies* 24 (1985): 110–31.

46. Cooper, Malcolm. *The Birth of Independent Air Power.* London: Collins, 1986.

47. Cooter, Roger, Harrison, Mark, and Sturdy, Steve, eds. *War, Medicine and Modernity.* Stroud: Sutton Publishing, 1998.

48. Crosthwait, Elizabeth. "The Girl behind the Man behind the Gun: The Position of the Women's Auxiliary Army Corps, 1914–18." In Davidoff, Leonore, and Westover, Belinda, eds., *Our Work, Our Lives, Our Words.* Totowa NJ: Barnes & Noble, 1986: 161–81.

49. Dallas, Glodden, and Gill, Douglas. *The Unknown Army: Mutinies in the British Army in World War One.* London: Verso, 1985.

50. Davis, Paul K. *Ends and Means: The British Mesopotamian Campaign and Commission.* Rutherford, NJ: Farleigh Dickinson University Press, 1994.

51. De Groot, Gerard. *Douglas Haig, 1861–1928.* London: Unwin Hyman, 1988.

52. De Groot, Gerard. *Blighty: British Society in the Era of the Great War.* London: Longman, 1996.

53. Denman, Terry. "The Catholic Irish Soldier in the First World War: The Racial Environment." *Irish Historical Studies* 27 (1991): 352–65.

54. Denman, Terry. *Ireland's Unknown Soldiers: The 16th (Irish) Division in the Great War, 1914–18.* Dublin: Irish Academic Press, 1992.

55. Dennis, Peter, and Grey, Jeffrey, eds. *1918: Defining Victory.* Canberra: Army History Unit, 1999.

56. Dewey, Peter. "Military Recruiting and the British Labour Force during the First World War." *Historical Journal* 27 (1987): 199–223.

57. Dewey, Peter. *British Agriculture in the First World War.* London: Routledge, 1989.

58. Dockrill, Michael, and Goold, Douglas. *Peace Without Promise: Britain and the Peace Conferences, 1919–23.* London: Batsford, 1981.

59. Dockrill, Michael, and French, David, eds. *Strategy and Intelligence: British Policy during the First World War.* London: Hambledon, 1996.

60. Dutton, David. *The Politics of Diplomacy: Britain and France in the Balkans in the First World War.* London: I B Tauris, 1998.

61. Dwork, D. *War Is Good for Babies and Other Young Children: A History of the Infant and Child Welfare Movement in England, 1898–1918.* London: Tavistock, 1986.

62. Egerton, G. W. *Great Britain and the Creation of the League of Nations: Strategy, Politics and International Organisation.* London: Scolar Press, 1979.

63. Englander, David, and Osborne, James. "Jack, Tommy and Henry Dubb: The Armed Forces and the British Working Class." *Historical Journal* 21 (1978): 593–621.

64. Englander, David. "Military Intelligence and the Defence of the Realm: The Surveillance of Soldiers and Civilians in Britain during the First World War." *Bulletin of the Society for the Study of Labour History* 52 (1987): 24–32.

65. Englander, David. "Troops and Trade Unions, 1919." *History Today* 37 (1987): 8–13.

66. Englander, David. "Public Order in Britain, 1914–18." In Emsley, Clive, and Weinberger, Barbara, eds, *Policing Western Europe: Politics, Professionalism and Public Order, 1850–1940.* New York: Greenwood Press, 1991: 90–138.

67. Englander, David. "Discipline and Morale in the British Army, 1917–18," in Horne, John, ed., *State, Society and Mobilisation in Europe during the First World War.* Cambridge: Cambridge University Press, 1997: 125–43.

68. Fedorowich, Kent. *Unfit for Heroes: Reconstruction and Soldier Settlement in the Empire between the Wars.* Manchester: Manchester University Press, 1995.

69. Ferguson. John. *The Arts in Britain in World War I.* London: Stainer & Bell, 1980.

70. Ferguson, Niall. *The Pity of War.* London: Allen Lane, 1998.

71. Ferguson, Niall. "The Kaiser's European Union: What if Britain Had Stood Aside in August 1914." In Ferguson, Niall, ed., *Virtual History: Alternatives and Counterfactuals.* London: Picador, 1997: 228–80.

72. Ferris, John. *The British Army and Signals Intelligence during the First World War.* Stroud: Alan Sutton, 1992.

73. Fest, Wilfried. *Peace or Partition: The Habsburg Monarchy and British Policy, 1914–18.* New York: St. Martin's Press, 1978.

74. Fitzpatrick, David. "The Logic of Collective Sacrifice: Ireland and the British Army, 1914–18." *Historical Journal* 38 (1995): 1017–30.

75. Fowler, Simon. "War Charity Begins at Home." *History Today* 49 (1999): 17–23.

76. Fowler, W. B. *British-American Relations, 1917–18.* Princeton: Princeton University Press, 1969.

77. Fraser, Peter. "British War Policy and the Crisis of Liberalism in May 1915." *Journal of Modern History* 54 (1982): 1–26.

78. Fraser, Peter. "The British Shells Scandal of 1915." *Canadian Journal of History* 18 (1983): 69–86.

79. French, David. "The Military Background to the Shell Crisis of May 1915." *Journal of Strategic Studies* 2 (1979): 192–205.

80. French, David. *British Economic and Strategic Planning, 1905–15.* London: Allen & Unwin, 1982.

81. French, David. "The Edwardian Crisis and the Origins of the First World War." *International History Review* 4 (1982): 207–21.

82. French, David. "Sir Douglas Haig's Reputation: A Note." *Historical Journal* 28 (1985): 953–60.

83. French, David. *British Strategy and War Aims, 1914–16.* London: Allen & Unwin, 1986.

84. French, David. "Official but Not History: Sir James Edmonds and the Official History of the Great War." *Journal of the Royal United Services Institute for Defence Studies* 121 (1986): 58–63.

85. French, David. "The Dardanelles, Mecca and Kut: Prestige as a Factor in British Eastern Strategy, 1914–18." *War and Society* 5 (1987): 45–61.

86. French. David. "The Meaning of Attrition, 1914–16." *Historical Journal* 103 (1988): 385–405.

87. French, David. *The Strategy of the Lloyd George Coalition, 1916–18.* Oxford: Oxford University Press, 1995.

88. French, David. "A One-man Show? Civil-military Relations in Britain during the First World War." In Smith, Paul, ed., *Government and the Armed Forces in Britain, 1856–1990.* London: Hambledon, 1996: 75–107.

89. Fry, M. "Political Change in Britain, August 1914 to December 1916: Lloyd George Replaces Asquith—The Issues Underlying the Drama." *Historical Journal* 31 (1988): 609–28.

90. Fuller, J. G. *Troop Morale and Popular Culture in the British and Dominion Armies, 1914–19.* Oxford: Oxford University Press, 1990.

91. Fussell, Paul. *The Great War and Modern Memory.* Oxford: Oxford University Press, 1975.

92. Gaffney, Angela. Aftermath: *Remembering the Great War in Wales.* Cardiff: University of Wales Press, 1998.

93. Gilbert, Martin. *Winston S. Churchill.* Vols III & IV, 1914–22. London: Heinemann, 1971, 1975.

94. Goldstein, Erik. *Winning the Peace: British Diplomatic Strategy, 1916–20.* Oxford: Oxford University Press, 1991.

95. Gooch, John. "Soldiers, Strategy and War Aims in Britain, 1914–18." In Hunt, Barry, and Preston, Adrian, eds., *War Aims and Strategic Policy in the Great War.* London: Croom Helm, 1977: 21–40.

96. Gordon, Andrew. *The Rules of the Game: Jutland and British Naval Command.* London: John Murray, 1997.

97. Graham, Dominick. "Sans Doctrine: British Army Tactics in the First World War," in Travers, Tim, and Archer, C., eds., *Men at War.* Chicago: Precedent, 1982: 69–92.

98. Graham, Dominick. "Observations on the Dialectics of British Tactics, 1904–45," in Haycock, Ronald, and Neilson, Keith, eds., *Men, Machines and War.* Waterloo: Wilfred Laurier University Press, 1988: 51–73.

99. Greasley, David, and Oxley, Les. "Discontinuities in Competitiveness: The Impact of the First World War on British Industry." *Economic History Review* 49 (1996): 82–100.

100. Greenhalgh, Elizabeth. "Why the British Were on the Somme in 1916." *War in History* 6 (1999): 147–73.

101. Gregory, Adrian. *The Silence of Memory: Armistice Day, 1919–46.* Oxford: Berg, 1994.

102. Grieves, Keith. *The Politics of Manpower, 1914–18.* Manchester: Manchester University Press, 1988.

103. Grieves, Keith. *Sir Eric Geddes.* Manchester: Manchester University Press, 1989.

104. Griffith, Paddy, ed. *British Fighting Methods in the Great War.* London: Frank Cass, 1996.

105. Griffith, Paddy. *Battle Tactics on the Western Front The British Army's Art of Attack, 1916–18.* New Haven: Yale University Press, 1994.

106. Grigg, John. *Lloyd George: From Peace to War, 1912–16.* London: Methuen, 1985.

107. Guinn, Paul. *British Strategy and Politics, 1914–18.* Oxford: Oxford University Press, 1965.

108. Harris. Paul. *Men, Ideas and Tanks: British Military Thought and Armoured Forces, 1903–19.* Manchester: Manchester University Press, 1995.

109. Harris, Paul, and Barr, Niall. *Amiens to the Armistice: The BEF in the Hundred Days Campaign, 8 August to 11 November 1918.* London: Brasseys, 1998.

110. Harrison, Mark. "The British Army and the Problem of Venereal Disease in France and Egypt during the First World War." *Medical History* 39 (1995): 133–58.

111. Harrison, Royden. "The War Emergency Workers National Committee." In Briggs, Asa, and Saville, John, eds., *Essays in Labour History, 1886–1924.* London: Archon Books, 1971: 211–60.

112. Hartley, Stephen. *The Irish Question as a Problem in British Foreign Policy, 1914–18.* London: Macmillan, 1987.

113. Harvey, A. D. *Collision of Empires: Britain in Three World Wars, 1793–1945.* London: Hambledon, 1992.

114. Hazelhurst, Cameron. *Politicians at War, July 1914 to May 1915: Prologue to the Triumph of Lloyd George.* London: Cape, 1971.

115. Heffernan, Michael. "For Ever England: The Western Front and the Politics of Remembrance in Britain." *Ecumene* 2 (1995): 293–323.

116. Hennessey, Thomas. *Dividing Ireland: World War I and Partition.* London: Routledge, 1998.

117. Holmes, Richard. *The Little Field Marshal: Sir John French.* London: Cape, 1981.

118. Holt, Sandra Stanley. *Feminism and Democracy: Women's Suffrage and Reform Politics in Britain, 1900–1918.* Cambridge: Cambridge University Press, 1986.

119. Horne, John. *Labour at War: France and Britain, 1914–18.* Oxford: Oxford University Press, 1991.

120. Hughes, Clive. "The Welsh Army Corps, 1914–15: Shortages of Khaki and Basic Equipment promote a 'National' Uniform." *Imperial War Museum Review* 1 (1986): 91–100.

121. Hughes, Colin. *Mametz: Lloyd George's Welsh Army at the Battle of the Somme.* Gerrards Cross: Orion Press, 1982.

122. Hughes, Matthew. *Allenby and British Strategy in the Middle East, 1917–19.* London: Frank Cass, 1999.

123. Hynes, Samuel. *A War Imagined: The First World War and English Culture.* London: Bodley Head, 1990.

124. Jaffe, Lorna. *The Decision to Disarm Germany: British Policy towards Postwar German Disarmament, 1914–19.* London: Allen & Unwin, 1985.

125. Jeffery, Keith. *The British Army and the Crisis of Empire, 1918–22.* Manchester: Manchester University Press, 1984.

126. Johnson, P. B. *Land Fit for Heroes: The Planning of British Reconstruction, 1916–19.* Chicago: University of Chicago Press, 1968.

127. Kavanagh, Gaynor. *Museums and the First World War: A Social History.* Leicester: Leicester University Press, 1994.

128. Keegan, John. *The Face of Battle.* London: Cape, 1976.

129. Kennedy, Paul. "Britain in the First World War." In Millett, Allan. R., and Murray, Williamson, eds., *Military Effectiveness: The First World War.* Boston: Unwin Hyman, 1988: 31–79.

130. Kennedy, T. C. *The Hound of Conscience: A History of the No-Conscription Fellowship.* Fayetteville: University of Arkansas Press, 1981.

131. Kernek, Sterling. *Distractions of Peace during War: The Lloyd George Government's Reaction to Woodrow Wilson, December 1916 to November 1918.* Philadelphia: American Philosophical Society, 1975.

132. Killingray, David. "All the King's Men: Blacks in the British Army in the First World War." In Lotz, R., and Pegg, I., eds., *Under the Imperial Carpet.* Crawley: Rabbit Press, 1986: 164–81.

133. King, Alex. *Memorials of the Great War in Britain: The Symbolism and Politics of Remembrance.* Oxford: Berg, 1998.

134. Koven, Seth. "Remembering and Dismemberment: Crippled Children, Wounded Soldiers and the Great War in Britain." *American Historical Review* 99 (1994): 1167–202.

135. Lawlor, Sheila. *Britain and Ireland, 1914–23.* Dublin: Gill & Macmillan, 1983.

136. Leese, Peter J. "Problems Returning Home: The British Psychological Casualties of the Great War." *Historical Journal* 40 (1997): 1055–67.

137. Lentin, A. *Lloyd George, Woodrow Wilson and the Guilt of Germany: An Essay in the Prehistory of Appeasement.* Leicester: Leicester University Press, 1984.

138. Levine, Philippa. "Walking the Streets in a Way No Decent Woman Should: Women Police in World War One." *Journal of Modern History* 66 (1994): 34–78.

139. Liddle, Peter (ed). *Home Fires and Foreign Fields.* London: Brasseys, 1985.

140. Liddle, Peter (ed). *Passchendaele in Perspective: The Third Battle of Ypres.* London: Leo Cooper, 1997.

141. Lloyd, David W. *Battlefield Tourism: Pilgrimage and the Commemoration of the Great War in Britain, Australia and Canada, 1919–39.* Oxford: Berg, 1998.

142. Louis, William Roger. *Great Britain and Germany's Lost Colonies, 1914–19.* Oxford: Oxford University Press, 1967.

143. Lovelace, Colin. J. "British Press Censorship during the First World War." In Boyce, George, Curran, James, and Wingate, Pauline, eds., *Newspaper History: From the Seventeenth Century to the Present Day.* London: Sage, 1978: 307–19.

144. Lowe, Rodney. "The Erosion of State Intervention in Britain. 1917–24." *Economic History Review* 31 (1978): 270–86.

145. Macdonald, Catriona, and McFarland, E. W., eds. *Scotland and the Great War.* East Linton: Tuckwell Press, 1999.

146. Mackenzie, S. P. *Politics and Military Morale: Current Affairs and Citizen Education in the British Army, 1914–50.* Oxford: Oxford University Press, 1992.

147. McDermott, J. "Total War and the Merchant State: Aspects of British Economic Warfare against Germany, 1914–16." *Canadian Journal of History* 21 (1986): 61–76.

148. McEwen, J. M. "The Press and the Fall of Asquith." *Historical Journal* 21 (1978): 863–83.

149. McEwen, J. M. "Brass Hats and the British Press during the First World War." *Canadian Journal of History* 18 (1983): 43–67.

150. McKibbin, Ross. *The Evolution of the Labour Party, 1910–24.* Oxford: Oxford University Press, 1974.

151. Marder, Arthur J. *From the Dreadnought to Scapa Flow: The Royal Navy in the Fisher Era, 1904–19.* Oxford: Oxford University Press, 1961–70: 5 vols.

152. Marwick, Arthur. *The Deluge.* London: Bodley Head, 1965 (2nd edition, London: Macmillan, 1991).

153. Marwick, Arthur. *Women at War, 1914–18.* London: Croom Helm, 1977.

154. Melling, Joseph. "Whatever Happened to Red Clydeside? Industrial Conflict and the Politics of Skill in the First World War." *International Review of Social History* 35 (1990): 3–32.

155. Messinger, Gary. *British Propaganda and the State in the First World War.* Manchester: Manchester University Press, 1992.

156. Milward, Alan. *The Economic Effects of Two World Wars on Britain.* London: Macmillan, 1970.

157. Moorhouse, Geoffrey. *Hell's Foundations: A Town, Its Myths and Gallipoli.* London: Hodder & Stoughton, 1993.

158. Morgan. Kenneth O. *Consensus and Disunity: The Lloyd George Coalition Government, 1916–22.* Oxford: Oxford University Press, 1979.

159. Mor-O'Brien, A. "Patriotism on Trial: The Strike of South Wales Miners, July 1915." *Welsh History Review* 12 (1984): 76–104.

160. Murphy, R. "Walter Long, the Unionist Ministers and the Formation of Lloyd George's Government in December 1916." *Historical Journal* 29 (1986): 735–45.

161. Neilson, Keith. "Kitchener: A Reputation Refurbished." *Canadian Journal of History* 15 (1980): 207–27.

162. Neilson, Keith. *Strategy and Supply: The Anglo-Russian Alliance, 1914–17.* London: Harper Collins, 1984.

163. Nelson, Harold. *Land and Power: British and Allied Policy on Germany's Frontiers, 1916–19.* London: Routledge & Kegan Paul, 1963.

164. Occleshaw, Michael. *Armour Against Fate: British Military Intelligence in the First World War.* London: Columbus Books, 1988.

165. Offer, Avner. *The First World War: An Agrarian Interpretation.* Oxford: Oxford University Press, 1989.

166. Onions, John. *English Fiction and Drama of the Great War, 1918–39.* Basingstoke: Macmillan, 1990.

167. Oram, Gerard, *Worthless Men: Race, Eugenics and the Death Penalty in the British Army during the First World War.* London: Francis Boutle, 1998.

168. Orbach, L. F. *Homes for Heroes: A Study of the Evolution of British Public Housing, 1915–21.* London: Seeley Service, 1977.

169. Orr, Philip. *The Road to the Somme.* Belfast: Blackstaff Press, 1987.

170. Osborne, J. M. *The Voluntary Recruiting Movement in Britain, 1914–16.* New York: Garland, 1982.

171. Osborne, J. M. "Defining Their own Patriotism: British Volunteer Training Corps in the Great War." *Journal of Contemporary History* 23 (1988): 59–75.

172. Paget, Derek. "Remembrance Play: *Oh! What a Lovely War* and History." In Howard, Tony, and Stokes, John, eds., *Acts of War: The Representation of Military Conflict on the British Stage and Television since 1945.* Aldershot: Ashgate Publishing, 1996: 82–97.

173. Panayi, Panikos. *The Enemy Within: Germans in Britain during the First World War.* Leamington Spa: Berg, 1990.

174. Paris, Michael. *Winged Warfare: The Literature and Theory of Aerial Warfare in Britain, 1859–1917.* Manchester: Manchester University Press, 1992.

175. Paris, Michael. "Enduring Heroes: British Feature Films and the First World War," in Paris, Michael, ed., *The First World War and Popular Cinema. 1914 to the Present.* Edinburgh: Edinburgh University Press, 1999: 51–73.

176. Parry, C. "Gwynedd and the Great War." *Welsh History Review* 14 (1988): 78–117.

177. Pattison, Michael. "Scientists, Inventors and the Military in Britain. 1915–19: The Munitions Inventions Department." *Social Studies of Science* 13 (1983): 521–68.

178. Phillips, Gervase. "Dai Bach Y Soldiwr: Welsh Soldiers in the British Army, 1914–18." *Llafur* 6 (1993): 94–105.

179. Philpott, William J. *Anglo-French Relations and Strategy on the Western Front, 1914–18.* London: Macmillan, 1996.

180. Pollins, Harold. "Jews in the British Army in the First World War." *The Jewish Journal of Sociology* 37 (1995): 100–111.

181. Prior, Robin, and Wilson, Trevor. *Command on the Western Front.* Oxford: Blackwell, 1992.

182. Pugh, M. D. *Electoral Reform in War and Peace, 1906–18.* London: Routledge & Kegan Paul, 1978.

183. Rae, John. *Conscience and Politics: The British Government and the Conscientious Objector to Military Service, 1916–19.* Oxford: Oxford University Press, 1970.

184. Reid, Alastair. "Dilution, Trade Unionism and the State in Britain during the First World War." In Tolliday, S., and Zeitlin, J., eds., *Shop Floor Bargaining and the State.* Cambridge: Cambridge University Press, 1985: 46–74.

185. Reid, Alastair. "World War One and the Working Class in Britain." In Marwick, Arthur, ed., *Total War and Social Change.* London: Macmillan, 1988: 16–24.

186. Reeves, Nicholas. *Official British Film Propaganda during the First World War.* London: Croom Helm, 1986.

187. Richter, Donald. *Chemical Soldiers: British Gas Warfare in World War One.* Lawrence: Kansas University Press, 1992.

188. Robert, Krisztina. "Gender, Class and Patriotism: Women's Para-military Units in First World War Britain." *International History Review* 19 (1997): 32–51.

189. Robbins, Keith. *The Abolition of War. The Peace Movement in Britain, 1914–19.* Cardiff: University of Wales Press, 1976.

190. Rose, M. "The Success of Social Reform? The Central Control Board (Liquor Traffic), 1915–21." In Foot, M. R. D., ed., *War and Society.* London: Paul Elek, 1973: 71–84.

191. Rothstein, Andrew. *The Soldier's Strikes of 1919.* London: Journeyman, 1985.

192. Rothwell, V. H. *British War Aims and Peace Diplomacy, 1914–18.* Oxford: Oxford University Press, 1987.

193. Rubin, Gerry. War, *Law and Labour: The Munitions' Acts, State Regulation and the Unions, 1915–21.* Oxford: Oxford University Press, 1987.

194. Sanders, Michael. L., and Taylor, Philip. M. *British Propaganda during the First World War, 1914–18.* London: Macmillan, 1982.

195. Schneider, Eric. "The British Red Cross Wounded and Missing Enquiry Bureau: A Case of Truth-telling in the Great War." *War in History* 4 (1997): 296–315.

196. Schweitzer, Rich. The Cross and the Trenches: Religious Faith and Doubt among some British Soldiers on the Western Front." *War and Society* 16 (1998): 33–58.

197. Sheffield, Gary. "The Effect of the Great War on Class Relations in Britain: The Career of Major Christopher Stone, MC." *War and Society* 7 (1989): 87–105.

198. Sheffield, Gary. "The Shadow of the Somme: The Influence of the First World War on British Soldiers' Perceptions and Behaviour in the Second World War." In Addison, Paul, and Calder, Angus, eds., *Time to Kill.* London: Pimlico, 1997: 29–39.

199. Sheffield, Gary. "Oh! What a Futile War: Representations of the Western Front in Modern British Media and Popular Culture." In Stewart, Ian, and Carruthers, Susan, eds., *War, Culture and the Media.* Trowbridge: Flicks Books, 1996: 54–74.

200. Sheffy, Yigal. *British Military Intelligence in the Palestine Campaign, 1914–18.* London: Frank Cass, 1998.

201. Sillars, Stuart. *Art and Survival in First World War Britain.* New York: St. Martin's Press, 1987.

202. Simkins, Peter. *Kitchener's Army: The Raising of the New Armies, 1914–16.* Manchester: Manchester University Press, 1988.

203. Steiner, Zara. *Britain and the Origins of the First World War.* London: Macmillan, 1977.

204. Strachan, Hew. "The Battle of the Somme and British Strategy." *Journal of Strategic Studies.* 21 (1998): 79–95.

205. Stubbs, J. 0. "The Impact of the Great War on the Conservative Party." In Peele, G., and Cook, C., eds., *The Politics of Reappraisal, 1918–39.* London: Macmillan, 1975: 14–38.

206. Tanner, Duncan. *Political Change and the Labour Party, 1900–18.* Cambridge: Cambridge University Press, 1990.

207. Terraine, John. *Douglas Haig: The Educated Soldier.* London: Hutchinson, 1963.

208. Thom, Deborah. *Nice Girls and Rude Girls: Women Workers in World War One.* London: I B Tauris, 1998.

209. Travers, Tim. *The Killing Ground: The British Army, the Western Front and the Emergence of Modern Warfare, 1900–1918.* London: Allen & Unwin, 1987.

210. Travers, Tim. "A Particular Style of Command: Haig and GHQ 1916–18." *Journal of Strategic Studies* 10 (1987): 363–376.

211. Travers, Tim. "Could the Tanks of 1918 Have Been War-winners for the British Expeditionary Force?" *Journal of Contemporary History* 27 (1992): 389–406.

212. Travers, Tim. *How the War Was Won: Command and Technology in the British Army on the Western Front, 1917–18.* London: Routledge, 1992.

213. Travers, Tim. "Command and Leadership Styles in the British Army: The 1915 Gallipoli Model." *Journal of Contemporary History* 29 (1994): 403–42.

214. Turner, John. "State Purchase of the Liquor Trade in the First World War." *Historical Journal* 23 (1980): 589–615.

215. Turner, John, ed. *Britain in the First World War.* London: Unwin Hyman, 1988.

216. Turner, John. *British Politics and the Great War: Coalition and Conflict, 1915–18.* New Haven: Yale University Press, 1992.

217. Valone, Stephen. J. "There Must Be Some Misunderstanding: Sir Edward Grey's Diplomacy of August 1, 1914." *Journal of British Studies* 27 (1988): 405–24.

218. Waites, Bernard. *A Class Society at War: England, 1914–18.* Leamington Spa: Berg, 1988.

219. Wall, Richard, and Winter, J. M., eds. *The Upheaval of War: Family, Work and Welfare in Europe, 1914–18.* Cambridge: Cambridge University Press, 1988.

220. Wallace, S. *War and the Image of Germany: British Academics, 1914–18.* Edinburgh: John Donald, 1988.

221. Ward, S. R., ed. *The War Generation: Veterans of the First World War.* Port Washington: Kennikat Press, 1975.

222. Whiteside, Noel. "Industrial Welfare and Labour Regulation in Britain at the Time of the First World War." *International Review of Social History* 25 (1980): 307–31.

223. Whiteside, Noel. "Welfare Legislation and the Unions in Britain during the First World War." *Historical Journal* 23 (1980): 857–74.

224. Wilkinson, Alan. *The Church of England and the First World War.* London: SPCK, 1978.

225. Williams, M. J. "The Treatment of the German Losses on the Somme in the British Official History." *Journal of the Royal United Services Institute for Defence Studies* 111 (1966): 69–74.

226. Williams, Rhodri. "Lord Kitchener and the Battle of Loos: French Politics and British Strategy in the summer of 1915." In Freedman, Lawrence, Hayes, Paul, and O'Neill, Robert, eds., *War, Strategy and International Politics.* Oxford: Oxford University Press, 1992: 117–32.

227. Williamson, Samuel. *The Politics of Grand Strategy: Britain and France Prepare for War.* Cambridge, MA: Harvard University Press, 1969.

228. Wilson, Keith. *The Policy of the Entente: Essays on the Determinants of British Foreign Policy, 1904–14.* Cambridge: Cambridge University Press, 1985.

229. Wilson, Keith, ed. *Empire and Continent Studies in British Foreign Policy before the First World War.* London: Mansell, 1987.

230. Wilson, Keith. "Britain." In Wilson, Keith, ed., *Decisions for War, 1914.* London: UCL Press, 1995: 175–208.

231. Wilson, Trevor. *The Downfall of the Liberal Party, 1914–35.* London: Collins, 1966.

232. Wilson, Trevor. "Britain's Moral Commitment to France in August 1914." *History* 44 (1979): 380–90.

233. Wilson, Trevor. *The Myriad Faces of War: Britain and the Great War, 1914–18.* Cambridge: Polity Press, 1986.

234. Wilson, Trevor, and Prior, Robin. *Passchendaele: The Untold Story.* New Haven: Yale University Press, 1996.

235. Winter, J. M. *Socialism and the Challenge of War: Ideas and Politics in Britain, 1912–28.* London: Routledge, 1974.

236. Winter, J. M., ed. *War and Economic Development.* Cambridge: Cambridge University Press, 1975.

237. Winter, J. M. *The Great War and the British People.* London: Macmillan, 1985.

238. Winter, J. M. *Sites of Memory, Sites of Mourning: The Great War in European Cultural History.* Cambridge: Cambridge University Press, 1995.

239. Winter, J. M., and Robert, Jean-Louis, eds. *Capital Cities at War: London, Paris, Berlin, 1914–19.* Cambridge: Cambridge University Press, 1997.

240. Winter, J. M. "Popular Culture in Wartime Britain." In Roshwald, Aviel, and Stites, Richard, eds., *European Culture in the Great War: The Arts, Entertainment and Propaganda, 1914–18.* Cambridge: Cambridge University Press, 1999: 330–48.

241. Winter, J. M., and Sivan, Emmanuel, eds. *War and Remembrance in the Twentieth Century.* Cambridge: Cambridge University Press, 1999.

242. Wolff, Leon. *In Flanders Fields.* London: Longman, 1959.

243. Woollacott, Angela. "Khaki Fever and its Control: Gender, Class, Age and Sexual Morality on the British Home Front in the First World War." *Journal of Contemporary History* 29 (1994): 325–48.

244. Woollacott, Angela. *On Her Their Lives Depend: Munitions Workers in the Great War.* Berkeley: University of California Press, 1994.

245. Woodward, David. *Lloyd George and the Generals.* Newark: University of Delaware Press, 1983.

246. Woodward, David. *Field Marshal Sir William Robertson, Chief of the Imperial General Staff in the Great War.* Westport, CT: Praeger, 1998.

247. Woodward, Sir Llewellyn. *Great Britain and the War of 1914–18.* London: Methuen, 1967.

248. Wrigley, Chris. "The First World War and State Intervention in Industrial Relations, 1914–18." In Wrigley, Chris, ed., *A History of British Industrial Relations, 1914–39.* Brighton: Harvester, 1987: 23–70.

249. Wrigley, Chris. "Trade Unions and Politics in the First World War." In Pimlott, Ben, and Cook, Chris, eds., *Trade Unions in British Politics.* London: Longman, 1991: 69–87.

250. Wrigley, Chris. "The State and the Challenge of Labour in Britain, 1917–20." In Wrigley, Chris, ed., *Challenges of Labour: Central and Western Europe, 1917–20.* London: Routledge, 1993: 262–88.

5

Italy

Brian R. Sullivan

Italian participation in the Great War stands out as the paramount event in the history of united Italy. The victory of November 1918 completed the Risorgimento by dealing the death blow to the national enemy, the Hapsburg Monarchy, and allowing the incorporation of 750,000 Italians of the Trentino, Istria, and Dalmatia into the Kingdom of Italy.

Yet, perhaps more influential on the Italians were the negative aspects of their involvement in the First World War. These included the 41 months of nationwide deprivation, painfully won advances on the battlefield and the singular disaster of Caporetto, which preceded the final triumph of Vittorio Veneto; the 2.3 million military casualties (including 709,000 dead, 271,000 amputees and blinded, 829,000 other wounded, 506,000 surviving prisoners of war); the severe disappointment with the peace settlement and the consequent anger toward both Italy's wartime allies and its governments of 1919–1922.

Reaction to these wounds upon the national psyche led directly to the formation of the Fascist dictatorship, with the eventual consequences of Italian alliance with Nazi Germany and military collapse in 1943, followed by 20 months of enemy occupation and vicious civil war. It seems evident that the decision to intervene in World War I was the necessary—if not the sufficient—cause of the 30 years of national tragedy that followed. As a result, Italian-language scholarly and literary works about the 1915–1918 war experience have grown constantly more abundant.

In sharp contrast, the relative paucity of English-language studies of Italy in World War I and the even smaller number of publications about that subject in other languages, reflects its insignificance to most non-Italians. This stark difference is quite puzzling, especially since over 25 million Italians have settled or worked in the United States, Canada, Argentina, Britain, France, Switzerland, Germany, Tunisia, Egypt, and Australia since the late nineteenth century. One would expect far more interest in the countries that received such a flood of immigrants about why so many Italians left their country for decades or forever. That is especially so since such Italian migration was directly connected to the causes and consequences of Italy's participation in World War I. Explaining this paradoxical disregard would require a different essay than the historiographical guide that follows. But having raised the question of such lack of historical curiosity some brief answers are in order: the relatively small numbers of British, French and even fewer Americans who fought in Italy in World War I; the correspondingly limited Italian participation in the war beyond its peninsula; the geographic isolation of the Italian Front; the lack of widespread knowledge of the Italian language by English, French, and German speakers; perhaps most important, excessive Fascist propaganda about the significance of Italy's role in the Great War and non-Italian rejection of such inflated claims, followed by the collapse of Italian world influence during World War II.

The absurd boasts by Mussolini and his minions that Italy won World War I for the Allies can be confidently dismissed. Nonetheless, while the assertion might strike some experts on the Great War as implausible, Italian contribution to the Allied war effort probably brought the conflict to an end in November 1918, rather than sometime in 1919. Less certain but still arguable is the hypothesis that without Italy's participation in the struggle against Austria-Hungary in 1915 and 1916, the Russian Empire might have collapsed a year earlier than it did. In turn, the consequent ability of the Germans and Austro-Hungarians to concentrate their forces on the Western Front in 1917 might have meant a compromise peace or even a victory for the Central Powers. Furthermore, the conduct of the aerial war over the Alps and Adriatic would inspire concepts of air power with enormous influence on the nature of both World War II and the Cold War. In short, while less important than the gigantic contests on the Western and Eastern Fronts both for the outcome and the consequences of the conflict, the Italian Front affected the Great War far more than did the fighting in the Balkans, Near East, Caucasus, or Mesopotamia. Thus, examination of the literature on Italy in the Great War is a rewarding endeavor for a student of contemporary history. Moreover, it is imperative for one seeking a comprehensive understanding of World War I and modern warfare.

As an examination of the bibliography that follows this text reveals, however, scholarship on Italian participation in World War I strongly reflects the factors mentioned in preceding paragraphs. Only one-seventh of the entries are in English. While a study of these non-Italian books and articles will provide a sound understanding of the subject, there is no question that gaining expertise on Italy's part in the Great War requires a reading knowledge of Italian. The Italian sources themselves mostly fall into two distinct chronological groupings: works produced from the end of the First World War until the outbreak of the second global conflict and a second group published since 1965. This division reflects the support given by the Fascist regime to the study of the Italian effort in World War I, followed by a revulsion against military history in the postwar period and then a revival of interest encouraged by the fiftieth anniversary of Italian intervention in World War I, an interest that has grown considerably since.

Many publications on the Great War that appeared in Italian during the 20-odd years of Fascist rule (the *Ventennio*) presented little more than bombastic propaganda or were, at least, heavily influenced by the ideology of Mussolini's regime. With a few exceptions made for illustrative purposes, none such are listed in the bibliography. Still, a good deal of solid history on the war did appear in the period 1922–1943. So long as certain sensitive subjects were avoided—such as the earlier responsibility of prominent military servants of the Fascist regime for the Caporetto disaster or the particularly brutal nature of Italian military justice—censorship of the extreme kind exercised by the Soviet or Nazi dictatorships on the publication of scholarship dealing with the First World War did not have a parallel in Fascist Italy. As a result, much sound work on the 1915–1918 conflict, particularly by professional military officers and especially by the army and navy historical offices, came out in Italy in the 1920s and 1930s. The great majority of these were operational histories, memoirs, or technical studies.

Both the regime and the armed forces encouraged the concept that purely military histories of the war were the province of professional officers, serving or retired. Thus, studies by civilian authors of Italy's part in World War I that appeared in print between 1922 and 1943 tended toward economic, social, or diplomatic subjects. Such a concentration was not only in response to political pressure but reflected a long tradition in Italian historiography, one that has continued long after the collapse of the Fascist rule. Painful awareness by eighteenth- and nineteenth-century Italian intellectuals of the economic and technological backwardness of their society, in contrast with those of northern and northwestern Europe, the marked differences in the standard of living of northern and southern Italians, and the centuries-long division of the peninsula into a dozen or more antagonistic states pursuing rival foreign policies made the study of economic, social, and diplomatic history compelling and practical for Italians.

After 1945, the great influence of Marxist (and Gramscian) theory on Italian intellectual life added a new stimulus to the study of economic and social history, while Italy's pivotal place in Cold War Europe continued to encourage studies of diplomatic history by scholars ranged across the political spectrum. When widespread interest in the history of Italian involvement in World War I revived in the mid-1960s, it resulted in a concentration of publications dealing with the economic, social, and diplomatic history of the period. At the same time, widespread revulsion by many Italians against the Vietnam War and the influence of pacifism on Italian Catholic thought made the study of military history in the narrow sense distasteful or even anathema in most of Italian academe. While many popular histories of Italian military participation in World War I appeared throughout the 1960s and increasingly so thereafter, scholarly treatments of the technological, tactical, operational, and strategic aspects of the conflict by civilian authors began to be published in significant numbers only from the early 1980s.

Nonetheless, the historical offices of the armed forces had continued to produce works on Italy in World War I from the 1950s onward. In addition to a professional interest in producing such publications at a time when few Italian civilian scholars dealt with contemporary military history, the army and navy historical offices enjoyed a great advantage in such regards: access to the archives. With very few exceptions, Italian military archives for the twentieth century were closed to outsiders until the 1970s. Even at the beginning of the twenty-first century, documents in these collections are far more difficult for civilians to study than is the case for military archives in the United States, Britain, or Germany. The Italian state remains far more sensitive to the possibility of embarrassing disclosures, even in regard to official actions of nearly a century ago, than do other Western governments. The end of the influence of the Cold War on domestic Italian politics has eased such official concern. Nonetheless, old habits die hard in Italy.

Qualified historians can now study the official records of the Italian armed forces in the Great War. But obtaining permission to do so requires passage through a series of bureaucratic passageways. Non-Italians interested in conducting such research should contact the cultural attaché at the Italian embassy in their country. Such foreign service officers can provide advice on gaining official agreement for such access. Failure to do so prior to embarking on a research endeavor in Italy would be a guarantee of maddening frustration. The same holds true for entry to the archives of the ministry of foreign affairs and to the *Archivio Centrale dello Stato* (Central State Archives), which stores the records of the other nonmilitary ministries. However, the tight control held by the Italian government over its records does offer researchers one advantage. All World War I–era papers held by the state are located in archives in Rome.

On the other hand, Italian newspapers and journals from the years 1914–1919 are kept in the National Library in Florence. Most unfortunately, the contents of this great national repository suffered devastating damage in the terrible Arno flood of 1966. The journalistic collection was housed in the Library basement, located along the banks of the river. Much was lost beyond hope of reclamation. However, a good deal of the collection has been restored, either through preservation or acquisition of copies of lost publications from other sources.

Another difficulty facing those seeking to study primary sources dealing on Italy in the First World War arises from the deep pride in family encouraged by Italian culture. Unlike the situation in the United States and Britain, it is virtually unheard of for prominent Italians or their heirs to donate private papers to the government, universities, or private institutions. With very few exceptions, the papers of the leading Italian generals, admirals, diplomats, and statesmen active in the 1914–1919 period remain in the hands of their descendants. Furthermore, there is no Italian equivalent to the National Catalogue of Manuscript Collections. Discovering who controls the papers of historical Italian figures is difficult. The best available guides are the bibliographies at the end of those entries in the *Dizionario Biografico degli Italiani* [109] published so far. However, acquiring permission to consult such documents can require surmounting major psychological and emotional obstacles. As a general rule, if a prospective researcher can locate such private collections, she or he needs the services of a mutual acquaintance to even hope to see family papers. Obtaining permission to copy or even quote from papers can be even more problematic. Obviously, these are not easy tasks and they demand almost infinite patience, persistence, and tact to accomplish.

Given these circumstances, the products of the armed forces historical offices are of greater than normal value to students of Italian participation in the First World War. Perhaps the most significant of these efforts was the ongoing publication of the Italian army's monumental official history of the Great War, completed only in 1981 [179]. But while other official books and pamphlets on the subject worthy of study came out in the period between 1950 and 1980—which will be noted below—the overall quality of such official military publications improved markedly in the last two decades of the twentieth century. The appearance of revisionist and critical accounts of Italian military operations and strategy in the Great War by civilian authors clearly stimulated the improvement of official history as well. So did the increase in government revenues made available for the publication of official histories from the late 1970s onward, as the Italian standard of living rose to the level of that of the British, French, and Germans.

Increased budgets benefited not only the military historical offices but that of the Ministry of Foreign Affairs as well. Publication of nine series of Italian diplomatic documents, dating from Unification until 1943, began in the early 1950s. However, the pace of the appearance of these volumes was painfully slow for the first quarter century of the project. Matters improved considerably in the late 1970s, allowing for the completion in 1986 of Series Five, covering 1914–1918 [175]. Regrettably, only the first two volumes of Series Six for the 1918–1922 years [176] have come out to date, leaving coverage of Italian participation in the post–World War I peace conferences incomplete. However, the printing of the entire series can be confidently expected during the present decade.

Beginning with general histories of the subject, what awaits a reader seeking knowledge of Italy and the Italians in the Great War? While it covers the half century between the capture of Rome by the Italian army in 1870 and the establishment of Mussolini's dictatorship in 1922, Christopher Seton-Watson's superb history of Liberal Italy [296] devotes ample space and a wealth of detailed analysis to the World War I period, as well as to the events preceding and following it. Another book covering a wider sweep of time than the war years but which describes the military events of 1915–1918 with great insight is Lucio Ceva's pioneering and magisterial history of the Italian armed forces [83].

Other works providing an overview of modern Italian history, as well as of the First World War itself, include the politically oriented *Dictionary of Modern*

Italian History [91]; a number of army-focused histories [51, 81, 85, 86, 101, 115, 212, 265, 270, 303, 304, 308, 325], including an excellent recent history of the Italian army [51]; the famous six-volume *Enciclopedia militare* of 1929–1931 sponsored by Mussolini [115]; the annual—since 1978—collection of military history articles published by the army historical office [212], which always contains at least one piece devoted to World War I; two collections of relevant articles by the leading military historian Giorgio Rochat [265, 270]; a volume from Filippo Stefani's authoritative multipart series on the doctrine and organization of the Italian army [303]; John Whittam's English-language survey of the Italian army from the Risorgimento through World War I [325]; the navy-focused works [103, 110, 229, 263], which include an explication of Italian naval doctrine from unification to the present [110] and the published version of Marco Rimanelli's study in English of Italian navy strategy and its influence over national foreign policy [263]; the studies of Italian aerial warfare theory from the late nineteenth century to the outbreak of World War II [50] and of military aviation from the 1880s to 1925 [135]; as well as the 1936 Italian-language aeronautical encyclopedia [195].

A general understanding of the interplay between political and military factors in the conduct of the war is given in Olindo Malagoli's invaluable records of candid conversations with the major Italian participants [193] and Piero Melograni's unsurpassed history of domestic politics during the conflict [211]. Largely or strictly devoted to Italian armed involvement in the conflict on a general level are a number of publications by both Italian and non-Italian historians dealing with the *Regio Esercito* (Royal Italian Army): [122, 174, 244, 245, 246, 267, 326], *Regia Marina* (Royal Italian Navy): [30, 31, 48, 163, 196, 197], and the air services of both [10, 90, 127, 252]. Particularly noteworthy are Emilio Faldella's two-volume history of the war [122]; the recent history of the entire conflict by Mario Isnenghi and Giorgio Rochat, with emphasis on the Italian Front [174]; Piero Pieri's classic history [244]; Romeo Bernotti's prescient 1920s studies of World War I at sea, including a detailed analysis of the naval war in the Adriatic [30, 31]; Paul Halpern's superb study of the naval war in the Mediterranean, 1914–1918 [163]; Camillo Manfroni's pioneering naval histories from 1925 and 1927 [196, 197]; Gregory Alegi's English-language synopsis of the Italian air war [10]; and the collection of excellent articles on the same subject edited by Paolo Ferrari [127]. Two English-language atlases [2, 116] well illustrate terrain, lines of communication, operations, and strategic options on the Italian Front during the conflict. Several books [92, 125, 156, 174, 238] provide excellent photographs of the same. Fine illustrations of Italian air, sea and land armaments manufacturing processes in the Great War can be found in the histories of the Caproni and Ansaldo corporations [1, 72a].

Other works that provide an overview of the Italian war and the events surrounding it include biographies, memoirs, diaries, correspondence, and speeches of the major political and military leaders involved. Biography in the strict sense enjoys a stronger tradition in English than in Italian. But the memoirs and collected papers of statesmen and generals have long formed a pillar of

Italian historiography. One or more biographies or biographical studies covering the period of their subjects' lives in 1914–1919 have been published for Mussolini [63, 96], the industrialist Giovanni Agnelli [71], pre- and postwar prime minister Giovanni Giolitti [97], 1914–1919 foreign minister Sidney Sonnino [164], King Vittorio Emanuele III [191] and treasury minister Francesco Saverio Nitti [222]. One for Mussolini [63] and those for Giolitti, Sonnino and Vittorio Emanuele III—the latter part of Denis Mack Smith's larger book on the Italian monarchy—are in English. Biographies or related studies of military leaders include those for 1917–1918 army chief of staff Armando Diaz [21, 159]; air war prophet Giulio Douhet [66, 129, 275, 290]; army commanders Emanuele Fili-berto, Duke of Aosta [78], Luigi Capello [215] and Enrico Caviglia [79]; navy chief of staff Paolo Thaon di Revel [126]; corps commanders Emilio De Bono [136] and Francesco Saverio Grazioli [186]; the aviator-demagogue-poet Gabriele D'Annunzio [184]; arms minister Alfredo Dallolio [213]; Diaz's deputy chief of staff, Pietro Badoglio [247]; prewar minister of war General Paolo Spingardi [275]; as well as for Otto von Below, commander of the Fourteenth Army at Caporetto [119]. Of these, only Diaz has a mediocre book-length biography [21] and Douhet a good article-length and an excellent dissertation-length biography in English [66, 290].

Douhet's publications up to 1915 have been edited by Andrea Curami and Giorgio Rochat [94]. One remarkable insight that emerges from this volume is how many of Douhet's fundamental ideas on air power, widely assumed to have resulted from his World War I experiences as reflected in his wartime diary [111], had originated in fact prior to May 1915. It is all the more lamentable, therefore, that the original air force historical office project to produce a multi-volume complete edition of Douhet's works has been abandoned.

Giolitti [151] and wartime prime ministers Antonio Salandra [277, 278, 279, 280] and Vittorio Emanuele Orlando [232] all left memoirs, with those by Giolitti and part of those by Salandra translated into English. Military memoirs are dominated by those of 1914–1917 army chief of staff Luigi Cadorna [57, 58, 60], Caporetto scapegoat Capello [64, 65], corps commander Antonino Di Giorgio [108], and army commander Gaetano Giardino [150]. Recently Badoglio's long-suppressed *apologia* for his actions before and during Caporetto has also appeared [19]. All these are in Italian only.

There are three excellent sources for article and entry-length biographies of Italian statesmen and military leaders in the Great War period. Foremost is the *Dizionario Biografico degli Italiani,* 56 massive volumes reaching to the Gs by 2001 [109]. The entries are by experts on their subjects, extremely detailed for their five-to-ten-page length, packed with information unavailable elsewhere and concluded with excellent bibliographies of unpublished, as well as published, sources. Obviously, only those World War I–era figures with last names beginning with the first seven letters of the alphabet are included to date. But the pace of publication of new volumes is regular and accelerating. Herwig and Heyman's *Biographical Dictionary of World War I* [167] contains a number of fine entries on Italians. Frank Coppa's previously cited *Dictionary of Modern*

Italian History [91] offers shorter coverage of subjects but nonetheless of many relevant individuals not mentioned in the other two works.

Many of the above-mentioned men, as well as a number of other prominent Italians of the period, left diaries, correspondence, and papers that have been published. These include the highly influential publisher of Italy's leading newspaper, *Corriere della Sera,* Luigi Albertini [4, 5]; the leading Interventionist and Irredentist martyr, Cesare Battisti [25]; another leading Interventionist and maverick Socialist, Leonida Bissolati [39]; Cadorna [59]; the Futurist and Interventionist, Tommaso Filippo Marinetti [204]; Colonial Minister Ferdinando Martini [205]; Mussolini [227, 228]; Salandra [276, 281]; and Sonnino [297]. Orlando and Sonnino's speeches [297] have also been published, the former's in English translation [231].

A number of bibliographies, either specifically devoted to Italy in World War I or containing sections on the subject, are available in print. Dedicated bibliographies [34, 174, 244, 246, 267], those on aerial military topics [41, 42, 305]—([41, 42] contain all publications, including journal articles, [305] cites only books)—and those on Italian military history in general [15, 52, 83, 102, 183, 269] are all excellent. Unfortunately, with the exception of that at the end of the 1964 volume in which Piero Pieri's English-language article appears [245], all of these are in Italian only.

There is a voluminous literature on the diplomatic and political background to Italy's part in the Great War. Only those considered among the best will be cited. Such works on foreign policy and diplomacy include a good many English-language studies or translations, as well as many more only in Italian. Perhaps the most impressive—certainly the lengthiest—is Luigi Albertini's three-volume study of the outbreak of the First World War, based on the published diplomatic documents of the powers. After Albertini's anti-Fascism led to his removal from the ownership of his prestigious newspaper, he devoted his time to the enormous labor of reading and analyzing the massive collections of diplomatic correspondence published during the 1920s and 1930s. He then wrote a critical narrative of the events of the summer of 1914, which appeared in Italian in the early 1940s and in English 10 years later [6]. Since the Italian diplomatic documents for the period were not yet available to scholars and the papers of Sonnino remained to be discovered, the portions of Albertini's work devoted to Italian foreign policy make up the least authoritative section of these volumes. Furthermore, thoroughly disillusioned by the disasters resulting from Fascist diplomacy and disgusted by the early adherence of many in the Italian foreign service to Mussolini's regime, Albertini transferred much of his quiet rage to his depiction of Italian diplomatic moves in mid-1914. This resulted in a more negative depiction of Salandra and his first foreign minister San Giuliano's actions than now appears justified. However, despite its composition nearly three quarters of a century ago, Albertini's work remains the classic work on the subject and its high reputation has survived more recent scholarship far better than the efforts of Sidney Fay, George Gooch, Pierre Renouvin, Bernadotte Schmitt, and even Fritz Fischer.

Other older but still impressive works in English include Albrecht-Carrié's study of Italian diplomacy at Versailles, which contains much on the 1914–1918 period [7]; Richard Bosworth's dissection of the achievements of San Giuliano in the years from the Italian-Turkish War to the early months of the Great War [46] and his later encapsulation of much of the same in a shorter book [45]; and the diary of Gino Speranza, the press attaché at the American embassy in Rome, 1915–1919 [299]. William Renzi's *In the Shadow of the Sword* provides an outstanding analysis of Italy's passage from alliance with Germany and Austria-Hungary to neutrality to war, June 1914–May 1915 [261]. James Burgwyn's more recent examination of Sonnino's foreign policy and conduct of diplomacy from Italian intervention in the war through the Paris Peace Conference provides a great deal of information in English for the first time [54]. Angelo Gatti, *Un italiano a Versailles,* offers a revealing firsthand look at the military aspects of Italy's relations with its allies in the immediate aftermath of Caporetto [144]. Robert Hess provides a fine analysis of Italian goals for African colonial aggrandizement in his 30-year-old article that remains the best on the subject in English [168]. While the relevant sections of Haywood's previously mentioned biography of Sonnino rely heavily on Burgwyn, he does offer additional insights into the actions and thoughts of the stubborn and ultimately tragic foreign minister [164].

Untranslated into English are the memoirs and diary extracts of foreign ministry *capo di gabinetto* (1914–1919) Luigi Aldrovandi Marescotti [8, 9]; the French-language recollections of the first secretary at France's Rome embassy in 1914–1915, Robert de Billy [38]; the aforementioned papers of Sonnino [297]; and the officially published Italian documents for the 1914–1919 period [175, 176]. Among the better secondary sources a dozen stand out: a study of the Italian military mission to Russia [32]; the relevant essays in Bosworth and Sergio Romano's excellent anthology on Italian foreign policy, 1860–1985 [47]; two fine French-language studies of Italian-French relations during the periods of Italian neutrality and the conflict itself [161, 257]; Monticone's masterful history of 1914–1915 German efforts to keep Italy neutral [220]; Pietro Pastorelli's work on Italian wartime and postwar policy toward Albania [239]; two articles on the origins of Woodrow Wilson's wartime diplomacy toward the Italians [271, 272]; two works by the greatest of Italy's diplomatic historians, Mario Toscano, on the Pact of London and various aspects of Italian foreign policy during and immediately after the conflict [312, 313]; and Brunello Vigezzi's two earlier studies of the diplomacy of the Giolitti-Salandra period and his recent historical overview of his country's international relations, including much on the 1914–1919 years [319, 320, 321].

Works on Italian politics in the World War I period obviously include many already noted above. In that context, Melograni's brilliant political history of the war [211] warrants additional notice, as do two histories of the Italian Socialists in the period of neutrality and of war [14, 317]. Other outstanding publications are offered by the following: a study of the influence of anarchism on the Italian anti-militarist movement [77], Simon Jones' English-language analysis of the influence of domestic political factors on Italian intervention [182], Massimo Mazzetti's study of national politics during the crisis following Caporetto [207], a detailed revelation of secret French subsidies to Mussolini for support of his prowar activities [230], and an older but still outstanding collection of essays by leading Italian historians on the trauma of intervention [315].

As discussed in the opening paragraphs of this essay, a wealth of economic and industrial history deals with Italy in World War I. These include a small number of high-quality works in English: Douglas Forsyth's comprehensive, if somewhat biased—among his advisers in writing the book were Arno Mayer and David Abraham (!)—examination of Italian government finance in the years 1914–1922 [132], Thomas Row's dissertation on the Ansaldo armaments firm [273], Gianni Toniolo's economic history of Italy from the Risorgimento to 1918 [311], Webster's now-classic study of Italian industrial imperialism in the immediate prewar period [324], and Vera Zamagni's brilliant economic history of united Italy [327].

Italian-language books and articles on these subjects are voluminous. Topics covered include the origins and early development of military aircraft design and production [17, 160, 190, 199], the arms industry on the eve of war [24, 128, 209], the establishment and expansion of Italian steelworks for armaments [44, 68, 233], the role of the Ansaldo corporation in World War I [72], wartime economic and taxation legislation [106, 114], Luigi Einaudi's classic study for the Carnegie Institution of the economic conduct and social effects of the Great War in Italy [113], the financing of the Italian war effort [120, 310], the future general Carlo Geloso's study of artillery ammunition manufacture [146], the creation and functioning of the ministry for arms and ammunition [206, 291], the general role of Italian industry in the conflict [36, 208, 214, 224, 243, 253, 309], the monetary cost of Italian participation in World War I [262, 329], and economic relations with Germany during the period of Italian neutrality [292].

As previously described, a number of solid studies have been written on Italian society during the war. Some have been cited already, including Einaudi's analysis of the social influence of the war. Other topics that have received attention include diet and rationing policy for the civilian population [18], the exploitation of child labor [33], relations among workers, technicians, managers and government officials in war industries [36, 62, 259, 301], the role of the peasantry in wartime food production [172], the relationship of various classes within the armed forces [221], physical and mental health conditions among the civilian population [226, 256], and urban life under wartime conditions [301, 302]. Manpower utilization and conscription policies are well covered in the relevant volume of Virgilio Ilari's four-part study of military service in Italy [169]. The influence on Italian society of the painful contrast between the reality of the conflict and the fantasies that preceded and followed it are explored by Isnenghi in *Il mito della Grande Guerra da Marinetti a Malaparte* [171].

Several books dealing with military preparations for war and mobilization have been noted previously under other categories. Prewar armaments procurement [128, 165, 209, 275, 306], naval planning and the influence of prewar operations [138, 139, 140, 162, 180], and army planning [157, 274, 275] are discussed in a number of publications, including several in English [157, 162, 165, 306, 325]. In the latter category, two articles by Michael Palumbo deserve special mention [234, 235]. These consider the prewar relations and military planning between the *Regio Esercito* leadership and that of the armies of Italy's German and Austro-Hungarian allies.

Obviously, for those capable of reading Italian, the richest source of information on the military conduct of the war is the 37-part army official history [179]. Two highly useful supplementary works are the army historical office's summaries of division, corps, and army level command activities [177, 178]. In addition to official histories, the largest number of books dealing with the Italians in the Great War are concerned with tactics, operations, and weaponry. Only a portion of the very best can be mentioned, although a number have been already cited in regard to other subjects. The Italian navy historical office has published and continues to update a series of superb publications on the various classes of warships that have seen service in the *Regia Marina* [20, 22, 130, 152, 153, 249, 250]. A shorter but excellent English-language photographic reference book on Italian warships of World War I has been created by Aldo Fraccaroli [134]. Italian aircraft, dirigibles, and observation balloons of World War I are pictured and described in several works [1, 37, 89, 103, 160, 187, 190, 195, 216, 240]. Other books have been devoted to First World War–era Italian army small arms, crew-served weapons, and military equipment [200]; artillery and shells [93, 146, 218, 223]; and motor vehicles [88].

The best English-language study of operations and tactics is the detailed and revealing article by John Gooch [158]. Land warfare tactics in the area of the major fighting on the Italian Front, the Isonzo River Valley, are analyzed in careful detail and with considerable intelligence in Antonio Sema's three-volume study [293]. Other views of the bloody combat in that region are furnished by [12, 39, 117, 282, 285]. Tactical and operational mountain warfare, another form of combat that distinguished the Italian Front, is described and discussed in a number of fine works [67, 107, 123, 189, 210, 254, 255]. Three of these works deserve special mention: *La conquista delle Alpi Fassia* [67] by Giacomo Carboni, who would later head the Italian military intelligence service on two occasions and command the defense of Rome in September 1943; the history of the *Alpini* by Emilio Faldella (1943 chief of staff of Italian forces on Sicily); and Emilio Lussu's *Un'anno sull'Altopiano* [189]—translated into English as *Sardinian Brigade*—a nightmare hallucination of a memoir under novelistic camouflage, written in exile by one of the leaders of the anti-Fascist resistance in the 1930s and 1940s.

By decision under Cadorna and by necessity under Diaz, the *Regio Esercito* concentrated the overwhelming majority of its resources on the Italian Front. Nonetheless, the Arab revolt in Libya and the Ethiopian threat to Eritrea tied down considerable numbers of Italian *Askaris,* native levies, in Africa, while weakening Italy's claims for postwar colonial expansion. These events are described briefly in Angelo Del Boca's two excellent books on the Italian

colonies in the World War I period [98, 99]. The Salandra government had intervened militarily in Albania prior to Italian entry into the Great War. The operations that resulted are well narrated in Montanari's official history of that
four-year campaign and its postwar denouement, 1914–1920 [217].

James Farrill Gentsch has recently produced a creative and provocative dissertation on the influence of military geography on operations on the Italian
Front [148]. Another commendable dissertation by Pierluigi Scolè [289],
directed by Lucio Ceva, partly explains the almost inexplicable failure on the
part of the Italian high command in 1915–1917 to learn and apply tactical and
operational lessons from the Western Front. Other insights into that failure come
from Ceva's article contrasting the poor quality of the Italian army's noncommissioned officers with those of the British, French, and Germans [87]. Gas
warfare in the Italian context is analyzed in [201]. Italy's crack assault troops,
the *Arditi,* are the subject of two books [186, 264]. The actions of the heroic
marines of the *San Marco* regiment are described in [149]. While hardly their
original purpose, a great deal about Italian infantry tactics in 1915–1918 can be
gleaned from the citations for Italy's highest award for military courage, the
Medaglie d'oro per valore militare [314]. One of the preconditions for all operations on the First World War Italian Front, although one rarely written about for
any conflict, forms the subject of one of the volumes of Botti and Cermelli's
study of the logistics of the Italian army [49]. Finally, three books in English on
British Army operations on the Italian Front offer not only information on that
subject but also a broader view of the war in that theater [70, 112, 155].

Air warfare tactics and operations are discussed in a number of books, all in
Italian and all cited already in other contexts [10, 187, 188, 216]. Perhaps even
more on such topics can be found in the biographies and memoirs of the leading
Italian pilots of the war, including the ace-of-aces, Francesco Baracca [11, 133,
194], as well as other legendary fliers, such as Francesco Pricolo [16]; Ernesto
Cabruna [69]; Mario Fucini [137]; Gabriele D'Annunzio [184]; Umberto Maddalena [192]; the only Italian ever to win three *medaglie d'oro,* Antonio
Locatelli [248]; Natale Palli [251]; Baracca's closest rival in enemy aircraft
brought down, Silvio Scaroni [287, 288]; and the former dirigible pilot and
1930s Fascist air force chief of staff, Giuseppe Valle [318]. Air unit histories on
the squadron and group level can be found in [23, 103, 187, 216, 241].

Not even the British and the Russians are as secretive regarding intelligence
matters as are the security-minded Italians. Over three quarters of a century
after its end, very little has been revealed by the Italian government about the
activities of its army and navy intelligence services in the Great War. The little
on the subject in print includes the memoirs of several army intelligence officers
[104, 105, 202, 203]; a short study of the major naval intelligence operation of
the conflict, the burglary of the Austro-Hungarian consulate in Zurich [147]; an
excellent if guarded history of the *Carabinieri* (the Italian national police),
including its counterespionage activities in 1914–1918 [61]; a rather superficial
history of Italian intelligence from Unification to the 1980s [40]; and a ground-

breaking study of Italian cryptanalysis in World War I by the leading expert on the subject in general, David Alvarez [13].

The largest battles on the Italian front are each the subjects of one or more particularly noteworthy books (some previously cited): Asiago-Gorizia, May–August 1916 [26, 328]; Bainsizza, August–September 1917 [73]; Caporetto, October–December 1917 [19, 27, 58, 64, 74, 95, 119, 121, 124, 141, 143, 173, 207, 219, 295, 307, 323]; Piave, June 1918 [75, 155, 185]; and Vittorio Veneto, October–November 1918 [3, 28, 80, 82, 155, 185]. Of these, some deserve specific mention: the particularly objective works by anti-Fascist General Roberto Bencivenga, recently reissued [26, 27]; the 1925 study of the capture of Gorizia by the World War II North African armor commander, Francesco Zingales [328]; Marshal Enrico Caviglia's honest and self-critical accounts of the major battles of August 1917–June 1918 [73, 74, 75]—that on Caporetto was not published until 20 years after the marshal's death, due to his critical examination of the responsibility of both the army high command and of then-corps commander Badoglio. Remarkable in a negative sense is Cyril Falls' study of Caporetto [124]—in reality a short history of the war on the Italian Front—written without benefit of a knowledge of Italian, based largely on German-language sources and filled with the most blatant anti-Italian prejudices. The English historian Ronald Seth's *Caporetto: The Scapegoat Battle* [295] offers a refreshingly objective contrast. Other particularly noteworthy works on Caporetto include Capello's posthumous arguments against his primary responsibility for the disaster [64]; Faldella's careful analysis of the reasons for the Italian defeat [121]; and Monticone's recently reissued study of the battle [219], which provides a paragon of careful historical balance. Last chronologically but hardly least of such battle histories is Lucio Ceva's highly original and revealing 1998 article on the strategic consequences of Vittorio Veneto and the armistice of Villa Giusti. Ceva argues convincingly that Italian access to the Brenner Pass, and thus to Bavaria, provided a major factor in the German decision to seek an end to the war in November 1918 [82].

The post-1945 Italian predilection for social history has resulted in a number of outstanding studies of day-to-day life between battles for enlisted men and junior officers, the effects of combat on soldiers, as well as post-Caporetto *Regio Esercito* efforts to improve the army's shattered morale. These works—some already mentioned in other regards—are complemented by published correspondence, diaries, memoirs by frontline journalists, soldiers, and company-grade officers that began appearing in the interwar period [12, 55, 95, 141, 143, 237, 282]. The secondary sources deal with military psychiatry [35, 154]; the work of the military chaplain corps [53, 225, 268]; diaries and memoirs [55, 84, 237, 260, 282, 298]; the military postal service [56]; propaganda and newspapers for the troops [100, 145, 170, 322]; soldiers' songs [284]; trench life [117, 286]; desertion, self-inflicted wounds and military justice [118, 131, 221]; and prisoners of war [258, 300]. The memoir by Spagnol [298] presents a unique view of the functioning of the high command and of soldier-officer relations as seen by an unusually observant enlisted man posted to *comando supremo* for his technical skills. This little-known work includes an intriguing sketch of the man who provided the operational brains of the Italian high command throughout the entire war, then-Colonel Ugo Cavallero, later head of *comando supremo* for Mussolini in 1941–1943.

As in the army's case, the logical starting place for a study of the navy's operations is the official history [181], as well as the navy historical office's studies of the Central Powers' submarine war on Italian shipping [43] and *Regia Marina* operations to occupy Istria and Dalmatia in 1918–1919 [76]. Other works on the subject have been mentioned already in other contexts with the exception of Romeo Bernotti's studies of aeronaval warfare edited by Ferruciio Botti [48]. The experiences of lower-ranking naval officers also provide much useful information on *Regia Marina* operations in the Great War in the memoirs by Romeo Bernotti [29], Raffaele Paolucci [236] and Vittorio Tur [316], and the biography of Costanzo Ciano [283].

The process of armed forces and national demobilization is described in a number of works mentioned above. Once again, Seton-Watson's history of Italy until 1925 [296] is the best starting place, thanks to its comprehensive nature, careful research, balance, and added advantage of being in English. Economic history continues to receive emphasis in Italian studies of the post-1918 period. Previously cited works include discussions of industrial restructuring [36, 44, 71, 233, 243, 273, 327] and government finances [120, 132]. Two other books on the topic deserve special mention: Peter Hertner and Giorgio Mori's comparison of the Italian and German transitions from war to peace economies [166] and Gabriele De Rosa's contribution to the well-researched, written, and illustrated multivolume history of the Ansaldo corporation [72].

Italian diplomacy at Versailles forms part of the subject matter for the study by Burgwyn [54] and, of course, for the two volumes published so far of diplomatic documents for 1918–1922 period [176]. The state of public health after the war in examined in the aforementioned [226]. Biographies and memoirs that devote considerable space to the immediate postwar lives of their subjects include those already noted for Bernotti, Mussolini, Giolitti, De Bono, Sonnino, Grazioli, Costanzo Ciano, Spagnol, and Tur [29, 63, 96, 97, 136, 164, 186, 283, 298, 316], as well as Marinetti's diary to 1921 [204]. Aspects of the military draw down after Vittorio Veneto are discussed in works cited above [88, 89, 135] as well as in two other outstanding works: Rochat's political study of the *Regio Esercito* from 1918 to 1925 [266] and Vincenzo Gallinari's more technical analysis of the same subject for the 1918–1920 years [142].

SUGGESTIONS FOR FURTHER RESEARCH

The response to the question of what *further research* can be suggested for Italy and the Italians in the Great War depends on the language in which the results would be published. Obviously, many topics that have formed the basis for extensive research in Italian-language publications have been barely touched upon or not at all by historians writing in English. It would be otiose in the extreme to mention those again. What is lacking in Italian—and therefore, in any other language—falls into a number of broad categories.

Even in the cases of individuals for whom biographies exist, many lack well-researched and probing life histories. Pieri and Rochat have written a fine biography of Badoglio with considerable space devoted to his 1915–1919 years. While Richard Bosworth has not written a biography of San Giuliano per se, his book does offer a good deal of biographical information. Geoffrey Haywood had recently produced what will surely remain the definitive biography of Sonnino. Both of the latter works are in English. But other deserving figures lack sound studies, including the Duke of Aosta, Cadorna, Cavallero, Dallolio, Diaz, Orlando, Salandra, Thaon di Revel, Vittorio Emanuele III, to mention only the most prominent.

A more important biographical question is the degree of mutual intellectual influence between Douhet and the aircraft designer and manufacturer, Giovanni Battista Caproni. Given the refusal of Caproni's children to allow access to their father's voluminous diaries and correspondence, and the little other information on the man's life up to 1919 [1, 17, 50, 127], the origins of one of the major factors in twentieth-century history remains largely unexplored in print. The death of Claudio Segrè, who was working on a biography of Douhet at the time of his premature demise, shut another avenue toward the resolution of this mystery. Perhaps Gianni Caproni's heirs can be prevailed upon to open his papers and someone else will take up Segrè's Douhet biography project.

Among other neglected topics, the paucity of intelligence histories has already been mentioned. Other glaring *lacunae* include the Italian prisoner of war experience; secret Italian–Austro-Hungarian negotiations for a separate peace after Caporetto; the fates of the thousands of naturalized Italian-American visitors forcibly conscripted into the *Regio Esercito;* the peculiar failure of the outstanding Italian junior and field grade officers in World War I to carry the lessons they learned from the earlier conflict into World War II; the critical (and deficient) role of noncommissioned officers in training and combat; graft and other corruption in the armaments industry; detailed analyses of the Italian campaigns in the air, the Adriatic, Libya, East Africa and Macedonia; the role of the royal family (perhaps an impossible task, however, if rumors of the burning of family papers by Vittorio Emanuele III's heir, Umberto II, are true); the conduct of the Italian war on the grand-strategic level; the failure to mesh political goals with strategy, and the latter with operations and tactics; and, perhaps most important, the disjunction of moral, religious, political, diplomatic and military leadership in the 29 months of war prior to Caporetto.

One final topic virtually calls out for a well-researched and well-written book in English: an objective study of the Italian combatant in World War I. Ernest Hemingway's *A Farewell to Arms* probably represents his finest novel and certainly is a monument of twentieth-century American literature. But the book was written by a man who, despite his later claims, did not actually witness the events described. The novel hardly presents a balanced picture of the *Regio*

Esercito at war in 1917. Nonetheless, Hemingway's fantasy has come to epitomize the reputation of the World War I Italian fighting man throughout the world. It is true that much negative criticism can be honestly directed at the Italian military leadership in the Great War, especially until the final year of the conflict. But Italian soldiers, sailors, and airmen fought as bravely as any others; they won more victories than they suffered defeats; and, in the end, they smashed their enemies on the field, at sea, and in the air. The time is long overdue for the true story of their historical accomplishments to be written, read, and appreciated in the English-speaking world and beyond.

BIBLIOGRAPHY

Abbreviations

USMM: Ufficio Storico della Marina Militare [Historical Office of the Navy]

USSMA: Ufficio Storico, Stato Maggiore dell'Aeronautica [Historical Office, Air Force General Staff]

USSME: Ufficio Storico, Stato Maggiore dell'Esercito [Historical Office, Army General Staff]

1. Abate, Rosario, Gregory Alegi, and Giorgio Apostolo. *Aeroplani Caproni. Gianni Caproni and His Aircraft, 1910–1983*. Trento: Museo Caproni, 1992.

2. Agnew, James B., Clifton R. Franks, and William R. Griffiths. *The Great War; Atlas for the Great War*. 2 vols. Wayne, NJ: Avery, 1986.

3. Alberti, Adriano. *L'armistizio di Villa Giusti* [*The Villa Giusti Armistice*]. Rome: USSME, 1925.

4. Albertini, Luigi. *Epistolario 1911–1926* [*Correspondence 1911–1926*]. Ottavio Barié, ed. 4 vols. Milano: Mondadori, 1968. 1. *Dalla guerra di Libia alla Grande Guerra* [*From the Libyan War to the Great War*]. 2. *La Grande Guerra.*

5. Albertini, Luigi. *I giorni di un liberale. Diari 1907–1925* [*The Days of a Liberal. Diaries 1907–1925*]. Bologna: il Mulino, 2000.

6. Albertini, Luigi. *Le origini della guerra del 1914.* 3 vols. Milan: Bocca, 1942–43. Translated as: *The Origins of the War of 1914.* 3 vols. Oxford University: London, 1952–53.

7. Albrecht-Carrié, René. *Italy at the Paris Peace Conference.* New York: Columbia University Press, 1938.

8. Aldrovandi Marescotti, Luigi. *Guerra diplomatica. Ricordi and frammenti di diario (1914–1919)* [*Diplomatic War. Recollections and Diary Excerpts (1914–1919)*]. Milan: Mondadori, 1936.

9. Aldrovandi Marescotti, Luigi. *Nuovi ricordi e frammenti di diario* [*Additional Recollections and Diary Excerpts*]. Milan: Mondadori, 1938.

10. Alegi, Gregory. "Above the Alps" in Norman L. R. Franks, Russell Guest, and Gregory Alegi. *Above the War Fronts.* London: Grub Street, 1997.

11. Alegi, Gregory, and Cesare Falessi. *L'Asso di assi* [*The Ace of Aces*]. Rome: Bariletti, 1992.

12. Alessi, Rino. *Dall'Isonzo al Piave. Lettere clandestine di un corrispondente di guerra* [*From the Isonzo to the Piave: Secret Letters of a War Correspondent*]. Milan: Mondadori, 1966.

13. Alvarez, David. "Italian Diplomatic Cryptanalysis in World War I." *Cryptologia,* Jan. 1996.

14. Ambrosoli, Luigi. *Né aderire né sabotare 1915–18* [*To Neither Support nor Sabotage 1915–18*]. Milan: Avanti! 1961.

15. Arpino, Alberto, Antonello Biagini, and Francesca Grispo, eds. *Le fonti per la storia militare italiana in età contemporanea* [*Sources for Italian Military History in the Contemporary Era*]. Rome: Ministero per I Beni Culturali e Ambientali, 1993.

16. *Ascensioni di guerra compiute dal pilota Francesco Pricolo 1915–18* [*War Flights Carried Out by the Pilot Francesco Pricolo 1915–18*]. Rome: USSMA, 1968.

17. *Aviazione in Lombardia. Pioneri, artigianato, industria* [*Aviation in Lombardy. Pioneers, Craftsmanship, Industry*]. Milan: Cariplo, 1982.

18. Bacchi, Riccardo. *L'alimentazione e la politica annonaria in Italia* [*Diet and Rationing Policy in Italy*]. Bari: Laterza, 1926.

19. Badoglio, Gian Luca, ed. *Il Memoriale di Pietro Badoglio su Caporetto* [*The Caporetto Memoir of Pietro Badoglio*]. Udine: Gaspari, 2000.

20. Bagnasco, Erminio. *I M.A.S. e le motosiluranti italiane, 1908–1968* [*The Italian Submarine Chasers and Motor Torpedo Boats, 1908–1968*]. Rome: USMM, 1969.

21. Baldini, Alberto. *Diaz.* Florence: Barbera, 1929. Translated as: *Diaz.* London: Humphrey Toulmin, 1935.

22. Bargoni, Franco, and Franco Gay. *Gli esploratori italiani (1861–1938)* [*The Italian Scout Cruisers (1861–1938)*]. 2nd ed. Rome: USMM, 1996.

23. Barozzi, Giovanni. *87a squadriglia La Serenissima* [*The 87th Squadron "La Serenissima"*]. Rovereto: Museo storico italiano della guerra, 1969.

24. Battistelli, Fabrizio. *Armi: nuovo modello di sviluppo. L'industria militare in Italia* [*Arms: New Model of Development. Military Industry in Italy*]. Turin: Einaudi, 1980.

25. Battisti, Cesare. *Scritti politici e epistolario* [*Political Writings and Correspondence*]. Paolo Alatri and Renato Monteleone, eds. Florence: La Nuova Italia, 1966.

26. Bencivenga, Roberto. *La campagna del 1916. La sorpresa di Asiago e quella di Gorizia* [*The 1916 Campaign. The Surprise of Asiago and of Gorizia*]. 2nd ed. Udine: Gaspari, 1998.

27. Bencivenga, Roberto. *La sorpresa strategica di Caporetto* [*The Strategic Surprise of Caporetto*]. 2nd ed. Udine: Gaspari, 1997.

28. Bernardi, Mario. *Di qua and di là dal Piave. Da Caporetto a Vittorio Veneto* [*On This and That Side of the Piave. From Caporetto to Vittorio Veneto*]. Milan: Mursia: 1989.

29. Bernotti, Romeo. *Cinquant'anni nella Marina militare* [*Fifty Years in the Navy*]. Milan: Mursia, 1971.

30. Bernotti, Romeo. *La guerra marittima. Studio critico sull'impiego dei mezzi nella Grande Guerra* [*The Maritime War. Analytical Study of the Employment of Resources in the Great War*]. Florence: Carpigiani & Zipoli, 1923.

31. Bernotti, Romeo. *Il potere marittimo nella Grande Guerra* [*Maritime Power in the Great War*]. Florence: Giusti, 1920.

32. Biagini, Antonello. *In Russia tra guerra e rivoluzione, la missione militare italiana 1915–1918* [*In Russia Between War and Revolution. The Italian Military Mission 1915–1918*]. Rome: USSME, 1983.

33. Bianchi, Bruna. *Crescere in tempo di guerra. Il lavoro e la protesta dei ragazzi in Italia 1915–1918* [*To Grow Up in Wartime. Labor and Childrens' Protest in Italy 1915–1918*]. Venice: Cafoscarina, 1995.

34. Bianchi, Bruna. "La grande guerra nella storiografia italiana dell'ultimo decennio" ["The Great War in Italian Historiography of the Last Decade"]. *Ricerche storiche,* 1991, no. 3.

35. Bianchi, Bruna. "Predisposizione, commozione o emozione? Natura e terapia delle neuropsicosi di guerra (1915–1918)" ["Predispostion, Concussion or Emotion? The Nature of and Therapy for War Psychosis (1915–1981)"]. *Movimento operaio e socialista,* 1983, no. 6.

36. Bigazzi, Duccio. *Il Portello. Operai, tecnici e imprenditori all'Alfa Romeo, 1906–1926* [*The Hatch Door. Workers, Technicians and Entrepreneurs at Alfa Romeo, 1906–1926*]. Milan: Franco Angeli, 1988.

37. Bignozzi, Giorgio, and Roberto Gentilli. *Aeroplani S.I.A.I. 1915–1935.* Florence: Edizioni Aeronautiche Italiane, 1982.

38. Billy, Robert de. "L'entrée en guerre de l'Italie vue de Rome (1914–1916)" ["The Entry of Italy into the War Seen from Rome (1914–1916)"]. *Revue d'histoire diplomatique,* 1985, nos. 1–2.

39. Bissolati, Leonida. *Diario di guerra. Appunti presi sulle linee, nei comandi, nei consigli interalleati* [*War Diary. Notes Taken in the Lines, in Command Posts, in Inter-Allied Councils*]. Turin: Einaudi, 1935.

40. Boatti, Giorgio. *Le spie imperfette* [*The Defective Spies*]. Milan: Rizzoli, 1987.

41. Boffito, Giuseppe. *Bibliografia aeronautica italiana illustrata* [*Illustrated Italian Aeronautical Bibliography*]. Florence: Olschki, 1929.

42. Boffito, Giuseppe. *Bibliografia aeronautica italiana illustrata. Primo supplemento decennale (1927–36).* Florence: Olschki, 1937.

43. Bollati di Saint Pierre, Eugenio. *La guerra al traffico marittimo* [*The War on Shipping*]. Rome: USMM, 1938.

44. Bonelli, Franco. *Lo sviluppo di una grande impresa in Italia. La Terni dal 1884 al 1962* [*The Development of a Great Firm in Italy. The Terni Steelworks from 1884 to 1962*]. Turin: Einaudi, 1975.

45. Bosworth, Richard J. B. *Italy and the Approach of the First World War.* New York: St. Martin's, 1983.

46. Bosworth, Richard J. B. *Italy, the Least of the Great Powers. Italian Foreign Policy before the First World War.* New York and Cambridge: Cambridge University, 1979.

47. Bosworth, Richard J. B. and Sergio Romano, eds. *La politica estera italiana (1860–1985)* [*Italian Foreign Policy (1860–1985)*]. Bologna: il Mulino, 1991.

48. Botti, Ferruccio, ed. *La guerra marittima e aerea secondo Romeo Bernotti* [*Naval and Air War According to Romeo Bernotti*]. Rome: Edizioni Forum di Relazioni Internazionali, 2000.

49. Botti, Ferruccio, ed. *La logistica dell'Esercito italiano (1831–1981).* 4 vols. Rome: USSME, 1991–95. *Vol. II. Dalla nascita dell'Esercito italiano alla Prima Guerra Mondiale (1861–1918)* [*The Logistics of the Italian Army (1831–1981). Vol. II. From the Birth of the Italian Army to the First World War*].

50. Botti, Ferruccio, and Mario Cermelli. *La teoria della guerra aerea in Italia dalle origini alla seconda guerra mondiale (1884–1939)* [*Air War Theory in Italy from its Origins to the Second World War (1884–1939)*]. Rome: USSMA, 1989.

51. Bovio, Oreste. *Storia dell'esercito italiano (1861–1990)* [*History of the Italian Army (1861–1990)*]. Rome: USSME, 1996.

52. Bovio, Oreste. *L'Ufficio storico dell'esercito. Un secolo di storiografia militare* [*The Army Historical Office. A Century of Military Historiography*]. Rome: USSME, 1987.

53. Bruti Liberati, Luigi. *Il clero italiano nella grande guerra* [*Italian Clergy in the Great War*]. Rome: Riuniti, 1982.

54. Burgwyn, H. James. *The Legend of the Mutilated Victory. Italy, the Great War, and the Paris Peace Conference, 1915–1919.* Westport, CT: Greenwood, 1993.

55. Caccia Dominioni, Paolo. *1915–1919. Diario di guerra.* 2nd ed. Milan: Mursia, 1993.

56. Cadioli, Beniamino, and Aldo Cecchi. *La posta militare italiana nella prima Guerra Mondiale* [*The Italian Military Postal Service in the First World War*]. Rome: USSME, 1978.

57. Cadorna, Luigi. *Altre pagine sulla grande guerra* [*Other Pages on the Great War*]. Milan: Mondadori, 1925.

58. Cadorna, Luigi. *La guerra alla fronte italiana fino all'arresto sulla linea del Piave e del Grappa* [*The War on the Italian Front until the Halt on the Piave-Monte Grappa Line*]. 2 vols. Milan: Treves, 1921.

59. Cadorna, Luigi. *Lettere famigliari* [*Family Letters*]. Rafaele Cadorna, ed. Milan: Mondadori, 1967.

60. Cadorna, Luigi. *Pagine polemiche* [*Polemical Pages*]. Milan: Garzanti, 1950.

61. Calanca, Alvaro. *Storia dell'Arma dei Carabinieri* [*History of the Italian Military Police*]. 3 vols. Foggia: Bastogi di Angelo Manuali, 1983–88.

62. Camarda, Alessandro, and Santo Pelli. *L'altro esercito. La classe operaia durante la prima guerra mondiale* [*The Other Army. The Working Class during the First World War*]. Milan: Feltrinelli, 1980.

63. Cannistraro, Philip V., and Brian R. Sullivan. *Il Duce's Other Woman.* New York: Morrow, 1993.

64. Capello, Luigi. *Caporetto, perché? La 2a armata e gli avvenimenti dell'ottobre 1917* [*Why Caporetto? The 2nd Army and the Events of October 1917*]. Turin: Einaudi, 1967.

65. Capello, Luigi. *Un militare nella storia d'Italia* [*A Soldier in Italian History*]. Cuneo: L'Arciere, 1987.

66. Cappelluti, Frank J. "The Life and Thought of Giulio Douhet." Ph.D. dissertation, Rutgers University, 1967.

67. Carboni, Giacomo. *La conquista delle Alpi Fassia* [*The Conquest of the Alps at Fassia*]. Rome: USSME, 1935.

68. Carparelli, Antonella. "La siderurgia italiana nella prima guerra mondiale: il caso di ILVA" ["The Italian Iron and Steel Industry in the First World War: The Case of ILVA"]. *Ricerche storiche,* 1978, no. 1.

69. Cartosio, Tomaso. *Vita eroica di Ernesto Cabruna* [*The Heroic Life of Ernesto Cabruna*]. Rome: USSMA, 1972.

70. Cassar, George. *The Forgotten Front: Britain and the Italian Campaign, 1917–1918.* London: Hambledon, 1998.

71. Castronovo Valerio. *Giovanni Agnelli. La FIAT dal 1899 al 1945.* Turin: Einaudi, 1977.

72. Castronovo Valerio. Series ed. *Storia dell'Ansaldo.* 7 volumes to date. Bari: Laterza, 1994. 4. Castronovo, ed., *L'Ansaldo e la Grande Guerra 1915–1918* [*History of Ansaldo. 4. Ansaldo and the Great War 1915–1918*]. 5. Gabriele De Rosa, ed., *Dal crollo alla ricostruzione 1919–1929* [*From Collapse to Reconstruction 1919–1929*].

73. Caviglia, Enrico. *La battaglia della Bainsizza* [*The Battle of the Bainsizza*]. Milan: Mondadori, 1930.

74. Caviglia, Enrico. *La dodicesima battaglia. Caporetto* [*The Twelfth Battle. Caporetto*]. Milan: Mondadori, 1965.

75. Caviglia, Enrico. *Le tre battaglie del Piave* [*The Three Battles of the Piave*]. Milan: Mondadori, 1934.

76. Ceci, Udalrigo. *Le occupazioni adriatiche* [*The Occupation of the Adriatic*]. Rome: USMM, 1932.

77. Cerrito, Gino. *L'antimilitarismo anarchico in Italia nel primo ventennio del secolo* [*Anarchic Antimilitarism in Italy in the First Twenty Years of the Century*]. Pistoia: RL, 1968.

78. Cervi, Mario. *Il Duca invitto. La vita di Emanuele Filiberto di Savoia Aosta principe e condottiero* [*The Invincible Duke. The Life of Emanuele Filiberto of Savoia-Aosta, Prince and Military Leader*]. Novara: De Agostini, 1987.

79. Cervone, Pier Paolo. *Enrico Caviglia. L'anti Badoglio.* Milan: Mursia, 1992.

80. Cervone, Pier Paolo. *Vittorio Veneto, l'ultima battaglia* [*Vittorio Veneto, the Final Battle*]. Milan: Mursia, 1994.

81. Ceva, Lucio. "Aspetti politici e giuridici dell'alto comando militare in Italia 1848–1941" ["Political and Legal Aspects of the Military High Command in Italy 1848–1941"]. *Il Politico,* 1984.

82. Ceva, Lucio. "La fine della Grande Guerra ad Occidente (Villa Giusti e Compiègne, 3–11 November 1918)" ["The End of the Great War in the West (Villa Giusti and Compiègne, 3–11 November 1918)"]. *Nuova Antologia,* Oct.–Dec. 1998.

83. Ceva, Lucio. *Le forze armate* [*The Armed Forces*]. Turin: UTET, 1981.

84. Ceva, Lucio. "La Grande Guerra nel Veneto: Scrittori e memorialisti" ["The Great War in the Veneto: Writers and Memoirists"]. *La Cultura,* 1988, no. 1.

85. Ceva, Lucio. "Ministro e Capo di Stato Maggiore" ["The Minister and the Chief of Staff"]. *Nuova Antologia,* Oct.–Dec. 1986.

86. Ceva, Lucio. "Monarchia e militari dal Risorgimento alla grande guerra" ["The Monarchy and the Military from the Risorgimento to the Great War (1848–1915)"]. *Nuova Antologia,* Jan.–March 1996.

87. Ceva, Lucio. "Riflessioni e notizie sui sottufficiali" ["Reflections and Notes on Non-Commissioned Officers"]. *Nuova Antologia,* Apr.–June 1992.

88. Ceva, Lucio, and Curami, Andrea. *La meccanizzazione dell'esercito italiano dalle origini al 1943* [*The Mechanization of the Italian Army from its Origins to 1943*]. 2 vols. Rome: USSME, 1989.

89. Chiusano, Amadeo, and Maurizio Saporiti. *Palloni, dirigibili ed aerei del Regio Esercito (1884–1923)* [*Balloons, Dirigibles and Aircraft of the Royal Italian Army (1884–1923)*]. Rome: USSME, 1998.

90. Contini, Luigi. *L'aviazione italiana in guerra.* Milan: Marangoni, 1934.

91. Coppa, Frank, ed. *Dictionary of Modern Italian History.* Westport, CT: Greenwood, 1985.

92. Corni, Gustavo, Eugenio Bucciol, and Arturo Schwarz. *Inediti della Grande Guerra. Immagini dell'invasione austrogermanico in Friuli e nel Veneto orientale* [*Unpublished Photographs of the Great War. Images of the Austro-German Invasion in Fiuli and Eastern Veneto*]. Padua: Ediciclo, 1992.

93. Curami, Andrea and Alessandro Massignani, eds. *L'artiglieria italiana nella grande guerra* [*Italian Artillery in the Great War*]. Valdagno (Vicenza): Gino Rossato, 1998.

94. Curami, Andrea, and Giorgio Rochat, eds. *Giulio Douhet. Scritti 1901–1915* [*Giulio Douhet. Written Works 1901–1915*]. Rome: USSMA, 1993.

95. D'Amico, Silvio. *La vigilia di Caporetto. Diario di guerra 1916–1917* [*On the Vigil of Caporetto. War Diary 1916–1917*]. Florence: Giunti, 1996.

96. De Felice, Renzo. *Mussolini il rivoluzionario 1883–1920.* Turin: Einaudi, 1965.

97. De Grand, Alexander. *The Hunchback's Tailor. Giovanni Giolitti and Liberal Italy from the Challenge of Mass Politics to the Rise of Fascism, 1882–1922.* Westport, CT: Praeger, 2001.

98. Del Boca, Angelo. *Gli italiani in Africa Orientale. I. Dall'Unità alla marcia su Roma* [*The Italians in East Africa. I. From Unification to the March on Rome*]. Bari: Laterza, 1976.

99. Del Boca, Angelo. *Gli italiani in Libia. I. Tripoli bel suol d'amore 1860–1922* [*The Italians in Libya. I. Tripoli "Beautiful Land of Love"*]. Bari: Laterza, 1986.

100. Della Volpe, Nicola. *Esercito e Propaganda nella Grande Guerra* [*The Army and Propaganda in the Great War*]. Rome: USSME, 1989.

101. Del Negro, Piero. "Army, State and Society in the Nineteenth and Early Twentieth Century: The Italian Case." *The Journal of Italian History,* Autumn 1979.

102. Del Negro, Piero. ed. *Guida alla storia militare italiana* [*Guide to Italian Military History*]. Naples: Edizioni Scientifiche Italiane, 1997.

103. De Risio, Carlo. *L'aviazione di Marina* [*Naval Aviation*]. Rome: USMM, 1995.

104. de'Rossi, Eugenio. *Ricordi di un agente segreto* [*Recollections of a Secret Agent*]. Milan: Alpes, 1929.

105. de'Rossi, Eugenio. *Vita di un ufficiale italiano sino alla guerra* [*Life of an Italian Officer until the War*]. Milan: Mondadori, 1927

106. De Stefani, Alberto. *La legislazione economica della guerra.* Bari: Laterza, 1926.

107. Di Giorgio, Antonino. *La battaglia dell'Ortigara.* Rome: Ardita, 1935.

108. Di Giorgio, Antonino. *Ricordi della Grande Guerra 1915–1918* [*Memories of the Great War 1915–1918*]. Palermo: Fondazione G. Whitaker, 1978.

109. *Dizionario Biografico degli Italiani* [*Biographical Dictionary of Italians*]. 56 vols. to date. Rome: Istituto della Enciclopedia Italiana, 1960.

110. Donolo, Luigi. *Storia della dottrina navale italiana* [*History of Italian Naval Doctrine*]. Rome: USMM, 1996.

111. Douhet, Giulio. *Diario critico di guerra, 1915–1916* [*Analytical War Diary, 1915–1916*]. 2 vols. Turin: Paravia, 1921–22.

112. Edmonds, James E., and H. R. Davies. *Military Operations Italy 1915–1919.* 2nd ed. London: Imperial War Museum, 1991.

113. Einaudi, Luigi. *La condotta economica e gli effetti sociali della guerra italiana* [*The Economic Conduct and Social Effects of the Italian War Effort*]. Bari: Laterza, 1933.

114. Einaudi, Luigi. *La guerra e il sistema tributario italiano* [*The War and the Italian Tax System*]. Bari: Laterza, 1927.

115. *Enciclopedia militare.* 6 vols. Milan: Istituto Editoriale Scientifico, 1929–31.

116. Esposito, Vincent J., ed. *The West Point Atlas of American Wars.* 2 vols. New York: Praeger, 1959. Vol. II. 1900–1953.

117. Fabi, Lucio. *Gente di trincea. La grande guerra sul Carso e sull'Isonzo* [*People of the Trenches. The Great War on the Carso Plateau and the Isonzo River*]. Milan: Mursia, 1994.

118. Fabi, Lucio. ed. *1914–1918 scampare la guerra. Renitenza, autolesionismo, comportamenti individuali e collettivi di fuga e la giustizia militare nella Grande Guerra* [*1914–1918: To Escape the War. Draft Evasion, Self-Inflicted Wounding, Individual and Group Flight, and Military Justice in the Great War*]. Monfalcone: Centro culturale pubblico polivalente, 1994.

119. Fadini, Francesco, ed. *Caporetto dalla parte del vincitore. La biografia del generale Otto von Below e il suo diario inedito sulla campagna d'Italia del 1917* [*Caporetto from the Winner's Side. The Biography of General Otto von Below and His Unpublished Diary on the Italian Campaign of 1917*]. Florence: Vallecchi, 1974.

120. Falco, Giancarlo. *L'Italia e la politica finanziaria degli alleati 1914–1920* [*Italy and Allied Financial Policy 1914–1920*]. Pisa: ETS, 1983.

121. Faldella, Emilio. *Caporetto: le vere cause di una tragedia* [*Caporetto: The True Causes of a Tragedy*]. Bologna: il Mulino, 1967.

122. Faldella, Emilio. *La grande guerra* [*The Great War*]. 2 vols. Milan: Longanesi, 1965.

123. Faldella, Emilio. ed. *Storia delle truppe alpine, 1872–1972* [*History of the Alpine Troops, 1872–1972*]. 3 vols. Milan: Cavallotti, 1972. Vol. II.

124. Falls, Cyril. *The Battle of Caporetto.* Philadelphia and New York; Lippincott, 1966.

125. Falzone del Barbarò, Michele, ed. *Vittorio Emanuele III. Album di guerra 1915–1918* [*Vittorio Emanuele III. War Album 1915–1918*]. Venice: Alinari, 1989.

126. Ferrante, Ezio. *Il Grande Ammiraglio Paolo Thaon di Revel* [*Grand Admiral Paolo Thaon di Revel*]. Rome: Rivista Marittima, 1989.

127. Ferrari, Paolo, ed. *La Grande Guerra aerea 1915–1918* [*The Great War in the Air 1915–1918*]. Valdagno (Vicenza): Gino Rossato, 1994.

128. Ferrari, Paolo, ed. "La produzione di armamenti nell'età giolittiana" ["Armaments Production in the Era of Giolitti"]. *Italia contemporanea,* 1986.

129. *La figura e l'opera di Giulio Douhet. Atti del convegno (12–14 Aprile 1987)* [*The Character and the Work of Giulio Douhet. Proceedings of the Conference (12–14 April 1987)*]. Caserta: Società di storia patria di terra di lavoro, 1988.

130. Fioravanzo, Giuseppe, Paolo Pollina and Franco Gnifetti. *I cacciatorpediniere italiani (1900–1971)* [*Italian Destroyers (1900–1971)*]. Rome: USMM, 1971.

131. Forcella, Enzo, and Alberto Monticone. *Plotone di esecuzione. I processi della prima guerra mondiale* [*Firing Squads. The Courts Martial of the First World War*]. Bari: Laterza, 1968.

132. Forsyth, Douglas J. *The Crisis of Liberal Italy: Monetary and Financial Policy, 1914–1922.* New York and Cambridge: Cambridge University, 1993.

133. Fossà, Angelo. *Duelli aerei. Le 34 vittorie aeree di F. Baracca* [*Air Duels. The 34 Aerial Victories of F. Baracca*]. Gambellara: Edle, 1968.

134. Fraccaroli, Aldo. *Italian Warships of World War I.* London: Ian Allan, 1970.

135. Fraschetti, Alessandro. *La prima organizzazione dell'aeronautica militare in Italia dal 1884 al 1925* [*The Original Organization of Military Aviation in Italy from 1884 to 1925*]. Rome: USSMA, 1986.

136. Fucci, Franco. *Emilio De Bono: il Maresciallo fucilato* [*Emilio De Bono: The Executed Marshal*]. Milan: Mursia, 1989.

137. Fucini, Mario. *Voli sul nemico* [*Flights over the Enemy*]. Florence: Bemporad, 1932.

138. Gabriele, Mariano. *Le convenzioni navali della Triplice* [*The Naval Conventions of the Triple Alliance*]. 3rd ed. Rome: USMM, 1999.

139. Gabriele, Mariano. *La marina nella guerra italo-turca. Il potere marittimo strumento militare e politico (1911–1912)* [*The Navy in the Italian-Turkish War. Maritime Power as a Military and Political Tool (1911–1912)*]. Rome: USMM, 1998.

140. Gabriele, Mariano, and Giuliano Friz. *La politica navale italiana dal 1885 al 1915* [*Italian Naval Policy from 1885 to 1915*]. Rome: USMM, 1982.

141. Gadda, Carlo Emilio. *Taccuino di Caporetto. Diario di guerra e di prigionia (Ottobre 1917–Aprile 1918)* [*Caporetto Notebook. War and Prison Diary (October 1917–April 1918)*]. Milan: Garzanti, 1991.

142. Gallinari, Vincenzo. *L'Esercito Italiano nel primo dopoguerra 1918–1920* [*The Italian Army in the Post–First World War Period 1918–1920*]. Rome: USSME, 198

143. Gatti, Angelo. *Caporetto. Diario di guerra (maggio-dicembre 1917).* Alberto Monticone, ed. 2nd ed. Bologna: il Mulino, 1997.

144. Gatti, Angelo. *Un italiano a Versailles, Dicembre 1917–Febbraio 1918* [*An Italian at Versailles, December 1917–February 1918*]. Milan: Cescina, 1957

145. Gatti, Gian Luigi. *Dopo Caporetto. Gli ufficiali P nella Grande guerra: propaganda, assistenza, vigilanza* [*"P" Officers in the Great War: Propaganda, Welfare, Surveillance*]. Gorizia: LEG, 2000.

146. Geloso, Carlo. "Produzione, rifornimento and consumo di munizioni per artiglierie durante la guerra italo-austriaca 1915–1918" ["Production, Resupply and Consumption of Artillery Ammunition during the Italian-Austrian War 1915–1918"]. *Rivista d'artiglieria e genio,* March and April 1928.

147. Gemignano, Marco. "Zurigo 1916: un colpo risolutivo. Il Servizio Segreto della R. Marina in azione" ["Zurich 1916: A Decisive Blow. The Royal Italian Navy Secret Service in Action"]. *Bollettino d'archivio dell'Ufficio storico della Marina militare,* Sept. 1989.

148. Gentsch, James Farrill. "Italy, Geography, and the First World War." Ph.D. dissertation, King's College, University of London, 1999.

149. Giordani, Antonio. *Il reggimento "San Marco." Memorie* [*The San Marco Regiment. Memoirs*]. Milan: Berterelli, 1920.

150. Giardino, Gaetano. *Rievocazioni e riflessioni di guerra* [*Recollections and Reflections on the War*]. 3 vols. Milan: Mondadori, 1929–32.

151. Giolitti, Giovanni. *Memorie della mia vita.* 2 vols. Milan: Treves, 1922. Translated as: *Memoirs of My Life.* London: Chapman and Dodd, 1923.

152. Giorgerini, Giorgio. *Gli incrociatori italiani (1861–1975)* [*Italian Cruisers (1861–1975)*]. 4th ed. Rome: USMM, 1976.

153. Giorgerini, Giorgio. *Le navi di linea italiane (1861–1969)* [*Italian Ships of the Line (1861–1969)*]. Rome: USMM, 1969.

154. Giovannini, Paolo. "La psichiatria italiana e la grande guerra. Ideologia e terapia psichiatrica alle prese con la nuova realtà bellica" ["Italian Psychiatry and the Great War. Ideology and Psychiatric Therapy in Confrontation with the New Reality of War"]. *Società, scienza e storia,* 1987, no. 1.

155. Gladden, Norman. *Across the Piave. A personal account of the British forces in Italy, 1917–1919.* London: HMSO, 1971.

156. Goglia, Luigi, ed. *Momenti di guerra 1915–1918 nella fotografia di Carlo Balelli* [*Moments of War, 1915–1918, in the Photography of Carlo Balelli*]. Rome: Editalia, 1995.

157. Gooch, John. *Army, State and Society in Italy, 1870–1915.* London: Macmillan, 1989.

158. Gooch, John. "Italy during the First World War" in Millett, Allan R., and Murray, Williamson, eds. *Military Effectiveness. Volume I: The First World War.* Boston: Allen & Unwin, 1988.

159. Gratton, Luigi. *Armando Diaz nell'ultimo anno della Grande Guerra. Testimonianze e giudizi* [*Armando Diaz in the Final Year of the Great War. Testimony and Judgements*]. Rome: Rivista Militare, 1994.

160. Guidi, Guido. *Sviluppo e attività della C.M.A.S.A.* [*Development and Activity of the Corporation for Aeronautical Mechanical Construction*]. Rome: USSMA, 1973.

161. Guillen, Pierre, ed. *La France e l'Italie pendant la première guerre mondiale* [*France and Italy during the First World War*]. Grenoble: Presses Universitaires di Grenoble, 1976.

162. Halpern, Paul G. *The Mediteranean Naval Situation, 1908–1914.* Cambridge: Harvard University, 1971.

163. Halpern, Paul G. *The Naval War in the Mediterranean, 1914–1918.* Annapolis: Naval Institute Press, 1987.

164. Haywood, Geoffrey A. *Failure of a Dream. Sidney Sonnino and the Rise and Fall of Liberal Italy 1847–1922.* Florence: Olschki, 1999.

165. Herrmann, David. *The Arming of Europe and the Making of the First World War.* Princeton: Princeton University, 1996.

166. Hertner, Peter, and Giorgio Mori, eds. *La transizione dall'economia di guerra all'economia di pace in Italia e in Germania dopo la Prima guerra mondiale* [*The Transition from a War Economy to a Peace Economy in Italy and Germany after the First World War*]. Bologna: il Mulino, 1983.

167. Herwig, Holger, and Neil M. Heyman. *Biographical Dictionary of World War I.* Westport, CT: Greenwood, 1982.

168. Hess, Robert L. "Italy and Africa: Colonial ambitions in the First World War." *Journal of African History,* 1963, no. 1.

169. Ilari, Virgilio. *Storia del servizio militare in Italia.* [*History of Military Service in Italy*]. 4 vols. Rome: Centro Militare di Studi Strategici/Rivista Militare, 1989–91. II. *La "nazione armata" (1871–1918)* [*The "Nation in Arms" (1871–1918)*]. III. *"Nazione militare" e "fronte del lavoro" (1919–1943)* [*"Military Nation" to "Labor Front" (1919–1943)*].

170. Isnenghi, Mario. *Giornali di trincea 1915–1918* [*Trench Newspapers 1915–1918*]. Turin: Einaudi, 1977.

171. Isnenghi, Mario. *Il mito della Grande Guerra da Marinetti a Malaparte* [*The Myth of the Great War from Marinetti to Malaparte*]. Bari: Laterza, 1970.

172. Isnenghi, Mario, ed. *Operai e contadini nella grande guerra* [*Workers and Peasants in the Great War*]. Bologna: Capelli, 1982.

173. Isnenghi, Mario. *I vinti di Caporetto nella letteratura di guerra* [*The Defeated Soldiers of Caporetto in War Literature*]. Padua: Marsilio, 1967.

174. Isnenghi, Mario, and Giorgio Rochat. *La Grande Guerra 1914–1918* [*The Great War 1914–1918*]. Milan: La nuova Italia, 2000.

175. Italy. Ministero degli Affari Esteri. Commissione per la pubblicazione dei documenti diplomatici. *I documenti diplomatici italiani. Quinta Serie: 1914–1918* [*The Italian Diplomatic Documents. Fifth Series: 1914–1918*]. Augusto Torre, Ettore Anchieri, Pietro Pastorelli and Federico Curato, eds. 11 vols. Rome: Istituto Poligrafico dell Stato, 1954–86.

176. Italy. Ministero degli Affari Esteri. Commissione per la pubblicazione dei documenti diplomatici. *Sesta Serie: 1918–1922.* Rodolfo Mosca and Renato Grispo, eds. 2 vols. to date. Rome: Istituto Poligrafico dello Stato, 1956.

177. Italy. Ministero di Guerra. *Le grandi unità nella guerra italo-austriaca 1915–1918* [*The Large Units* [armies, corps and divisions] *in the Italo-Austrian War 1915–1918*]. 2 vols. Rome: USSME, 1926.

178. Italy. Ministero di Guerra. *Riassunti storici dei corpi e comandi nella guerra 1915–1918* [*Historical Summary of the Corps and Commands in the War, 1915–1918*]. 11 vols. Rome: USSME, 1926–31.

179. Italy. Ministro di Guerra/della Difesa. *L'esercito italiano nella Grande Guerra (1915–1918)* [*The Italian Army in the Great War (1915–1918)*]. 7 vols. in 37 parts. Rome: USSME, 1927–81.

180. Italy. Ministero della Marina. *L'attività della R. Marina dalla guerra libica a quella italo-austriaca* [*The Activity of the Royal Italian Navy from the Libyan War to the Italo-Austrian War*]. Rome: USMM, 1931.

181. Italy. Ministero della Marina. *La Marina italiana nella grande guerra* [*The Italian Navy in the Great War*]. 8 vols. Florence: Vallecchi/USMM, 1935–42.

182. Jones, Simon Mark. *Domestic Factors in Italian Intervention in the First World War.* New York: Garland, 1986.

183. Labanca, Nicola; Piero Del Negro, Giorgio Rochat, Filippo Frassati, and Giuseppe Caforio, eds. *Bibliografia italiana di storia e studi militari 1960–1984* [*Bibliography of Italian Military History and Studies 1960–1984*]. Milan: Franco Angeli, 1987.

184. Laredo de Mendoza, Saverio. *Gabriele D'Annunzio combattente nella grande guerra (1915–1918)* [*Gabriele D'Annunzio, Combatant in the Great War (1915–1918)*]. Milan: Impresa Editoriale Italiana, 1964.

185. Lioy, Vincenzo. *1918–1958. Nel 40. Anniversario delle battaglie del Piave e di Vittorio Veneto* [*1918–1958. On the 40th Anniversary of the Battles of the Piave and Vittorio Veneto*]. Rome: USSMA, 1958.

186. Longo, Luigi Emilio. *Francesco Saverio Grazioli.* Rome: USSME, 1989.

187. Ludovico, Domenico. *Gli aviatori italiani del bombardamento nella guerra 1915–1918* [*Italian Bomber Aircrew in the War of 1915–1918*]. Rome: USSMA, 1980.

188. Ludovico, Domenico. *L'incursione aerea su Cattaro da Gioa del Colle (4 Ottobre 1917)* [*The Aerial Incursion over the Bay of Cattaro from the Gioa del Colle Airbase (4 October 1917)*]. Rome: Museo Caproni, 1981.

189. Lussu, Emilio. *Un'anno sull'Altopiano* [*A Year on the High Plateau*]. 2nd ed. Turin: Einaudi, 1964. Translated as: *Sardinian Brigade.* London: Prion, 2000.

190. Macchione, Pietro. *L'aeronautica Macchi. Dalla leggenda alla storia* [*Macchi Aeronautics. From Legend to History*]. Milan: Franco Angeli, 1985.

191. Mack Smith, Denis. *Italy and its Monarchy.* New Haven: Yale University, 1989.

192. Maddalena, Umberto. *Lotte e vittorie sul mare e nel cielo* [*Fights and Victories over the Sea and in the Sky*]. Milan: Mondadori, 1930.

193. Malagodi, Olindo. *Conversazioni della guerra 1914–1919* [*War Conversations 1914–1919*]. Brunello Vigezzi, ed. 2 vols. Milan: Ricciardi, 1960.

194. Manca, Vincenzo. *L'idea meravigliosa di Francesco Baracca* [*The Wonderful Idea of Francesco Baracca*]. Rome: Dell'Ateneo, 1980.

195. Mancini, Luigi. *Grande enciclopedia aeronautica.* Milan: Aeronautica, 1936.

196. Manfroni, Camillo. *Nostri alleati navali: ricordi della guerra Adriatica, 1915–1918* [*Our Naval Allies: Records of the War in the Adriatic, 1915–1918*]. Milan: Mondadori, 1927.

197. Manfroni, Camillo. *Storia della Marina italiana durante la guerra mondiale 1914–1918* [*History of the Italian Navy during the World War 1914–1918*]. 2nd ed. Bologna: Zanichelli, 1925.

198. Mangone, Angelo. *Diaz. Da Caporetto al Piave a Vittorio Veneto* [*Diaz. From Caporetto to the Piave to Vittorio Veneto*]. Milan: Frassinelli, 1987.

199. Mantegazza, Amilcare. "La formazione del settore aeronautica italiano" ["The Formation of the Aeronautical Sector of Italian Industry"]. *Annali di storia dell'impresa.* Vol. 2. Milan: Franco Angeli, 1986.

200. Mantoan, Nevio. *Armi e equipaggiamenti dell'esercito italiano nella Grande Guerra (1915–1918) Arms and Equipment of the Italian Army in the Great War (1915–1918)*]. Valdagno (Vicenza): Gino Rossato, 1996.

201. Mantoan, Nevio. *La guerra dei gas* [*The Poison Gas War*]. Udine; Gaspari, 1999.

202. Marchetti, Odoardo. *Il servizio informazione dell'esercito italiano nella grande guerra* [*The Italian Army Intelligence Service in the Great War*]. Rome: Tipografia regionale, 1937.

203. Marchetti, Tullio. *Ventotto anni nel Servizio Informazioni Militari* [*Twenty-Eight Years in the Military Intelligence Service*]. Trento: Temi, 1960.

204. Marinetti, Filippo Tommaso. *Taccuini (1915–1921)* [*Notebooks (1915–1921)*]. A. Bertoni, ed. Bologna: il Mulino, 1987.

205. Martini, Ferdinando. *Diario 1914–18.* Verona: Mondadori, 1966.

206. Mascolini, Loredana. "Il ministro per le armi e munizioni (1915–1918)" [The Ministry for Arms and Munitions (1915–1918)"]. *Storia contemporanea,* 1980, no. 6.

207. Mazzetti, Massimo. *Da Caporetto al Monte Grappa (la crisi nazionale del 1917)* [*From Caporetto to Monte Grappa (The National Crisis of 1917)*]. Naples: Libreria scientifica, 1970.

208. Mazzetti, Massimo. *L'industria italiana nella Grande Guerra* [*Italian Industry in the Great War*]. Rome: USSME, 1979.

209. Mazzetti, Massimo. "Spese militari italiane e preparazione bellica nel 1914" [Italian Military Expenditures and War Preparations in 1914"]. *Clio,* Oct.–Dec. 1972.

210. Mazzetti, Ottorino. *Dal piede alla cima del Col di Lana* [*From the Foot to the Summit of the Col di Lana*]. Rome: USSME, 1934.

211. Melograni, Piero. *Storia politica della Grande guerra 1915–1918* [*Political History of the Great War 1915–1918*]. Bari: Laterza, 1971.

212. *Memorie/Studi Storico Militari 1977*. Rome: USSME, 1978.

213. Minniti, Fortunato. "Protagonisti dell'intervento pubblico: Alfredo Dallolio" [Champions of Public Intervention: Alfredo Dallolio]. *Economia pubblica,* June 1976.

214. Miozzi, Umberto Massimo. *La mobilitazione industriale italiana (1915–1918)* [*Italian Industrial Mobilization (1915–1918)*]. Rome: La Goliardica, 1980.

215. Mola, Aldo Alessandro, ed. *Luigi Capello. Atti del convegno di Cuneo, 3–4 Aprile 1987* [*Luigi Capello. Proceedings of the Conference at Cuneo, 3–4 April 1987*]. Cuneo: L'Arciere, 1987.

216. Molfese, Manlio. *L'aviazione da ricognizione italiana durante la guerra europea (Maggio 1915-Novembre 1918)* [*Italian Reconnaissance Aviation during the European War (May 1915-November 1918)*]. Rome: Provveditorata generale dello Stato, 1925.

217. Montanari, Mario. *Le truppe italiane in Albania (Anni 1914–20 e 1939)* [*Italian Troops in Albania (1914–20 and 1939)*]. Rome: USSME, 1978.

218. Montefinale, Tito. "L'artiglieria italiana durante e dopo la guerra europea" ["The Italian Artillery during and after the European War"]. *Rivista d'artiglieria e genio,* 3 parts, Aug.–Nov. 1933.

219. Monticone, Alberto. *La battaglia di Caporetto* [*The Battle of Caporetto*]. 2nd ed. Udine: Gaspari, 1999.

220. Monticone, Alberto. *La Germania e la neutralità italiana: 1914–1915* [*Germany and Italian Neutrality: 1914–1915*]. Bologna: il Mulino, 1971.

221. Monticone, Alberto. *Gli italiani in uniforme 1915–1918. Intellettuali, borghesi, disertori* [*Italians in Uniform 1915–1918. Intellectuals, Bourgeoisie, Deserters*]. Bari: Laterza, 1972.

222. Monticone, Alberto. *Nitti e la grande guerra 1914–1918.* Milan: Giuffré, 1961.

223. Montù, Carlo et al. *Storia dell'Artiglieria Italiana.* 16 vols. Rome: Rivista d'artiglieria e genio/Biblioteca d'artiglieria e genio, 1934–55. Vols. IX–XI.

224. Mori, Giorgio. "Le guerre parallele. L'industria elettrica in Italia nel periodo della grande guerra, 1914–1918" ["The Parallel Wars. The Electrical Industry in Italy in the Period of the Great War, 1914–1918"]. *Studi storici,* 1973, no. 2.

225. Morozzo della Rocca, Roberto. *La fede e la guerra. Cappellani militari e preti-soldati (1915–1919)* [*Faith and War. Military Chaplains and Soldier-Priests (1915–1919)*]. Rome: Studium, 1980.

226. Mortara, Giorgio. *La salute pubblica in Italia durante e dopo la guerra* [*Public Health in Italy during and after the War*]. Bari: Laterza, 1925.

227. Mussolini, Benito. *Opera omnia di Benito Mussolini.* Edoardo and Duilio Susmel, eds. 36 vols. Florence: La Fenice, 1951–62. Vols. VI–XI, XXXIV.

228. Mussolini, Benito. *Opera omnia di Benito Mussolini. Appendici.* Edoardo and Duilio Susmel, eds. 8 vols. Rome: Giovanni Volpe, 1978–80. Vol. XVIII.

229. Nassigh, Riccardo. *La Marina italiana e l'Adriatico. Il potere marittimo in un teatro ristretto* [*The Italian Navy and the Adriatic. Maritime Power in a Restricted Theater*]. Rome: USMM, 1998.

230. Nemeth, Luc. "Dolci corrispondenze. La Francia e I finanziamenti al 'Il Popolo d'Italia' 1914–1917 ["Letters with Sweets. France and the Subsidies for *Il Popolo d'Italia* 1914–1917"]. *Italia contemporanea,* 1998, no. 212.

231. Orlando, Vittorio Emanuele. *Discorsi per la guerra e per la pace* [*Speeches for War and for Peace*]. Foligno: Campitelli, 1923. Previously published in translation as: *War Speeches.* Rome: F. S. Arnold, 1919.

232. Orlando, Vittorio Emanuele. *Memorie (1915–1919).* Rodolfo Mosca, ed. Milan: Rizzoli, 1960.

233. Pagani, Giovanni. *Lo sviluppo dell'industria bellica a La Spezia dalla costituzione della Società Anonima degli Alti Forni Fonderie e Acciaierie di Terni (1884–1985). L'Oto Melara verso il centenario* [*The Development of War Industry at La Spezia from the Establishment of the Corporation for Blast-Furnaces and Steelworks at Terni (1884–1985). Oto-Melara Toward its Centenary*]. La Spezia: Unitech, 1991.

234. Palumbo, Michael. "German-Italian Military Relations on the Eve of World War I." *Central European History,* 1979, no. 4.

235. Palumbo, Michael. "Italian—Austro-Hungarian Military Relations before World War I" in Samuel R. Williamson Jr. and Peter Pastor, eds. *Essays on World War I: Origins and Prisoners of War.* New York: Brooklyn College, 1983.

236. Paolucci, Raffaele. *Il mio piccolo mondo perduto* [*My Little Lost World*]. Bologna: Cappelli, 1947.

237. Parri, Ferruccio. *Scritti 1915–1975.* Milan: Feltrinelli, 1976.

238. Passarin, Mauro, and Glauco Viazzi, eds. *Panorami della Grande Guerra sul fronte dall Stelvio al Garda* [*Panoramas of the Great War on the Front from Stelvio to Lake Garda*]. Vicenza: Museo del Risorgimento e della Resistenza, 1998.

239. Pastorelli, Pietro. *L'Albania nella politica estera italiana, 1914–1920* [*Albania in Italian Foreign Policy, 1914–1920*]. Naples: Jovene, 1970.

240. Pesce, Giuseppe. *I dirigibili italiani* [*Italian Dirigibles*]. Modena: STEM Mucchi, 1982.

241. Pesce, Giuseppe. *L'8° gruppo caccia in due conflitti mondiali* [*The 8th Fighter Group in Two World Conflicts*]. Modena: STEM Mucchi, 1974.

242. Petra di Caccuri, Carlo. "L'industria degli esplosivi in Italia durante la guerra e loro utilizzazione nel dopoguerra" ["The Explosives Industry in Italy during the War and Their Use in the Postwar Period"]. *Rivista d'artiglieria e genio,* July–Aug. 1923.

243. Pianta, Mario, and Giulio Perani. *L'industria militare in Italia. Ascesa e declino della produzione di armamenti* [*Military Industry in Italy. The Rise and Fall of Armaments Production*]. Rome: Edizioni associate, 1991.

244. Pieri, Piero. *L'Italia nella prima guerra mondiale (1915–1918)* [*Italy in the First World War (1915–1918)*]. Turin: Einaudi, 1968.

245. Pieri, Piero. "Italian Front" in Esposito, Vincent J., ed. *A Concise History of World War I.* New York and London: Praeger, 1964.

246. Pieri, Piero. *La prima guerra mondiale 1914–1918. Problemi di storia mondiale* [*The First World War 1914–1918. Problems of Military History*]. 3rd ed. Udine: Gaspari, 1998

247. Pieri, Piero, and Giorgio Rochat. *Badoglio.* Turin: UTET, 1974.

248. Polli, Vittorio. *Antonio Locatelli. Vita e documenti* [*Antonio Locatelli. Life and Documents*]. Bergamo: Bolis, 1986.

249. Pollina, Paolo. *I sommergibili italiane (1895–1971)* [*Italian Submarines (1895–1971)*]. Rome: USMM, 1971.

250. Pollina, Paolo. *Le torpediniere italiane (1881–1964)* [*Italian Torpedo Boats (1881–1964)*]. Rome: USMM, 1974.

251. Porro, Alberto. *Natale Palli.* Rome: USSMA, 1973.

252. Porro, Felice. *La guerra nell'aria* [*The War in the Air*]. 4th ed. Milan: MATE, 1965.

253. Porsini, Giorgio. *Il capitalismo italiano nella prima guerra mondiale* [*Italian Capitalism in the First World War*]. Florence: La Nuova Italia, 1975.

254. Porta, Gianfranco. *I giorni di guerra sull'Adamello-Kriegstage am Adamello* [*Days of War on the Adamello Plateau*]. Brescia: Grafo, 1996.

255. *La prima guerra mondiale e il Trentino. (Atti del Convegno Internazionale, Rovereto 25–29 Giugno 1978)* [*The First World War and the Trentino. (Proceedings of the International Conference, Rovereto 25–29 June 1978)*]. Rovereto: Comprensorio della Val Laraina, 1980.

256. Procacci, Giuliana. "Gli effetti della Grande guerra sulla psicologia della popolazione civile" ["The Influence of the Great War on the Psychology of the Civilian Population"]. *Studi e problemi contemporanei,* 1992, no. 10.

257. Procacci, Giuliana. "La neutralité italienne et l'entrée en guerre" ["Italian Neutrality and Entry into the War"]. *Guerres mondiales et conflits contemporains,* July 1995.

258. Procacci, Giuliana. *Soldati e prigioneri italiani nella Grande guerra. Con una raccolta di lettere inediti* [*Soldiers and Italian Prisoners in the Great War. With a Collection of Unpublished Letters*]. Rome: Riuniti, 1993.

259. Procacci, Giuliana. ed. *Stato e classe operaia durante la prima guerra mondiale* [*State and Working Class during the Great War*]. Milan: Franco Angeli, 1983.

260. Procacci, Giovanna, and Bruna Bianchi. "Diari di guerra 1915–1918" ["War Diaries 1915–1918"]. *Ricerche storiche,* 1993, no. 3.

261. Renzi, William A. *In the Shadow of the Sword: Italy's Neutrality and Entrance into the Great War, 1914–1915.* New York: Peter Lang: 1987.

262. Répaci, Francesco A. "Il costo finanziario della prime guerra mondiale in Italia" ["The financial cost of the First World War in Italy"]. *Statistica,* 1954, no. 4 (*Studi in onore di G. Pietra*).

263. Rimanelli, Marco. *Italy between Europe and the Mediterranean. Diplomacy and Naval Strategy from Unification to NATO.* New York: Peter Lang, 1997.

264. Rochat, Giorgio. *Gli Arditi della grande guerra. Origini, battaglie e miti* [*The Italian Storm Troops of the Great War. Origins, Battles and Myths*]. 2nd ed. Gorizia: Edizione Goriziana, 1990.

265. Rochat, Giorgio. *L'esercito italiano in pace e in guerra: studi di storia militare* [*The Italian Army in Peace and War: Studies in Military History*]. Milan: RARA, 1991.

266. Rochat, Giorgio. *L'esercito italiano da Vittorio Veneto a Mussolini (1919–1925)* [*The Italian Army from Vittorio Veneto to Mussolini (1919–1925)*]. Bari: Laterza, 1967.

267. Rochat, Giorgio. *L'Italia nella prima guerra mondiale. Problemi d'interpretazione e prospettive di ricerca* [*Italy in the First World War. Problems of Interpretation and Prospects for Research*]. Milan: Feltrinelli, 1976.

268. Rochat, Giorgio. ed. *La spada e la croce. I cappellani italiani nelle due guerre mondiali* [*The Sword and the Cross. Italian Military Chaplains in the Two World Wars*]. Torre Pellice: Società di studi valdesi, 1995.

269. Rochat, Giorgio. ed. *La storiografia militare italiana negli ultimi venti anni* [*Italian Military Historiography in the Last Twenty Years*]. Milan: Franco Angeli, 1985.

270. Rochat, Giorgio. *Ufficiali e soldati. L'esercito italiano dalla prima alla seconda guerra mondiale* [*Officers and Soldiers. The Italian Army From the First to the Second World War*]. Udine: Gaspari, 2000.

271. Rossini, Daniela. "Le radici del Wilsonismo in Italia 1917–18: la campagna della Croce Rossa Americana e dell'YMCA nel dopo-Caporetto" [The Roots of Wilsonianism in Italy 1917–18: The Campaign of the American Red Cross and YMCA in the Period after Caporetto"]. *Storia delle relazioni internazionali,* 1993, no. 1.

272. Rossini, Daniela. "Wilson e il patto di Londra nel 1917–18." *Storia contemporanea,* 1991, no. 3.

273. Row, Thomas. "Economic Nationalism in Italy: The Ansaldo Company 1882–1921." Ph.D. dissertation, Johns Hopkins University, 1988.

274. Ruffo, Maurizio. *L'Italia nella Triplice Alleanza. I piani operativi dell S.M. verso l'Austria-Ungheria dal 1885 al 1915* [*Italy in the Triple Alliance. The Operational Plans of the General Staff Against Austria-Hungary from 1885 to 1915*]. Rome: USSME, 1998.

275. Saccoman, Andrea. *Il gen. Paolo Spingardi ministero della guerra 1909–1914* [*Gen. Paolo Spingardi, Minister of War 1909–1914*]. Rome: USSME, 1995.

276. Salandra, Antonio. *Il diario di Salandra.* Giambattista Gifuni, ed. Milan: Pan, 1969.

277. Salandra, Antonio. *L'intervento (1915): Ricordi e pensieri* [*The Intervention (1915): Recollections and Thoughts*]. Milan: Mondadori, 1930. Translated as the second half of: *Italy and the Great War.* London: Edward Arnold, 1932.

278. Salandra, Antonio. *Memorie politiche 1916–1925* [*Political Memoirs 1916–1925*]. Milan: Garzanti, 1951.

279. Salandra, Antonio. *La neutralità italiana 1914* [*Italian Neutrality 1914*]. Milan: Mondadori, 1928. Translated as the first half of: *Italy and the Great War.* London: Edward Arnold, 1932.

280. Salandra, Antonio. *I retroscena di Versailles* [*Behind the Scenes at Versailles*]. Giambattista Gifuni, ed. Milan: Pan, 1971.

281. Salandra, Antonio. *Salandra inedito* [*Unpublished Salandra Papers*]. Giambattista Gifuni, ed. Milan: Pan, 1973.

282. Salsa, Carlo. *Trincee: confidenze di un fante* [*Trenches: Revelations of an Infantryman*]. Milan: Sonzogno, 1924.

283. Santini, Aldo. *Costanzo Ciano, il ganascia del fascismo* [*Costanzo Ciano, the Hungry Jaw of Fascism*]. Milan: Camunia, 1993.

284. Savona, Virgilio, and Michele Straniero. *Canti della Grande Guerra* [*Songs of the Great War*]. 2 vols. Milan: Garzanti, 1981.

285. Scala, Edoardo. *Storia delle fanterie italiane* [*History of the Italian Infantry*]. 10 vols. Rome: USSME, 1950–56, vol. V, *Le fanterie nella prima guerra mondiale.*

286. Scardigli, Marco. "Superstizione, alcolismo e fuga nelle trincee italiane: 1915–1917" ["Superstition, Alcoholism and Flight in the Italian Trenches: 1915–1917"]. *Il Politico,* 1986, no. 1.

287. Scaroni, Silvio. *Battaglie nel cielo* [*Battles in the Sky*]. Milan: Mondadori, 1934.

288. Scaroni, Silvio. *Impressioni and ricordi di guerra aerea* [*Impressions and Memories of Aerial War*]. Rome: Danesi, 1922.

289. Scolè, Pierluigi. "Le lezioni tattiche del fronte occidentale e il loro mancato riflesso sulla guerra italiana (1915–17)" ["The Tactical Lessons of the Western Front and Their Lack of Influence on the Italian War Front (1915–17)"]. Ph.D. dissertation, University of Pavia, 1990.

290. Segrè, Claudio. "Douhet in Italy: Prophet Without Honor?" *Aerospace Historian,* 1979, no. 2.

291. Segreto, Luciano. "Armi e munizioni. Lo sforzo bellico tra sperimentazione e progresso tecnico" ["Arms and Munitions. The Italian War Effort between Experimentation and Technical Progress"]. *Italia contemporanea,* 1982, nos. 146–47.

292. Segreto, Luciano. "Aspetti delle relazioni economiche tra Italia e Germania nel periodo della neutralità (1914–1915)' ["Aspects of the Economic Relations Between Italy and Germany in the Period of Neutrality (1914–1915)"]. *Annali della Fondazione Luigi Einaudi. Vol. XVIII-1984.* Turin: Fondazione Luigi Einaudi, 1985.

293. Sema, Antonio. *La Grande Guerra sul fronte dell'Isonzo* [*The Great War on the Isonzo Front*]. 3 vols. Gorizia: Editrice Goriziana, 1995–97.

294. Serpieri, Arrigo. *La guerra e le classi rurali italiane* [*The War and the Italian Rural Classes*]. Bari: Laterza, 1921.

295. Seth, Ronald. *Caporetto: The Scapegoat Battle.* London: Macdonald, 1965.

296. Seton-Watson, Christopher. *Italy from Liberalism to Fascism: 1870–1925.* London: Methuen, 1967.

297. Sonnino, Sidney. *Opera omnia di Sidney Sonnino* [*Complete Works of Sidney Sonnino*]. Benjamin F. Brown and Pietro Pastorelli, eds. 8 vols. Bari: Laterza, 1972–81.

298. Spagnol, Tito A. *Memoriette marziali e veneree* [*Memoirs of War and Love*]. Vicenza: Mario Spagnol, 1970.

299. Speranza, Gino. *The Diary of Gino Speranza 1915–1919.* 2 vols. New York: Columbia University, 1941.

300. Spitzer, Leo. *Lettere di prigionieri di guerra italiani 1915–1918* [*Letters of Italian Prisoners of War 1915–1918*]. Turin: Boringheri, 1976.

301. Spriano, Paolo. *Torino operaia nella grande guerra 1914–1918* [*Working Class Turin in the Great War 1914–1918*]. Turin: Einaudi, 1960.

302. Staderni, Alessandra. *Combattenti senza divisa. Roma nella Grande Guerra* [*Combatants Without Uniforms. Rome in the Great War*]. Bologna. il Mulino, 1995.

303. Stefani, Filippo. *La storia della dottrina e degli ordinamenti dell'esercito italiano. I. Dall'esercito piemontese all'esercito di Vittorio Veneto* [*The History of the Doctrine and Regulations*

of the Italian Army. I. *From the Piedmontese Army to the Army of Vittorio Veneto*]. Rome: USSME, 1984.

304. *Storia militare d'Italia 1796–1975*. Rome: Editalia, 1990.

305. Straulino, Luigi. *Bibliografia aeronautica italiana dal 1937 al 1981* [*Italian Aeronautical Bibliography from 1937 to 1981*]. Rome: USSMA, 1982.

306. Stevenson, David. *Armaments and the Coming of War. Europe, 1904–1914*. Oxford: Clarendon Press, 1996.

307. Sullivan, Brian R. "Caporetto: Causes, Recovery and Consequences" in George Andreopoulos and Harold E. Selesky, eds. *The Aftermath of Defeat. Societies, Armed Forces and the Challenge of Recovery*. New Haven: Yale University, 1994.

308. Sullivan, Brian R. "The strategy of the decisive weight: Italy, 1882–1922" in Williamson Murray, MacGregor Knox, and Alvin Bernstein, eds., *The Making of Strategy. Rulers, States and War*. Cambridge and New York: Cambridge University, 1994.

309. Tomassini, Luigi. "Guerra e scienza. Lo stato e l'organizzazione della ricerca in Italia 1915–1919" ["War and Science. The State and the Organization of Research in Italy 1915–1919"]. *Ricerche storiche*. 1991, no. 3.

310. Toniolo, Gianni, ed. *La Banca d'Italia e l'economia di guerra (1914–1919)* [*The Bank of Italy and the War Economy (1914–1919)*]. Bari: Laterza, 1989.

311. Toniolo, Gianni, ed. *An Economic History of Liberal Italy 1850–1918*. London and New York: Routledge, 1990.

312. Toscano, Mario. *Pagine di storia diplomatica contemporanea* [*Pages from Contemporary Diplomatic History*]. 2 vols. Milan: Giuffrè, 1963. Vol. I.

313. Toscano, Mario. *Il patto di Londra. Storia diplomatica dell'intervento italiano (1914–1915)* [*The Pact of London. The Diplomatic History of Italian Intervention (1914–1915)*]. 2nd ed. Bologna: Zanichelli, 1934.

314. Tosti, Amedeo. *Le medaglie d'oro* [*The Gold Medals*]. 4 vols. Rome: USSME, 1934.

315. *Il Trauma dell'intervento: 1914/1919* [*The Trauma of Intervention: 1914–1919*]. Florence: Vallecchi, 1968.

316. Tur, Vittorio. *Plancia ammiraglio* [*Admiral's Bridge*]. 3 vols. Rome: Canesi, 1958–63. Vol. I.

317. Valiani, Leo. *Il partito socialista italiano nel periodo della neutralità 1914–15* [*The Italian Socialist Party in the Period of Neutrality 1914–15*]. 2nd ed. Milan: Feltrinelli, 1977.

318. Valle, Giuseppe. *I miei trent'anni di volo* [*My Thirty Years of Flight*]. Milan: Mondadori, 1939.

319. Vigezzi, Brunello. *Da Giolitti a Salandra*. Florence: Vallecchi, 1969.

320. Vigezzi, Brunello. *L'Italia di fronte alla prima guerra mondiale* [*Italy Confronted with the First World War*]. 2 vols. Milan: Ricciardi, 1966.

321. Vigezzi, Brunello. *L'Italia unita e le sfide della politica estera. Dal Risorgimento all Repubblica* [*United Italy and the Challenge of Foreign Policy. From the Risorgimento to the Republic*]. 2 vols. Milan: Unicopli, 1997.

322. Viggiani, Carmine. "Arturo De Riseis, capo dell'Ufficio speciale del Ministero della Marina e is suoi corrispondenti di guerra (Novembre 1917–Novembre 1918)" ["Arturo De Riseis, Head of the Special Office of the Ministry of the Navy and His War Correspondents (November 1917–November 1918)"]. *Bollettino d'archivio dell'Ufficio storico della Marina militare,* March 1994.

323. Volpe, Gioacchino. *Caporetto*. Rome: Canini, 1965.

324. Webster, R. A. *Industrial Imperialism in Italy, 1908–1915*. Berkeley: University of California, 1975.

325. Whittam, John. *The Politics of the Italian Army, 1861–1918*. London: Croon Helm, 1977.

326. Whittam, John. "War Aims and Strategy: the Italian Government and High Command 1914–1919" in Barry Hunt and Adrian Preston, eds. *War Aims and Strategic Policy in the Great War 1914–1918*. London: Croon Helm, 1977.

327. Zamagni, Vera. *The Economic History of Italy 1860–1999*. Oxford: Clarendon Press, 1993.

328. Zingales, Francesco. *La conquista di Gorizia* [*The Conquest of Gorizia*]. Rome: USSME, 1925.

329. Zugaro, Fulvio. *Il costo della guerra italiana. Contributo alla storia economica della guerra mondiale* [The Cost of the Italian War. A Contribution to the Economic History of the World War]. Rome: Stabilimento poligrafico per l'amministrazione della guerra, 1921.

6

Austria-Hungary

John R. Schindler

Austria-Hungary's final struggle remains the least studied war effort of all the major belligerents. Although the problems of the Habsburg Monarchy contributed directly to the First World War, it has been neglected, particularly in English-language scholarship, for the past eight decades.

For most historians, the Dual Monarchy has presented a subject too complex to study without unusual effort: the names are foreign, the words unpronounceable, the issues often numbingly obscure. As a result, there is a critical dearth of quality historical works on most aspects of the Austro-Hungarian war effort; much more remains to be done than has yet been accomplished. Additionally, studies of the Habsburgs' last war seem preternaturally prone to ideological or ethnic bias. More than anywhere else in Europe, the lands of the former Dual Monarchy have been sadly deficient in producing meaningful historical works on the disaster of 1914–1918, due in no small part to the decades of sufferings visited on those lands in the aftermath of Habsburg defeat. In addition to the linguistic difficulty—a true *Meisterwerk* on the Austro-Hungarian war effort would require a scholar to read a dozen languages—the national particularisms of the Danubian basin frequently remain impenetrable to outsiders.

For decades after 1918, misplaced determinism haunted most scholarship on the topic. While accounts by German-Austrians, Hungarians, Czechs, Romanians, and others rarely coincided in the details, they mostly agreed that the monarchy was doomed to lose the war. The reasons attributed varied—from alleged Slavic disloyalty to supposed Habsburg militarism—but on the essential hopelessness of the cause most authors agreed. Unsurprisingly, this bias crept into histories of the monarchy's war effort in the English-speaking world too, second- or third-hand.

That most of the post-1918 Danubian governments—Czechoslovakia, Yugoslavia, Romania—were deeply hostile to the defunct Dual Monarchy hardly helped serious scholarship; depicting Austria-Hungary simply as the "prison of nations," while satisfying to victorious nationalists, did little to promote understanding of what kind of war the Habsburgs actually fought. No less, the National Socialist predilection of some German-Austrian historians led to deceptions in the opposite direction, amounting to a uniquely Austrian *Dolchstoßlegende* ("stab-in-the-back" legend): namely, that loyal *Deutschösterreicher* (German-Austrians) had been betrayed by Slavic comrades-in-arms, thus undoing the army. Horthyist Hungary affected similar conclusions, with the "heroic Magyar race" being substituted for Germans, naturally.

Communist historiography, which was mandated in all the Habsburg successor states save Austria after 1945, similarly depicted the Dual Monarchy as retrograde and doomed, though for different reasons. Overnight many nationalist revolts against the monarchy and its army predictably became heroic socialist uprisings in official accounts. The essential willingness to ignore inconvenient facts remained unchanged. For want of other sources—or at least seeking books in familiar tongues—most English-language historians fell back on Reich German works detailing the Austro-Hungarian war effort, writings that were filled with traditional Prussian distaste for Habsburg inefficiencies. In tone, if not content or enjoyability, they resembled the fictional yet unforgettable *Good Soldier švejk*. Reading such works, one would conclude that the Austro-Hungarian Army was an extended exercise in *Schlamperei* (slackness) and little else, leaving open the vital question of how the muddling-through Habsburgs managed to stay in the war for over four years.

The fall of Communism in the ex-Habsburg lands since 1990 has at last opened up grounds for historiographical optimism. The old prejudices, while not evaporating, have moderated over decades; after living under Nazism and Communism, it is hard to convince many Central Europeans that the Dual Monarchy was an oppressive place. Indeed, with hindsight over a terrible century, the *Schlamperei* that infected the Austro-Hungarian bureaucracy, military and civil, seems more charming than annoying, and definitely not deadly. Achieving a scholarly balance between denunciations of "Kakania" (Robert Musil's term for the empire, a play on the ubiquitous abbreviation *k.u.k.,* i.e., Imperial-and-Royal) and mere Mitteleuropean nostalgia is the current historical necessity for Austria-Hungary's last war to be seen in proper perspective, a formidable task that has only recently begun. This essay offers some often overlooked places were scholars may start down that road.

GENERAL TEXTS

The ethnic and political diversity of the Danubian basin, not to mention the problem of dealing with a dozen national viewpoints, has created a poor climate for producing general overviews of the war. Unsurprisingly, the first serious examination of the topic came from abroad with Gunther Rothenberg's *Army of Francis Joseph* in 1976 [78]. This work, while more military than political in focus, and covering the entire reign of Emperor Francis Joseph (1848–1916), remains a serviceable overview of the relevant issues, very solid in its premise and conclusions; for English-speakers it remains the obvious jumping-off point for any study of the topic. Rothenberg's work, whatever its shortcomings, is devoid of ethnic bias and obvious political inclination in a manner nearly impossible to find in Europe before the end of the Cold War.

Happily, Rothenberg's work was joined in 1994 by Manfried Rauchensteiner's magisterial *Der Tod des Doppeladlers* (*The Death of the Double Eagle*) [72]. Written by an eminent Austrian historian, this substantial book successfully addresses politico-military factors, strategic, and some tactical issues, as well as the broader multiethnic context of the Dual Monarchy. In it, the causes of Habsburg defeat become plainly and painfully apparent. No less, Rauchensteiner is appropriately scathing in his indictments of Viennese leadership, civilian and military; the author clearly departs from any Austrian tradition of covering up disasters, and his work is archivally excellent. *Der Tod des Doppeladlers* is unquestionably the starting point for general yet in-depth reading in the subject.

Mention must also be made of the Austrian official history, *Österreich-Ungarns letzter Krieg* (*ÖUlK*), written in seven volumes between 1930 and 1938 by the staff of Vienna's Kriegsarchiv. Supervised by the respected scholar Edmund Glaise-Horstenau (a wartime General Staff officer and, controversially, an early Austrian National Socialist later executed by Tito's regime for his role as the senior Wehrmacht general in occupied Croatia, 1941–1945), *ÖUlK* was actually written by a stable of skilled historians, most of them wartime confidants of Glaise-Horstenau. In a real sense, the official history was authored by the defunct Habsburg General Staff itself, with the intent of protecting sacred reputations.

That said, *ÖUlK* is both better and fairer than its provenance might imply. There is no doubt that its authors were careful to shield certain top generals, pre-eminently Field Marshal Franz Conrad von Hötzendorf, General Staff chief for most of the war. However, it is arguably less politicized and polemical than most of the other official histories to come out of the First World War; certainly Basil Liddell Hart's verdict that it was "probably the best and most unbiased of the General Staff histories" seems essentially correct more than six decades on. Its only consistent shortcoming is a general willingness to blame battlefield reverses on the "ethnic question"—that is, alleged disloyalty, particularly on the part of Czechs, Serbs, and Ukrainians—rather than on incompetent leadership, poor tactics, or simple bad luck; yet in this, the official history only reflected the core *déformation professionelle* (professional deformation) of too much of the Habsburg officer corps.

In its favor, *Österreich-Ungarns letzter Krieg* remains indispensable to the historian for its exceptional detail on issues great and small; especially helpful are the seven supplementary volumes that accompany the text, filled with maps, graphs, and charts impossible to find outside the recesses of the Kriegsarchiv. For these alone, Glaise-Horstenau's history-by-committee has stood the test of time, even allowing for its shortcomings. Any serious examination of the war the Habsburgs fought must include its seven volumes, though the reader ought to have digested Rauchensteiner first to have gained a solid—and far less biased—grounding in the essential factors, places, and players. (N.B. The complex background to the official history is elaborated in Kurt Peball's "Österreichische Militärgeschichtliche Forschung zum Ersten Weltkrieg zwischen 1918 und 1960.") [62]

There are few other general works that can be recommended. József Galántai's *Hungary in the First World War* [37] is a comparatively recent (1989) and serviceable review of the political tribulations of Budapest's doomed realm during the war, admittedly from a Hungarian perspective; its details on the politico-economic weakness of the Danubian empire are helpful. Z. A. B. Zeman's *The Break-Up of the Habsburg Empire, 1914–1918* [109], though not new (1961), covers the rising and ultimately insurmountable political difficulties faced by Vienna better than most works, while Alan Sked's more recent *Decline and Fall of the Habsburg Empire 1815–1918* (1989) [92], though reaching far beyond the period of the Great War, nevertheless offers the newcomer a commendable examination of the essential political and even military issues, all handled freshly and concisely.

POLITICAL AND DIPLOMATIC BACKGROUND

The unenviable political and diplomatic circumstances of the Dual Monarchy are expansive fields of study all their own, yet they must be understood, at least in outline, to gain any appreciation for the military situation faced by the Habsburgs in their last war. A full understanding of these issues can be gained by studying the thousands of pages of the six volume (to date) study undertaken by the Austrian Academy of Arts and Sciences, *Die Habsburgermonarchie 1848–1918* (*The Habsburg Monarchy 1848–1918*). Each weighty volume addresses a particular topic (e.g., foreign policy, the nationalities, and the armed forces) and is composed of review articles by leading experts, based mostly on secondary sources (in German and other languages) and impressively footnoted. For gaining an understanding of the political and diplomatic predicament confronting the Dual Monarchy, as well as finding countless citations to even more detailed sources, *Die Habsburgermonarchie* cannot be improved upon. For English-speakers, the many works by the estimable Robert Kann [47] detailing the Austro-Hungarian system in all its politico-ethnic complexities offer a worthwhile substitute.

For Vienna, there were few purely domestic issues; most of its political debates—and particularly those involving fractious minority issues—were foreign policy questions too, and often dangerous ones. This hazardous complexity is elaborated effectively in Samuel Williamson's concise *Austria-Hungary and the Origins of the First World War* (1991) [106], while a more traditional diplomatic approach is offered in F. R. Bridge's *The Habsburg Monarchy among the Great Powers* (1990) [16]. Interestingly, the weighty question of the degree of prewar cooperation between Austria-Hungary and her all-important German ally is taken up by Holger Herwig in the article "Disjointed Allies: Coalition Warfare in Berlin and Vienna, 1914" (1990) [43], in which the author concludes that there really wasn't any. Revealing much about Habsburg understandings with its only worthwhile ally, Norman Stone's earlier article "Moltke and Conrad: Relations between the Austro-Hungarian and the German General Staffs, 1910–1914" (1969) [99] reaches much the same conclusion. Also useful is Gary Shanafelt's *The Secret Enemy* (1985) [88], which explains the convoluted and difficult relationship between Berlin and Vienna under the pressures of war, while the fateful role played by Vienna's top generals in foreign policymaking is revealed in Gerard Silberstein's "The High Command and Diplomacy in Austria-Hungary, 1914–1916" (1970) [90].

ECONOMIC AND INDUSTRIAL MATTERS

In the end, the Habsburg military machine cracked under the economic weight of total war. Despite its myriad political and military shortcomings, the Austro-Hungarian military was undone more by material weakness than by any other factor. Simply put, the only semi-industrialized Dual Monarchy (composed, in economic as well as political terms, of a well developed western or Austrian half and a more backwards eastern or Hungarian half) was unable to sustain a prolonged fight, much less the extended three-front war which it found itself in. Prewar economic preparations had been sadly lacking, and improvisations under the pressures of repeated defeats served barely to keep the army in the war; they were never sufficient to produce the first-rank military machine Vienna needed to deliver victory. There was never a real manpower shortage until the last months of the war, but Austria-Hungary's shortage of weapons, ammunition, and materiel was a constant. In the end, during the war's last campaigns in Italy in 1918, the once magnificently uniformed *k.u.k. Armee* was dressed literally in rags, its depleted regiments underfed, underarmed, undersupplied, and critically underequipped.

A sense of this pervasive deprivation, which hit civilians harder even than most soldiers, is captured well in Reinhard Sieder's "Behind the Lines: Working-Class Family Life in Wartime Vienna" (1988) [89]. More broadly, J. Robert Wegs detailed effectively a preeminent, though oft-overlooked, Habsburg economic shortcoming in his article "Transportation: The Achilles' Heel of the Habsburg War Effort" (1977) [105], while Horst Haselsteiner's related piece, "The Habsburg Empire in World War I: The Mobilization of Food Supplies" (1985) [41], rounds out a depressing tale.

On a broader scale, the Dual Monarchy's economic downfall in 1918, with emphasis on military concerns, is explained in some detail in the official history, *Österreich-Ungarns letzter Krieg,* Volume VII (1938) [64]. Useful to understanding the role of the military in politico-economic decision-making is

Christoph Führ's *Das k.u.k. Armeeoberkommando und Innenpolitik in Österreich 1914–1917* (*The Imperial-and-Royal High Command and Domestic Politics
in Austria 1914–1917*) (1968) [34]. Similar issues are described in more detail,
and with less desire to explain away than in the official history, in the excellent
two-volume work *Innere Front: Militärassistenz, Widerstand und Umsturz in
der Donaumonarchie 1918* (*Internal Front: Military Assistance, Resistance,
and Subversion in the Danubian Monarchy 1918*) (1974) [70] by Richard Georg
Plaschka et al., which explains lucidly the economic and social as well as political causes of Austro-Hungarian collapse during the war's last year. Back at the
front, Peter Fiala's *Die letzte Offensive Altösterreichs* (*Old Austria's Last Offensive*) (1967) [30] offers an examination of the waning months of the Habsburg
army in the field, revealing precisely how poorly equipped it actually was.

NATIONALISM AND MINORITIES

If the Dual Monarchy's economic weakness has been given too little historiographical emphasis, its problems with its minorities surely have not. Nevertheless, despite the plethora of works in many languages that elaborate the ethnic
woes of the Habsburg military, the actual role of ethnicity and nationalism in
Austria-Hungary's last war remains surprisingly vexing and controversial. Long
the bugbear of Habsburg generals and anti-Austrian nationalists alike—admittedly for altogether different reasons—the vaunted "ethnic question" is still very
much alive, due in part to a dearth of well-researched and level-headed published works. The result has been an overwhelming tendency to stereotype—
cowardly Czechs, heroic Alpine Germans, timid Ukrainians, for example—in
even otherwise commendable works, particularly in English. The temptation to
blame all on "traitorous Slavs" seems no less tempting to many historians than
to wartime generals eager to explain away routs and retreats.

In contrast, the official records bear out a complex saga filled with contradictions and controversy. The essential problem, from the war's troubled beginning
in Serbia to its traumatic end in Venetia, was one of leadership: units that were
commanded by well-trained, energetic, and thoughtful officers generally performed well on all fronts; however, the army's catastrophic losses in its opening
battles, particularly among trained officers, meant that such battalion-and-under
combat leaders were in critically short supply from fall 1914 on.

There can be no doubt that the Habsburg military unofficially rated its troops
by broad categories: German-Austrians, Magyars, Bosnians—always reliable;
Slovenes, Croats—nearly always reliable; Poles, Slovaks, Romanians—often
dependable; Czechs, Serbs, Ukrainians, Italians—effective if well led, but not to
be trusted when fighting against ethnic kin. With hindsight, such groupings can
be viewed as accurate in a most generalized way. However, the reliability of
given regiments (keeping in mind that the army recruited regionally, so that
units often closely reflected the ethnicity of their home regions) had much to do
with who the enemy was. For instance, Serb units fought like lions against the
Italians, but were shaky on the Eastern front and were useless when employed

against fellow Serbs. Similarly, Prague's 28th Regiment, the army's worst unit (and certainly its most widely lamented: it went over to the Russians in early 1915 *en masse,* an incident clarified by Richard Georg Plaschka in his article "Zur Vorgeschichte des Übergangs von Einheiten des IR.Nr.28 an der Russischen Front 1915" ["On the Prehistory of the Defection of Elements of the 28th Infantry Regiment on the Russian Front 1915"]) [69] wholly redeemed itself against the Italians, earning a reputation for tenacity and effectiveness on the Isonzo front.

Such nuances are captured well in Robert Nowak's unfortunately unpublished multivolume work "Die Klammer des Reichs" ("The Hinge of the Empire") [60], available at the Kriegsarchiv. The author, a wartime officer, was unusually sympathetic and informed about the army's Slavic troops (47 percent of the forces), and his long-labored volumes include a comprehensive examination of each ethnic group and its performance through the vicissitudes of total war. Its details about specific units and incidents render Nowak's manuscript a unique resource for historians. The work stands as a special contribution to studies of the Habsburg war effort, as well as a useful antidote to prevailing wisdoms.

"Das Nationalitätenproblem in Habsburgs Wehrmacht 1848–1918" ("The Nationality Problem in the Habsburg Military 1848–1918") (1959) [53] by the noted historian Rudolf Kiszling, an author of the official history, is a serviceable introduction to the basic issues, while the topic of ethnicity in the military is handled eruditely—if perhaps overly sympathetically—by István Deák in his tellingly titled *Beyond Nationalism* (1990) [22], a thorough sociopolitical survey of the all-important officer corps, an account marred by its inattention to the actual conduct of the war. However, Deák's article "Pacesetters of Integration" (1989) [24] tells the revealing story of the many Jewish officers in the *k.u.k. Armee,* an important topic given the effects of Danubian anti-Semitism on recent European history. Additional detail can be found in Erwin Schmidl's *Juden in der k.(u.)k. Armee 1788–1918* (Jews in the Imperial-[and]-Royal Army 1788–1918) (1989) [85].

The impact of ethnicity on the fighting—the core historiographical problem—is treated comprehensively, at least on the Italian front, in this author's *Isonzo: The Forgotten Sacrifice of the Great War* (2001). Relatedly, two of his articles forthcoming in *War in History* elaborate on Habsburg combat performance in Serbia in 1914 and in Galicia in 1916, respectively, with particular emphasis on ethnicity and battlefield effectiveness. Although the official history and its many *Ergänzungshefte* (supplementary volumes) are often fair in their renderings of battle, they have a tendency to find fault with "politically unreliable" nationalities (Czechs, Serbs, sometimes Ukrainians) when not always warranted, and must be read with caution whenever ethnic questions arise.

Removed from the firing line, "Um das Erbe: Zur Nationalitätenpolitik des k.u.k. Armeeoberkommandos während der Jahre 1914 bis 1918" ("About the Inheritance: On the Nationalities Policy of the Habsburg High Command from 1914 to 1918") (1967) [63] by Kurt Peball details the High Command and its changing policies toward Austria-Hungary's increasingly disgruntled minorities as the war headed to disaster. The usually overstated impact of nationalism on the army's collapse is handled well in *Cattaro-Prag: Revolte und Revolution* (*Cattaro-Prague: Revolt and Revolution*) (1963) [68] by Richard Georg Plaschka, who argues convincingly that socio-economic concerns weighed much more heavily on the creaking military machine than purely ethnic ones. Individual ethnic groups are discussed in Lawrence Sondhaus' *In the Service of the Emperor* (1990) [93], which tells the not overlarge story of Italians in Habsburg uniform, by far the empire's smallest minority, while Richard Spence does a more valuable job with "The Yugoslav Role in the Austro-Hungarian Army, 1914–1918" (1985) [95], taking on a nuanced subject with clarity. Edward Kelleher helpfully demolishes the myth of unquestioning German-Austrian loyalty in his 1992 article "Emperor Karl and the Sixtus Affair" [48].

Numerous well-presented unit histories collectively illustrate the relative unimportance of the "ethnic question" in the front lines (for instance, von Berndt [15], von Hubka [44], Schön [87], Zanantoni [108]), while the prickly issue of who sacrificed most is settled in admirable detail in Wilhelm Winkler's *Die Totenverluste der öst.-ung. Monarchie nach Nationalitäten* (*The Fatal Casualties of the Austro-Hungarian Monarchy by Nationality*) (1934) [107], which leaves no doubt that, stereotypes aside, German-Austrians and Bosnian Muslims gave their lives in proportionally greater numbers than other nationalities in Habsburg uniform.

SOCIAL HISTORY AND MANPOWER

The attention devoted to ethnic issues in the Habsburg war effort has detracted from the development of a genuine history-from-below on the topic. There are promising signs that this, like so much else in the historiography of the region, is set to change, a decade after the fall of the Soviet empire. Two generations of Marxist orthodoxy have left a bad taste in the mouths of many Central European scholars, and constructing usable conventional histories of the Great War is still the primary task at hand. However, there is much left undone with respect to social history; and, sadly, with the small number of veterans still living, opportunities have been lost permanently.

For scholars seeking a flavor of Austro-Hungarian wartime *Alltagsgeschichte* (history of daily life), there are memoir accounts available in English which offer insights into the experience of the Habsburg everyman at war: Joseph Gál's bitter *In Death's Fortress* (1991) [36] recounts the horrors of static fighting against the Italians, while Jan Triska's recent *The Great War's Forgotten Front* (1998) [101] tells a similar story; though everything but the diary itself should be ignored. *Four Weeks in the Trenches* (1917) [57] by the noted violinist Fritz Kreisler ought not be overlooked, despite its age, as its handling of the opening campaigns in Galicia is detailed and insightful.

There are numerous memoir accounts, mostly in German, by low-ranking soldiers who provide valuable glimpses into the war the army actually fought. Among the more valuable of this genre are Karl Bergmann's *Am Niemandslande*

(*In No Man's Land*) (1930) [13], an account of frontline life with a well-rated Sudentendeutsche regiment; Hans Fritz's *Bosniak* (*Bosnian Soldier*) (1931) [33], a vivid story told by one of the few German-Austrian rankers serving in the army's elite Bosnian regiments; Wilhelm Czermak's *In deinem Lager war Österreich* (*Austria Was in Your Camp*) (1938) [20], which is valuable despite the author's ideological bias; among recently published works, and beyond the German-Austrian realm, Josef Váchal's *Malířna fronte* (*A Painter at the Front*) (1996) [102] is a sensitive portrayal of the war's last year on the Italian front. For a junior officer's perspective, Rudolf Martinek's *Kriegstagebuch eines Artillerie-Offiziers* (*War Diary of an Artillery Officer*) (1975) [59] should not be missed; in addition to its value as a memoir, its descriptions of early war artillery tactics are unique, as are its many detailed battlefield sketches.

The issue of manpower loomed large during the war, not surprisingly for an army that mobilized over eight million soldiers, five million of whom became casualties. The Habsburg Army's enormous losses in the war's opening months—1,269,000 lost to all causes by New Year's 1915, a total well in excess of the total infantry strength mobilized five months earlier—crippled the military machine ever after; deficits of trained officers in particular were never made good. In retrospect, that the army stayed in the war as long as it did, through over four years of fighting, appears remarkable. This rollercoaster saga is elaborated in all its complexity in an unpublished dissertation, Rudolf Hecht's "Fragen zur Heeresergänzung der gesamten bewaffneten Macht Österreich-Ungarns während des Ersten Weltkrieges" ("Questions Regarding the Military Organization of Austria-Hungary's Joint Armed Forces during the First World War") (1969) [42].

Also useful are two articles by the highly decorated veteran and perceptive historian Fritz Franek from *Ergänzungshefte* [31, 32] of the official history (see bibliography), which explain the army's sometimes creaking reaction to the onslaught of total war. Recommended also is an article from another *Ergänzungsheft* by Emil Ratzenhofer "Verlustkalkül für den Karpathenwinter 1915" ("Casualty Calculation for the Carpathian Winter of 1915") (1930) [73], which tabulates the army's loss of an additional three-quarters of a million soldiers in the first four months of 1915 in the terrible battles for the Carpathian passes, which makes the survival of the Habsburg military appear even more miraculous. As these sources make painfully clear, what little of the prewar army outlived the opening campaigns in Galicia and Serbia was finished off during the war's first winter. What replaced it, sometimes awkwardly, was a completely new, war-raised, improvised military, a force of teenagers and middle-aged militiamen led by reserve lieutenants.

MILITARY PREPARATIONS AND MOBILIZATION

That the Habsburg Army was unready for war in 1914—certainly for the prolonged multifront war it got—seems beyond debate. Given the Dual Monarchy's population and economy, its prewar military was both undersized and undergunned, with fatal consequences when war actually arrived. Political paralysis and the general lack of interest prevailing in official circles willed a military machine incapable of standing up to the Dual Monarchy's many adversaries, much less occupying their terrain. This essential reality is explained playfully in Norman Stone's "Army and Society in the Habsburg Monarchy, 1900–1914" (1966) [96], and more substantively in "Die bewaffnete Macht in Staat und Gesellschaft" ("The Armed Forces in State and Society") (1987) by Christoph Allmayer-Beck [2]. Taken together, Peter Broucek's "Taktische Erkentnisse aus dem russisch-japanischen Krieg und deren Beachtung in Österreich-Ungarn" ("Tactical Insights from the Russo-Japanese War and Their Impact on Austria-Hungary") (1977) [17] and Erwin Schmidl's "Paardeberg to Przemysl" (1988) [86] portray a military machine that, while not significantly blinder than any of the other major powers, nevertheless failed to learn the proper tactical lessons from recent conflicts. In a typical case, reforms shortly before the war provided the infantry with drab uniforms, machine guns, and improved organization, but were politically impotent to deprive the cavalry of its brightly colored uniforms and wholly outmoded tactics. Max Pitreich's *1914: Die militärische Probleme unseres Kriegsbeginnes* (*1914: The Military Problems of Our War's Beginning*) (1934) [67] lays bare many of the operational shortcomings that stymied Habsburg battlefield lessons at the war's outset. The actual disposition of the army when war came is found in admirable detail in Max Ehnl's "Die öst.-ung. Landmacht" ("Austro-Hungarian Land Forces") (1934) [25].

Perhaps the worst example of bad generalship and all-purpose *Schlamperei* to befall the Austro-Hungarian military at war was the thoroughgoing disaster made of mobilization in 1914. Against the expectations of informed opinion—inside the army as well as outside its ranks—there were no notable ethnic problems during the summer of 1914; to the profound shock of many generals, Czechs and other "suspect Slavs" reported for duty, frequently with real enthusiasm. However, the High Command nullified this by succumbing to delusion and deceit when it came to actually placing divisions and corps where they needed to be. The result was strategic calamity and the loss of hundreds of thousands of troops. Norman Stone deconstructs the official history's convenient, if meretricious, verdict in his noteworthy "Die Mobilmachung der öst.-ung. Armee 1914" ("The Mobilization of the Austro-Hungarian Army in 1914") (1974) [98], which elaborates the farce-as-tragedy of Austro-Hungarian mobilization and is a necessary article for anyone wishing to comprehend why the Habsburg military met the terrible fate it did in Galicia in the summer of 1914.

FIGHTING THE WAR

The Habsburg Army's battlefield performance remains a large and complex subject meriting careful treatment. Overall assessments of the army's capabilities can be found in Alfred Krauss' *Die Ursachen unserer Niederlage* (*The Causes of Our Defeat*) (1920) [55]; its often scathing tone is more than compensated for with the insights of the author, perhaps the army's finest tactician and one of its most successful generals. Interesting too is *Unser österreichisch-ungarischer Bundesgenosse im Weltkrieg* (*Our Austro-Hungarian Ally in the World War*) (1920) by August von Cramon [19], the wartime Prussian liaison at the Habsburg High Command: the author, while more understanding of Austro-Hungarian particularisms than most Reich German officers, still paints an often disturbing picture. The High Command's viewpoint can be found in Franz Conrad von Hötzendorf's five-volume apologia, *Aus meiner Dienstzeit* (*From My Time of Service*) (1921–1925) [18], which is valuable if utterly self-serving; it should be imbibed with the less unctuous memoir of his successor, Arthur Arz von Straußenburg: *Zur Geschichte des großen Krieges 1914 bis 1918* (*On the History of the Great War 1914 to 1918*) (1924) [6].

Among campaign histories, Norman Stone's *The Eastern Front 1914–1917* (1975) [97] is indispensable to understanding the Habsburg-Romanov war, which ultimately proved fatal to both parties; the book deals intensely with Austro-Hungarian issues (unlike most works on the Eastern front), to good—if frequently scathing—effect. Max Pitreich's *Lemberg 1914* (1929) [66] explains how the war against Russia got off on a painfully wrong foot, while Rudolf Kiszling's "Die Brussilow-Offensive bei Łuck-Olyka" ("The Brusilov Offensive at Łuck-Olyka") (1966) [51] gives a thorough, if decidedly "official," view of the worst disaster ever to befall Habsburg arms (which is explained in a less biased fashion in Stone's book). Kiszling's "Der Krieg gegen Rumänien 1916" ("The War Against Romania, 1916") (1966) [52] is a serviceable overview of the only success enjoyed by Austro-Hungarian forces in the East during that terrible year. Michał Klimecki's *Gorlice 1915* (1991) [54] covers the sole decisive Habsburg defeat of Russian forces, the Gorlice-Tarnów breakthrough, admittedly with extensive Imperial German assistance.

The Balkan front, specifically the ill-starred war against Serbia, is explained in Gunther Rothenberg's "The Austro-Hungarian Campaign Against Serbia" (1989) [79] and relatedly by Kurt Peball's "Der Feldzug gegen Serbien und Montenegro im Jahre 1914" ("The Campaign Against Serbia and Montenegro in 1914") (1965) [61]: neither leaves any doubt as to why the Serbs gave the Entente its first victory. The role of the military once Serbia was finally vanquished is explained in Hugo Kerchnawe's *Die Militärverwaltung in den von den österreichisch-ungarischen Truppen besetzten Gebieten* (*Military Administration in Territories Occupied by Austro-Hungarian Troops*) (1928) [49], a necessary antidote to wartime claims of constant Habsburg atrocities against Serbia.

The war with Italy saw the Habsburg military in its best light; indeed, before late October 1918, Austro-Hungarian arms never suffered a genuine defeat at the hands of the Italians. *Isonzo 1915–1917: Krieg ohne Wiederkehr* (*Isonzo 1915–1917: War Without Recurrence*) (1993) [82] by Walther Schaumann and Peter Schubert is a pleasing introduction to the most important campaign of the Austro-Italian conflict, the dozen battles waged on the Isonzo river—11 of them being failed Italian offensives. Georg Veith provides helpful tactical detail on how the army withstood repeated Italian onslaughts in his "Die Isonzoverteidigung" ("The Isonzo Defense") (1932) [103], while in her *Dem Tod geweiht und doch gerettet* (*Doomed by Death and Still Saved*) (1995), Daniela Angetter [4] explains how Habsburg military medicine functioned in the difficult and often deadly Alpine terrain. The "Caporetto Miracle" of October 1917, the epic breakthrough of the Twelfth Battle of the Isonzo, is handled superlatively in Alfred Krauss' *Das Wunder von Karfreit* (*The Caporetto Miracle*) (1926) [56] as well it should be, as the author commanded the spearhead Habsburg corps during the offensive.

Other aspects of the frequently brutal Italian front are covered in Gerhard Artl's *Die österreichisch-ungarische Südtiroloffensive 1916* (*The Austro-Hungarian South Tyrol Offensive, 1916*) (1983) [5], which contends with one of the preeminent what-ifs of Austria-Hungary's war. Peter Fiala's previously mentioned *Die letzte Offensive Altösterreichs* (*Old Austria's Last Offensive*) (1967) [30] explains the inevitable and costly failure of the army's final offensive on the Piave river in June 1918. Erich Gabriel details the changing firepower available to the army by the war's final battles in his "Die wichtigsten Waffen der öst.-ung. Armee 1918" ("The Most Important Weapons of the Austro-Hungarian Army, 1918") (1968) [35], while the extensive tactical lessons the army had learned by 1917–1918 at great cost are elaborated in Christoph Allmayer-Beck's "Heeresreorganization vor 50 Jahren" ("The Army Reorganization 50 Years Ago") (1967) [3].

There are far too few biographies of Habsburg generals, and many of those that exist are substandard. Among the few recent works are two by Ernest Bauer, *Der Löwe vom Isonzo* (*The Lion of the Isonzo*) (1985) [12] and *Der letzte Paladin des Reiches* (*The Last Paladin of the Empire*) (1988) [11], which recount the lives of two of the army's top Croatian officers, the legendary Field Marshal Svetozar Borojević and Colonel-General Stefan Sarkotić, respectively; these biographies, though close to hagiographies, are still valuable due to their detail and the critical lack of other secondary sources; they also have excellent pictures. Much better is Rudolf Jeřábek's well researched *Potiorek: General im Schatten von Sarajevo* (*Potiorek: General in the Shadow of Sarajevo*) (1991) [46], which illuminates the life of the general who had the misfortune of overseeing both the assassination of Archduke Franz Ferdinand and the débâcle in Serbia in 1914.

There are numerous unit histories available, most of them written in the decade after the war and therefore of relatively low value to the serious scholar (though their ability to communicate the "feel" of the *k.u.k. Armee* is often excellent). Three works on the famed *Bosniaken* are cited below: one is an official regimental history produced by the Defense Ministry in Vienna, Schachinger's [81] is strictly drum-and-trumpet, while Spence's [94] is more nuanced and analytic. Additional unit histories mentioned in the bibliography are also to be recommended, allowing for the shortcomings of the "regimental" style of military history. Together they help explain how and why the army stayed in the field as long as it did, against all odds, despite appalling losses, often dismal equipment and rations, and scant hope of eventual victory.

One of the fields of study unjustly neglected by historians has been Austro-Hungarian military intelligence during the Great War. Comprehending the role of intelligence is vital in gaining a complete picture of military operations, tactical or strategic. This was especially true in the case of the *k.u.k. Armee,* as its intelligence arm was among its few consistent strongpoints; it is no exaggeration to state that the *Nachrichtenabteilung* (Intelligence Department) of the General Staff at several points kept the Dual Monarchy in the war by its innovative and profitable efforts. Indeed, Austria-Hungary's espionage effort has a good claim to being the most effective of any belligerent during the Great War, a point made well in the recent *Agenten für den Doppeladler* (*Agents for the Double Eagle*) (1998) [65] by Albert Pethö, which is exceptionally detailed; it ranks among the most important works in the past two decades in improving understanding of the Habsburgs' last war. Vienna's intelligence service was by no means free of shortcomings, as illustrated by the humiliating prewar scandal surrounding Colonel Alfred Redl, deputy chief of espionage and the head of counterintelligence, who was actually a Russian agent for a dozen years before his death by suicide in 1913. The sensational case, much distorted by repeat film and stage presentations, is elaborated mainly accurately and fully entertainingly in Robert Asprey's *The Panther's Feast* (1959) [7]. Georg Markus' *Der Fall Redl* (*The Redl Case*) (1984) [58] is better on the details and more extensively researched.

Mention must also be made of the two books authored by Max Ronge, *Kriegs- und Industrie-Spionage* (*War and Industrial Espionage*) (1930) [76] and *Meister der Spionage* (*Master of Espionage*) (1935) [77]. Ronge was the last chief of army intelligence, and his engaging writings provide useful—if sometimes guarded—detail about how Vienna's spies endeavored to compensate for the Dual Monarchy's weaknesses with clever intelligence work. The nascent discipline of signals intelligence was a particular Habsburg "force multiplier," as explained by the author in "A Hopeless Struggle: Austro-Hungarian Cryptology during World War I" (2000), and even more comprehensively in the recently published *Emlékeim (Memories)* (2000) [71], a memoir by Hermann Pokorny, Austria-Hungary's most decorated intelligence officer and the chief of signals intelligence; Pokorny's legendary successes, notably against the Russians, at last have received some of the historical attention they deserve.

DEMOBILIZATION

The Austro-Hungarian Army never properly demobilized. In the chaos of October-November 1918, while the ancient empire of the Habsburgs evaporated, and the military tried vainly to resist the long-awaited Italian "victory offensive," there was no coherent demobilization. While some regiments and divisions made it home in good order—without the benefit of instructions from the High Command—many others were captured *en masse* by the victorious Allies. This confusing saga is elucidated in works such as Otto von Berndt's *Letzter Kampf und Ende der 29.ID.* (*The Last Battle and End of the 29th Infantry*

Division) (1928) [15], which tells the story of a division that got away; Emil Ratzenhofer's "Der Waffenstillstand von Villa Giusti und die Gefangnahme Hunderttauseender" ("The Armistice of Villa Giusti and the Hundreds of Thousands Taken Captive") (1932) [74], which exposes underhanded Italian diplomacy; and the more balanced "Vae Victis! The Austro-Hungarian Armeeoberkommando and the Armistice of Villa Giusti" (1978) by R. Wayne Hanks. [40]

Mostly feeble Austro-Hungarian efforts to extricate the Dual Monarchy from the war as disaster loomed are elaborated in Robert Kann's *Die Sixtusaffäre und die geheimen Friedensverhandlungen Österreich-Ungarns im ersten Weltkrieg* (*The Sixtus Affair and Austria-Hungary's Secret Peace Negotiations in the First World War*) (1966) [47] and Tamara Griesser-Pečar's more recent *Die Mission Sixtus: Österreichs Friedenversuch im 1. Weltkrieg* (*The Sixtus Mission: Austria's Peace Attempt in the First World War*) (1988) [39]. The circumstances of the empire's disintegration are explained, with detail though not without bias, in Edmund Glaise-Horstenau's *Die Katastrophe* (*The Catastrophe*) (1929) and Hugo Kerchnawe's *Der Zusammenbruch der öst.-ung. Wehrmacht im Herbst 1918* (*The Collapse of the Austro-Hungarian Armed Forces in Autumn 1918*) (1921) [38], with the latter emphasizing military concerns. The army's hopeless predicament is likewise covered in Márton Farkas' *Katonai összeomlás és forradalom 1918-ban* (*Military Collapse and Revolution in 1918*) (1969) [26].

For sources on the last months of fighting and the process of dissolution, one cannot do better than *Die Auflösung des Habsburgerreiches* (*The Dissolution of the Habsburg Empire*) (1970), a superlative collection of essays detailing the politico-economic as well as military collapse of the Dual Monarchy, edited by Richard Georg Plaschka and Karlheinz Mack. Oskar Regele finds much fault with the High Command's performance in the war's last year in *Gericht über Habsburgs Wehrmacht* (*Judgement on the Habsburg Armed Forces*) (1968) [75], mostly fairly. Another viewpoint on the role of the High Command can be found in Christoph Allmayer-Beck's solid article "AOK und 'Armeefrage' im Jahre 1918" ("The High Command and the 'Army Question' in 1918") (1968) [1]. The general spirit of chaos and tumult prevalent in much of Austria-Hungary by the latter half of 1918 is captured well in "Emperor Karl Has Become a Comitadji" (1992) by Ivo Banac [9], which makes clear that, regardless of what was happening at the front, Habsburg authority was collapsing at home in a rapid fashion, rendering battlefield events in the end almost irrelevant on their own.

FURTHER RESEARCH NEEDED

Much research remains to be done on the war waged by the Dual Monarchy from 1914 to 1918. What we know is still dwarfed by what has yet to receive rigorous scholarly attention. Although conditions for writing the history of the Great War from a broadly Central European perspective are much more promising than they have ever been, it will be years, if not decades, before the historiography of Austria-Hungary during the war reaches the level and diversity of studies currently available on Germany, Great Britain, or France, for instance.

That said, areas needing particular scholarly attention can be easily defined. More complex and nuanced works on the actual conduct of the *k.u.k. Armee* in battle are long overdue; historians must be willing to dispense with shopworn stereotypes and head for the sound of the guns, archives and memoirs in hand. Campaign studies on all fronts—Eastern, Italian, Balkan—are needed, at a minimum. Additionally, historians must be willing to tackle the vaunted "ethnic question" with fresh approaches, employing aspects of sociology and ethnic studies, so that the real role of nationalism and ethnicity on that most complex and multinational of militaries can be properly evaluated. That said, works that deal solely with peacetime or the home front, though welcome, are less necessary than determining how the polyglot regiments of the Habsburgs actually waged war against a host of enemies. The infantrymen of 1914–1918 remain in a real sense "unknown soldiers" to most historians, and none more so than those who battled under the black-and-yellow standard of the House of Habsburg.

Secondarily but also importantly, more research into Habsburg military-industrial performance during wartime is needed, as is an examination of the home front and its impact on military effectiveness; the latter will be particularly challenging, as a worthwhile survey of the topic would have to address all the nations of the empire. Biographies of major war leaders, military and civilian, are likewise long overdue. Welcome too would be works detailing the fate of Habsburg veterans after 1918, when the majority found themselves in states hostile to the defunct empire; certainly the large number of Austro-Hungarian ex-soldiers who rose to prominence in Central European politics—not least communist and fascist—for decades after 1918 indicates there is quite a story waiting to be told.

In the end, the fundamental question remains: not—Why did Austria-Hungary lose World War One? but rather—How did the Dual Monarchy stay in the war as long as it ultimately did? To answer that, historians will need to employ not only the most up-to-date awareness of the emerging historiography of the Great War, but also multiple languages and an understanding of a complex military and civil culture. It is no small order, but fulfilling it will significantly advance our understanding of the First World War and European history.

BIBLIOGRAPHY

1. Allmayer-Beck, Christoph. "AOK und 'Armeefrage' im Jahre 1918" ("The High Command and the 'Army Question,' 1918"). *Österreichische Militärische Zeitschrift* 1968.

2. Allmayer-Beck, Christoph. "Die bewaffnete Macht in Staat und Gesellschaft" ("The Armed Forces in State and Society") in *Die Habsburgermonarchie 1848–1918: Band V: Die bewaffnete Macht. (The Habsburg Monarchy 1848–1918: Vol. V: The Armed Forces)* (Wandruszka, A., and Urbanitsch, P., eds.) (Vienna, 1987).

3. Allmayer-Beck, Christoph. "Heeresreorganization vor 50 Jahren." ("Army Reorganization 50 Years Ago") *Österreichische Militärische Zeitschrift* 1967/Sonderheft.

4. Angetter, Daniel Claudia. *Dem Tod geweiht und doch gerettet: Die Sanitätsversorgung am Isonzo und in den Dolomiten 1915–1918.* (*Doomed by Death and Still Saved: Medical Care on the Isonzo and in the Dolomites, 1915–1918*) (Frankfurt am Main, 1995).

5. Artl, Gerhard. *Die österreichisch-ungarische Südtiroloffensive 1916.* (*The Austro-Hungarian South Tyrol Offensive, 1916*) (Vienna, 1983).

6. Arz von Straußenburg, Arthur. *Zur Geschichte des großen Krieges 1914 bis 1918.* (*On the History of the Great War, 1914 to 1918*) (Vienna, 1924).

7. Asprey, Robert. *The Panther's Feast.* (London, 1959).

8. Ajtay, Endre. *A volt cs. és kir. 46. gyalogezgred világháborús története 1914–1918.* (*The History of the Former Imperial-and-Royal 46th Infantry Regiment in the World War, 1914–1918*) (Szeged, 1933).

9. Banac, Ivo. "'Emperor Karl Has Become a Comitadji': The Croatian Disturbances of Autumn 1918." *Slavonic and East European Review.* Vol. 70, No. 2, April 1992.

10. Banac, Ivo. "South Slav Prisoners of War in Revolutionary Russia." In *War and Society in East Central Europe: Vol. V: Essays on World War I: Origins and Prisoners of War.* (Williamson, S., and Pastor, P., eds.) (New York, 1983).

11. Bauer, Ernest. *Der letzte Paladin des Reiches: Generaloberst Stefan Freiherr Sarkotić von Lovćen* (*The Last Paladin of the Empire: Colonel-General Stefan [Baron] Sarkotić von Lovćen*) (Graz, 1988).

12. Bauer, Ernest. *Der Löwe vom Isonzo: Feldmarschall Svetozar Borojević de Bojna.* (*The Lion of the Isonzo: Field Marshal Svetozar Borojević de Bojna*) (Graz, 1985).

13. Bergmann, Karl. *Am Niemandslande: Fronterleben bei einem sudetendeutschen Regimente.* (*In No Man's Land: Front Experiences with a Sudeten German Regiment*) (Reichenberg, 1930).

14. Berkó, István. *A magyar királyi honvédség története 1868–1918.* (*The History of the Royal Hungarian Honvéd, 1868–1918*) (Budapest, 1928).

15. Berndt, Otto von. *Letzter Kampf und Ende der 29.ID.: Meine Erinnerungen aus der Zeit des Zusammenbruches.* (*Last Battle and End of the 29th Inf. Div.: My Memories of the Time of the Collapse*) (Reichenberg, 1928).

16. Bridge, F. R. *The Habsburg Monarchy among the Great Powers, 1815–1918.* (Providence, 1990).

17. Broucek, Peter. "Taktische Erkentnisse aus dem russisch-japanischen Krieg und deren Beachtung in Österreich-Ungarn." ("Tactical Insights From the Russo-Japanese War and Their Impact on Austria-Hungary") *Mitteilungen des österreichischen Staatsarchives* 30, 1977.

18. Conrad von Hötzendorf, Franz. *Aus meiner Dienstzeit 1906–1918.* (*From My Time of Service, 1906–1918*) (5 vols.) (Vienna, 1921–1925).

19. Cramon, August von. *Unser österreichisch-ungarischer Bundesgenosse im Weltkrieg: Erinnerungen aus meiner vierjährigen Tätigkeit als bevollmächtiger deutscher General beim k.u.k. Armeeoberkommando.* (*Our Austro-Hungarian Ally in the World War: Memories From My Four-Year Work as the Plenipotentiary German General at the Imperial-and-Royal High Command*) (Berlin, 1920).

20. Czermak, Wilhelm. *In deinem Lager war Österreich: Die österreichisch-ungarische Armee, wie man sie nicht kennt.* (*Austria Was in Your Camp: The Austro-Hungarian Army No One Knows*) (Breslau, 1938).

21. *Das bosnisch-herzegovinische Infanterie-Regiment Nr.2 im Weltkrieg 1914 bis 1918.* (*The 2nd Bosnian-Hercegovinian Infantry Regiment in the World War, 1914 to 1918*) (Vienna, 1970).

22. Deák, István. *Beyond Nationalism: A Social and Political History of the Habsburg Officer Corps, 1868–1918.* (New York, 1990).

23. Deák, István. "Comparing Apples and Pears: Centralization, Decentralization and Ethnic Policy in the Habsburg and Soviet Armies." In *Nationalism and Empire: The Habsburg Empire and the Soviet Union.* (Rudolph, R., and Good, D., eds.) (New York, 1992).

24. Deák, István. "Pacesetters of Integration: Jewish Officers in the Habsburg Monarchy." *East European Politics and Societies.* Vol. 3, No. 1, Winter 1989.

25. Ehnl, Max. "Die öst.-ung. Landmacht nach Aufbau, Gliederung, Friedensgarnison, Einteilung and nationaler Zusammensetzung im Sommer 1914." ("The Austro-Hungarian Land Power by Structure, Deployment, Peacetime Garrison, Organization, and National Composition in the Summer of 1914") *Ergänzungsheft 9 zum Werke Österreich-Ungarns letzter Krieg 1914–1918 (ÖUlK)* (Vienna, 1934).

26. Farkas, Márton. *Katonai összeomlás és forradalom 1918-ban.* (*Military Collapse and Revolution in 1918*) (Budapest, 1969).

27. Farkas, Márton. "Die politische Erziehungsarbeit in die Armee am Ende des ersten Weltkrieges." (Political Propaganda Work in the Army at the End of the First World War") *Die Auflösung des Habsburgerreiches: Zusammenbruch und Neuorientierung im Donauraum.* (Plaschka, R. G., and Mack, K., eds.) (Vienna, 1970).

28. Fejtő, François. *Requiem pour un Empire défunt: Histoire de la destruction de l'Autriche-Hongrie.* (*Requiem for a Defunct Empire: A History of the Destruction of Austria-Hungary*) (Paris, 1988).

29. *Feuerbereit! Kriegsalbum des Feldartillerieregiments Nr.104, Wien.* (*Ready to Fire! War Album of the Viennese 104th Field Artillery Regiment*) (Vienna, 1919).

30. Fiala, Peter. *Die letzte Offensive Altösterreichs: Führungsprobleme und Führerverantwortlichkeit bei der öst.-ung. Offensive in Venetien, Juni 1918.* (*The Last Offensive of Old Austria: Command Problems and Responsibility in the Austro-Hungarian Offensive in Venetia, June 1918*) (Boppard am Rhein, 1967).

31. Franek, Fritz. "Die Entwicklung der öst.-ung. Wehrmacht in den ersten zwei Kriegsjahren." ("The Development of the Austro-Hungarian Armed Forces in the First Two War Years") *Ergänzungsheft 5 zum Werke ÖUlK.* (Vienna, 1933).

32. Franek, Fritz. "Probleme der Organization im ersten Kriegsjahren." ("Organizational Problems in the First War Years") *Ergänzungsheft 1 zum Werke ÖUlK* (Vienna, 1930).

33. Fritz, Hans. *Bosniak.* (Waidhofen a.d. Ybbs, 1931).

34. Führ, Christoph. *Das k.u.k. Armeeoberkommando und Innenpolitik in Österreich 1914–1917.* (*The Imperial-and-Royal High Command and Domestic Politics in Austria 1914–1917*) (Graz, 1968).

35. Gabriel, Erich. "Die wichtigsten Waffen der öst.-ung. Armee 1918." ("The Most Important Weapons of the Austro-Hungarian Army 1918") *Österreichische Militärische Zeitschrift* 1968.

36. Gál, Joseph. *In Death's Fortress.* (New York, 1991).

37. Galántai, József. *Hungary in the First World War.* (Budapest, 1989).

38. Glaise-Horstenau, Edmund. *Die Katastrophe: Die Zertrümmerung Österreich-Ungarns und das Werden der Nachfolgestaaten.* (*The Catastrophe: The Collapse of Austria-Hungary and the Coming of the Successor States*) (Zürich, 1929).

39. Griesser-Pečar, Tamara. *Die Mission Sixtus: Österreichs Friedenversuch im 1. Weltkrieg.* (*The Sixtus Mission: Austria's Peace Attempt in the First World War*) (Vienna, 1988).

40. Hanks, R. Wayne. "Vae Victis! The Austro-Hungarian Armeeoberkommando and the Armistice of Villa Giusti." *Austrian History Yearbook* Vol. XIV, 1978.

41. Haselsteiner, Horst. "The Habsburg Empire in World War I: The Mobilization of Food Supplies" in: *War and Society in East Central Europe: Vol. XIX: East Central European Society in World War I.* (Király, B., Dreisziger, N., and Nofi, A., eds.) (New York, 1985).

42. Hecht, Rudolf. "Fragen zur Heeresergänzung der gesamten bewaffneten Macht Österreich-Ungarns während des Ersten Weltkrieges." ("Questions on Army Organization of the Joint Armed Forces of Austria-Hungary during the First World War") (University of Vienna diss., 1969).

43. Herwig, Holger. "Disjointed Allies: Coalition Warfare in Berlin and Vienna, 1914." *Journal of Military History* 54 July 1990.

44. Hubka, Gustav von. *Geschichte des k.u.k. IR. Graf von Lacy Nr.22 vom Jahre 1902 bis zu seiner Auflösung.* (2 vols.) (*The History of the Imperial-and-Royal 22nd Infantry Regiment Count von Lacy from 1902 to its Disbandment*) (Vienna, 1938).

45. Jedlicka, Ludwig. "Die Tradition der Wehrmacht Österreich-Ungarns und die Nach-folgestaaten." ("The Tradition of the Austro-Hungarian Military and the Successor States") *Öster-reichsiche Militärische Zeitschrift* 1968.

46. Jeřábek, Rudolf. *Potiorek: General im Schatten von Sarajevo.* (Potiorek: General in the Shadow of Sarajevo) (Graz, 1991).

47. Kann, Robert. *Die Sixtusaffäre und die geheimen Friedensverhandlungen Österreich-Ungarns im ersten Weltkrieg.* (*The Sixtus Affair and Austria-Hungary's Secret Peace Efforts in the First World War*) (Munich, 1966).

48. Kelleher, Edward P. "Emperor Karl and the Sixtus Affair: Politico-Nationalist Repercus-sions in the Reich German and Austro-German Camps, and the Disintegration of Habsburg Aus-tria." *East European Quarterly* XXVII, No. 2, June 1992.

49. Kerchnawe, Hugo. *Die Militärverwaltung in den von den österreichisch-ungarischen Truppen besetzten Gebieten.* (*Military Administration in Territories Occupied by Austro-Hungarian Troops*) (Vienna, 1928).

50. Kerchnawe, Hugo. *Der Zusammenbruch der öst.-ung. Wehrmacht im Herbst 1918.* (*The Collapse of the Austro-Hungarian Armed Forces in Autumn 1918*) (Munich, 1921).

51. Kiszling, Rudolf. "Die Brussilow-Offensive bei Łuck-Olyka." ("The Brusilov Offensive at Łuck-Olyka") *Österreichische Militärische Zeitschrift* 1966.

52. Kiszling, Rudolf. "Der Krieg gegen Rumänien 1916." ("The War Against Romania 1916") *Österreichische Militärische Zeitschrift* 1966.

53. Kiszling, Rudolf. "Das Nationalitätenproblem in Habsburgs Wehrmacht 1848–1918." ("The Nationalities Problem in the Habsburg Military 1848–1918") *Der Donauraum* 4. Jahrg, 2. Heft, 1959.

54. Klimecki, Michał. *Gorlice 1915.* (Warsaw, 1991).

55. Krauss, Alfred. *Die Ursachen unserer Niederlage.* (*The Causes of Our Defeat*) (Munich, 1920).

56. Krauss, Alfred. *Das Wunder von Karfreit: im besonderen der Durchbruch bei Flitsch und die Bezwingung des Tagliamento.* (*The Caporetto Miracle: Particularly the Breakthrough at Flitsch and the Crossing of the Tagliamento*) (Munich, 1926).

57. Kreisler, Fritz. *Four Weeks in the Trenches.* (Boston, 1917).

58. Markus, Georg. *Der Fall Redl.* (*The Redl Case*) (Vienna, 1984).

59. Martinek, Rudolf. *Kriegstagebuch eines Artillerie-Offiziers.* (*The War Diary of an Artillery Officer*) (Vienna, 1975).

60. Nowak, Robert. "Die Klammer des Reichs: Das Verhalten der elf Nationalitäten in der k.u.k. Wehrmacht 1914–1918." ("The Hinge of the Empire: The Conduct of the Eleven Nationalities in the Austro-Hungarian Armed Forces 1914–1918") Nachlaß B/726, Nr.1/I,II,III, Kriegsarchiv Vienna.

61. Peball, Kurt. "Der Feldzug gegen Serbien und Montenegro im Jahre 1914." ("The Cam-paign Against Serbia and Montenegro in 1914") *Österreichische Militärische Zeitschrift* 1965/Sonderheft.

62. Peball, Kurt. "Österreichische Militärgeschichtliche Forschung zum Ersten Weltkrieg zwischen 1918 und 1960." ("Austrian Military Historical Research Between 1918 and 1960") in *Geschichte und Militärgeschichte: Wege der Forschung.* (Von Gersdorff, U., ed.) (Frankfurt/Main, 1974).

63. Peball, Kurt. "Um das Erbe: Zur Nationalitätenpolitik des k.u.k. Armeeoberkommandos während der Jahre 1914 bis 1918." ("About the Inheritance: On the Nationalities Policy of the Habsburg High Command from 1914 to 1918") *Österreichische Militärische Zeitschrift* 1967/Sonderheft.

64. *Österreich-Ungarns letzter Krieg 1914–1918.* (*Austria-Hungary's Last War 1914–1918*) (7 vols. and 7 supp.vols.) (Glaise-Horstenau, E., ed.) (Vienna, 1930–1938).

65. Pethö, Albert. *Agenten für den Doppeladler: Österreich-Ungarns geheimer Dienst im Weltkrieg.* (*Agents for the Double Eagle: Austria-Hungary's Secret Service in the World War*) (Graz, 1998).

66. Pitreich, Max. *Lemberg 1914.* (Vienna, 1929).

67. Pitreich, Max. *1914: Die militärische Probleme unseres Kriegsbeginnes.* (*1914: The Military Problems of Our War's Beginning*) (Vienna, 1934).

68. Plaschka, Richard Georg. *Cattaro-Prag: Revolte und Revolution.* (*Cattaro-Prague: Revolt and Revolution*) (Graz, 1963).

69. Plaschka, Richard Georg. "Zur Vorgeschichte des Übergangs von Einheiten des IR.Nr.28 an der Russischen Front 1915." ("On the Background of the Defection of Units of the 28th Infantry Regiment on the Russian Front 1915") in *Österreich und Europa: Festgabe für Hugo Hantsch zum 70. Geburtstag.* (Vienna, 1965).

70. Plaschka, Richard Georg, Horst Haselsteiner, and Arnold Suppan. *Innere Front: Militärassistenz, Widerstand und Umsturz in der Donaumonarchie 1918.* (2 vols.) (*Internal Front: Military Assistance, Resistance, and Downfall in the Danubian Monarchy 1918*) (Vienna, 1974).

71. Pokorny, Hermann. *Emlékeim.* (*Memories*) (Budapest, 2000).

72. Rauchensteiner, Manfried. *Der Tod des Doppeladlers: Österreich-Ungarns und der Erste Weltkrieg.* (*The Death of the Double Eagle: Austria-Hungary and the First World War*) (Graz, 1994).

73. Ratzenhofer, Emil. "Verlustkalkül für den Karpathenwinter 1915." ("Casualty Estimates for the Carpathian Winter 1915") *Ergänzungsheft 1 zum Werke ÖUlK.* (Vienna, 1930).

74. Ratzenhofer, Emil. "Der Waffenstillstand von Villa Giusti und die Gefangnahme Hunderttausender." ("The Armistice of Villa Giusti and the Captured Hundreds of Thousands") *Ergänzungsheft 2 zum Werke ÖUlK* (Vienna, 1932).

75. Regele, Oskar. *Gericht über Habsburgs Wehrmacht: Letzte Siege und Untergang unter dem Armee-Oberkommando Kaiser Karls I.* (*Judgment on the Habsburg Military: Last Victories and Defeat under the Army Command of Emperor Karl I*) (Vienna, 1968).

76. Ronge, Max. *Kriegs- und Industrie-Spionage: Zwölf Jahre Kundschaftsdienst.* (*War and Industrial Espionage: Twelve Years Intelligence Service*) (Vienna, 1930)

77. Ronge, Max. *Meister der Spionage.* (*Master of Espionage*) (Vienna, 1935).

78. Rothenberg, Gunther E. *The Army of Francis Joseph.* (West Lafayette, IN, 1976).

79. Rothenberg, Gunther E. "The Austro-Hungarian Campaign Against Serbia." *Journal of Military History* 53, April 1989.

80. Rothenberg, Gunther E. "Toward a National Army: The Military Compromise of 1868 and its Consequences." *Slavic Review.* Vol. 31, No. 4, December 1972.

81. Schachinger, Werner. *Die Bosniaken kommen! Elitetruppe in der k.u.k. Armee, 1879–1918.* (*The Bosnians Are Coming! Elite Units in the Austro-Hungarian Army, 1879–1918*) (Graz, 1989).

82. Schaumann, Walther, and Peter Schubert. *Isonzo 1915–1917: Krieg ohne Wiederkehr.* (*Isonzo 1915–1917: War Without Recurrence*) (Bassano del Grappa, 1993).

83. Schindler, John R. "A Hopeless Struggle: Austro-Hungarian Cryptology during World War I" *Cryptologia.* Vol. XXIV, No. 4, October 2000.

84. Schindler, John R. *Isonzo: The Forgotten Sacrifice of the Great War* (Westport, CT, 2001).

85. Schmidl, Erwin A. *Juden in der k.(u.)k. Armee 1788–1918.* (*Jews in the Imperial [-and-] Royal Army, 1788–1918*) (Eisenstadt, 1989).

86. Schmidl, Erwin A. "Paardeberg to Przemysl: Austria-Hungary and the Lessons of the Boer War, 1899–1902." In *War and Society in East Central Europe: Vol. XXVIII: The Boer War and Military Reforms.* (Stone, J., and Schmidl, E., eds.) (Lanham, MD, 1988).

87. Schön, Joseph. *Šabac! Der Kampf der deutschböhmischen 29.ID., des Prager VIII.Korps und des Budapester IV.Korps im August 1914 in Nordwest-Serbien.* (*Šabac! The Battle of the German-Bohemian 29th Inf. Div., the Prague VIII Corps, and the Budapest IV Corps in August 1914 in Northwest Serbia*) (Reichenberg, 1928).

88. Shanafelt, Gary. *The Secret Enemy: Austria-Hungary and the German Alliance, 1914–1918.* (New York, 1985).

89. Sieder, Reinhard. "Behind the Lines: Working-Class Family Life in Wartime Vienna." In *The Upheaval of War: Family, Work and Welfare in Europe, 1914–1918.* (Wall, R., and Winter, J., eds.) (Cambridge, 1988).

90. Silberstein, Gerard. "The High Command and Diplomacy in Austria-Hungary, 1914–1916." *Journal of Modern History.* Vol. 42, No. 4, December 1970.

91. *61 in Waffen: Kriegsalbum des k.u.k. IR.61, 1914–1917. (61 in Arms: War Album of the Imperial-and-Royal 61st Inf. Regt., 1914–1917)* (Budapest, 1918).

92. Sked, Alan. *The Decline and Fall of the Habsburg Empire, 1815–1918.* (New York, 1989).

93. Sondhaus, Lawrence. *In the Service of the Emperor: Italians in the Austrian Armed Forces, 1814–1918.* (New York, 1990).

94. Spence, Richard B. "*Die Bosniaken kommen!* The Bosnian-Hercegovinian Formations of the Austro-Hungarian Army, 1914–1918." in *Scholar, Patriot, Mentor: Historical Essays in Honor of Dimitrije Djordjević.* (Spence, R., and Nelson, L., eds.) (New York, 1992).

95. Spence, Richard B. "The Yugoslav Role in the Austro-Hungarian Army, 1914–1918." In *War and Society in East Central Europe: Vol. XIX: East Central European Society in World War I.* (Király, B., Dreisziger, N., and Nofi, A., eds.) (New York, 1985).

96. Stone, Norman. "Army and Society in the Habsburg Monarchy, 1900–1914." *Past and Pres-ent.* No. 33, April 1966.

97. Stone, Norman. *The Eastern Front 1914–1917.* (New York, 1975).

98. Stone, Norman. "Die Mobilmachung der öst.-ung. Armee 1914." ("The Mobilization of the Austro-Hungarian Army, 1914") *Militärgeschichtliche Mitteilungen* 16, Bd.2/1974.

99. Stone, Norman. "Moltke and Conrad: Relations between the Austro-Hungarian and the German General Staffs, 1910–1914." In *The War Plans of the Great Powers, 1880–1914.* (Kennedy, P., ed.) (Boston 1979).

100. Švajncer, Janez. *Svetovna vojna 1914–18: Slovenci v avstro-ogrski armadi. (The World War 1914–18: Slovenes in the Austro-Hungarian Army)* (Maribor, 1988).

101. Triska, Jan. *The Great War's Forgotten Front: A Soldier's Diary and a Son's Reflections.* (New York, 1998).

102. Váchal, Josef. *Malíř na fronte: Soča a Italie 1917–18. (A Painter at the Front: Isonzo and Italy, 1917–1918)* (Prague, 1996).

103. Veith, Georg. "Die Isonzoverteidigung." ("The Isonzo Defense") *Ergänzungsheft 3 zum Werke ÖUlK.* (Vienna, 1932).

104. Wagner, Richard. *Geschichte des ehemaligen Schützen-Regiment Nr.6. (History of the For-mer 6th Rifle Regiment)* (Karlsbad, 1932).

105. Wegs, J. Robert. "Transportation: The Achilles' Heel of the Habsburg War Effort." In *The Habsburg Empire in World War I.* (Kann, R., Király, B., and Fichtner, P., eds.) (Boulder, CO, 1977).

106. Williamson, Samuel R. *Austria-Hungary and the Origins of the First World War.* (New York, 1991).

107. Winkler, Wilhelm. *Die Totenverluste der öst.-ung. Monarchie nach Nationalitäten. (The Fatal Casualties of the Austro-Hungarian Monarchy by Nationality)* (Vienna, 1934).

108. Zanantoni, Eduard. *Die Geschichte der 29.ID. im Weltkrieg 1914–1918. (The History of the 29th Inf. Div. in the World War, 1914–1918)* (Reichenberg, 1929).

109. Zeman, Z. A. B. *The Break-Up of the Habsburg Empire, 1914–1918: A Study in National and Social Revolution.* (London, 1961).

7

Russia

David R. Jones

In 1913 the wealthy Polish-Russian aristocrat Princess Catherine Radziwill, writing as "Count Paul Vasili," published in London her *Behind the Veil of the Russian Court.* Although largely a collection of gossip and tittle-tattle, this supposed "insider's account" found avid readers. Indeed, the appetite for glimpses of the lifestyles and scandals of the rich and famous of that era's European courts was as insatiable as is today's for accounts of goings-on in the Kremlin, the White House, and Buckingham Palace. And at that time, despite the rise of democratic institutions and a popular press, European diplomacy was conducted *in camera,* monarchs remained important political actors, and their courts kept their secrets.

Nowhere was this truer than in Imperial Russia. Although long described as an autocracy, the October Manifesto of 1905 had introduced a bicameral legislature and so formally converted the empire into a "limited autocracy." But the cabinet still remained responsible to the Tsar-Emperor Nicholas II, not to the new Duma or lower house, and the monarch retained full powers in military-naval and foreign affairs. Consequently, as was also true in Germany and Austro-Hungary, most decisions in these areas were made behind the closed doors of the court, doors that in Russia were sealed especially tight due to the need to preserve the state secret of the heir's hemophilia. Consequently, the motives and actions of Nicholas II remained as obscure to outside observers as did those of his predecessors Alexander I, "the Russian Sphinx," and his enigmatic grandfather Alexander II.

Not unnaturally, "liberal" proponents of a fully "democratic" parliamentary regime, who were united in Constitutional Democratic Party (Kadets) and more conservative Union of October Seventeen (Octobrists), remained dissatisfied. Their continuing drive for further concessions produced a growing political crisis that paralleled a mounting wave of labor and peasant unrest, which the various revolutionary groups encouraged whenever possible. All these strains seemed to peak in the summer of 1914. Yet when war broke out in July–August 1914, most members of Russian "society," like their compatriots in the other warring powers, supported their government. Formal opposition practically disappeared with the proclamation of a "sacred union" in support of the country's war effort. Even many striking workers seemed caught up in the nationalist enthusiasm that apparently gripped St. Petersburg, Moscow, and other urban centers, and to a much lesser extent, the rural peasantry. Despite informed expectations, however, the war was not over by Christmas. The fighting instead wore on, casualties mounted, and the mood began to change dramatically, especially after the defeats and Great Retreat of the spring and summer of 1915. In this atmosphere, the political battles resumed and after a period of seeming reconciliation in June–July 1915, a battle to the death opened between the Tsar and his government on one hand, and the "loyal" opposition on the other.

HISTORIOGRAPHIC INTRODUCTION

Thanks to this internal wartime conflict, the history of all aspects of Imperial Russia's war effort emerged as an intertwined mix of truths, half-truths, and outright myths. These last in particular have proven to be remarkably long-lived. As a result, even many of today's informed readers still accept that on the Eastern Front, an economically backward Tsarist empire collapsed militarily and politically in part thanks to its economy's inability to sustain its armies, but even more so because of the ease with which an hysterical empress, influenced by the manipulative healer Rasputin, controlled the weak-willed, stubborn, and mystical Nicholas II. Their influence, we have been told, kept honest "liberal" reformers out of power, ensured that venal if not traitorous bureaucrats ran the war effort, prevented the social and economic mobilization necessary to forestall defeat, and inevitably brought Russia to ruin and revolution. And since Rasputin's authority rested on his uncanny abilities to heal the Tsar's young son, many not unnaturally believe that Imperial Russia collapsed largely due to one child's tragic illness.

If serious historians reject this simplistic conclusion, the more general themes associated with it nonetheless became intertwined with fact during the 1920s to create an interpretative orthodoxy which underlies much of the literature published since 1917. To some extent this is because the tale of a doomed ruler (a true-life "Fisher King," if only by proxy) and his suffering land is the stuff of myths, and thus compelling is in its own right. Furthermore, linguistic barriers and inaccessible archives often hindered the efforts of those seeking to probe more. Most importantly, this interpretation reflects the fact that the story of Imperial Russia's war effort is inextricably mixed with that of the downfall of the Tsarist regime and the birth of Soviet Russia, events that laid the basis for the subsequent course of East-West relations and the so-called Cold War.

For Marxist-Leninists, on the one hand, the accepted chronicle of military defeat combined with industrial backwardness, capitalist exploitation and bureaucratic incompetence became an integral component of a myth that justified the Bolshevik Revolution and Communist regime in general, and the Stalinist programs of industrialization and collectivization in particular. Their liberal opponents, on the other hand, stressed the same factors in an effort to prove the empire fell because of its own follies, represented mainly by Nicholas II, his wife, and the covey of court favorites (the "Dark Forces") headed by the misnamed "mad monk" Rasputin. In his way the erstwhile opponents of the Tsarist regime sought to escape all responsibility for the collapse of the Imperial war effort, for their own failure to establish democracy in 1917, and for Lenin's subsequent triumph. What began as unsubstantiated wartime gossip and liberal propaganda thus was transformed into an article of faith and "received" historical truth. And since the first generations of Western scholars were trained mainly by liberal émigrés such as Michael Karpovich and George Vernadsky, or their Western supporters such as Bernard Pares in Britain and Samuel Harper in the United States, the liberal account of Russia's political and social development has had a remarkably long life.

Recent developments in international relations undoubtedly will open the way for a full reassessment of Russia's history during the years 1914–1917. In the first place, scholars now are obtaining full access to archives that long remained almost completely closed to Western (and many Russian) researchers. The possible impact of this access is as yet unclear and will be addressed more fully at the close of this discussion. It is equally significant, however, that the collapse of Communism removed many of the ideological timbers buttressing the two major variants of the myth just mentioned, the Marxist-Leninist-Socialist and the anti-Communist Liberal-Democratic. This most obviously affects historians working within the ex–Soviet Union, historians who will no longer be bound by the restraints of the Party's ideological censorship. Yet if the implications for Western scholars probably will be superficially more subtle, the long-run impact on their interpretations may be no less fundamental. More precisely, once they abandon the perspective of World War I as being predominantly a "prelude to Bolshevism," other neglected aspects of the story may gain greatly in interpretative stature.

Such considerations make this an appropriate moment to review the historical literature published over the last eight decades. In general, it comprises the categories familiar to all historians: research, bibliographic, and archival guides; published primary sources (documents, memoirs, and contemporary accounts); and secondary, ex post facto popular and scholarly studies. All these groupings, listed and numbered alphabetically, are included in the appended bibliography and discussed thematically below. This, it is hoped, will make this essay useful for the average, English-speaking student seeking an introduction to this often neglected aspect of World War I.

This said, we also should note that this literature again can be subdivided into three other, distinct main classes according to the origins of the writers: the émigré or "White" Russians, the Soviet or "Red" Russians (and their adherents), and the non-Russian (mainly Western travelers, journalists and later scholars). In its own way, each group made a unique contribution to our understanding of Russia's war effort. Yet a survey of the literature produced by all these groups also illustrates the extent to which the above-mentioned wartime political conflicts and associated myths continue to affect our accepted historiography. Such a survey reveals as well that after the mid-1960s, cracks in these interpretative monoliths became increasingly visible, cracks that in recent decades have widened when a range of researchers finally gained access, albeit limited, to the Imperial archives.

Finally, any attempt to outline the developing historiography of Russia's role in World War I is complicated by the difficulty of setting chronological boundaries. In Russia, of course, the military effort was interrupted in 1917—first by the February–March Revolution, and then by the October–November Revolution, after which the "imperialist war" (as the Soviets called it) was transformed into a civil conflict. Yet in practice, matters are not so simple. For example, one may consider the Central Powers' intervention of 1918 in the Ukraine, South Russia, and Caucasus to be part of the continuing overall "world struggle." But if so, can one legitimately ignore the corresponding Allied efforts to compensate by attempting to restore the Eastern Front, first by supporting the Bolsheviks and subsequently by aiding their White opponents?

Any decision on such issues must be somewhat arbitrary. Even so, for our immediate purposes we may take note of the Central Powers' actual military operations in the East from the signing of the Brest-Litovsk treaty in March 1918 to their collapse in the autumn of 1918, but largely ignore Allied initiatives after the demobilization of the old Imperial Army in December 1917. Similarly, this essay makes no attempt to discuss the purely Red-White Civil War. While this struggle did affect Allied planning during the World War's last seven months, it nonetheless involved the creation of new Russian armies that are of only marginal significance for our discussion.

GENERAL TEXTS AND BIBLIOGRAPHICAL GUIDES

The continuing influence of the historiographic orthodoxy described above explains the prevailing consensus in tone and themes found in the numerous standard texts devoted to late Imperial Russia. Typical of these are such relatively recent works as Bruce Lincoln's *War's Dark Shadow* [210] and *Passage through Armageddon* [211], Hans Rogger's "Russia in 1914" [308] and later longer study [308], and to a lesser extent, Richard Pipes' *Russian Revolution* [286]. Although these recount the familiar and dismal litany of defeats, punctuated by occasional but costly victories, these authors' interest in military events is only secondary to the themes of the empire's political, social, and economic disintegration. Otherwise, Edward Pearlstein's *Revolution in Russia* [279] provides an insight into the view from abroad through a published selection of reports from the New York press for the years 1894–1921.

More surprisingly, perhaps, Western military historians long paid equally scant attention to the Eastern Front of World War I. This is immediately evident from even a cursory glance at the standard histories of the conflict. While the Russian and Turkish theaters did received their fair share of attention in contemporary accounts such as French General Malleterre's *Les campagnes de 1915* (Paris, 1918), postwar histories were far less generous. This is illustrated by the works of the celebrated English writer B. H. Liddell Hart. Although he devotes a full chapter of his widely read *The Real War, 1914–1918* (London, 1930) to the disaster of "Tannenberg—The Field of Legend," Russia's other campaigns are treated as sideshows. For example, he allows less than three pages to the surprisingly successful "Brusilov offensive" of 1916, as compared to four to the British capture of Baghdad. That his focus was not eccentric is evident from such representative later studies as Cyril Falls' *The Great War, 1914–1918* (London, 1959), V. J. Esposito's *A Concise History of World War* (New York, 1964), and General L. Koeltz's *La Guerre de 1914–1918: Les Operations militaires* (Paris, 1966). In these and most other non-Russian general histories, the Western Front takes pride of place while the massive struggle in the East is accorded a position not dissimilar to the Balkan or Turkish theaters.

A glance at the standard Western bibliographies devoted to World War I makes the Western Theater's continuing domination equally apparent. When Cyril Falls compiled *War Books: A Critical Guide* (London, 1930), he hoped that no critic would find "that any aspect or point of view has been ignored." Nonetheless, Falls included only a handful of titles dealing directly with the Russian war effort. This gap remained unplugged in both R. J. Wyatt's expanded reissue (London, 1989), and in *The Two World Wars: Selective Bibliography* (Brussels, 1964) of the Commission Internationale pour l'Enseignment de l'Histoire. Also indicative is David Shapiro's *A Select Bibliography of Works in English on Russian History* [335], published in 1962. If he does list ten entries on the Imperial Army during World War I, only two—Winston Churchill's *Unknown War* [39] and Edmund Ironside's *Tannenberg* [148]—are English-language military studies by non-Russians. A fuller but still only a partial listing of Western works published before 1943 is available in Philip Gierson's *Books on Soviet Russia* [100], but in recent decades this literature has expanded considerably in a number of areas.

Students seeking further guidance to both Western and Russian studies of the war effort will find full bibliographical details in many of the more recent works, as well as in the relevant entries in the encyclopedias edited by David R. Jones [160] and Joseph L. Wieczynski [401]. Equally useful is the bibliography edited by Alexandra Dumesnil and Wilfrid Lerat [64] and Marvin Lyons' listing of regimental histories [221]. For those reading Russian, Aleksei Gering [99] provides an excellent guide to émigré "White" Russian memoirs and studies while other emigre and Soviet bibliographers have published volumes listing the most important studies of the 1920s and 1930s. Of special value are those of M. Dobranitskii [57], G. Khmelevskii [183], M. S. Seleznev [333], and Yan Slavik [343], as well as the collectively edited volume *Mirovaia voina* [244]. Information on both early and later Soviet scholarship is also available in more recent Soviet works such as those of R. E. Rutman [321] and I. I. Rostunov [317], among others. In addition, Charles G. Palm and Dale Reed describe the major early holdings of the Hoover Institution's important archives [268], and their survey was recently updated in a volume edited by Peter Duignan [61].

POLITICAL BACKGROUND

In its most popular form, the traditional version of the political processes bringing about the collapse of Imperial Russia found expression in the numerous memoirs and biographies of Tsar Nicholas and his wife by both Russian and foreign authors. Typical are those of Sophie Buxhoevdon [34], Lili Dehn [52], Mohammed Essad-Bey [70], G. V. Marsden [226], Marfa Mouchanow [232], Vladimir Poliakoff [288], and Catherine Radziwill [297–299]. Apart from Robert Massie's best-seller *Nicholas and Alexandra* of 1960 [228], this tradition has since been reinforced by the more recent biographies (of varying quality) devoted to Nicholas II and Alexandia by E. M. Almedingen [8], Constantin de Grunwald [126], Greg King [186], Edward Radzinsky [295], and Robert Warth [391]. The same theme is even more strongly stressed in accounts of the life of Rasputin, and of the supposed influence of the "Dark Forces," penned by Alex de Jong [53], Joseph T. Fuhrmann [88], Geoffrey Hosking [124], Brian Moynahan [251], Edward Radzinsky [296], and a host of others. All, in fact, basically repeat the story as told by Polish Princess Catherine Radziwill [298] and the popular writer Rene Fullop-Miller [92] in the late 1920s. As already noted, Soviet historians adopted a similar interpretative lens, which received canonical status in the first volume of the Stalinist *History of the Civil War in the USSR* of 1935 [107], and which was still firmly in place in the 1960s [e.g., see A. Grunt, 125.]

The dominating tone in later Western accounts of Imperial Russia's war effort was set by a number of émigré and Western authors during the decade following 1917. This received full scholarly sanction from Bernard Pares in his major article of 1927 [273] and subsequent full-scale study, *The Fall of the Russian Monarchy* [275], which appeared first in London in 1931 and was repeatedly republished thereafter. Pares' authority was buttressed by his own frequent visits to, and service in, Imperial Russia both before and during the war, experiences which he recounted both at the time [271] and in his subsequent memoirs [270, 274]. He further promoted his case by the use of highly selective quotations from the published wartime correspondence of the Tsar and Tsarina [374], and by his occasional pen portraits and obituaries of members of the opposition [e.g., 272]. In addition, Pares' position received general support from the memoirs of diplomats such as British Ambassador Sir George Buchanan [30], French Ambassador George Paleologue's gossipy and unreliable three-volume, alleged day-by-day account of events in wartime Petrograd [266], and the works of Americans David Francis [87] and George Mayre [227], among others. So while Michael Florinsky's *The End of the Russian Empire* [84], which appeared in the same year as Pares' study, provided a somewhat more complex and scholarly overview of the Russian war effort, it was the Englishman who set future trends.

Overall, Pares' view reflected that found in many of the translated and usually self-serving memoirs of the many former politicians driven into exile after the Soviet victory. Although the recollections of Mikhail V. Rodzianko [306] are perhaps the most notorious example, similarly gloomy interpretations are found in the accounts left by a wide range of leading political figures and bureaucrats. Of these, the most informative perhaps are those of senior officials Vladimir I. Gurko (Gourko) [128] and George C. Guins [127], and of Finance Minister and Premier Vladimir N. Kokovtsov [192]. But others of value include the memoirs of Air Fleet commander Grand Duke Aleksandr Mikhailovich Romanov [311] and Foreign Minister Sergei D. Sazonov [330], of liberal leaders Pavel N. Miliukov [243] and Vasilii A. Mallakov [222], of rightist politicians Vasilii V. Shulgin [338–340] and Vladimir M. Purishkevich (Pourichkevitch) [294], of socialist politicians such as Victor Chernov [37] and Alexander F. Kerensky [176–179] and, to a lsser extent, those of the aristocrat and murderer of Rasputin Felix F. Yusupov (Youssoupoff) [411, 412]. In addition, the same tone of futility in the face of court stupidy pervades the accounts of a host of lesser figures, both Russian and non-Russian. They include the anonymous author of the early *Fall of the Romanovs* [9], emigre aristocrats such as Baron Graevinitz [108], Countess Kleinmichel [189] and Princess Paley [267], and English observers like the *Times's* correspondent Robert Wilton [405], junior diplomat Robin Bruce Lockhart [214, 215], and many others (e.g., E. J. Dillon, [56], Bertie Stopford [365] and so on).

This same tendency informed the editorial policies behind the collections of translated documents published by Frank Golder [104], Colwyn Vuilliamy [387] and V. P. Semennikov [334], as well as those that occasionally appeared in various journals. Yet given the vast quantities of documents published by Soviet archivists, especially in the journal *Krasnyi arkhiv* [see 333], surprisingly few have appeared in Western languages. Apart from the above-mentioned private correspondence of the Tsar and Tsaritsa, Nikolai Mikhailovich Romanov's letters to Frederic Mason [315] are worthy of note. More importantly, the governmental crisis of 1915 can be studied in Michael Cherniavsky's edition of A. N. Yakhontov's notes on the secret meetings of the council of ministers during the crisis of mid-1915 [36], and the year 1917 through R. P. Browder's and A. F. Kerensky's *The Provisional Government* [28], a three-volume collection. Documents on the fall of the Tsarist regime as such recently were recently edited and published by Mark D. Steinburg and Vladimir M. Khrustalev [358], and extracts from the Nicholas-Alexandra correspondence, along with other materials, also appear in a new but badly edited collection, *A Lifelong Passion,* of Andrei Maylunus and Sergei Mironenko [230].

Not surprisingly, all these traditions have left their imprint on many, otherwise excellent scholarly works published in the West. This aside, a number of these studies do provide useful accounts of Russia's prewar and wartime political battles. Apart from the more general accounts noted above, useful introductions to the constitutional system established in 1905 and subsequent political battles are found in the relatively recent works of Geoffrey Hosking [143], Robert Edelman [67], Roberta Manning [223], Michael Taube [373], and Theodore von Laue [384], among others. Again, the political scene as of July 1914 has been described by Hans Rogger [308], Dominic Lieven [208] and, in more depressing shades, by Leopold Haimson [131]. For military historians, John D. Walz's pioneering dissertation on the politics of Russian defense [390], William Fuller's later study of civil-military interactions [91], and John Steinberg's forthcoming *War and Society* [357], are especially significant. Also deserving of attention are the biographies of various political leaders, such as Eleanor Eddy's study of Rodzianko [66], Thomas Riha's [304] and Melissa Stockdale's [362] of Miliukov, William Gleason's of Alexander Guchkov [102], Leonid Strakovsky's of Count Pavel Ignatiev [366, 367], and T. John Thompson's of Boris Sturmer [373]. Less valuable, but still of "atmospheric" interest are the biographies of the Prince Yusupov [59, 187], the Dowager Empress [288, 375], the Tsar's sister Olga (283, 386), and of other members of the dynasty [see 7, 45, 119, 371].

Apart from the earlier, more general histories mentioned, the course of Russia's wartime politics is outlined in the contribution of 1929 by Paul Gronsky and Nicholas Astrov [116] to the Carniegie Foundation's studies of the war [124], and more recently Raymond Pearson's study [280] and in the unpublished dissertations of Jamie Cockfield [41] and Robert Coonrod [44]. Western students have been especially interested in the opposition liberals, and in the Progressive Bloc they formed in the late summer of 1915. This is the subject of full-scale dissertations by Elizabeth Greicus [123] and Michael Hamm [133], and articles by Hamm [132] and Riha [305]. Equal attention has been devoted to the local town and *zemstvo* (rural) administrations, their contribution to the war effort, and their own claims to political authority. Apart from the Carnegie volume by T. J. Polner, V. A. Obolensky and S. P. Turin [283], the work of the Union of Towns and Zemstvos is the subject of detailed studies by Thomas Fellows [78] and William Gleason [103]. But if all this adds needed texture to the picture presented by less scholarly examinations of the role of Rasputin and the court's supposed "Dark Forces," the latter view long continued to influence the assessments of even such eminent analysts as George Kennan [173]. Consequently, the picture that emerges was usually one of Russia's "vital forces," represented by the patriotic liberal opposition, being left hopelessly constrained by economic backwardness in their hopeless battle with the Central Powers on the one hand, and by a corrupt, incompetent and stupid government on the other.

True, some doubt was cast on particular details of this accepted view of Russian conditions by collections of shorter, detailed studies like those edited by Theofanis Stavrou in 1969 [355] and Erin Oberlander in 1971 [262]. Even so, the only attempted challenge to the orthodoxy of the liberal and Marxist schools came initially from former court officials and conservatives (or reactionaries) forced into emigration after 1917. Their views are illustrated by the memoirs of court doctor Gleb Botkin [25], the Tsarevitch's tutor Pierre Gilliard [101], Generals Vasilii Gourko [129], A. A. Mossolov [248] and A. A. Noskov [261], and the American-born wife of a Guards colonel, Princess Cantacuzene (nee Grant) [35], as well as by the brief studies of monarchist exiles like Boris Brasol [26] or Vladimir Rudnev [319]. Such memoirs, however, usually were discounted as credulous, if not dishonest while the pro-monarchist studies (those mentioned excepted) appeared only in small, Russian-language editions. Only in 1967 did English-language readers gain access to a new version of events when George Katkov, a Russian-born Oxford don, published his full-scale, revisionist account of Russia's wartime politics and subsequent February Revolution [166]. Then, in 1979, Patrick Rollins finished translating into English S. S. Oldenburg's major study of Nicholas II's reign (1949) [264], which appeared with an introduction [310] that challenged earlier accounts. If the impact of these alternative views took time to be felt, by the 1980s this revisionism was influencing the work of scholars such as David R. Jones [154, 146], Dominic Lieven [207–209], and Marc Ferro [79]. Even so, the Western reading public still awaits a full and balanced narrative of the politics of wartime Russia.

DIPLOMATIC BACKGROUND

Unlike the situation in other areas, the debates over "war guilt" that followed the war ensured the publication of many of the most important Russian documents on foreign affairs and wartime inter-Allied cooperation. These appeared in French in 16 volumes [381] and in French, as edited by Rene Marchand, in three volumes (covering 1910–1917) [225]. Apart from numerous general studies on the diplomatic background to the war, and the final crisis of June–August 1914, the forging and development of the Franco-Russian alliance is the subject of special document collection, published by the French Foreign Ministry in 1918 [86]. The diverse historiography surrounding this alliance is illustrated by the studies of R. H. Allshouse [6], George F. Kennan [174], Donald Mathieu [229], Georges Michon [242], Boris Nolde [258], Derek Spring [351], and Friedrich Stieve [361], and the many others listed in Shapiro [340]. In particular, Rogers Churchill [38] traces the formation of the Anglo-Russian Convention that completed the Triple Entente, the basis for the later wartime alliance. Apart from such standard works as Luigi Albertini's study of the outbreak of World War I [3], Dominic Lieven [208] provides an updated account of both the background and Russia's conduct in July–August 1914. The final stages of that crisis in St. Petersburg can be followed in detail in the Russian Foreign Ministry's official diary [331], in the memoirs of German Ambassador F. Pourtales [292], and in those of the French and English diplomats [266, 30] mentioned above. As the still expanding scholarly literature indicates, both Russia's prewar foreign policy and the August disaster continue to provoke debate.

Imperial Russia's overall wartime diplomacy and inter-Allied relations are dealt with in C. Jay Smith, Jr. [344], and specific aspects in Marjorie Snively [345], Peter Berton [21], Alexander Dallin [48], and Robert J. Kerner [180, 181], as well as in broader studies like Harry Howard's discussion of Allied plans to partition Turkey [144]. Overall Russo-Allied relations are the subject of a dissertation by Ioannis Sinanoglou [342], while Keith Neilson [236] focuses on issues of wartime supply [236]. American-Russian relations between 1911 and 1918 are examined in Edward Finnegan's dissertation of 1947 [82], which, although outdated, is still a useful guide to the American sources. Otherwise, the once debated issue of alleged negotiations for a Russo-German separate peace is reviewed by both V. V. Lebedev [202] and L. L. Farrar [73]. There also is the particularly extensive memoir literature penned by the numerous Tsarist diplomats who chose emigration after the Revolution. These include Dmitrii Abrikossow [2], Nicholas Basily [15], A. D. Kalymkov [163], Konstantin Nabokov [253], Alexander Nekliudov [255], Roman Rosen [316] and, of course, Foreign Minister Sergei Sazonov [330].

Of equal if tangential interest are the documents on Germany's efforts to stir up revolution among the empire's non-Russian nationalities. Published by Z. A. B. Zeeman [414], these are discussed by George Katkov [164], and in German historian Fritz Fischer's controversial *Germany's Aims in the First World War* (New York, 1967). Rex A. Wade [388] provides an excellent study of the Provisional Government's foreign policy after February 1917, as well as a useful introduction to the literature on inter-Allied relations during that year. Petrograd's Balkan policies during the Revolution are detailed in Robert Johnston's dissertation of 1966 [150]. Although far too extensive to be fully considered here, the Soviet regime's revolutionary "diplomacy" of October 1917–November 1918, as well as the last stages of Russia's participation in World War I are chronicled in a wide-ranging literature. Representative in this regard are the works of Robert Warth [388], Michael Kettle [182] and Richard K. Debo [51]. The Treaty of Brest-Litovsk, Russia's departure from the ranks those fighting World War I, and the Central Powers's intervention in South Russia are examined in detail by a classic study of John W. Wheeler-Bennett [399], in Oleh S. Fedyshyn's monograph on intervention in the Ukraine [76], and in German-language studies such as those by Winfried Baumgart [16], Kurt Fischer [83], Otto Hennicke [139], Werner Hahlweg [130], and so on.

ECONOMIC WAR AND INDUSTRIAL MOBILIZATION

In many cases the existing Western-language literature on Russia's wartime economy long appeared to confirm the image of Russian underdevelopment. This was especially true of the series of émigré-authored studies published in the late 1920s and early 1930s by Yale University Press, in cooperation with the Carnegie Peace Endowment. It includes the volume of Stanislas Kohn and Alexander F. Meyendorf on the overall costs of the conflict [191], that of Alexander M. Michelson, Paul N. Apostol and Michael W. Bernatzky on public finance [241], B. E. Nolde's account of Russia's economic war [259], Peter B. Struve's on food supply [369], Eugene M. Kayden and Alexis N. Antsiferov's on the co-operative movement [167], and Semen A. Zagorsky's on the state control of industry [413]. The development of Russian agriculture is outlined in George Pavlovsky's parallel volume [278], one of the first in a number of analyses of the wartime countryside.

Despite the prevailing orthodoxy of Pares and company, the more recent economic studies of Roger Portal [291] and Peter Gatrell [97], among others, suggest that the Tsarist economy was stronger than generally believed. Edward Goldstein [105] and, more recently Gatrell [95, 96] as well, also examine the extent to which this economy was devoted to military ends, and Norman Stone [364, 365] demonstrates Imperial Russia's considerable success in mobilizing its resources and expanding production to meet wartime demands. Apart from the profits reaped [see T. Cohen, 42], administrative conflict over this industrial mobilization rapidly emerged as only another aspect of the political struggle between the government and the opposition. In this case the regime's opponents were represented by the War Industries Committees (WICs), which in 1918 presented the English-speaking public with a reckoning of their alleged successes [377]. Since official rebuttals appeared almost exclusively in the Russian émigré press, such claims long went largely uncontested. Again, it is only recently that this and related issues have been addressed in a scholarly manner by Lewis H. Siegelbaum [341], among others.

Meanwhile, the burden laid by the war effort upon the economy, and on the empire's manpower, brought the inflation, temporary shortages, and other social problems enumerated in most of the general and specialized studies already mentioned. This said, a proper Western-language social history devoted to the war years has yet to appear. True, special studies do exist, and include those devoted to the Orthodox Church [47], the education system [146], the Secret Police [383], and the Kazakh-Kirghiz uprising provoked by conscription that exploded in Central Asia in 1916 [347]. But while many followers of the "New Social History" examine the conditions and attitudes of Russia's wartime workers and peasants, they did so largely in an attempt to elucidate their subjects' role in the revolutionary events of 1917. Only recently have scholars focused attention on the war years as such, and often with considerable profit. This is the case, for example, with H. F. Jahn's study of Russian "patriotic culture" [149], Karen Petrone's discussion of the symbolism employed in wartime propaganda posters [282], and Peter Gatrell's recent *Whole Empire Walking* [94], a long-needed examination of the refugee issue. For the military historian's purpose, the work of Joshua Sandborn [325, 326] is especially relevant and his forthcoming monograph, *Drafting the Russian Nation* [324], should prove particularly stimulating for future researchers.

MILITARY PREPARATIONS AND MOBILIZATION

As might be expected, the problems bedeviling the more purely military historiography parallel those in the political and other areas. Overall, any attempt to demonstrate Tsarist competence in organizing the empire for war clearly runs counter to the old and long-dominating political myths outlined above. Yet surprisingly, most are constrained to admit the actual mobilization and concentration of Russia's forces during July–August 1914 went smoothly enough. This is reviewed by Michael Florinsky [85], L. C. F. Turner [379], Alfred von Wegerer

[397] and, in greater detail, by Sergei Dobrorolski [58]. But if the mobilization has never been the object of sustained criticism from the military-technical point of view, Joshua Sanborn [326] rightly points out that there was more opposition to the prcess than is usually admitted, and that the nationalist or "patriotic" mood was less real than is often assumed.

Even so, the mobilization was a success and the Tsarist regime's military preparations for war therefore deserve careful examination. These preparations, the prewar strategic planning included, obviously took place within the wider context of what David Hermann calls the general "arming of Europe" [140], and they were shaped by the Franco-Russian alliance in particular. This pact's military-strategic dimensions are outlined by F. M. Laney [200] and in the recent excellent monograph of William C. Fuller, Jr. [90], while its specific impact on Tsarist strategic railway policy is delineated by David Collins [43]. Issues of military thought and changing tactics are covered extensively by Peter Von Wahlde [385], Jack Snyder [346], Bruce W. Menning [238], David R. Jones [154–155], and Jacob W. Kipp [188]. Jones [151] also outlines the military's bureaucratic-planning framework, while Nikolai N. Golovin [110] details the actual plans implemented in 1914. The specific structure and conduct of the General Staff, the "brain of the army" that developed these concepts, is the topic of studies by John Erickson [69], M. Mayzal [234, 235], Carl Van Dyke [382], and David Rich [303]. Also of use are the many reports, collected by Gustav Lambsdorff [198], of the German Emperor's personal military representatives attached to the Russian Court until the outbreak of war. In addition, Fuller [89] also examines the effectiveness of prewar Russian military intelligence.

The Russian military's poor performance in the Japanese War of 1904–1905 naturally forced a series of reforms which, after a number of false starts, did much to modernize the Imperial Army. These are described in general by S. P. Andolenko [9] and Bruce Menning [238, 239], and in greater detail in the dissertations of Peter T. Wilfong [403] and Christopher D. Bellamy [17]. The last deals with the measures implemented after 1908 by the controversial and later discredited War Minister V. A. Sukhomlinov, who earlier was the subject of a mimeographed study by the French analyst Leon Agourtine [4]. Robert McNeal [237] meanwhile examines the impact of the reforms on the famed Cossack light cavalry. Equally worthy of attention are John Screen's account of Gustav Mannerheim's early career [332], Dimitry Lehovich's biography of A. I. Denikin [205], and Alexis Wrangel's of P. N. Wrangel [408], as well as the relevant sections of the memoirs of Mannerheim [223], Denikin [55, 277], Vladimir Littauer [210], and other prewar military professionals. But the officer-reformers faced immense obstacles and some indication of their nature, at least in the average line infantry regiment, is evident in an interesting study by John Bushnell [32].

There is a considerable literature on the officer question. Richard Luckett summarizes this in his study of the later White generals [212], which he recently revised and republished, and the ideological atmosphere of army service is illuminated by John Keep's [169] and Peter Kenez's [171] essays on Romanov military "style." The traditional view of the officer corps, as set forth by Oliver A. Ray [300], also must be considered within the context of John Bushnell's some-what one-sided study [33], and that of Peter Kenez's more wide-ranging profile [170]. In addition, Cossack General Pavel N. Krasnov's once-celebrated novel, *From Double-Headed Eagle to Red Flag* [194], provides personal insights into many aspects of army life both before and after 1914, and this despite its vicious antisemitism.

FIGHTING THE WAR

Although concerned primarily with political events, the prevailing orthodoxy of the "Pares-emigre" school long influenced Western historians' accounts of Russia's military effort as well. Its portrayal of a reactionary, corrupt, and deca-dent regime dictated that the Imperial Army's Galician victories of 1914 remain overshadowed by the East Prussian disaster of Tannenberg, that the Great Retreat of 1915 be blamed on the regime's alleged inability to provide muni-tions, that the unexpected success of the A. A. Brusilov's offensive in 1916 be treated as the dying gasp of a ruined army, that the Caucasian Army's brilliant campaigns against Turkey be regarded as irrelevant sideshows, and so on. This view was propagated by most of the above-mentioned exiled politicians, by the émigré military followers of Grand Duke Nikolai Nikolaevich in Belgrade and Paris (e.g., Generals N. N. Golovin and Yuri Danilov), and by many influential Allied observers. The generals in particular absolved their leader, the Tsar's oversized uncle who had served as Supreme Commander-in-Chief during the war's first year, of responsibility for the disasters suffered by his armies. Instead, they made the hated War Minister Sukhomlinov a scapegoat for these defeats, which in turn permitted them to portray the reactionary and antisemitic Grand Duke as a competent commander at the front. Even less deservedly, their politi-cal compatriots sought to depict Nikolai Nikolaevich as a prop of reform at home, and to transform him into a minor liberal icon. True, careful historical studies by Red Army staff officers during the 1920s and 1930s, as well as more polemical contributions from a handful of monarchist émigrés, demonstrated the absurdity of such claims. Yet these latter usually appeared only in small edi-tions while the Red Army studies remained equally scarce on the ground, and both were politically suspect. Consequently, until recently the orthodox histori-ography dictated that these correctives remain largely untranslated, that they be viewed through the lens prvided by Golovin and company, and that they be oth-erwise ignored by the majority of Western scholars.

Pares [275] and Florinsky [84] aside, the basic "line" of this school of mili-tary historiograhy was codified in 1931 by General Golovin in his *The Russian Army in the World War* [109]. This was the first full, and until the 1970s, the only comprehensive study of all aspects (manpower, supply, etc.) of the war effort available to the non-Russian reader. Subsequently republished (and issued in an expanded Russian edition in 1939), the influence of his study became immedi-ately evident in works such as Winston S. Churchill's account of operations on

the Eastern Front [39], which appeared in 1932. As a staunch supporter of
Grand Duke Nikolai Nikolaevich, Golovin had views that views naturally
reflected those of other émigré military-historians of the Paris-Belgrade circle.
These included the above-mentioned Sergei Dobrorolski [58] and, more importantly, the Grand Duke's close wartime associate, Quartermaster-General Yuri
N. Danilov [49, 50], and the influential British attaché, Alfred W. F. Knox [190].
This last writer's two volumes of memoirs (with documents) appeared in 1921
and, despite his own bias, they remain an important contribution. As for
Golovin, he also penned two major studies of Russia's campaigns of 1914 [107,
108], and a briefer account of the Brusilov spring offensive of 1916 [106]. Significantly, all neatly dovetail with the Pares school's vision of the politics and
course of the war.

The degree to which Golovin and his fellows influenced later writers is evident in the account of Tannenberg presented in Alexander Solzhenitsyn's much
acclaimed novel *August 1914* [348]. The same is true of the military-historical
studies of Western military historians such as Trevor N. Dupuy and Woldzimiez
Onacewicz [62, 63], Geoffrey Evans [71], Geoffrey Jukes [162], Alan Clark
[40], and Ward Rutherford [320], the last of whose account appeared in a
revised edition in 1992. Indeed, the basic tenets of the Pares and Golovin school
remain unchallenged even in S. P. Andolenko's otherwise excellent history of
the Russian Army [9], or such major and important studies as Daniel W. Graf's
on the relations between the Grand Duke's headquarters and the civil authorities
[115, 116], and Alan K. Wildman's two-volume account of the Army's collapse
during 1917 [402].

All in all, then, challenges to the established orthodoxy long remained occasional at best in the non-Russian historiography. As noted, those that did appear
were often penned by rightist émigrés (like Krasnov), whose overt antisemitic
tone made them unpalatable to most Western scholars, or were late on the scene,
as was the case with the translation of Sergei S. Oldenburg's above-mentioned
history of the last Tsar's reign [266]. Similarly, memoirs that bucked the liberal
trend in historiography (e.g., Princess Cantacuzene, 35], remained largely
ignored while others, such as those of the discredited War Minister Sukhomlinov [370], or of the military-police official Pavel G. Kurlov [197], appeared in
Russian and German, but not in English or French. Consequently, W. E. D.
Allen's and Paul Muratoff's careful and detailed, 270-page account of the Caucasian theater [5] is a shining exception in the earlier Western literature and,
recently republished, it remains a model for today's scholars.

Meanwhile, only one example of the Red Army's numerous historical studies
of the 1920s and 1930s became available to non-Russian readers. This was a
French translation of the Red Army General Staff's study of the East Prussian
and Galician campaigns of August–November 1914 [380]. Despite this, the only
battle to receive repeated and detailed study in the West is the Tannenberg disaster. Apart from the impact of the Pares-Golovin school, this focus also illustrates
the influence of the heroic German historiography centered on Field Marshals
Hindenburg and Ludendorff. Being readily accessible to Western scholars,

works of this school rapidly established the myth of the Germans' near-invincibility that permeates many military histories of the Eastern Front. While the German memoir and historical literature regarding Tannenberg and other battles need not concern us here, readers can assess their value through the careful studies of Dennis Showalter [337] and Holger Herwig [141], both of which shed light on Russian operations as well. In any case, the works of A. A. Noskov [260] and Golovin [107] aside, other early, non-German studies of Tannenberg include those of British General Edmund Ironside [148] and of J. von Kurenberg [196]. Both are notable for their extensive use of the available Russian as well as German sources. These were then supplemented by the analyses of Alexander Kearsey [168] and J. Argueyrolles [11], as well as Jean Savant's revisionist defense of General Pavel Rennenkampf [329]. The continuing fascination exerted by this battle is also evident from Geoffrey Evens's study of 1970 [71], the success of the above-mentioned novel by Solzhenitsyn [348], and by Richard Harrison's still more recent sketch of the doomed General Aleksandr Samsonov [1379].

Apart from this handful of studies, before 1960 there was little to Western students of the Russian "side of the hill." They remained virtually prisoners of the Pares school until the first serious assault on the "Rasputin myth" was launched by Martin Kilcoyne [184] in 1961. Unfortunately, his important and carefully argued dissertation has remained unpublished. As noted above, only in 1967 did the broader Western public finally gain access to a full-scale, academically respectable alternative to the Pares-Golovin orthodoxy in the form of George Katkov's above-mentioned *Russia 1917: The February Revolution* [165]. In his revisionist study of wartime Russian politics and fall of the monarchy, Katkov also raised doubts about the accepted military-historical conclusions drawn by his predecessors. Many remained skeptical of his anti-liberal interpretation but, in 1975–1978, Katkov's brief review of military issues soon received considerable support from Norman Stone's important essay [363] and full-scale *The Eastern Front* [333], and later from the dissertation and subsequent extended articles of David R. Jones [154, 158]. As well, a parrallel reassessment was under way within the Soviet Union, an excellent example of which is the major monograph of I. I. Rostunov [317]. Jones meanwhile also challenged the traditional view of the respective roles and merits of Grand Duke Nikolai and Nicholas II as wartime leaders [156]. If his controversial conclusions have not won full acceptance, they nonetheless influenced the subsequent work of scholars such as Marc Ferro [76] and Dominic Lieven [196]. Consequently, the historiography of Russia's war effort is today in a state of flux and readers can sample the broad range of subjects considered, including the issue of the "subject nationalities," as well as the varied interpretations proposed by contemporary scholars, by perusing the papers presented at the Great War Society's annual seminars for 2001 and 2002 [120, 121].

Despite the influence of Pares-Golovin, Western students from the first were well served by numerous translations from the extensive military-memoir literature, despite the fact that this largely reflects the experience of "White" officers who found refuge abroad after 1920. Of these, the most important were generals A. I. Denikin [54, 55, 277], A. S. Lukomsky [220], and P. N. Wrangel [410] (whose memoirs were reissued in 1957). From the Soviet side, their recollections are supplemented by translations of those penned by the celebrated A. A. Brusilov [29], Aleksei Ignatiev [145] and, later, by General M. D. Bonch-Bruevich [23], all of whom had joined the Red Army. Worthy of special note are the memoirs of Basil (Vasili) I. Gourko (Gurko) [129], the only Front commander to resign when Nicholas II abdicated in March 1917. The accounts of that same event by Finance Minister P. A. Bark [14] and diplomat Nicolas de Basily (Bazili) [15] are also sympathetic to the Tsar and his situation. Equally so are the portraits left by English King George V's personal delegates to Stavka—John Hanbury-Williams [134], W. H. H. Waters [395], and Richard Phillimore [285], all of which have been too long ignored by most scholars of wartime Russia.

Of the accounts left by French representatives, those of Jules Legras [203, 204] and Pierre Pascal [276] are well worth consideration. So too are the memoirs left by more junior, anti-Red Russian officers, representative of whom are Sergei Kournakoff [193], Vladimir Littauer [212], A. Lobanov-Rostovsky [213], Gustav Mannerheim [223], V. M. Moltchanov [249], Serge Obolensky [263], P. A. Polovtsov [290], Paul Rodzyanko [307], Gregory P. Tschebotarioff [376], and the flier Alexander Riaboff [302]. Also valuable are the published letters of the young artillery officer and later émigré writer Fedor Stepun [359], as well as the recollections of naval officers D. Fedotoff White [75], C. Benckendorff [20], and G. Graf [117]. Later Soviet commanders who recall their service as noncomissioned officers before 1917 include Stalin's colleague S. M. Budyonny [31], purge victim A. V. Gorbatov [112], and the famous Georgii K. Zhukhov [415]. Of particular note are the little-known accounts of the soldiers Nuhum Sabay [322] and Max Star [353]. As a Jewish refugee conscripted during the war, and later an American businessman, Star had no real knowledge of politics, but he still provides a unique bird's-eye view of military service. Equally interesting are the memoirs of nurses, who saw events from their own, somewhat particular view. Among these are the accounts of S. Botcharsky and F. Pier [24], Florence Farmborough [72], Sofia Fedorchenko [74], Olga Poutiatine [293], and the Tsar's younger sister, Grand Duchess Olga [386].

Other reminiscences deserving special attention are those of Vladimir N. Ipatiev [147], a noted chemist who worked with the military, as well as those of George V. Lomonosov [216], Viktor Shklovsky [336], W. S. Woytinsky (Voitinskii) [407], and Pitrim Sorokin [349]. All are written by civilians drawn into the military by the war, and all record the impact of the 1917 revolutions on the army. Although of various utility, there also are a number of wartime English-language accounts of experiences on the Eastern Front. Aside from Bernard Pares's *Day by Day with the Russian Army* [271], these include V. Doroshevitch's account of refugees during the Great Retreat of 1915 [60], and the works of Stephen Graham [118]; M. C. Lethbridge [206]; Robert R. McCormick [236]; John Morse [247]; Marr Murray [252]; the later famous American leftist journalist John Reed [301]; Percy Cross Standing [352]; W. Barnes Steveni

[360]; Bertie Stopford [365]; and *The Times* (London) correspondent Stanley Washburn [393]. The English writer A. G. Gardiner [93, pp. 131–138] provided his readers with a propagandistic and flattering sketch of Grand Duke Nikolai Nikolaevich that typifies the articles and pamphlets that circulated throughout Russia and abroad in 1914–1915. Like Pares, Washburn later published his memoirs [394], as did his more conservative colleague Robert Wilton [405]. Otherwise, students of Russia's naval efforts will profit from consulting F. N. A. Cromie's all-too-long ignored letters concerning his submarine service in the Baltic [46], as well as Admiral Richard Phillimore's memoirs [285] and extensive biographical sketch of Admiral Kolchak [284], Russia's commander in the Black Sea after 1915 and the later Siberian "White dictator."

Although not as yet the subject of a special study, the overall problems of manpower raised by the high rate of wartime casualties, and the issue of supplying the forces with arms, munitions and material, are all discussed—in varying length—by Golovin [109], Stone [364], Jones [154], and Sanborn [323, 324], as well as by the works on economic mobilization mentioned above. The nature of the wartime officer corps receives particular attention from Kenez [172], Jones [159, 161], and (for the navy) David A. Longley [217, 218]. In this regard, many of the biographies and memoirs already mentioned merit careful reading.

Western students of the Russian military have examined a number of the individual arms and services. For example, wartime developments in artillery are briefly but expertly examined by Christopher Bellamy [18, 19], Alexis Wrangel [409] deals with the cavalry, and Michael Harmer's essay on the work of an English hospital in wartime Russia provides insights into the operation of the military's medical support [136]. John Milsom [245] meanwhile outlines developments in early armor and armored-car actions are the subject of Bryan Perrett's and Anthony Lord's account of a British squadron in Russia [281]. Studies of another technical arm, the Tsarist air service, vary in value but are surprisingly extensive. Those readily available now include the book-length works of V. Hardesty and G. Sikorskii [136] and Alan Durkota, Thomas Darcey and Victor Kulikov [65], as well as B. Roustem-Bek's [318] contemporary account of 1916. These are supplemented by a host articles that include contributions from August Blume [22], Mark George and Vic Shepherd [98], David Jones [152, 157], Robert Kilmarx [185], Victor Kulikov [195], R. D. Layman [210], E. Meos [240], T. Stariparloff [354], and David Waligora [389]. Rene Greger [122] and chapters 13–15 in Donald W. Mitchell [246] provide reliable surveys of wartime naval operations. While George Nekrasov [256] focuses on the Black Sea and G. Graf [117] on the Baltic, Jan Breemer [28] is especially interesting with regard to Russia's early submarines in both theaters.

REVOLUTION AND COLLAPSE

Given the breakdown of the old army in 1917, many scholars have attempted to identify the origins of this process. Here General L. G. Spannocchi's pionering, German-language account [350] of the collapse of the Imperial Army, published in 1932, still may be perused with profit. For English readers there is Dean Lambert's [199] careful but unpublished chronicle of the army's apparent decline in fighting power and eventual deterioration, and Alan K. Wildman's more recent two-volume account [402] similarly chronicles the army's disintegration, both before and after the February Revolution. Most Soviet studies, such as that of P. A. Golub [105], focus more narrowly on, and exaggerate, the role of the Bolsheviks in this process. Apart from other works already mentioned, those interested in the Revolution's direct impact on the armed forces can consult A.M. Nikolaieff [257], John White (400), Richard Abraham [1], Gerhard Wettig [398], Marc Ferro [80, 81], and M. Mayzal [232, 233, 235]. Events in the navy are well-covered by David Longley [217, 218], Evan Maudsley [231], and Norman E. Saul [323]. Similarly, Robert S. Feldman [77], and Louise Heenan [138] provide overviews of the origins and course of the failed "Kerensky" offensive of June 1917. Those seeking an introduction to the debate over General L. G. Kornilov's much-debated attempt to "restore" military discipline can consult a range of works. Of these latter, the contributions of Leonid I. Strakhovsky [368], Alexander Kerensky [175, 176, 178], Harvey Asher [12, 13], Norman Saul [327], and George Katkov [166] provide an introduction to the contending views, while John Steinberg [356] continues the story into 1918. By that time the Imperial Army in effect had demobilized by itself, a process described in a multitude of studies devoted to the October Revolution and creation of the new Red Army. Although neither of the details of these events, nor the German operations in the East after 1917 need concern us here, those seeking an indication of the extensive literature on this subject can consult the articles by John Erickson [68] and David Jones [153], as well as the relevant works mentioned in the above sections on bibliography and foreign affairs. Otherwise, the impact of the revolutions at home on the often forgotten Russian detachments in France is recounted by Pierre Poitevin [287], John Williams [404], and Richard Watt [396], and Alan Palmer [269] details the fate of the similar expeditionary force serving with the other Allies on the Salonika Front.

AREAS FOR FURTHER RESEARCH

Given the extent to which liberal apologetics and Communist myths have dominated both the political and military historiography of this period, a serious re-examination of Russia's war effort has only just began. This process now is being fueled by the opening of long inaccessible archives. This, in time, should permit a complete reassessment of both the wartime, domestic political struggle, and of the impact of the war effort on all levels of Imperial society, the non-Russian nationalities included. Research by military historians meanwhile should proceed in a number of directions. For example, both the Galician campaigns of the war's first period and the campaigns of 1915–1916, deserve the same detailed attention long lavished on the initial East Prussian operations and the Tannenberg disaster. Again, it is time Western historians abandoned their traditional preconceptions and examined the real effectiveness of the leadership provided by the headquarters of Grand Duke Nikolai as compared to that of Nicholas II and his Chief of Staff M. V. Alekseev. Another area demanding careful analysis is the interaction between the supporting networks established by both official agencies and the "voluntary organizations" in the army's immediate rear, and the latter's role in sustaining or undermining morale during the years 1915–1917. And finally, Russia's wartime successes and failures should at last be viewed comparatively with those of the other combatants, and especially with regard to the records of Italy, Turkey, and Austro-Hungary. For from this viewpoint, the Imperial Army's record may appear much brighter than is usually expected.

In these and other respects, another comment is necessary. The above review of even the Western literature suggests that the material already available is much greater than often is realized. It also suggests that the majority of Western scholars of Russia's war effort have done little more than scratch the surface of the available sources. Before George Katkov and Norman Stone, for example, most writers based their conclusions on the works of Danilov, Golovin, and Denikin, and paid scant attention to the numerous Soviet documentary and scholarly publications that had appeared before 1939. Again, with the exception of Alan Wildman, few have used the extensive Russian-language, émigré literature as listed in Gering [99]. And even Wildman does not begin to plumb the depths of such prominent émigré periodicals as *Chasovoi* (Paris-Brussels), *Voennaia byl'* (Brussels), *Russkii invalid* (Paris), *Morskoi zhurnal* (Prague), and let alone a score of lesser rivals. Indeed, on occasion scholars seem to have used their often hurried and limited access to Soviet archives as an excuse for ignoring even the available, though often flawed, Soviet sources published over the last forty years. So if newly opened archives undoubtedly do extend our understanding in some areas, in others there remains much to be gained from an open-minded examination of an extensive range of published materials that, although long available, have seldom been used by scholars in both East and West.

BIBLIOGRAPHY

1. Abraham, Richard, *Alexander Kerensky: The First Love of the Revolution.* New York and London: Columbia University Press and Sidgewick and Jackson, 1987.

2. Abrikossow, Dimitri I., *Revelations of a Russian Diplomat.* Seattle: University of Washington, 1964.

3. Albertini, Liugi, *The Origins of the War of 1914.* 3 vols. Oxford, UK: Oxford University, 1952–57.

4. Agourtine, Leon, *Le general Soukhomlinov.* Preface Gen. Carolet. Clichy (Seine): Author, 1951. Mimeographed.

5. Allen, W. E. D., and Muratoff, Paul, *Caucasian Battlefields: A History of the Wars on the Turco-Caucasian Border, 1828–1921.* Cambridge: Cambridge University Press, 1953. Reprint: London: Curzon, 2002. Especially pp. 221–496.

6. Allshouse, R. H., *Alexander Isvokskii and Russian Foreign Policy, 1910–1914.* Unpublished Ph.D. Dissertation: Case Western Reserve University, 1976.

7. Almedingen, E. M., *An Unbroken Unity: A Memoir of Grand-Duchess Serge of Russia, 1864–1918.* London: Bodley Head, 1964.

8. Almedingen, E. M., *The Empress Alexandra.* London: Hutchinson, 1961.

9. Andolenko, S. P., *Histoirie de l'Armee russe.* Paris: Flammarion, 1967.

10. [Anonomyous], *The Fall of the Romanoffs: How the Ex-Empress and Rasputine Caused the Russian Revolution.* New York: Dutton, 1917.

11. Argueyrolles, J., *Le coup de des de Tannenberg (aout 1914). La tragique campagne de Prusse-Orientale.* Preface by M. Weygand. Paris: N.R.C., 1937.

12. Asher, Harvey, *The Kornilov Affair: A History and Interpretation.* Unpublished Ph.D. dissertation, Indiana University, 1967.

13. Asher, Harvey, "The Kornilov Affair: A Reinterpretation," *Russian Review* 29 (1970), 286–300.

14. Bark, Peter A., "The Last Days of the Russian Monarchy—Nicholas II at Army Headquarters," *Russian Review,* 16 (July 1957), no. 3, 35–44.

15. Basily [Bazili], Nicolas de, *Memoirs: Diplomat of Imperial Russia, 1903–1917.* Stanford, CA: Hoover Institution, 1973. Reprinted as *The Abdication of Emperor Nicholas II of Russia. A Memoir.* Princeton: Kingston Press, 1984.

16. Baumgart, Winfried, *Deutsche Ostpolitik 1918: Von Brest-Litowsk bis zum Ende des ersten Weltkrieges.* Vienna and Munich: R. Oldenbourg, 1966.

17. Bellamy, Christopher D., *Sukhomlinov's Army Reforms, 1908–1915.* Unpublished M.A. essay: King's College, University of London, 1978.

18. Bellamy, Christopher D., *The Red God of War.* London: Brassey's, 1986.

19. Bellamy, Christopher D., "The Russian Artillery and the Origins of Indirect Fire." *Army Quarterly and Defence Journal* 112 (April 1982), no. 3, 330–337.

20. Benckendorff, Constantine, Count, *Half a Life.* London: Richards, 1954.

21. Berton, Peter A., *The Secret Russo-Japanese Alliance of 1916.* Unpublished Ph.D. dissertation, Columbia University, 1956.

22. Blume, August G., "The Eastern Front War Episodes of Russian Aviation 1914–1917." *Over the Front Journal USA* 5 (1990), no. 4, 340–55.

23. Bonch-Bruevich, Mikhail Dmitrievich, *From Tsarist General to Red Army Commander.* Moscow: Progress, 1966.

24. Botcharsky, S. and Pier, F., *They Knew How to Die. Being a Narrative of the Personal Experiences of a Red Cross Sister on the Russian Front.* London: Peter Davies, 1931.

25. Botkin, Gleb, *The Real Romanovs.* New York: Fleming H. Revell, 1931.

26. Brasol, Boris, *The Reign of Emperor Nicholas II (1894–1917) in Facts and Figures: A Reply to the Slanderers of Imperial Russia and the Martyred Czar Nicholas II,* 1st ed. New York: All-Russian Monarchist Front, 1959); 2nd rev. ed. Bridgeport, CT: The Order of Imperial Russian Union, 1975. [Pamphlet]

27. Breemer, Jan, *Soviet Submarines. Design, Development and Tactics.* London: Jane's Information Group, 1989. Especially chapters 1–2.

28. Browder, Robert Paul, and Kerensky, Alexander F., eds., *The Russian Provisional Government, 1917: Documents.* 3 vols. Stanford, CA: Hoover Institute, 1961.

29. Brusilov (Brussilov), Aleksei Aleksievich, *A Soldier's Note-Book, 1914–1918.* London, 1930. Reissued: Westport, CT: Greenwood, 1971. In French: *Memoirs du General Broussilov. Guerre 1914–1918.* Paris: Payot, 1929.

30. Buchanan, George [Sir], *My Mission to Russia and Other Diplomatic Memories.* 2 vols. Boston: Little, Brown and Co., 1923. Republished, 2 vols. in one, New York: Arno Press, 1970.

31. Budennyi (Budyonny), S. M., *The Path of Valour.* Moscow: Progress, 1972.

32. Bushnell, John, "Peasants in Uniform: The Tsarist Army as a Peasant Society." *Journal of Social History* 13 (Summer 1980), no. 4, 565–76.

33. Bushnell, John. "The Tsarist Officer Corps, 1881–1914: Customs, Duty, Inefficiency," *American Historical Review* 86 (October 1981), no. 4, 753–80.

34. Buxhoeveden, Sophie, Baroness, *The Life and Tragedy of Alexandra Feodorovna, Empress of Russia. A Biography.* London-New York: Longmans, Green, 1928.

35. Cantacuzene (nee Grant), Princess, *Revolutionary Days. Recollections of Romanoffs and Bolsheviki, 1914–1917*. London: Chapman and Hall, 1920.

36. Cherniavsky, Michael, ed., *Prologue to Revolution: Notes of A. N. Iakhontov on the Secret Meetings of the Council of Ministers, 1915*. Englewood Cliffs, NJ: Prentice-Hall, 1967.

37. Chernov, Viktor, *The Great Russian Revolution*. Trans. and abridged Philip E. Moseley. New Haven: Yale, 1936.

38. Churchill, Rogers Platt, *The Anglo-Russian Convention of 1907*. Cedar Rapids, IA: Torch Press, 1939.

39. Churchill, Winston S., *The Unknown War: The Eastern Front*. New York: Charles Scribner's, 1932.

40. Clark, Alan, *Suicide of the Empires: The Battles on the Eastern Front 1914–1918*. London: BPC Unit; 1971.

41. Cockfield, Jamie H., *The Union Sacre: Tsarism and the Constitutional Democratic Party, 1914–1917*. Unpublished Ph.D. dissertation: University of Virginia, 1972.

42. Cohen, T., "Wartime Profits of Russian Industry, 1914–1916," *Political Science Quarterly* 58 (June 1943), 217–38.

43. Collins, David N., "The Franco-Russian Alliance and Russian Railways, 1891–1914." *Historical Journal* (December 1973), no. 16/4, 747–88.

44. Coonrod, Robert W., *The Fourth Duma and the War, 1914–1917*. Unpublished Ph.D. dissertation, 1950.

45. Crawford, Rosemary, and Crawford, Michael, *Michael and Natasha: The Life and Love of Michael II, the Last of the Romanov Tsars*. New York: E. Drew/Scribner's, 1997.

46. Cromie, F. N. A., *Letters on Russian Affairs from Captain F. N. A. Cromie, G.B., D.S.O., R.N.* N.p. [London]: Private; 1919). Letters from 1916–1918, with those for 1917 being republished in David R. Jones, ed., Documents on British Relations with Russia, 1917–1918: F. N. A. Cromie's Letters," *Canadian-American Slavic Studies,* 7 (Fall 1973), no. 3, 350–375; (Winter 1973), no. 4, 498–511.

47. Curtiss, John Shelton, *Church and State in Russia. The Last Years of the Empire, 1900–1917*. New York: Columbia University, 1940.

48. Dallin, Alexander, *Russian Diplomacy and Eastern Europe, 1914–1917*. New York: King's Crown Press, 1963.

49. Danilov, Yuri N., "La decomposition de l'armee Russe au debut de la revolution," *Revue des deux mondes,* 60 (1930), 66–93.

50. Danilov, Yuri N., *La Russie dans la guerre mondiale, 1914–1917*. Paris: Payot, 1927.

51. Debo, Richard K., *Revolution and Survival: The Soviet Policy of Soviet Russia 1917–18*. Liverpool: Liverpool University, 1979.

52. Dehn, Lili, *The Real Tsaritsa*. London: Thornton, Butterworth, 1922; Boston: Little, Brown, 1932.

53. de Jong, Alex, *The Life and Times of Grigorii Rasputin*. New York: Coward, McCann and Geoghegan, 1982.

54. Denikin, Anton I., *The Russian Turmoil*. London: Hutchinson, 1922.

55. Denikin, Anton I., *The Career of a Tsarist Officer: Memoirs, 1872–1916*. Trans. M. Patoski. Minneapolis: University of Minnesota, 1975.

56. Dillon, E. J., *The Eclipse of Russia*. London: J. M. Dent & Sons, 1918.

57. Dobranitskii, M., *Sistematicheskii ukazatel literatury po istorii russkoi revoliutsii*. Moscow-Leningrad: Gosizdat, 1926.

58. Dobrorolski, Sergei, *Die Mobilmachung der russischen Armee 1914*. Berlin: Deutsche Verlagsgesellschaft für politik und geschichte, 1922.

59. Dobson, Christopher, *Prince Felix Yusupov. The Man Who Killed Rasputin*. London: Harrap, 1989.

60. Doroshevitch, V., *The Way of the Cross*. London: Constable, 1916.

61. Duignan, Peter, ed., *The Library of the Hoover Institution on War, Revolution and Peace*. Stanford, CA: Hoover Institution; 1985.

62. Dupuy, Trevor N., *1914: The Battles in the East.* New York: Franklin Watts, 1967.

63. Dupuy, Trevor N., and Onacewicz, Woldzimiez, *Triumphs and Tragedies in the East, 1915–1917.* New York: Franklin Watts, 1967.

64. Dumesnil, Alexandra, and Lerat, Wilfrid, *Catalogue methodique du Fonds Russe de la Bibliotheque.* Paris: Societe de l'Histoire de la Guerre, 1932.

65. Durkota, Alan, Darcey, Thomas, and Kulikov, Victor, *The Imperial Russian Air Service. Famous Pilots and Aircraft of World War I.* Mountain View, CA: Flying Machine Press, 1995.

66. Eddy, Eleanor Madeleine, *The Last President of the Duma: A Political Biography of M. V. Rodzianko.* Unpublished Ph.D. dissertation: Kansas State University, 1975.

67. Edelman, Robert, *Gentry Politics on the Eve of the Russian Revolution: The Nationalist Party, 1907–1917.* New Brunswick: Rutgers University, 1980.

68. Erickson, John, "The Origins of the Red Army." In Richard Pipes, ed., *Revolutionary Russia.* New York, Columbia University, 1969, 224–56.

69. Erickson, John, "The Russian Imperial/Soviet General Staff," *College Station Papers No. 3.* College Station, TX: Center for Strategic Technology, Texas A&M University, 1981.

70. Essad-Bey, Mohammed [pseudonym], *Nicholas II: Prisoner of the Purple.* Trans. P. M. and Elsa Brandan. New York and London: Funk & Wagnalls, 1937.

71. Evans, Geoffrey, *Tannenberg, 1410/1914.* London: Hamish Hamilton, 1970.

72. Farmborough, Florence, *Nurse at the Russian Front: A Diary, 1914–18.* London: Constable, 1974.

73. Farrar, L. L., Jr., " 'This Unfathomable Sphinx': German Efforts during 1916 to Conclude a Separate Peace with Russia," *New Review of East-European History* 15 (June 1975), no. 1/2, 65–90.

74. Fedorchenko, Sofia, *Der Russe redet: Aufzeichnungen der Krankenschwester Sofja Fedortschenko nach dem Srenogramm.* Trans. Alexander Eliasberg. Heidelberg: Verlag Lambert Schneider, 1961. Reissue of 1923 edition.

75. Fedotoff White, D., *Survival through War and Revolution in Russia.* London-Philadelphia: Oxford/Pennsylvania University Press, 1939.

76. Fedyshyn, Oleh S., *Germany's Drive to the East and the Ukrainian Revolution, 1917–1918.* New Brunswick: Rutgers University, 1971.

77. Feldman, Robert S., "The Russian General Staff and the June 1917 Offensive," *Soviet Studies,* 19 (1968), no. 4, 526–43.

78. Fellows, Thomas, "Politics and the War Effort in Russia: The Union of Zemstvos and the Organization of Food Supply, 1914–1916," *Slavic Review* 37 (1978), no. 1, 71–87.

79. Ferro, Marc, *Nicholas II: The Last of the Tsars.* London: Oxford, 1991.

80. Ferro, Marc, *The Russian Revolution of February 1917.* Trans. J. R. Richards. London: Routledge and Kegan Paul, 1972.

81. Ferro, Marc, "The Russian Soldier in 1917: Undisciplined, Patriotic and Revolutionary," *Slavic and East European Review* 30 (1971), 483–512.

82. Finnegan, Edward H., *The United States Policy toward Russia, March 1911–March 1918.* Unpublished Ph.D. dissertation, Fordham University, 1947.

83. Fischer, Kurt, *Deutsche Truppen und Entente-Intervention in Sudrussland 1918/19.* Boppard am Rhein: Harald Boldt Verlag, 1973.

84. Florinsky, Michael T., *The End of the Russian Empire.* New Haven: Yale University, 1931. Republished with new introduction. New York: Collier Books, 1961.

85. Florinsky, Michael T., "The Russian Mobilization in 1914." *Political Science Quarterly* 42 (June 1927), 203–27.

86. France. Ministere des affaires etrangeres. *Documents diplomatiques l'Alliance Franco-Russe.* Paris, 1918.

87. Francis, David R., *Russia from the American Embassy.* New York: Scribner's Sons, 1928.

88. Fuhrmann, Joseph T., *Rasputin: A Life.* New York: Praeger, 1990.

89. Fuller, William C., Jr., "Imperial Russia." In: Ernest R. May, ed., *Knowing One's Enemies. Intelligence Assessment before the Two World Wars.* Princeton: Princeton University, 1984, 98–126.

90. Fuller, William C., Jr., *Strategy and Power in Russia, 1600–1914.* New York: Free Press, 1992.

91. Fuller, William C., Jr., *Civil-Military Conflict in Imperial Russia, 1881–1914.* Princeton: Princeton University, 1985.

92. Fullop-Miller, Rene, *Rasputin, the Holy Devil.* Translated by F. Flint and D. Tait. New York: Doubleday, 1928.

93. Gardiner, A. G., *The War Lords.* London: J. M. Dent, 1917.

94. Gatrell, Peter, *A Whole Empire Walking: Refugees in Russia during World War I.* Bloomington, IN: Indiana University, 1999.

95. Gatrell, Peter, "Defense Industries in Tsarist Russia, 1908–1913: Production, Employment and Military Procurement," in Linda Edmondson and Peter Waldron, eds., *Economy and Society in Russia and the Soviet Union, 1860–1930. Essays for Olga Crisp.* Houndmills, UK: Macmillan, 1992, 131–51.

96. Gatrell, Peter, *Government, Industry and Rearmament in Russia, 1900–1914: The Last Argument of Tsarism.* Cambridge, UK: Cambridge University, 1994.

97. Gatrell, Peter, *The Tsarist Economy, 1850–1917.* London: Batsford, 1986.

98. George, Mark, and Sheppard, Vic, "Russia's Air Forces in War and Revolution." *Cross and Cockade Journal GB,* 17 (1985), no. 4, 145–53; 18 (1987), no. 2, 49–54.

99. Gering, Aleksei, *Materialy k bibliografii russkoi voennoi pechati za rubezhom.* Paris: "Voennaia Byl," 1968.

100. Gierson, Philip, *Books on Soviet Russia, 1917–1942: A Bibliography and a Guide to Reading.* London: Methuen, 1943.

101. Gilliard, Pierre, *Thirteen Years at the Russian Court.* Trans. F. Appleby Holt. London: Hutchinson, 1921. New York: Doran, 1921. In French: Gilliard, Pierre, *La tragique destin de Nicolas II et de sa famille.* Paris: Payot, 1922.

102. Gleason, William E., *Alexander Guchkov and the End of the Russian Empire.* Philadelphia: Pennsylvania State University, 1983.

103. Gleason, William E., *The All-Russian Union of Towns and All-Russian Union of Zemstvos in World War I: 1914–1918.* Unpublished Ph.D. dissertation: Indiana University, 1972.

104. Golder, Frank Alfred, ed., *Documents of Russian History, 1914–1917,* translated by Emanuel Aronsberg. New York-London: Century Co., 1927. Reprint: Gloucester, MA: Peter Smith, 1964.

105. Goldstein, Edward Ralph, *Military Aspects of Russian Industrialization: The Defense Industries, 1890–1917.* Unpublished Ph.D. dissertation: Case Western Reserve University, 1971.

106. Golovin, Nikolai N., "Brusilov's Offensive," *Slavonic and East European Review* 13 (April, 1935), 571–96.

107. Golovin, Nikolai N., *The Russian Campaign of 1914.* Translated by A. G. S. Muntz. Fort Leavenworth: Command and General Staff School, 1933.

108. Golovin, Nikolai N., "The Great Battle of Galacia (1914), *Slavonic and East European Review,* V (June 1926), 25–47.

109. Golovin, Nicholas N., *The Russian Army in the World War.* New Haven: Yale University, 1931.

110. Golovin, Nikolai N., "The Russian War Plan of 1914," *Slavonic and East European Review,* XIV (1936), April 564–84; July 70–90.

111. Golub, P. A., *The Bolsheviks and the Armed Forces in Three Revolutions: Problems and Experience of Military Work.* Moscow: Progress, 1979.

112. Gorbatov, A. V., *Years Off My Life: The Memoirs of General of the Soviet Army A. V. Gorbatov.* London: Constable, 1964.

113. Gorky, M., Molotov, V., et al., eds., *History of the Civil war in the USSR* 1: *Preparation of the Great Proletarian Revolution (From the Beginning of the War to the Beginning of October 1917).* Moscow: International Publishers, 1935. Numerous subsequent editions in Russian, English, and other languages.

114. Graevenitz, P., Baron, *From Autocracy to Bolshevism.* London: Allen and Unwin, 1918.

115. Graf, Daniel William, "Military Rule Behind the Russian Front, 1914–1917: The Political Ramifications," *Jahrbucher fur Geschiichte Osteoropas* 20 (1974), no. 3, 390–411.

116. Graf, Daniel William, *The Reign of the Generals: Military Government in Western Russia, 1914–1915.* Unpublished Ph.D. Dissertation: University of Nebraska, 1972.

117. Graf, G., *La Marine russe dans la Guerre et dans la Revolution, 1914–1918.* Paris: Payot, 1928.

118. Graham, Stephen, *Russia in 1916.* New York: MacMillan, 1917.

119. Gray, Pauline, *The Grand Duke's Woman.* London: Macdonald, 1976.

120. Great War Society, *The Imperial Russian Army in World War I.* Papers presented to the Tenth Annual Seminar, Philadelphia, PA, 27–29 April 2001, on CD-ROM. Stanford, CA: Great War Society, 2001.

121. Great War Society, *The Russian Civil War, 1917–1921.* Papers presented to the Eleventh Annual Seminar, Boston, MA, 26–28 April 2002, on CD-ROM. Stanford, CA: Great War Society, 2002.

122. Greger, Rene, *Die Russische Flotte im Ersten Weltkrieg 1914–17.* Munich: J. F. Lehmanns Verlag, 1972. Translated by Jill Gearing as *The Russian Fleet, 1914–1917.* London: Ian Allen, 1972.

123. Greicus, Elizabeth A. McK., *Efforts of the Progressive Bloc to Influence the Conduct of the War in Russia, 1915–1917.* Unpublished Ph.D. dissertation, Tulane University, 1969.

124. Gronsky, Paul P., and Astrov, Nicholas J., *The War and the Russian Government.* New Haven: Yale University, 1929.

125. Grunt, A., "Russia at War." In *History of the 20th Century.* Bristol, UK, 1970, no. 25, 674–83.

126. Grunwald, Constantin de. *Le Tsar Nicholas II.* Paris: Berger-Levrault, 1965.

127. Guins, George C., *Impressions of the Russian Imperial Government.* Oral history interview conducted by Richard A. Pierce. Berkeley, CA: Bancroft Library, 1971.

128. Gurko (Gourko), Vladimir I., *Features and Figures of the Past: Government and Opinion in the Reign of Nicholas II.* Translated by Laura Matveev. Edited by J. E. Wallace Sterling, Xenia Joukoff Eudin and H. H. Fisher. Stanford, CA: Hoover Institute, 1939. Reprinted New York: Russell & Russell, 1970.

129. Gurko (Gourko), Vasili (Basil) I., *Memoirs and Impressions of War and Revolution in Russia, 1914–1917.* London-New York: Lane/Macmillan, 1918–1919.

130. Hahlweg, Werner, ed., *Der Friede von Brest-Litowsk.* Dusseldorf: Droste Verlag, 1971.

131. Haimson, Leopold, "The Problem of Social Stability in Urban Russia, 1905–1917." *Slavic Review* 23 (1964), 619–42; 24 (1965), 1–22.

132. Hamm, Michael F., "Liberal Politics in Wartime Russia: An Analysis of the Progressive Bloc," *Slavic Review* 33 (September 1975), no. 3, 453–68.

133. Hamm, Michael F., *The Progressive Bloc of Russia's Fourth Duma.* Unpublished Ph.D. dissertation: Indiana University, 1971.

134. Hanbury-Williams, John, *The Empress Nicholas II as I Knew Him.* London: Humphreys, 1922.

135. Hardesty, V., and Sikorskii G., *Igor Sikorskii: The Russian Years.* Seattle: University of Washington, 1988.

136. Harmer, Michael, *The Forgotten Hospital. An Essay.* Chichester: Springwood Books, 1982.

137. Harrison, Richard W., "Alexander Samsonov and the Battle of Tannenberg, 1914." In: Brian Bond, ed., *Fallen Stars. Eleven Studies of Twentieth Century Military Disasters.* London: Brassey's; 1991, 13–28.

138. Heenan, Louise Erwin, *Russian Democracy's Fatal Blunder: The Summer Offensive of 1917.* New York: Praeger, 1987.

139. Hennicke, Otto, et al., *Militarismus gegen Sowjetmacht 1917 bis 1919. Das Fiasko der ersten antisowjetischen Aggression des deutschen Militarismus.* Berlin: Deutscher Militarverlag, 1967.

140. Hermann, David Gaius, *The Arming of Europe and the Making of the First World War.* Princeton: Princeton University, 1996.

141. Herwig, Holger H., *The First World War. Germany and Austria-Hungary, 1914–1918.* London: Arnold, 1997.

142. Hosking, Geoffrey A., "Rasputin and the Dark Forces." In *History of the 20th Century,* (Bristol, UK, 1970), no. 25, 698–91.

143. Hosking, Geoffrey A., *The Russian Constitutional Experiment. Government and Duma 1907–1914.* Cambridge, UK: Cambridge University, 1973.

144. Howard, Harry N., *The Partition of Turkey, 1913–1923.* Norman, OK: University of Oklahoma, 1931.

145. Ignat'ev, Aleksei A., *A Subaltern in Old Russia.* London: Hutchinson, 1944.

146. Ignatieff (Ignatiev), Paul N., Odinetz, Dimitry M., and Novgorotsev, Paul J., *Russian Schools and Universities in the World War.* New Haven: Yale University, 1929.

147. Ipat'ev (Ipatiev), Vladimir N., *Life of a Chemist: Memoirs.* Trans. V. Haensel and R. H. Lusher. Stanford: Stanford University; 1946.

148. Ironside, Edmund (Sir), *Tannenberg: The First Thirty Days in East Prussia.* Edinburgh: William Blackwood, 1933.

149. Jahn, Hubertus F., *Patriotic Culture in Russia during World War I.* Ithaca: Cornell University, 1995.

150. Johnston, Robert H., *Continuity versus Revolution: The Russian Provisional Government and the Balkans, March–November 1917.* Unpublished Ph.D. dissertation, Yale University, 1966.

151. Jones, David R., "Administrative and Policy-Making System." In: *Military Encyclopedia of Russia and Eurasia* (cited hereafter as MERE), II, 34–169.

152. Jones, David R., "Aerial Armament (Aviatsionnoe Vooruzhenie)." In MERE, V, 63–191 (especially pp. 67–98).

153. Jones, David R., "From Imperial to Red Army: The Rise and Fall of the Bolshevik Military Tradition." In Carl Reddel, ed., *Transformation in Russian and Soviet Military History.* Washington, DC: U.S. Air Force Academy, 1990, 61–74.

154. Jones, David R., *Imperial Russia's Armed Forces at War, 1914–1917: An Analysis of Combat Effectiveness.* Ph.D. dissertation: Dalhousie University, 1986. Published in an edited form as "Imperial Russia's Forces at War," in A. R. Millet and W. Murray, eds., *Military Effectiveness.* 3 vols. London and Boston: Allen and Unwin, 1988, I: *The First World War,* 429–328.

155. Jones, David R., *Mobility and Advanced Units in Russian and Soviet Military Thought and Practice, 1870–1985.* Gulf Breeze, FL: Academic International Press, 1985.

156. Jones, David R., "Nicholas II and the Supreme Command: An Investigation of Motives." In: Study Group on the Russian Revolution, *Sbornik 11.* Durham, UK, 1985, 47–83.

157. Jones, David R., "The Beginnings of Russian Air Power, 1907–1922." In R. Higham and J. Kipp, eds. *Soviet Aviation and Air Power: A Historical View.* London and Boulder, CO: Brassey's and Westview, 1977/1978.

158. Jones, David R., "The Imperial Army in World War I, 1914–1917," in Frederick W. Kagan and Robert Higham, eds., *The Military History of Tsarist Russia.* New York: St. Martin's Press/Palgrave, 2002, 227–48.

159. Jones, David R., "The Imperial Russian Life Guards Grenadier Regiment, 1906–1917: The Disintegration of an Elite Unit," *Military Affairs* 33 (October 1969), no. 2, 289–301.

160. Jones, David R., ed., *The Military Encyclopedia of Russia and Eurasia,* formerly *The Military-Naval Encyclopedia of Russia and the Soviet Union.* Gulf Breeze, FL: Academic International Press, 1978. 8 volumes to date.

161. Jones, David R., "The Officers and the October Revolution," *Soviet Studies* XXVIII (April 1976), no. 2, pp. 207–23.

162. Jukes, Geoffrey, *Carpathian Disaster: The Death of an Army.* New York: Ballantine, 1971.

163. Kalmykov, A. D., *Memoirs of a Russian Diplomat: Outposts of Empire, 1893–1917.* New Haven: Yale University, 1971.

164. Katkov, George, "German Political Intervention in Russia During World War I." In Richard Pipes, ed., *Revolutionary Russia.* New York: Columbia University, 1969, 63–93.

165. Katkov, George, *Russia 1917: The February Revolution.* London: Longmans, 1967.

166. Katkov, George, *Russia 1917: The Kornilov Affair. Kerensky and the Break-up of the Russian Army.* London: Longman, 1980.

167. Kayden, Eugene M., and Antsiferov, Alexis N., *The Cooperative Movement in Russia during the War.* New Haven: Yale University, 1929.

168. Kearsey, Alexander H. C., *A Study of the Strategy and Tactics of the East Prussian Campaign, 1914.* London: Sifton, Praed, & Company; 1932.

169. Keep, John L. H., "The Military Style of the Romanov Rulers." *War & Society* 1 (September 1983), no. 2, 61–84.

170. Kenez, Peter, "A Profile of the Prerevolutionary Officer Corps." *California Slavic Studies* (1973), no. 8, 121–58.

171. Kenez, Peter, "Autocracy and the Russian Army." *Russian Review* 13 (July 1974), no. 5, 201–05.

172. Kenez, Peter, "Changes in the Social Composition of the Officer Corps during World War I," *Russian Review* (October 1972), pp. 369–75.

173. Kennan, George, "The Breakdown of the Tsarist Autocracy." In Richard Pipes, ed., *Revolutionary Russia.* New York: Columbia University, 1969, pp. 1–19.

174. Kennan, George F., *The Fateful Alliance: France, Russia, and the Coming of the First World War.* New York: Pantheon Books, 1984.

175. Kerenskii, Alexander F., *Delo kornilova.* Moscow: "Zadruga," 1918, translated as *Prelude to Bolshevism: The Kornilov Rebellion.* New York: Unwin, 1919.

176. Kerensky, Alexander F., *Russia and History's Turning Point.* New York: Duell, Sloane and Pearce, 1965.

177. Kerensky, Alexander F., "Russia on the Eve of World War I," *Russian Review* 5, no. 1 (1945), 10–30.

178. Kerensky, Alexander F., *The Cruxification of Liberty.* New York: John Day, 1934.

179. Kerensky, Alexander F., "Why the Russian Monarchy Fell," *Slavonic and East European Review* 8 (March 1930), 496–513.

180. Kerner, Robert J., "Russia, the Straits and Constantinople, 1914–1915," *Journal of Modern History* 1 (September 1929), 400–15.

181. Kerner, Robert J., "Russia and the Straits Question, 1915–1917," *Slavonic and East European Review* 8 (March 1930), 589–600.

182. Kettle, Michael, *The Allies and the Russian Collapse, March 1917–March 1918.* London: Andre Deutsch, 1981.

183. Khmelevskii, G., *Mirovaia imperialisticheskaia voina 1914–18 gg. Sistematicheskii ukazatel'knizhnoi i stateinoi voenno-istoricheskoi literatury za 1914–1935 gg.* Moscow: Voennaia akademiia RKKA im. M.V. Frunze, 1936. Reprinted by Oriental Research Partners, London, 1973.

184. Kilcoyne, Martin, *The Political Influence of Rasputin.* Ph.D. Dissertation, University of Washington, 1961.

185. Kilmarx, Robert A., "The Imperial Air Forces in World War I." *Airpower Historian* 10 (July 1963), no. 3, 90–95.

186. King, Greg, *The Last Empress: The Life and Times of Alexandra Fedorovna, Tsarsina of Russia.* New York: Birch Lane, 1994.

187. King, Greg, *The Man Who Killed Rasputin. Prince Felix Youssoupov and the Murder that Helped Bring Down the Russian Empire.* New York: Birch Lane, 1995.

188. Kipp, Jacob W., "The Beginning: Imperial Russian and Soviet Mobile Warfare to 1920." Section I in: Historical Analysis of the Use of Mobile Forces by Russia and the USSR," *Occasional Papers Series No. 10.* College Station, TX: Center for Strategic Technology, Texas A & M University, 1985, 15–115.

189. Kleinmichel, (Countess), *Memoirs of a Shipwercked World*. Trans. Vivian le Grand. London: Bretano's, 1923.

190. Knox, Alfred W. F., *With the Russian Army, 1914–1917*. 2 vols. in one. New York: Arno Press, 1971. Reprint of two-volume London, 1921, edition.

191. Kohn, Stanislas, and Meyendorf, Alexander F. (Baron), *The Cost of the War to Russia*. New Haven: Yale, 1932. Reissued: New York: Howard Fertig, 1973.

192. Kokovtsov, Vladimir N., *The Memoirs of Count Kokovtsov: Out of My Past*. Translated by Laura Matveev and edited by H. H. Fisher. Stanford, CA: Hoover Institution, 1935.

193. Kournakoff, Serge, *Savage Squadrons*. London: Harrap, 1936.

194. Krasnov, Pavel N., *From Double-Headed Eagle to Red Flag*. New York: Duffield and Company, 1926.

195. Kulikov, Viktor, "Chronicle of the Operations of the 1st Corps of the Imperial Russian Air Service, 1914–1917." *Over the Front Journal USA* 10 (1995), no. 2, 149–61.

196. Kurenberg, Joachim von, *Russlands Weg nach Tannenberg*. Berlin: Universitas; 1934.

197. Kurlov, Pavel G., *Das End des russischen Kaisertums. Personliche Erinnerungen des Chefs der russischen Geheimpolizei, Generals der Kavallerie Komaroff-Kurloff*. Berlin: A. Scherl 1929.

198. Lambsdorff, Gustav Graf von, *Die Militarbevollmachtigten Kaiser Wilhelms II. am Zarenhofe, 1904–1914*. Berlin: Schlieffen, 1937.

199. Lambert, Dean W., *The Deterioration of the Imperial Russian Army in the First World War, August 1914–March 1917*. Unpublished Ph.D. dissertation: University of Kentucky, 1975.

200. Laney, F. M., *The Military Implementation of the Russian Alliance, 1890–1914*. Unpublished Ph.D. dissertation, University of Virginia, 1975.

201. Layman, R. D., "Euxine Wings—Russian Shipboard Aviation in the Black Sea: 1913–1917." *Cross and Cockade Journal USA* 15 (1974), no. 2, 143–78.

202. Lebedev, V. V., "A Contribution to the Historiography of the Problem of Russia's Leaving the War on the Eve of the February Revolution." *Soviet Studies in History* 11 (Fall 1972), no. 2, 178–92.

203. Legras, Jules, *Memoires de Russie*. Paris: Payot, 1921.

204. Legras, Jules, "Souvenirs sur la Guerre en Russe," *Revue d'Histoire de la Guerre* 11 (Paris, 1933), 222–39.

205. Lehovich, Dimitry V., *White Against Red: The Life of General Anton Denikin*. New York: Norton, 1974.

206. Lethbridge, M. C., *Russian Chaps*. London: John Lane, 1916.

207. Lieven, Dominic C. B., *Nicholas II: Emperor of All the Russias*. London, John Murray; 1993.

208. Lieven, Dominic C. B., *Russian and the Origins of the First World War*. New York-London: St. Martin's Press/Macmillan, 1983. Corrected edition 1984.

209. Lieven, Dominic C. B., *Russia's Rulers under the Old Regime*. New Haven: Yale University; 1989.

210. Lincoln, W. Bruce, *In War's Dark Shadow*. New York: Dial, 1983.

211. Lincoln, W. Bruce, *Passage Through Armageddon: The Russians in War and Revolution, 1914–1918*. New York: Simon and Schuster, 1986.

212. Littauer, Vladimir, *Russian Hussar*. London: J. A. Allen, 1965.

213. Lobannov-Rostovsky, A., *The Grinding Mill*. New York: Macmillan; 1935.

214. Lockhart, Robert Bruce, *Memoirs of a British Agent*. London: Macmillan, 1938.

215. Lockhart, Robin Bruce, *The Diaries of Sir Robert Bruce Lockhart*. I: *1915–1938*. Ed. Kenneth Young. London: Macmillan, 1973.

216. Lomonosov, George V., *Memoirs of the Russian Revolution*. Trans. D. H. Dubrowsky and Robert T. Williams. New York: Rand School of Social Science, 1919.

217. Longley, David A., "Officers and Men: A Study of the Development of Political Attitudes Among the Sailors of the Baltic Fleet in 1917," *Soviet Studies* 25 (July 1973), no. 1, 28–50.

218. Longley, David A., "The February Revolution in the Baltic Fleet at Helsingfors: *Vosstanie* or *Bunt?*" *Canadian Slavonic Papers* 20 (March 1978), no. 1, 1–23.

219. Luckett, Richard, *The White Generals: An Account of the White Movement and the Russian Civil War.* London: Longman, 1971.

220. Lukomskii [Loukomsky], A. S., *Memoirs of the Russian Revolution.* Translated by Mrs. Vitali. London: Allen and Unwin, 1922. Republished: Westport, CT: Hyperion, 1975.

221. Lyons, Marvin, *The Imperial Russian Army: A Bibliography of Regimental Histories and Related Works.* Stanford, CA: Hoover Institution, 1968.

222. Maklakov, Vasilii A., "On the Fall of Tsardom," *Slavonic and East European Review* 18 (July 1939), 73–92. [Discusses B. Pares, *Fall of the Russian Monarchy* (1939).]

223. Mannerhdeim, Gustav, *The Memoirs of Marshal Mannerheim.* Trans. E. Lewenhaupt. New York: Dutton, 1954.

224. Manning, Roberta T., *The Crisis of the Old Order in Russia: Gentry and Government.* Princeton: Princeton University, 1982.

225. Marchand, Rene, ed., *Un livre noire. Diplomatie d'avant guerre a'apres les documents des Archives Russes, 1910–1917.* 3 vols. Paris: Librairie du travail, 1922–34.

226. Marsden, G.V., *Rasputin and Russia. The Tragedy of a Throne.* London: F. Bird, 1920.

227. Marye, George Thomas, *Nearing the End in Imperial Russia.* Philadelphia: Dorrance, 1929.

228. Massie, Robert K., *Nicholas and Alexandra.* New York: Atheneum, 1960.

229. Mathieu, Donald R., *The Role of Russia in French Foreign Policy, 1908–1914.* Unpublished Ph.D. dissertation: Stanford University, 1968.

230. Maylunus, Andrei, and Mironenko, Sergei, *A Lifelong Passion: Nicholas and Alexandra: Their Own Story.* New York: Doubleday, 1997.

231. Mawdsley, Evan, *The Russian Revolution and the Baltic Fleet: War and Politics, February 1917–April 1918.* London: Macmillan, 1978.

232. Mayzel, Matitiahu, "An Army in Transition: The Russian High Command, October 1917– May 1918," *Slavic and Soviet Series, No. 5.* Tel-Aviv: Russian and East European Research Center, September 1976.

233. Mayzel, M., *Generals and Revolutionaries. The Russian General Staff During the Revolution: A Study in the Transformation of Military Elite.* Osnabruck: Biblio Verlag. Studien zur Militargeschichte, Militarwissenshaft and Kobfliktforschung, 1979.

234. Mayzal, M., "The Formation of the Russian General Staff, 1880–1917: A Social Study." *Cahiers du Monde russe et sovietique,* 16 (July-December, 1973), nos. 3–4, 297–321.

235. Mayzel, Matitiahu, *The Russian General Staff during the Revolution.* Unpublished Ph.D. dissertation: University of Rochester, 1975.

236. McCormick, Robert R., *With the Russian Army.* New York: Macmillan, 1915.

237. McNeal, Robert H., *Tsar and Cossack, 1855–1914.* London: Macmillan, 1987.

238. Menning, Bruce W., *Bayonets before Bullets. The Imperial Russian Army, 1861–1914.* Bloomington and Indiana: Indiana University, 1992.

239. Menning, Bruce W., "Mukden to Tannenberg: Defeat to Defeat, 1905–1914," in Frederick W. Kagan and Robert Higham, eds., *The Military History of Tsarist Russia.* New York: St. Martin's Press/Palgrave, 2002, 203–5.

240. Meos, E., "Allies on the Eastern Front." *Cross and Cockade Journal USA,* 10 (1969), no. 4, 314–27.

241. Michelson, Alexander M., Apostol, Paul N. and Bernatzky, Michael W., *Russian Public Finance during the War.* New Haven: Yale University, 1928.

242. Michon, Georges, *The Franco-Russian Alliance, 1891–1917.* London: Allen and Unwin, 1929. Reprint: New York: Howard Fertig, 1969.

243. Miliukov, Pavel N., *Political Memoirs, 1905–1917.* Translated by Carl Goldberg and edited by Arthur P. Mendel. Ann Arbor: University of Michigan, 1967.

244. *Mirovaia voina: ukazatel' literatury.* Leningrad: Bibliotech. metod. baza Leningr. oblprofsoveta. Bibliotech. kollektor Kogiza, 1934.

245. Milsom, John, *Russian Tanks, 1900–1970: The Complete Illustrated History of Soviet Armoured Theory and Design.* New York: Galahad Books, 1970.

246. Mitchell, Donald W., *A History of Russian and Soviet Sea Power.* New York: Macmillan, 1974. Chapters 13–16.

247. Morse, John, *An Englishman in the Russian Ranks. Ten Months' Fighting in Poland.* London: Duckworth, 1915.

248. Mosolov [Mossolov], A. A., *At the Court of the Last Tsar. Being the Memoirs of A. A. Mosolov, Head of the Court Chancellory, 1900–1916.* Trans. E. W. Dickes and ed. A. A. Pilenco. London: Methuen, 1935.

249. Moltchanoff, Victorin M., *The Last White General.* Oral History Interview conducted by Boris Raymond, University of California, Berkeley, 1972.

250. Mouchanow, Marfa, Madame, *My Empress.* New York and London: Lane, 1918.

251. Moynahan, Brian, *Rasputin: The Saint Who Sinned.* New York: Random House, 1997.

252. Murray, Marr, *The Russian Advance.* London and New York: Hodder and Stoughton, 1914.

253. Nabokov, Konstantin, *Ordeal of a Diplomat.* London: Duckworth, 1921.

254. Neilson, Keith, *Strategy and Supply: The Anglo-Russian Alliance, 1914–17* London: Allen and Unwin, 1984.

255. Nekliudov, Alexander I., *Diplomatic Remeniscences before and during the World War, 1911–1917.* Trans. Alexandra Paget. London: Murray, 1920.

256. Nekrasov, George, *North of Gallipoli: The Black Sea Fleet at War 1914–1917.* Boulder, CO: East European Monographs, 1992.

257. Nikolaieff, A. M., "The February Revolution and the Russian Army," *Russian Review* 6 (1946), 1, 17–25.

258. Nolde, B. E., *L'Alliance franco-russe. Les Origines du Systeme diplomatique d'Avant-Guerre.* Paris: Institut d'Etudes Slaves, 1936.

259. Nolde, B. E., *Russian in the Economic War.* New Haven: Yale University, 1928.

260. Noskov, A. A., *Le Mystere de Tannenberg.* Paris: Payot, 1935.

261. Noskov, A. A., *Nicholas II inconnu.* Paris: Plon, 1920.

262. Oberlander, Erwin, et al., *Russia Enters the Twentieth Century, 1984–1917.* New York: Schocken Books, 1971.

263. Obolensky, Serge, *One Man in His Time.* New York: McDowell, 1958.

264. Oldenburg, S. S., *Last Tsar. Nicholas II. His Reign and his Russia.* 4 vols. Translated and edited by Patrick J. Rollins with Leonid I. Mihalap. Gulf Breeze, FL: Academic International Press, 1978. Volume 4 covers 1914–1918.

265. Paleologue, Georges Maurice, *Alexandra-Feodorowna, imperatrice de Russie.* Paris: Plon, 1932.

266. Paleologue, Georges Maurice, *La Russie des Tsars pendant la Grande Guerre.* 3 vols. Paris: Plon, 1922. Published in English as *An Ambassador's Memoirs.* 3 vols. London: Hutchinson, 1923–1925.

267. Paley (Palei), Princess (Morhange, Zinaida), *Memoirs of Russia, 1916–1919.* London: Jenkins, 1924.

268. Palm, Charles G., and Reed, Dale, *Guide to the Hoover Institution Archives.* Stanford: Hoover Institution, 1980.

269. Palmer, Alan, *The Gardeners of Salonika.* London: Andre Deutsch, 1965.

270. Pares, Bernard, Sir, *A Wandering Student: The Story of a Purpose.* New York: Syracuse University, 1948.

271. Pares, Bernard, Sir, *Day by Day with the Russian Army.* Boston and New York, Constable, 1915.

272. Pares, Bernard, "Alexander Guchkov," *Slavonic and East European Review* 15 (July 1936), 121–34.

273. Pares, Bernard, "Rasputin and the Empress: Authors of the Russian Collapse," *Foreign Affairs* VI (1927), 140–54.

274. Pares, Bernard, Sir, *My Russian Memoirs.* London, 1931. Reprinted: New York: AMS Press, 1969.

275. Pares, Bernard, *The Fall of the Russian Monarchy.* (London, 1931; New York: Alfred A. Knopf, 1939; New York: Vintage, 1961.

276. Pascal, Pierre, *Mon Journal de Russie a la Mission Militaire Francaise, 1916–1918.* Lausanne: Editions l'Age d'Homme, 1975.

277. Patoski, Margaret, *The Career of a Russian Officer: The Memoirs of General A. I. Denikin, an Annotated Translation from the Russian.* Unpublished Ph.D. dissertation, Texas Christian University, 1973.

278. Pavlovsky, G. P., *Agricultural Russia on the Eve of the Revolution.* London: G. Routledge, 1930.

279. Pearlstein, Edward W., ed., *Revolution in Russia! As Reported by the New York Tribune and the New York Herald, 1894–1921.* New York: Viking, 1967.

280. Pearson, Raymond, *The Russian Moderates and the Crisis of Tsarism, 1914–1918.* London: Macmillan, 1977.

281. Perrett, Bryan, and Lord, Anthony, *The Czar's British Squadron.* London: William Kimber, 1981.

282. Petrone, Karen, "Family, Masculinity, and Heroism in Russian War Posters of the First World War" in Billie Melman, ed. *Borderlines: Genders and Identities in War and Peace, 1870–1930.* New York–London: Routledge, 1998, 95–115.

283. Phenix, Patricia, *Olga Romanov, Russia's Last Grand Duchess* (Toronto-London: Viking-Penguin, 1999).

284. Phillimore, Richard E., Sir, "Kolchak. Arctic Explorer, Russian Admiral, and Siberian Dictator," *Naval Review* 24 (May 1936), 2, 474–79; (August), 3, 489–94; (November), 4, 659–65; 25 (February 1937), 1, 133–35; (May), 2, 312–17.

285. Phillimore, Richard F., Sir, "Some Russian Experiences, 1915–16," *Naval Review* 22 (May 1935), 2, 351–60; (August), 3, 487–94; (November), 4, 692–700; 24 (February, 1936), 1, 92–99; (May) 2, 320–27; (August), 3, 489–94; (November), 4, 679–84; 25 (February 1937), 1, 126–32; (May), 2, 306–17; (August), 3, 534–41.

286. Pipes, Richard, *The Russian Revolution 1899–1919.* London: Collins Harvill, 1990.

287. Poitevin, Pierre, *Une Bataille au centre de la France en 1917.* Limoges: Impr. Soc. des Journaux & Publ. du Centre, 1937.

288. Poliakoff, Vladimir, *The Empress Marie of Russia and Her Times.* London: Thornton, 1926.

289. Polner, T. J., Obolensky, V. A. (Prince), and Turin, S. P., *Russian Local Government During the War.* New Haven: Yale University, 1930.

290. Polovtsov (Polovtsoff), P. A., *Glory and Downfall. Reminiscences of a Russian General Staff Officer,* London: Bell, 1935.

291. Portal, Roger, *La Russie industrielle de 1881 a 1927.* Paris: Centre de Documentation universitaire, 1926.

292. Pourtales, F., Count, *Mes dernieres Negociations a Saint-Petersbourg en juillet 1914.* Paris: Payot, 1929.

293. Poutiatine, Olga, *War and Revolution: Excerpts from the Letters and Diaries of Countess Olga Poutiatine.* Trans. and ed. by G. A. Lensen. Tallahassee: Diplomatic Press, n.d. [c. 1971].

294. Purishkevich [Pourichkevitch], Vladimir M., *Comme j'ai tue Raspoutine* Paris, 1923. In English: *The End of Rasputin.* Ann Arbor: Ardis Press, 1985.

295. Radzinsky, Edward, *The Last Tsar: The Life and Death of Nicholas II,* trans M. Schwartz. New York: Doubleday, 1992.

296. Radzinsky, Edward, *The Rasputin File.* New York: Doubleday, 1999.

297. Radziwill, Catherine, Princess, *Nicholas II: The Last of the Tsars.* London: Cassell, 1931.

298. Radziwill, Catherine, Princess, *Rasputin and the Russian Revolution.* New York: Lane, 1918.

299. Radziwill, Catherine, Princess, *The Intimate Life of the Last Tsarina.* London: Cassell, 1929.

300. Ray, Oliver Allen, "The Imperial Russian Army Officer." *Political Science Quarterly,* 76 (December 1961), no. 4, 575–90.

301. Reed, John, *The War in Eastern Europe.* New York: Boni & Liveright, 1919.

302. Riaboff, Alexander, *Gatchina Days: Reminiscences of a Russian Pilot,* ed. Von Hardesty. Washington, DC: Smithsonian, 1986.

303. Rich, David Alan, *The Tsar's Colonels: Professionalism, Strategy, and Subversion in Late Imperial Russia.* Cambridge: Harvard University, 1998.

304. Riha, Thomas, *A Russian European: Paul Miliukov in Russian Politics.* Notre Dame: Notre Dame University, 1969.

305. Riha, Thomas, "Miliukov and the Progressive Bloc in 1915: A Study in Last-Chance Politics," *Journal of Modern History* 32 (March 1960), 16–24.

306. Rodzianko, Mikhail V., *The Reign of Rasputin: An Empire's Collapse.* Trans. Catherine Zvegintoff. London: Philpot; 1927. Reissue: Hattiesburg, MS: Academic International Press, 1973, with a new introduction by David R. Jones.

307. Rodzianko (Rodzyanko), Paul, *Tattered Banners: An Autobiography.* 2nd ed. London: Seeley Service, 1939.

308. Rogger, Hans, *Russia in the Age of Modernization and Revolution, 1881–1917.* London: Longmans, 1983.

309. Rogger, Hans, "Russia in 1914." *Journal of Contemporary History* 1 (1966), 95–119.

310. Rollins, Patrick J., "Searching for the Last Tsar." In Oldenburg, *Last Tsar: Nicholas II, His Reign and His Russia,* 1, xiv–xxxi.

311. Romanov, Aleksandr Mikhailovich, Grand Duke, *Once a Grand Duke.* New York: Farrar and Rhinehart, 1932.

312. Romanov, Grand Duchess George (Marie Georgieevna), *Memoirs.* New York: Atlantic International Publishers, 1988.

313. Romanov, Marie [Maria Pavlovna], Grand Duchess, *A Princess in Exile.* New York: Viking, 1931.

314. Romanov, Marie [Maria Pavlovna], Grand Duchess, *Things I Remember.* Trans. under ed. supervision of Russell Lord. London: Cassell, 1930. American title: *Education of a Princess. A Memoir.* New York: Viking, 1931.

315. Romanov, Nikolai Mikhailovich, *La Fin du Tsarisme: Lettres inedites a Frederic Masson.* Paris: Bibliotheque Slave, 1969.

316. Rosen, Roman R., Baron, *Forty Years of Diplomacy.* 2 vols. New York: A. A. Knopf, 1922.

317. Rostunov, I. I., *Russkii front pervoi mirovoi voiny.* Moscow: "Nauka," 1976.

318. Roustem-Bek, B., *Aerial Russia.* London: J. Lane Company, 1916.

319. Rudnev, V. M., "The Truth concerning the Russian Imperial Family: Statement by Vladimir Michailovich Roudneff, appointed by Minister of Justice Kerensky." In: A. A. Vyrubova Taneeva), *Memoirs of the Russian Court.* New York: Macmillan, 1923, 383–99.

320. Rutherford, Ward, *The Russian Army in World War I.* London: Gordon Cremonesi, 1975. Revised edition: *The Tsar's War, 1914–1917: The Story of the Imperial Russian Army in the First World War.* Cambridge, UK: I. Faulkner, 1992.

321. Rutman, R. E., comp., *Rossiia v period pervoi mirovoi voiny i fevral'skoi burzhuazno-demokraticheskoi revoliutsii (iiul' 1914-fevral' 1917 g.). Bibliograficheskii ukazatel' sovetskoi literatury, izdannoi v 1953–1968 gg.* Leningrad: BAN, 1975.

322. Sabsay, Nahum, *A Moment of History: A Russian Soldier in the First World War.* Caldwell, ID: Caxton Printers, 1960.

323. Sanborn, Josh, "Conscription, Correspondence, and Politics in Late Imperial Russia," *Russian History/Histoire Russe* 24 (Spring–Summer 1997), no. 1–2, 27–40.

324. Sanborn, Josh, *Drafting the Russian Nation: Military Conscription, Total War, and Mass Politics, 1905–1925.* Forthcoming: DeKalb, IL: Northern Illinois University, forthcoming.

325. Sanborn, Josh, "Riots before Revolution," *Relevance: Journal of the Great War Society* 11 (Winter 2002), no. 1, 9–13.

326. Sanborn, Josh, "The Mobilization of 1914 and the Question of the Russian Nation: A Reexamination," *Slavic Review* 59 (Summer 2000), no. 2, 267–89.

327. Saul, Norman E., "British Involvement in the Kornilov Affair," *Rocky Mountain Social Science Journal* 10 (January, 1973), no. 1, pp. 43–50.

328. Saul, Norman E., *Sailors in Revolt: The Russian Baltic Fleet in 1917.* Lawrence: Regents Press of Kansas, 1978.

329. Savant, Jean, *Epopee russe: Campagne de l'armee Rennenkampf en Prusse-Orientale.* Paris: Calmann-Levy, 1945.

330. Sazonov, Sergei, *Fateful Years, 1909–1916.* London–New York: J. Cape, 1928. Reissued: *Fateful Years: The Reminiscences of Serge Sazonov.* New York, 1971.

331. [Schilling, M. F.], *How the War Began in 1914: Being the Diary of the Russian Foreign Office.* London, 1925. *How the War Began in 1914. Being the Diary of the Russian Foreign Office from the 3rd to the 20th of July 1914.* Forward by S. D. Sazanov. Introduction by Baron Schilling. London: G. Allen & Unwin, 1925.

332. Screen, John E. O., *Mannerheim: The Years of Preparation.* London: C. Hurst and Co., 1970.

333. Seleznev, M. S., ed., *"Krasnyi arkhiv." Sistematicheskii ukazatel' publikastii i statei.* Moscow: Moscow State Institute of Historical Archives, 1957.

334. Semennikov, V. P., ed., *Lettres des Grands-ducs a Nicolas II.* Trans M. Lichnevsky. Paris: Payot, 1926.

335. Shapiro, David, *A Select Bibliography of Works in English on Russian History, 1801–1917.* Oxford: Basil Blackwell, 1962.

336. Shklovsky, Viktor, *Sentimental Journey. Memoirs, 1917–1922.* Trans. Richard Sheldon. Ithaca: Cornell University, 1970.

337. Showalter, Dennis E., *Tannenberg: Clash of Empires.* Hamden, CT: Archon, 1991.

338. Shulgin, Vasilii V., *Days of the Russian Revolution. Memoirs from the Right, 1905–1917.* Gulf Breeze, FL: Academic International Press, 1990.

339. Shulgin, Vasilii V., "The Months Before the Russian Revolution," *Slavonic and East European Review* 1 (December 1922), 380–90.

340. Shulgin, Vasilii V., *The Years: Memoirs of a Member of the Russian Duma.* New York: Hippocrene Books, 1984.

341. Siegelbaum, Lewis H., *The Politics of Industrial Mobilization in Russia, 1914–17: A Study of the War Industries Committees.* London: Macmillan–St. Antony's College, 1983.

342. Sinanoglou, Ioannis, *France Looks Eastward: Perspectives and Prospects in Russia, 1914–1918.* Unpublished Ph.D. dissertation, Columbia University, 1975.

343. Slavik, Yan, ed., *Bibliografiia russkoi revoliutsii i grazhdanskoi voiny (1917–1921).* Prague: Russkii zagranichnyi istoricheskii arkhiv v Prage, 1938.

344. Smith, C. Jay, Jr., *The Russian Struggle for Power, 1914–1917: A Study of Russian Foreign Policy during the First World War.* New York: Philosophical Library, 1956.

345. Snively, Marjorie K., *Russia and the Straits, 1914–1932.* Unpublished Ph.D. dissertation, Ohio State University, 1932.

346. Snyder, Jack, *The Ideology of the Offensive.* Ithaca: Cornell University, 1984.

347. Sokol, Edward D., *The Revolt of 1916 in Russian Central Asia.* Baltimore: Johns Hopkins University, 1954.

348. Solzhenitsyn, Alexander, *Augusr 1914.* Trans M. Glenny. New York: Farrar, Straus & Giroux; 1972.

349. Sorokin, Pitrim, *A Long Journey.* New Haven: Yale University, 1962.

350. Spannicchi, Lelio Graf, *Das Ende des kaiserlich russischen Heeres.* Vienna-Leipzig: Elbenuehl-Verlag, 1932.

351. Spring, Derek W., "Russia and the Franco-Russian Alliance." *Slavonic and East European Review* 64 (1988), pp. 564–92.

352. Standing, Percy Cross, *The Campaign in Russian Poland.* London and New York: Hodder and Stroughton, 1914.

353. Star, Max, *In the Lion's Den.* Tampa: Florida Grower Press, 1964.

354. Stariparloff, T., "The Russian Military Air Services Up to the Time of the Revolution." *Air Power* (December 1918), 337–41.

355. Stavrou, Theofanis George, ed., *Russia under the Last Tsar.* Minneapolis: University of Minnesota Press, 1969.

356. Steinberg, John, "Russia Leaves the War," *Relevance: Quarterly Journal of the Great War Society* 11 (Winter 2002), no. 1, 14–20.

357. Steinberg, John, *War and Society during the Imperial Russian Epoch, 1613–1917.* Cambridge: Harvard University, 2002.

358. Steinberg, Mark D., and Khrustalev, Vladimir M., eds., *The Fall of the Romanovs: Political Dreams and Personal Struggles in a Time of Revolution.* New Haven: Yale University, 1995.

359. Stepun, Fedor, *Als ich russischer Offizier war.* Munich: Kosel Verlag, 1963.

360. Steveni, W. Barnes, *The Russian Army from Within.* London and New York: Hodder and Stoughton, 1914.

361. Stieve, Friedrich, *Izvolsky and the World War.* London: G. Allen & Unwin, 1926.

362. Stockdale, Melissa Kirschke, *Paul Miliukov and the Quest for a Liberal Russia, 1880–1918.* Ithaca and London: Cornell University, 1996.

363. Stone, Norman, "Organizing an Economy for War: The Russian Shell Shortage, 1914–1917." In: A. Wheatcroft and Geoffrey Best, eds., *War, Economy and the Military Mind.* London: Croom, Helm, 1976, 108–19.

364. Stone, Norman, *The Eastern Front, 1914–1917.* London: Hodder and Stoughton, 1975.

365. Stopford, Bertie, The Hon., *The Russian Diary of an Englishman.* London: William Heinemann, 1919.

366. Strakovsky, Leonid I., "Count Ignatiev's Efforts to Save the Monarchy of Nicholas II," *University of Toronto Quarterly* 23 (October 1953), no. 1, 64–83.

367. Strakovsky, Leonid I., "Count P.N. Ignat'yev, Reformer of Russian Education," *Slavonic and East European Review* 36 (December 1957), no. 86, 1–26.

368. Strakhovsky, Leonid I. "Was There a Kornilov Rebellion? A Reappraisal of the Evidence," *Slavonic and East European Review* 32 (June 1955), no. 81, 372–95.

369. Struve, P. B., *Food Supply in Russia during the World War.* New Haven: Yale University, 1930.

370. Sukhomlinov (Suchomlinow), V. A., *Erinnerungen.* Berlin: Reimar Hobbing, 1924.

371. Sullivan, Michael John, *A Fatal Passion: The Story of the Uncrowned Last Empress of Russia.* New York: Random House, 1996.

372. Taube, Michael de [Mikhail A.], Baron, *La Politique russe d'avant Guerre et la Fin de l'Empire des Tsars (1904–1917).* Paris, 1928. Expanded German edition: *Der grossen Katastrophe entgegen: Die russische Politik der Vorkriegszeit und das Ende des Zarenreiches (1904–1917).* Berlin-Leipzig: K. F. Koehler, 1937.

373. Thomson, Thomas John, *Boris Sturmer and the Imperial Russian Government, February 2–November 22, 1916.* Unpublished Ph.D. dissertation: Duke University, 1972.

374. *The Nicky-Sunny Letters: Correspondence of the Tsar and Tsaritsa, 1914–1917.* Hattiesburg, MS: Academic International Press, 1970. Republication in one volume of Bernard Pares, ed., *The Letters of the Tsaritsa to the Tsar, 1914–1916.* London, 1923, and Golwyn E. Vulliamy, *The Letters of the Tsar to the Tsaritsa, 1914–1917.* London and New York: 1929.

375. Tisdall, E. E. P., *The Dowager Empress.* London: Paul, 1957. American edition: *Maria Feodorovna: Empress of Russia.* New York: Day, 1958.

376. Tschebotarioff, Gregory P., *Russia, My Native Land: A U.S. Engineer Reminiscences and Looks at the Present.* New York: McGraw Hill, 1964.

377. Tsentral'nyi voenno-promyshlennyi komitet. American Delegation, *An Outline of Activities of the Central War Industries Committee of Russia.* New York: Am. Deleg. of Cent. War Indust. Com., 1918.

378. Tunstall, Graydon A., Jr., *Blood in the Snow: The Carpathian Winter War, 1914–1915.* Forthcoming.

379. Turner, L. C. F., "The Russian Mobilization in 1914." *Journal of Contemporary History* 3 (January 1968), no. 1, 65–88. Reprinted in Paul M. Kennedy, *The War Plans of the Great Powers, 1880–1914.* Foreward by Fritz Fischer. Boston: Allen and Unwin, 1985, 252–68.

380. USSR. General'nyi shtab RKKA, *La grande Guerre: Relation de l'etat major russe. Concentration des Armees. premiieres Operations en Prusse orientale, en Galicie et en Pologne (1er auot-24 novembre 1914),* trans. by Edouard Chapouilly. Paris: Charles-Lavauzelle, 1926.

381. USSR. NKID, *Die internationalen Beziehungen im Zeitalter des Imperialismus.* Edited by Otto Hoetzsch. 6 vols. Berlin: Deutsche Gesellschaft zum Studium Russlands, 1931–36.

382. Van Dyke, Carl, *Russian Imperial Military Doctrine, 1832–1914.* New York and Westport, CT: Greenwood, 1990.

383. Vasil'ev (Vassilyev), A. T., *The Ochrana: The Russian Secret Police.* Ed. Rene Fulop-Miller. Philadelphia and London: Lippincott, 1930.

384. Von Laue, Theodore H., "The Chances for Liberal Constitutionalism." *Slavic Review* 24 (1965), 34–46.

385. Von Wahlde, Peter, *Military Thought in Imperial Russia.* Unpublished Ph.D. dissertation: Indiana University, 1966.

386. Vorres, Ian, *The Last Grand-Duchess. Her Imperial Highness Grand-Duchess Olga Alexandrovna: 1 June 1882—24 November 1960.* London and New York: Hutchinson/Scribner's, 1964.

387. Vulliamy, Colwyn E., ed., *Red Archives: Russian State Papers and Other Documents relating to the Years 1915–1918.* Trans. A. L. Hynes. London: Geoffrey Bles, 1929.

388. Wade, Rex A., *The Russian Search for Peace, February–October 1917.* Stanford: Stanford University, 1969.

389. Waligora, David, "Le mission aeronatique francaise en Russie, 1916–1918." *Pegase* (January 1994), no. 72, 4–20.

390. Walz, J. D., *State Defense and Russian Politics Under the Last Tsar.* Unpublished Ph.D. Dissertation, Syracuse University, 1967.

391. Warth, Robert D., *Nicholas II: The Life and Reign of Russia's Last Monarch.* Westport, CT: Praeger, 1997.

392. Warth, Robert D., *The Allies and the Russian Revolution.* Durham, NC: Duke University, 1954.

393. Washburn, Stanley, *Field Notes from the Russian Front.* London: Andrew Melrose, 1915.

394. Washburn, Stanley, *On the Russian Front in World War I. Memoirs of an American War Correspondent.* New York: Robert Speller, 1982.

395. Waters, W. H. H., *Secret and Confidential. The Experiences of a Military Attache.* London: John Murray, 1926.

396. Watt, Richard M., *Dare Call It Treason.* London: Chatto and Windus; 1964.

397. Wegerer, Alfred von, "The Russian Mobilization of 1914." *Political Science Quarterly* 43 (1928), 201–28.

398. Wettig, Gerhard, "Die Rolle der russischen Armee im revolutionaren Machtkampf 1917," *Forschungen zur osteuropaischen Geschichte* (Berlin, 1967), Bd. 12, 46–389.

399. Wheeler-Bennett, John W., *Brest-Litovsk: The Forgotten Peace, March 1918.* London: Macmillan, 1963. First edition 1938.

400. White, Howard, "1917 in the Rear Garrisons," in Linda Edmondson and Peter Waldron, eds., *Economy and Society in Russia and the Soviet Union, 1860–1930. Essays for Olga Crisp.* Houndmills, UK: Macmillan, 1992. Pp. 152–68.

401. Wieczynski, Joseph L., ed., *The Modern Encyclopedia of Russian and Soviet History.* 58 vols. Gulf Breeze, FL.: Academic International Press, 1976.

402. Wildman, Allan K., *The End of the Russian Imperial Army.* 2 vols. Princeton: Princeton University Press, 1980–87.

403. Wilfong, Peter Thomas, *Rebuilding the Russian Army, 1904–1914: The Question of a Comprehensive Plan for National Defense.* Unpublished Ph.D. dissertation: Indiana University, 1977.

404. Williams, John, *Mutiny 1917*. London: Heinemann, 1962.

405. Wilton, Robert, *Russia's Agony*. New York: Dutton, 1919.

406. Wolkonsky [Volkonskii], *My Reminiscences*. 2 vols. Trans. A. E. Chamot. London: Hutchinson, n.d.

407. Woytinsky [Voitinskii], W. S., *Stormy Passage: A Personal History through Two Russian Revolutions to Democracy and Freedom, 1905–1960*. New York: Vanguard, 1961.

408. Wrangel, Alexis, *General Wrangel, 1878–1929: Russia's White Crusader*. London: Leo Cooper, 1987.

409. Wrangel, Alexis, *The End of Chivalry: The Last Great Cavalry Battles, 1914–1918*. New York: Hippocrene, 1982.

410. Wrangel [Vrangel], Petr N., *The Memoirs of General Wrangel, the Last Commander-in-Chief of the Russian National Army*. New York: Duffield, 1930. Reissued as *Always with Honour: Memoirs of General Wrangel*. New York: Robert Speller, 1957.

411. Yusupov [Youssoupoff], Felix F., Prince, *Avant l'Exil, 1887–1919* (Paris: Plon, 1952). English edition: *Lost Splendour*. Trans. Ann Green and Nicholas Katkoff. London: Cape, 1953.

412. Yusupov [Youssoupoff], Felix F., Prince, *Rasputin. His Malignant Influence and his Assassination*. New York: Dial, 1927. In French: *La Fin de Rasputine*. Paris, 1927.

413. Zagorsky, Semen A., *State Control of Industry during the War* New Haven: Yale University, 1928.

414. Zeman, Z. A. B., *Germany and the Revolution in Russia, 1915–1918. Documents from the Archives of the German Foreign Ministry*. London: Oxford University, 1958.

415. Zhukhov, Georgii K., *The Memoirs of Marshal Zhukov*. London: Jonathan Cape, 1971.

8

The Middle East

David L. Bullock

The Allies and Central Powers fought across several fronts in the Middle East during World War I. Invariably, campaigns involved the forces of the Ottoman Empire supported by small contingents of Germans and Austro-Hungarians pitted against the British Commonwealth, France, and Russia (the Triple Entente), and as the war progressed, against the ever-increasing number of nations known as the Allied Powers or "Allies." In one sense, World War I in the Middle East may be seen as one more round, but perhaps not the final round, of the historic Eastern Question. To quote the great Napoleon: "Who is to have Constantinople? That is always the crux of the problem."

The Eastern Question of course predated Napoleon and his unrealized ambitions. To better understand the diplomatic alignments as well as ethnic animosities in the Middle East during World War I, one should examine a few of the books that can provide insight into the historical background of the region.

Kemal Karpat [93] has edited a series of articles that examine Turkish culture and administration as well as the geopolitical position over which the Ottomans held sway. Paul Coles [34] surveys the period of Ottoman expansion from A.D. 1300 to the second siege of Vienna in 1683, a period in which the Ottoman Empire remained an aggressive dagger aimed at the Balkans and indeed, at the very heart of central Europe. After the cresting of the Turkish tide in 1683, the Ottoman Empire entered an age of stagnation and then chronic decline. The moribund Empire became known derisively in European and Russian circles as "The Sick Man of Europe." For Turkish official histories see [194].

J. A. R. Marriott [117] and M. S. Anderson [6] have evaluated the changing international relations caused by this gradual and habitual erosion of Ottoman military and political power. Marriott penned the pioneering study on the Eastern Question from the fourteenth to the seventh centuries, the question being how to fill the vacuum left behind by the centuries of Ottoman retreat as well as what to do with the ethnic minorities remaining within the Empire and how to balance major European power relationships between such strategic arteries as the Suez Canal and the Turkish Straits. Anderson continues Marriott's somewhat dated and even ethnocentric work with an examination of European-Ottoman relations from 1774 to 1923.

Understanding World War I in the Middle East additionally necessitates a look into the internal conditions of the Ottoman Empire. Lord Kinross [100] has written an excellent summary of the general course of Ottoman history. Several works notably catalog the problems attendant to an aging Empire, especially during the immediate years leading into the Great War. One Albanian-Turkish viewpoint is presented by reformer Ismail Kemal Bey [157]. Indispensable are the memoirs of Izzet Pasha [102], the Turkish Minister of War after Mahmud Sevket who served in this post until Enver Pasha took over in January 1914.

Sir Edwin Pears, a forty-year veteran of politics and diplomacy in Constantinople, has left his memoirs [139] as well as a scathing biography of Sultan Abdul Hamid II [140]. Bernard Lewis' *The Emergence of Modern Turkey* [108] should be consulted, as should the works of Stanford Shaw and his wife, Ezel Kural Shaw [152]. The Shaws are notable for their generally sympathetic portrayal of Abdul Hamid and for their elucidation of Turkish viewpoints and positions.

Demand for reform grew in the nineteenth century, particularly among young, progressive military officers. Dankwart Rustow has contributed an article depicting the army's role in reform [146]. The most serious challenge to the rule of the Ottomans in fact came from within the army and among similiar-minded officials in the civil service. Two works delve into the advent of the "Young Turks" who were represented politically through the Committee of Union and Progress (CUP). Ernest Ramsaur [143] focuses on the background to the revolution of 1908, while Feroz Ahmad [2] continues the chronicle to the beginning of World War I. Both are instrumental insights into the mindsets of the Turkish leaders who steered the Empire into the Great War.

Works on the Young Turk leaders are unforgivably scarce. Djemal Pasha, one of the ruling triumvirate along with Talaat and Enver from 1914 to 1918, has left memoirs [41] that include his service as Minister of Marine, Commander of 4th Army, and civil governor of Syria, Palestine, and the Hejaz. Written before his assassination by an Armenian in 1922, the memoirs are critical for understanding the Young Turk leadership, but they are flawed because they form the *corpus* of an *apologia* for his own actions. Von Kressenstein, the German commander of 8th Army who fought alongside him in Syria and Palestine [172], briefly details the life of Djemal Pasha in a multivolume yearbook of articles written by German veterans who served in the Middle East.

Talaat Pasha also has left a brief memoir [160], published posthumously after his assassination by an Armenian in 1921. Talaat, who served as Secretary-

General of the CUP, Minister of the Interior, and finally Grand Vizier, often has been blamed for the infamous Armenian massacres.

Enver Pasha, hero of the revolution of 1908 and successively military *attaché* to Berlin, Minister of War, Deputy Commander-in-Chief under the Sultan, then Chief of the General Staff, was virtually the generalissimo of the Turkish forces in World War I and the most powerful man in the Empire. Enver seems to have left no memoirs and, after exile, died a perhaps untimely death after a series of adventures in Central Asia in 1922. A synopsis of his life is presented in *The Encyclopedia of Islam* [109].

Conditions within the Ottoman Empire during the war are portrayed in several works. The standard has been Ahmed Emin [48], who recounts the deplorable conditions within the Empire that led progressively to defeat. Emin should be compared to the work of the Shaws and to that of M. Larcher [105]. The best accounts concerning medical conditions in the Middle East, which naturally affected the combatants of all sides, may be appreciated in two official histories, those edited by Butler [27] and MacPherson [115].

The war in the Middle East inevitably wrought stresses upon the diverse ethnic fabric underlying the far-flung Ottoman domains. The Armenian Question loomed large and has remained a subject of intense controversy throughout the course of the twentieth century. Beginning in 1915, reports reached the outside world that the Armenian population within the Empire was suffering deportation and loss of life. One early series of reports, by American diplomat Leslie Davis [38], recorded the disaster and offered pictorial evidence. Continuing this tradition, Donald and Lorna Touryan Miller [124] collected the testimonies of one hundred eyewitnesses.

The Turkish view of the Armenian Question is stated by the Shaws [152] and is covered in much more detail in the monumental compilation by Esat Uras [169]. Simply put, the Turks considered the Armenians subjects of the Ottoman Empire. When the Russians invaded the Empire through the Caucasus, a proportion of the Armenians joined the Russian forces or conducted acts of sabotage. Therefore it was necessary to deport them. Not surprisingly, the vast majority of Armenians reject this view and insist that the resulting massacres were purposeful genocide ordered by the Ottoman government. Two works provide an insightful journey into this point of view, those of Richard Hovannisian [84] and Christopher Walker [180].

The Turkish military remains a long-neglected subject. Fortunately, two excellent popular introductions have appeared in recent years. David Nicolle [135] has presented perhaps the first color depictions of the Ottoman armed forces in World War I. Paintings of Enver and Mustapha Kemal (the future president of Turkey) are included along with the uniforms of Turkish soldiers in the aviation, naval, and army branches. In 1995 The Naval Institute Press [104] published a highly illustrated book on the Ottoman Steam Navy from 1828 to 1923.

Alexander Aaronsohn [1], a Jew in the Turkish Army who deserted and later became a British spy in the Middle East, has testified to the inefficiency and injustice inherent in the Empire's system of recruitment in the early months of

World War I. Colonel Trevor Dupuy has statistically and very briefly analyzed the national combat effectiveness of the Turkish soldier in the 1917–1918 period [45]. Though highly colored by personal experiences and at least partially suspect, Rafael Nogales' account of his military services on behalf of the Ottomans in Syria and Palestine is worthy of note [136]. The account of Commandant M. Larcher remains perhaps the most complete attempt to portray the course of the war in a non-Turkish language [105].

Controversy lingers to the present day regarding the extent of German influence over the Young Turk leadership during World War I. Most of the Allies during and after the war generally assumed that influence was great. This assumption has been attacked in recent years by historian Ulrich Trumpener [166, 167, 168]. Trumpener portrays the checks and balances in the relationship between the Germans and Turks and, indeed, goes so far to conclude that by 1918 the Turks were calling the tune to the diplomatic dance, not the Germans.

Several additional books and articles have been written about the German Military Mission to the Ottomans. The works of von Steinitz [178], Solger [154], and Swanson [159] depict key figures important to the progress of the mission before the war. Jehuda Wallach [179] traces the origins of the mission and carries the story through the Great War, while Joseph Pomiankowski [141] relates his personal experiences inside the Austrian Military Mission at Constantinople.

Several German officers have left memoirs about their labors within the mission and in the field in support of their Turkish ally. Liman von Sanders [177] headed the military mission dispatched from Germany in 1913. Von Sanders commanded a Turkish army at Gallipoli and then an entire front in Palestine in 1918. These memoirs may be compared with the article on von Sanders' experiences written by C. T. Atkinson [12]. Kress von Kressenstein [172, 173, 174, 175] rose from chief-of-staff of 8th Corps in Palestine to commander of the Desert Force and 8th Army.

Erich von Falkenhayn followed his campaigns at Verdun and in Rumania with a tour of duty as commander of the Turkish Army Group F, popularly known as *Yilderim* or "Lightning." Cyril Falls [50] analyzes the redoubtable von Falkenhayn's advent in-theater and his eventual defeat at the hands of British General E. H. H. Allenby. Colonel Böhme describes his command of the 24th Ottoman Division in 1918 on the Palestine Front [20]. Captain Simon-Eberhard [153], Captain Merkle [122], and Dr. Steuber [155] relate their experiences in *Yilderim*. Field Marshal Paul von Hindenburg [170] and General Erich von Ludendorff [176], who did not serve in the Middle East, nevertheless briefly comment on the situation of the Ottoman Empire and its impact upon Germany.

Secondary German sources on the war in the Middle East are relatively scarce. The thirteenth volume of the German military history of the war [58] contains several short, general entries as do the works of Schwarte [150] and Foerster [57].

Much scholarship also needs to be accomplished regarding the small but lively air war within the Ottoman Empire, particularly on the Palestine front where aircraft dueled increasingly with the British Royal and the Australian Flying Corps from 1916 to 1917 and with the Royal Air Force from 1918. The reports of German Major Erich Serno [56], who headed the Turkish air force throughout the war, are by far the most informative sources. Serno address the conditions along each of the Ottoman fronts. Major Neumann [132, 133] includes reports on the air war in Palestine and Mesopotamia from veterans, with that from Palestine being written by the front air commander. German fliers Liebmann [110], Hentelburg [78], and Euringer [49] each have published colorful personal accounts of their aerial activities in the Middle East.

The war efforts of the Allied Powers in the Middle East also have been neglected. The Allies faced the Turks along fronts from the Dardanelles to the Caucasus to Mesopotamia to the Arabian Peninsula and to Egypt and Palestine. The Russians concentrated in the Caucasus, while France participated in the Dardanelles-Gallipoli and Salonika Campaigns, sent limited support to Arab rebels, and raised several small military units for service in Palestine. Alone among the Allies, Britain committed troops to every front engaging the Turks. (On the Salonika expedition see Chapter 9.)

A good understanding of British strategy and international politics during the war may be obtained through Paul Guinn [66]. David French [60] addresses three areas of particular concern to British war planners: the Dardenelles, the gateway to the Ottoman capital; Mecca, the spiritual fount of Islam; and Kut, the key to Mesopotamia. The memoirs of British Prime Minister David Lloyd George [112] are noteworthy because he was of the "Eastern" vein of strategic thought. While the "Western" school believed any diversion from the Western Front was folly, proponents of the "Eastern" school considered offensives on the Western Front too costly and looked for easier victories in the eastern theaters that might knock the props out from under the primary antagonist, Germany.

In 1914–1915 the strategic plum in the Easterner's dream was to force the Turkish Straits. Occupation of the Gallipoli Peninsula would have opened a direct path into Constantinople and probably would have achieved the direct surrender of the Ottoman Empire. Allied Russia would have been free to receive a steady flow of munitions and thereby could have exerted greater pressure on the Germans and Austro-Hungarians on the Eastern Front. Balkan neutrals might have been persuaded to join the Entente allies or at least to have remained neutral. Few plans of the war offered so much promise.

From the outset, Allied plans for the Dardenelles were hampered by argument and delay. Early in January 1915, First Lord of the Admiralty Winston Churchill became a strident champion of forcing the Straits [81]. This role cast him into increasing conflict with the First Sea Lord, Sir John Fisher, who believed that a purely naval attack was doomed to failure [555].

Ultimately, the joint British-French naval expedition went in against the Turkish forts in mid-February and had to be withdrawn in failure in mid-March. Four works illustrating the overall operations at the Dardanelles are highly recommended: volume two of Arthur Marder's monumental naval series [116], and the books of Richard Hough [83], Paul Halpern [70], and Thomas Frothingham

[61]. Six accounts by veterans additionally are recommended. Vice-Admiral Guépratte [65], commander of the French naval forces during the Dardanelles adventure, should be compared to the British points of view represented by Admiral Wemyss [184], H. M. Denham [40], Peter Shankland [151], Andrew Cunningham [35], and Roger Keyes [98]. Keyes, a relatively junior officer at the time, strongly desired to renew the naval assault after the failure of 18 March. Interestingly, German accounts, for example the testimony of Liman von Sanders [177], tended to support Keyes' belief that another determined naval attack might well have forced the Straits.

Even before the naval tragedy, opinion in the British war leadership gradually had been drifting toward landing troops on the Gallipoli Peninsula. The failure of the navy on 18 March produced a general if somewhat reluctant overall agreement to proceed with landings, which were carried out in fact on 25 April 1915. The ensuing debacle at Gallipoli remains perhaps the best-known event of the war in the Middle East during World War I.

Very little has appeared in English translation from the Turkish and German point of view. The memoirs of Djemal Pasha contain personal information [41] and are useful to compare to references made by the commander of the Turkish 2nd Army at Gallipoli, German General Liman von Sanders [177]. The memoirs of von Hindenburg and von Ludendorff clearly illustrate the concerns of the German higher command regarding the need to hold the Turkish Straits [170, 176]. German Major-General Hans Kannengiesser Pasha has left an account of his command of the Turkish 3rd Division at Gallipoli [92]. Lord Kinross has told the story of Mustafa Kemal, commander of the Turkish 19th Division [100].

The campaign from the British perspective has been served better by scholarship. C. F. Aspinall-Oglander and C. E. W. Bean have written respectively the official British [9] and Australian [17] histories. General Sir Ian Hamilton, the commander of the Mediterranean Expeditionary Force, which landed at Gallipoli, has left two reminiscences: his diary [71] and a record of his dispatches [72]. Lieutenant-General Sir George MacMunn [114], who was in charge of the lines of communications, and Lieutenant-General Sir William Marshall [118], who commanded a brigade of the 29th Division, then the entire division, and variously the 42nd and 53rd as well, have contributed to the *corpus* of first-hand accounts. Works by other veterans include that of an enlisted soldier, Joseph Murray [131], and that of an Intelligence officer, Aubrey Herbert [79].

Perennially, secondary sources are published on the Dardanelles Campaign. Included among the best received, best written, and better researched are the works of John Laffin [103], Robert James [87], and Alan Moorehead [128]. Two books point out the military "lessons" learned: Major-General Sir C. E. Callwell takes the British to task [28] while George Cassar analyzes French operations [30].

The front in Mesopotamia began when the British created a bridgehead at Basra in November 1914 to protect oilfields vital to the British economy. By late spring 1915, the British under Major-General Sir Charles Townshend [16, 165] began to advance on the regional capital of Ottoman administration, Baghdad.

After victories at Nasiriya and Kut-el-Amara, the British stalled against Turkish defenses at Ctesiphon in November and were forced to retire on Kut the following month. Besieged by the Turkish 6th Army and without hope of relief, Townshend finally felt compelled to surrender in April 1916. Major Charles Barber has described the experiences of the British during the siege [13], while Ronald Millar has published a secondary work describing the events surrounding the defense of Kut [123]. This disaster provoked the government into a special commission of inquiry, which recently has been scholastically reexamined by Paul Davis [39].

Kut soon was to be avenged by the British, however. Lieutenant-General Sir Stanley Maude [29] defeated the Turks at Kut in February 1917 and captured Baghdad in March. Lieutenant-General Sir William Marshall [118] assumed command in November 1917 after Maude died of cholera. Few serious operations transpired in 1918. The reader may understand the problems presented by the lines of communications by reading the firsthand account of General Mac-Munn [115] and may appreciate the stark terrain and harsh climate by referring to the work of the official war artist Donald Maxwell [121]. Three additional works are worthy of note: the official British account by Brigadier-General F. J. Moberly, the general study by Lieutenant-Colonel A. H. Burne [26] and Lieutenant-Colonel A. Kearsey's foray into the strategy and tactics of the Mesopotamian Campaign [95].

Perhaps the least well known British actions against the Turks were those sideshows undertaken by "Dunsterforce" [42, 44] and the associated Trans-Caspian force [47] in the Caucasus, northwest Persia and Central Asia during 1917–1919. The collapse of the allied Russian front in the Caucasus in 1917 due to revolution and subsequent civil war produced a power vacuum into which the Turks advanced. Originally dispatched into these strife-torn regions to oppose the Turks through the creation of pro-allied coalitions, both expeditions finally had to be withdrawn after varying degrees of success and failure in light of the impossible spiderweave of ethnic conflict. One official British volume, difficult to obtain because the India Office raised objections to its general publication after being printed in 1929, is a work by Brigadier F. J. Moberly concerning operations in Persia, 1914–1919 [127].

The Russians, of course, had been embattled heavily in this region. Scholarship has underestimated and under appreciated the immense Russian war effort against the Ottomans in the Caucasus. Early in 1915 the Russians destroyed the Turkish 3rd Army at Sarakamish in one of the most decisive engagements of World War I. Russian victories followed in 1915–1916 at Koprukoy, Erzerum, and Trebizond. A renewed Russian offensive then destroyed the reconstituted 3rd Army and sent the Turkish 2nd Army recoiling in defeat.

Probably only the advent of the Russian Revolution and Civil War saved the Ottomans in 1917. Even so, the legacy of the Russian contribution to the Allied effort continued. Enver Pasha, dreaming of a Pan-Turkish Empire, continued to dispatch troops to the Caucasus as late as autumn 1918 in an effort to replenish the many divisions previously decimated by the Russians. In so doing, he denuded other fronts, particularly in Palestine where General Sir Edmund (E. H. H.) Allenby was planning the final defeat of the Turks. The classic study of the Caucasian Front remains that of Paul Muratoff and W. E. D. Allen [4]. Other works, such as those of John Buchan [24] and Firuz Kazemzadeh [94], provide insights into the region overall.

In the final analysis, the British campaigns in Palestine arguably became the most decisive front in the Middle East during World War I. The British depended upon the strategic and logistical base in Egypt that they had established in 1882. For an appreciation of the British position in Egypt, see Sir Evelyn Baring [14] and the biographies of Lord Kitchener [8, 145]. For relations between the Egyptians and British, see Robert Tignor [164] and Keith Wilson [188]. Lieutenant Colonel P. G. Elgood deals with the loyalty and efficiency of the Egyptian Army, which was perhaps critical to the maintenance of the British base [46]. D. A. Farnie portrays the importance of the Suez Canal as a jugular vein between the far-flung corners of the British Empire [54].

The British front that started in Egypt and gradually extended to Palestine and the Arabian Peninsula conveniently may be organized into three periods. During the first, from autumn 1914 to summer 1916, the British strove to prevent the occupation of the Suez Canal. From summer 1916 to June 1917 the British advanced to the gates of Palestine and supported the Arabs who rose against the Ottoman Empire. In June 1917 General Allenby took command of the Egyptian Expeditionary Force (EEF) and inaugurated a series of campaigns in conjunction with his Arab allies that ultimately shattered the Turkish front just prior to the Armistice, which occurred in the Middle East on 31 October 1918.

The researcher is best served on this front by first delving into the several official histories documenting the ground campaigns. Captain Cyril Falls has produced the most monumental three-volume work from the British standpoint [50]. These volumes also include references and captured documents that illustrate Turkish and German actions and viewpoints. Two other official histories should be read in conjunction, those of H. S. Gullet [67] and C. Powles [142], who present the Australian and New Zealander operations respectively.

These official histories should be supplemented by the campaign analysis of Colonel A. P. Wavell (later Field Marshal), who was a senior officer in Palestine [182]. Heading the list of accounts by senior veterans are those of General Allenby [5] and General Sir Archibald Murray [130], both of whom commanded the EEF, Murray in 1916–1917 and Allenby in 1917–1918. Allenby, who carried the campaigns in Palestine to a victorious conclusion by capturing Jerusalem, Damascus, and Aleppo, has been the subject of several biographies including those of A. P. Wavell [181], Brian Gardner [62], Sir Basil Liddell Hart [77], and Raymond Savage [148]. Two biographies on Lieutenant-General Jan Smuts are notable [73, 125] because in 1918 Smuts visited Egypt as a special representative of His Majesty's Government and subsequently supported Allenby's plan for victory against the Turks in 1918.

Other British and Dominion veterans have left memoirs about their experiences in the ground campaigns in Egypt and Palestine. Junior officers of the cavalry and camelry who have left reminiscences include O. Teichman [161], Robert Wilson [189], and Geoffrey Inchbald [85, 86]. At least two Australian other ranks have written their stories while in the camel corps [82, 144]. War correspondent W. T. Massey's two books on the final campaigns reveal the perspective of a civilian who was at the front [119, 120]. Although Colonel Richard Meinhertzagen seems to have left no published memoirs, his life story inspired John Lord to pen a biography [113]. Meinhertzagen was one of Allenby's Intelligence advisers and the architect of the famous "haversack ruse," which allowed the British to trick the enemy as to the direction of the British attack at Beersheba and the Third Battle of Gaza in the summer of 1917.

Two brief general campaign summaries were published in the years following the war: those of war correspondent Edmund Dane [37] and the head of the signal corps of the EEF, Major General M. G. E. Bowman-Manifold [21]. More than two decades after finishing his prolific official volumes, Capt. Cyril Falls again covered Allenby's final campaign at Megiddo (site of the biblical Armageddon) in a book, although little new information seems to have been introduced [50]. Sadly, almost no recent work has appeared on the ground campaigns in Egypt-Palestine with the exception of David Bullock's general history published in 1988 [25]. Researchers wishing to study individual units should consult the regimental histories such as Lieutenant-Colonel R. R. Thompson's record of the 52nd Lowland Division [163] or the several articles appearing in *The Cavalry Journal;* for instance, the work of Lieutenant-Colonel W. J. Foster [59].

The air war over Egypt and Palestine, which began as an improvised effort in 1914–1915, culminated in a series of aerial engagements that wrought Royal Air Force theaterwide air superiority by the summer of 1918. Airpower played a vital part in Allenby's crushing of the Turkish front in the Megiddo Campaign. Two official histories remain the published standard on this air war. British historian H. A. Jones' multivolume work on Britain's air war contains three chapters on Palestine [90, 91]. Australian historian F. M. Cutlack [36] has covered the Australian Flying Corps' side of the story. These two works should be read in tandem to better appreciate a given action or period.

Published works by veterans of the air are rare. French Lieutenant Georges Douin [43] has recounted his experiences as a flier during the Turkish attack on the Suez Canal in 1915. Australian Air Marshal Sir Richard Williams recorded his experiences as commander of No. 67 (No. 1 Australian) Squadron and of 40th Wing in Palestine [186]. Frank Clune and L. W. Sutherland have published accounts that are especially illustrative of the daily life of Australian flyers in Egypt and Palestine [33, 158]. Air Commodore Charles Rumney Samson [147], Captain L. B. Weldon [183] and Captain Wedgwood Benn [19] have each left memoirs of their experiences in Egypt and in the Eastern Mediterranean aboard seaplane tenders. Stray articles can also be found; for example, in the 1960s and 1970s, *Cross and Cockade Journal* published a series of interviews with veterans of the air in the Middle East [111].

Unfortunately, the war in the air has been neglected by scholars. Some brief chapters or references occasionally appear in general or popular histories [137].

U.S. Air Force historian Richard Hallion [69] published a brief chapter on the role of the Royal Air Force during Allenby's final campaign that emphasized the value of battlefield interdiction. David Bullock's 1995 doctoral dissertation on the Royal Air Force in Palestine 1914–1918 remains sequestered, pending possible publication.

The revolt of the Arabs against the Ottoman Turks in June 1916 aided the advance of the Egyptian Expeditionary Force in Palestine, while British supplies and gold supported the Arab forces in return. Two books by Elie Kedourie [96, 97] and one by Rashid Khalid [99] provide insight into the background relations between Britain and Hussein ibn Ali (Amir of Mecca, Keeper of the Holy Cities, and later King of the Hejaz) that led to Arab participation in the Allied war effort. Zeine N. Zeine explains the relationship between the Arabs and Turks and its implications for Arab nationalism and ultimately, revolt [193].

The Arab Revolt, like Gallipoli, has continued to receive attention from popular historians. Works almost invariably focus on some aspect of the controversial mystique of Lawrence of Arabia. Of the many biographies of T. E. Lawrence, the work of Jeremy Wilson is perhaps the best [187]. The Lawrencian legend began when American world traveler Lowell Thomas visited Lawrence in Arabia. Thomas produced a romantic hero and offered him to a war-weary Allied public: the American and British response was enthusiastic, perhaps wildly so. After the war, Sir Basil Liddell Hart [76] portrayed Lawrence as a champion of guerrilla warfare, a theme that has continued to the present day in more recent publications [10].

Lawrence was indeed a brave and extraordinary man of great endurance with a sharp mind; but in the final analysis he seems to have been a dedicated and valuable liaison officer between the EEF and Prince Feisal's Arab Northern Army and not the architect of the Arab Revolt or its ultimate military victory. This is certainly the view of Suleiman Mousa [129] in his eloquently argued reinterpretation of Lawrence based on Arab sources. Richard Aldington [3] also is critical of the Lawrencian legend.

Lawrence wrote two books on his experiences, *Revolt in the Desert* [106] being a condensation, more or less, of his *Seven Pillars of Wisdom* [107]. These should be compared to the firsthand accounts of other veterans of Arabia, especially those of two British officers, Major N. N. E. Bray [22] and Major C. S. Jarvis [88]. Additionally, the head of the French Military Mission, Colonel Edouard Brémond, has provided a perhaps understandably pro-French perspective [23].

Lawrence, of course, was only one luminary in a larger group of British specialists generally known as the "Arab Bureau." Bruce Westrate's well-written and researched book on the Bureau amplifies the achievements of the several members largely ignored by scholarship [185]. H. V. F. Winstone has published several books on the Bureau as well as on the individuals who were a part of the larger British Intelligence apparatus in the Middle East; for example [190, 191]. Works by veterans associated with Intelligence include those of Sir Gilbert Falkingham Clayton [32], who brought the first coterie of specialists, the "Intrusives," to the Middle East, Gertrude Bell [18], and Sir Ronald Storrs, Oriental Secretary in Cairo [156].

Works on the Arabs themselves remain scarce. David Nicolle's illustrated book offers the first color depictions of Arab uniforms worn during World War I [134]. Some insight into the operations of Arab forces may be obtained through three books. Although partially suspect, the memoirs of Prince Abdullah (later King of the Transjordan) are necessary reading to understand the activities of the southern Arab forces besieging Turkish-held Medina [64]. George Antonius traces Arab operations in general [7]. By far the most important is Suleiman Mousa's account [129], which should be compared with British records.

FURTHER RESEARCH

Much work remains to be accomplished on the Middle East in World War I. Studies by Turkish, Arabic, and Russian scholars are particularly needed, and British and German sources could also be updated.

BIBLIOGRAPHY

1. Aaronsohn, Alexander. *With the Turks in Palestine.* London: Constable and Company, 1917.

2. Ahmad, Feroz. *The Young Turks: The Committee of Union and Progress in Turkish Politics, 1908–1914.* Oxford: The Clarendon Press, 1969.

3. Aldington, Richard. *Lawrence of Arabia: a Biographical Enquiry.* Westport, CT: Greenwood Press, 1976 (originally William Collins & Sons, 1955).

4. Allen, W. E. D., and Paul Muratoff. *Caucasian Battlefields.* Cambridge: University Press, 1953.

5. Allenby, Sir Edmund H. H., General. *A Brief Record of the Advance of the Egyptian Expeditionary Force: July 1917 to October 1918.* 2nd ed. London: His Majesty's Stationery Office, 1919.

6. Anderson, M. S. *The Eastern Question, 1774–1923: A Study in International Relations.* London: Macmillan, 1966.

7. Antonius, George. *The Arab Awakening: The Story of the Arab National Movement.* New York: Capricorn Books, 1965.

8. Arthur, George. *The Life of Lord Kitchener.* Vol. 3. London: Macmillan and Co., 1920.

9. Aspinall-Oglander, C. F. *History of the Great War: Military Operations, Gallipoli.* London: William Heinemann, 1929.

10. Asprey, Robert B. *War in the Shadows: the Guerrilla in History.* New York: William Morrow and Co., 1994.

11. Asquith, Herbert Henry. *Memories and Reflections, 1852–1927.* Vol. 2. Boston: Little Brown & Co., 1928.

12. Atkinson, C. T. "General Liman von Sanders on His Experiences in Palestine." *The Army Quarterly* 3, no. 2 (January 1922): 259–64.

13. Barber, Charles H., Major. *Besieged in Kut and After.* London: William Blackwood and Sons, 1917.

14. Baring, Evelyn, Earl of Cromer. *Modern Egypt.* 2 vols. New York: The Macmillan Co., 1908.

15. Barker, A. J. *The Neglected War: Mesopotamia, 1914–1918.* London: Faber & Faber 1967.

16. Barker, A. J. *Townshend of Kut: A Biography of Major-General Sir Charles Townshend.* London: Cassell & Co., Ltd., 1967.

17. Bean, C. E. W. *The Story of Anzac.* Vol. 1 and 2. Official history of Australia in the War of 1914–1918. 10th edition. Sydney: Angus & Robertson, Ltd., 1940 (originally 1921).

18. Bell, Gertrude. *The Arab War: Confidential Information for General Headquarters from Gertrude Bell: Being Despatches Reprinted from the Secret "Arab Bulletin."* Intro. by Sir Kinahan Cornwallis, director of the Arab Bureau, 1916–1920. England: The Golden Cockerel Press. Privately Printed, 1940.

19. Benn, Wedgwood, Capt. *In the Side Shows.* London: Hodder and Stoughton, 1919.

20. Böhme, Oberst. "Die 24. Osmanische Division in der 2. Jordanschlacht." *Zwischen Kaukasus und Sinai: Jahrbuch des Bundes der AsienKämpfer.* Vol. 2. Berlin: Mulzer and Cleeman, 1922.

21. Bowman-Manifold. M. G. E., Major General. *An Outline of the Egyptian and Palestine Campaigne, 1914–1918.* 8th ed. Chatham: Institute of Royal Engineers, 1932.

22. Bray, N. N. E., Major *Shifting Sands.* Foreword by Sir Austen Chamberlain. London: Unicorn Press, 1934.

23. Brémond, Edouard, Colonel. *Le Hedjaz dans la Guerre Mondiale.* Paris: Payot, 1931.

24. Buchan, John, ed. *The Baltic and Caucasian States.* The Nations of the World Today. Boston: Houghton Mifflin, 1923.

25. Bullock, David L. *Allenby's War: the Palestine-Arabian Campaigns, 1916–1918.* London: The Blandford Press, 1988.

26. Burne, A. H., Lieutenant-Colonel. *Mesopotamia: The Last Phase.* 2nd ed. London: Gale & Polden, Ltd., 1938.

27. Butler, A. G., Colonel, ed. *The Official History of the Australian Army Medical Services in the War of 1914–1918.* Vol. 1 *Gallipoli, Palestine and New Guinea.* 2nd ed. Melbourne: Australian War Memorial, 1938.

28. Callwell, Sir C. E., Major-General. *The Dardanelles: Campaigns and Their Lessons.* London: Constable and Co., 1919.

29. Callwell, Sir C. E. *The Life of Sir Stanley Maude.* Boston: Houghton Mifflin Company, 1920.

30. Cassar, George H. *The French in the Dardanelles: A Study of Failure in the Conduct of War.* London: George Allen and Unwin, 1971.

31. Churchill, Winston S. *The World Crisis, 1915.* London: Thornton Butterworth, 1923.

32. Clayton, Sir Gilbert Falkingham. *An Arabian Diary.* Intro. 2nd ed. by Robert O. Collins. Berkeley: University of California Press, 1969.

33. Clune, Frank. *D'Air Devil: The Story of "Pard" Mustar; Australian Air Ace.* Sidney: Angus and Robertson, 1941.

34. Coles, Paul. *The Ottoman Impact in Europe.* New York: Harcourt Brace and World, 1968.

35. Cunningham, Andrew Browne, Admiral of the Fleet. *A Sailor's Odyssey: The Autobiography of Admiral of the Fleet Viscount Cunningham of Hyndthorpe.* New York: E. P. Dutton and Co., 1951.

36. Cutlack, F. M. *The Australian Flying Corps in the Western and Eastern Theatres of War, 1914–1918.* Sydney: Angus and Robertson, 1939.

37. Dane, Edmund. *British Campaigns in the Nearer East, 1914–1918: From the Outbreak of War with Turkey to the Armistice.* Vol. I, *The Days of Adversity.* London: Hodder and Stoughton, 1919.

38. Davis, Leslie A. ed. and intro. by Susan K. Blair. *The Slaughterhouse Province: An American Diplomat's Report on the Armenian Genocide, 1915–1917.* New York: Aristide D. Caratzas, Publisher, 1990.

39. Davis, Paul K. *Ends and Means: The British Mesopotamian Campaign and Commission.* London: Associated University Presses, 1994.

40. Denham, H. M. *Dardanelles: A Midshipman's Diary, 1915–1916.* London: John Murray, Publisher, 1981.

41. Djemal Pasha. *Memories of a Turkish Statesman, 1913–1919.* New York: George H. Doran Co., 1922.

42. Donohoe, M. H. *With the Persian Expedition.* Edward Arnold, 1919.

43. Douin, Georges, Lieutenant de Vaisseau. *L'Attaque du Canal de Suez, 3 Fevrier 1915.* Paris: Librairie Delagrave, 1922.

44. Dunsterville, L. C., Maj. Gen. *The Adventures of Dunsterforce.* London: Edward Arnold, 1920.

45. Dupuy, T. N., Colonel. *Numbers, Predictions and War: Using History to Evaluate Combat Factors and Predict the Outcome of Armed Conflict.* Revised Edition. Fairfax, Virginia: Hero Books, 1985.

46. Elgood, P. G., Lieutenant-Colonel. *Egypt and the Army.* London: Oxford University Press, 1924.

47. Ellis, C. H. *The Transaspian Episode, 1918–1919.* London: Hutchinson & Co., 1963.

48. Emin, Ahmed. *Turkey in the World War: Economic and Social History of the World War.* Turkish Series. New Haven: Yale University Press, 1930.

49. Euringer, Richard. *Vortrupp "Pascha": Roman der ersten Expedition deutscher Flieger in die Wüste.* Hamburg: Hanseatische Verlagsanstalt, 1937.

50. Falls, Cyril. *Armageddon 1918.* Great Battles of History Series. London: Weidenfeld and Nicholson, 1964.

51. Falls, Cyril. "Falkenhayn in Syria." *The Edinburgh Review.* Vol. 250 (October 1929): 272, 276–78.

52. Falls, Cyril. *Military Operations: Egypt and Palestine. To June 1917.* London: His Majesty's Stationery Office, c. 1920s.

53. Falls, Cyril. *Military Operations: Egypt and Palestine. From June 1917. Parts 1 and 2.* London: His Majesty's Stationery Office, c. 1920s.

54. Farnie, D. A. *East and West of Suez: The Suez Canal in History 1854–1956.* Oxford: The Clarendon Press, 1969.

55. Fisher, John A., Admiral of the Fleet. *Memories and Records.* Vol. 1. New York: George H. Doran Co., 1920.

56. Flanagan, Brian P., ed. and trans. "The History of the Ottoman Air Force in the Great War: the Reports of Major Erich Serno." 2nd ed. *Cross and Cockade* 11, nos. 2, 3, 4 (Summer, Autumn, Winter 1970).

57. Foerster, Wolfgang, ed. *Kämpfer an vergessenen Fronten: Feldzugsbriefe, Kriegstagebücher und Berichte. Kolonialkrieg, Seekrieg, Luftkrieg, Espionage.* Berlin: Neufeld & Henius, 1931.

58. Forschungsanstalt des Heeres, Kriegsgeschichtlichen. *Der Weltkrieg 1914 bis 1918.* Dreizehnter Band. *Die militärischen Operationen zu Lande.* Berlin: Ernst Siegfried Mittler and Sohn, 1942.

59. Foster, W. J., Lieutenant-Colonel. "Operations of the Mounted Troops of the Egyptian Expeditionary Force." *The Cavalry Journal* Vol. XI (1921): pp. 8–10.

60. French, David. "The Dardanelles, Mecca and Kut: Prestige as a Factor in British Eastern Strategy, 1914–1916." *War and Society.* 5 (1987): 45–61.

61. Frothingham, Thomas G. *The Naval History of the World War: Offensive Operations, 1914–1915.* Cambridge: Harvard University Press, 1924.

62. Gardner, Brian. *Allenby of Arabia: Lawrence's General.* New York: Coward-McCann, 1965.

63. Golovin, N. H. *The Russian Army in the World War.* New Haven: Yale University Press, 1931.

64. Graves, Philip P., ed. *Memories of King Abdullah of Transjordan.* London: Jonathan Cape, 1950.

65. Guépratte, P. E., Vice Admiral. *L'Epédition des Dardanelles, 1914–1915.* Paris: Payot, 1935.

66. Guinn, Paul. *British Strategy and Politics: 1914–1918.* Oxford: at the Clarendon Press, 1965.

67. Gullett, H. S. *The Australian Imperial Force in Sinai and Palestine, 1914–1918.* Sydney: Angus and Robertson, 1944.

68. Haldane, Sir Aymer. *A Soldier's Saga.* London: Blackwood, 1948.

69. Hallion, Richard P. *Strike from the Sky: the History of Battlefield Air Attack, 1911–1945.* Smithsonian History of Aviation Series. Washington, DC: Smithsonian Institution Press, 1989.

70. Halpern, Paul G. *The Naval War in the Mediterranean, 1914–1918.* Annapolis: The Naval Institute Press, 1987.

71. Hamilton, Sir Ian. *Gallipoli Diary.* Vol 1 and 2. London: Edward Arnold, 1920.

72. Hamilton, Sir Ian. *Ian Hamilton's Despatches from the Dardanelles.* London: George Newnes, Ltd., 1917.

73. Hancock, W. K. *Smuts: The Sanguine Years, 1870–1919.* Cambridge: Cambridge University Press, 1962.

74. Hankey, Maurice. *The Supreme Command, 1914–1918.* Vol 1. London: George Allen and Unwin, 1961.

75. Hart, [Sir] Basil Liddell. *Reputations Ten Years After.* Boston: Little, Brown, and Co., 1928.

76. Hart, [Sir] Basil Liddell. *T. E. Lawrence: in Arabia and After.* Westport, Conn: Greenwood Press, 1974, (previously published 1934).

77. Hart, [Sir] Basil Liddell and Graves, Robert. *T. E. Lawrence to His Biographers.* New York: Doubleday & Co., 1938.

78. Hentelburg, Hans, Leutnant. *Als Kampflieger am Suez-Kanal.* Berlin: August Scherl, 1917.

79. Herbert, Aubrey. *Mons, Anzac and Kut.* London: Edward Arnold, 1919.

80. Herwig, Holger, and Neil M. Heyman. *Biographical Dictionary of World War I.* Westport, CT: Greenwood Press, 1982.

81. Higgins, Trumbull. *Winston Churchill and the Dardanelles.* London: William Heinemann, 1963.

82. Hogue, Oliver. *The Cameliers.* London: Andrew Melrose, 1919.

83. Hough, Richard. *The Great War at Sea, 1914–1918.* Oxford: Oxford University Press, 1983.

84. Hovannisian, Richard G., ed. *The Armenian Genocide in Perspective.* Oxford: Transaction Books, 1986.

85. Inchbald, Geoffrey. *Camels and Others.* London: Johnson Publications, 1968.

86. Inchbald, Geoffrey. *The Imperial Camel Corps.* London: Morrison and Gibb, Ltd., 1970.

87. James, Robert Rhodes. *Gallipoli.* New York: The Macmillan Co., 1965.

88. Jarvis, C. S., Major. *Arab Command: the Biography of Lieutenant-Colonel F. G. Peake Pasha.* London: Hutchinson and Co., 1942.

89. Jeffrey, K. "Sir Henry Wilson and the Defence of the British Empire, 1918–1922." *Journal of the Imperial and Commonwealth History.* 5 (1977): 273.

90. Jones, H. A. *Official History of the War: The War in the Air.* Vol. 5. Oxford: Clarendon Press, 1935.

91. *Official History of the War: The War in the Air.* Vol. 6. Oxford: Clarendon Press, 1935.

92. Kannengiesser Pasha, Hans, Major General. *The Campaign in Gallipoli.* Intro. by Marshal Liman von Sanders Pasha, and trans. by Maj. C. J. P. Ball, formerly 29th Div., Gallipoli. London: Hutchinson & Co., 1927.

93. Karpat, Kemal H., ed. *The Ottoman State and its Place in World History.* Leiden: E. J. Brill, 1974.

94. Kazemzadeh, Firuz. *The Struggle for Transcaucasia, 1917–1920.* New York: Philosophical Library, 1951.

95. Kearsey, A. *A Study of the Strategy and Tactics of the Mesopotamia Campaign, 1914–1917.* Aldershot, Gale & Polden, no date.

96. Kedourie, Elie. *England and the Middle East.* Hassocks, Sussex: The Harvester Press, 1956.

97. Kedourie, Elie. *In the Anglo-Arab Labyrinth: The MacMahon-Husayn Correspondence and its Interpretations, 1914–1939.* London: Cambridge University Press, 1976.

98. Keyes, Roger. *The Naval Memoirs of Admiral of the Fleet Sir Roger Keyes: The Narrow Seas to the Dardanelles, 1910–1915.* New York: E. P. Dutton and Co., 1934.

99. Khalid, Rashid Ismail. *British Policy Towards Syria and Palestine, 1906–1914, A Study of the Antecedents of the Hussein-McMahon Correspondence, the Sykes-Picot Agreement and the Balfour Declaration.* London: Ithaca Press, 1980.

100. Kinross, Lord Patrick Balfour. *Ataturk.* New York: William Morrow, 1964.

101. Kinross, Lord Patrick Balfour. *The Ottoman Centuries: The Rise and Fall of the Turkish Empire.* New York: Morrow Quill Paperbacks, 1977.

102. Klinghardt, Karl, ed. and trans. *Denkwürdigkeiten des Marschalls Izzet Pascha.* Leipzig: Verlag von K. F. Koehler, 1927.

103. Laffin, John. *Damn the Dardanelles.* London: Osprey Publishing Ltd., 1980.

104. Langensiepen, Bernd, and Ahmet Güleryüz. ed. and trans. by James Cooper. *The Ottoman Steam Navy, 1828–1923.* Annapolis: The Naval Institute Press, 1995.

105. Larcher M., Commandant. *La Guerre Turque dans la Guerre Mondiale.* Intro. by M. le Marechal Franchet D'Esperey. Paris: Berger-Levrault et Compagnie, 1926.

106. Lawrence, T. E. *Revolt in the Desert.* London: Jonathan Cape, 1927.

107. Lawrence, T. E. *Seven Pillars of Wisdom.* London: Jonathan Cape, 1946.

108. Lewis, Bernard. *The Emergence of Modern Turkey.* London: Oxford University Press, 1961.

109. Lewis, B., C. H. Pellat, and J. Schacht, eds. *The Encyclopedia of Islam.* New ed. Vol 2, C-G. Leiden: E. J. Brill, 1965.

110. Liebmann, Z. D. *Dardanellen Flieger.* Berlin: Boll u. Pickardt, 1918.

111. Lightall, W. S. "The Royal Air Force in the Palestine Campaign: 1917–1918." *Cross and Cockade Journal* 11, no. 2 (summer 1970): 175.

112. Lloyd George, David. *War Memoirs.* Vols. 1 and 2. London: Ivor Nicholson and Watson, 1923–1934.

113. Lord, John. *Duty, Honor, Empire: The Life and Times of Colonel Richard Meinhertzagen.* New York: Random House, 1970.

114. MacMunn, Sir George. *Behind the Scenes in Many Wars: Being the Military Reminiscences of Lieut.-General Sir George MacMunn.* London: John Murray, 1930.

115. MacPherson, Sir W. G., Major-General, et. al., eds. *Official History of the War. Medical Services. Diseases of the War.* Vol. 1. London: His Majesty's Stationery Office, ca. 1933.

116. Marder, Arthur J. *From Dreadnaught to Scapa Flow: The Royal Navy in the Fisher Era, 1904–1919.* Vol. 2, *The War Years to the Eve of Jutland.* London: Oxford University Press, 1965.

117. Marriott, J. A. R. *The Eastern Question: An Historical Study in European Diplomacy.* Oxford: Oxford University Press, 1940.

118. Marshall, Sir William, Lieutenant-General. *Memories of Four Fronts.* London: Ernest Benn Limited, 1929.

119. Massey, W. T. *Allenby's Final Triumph.* London: Constable and Company, 1920.

120. Massey, W. T. *The Desert Campaigns.* With illustrations from drawings by James McBey. London: G. P. Putnam's Sons, 1918.

121. Maxwell, Donald. *A Dweller in Mesopotamia: Being the Adventures of an Official Artist in the Garden of Eden.* New York: John Lane Company, 1921.

122. Merkle, Hauptmann "Die Deutsche Jildirim-Etappe." *Zwischen Kaukasus und Sinai: Jahrbuch des Bundes der Asien Kämpfer.* Band 1 (1921): 107.

123. Millar, Ronald. *Death of an Army: The Siege of Kut, 1915–1916.* Boston: Houghton Mifflin Company, 1970.

124. Miller, Donald E., and Lorna Touryan. *Survivors: An Oral History of the Armenian Genocide.* Berkeley: University of California Press, 1993.

125. Millin, Sarah G. *General Smuts.* Boston: Little, Brown and Co., 1936.

126. Moberly, F. J., Brigadier-General. *The Campaign in Mesopotamia, 1914–1918,* four vols. History of the Great War. London: His Majesty's Stationery Office, 1927.

127. Moberly, F. J. *Operations in Persia, 1914–1919.* London: His Majesty's Stationery Office, 1929 (reprinted 1987).

128. Moorehead, Alan. *Gallipoli.* New York: Harper & Brothers, Publishers, 1989.

129. Mousa, Suleiman. *T. E. Lawrence: an Arab View.* London: Oxford University Press, 1966.

130. Murray, Sir Archibald. *Sir Archibald Murray's Despatches, (June 1916–June 1917).* London: J. M. Dent and Sons, 1920.

131. Murray, Joseph. *Gallipoli as I Saw it.* London: William Kimber, 1965.

132. Neumann, Georg Paul, Major. *Die Deutschen Luftstreitkräfte im Weltkriege: unter Mitwirkung von 29 Offizieren und Beamten der Heeres und Marine Luftfahrt nach amtlichen Quellen herausgegeben.* Berlin: Ernst Siegfried Mittler und Sohn, 1920.

133. Neumann, Georg Paul. *The German Air Force in the Great War: From the Records and with the Assistance of 29 Officers and Officials of the Naval and Military Air Services.* Trans. by J. E. Gordon. London: Hodder and Stoughton, c. 1930.

134. Nicolle, David. *Lawrence and the Arab Revolts.* Osprey Men-at-Arms Series. London: Osprey Publishing Ltd., 1989.

135. Nicolle, David. *The Ottoman Army, 1914–1918.* Osprey Men-at-Arms Series. London: Reed International Books, Ltd., 1994.

136. Nogales, Rafael. *Four Years Beneath the Crescent.* Intro. by Lt. Col. Edward Davis, and trans. by Muna Lee. New York: Charles Scribner's Sons, 1926.

137. Owens, Colin A. "Aerial Observer, No. 1 Sqdn., Australian Flying Corps: An Interview with Lawrence H. Smith." *Cross and Cockade Journal: the Society of World War One Area Historians* 11, no. 2 (Summer 1970): 158.

138. Parnell, N. M., and C. A. Lynch. *The Australian Air Force Since 1911.* Sydney: A. H. and A. W. Reed, 1976.

139. Pears, Sir Edwin. *Forty Years in Constantinople.* New York: D. Appleton and Co., 1916.

140. Pears, Sir Edwin. *Life of Abdul Hamid.* The Middle East Collection. New York, Arno Press, 1973 (originally Constable and Co., 1917).

141. Pomiankowski, Joseph. *Der Zusammenbruch des Ottomanischen Reiches.* Graz: Akademische Druck-u. Verlagsanstalt, 1969; orig. Wien: Amalthea-Verlag, 1928.

142. Powles, C., Lieutenant Colonel. *The New Zealanders in Sinai and Palestine.* Auckland: Whitcome and Tombs Ltd., 1922.

143. Ramsaur, Jr., Ernest E. *The Young Turks: Prelude to the Revolution of 1908.* New York: Russell and Russell, 1957.

144. Reid, Frank. *The Fighting Cameliers.* Sydney: Angus & Robertson, 1934.

145. Royle, Trevor. *The Kitchener Enigma.* London: Michael Joseph, 1985.

146. Rustow, Dankwart A. "The Army and the Founding of the Turkish Republic." *World Politics: A Quarterly Journal of International Relations.* 11 (October 1958–October 1959): 516–17.

147. Samson, Charles Rumney, Air Commodore. *Fights and Flights.* London: Ernest Benn, Ltd., 1930.

148. Savage, Raymond. *Allenby of Armageddon.* Preface by David Lloyd George. London: The Diamond Press, 1925.

149. Schaedel, Charles. *Men and Machines of the Australian Flying Corps, 1914–1919.* Victoria: Kookaburra Technical Publications, 1972.

150. Schwarte, Max. *Der Grosse Krieg: 1914–1918.* Zehn Banden. Leipzig: Johann Ambrosius Barth, 1922.

151. Shankland, Peter, and Anthony Hunter. *Dardanelles Patrol.* New York: Charles Scribner's Sons, 1964.

152. Shaw, Stanford, and Ezel Kural Shaw. *History of the Ottoman Empire and Modern Turkey.* Vol. 2: *Reform, Revolution and Republic: The Rise of Modern Turkey, 1808–1875.* Cambridge: Cambridge University Press, 1977.

153. Simon-Eberhard, Max Hauptmann. *Mit dem Asien Korps zur Pälastina Front.* Geleitwort von General-Major a. D. v. Frankenberg und Proschlitz. Berlin: Selbstverlag des Verfassers, 1927.

154. Solger, A. D. "Colmar Freiherr v. d. Goltz." *Zwischen Kaukasus und Sinai: Jahrbuch des Bundes der Asien Kämpfer.* Band 2 (1922): 1–15.

155. Steuber, Dr. *"Jilderim." Deutsche Streiter auf heiligen Boden.* Schlachten des Weltkrieges, heft 5. Berlin: Gerhard Stalling, no date.

156. Storrs, Sir Ronald. *The Memoirs of Sir Ronald Storrs.* New York: G. P. Putnam's Sons, 1937.

157. Story, Sommerville, ed. *The Memoirs of Ismail Kemal Bey.* London: Constable and Co., 1920.

158. Sutherland, L. W. *Aces and Kings*. London: John Hamilton, no date.

159. Swanson, Glen W. "War, Technology and Society in the Ottoman Empire from the Reign of Abdulhamid II to 1913. Mahmud Sevket and the German Military Mission." In V. J. Parry and M. E. Yapp, *War Technology and Society in the Middle East*. London: Oxford University Press, 1975.

160. Talaat Pasha. "Posthumous Memoirs of Talaat Pasha." *The New York Times Current History*. Vol. 15. Trans. by M. Zekeria, 1921: 287–94.

161. Teichman, O., Captain. *The Diary of a Yeomanry M. O.: Egypt, Gallipoli, Palestine and Italy*. London: T. Fisher Unwin, 1921.

162. Thomas, Lowell. *With Lawrence in Arabia*. London: Hutchinson and Co., Ltd., c. 1921.

163. Thompson, R. R. *The 52nd Lowland Division*. Glasgow: Macelehose, Jackson & Co., 1923.

164. Tignor, Robert L. *Modernization and British Colonial Rule in Egypt, 1882–1914*. Princeton: Princeton University Press, 1966.

165. Townshend, Sir Charles V. F., Major-General. *My Campaign in Mesopotamia*. London: Thornton Butterworth Ltd., 1920.

166. Trumpener, Ulrich. *Germany and the Ottoman Empire, 1914–1918*. Princeton: Princeton University Press, 1968.

167. Trumpener, Ulrich. "German Military Aid to Turkey in 1914: an Historical Re-evaluation." *Journal of Modern History* 32 (1960): 145–49.

168. Trumpener, Ulrich. "Liman von Sanders and the German-Ottoman Alliance." *Journal of Contemporary History* 1, no. 4 (1966): 192.

169. Uras, Esat. *The Armenians in History and the Armenian Question*. Istanbul: Documentary Publications, 1988.

170. Von Hindenburg, Paul. *Out of My life*. Vols 1, 2. Trans. by F. A. Holt. New York: Harper and Bros., 1921.

171. Von Hoeppner, General der Kavellerie *Deutschlands Krieg in der Luft*. Leipzig: R. F. Koehler, 1921.

172. Von Kressenstein, Friedrich Freiherr Kress, Major-General. "Achmed Djemal Pascha." *Zwischen Kaukasus und Sinai: Jahrbuch des Bundes der AsienKämpfer*. Band 3, 1923.

173. Von Kressenstein, Friedrich Freiherr Kress. "The Campaign in Palestine from the Enemy's Side." *Journal of the Royal United Service Institution*. 67 (February 1922): 503–13.

174. Von Kressenstein, Friedrich Freiherr Kress. "*Mit den Türken zum SuezKanal*. Berlin: Verlag Otto Schlegel, 1938.

175. Von Kressenstein, Friedrich Freiherr Kress. "Uberblick uber die Ereignisse an der Sinai-Front von Kriegsbeginn bis zur Besetzung Jerusalems durch die Englander Ende 1917." *Zwischen Kaukasus und Sinai: Jahrbuch des Bundes der AsienKämpfer: 1921*. Berlin: Mulzer & Cleemann, 1921.

176. Von Ludendorff, Erich. *Ludendorff's Own Story, August 1914–November 1918*. New York, Harper and Bros., 1919.

177. Von Sanders, Liman. *Five Years in Turkey*. Trans. from the August Scherl Edition, Berlin, 1920. Annapolis: U.S. Naval Institute, 1927.

178. Von Steinitz, Ritter, General-Major, ed. *Zwei Jahrzehnte im Nahen Orient: Auf zeichnungen des Generals der Kavellerie Baron Wladimir Geisl*. Berlin: Verlag für Kultur Politik, 1927.

179. Wallach, Jehuda L. *Anatomie einer Militärhilfe: die Preussisch-deutschen Militärmissionen in der Turkei, 1835–1919*. Schriftenreihe des Instituts für Deutsche Geschichte Universität Tel Aviv. Dusseldorf: Droste Verlag, 1976.

180. Walker, Christopher. *Armenia: the Survival of a Nation*. Revised Second Edition. New York: St. Martin's Press, 1990.

181. Wavell, Archibald, Field Marshal Viscount. *Allenby: Soldier and Statesman*. London: Harrap and Co., 1946.

182. Wavell, Archibald. *The Palestine Campaigns*. London: Constable and Co., 1931 (orig. 1928).

183. Weldon, L. B., Captain. *Hard Lying: Eastern Mediterranean, 1914–1919*. London: Herbert Jenkins, 1925.

184. Wemyss, Viscount Rosslyn Erskine, Admiral. *The Navy in the Dardanelles Campaign.* London: Hodder and Stoughton, 1924.

185. Westrate, Bruce. *The Arab Bureau: British Policy in the Middle East, 1916–1920.* University Park: Pennsylvannia State University Press, 1992.

186. Williams, Sir Richard. *These Are Facts: The Autobiography of Air Marshal Sir Richard Williams KBE, CB, DSO.* Canberra: The Australian War Memorial and the Australian Government Publishing Service, 1977.

187. Wilson, Jeremy. *Lawrence of Arabia: The Authorised Biography of T. E. Lawrence.* London: William Heinemann, 1989.

188. Wilson, Keith M., ed. *Imperialism and Nationalism in the Middle East: The Anglo-Egyptian Experience, 1882–1982.* London: Mansell Publishing, 1983.

189. Wilson, Robert H. *Palestine 1917.* Edited by Helen D. Millgate. D. J. Costello, 1987.

190. Winstone, H. V. F., ed. *The Diaries of Parker Pasha.* London: Quartet Books, 1983.

191. Winstone, H. V. F., ed. *The Illicit Adventure: The Story of a Political and Military Intelligence Officer in the Middle East from 1896–1926.* London: Jonathan Cape, 1982.

192. Wood, Sir Evelyn, Field Marshal. *Ian Hamilton's Despatches from the Dardanelles, etc.* London: George Newnes, Ltd., 1917.

193. Zeine, Zeine N. *The Emergence of Arab Nationalism: With a Background Study of Arab-Turkish Relations in the Near East.* New York: Caraven Books, 1958.

194. Robin Higham, ed. *Official Histories,* pp. 474–79. Manhattan, KS: Sunflower University Press, 1970.

195. Robin Higham, ed. *Official Military Historical Offices and Sources I, Europe, Africa, the Middle East and India,* pp. 313–41. Westport, CT: Greenwood Press, 2000.

196. Bean, C. E. W. *Gallipolis Mission.* Canberra, ACT: Australian War Memorial, 1948 (reprinted Sydney, 1990).

197. Hughes, Matthew. *Allenby and British Policy in the Middle East, 1917–1919.* London: Frank Cass, 1999.

MOVIES

198. *Lawrence of Arabia* (Peter O'Toole) 1962–1963.

199. *Gallipoli* (Mel Gibson), 1983–1984.

200. *The Light Horsemen* (Australian film about the capture of Beersheba), 1988–1989.

POPULAR UNIFORM BOOKS

Each of these books has at least one pertinent plate on uniforms of the Middle Eastern Theater.

201. Nicolle, David. *Lawrence and the Arab Revolts.* Osprey Men-at-Arms Series. London: Osprey Publishing, Ltd. 1989.

202. Nicolle, David. *The Ottoman Army, 1914–1918.* Osprey Men-at-Arms Series. London: Reed International Books, Ltd. 1994.

203. Fosten, D. S. V., and R. J. Marrion. *The British Army, 1914–1918.* Osprey Men-at-Arms Series. London: Osprey Publishing, Ltd. 1978.

204. Fosten, D. S. V., and R. J. Marrion. *The German Army, 1914–1918.* Osprey Men-at-Arms Series. London: Osprey Publishing, Ltd. 1978.

9

The Balkans: Serbia, Bulgaria, Romania, and Greece

Glenn E. Torrey

World War I has been called, and not without reason, the Third Balkan War. Not only did an act of Balkan terrorism serve as a catalyst for the larger European conflict, but rivalry over this region had poisoned relations between the Great Powers for decades. The Balkans also posed perplexing problems for the conduct of the war. Both groups of belligerents sought to bolster their forces by recruiting new allies among the Balkan neutrals. Later, they came to question the price they paid for the assistance of these small powers as they required substantial aid, including the diversion of large contingents from the main battle fronts. Furthermore, the political concessions necessary to win their allegiance created difficulties for the peace conference at Paris in 1919. The consequences of some of these issues persist to the present day.

Proper understanding of the Balkans has been handicapped by the paucity of reliable, dispassionate studies. During the past generation, however, the situation has greatly improved. The opening of Western European archives in the 1960s not only stimulated researchers in the West to choose Balkan topics and produce solidly-based accounts, but also it encouraged Balkan scholars to travel to these same repositories to the great benefit of the credibility of their own writings. Perhaps more significant has been the trend among Balkan authorities to open their own archives to foreign scholars and to encourage international symposia. The revolutions of 1989 have accelerated these trends and have freed Balkan historians from their earlier dependence on Marxist presuppositions. Consequently, in addition to giving preference to scholarship based on archival research done during the last generation, special attention has been to seek out works published in the last decade. However, important older works have not been neglected. Although this section of the *Handbook* centers on Serbia, Bulgaria, Romania, and Greece, modest attention will be given to two other small Balkan countries: Montenegro, which was intimately involved with Serbia as Novica Rakočević shows [170]; and Albania, which was a special bone of contention in Balkan politics and diplomacy.

Whenever possible, literature in western languages will be suggested. But for many topics the inclusion of a substantial number of titles in Balkan languages was necessary. Fortunately, Balkan historians have made a concerted effort to ease the access of foreign readers to their scholarship through bilingual editions, translations of monographs and documentary collections, or at least through the inclusion of summaries in English, German, or French. In addition, historical journals in western languages are published regularly in Bulgaria [22, 56], Greece [8], and Romania [175, 217]. Occasionally, volumes of the *Revue internationale d'histoire militaire* [174], whose publication is rotated annually from country to country, are devoted to the Balkans. Furthermore there are a number of western-edited journals concerned with Balkan studies whose pages frequently contain articles on World War I [53, 181, 190, 197, 207]. Readers with appropriate language skills may also consult specialized military periodicals for Bulgaria [229], Romania [173], and Serbia [230].

General bibliographical assistance can be found in Clio's World Bibliographical Series [30, 74, 193, 225]. More detailed guides include: *Südost-Bibliographie* [206] and *Bibliographie Rumänien* [16] (both publications of the respected Südost Institut in Munich); *Bibliographie d'études balkaniques* [15] (Bulgaria); and the very complete and ongoing *Bibliografia istorica a României* [13] (Romania). Among military bibliographies, John E. Jessup's *Balkan Military History: A Bibliography* [86] is a beginning. Others include: *Bulgarskata armiia 1877–1944: bibliografiia* [88], *Bibliografia militara româneasca* [14] and its English recension, *Romanian Military Bibliography* [182]. Although now dated, two older bibliographies on Romania in the war retain some value [179, 214]. Another very helpful aid for the researcher is a four-volume biographical dictionary produced by the Südost Institut [17].

The complexity and turbulence of Balkan history necessitates discrimination, especially in selecting background texts. More than 40 years after its appearance, Leften Stavrianos' *The Balkans Since 1453* [203] remains the most reliable survey. For an understanding of the emergence of the Balkan national states in the nineteenth century, the writings of Charles and Barbara Jelavich are the best guides [83, 84]. Reliable surveys for individual countries are Richard Clogg [26] (Greece); R. J. Crampton [31] (Bulgaria), Michael Petrovich [149] (Serbia), and Keith Hitchins [73] (Romania). The latter two are the most comprehensive and are unequaled in any language. Miranda Vickers has a survey of modern Albania that gives substantial attention to World War I [227].

There is, as yet, no single satisfactory general survey of the Balkans during the war. However, several volumes in the series *War and Society in East Central Europe,* edited by Bela Király, are devoted to the war and contain many extremely helpful articles [91–93, 143, 231]. For an introduction to almost any subject and its relevant bibliography, it is prudent to consult these volumes, which draw upon the expertise of both western and Balkan specialists. For economic matters, the survey of Balkan economic history by John Lampe and Marvin Jackson contains a brief but authoritative coverage of the war period [102]. The same reliability can be found in Lampe's *Bulgarian Economy in the 20th Century* [103]. Also, there is an article on the Bulgarian economy in a Király volume [11]. The Carnegie series, *The Economic and Social History of the World War,* has volumes on Serbia [235], Greece [4], Romania [77], and Bulgaria [38]. In the same series, David Mitrany has contributed a general survey of the economic impact of the war in Southeastern Europe [121]. He has also produced a study of the Romanian peasant problem 1917–1921 [122]. Much of the Marxist literature on social and economic themes produced 1944–1989 needs to be revised.

For individual countries, general historical surveys do exist. For Serbia, volume 6 of a collective history is devoted to the war period [80]. Novica Rakočević has a survey of Montenegro in the war [169]. The South Slav specialist at the Institute of Balkan Studies in Moscow, Iuri Pisarev, has an account that covers both Serbia and Montenegro [154]. The Institute of History of the Bulgarian Academy is producing a lavish history of Bulgaria in 14 volumes [79]. The volumes on the war and events that immediately preceded it are forthcoming. There is also N. Nedev's older monograph on Bulgaria in the war [135]. Likewise, on Greece, there are older accounts in French, mostly political and diplomatic in nature, by Eduoard Driault [49] and A. F. Phrangoules [152]. In Greek there is a two-volume work by Georgios Ventiris [224]. For Romania there is the classic nationalistic account by Constantin Kirițescu [95] and its French recension [96], the unsympathetic but informed survey by the Russian Romanian specialist V. N. Vinogradov [228], and, most importantly, two quasi-official collective works [178, 177]. The first is more helpful on political-diplomatic issues while the second, written primarily by military historians and more than double in length, is able to give more extensive coverage of military operations. Helpful supplements to these Romanian titles are a collection of studies by Glenn Torrey [213] and a volume of symposium papers edited by Kurt Treptow [219].

Because the war period in each of the Balkan countries was dominated by strong political leaders, it is essential to consult accounts by or about them. For Serbia this means Premier Nicola Pašić [89, 202], for Greece, King Constantine and Premier Eleutherios Venizelos [222, 239], for Bulgaria, King Ferdinand [27, 115] and Premier Vasil Radoslavov [165], especially the recently edited version of the latter's 1914–1918 diary [166]. In addition to the biography of Romanian Premier Ion I. C. Brătianu by Anastasie Iordache [78], almost half of which is devoted to the war period, one should consult the memoirs of one of Brătianu's closest collaborators, I. C. Duca [50]. A number of important wartime Balkan leaders are evaluated in articles contained in the Király volume on *East Central European War Leaders: Civilian and Military* [93].

Turning to the diplomatic background of the involvement of the Balkan nations in the war, it is important to give some consideration to their prewar relationships with the Great Powers. Although some accounts, such as that of Pisarev [157], reach back to the Congress of Berlin (1878) whose decisions haunted Balkan history for decades, most studies begin a decade or so before 1914. This is the emphasis of a 1976 volume issuing from an international symposium on the Great Powers and Serbia on the eve of the First World War [34]. In addition to presenting the views of both Eastern and Western specialists, its contributions contain a significant number in western languages. This same period is also the starting point of books by Andrej Mitrović on Austro-German policy toward Serbia [124], Konstantin Loulos on German-Greek relations [109], Novica Rakočević [168] and John Treadway [218] on Montenegro's relations with Austria-Hungary, Şerban Rădulescu-Zoner [167] on the alliance between the Central Powers and Romania, and Vasile Vesa [226] on the latter's relationship with France. Andrew Rossos [184] traces the growth of Russia's influence in Southeastern Europe after 1908, climaxing with her sponsorship of the Balkan Alliance of 1912. But he demonstrates how the Second Balkan War (1913) exposed the danger inherent in a policy of attempting to court simultaneously Balkan nations with conflicting territorial ambitions. As a consequence, Russia's dominant position in the region fell apart and left her Balkan flank insecure in 1914.

But a more immediate influence on the involvement of Serbia, Bulgaria, Greece, and Romania in World War I were the two internecine Balkan wars (1912–1913) that preceded it. Early in 1912 the first three named joined together to take over what remained of Turkey-in-Europe. This was easily accomplished during a brief campaign in the autumn of that year. But after some months of wrangling over the division of the spoils, a second conflict broke out in the summer of 1913 among the victors. Bulgaria was defeated, not only by her former allies, but also by Romania (and then Turkey as well). From this Second Balkan War, Bulgaria emerged truncated and bitter, her Balkan neighbors enlarged but insecure about their gains. In addition, the outcome of these conflicts stimulated irredentist sentiment in Serbia and Romania that in turn evoked paranoia in Austria-Hungary, whose provinces they coveted. Ernest C. Helmreich's *The Diplomacy of the Balkan Wars,* although more than 60 years old, is still useful, especially on the involvement of the Great Powers and the conflict's impact on their attitudes toward war [72]. Its discussion of the roles of the Great Powers can be supplemented by Edward Thaden's study of Russian policy [209] and R. J. Crampton's monograph on the Balkans in British-German relations, 1911–1914 [32]. However, the new standard for understanding the interplay of Balkan ethnicity, politics, and nationalism 1912–1914 is the recent study, based on wide-ranging archival research, by Katrin Boeckh [18]. She emphasizes the ethnic basis of Balkan conflict and shows how longstanding problems were exacerbated by the territorial settlement following the Second Balkan War. Events on the battlefield are summarized succinctly while close attention is given to economic issues, frontier delineation, population dislocation, minorities, religious issues, and the attitudes of those involved. Also extremely valuable are the articles in the Király volume devoted to the Balkan Wars [91]. There is a recent Greek history of the Balkan Wars in English [242].

When the world war opened in August 1914, Serbia was the only Balkan nation involved. Bulgaria remained neutral until October 1915, Romania until August 1916, and Greece until June 1917. Consequently much of the history of World War I in the Balkans is diplomatic history. From the summer of 1914, these neutrals became the objects of intense competition between the opposing groups of belligerents, who were seeking new allies. The efforts that the Russians undertook are described on the basis of published documents in a book by C. Jay Smith, Jr. [196], and in a collective volume edited by Alexander Dallin [37]. Ineffective British initiatives in the Balkans during the early months of the war are described in a monograph by Lynn Curtright [35]. David Dutton, however, has the most recent and complete analysis of British-French policy, which he carries through to 1918 [52]. As well as being critical of the diplomacy of the Entente powers toward the Balkan neutrals, he offers an extremely negative judgment on their military campaign at Salonika as we will point out later. Italy's Balkan policy is explained in a long article by James Burgwyn [23]. The Balkan diplomacy of the Central Powers takes up a major portion of Gerard Silberstein's book on German-Austrian relations 1914–1917 [194].

From the perspective of the individual Balkan states themselves, there are many diplomatic studies. The prolific Pisarev has a monograph on Russian-Serbian relations 1914–1915 [156] and the Serb Nikola Popović has two books on the same subject [158, 159]. Popović's books, which benefit from access to the archives of the Quai d'Orsay in Paris, portray Serbia as struggling not only against an enemy on the battlefield but against her Entente allies diplomatically as they sought to convince her to buy off Bulgaria to keep the latter neutral. Milorad Ekmečić has a short, recent survey that is also critical of the Entente's attempts to facilitate the creation of a Balkan bloc based on Serbian concessions [54]. An even more recent monograph on Serb-Greek relations 1914–1918 by Miladin Milosěvić examines the futile attempt to persuade Greece to come to the aid of Serbia in 1914–1915 and the uneasy relationship that continued between these two nations throughout the war [119]. There are also several important articles on this subject in a volume produced by a Greek-Serbian symposium [162].

A host of monographs by both native and Western scholars trace the path Bulgaria, Romania, and Greece trod as they moved toward war. Bulgaria was close to a commitment to the Central Powers in the summer of 1914 but drew back until October 1915 when she joined in the attack on Serbia. Her policy during neutrality and her decision for war are analyzed in two studies by Western historians: Wolfgang-Uwe Friedrich [61] and Christopher Hall [70]. The latter devotes most of his attention to the background of Bulgaria's decision. Friedrich explains Bulgarian motivation on the basis of economic advantage, a burning hatred of Serbia, the venality of some Bulgarian leaders, and the simple fact that the Central Powers could offer unlimited amounts of Serbian territory while the Entente could not. In addition, a number of Bulgarian historians have written accounts that are likewise based, in part, on western European archives (as well as Bulgarian). These include Ivan Ilchev, who concentrates on relations with the

Entente [76]; Georgi Markov, who views the Bulgarian decision in a wider European perspective [118]; and Milcho Lalkov, who argues that the Central Powers would have been satisfied with Bulgaria's neutrality if she had refused to intervene [101]. A recent contribution by Mincho Semov [188] provides documents as well as commentary. All of these studies indicate that Bulgaria's leaders, anxious to avenge their defeat in the Second Balkan War, were persuaded that this could be accomplished by an alliance with the Central Powers, a "fatal illusion" as Gencho Kamburov has titled his book [87]. This led to Bulgaria's second military disaster in a decade. A third would come a generation later.

Romania, in turn, prolonged her neutrality for over two years before joining the Entente by invading Austria-Hungary on 27 August 1916. This delay was not due to indecision over which side she should range herself but over concern to secure a political convention guaranteeing her the annexation of Habsburg provinces inhabited by ethnic Romanians and a military convention which promised supporting offensives that would make intervention less of a gamble. For Premier Brătianu, who alone directed Romanian policy, the task was not easy. He had to placate the Central Powers with grain sales and lies while at the same time creating confidence among the Entente leaders that his ultimate loyalty was to them. Brătianu's brilliant management of Romania's "expectative neutrality," which involved controlling internal agitation for and against war as well as balancing between the belligerents, is described in Constantin Nuțu's survey [137]. Romania's relations with the Central Powers are documented in Ema Nastovici's monograph [130] and those with France in the work of Vasile Vesa [226]. Victor Atanasiu discusses the military aspects of Romanian neutrality [6]. Several articles in the collection by Glenn Torrey are relevant to these Romanian accounts [213].

The story of Greece's turbulent neutrality, 1914–1917, which involved internal division and the violation of her sovereignty by an Allied expeditionary force at Salonika, is the focus of a number of studies. Among the most important, based on archival research, are those by Christo Theodoulou [210] and George Leon [108]. Both concentrate on the early years of the war. Also valuable are Greek-British [68] and Greek-French [100] symposium volumes that contain a number of pertinent essays.

The war in the Balkans was markedly different from that on other fronts not only in prolonged periods of diplomatic maneuvering but in that the fighting was divided among three theaters of operations whose campaigns were brief and relatively unrelated to one another. There is no satisfactory survey covering all of these. Commandant Maurice Larcher's *La grande guerre dans les Balkans* [105] is dated. So is a volume by Nicolai Korsun that gives a short, year-by-year summary of military operations [98]. Carl Mühlmann's informed study based on the German military archives subsequently destroyed in World War II covers only Germany's strategy and operations [129]. Norman Stone's survey of the Eastern Front is well researched and full of insight but has only two chapters on the Balkans and it ends in 1917 [204]. Multivolume, concurrent accounts, such as *The Times* (*London*) *History of the War* [211], do give coverage to all theaters but have the limitations inherent in contemporary writing. However, one should not neglect to consult them. They are based, to a degree, on the reports of war correspondents in the Balkans, many of whom were longtime residents there and well informed. In contrast to a paucity of overviews, specialized accounts of individual campaigns in the Balkans are numerous. It is to these that we now turn, dealing with each of the three theaters of operations in chronological order.

Fighting began in the Balkans in August 1914 with an Austrian "punitive expedition" against Serbia as a retaliation for the assassination of the Habsburg Heir Apparent, Archduke Francis Ferdinand, by a Bosnian Serb at Sarajevo on 28 June. The roots of this tragedy have attracted much attention with books by the American Joachim Remak [172] and the Yugoslav Vladimir Dedijer [39] being considered the standard accounts. Remak emphasizes the complicity of Serbian officials in recruiting, training, arming, and otherwise facilitating the work of the young assassins. Dedijer, on the other hand, stresses the initiative of the young student radicals, especially Gavrilo Princip. A trilogy by David MacKenzie on the subversive Serbian terrorist organization, the Black Hand, and its guiding spirit, Colonel Dragutin T. Dimitrijević, nicknamed "Apis," brings new and perhaps definitive answers [112–114]. With Remak, he affirms the responsibility of Dimitrijević, who was at the time Chief of Serbian Military Intelligence, in conceiving and planning the deed. But he also emphasizes the determination of Princip and his young colleagues to carry it through despite Dimitrijević's last-minute attempt to stop them in favor of other means. Several articles in a collection edited by Keith Wilson [232], update our understanding of the transition from the assassination to war. The detailed and insightful con-tribution of Mark Cornwall [29] on Serbia emphasizes that the government in Belgrade was aware of rumors regarding a plot but did little in a concrete way to stop it beforehand or to investigate it afterward. Yet, as he shows, Pašić and most responsible Serbian leaders dearly wanted to avoid war with Austria but not at the expense of compromising Serbian sovereignty.

The story of the three unsuccessful attempts of the Austro-Hungarian army to invade Serbia in 1914 are, of course, covered in detail in the official military his-tories of Serbia [236] and Austria [7]. But there are also many other accounts to consult. A number of these are in English. Graydon Tunstall analyzes Austro-German war plans, showing how muddled priorities, incompetence, and per-sonal egos doomed the initial attack in August [221]. Gunther Rothenberg has an article, "The Austro-Hungarian Campaign Against Serbia in 1914" [185], but James B. Lyon's dissertation, based on research in both Belgrade and Vienna, is the most recent and most complete account in English [111]. Among other things, Lyon argues that the Austro-Hungarian army was not so weak or poorly prepared as is often assumed. This fact underscores the desperate patriotism of the Serbs, hopelessly outclassed in numbers and equipment, which allowed them to repel their invader. A more accessible introduction to Lyon's work is available in a journal article [110]. Among many Serbian accounts of the battles of 1914, one could mention one on the Battle of Jadra by Živko Pavlović [145] and one on the Battle of Drina by Mitar Djurišic [46]. Pavlović, chief of the operations section of the Serbian army who turned historian after the war, also has a detailed operational history of the third humiliating defeat administered to the Habsburg army in December 1914 at Kolubara [146]. What Pavlović's writings lack in detached analysis, they compensate for in intimate familiarity with operational issues and in his personal observations. Essential insight into the two opposing military leaders and their strategy can be found in recent and authoritative biographies of the much maligned General Oskar Potiorek [85] and the legendary Voyvode Radomir Putnik [195]. Two articles by Professor Djordjević evaluate Putnik and Serbian strategy [44, 45]. Naval operations in the Serbian campaigns are recounted by Olaf Wulff [234] and Charles Fryer [63].

Following the third Austro-Hungarian failure at Kolubara in December 1914, the Serbian front was relatively quiet until October 1915, when Bulgarian and German forces joined with the Habsburg army in a new and decisive assault. At this point the Bulgarian [21] and German [65] official military histories become relevant. The greatly outnumbered and under-equipped Serbian army, attacked from two directions, was forced to retreat to the south and then westward. Among the Serbian accounts there is another detailed operational narrative by Pavlović, which carries the story to the end of 1915 [147]. The sources for the important Battle of Mojkovacka, which took place as the pursuit passed through Montenegro, include a monograph by Aleksandar Drašković [46] and a recent symposium volume [127]. Montenegro had been closely aligned with Serbia from the beginning of the war in 1914, but her army played little role in the initial fighting. However in 1915–1916 her forces served as the rear guard of the Serbian army; a recent monograph gives due credit [237]. The classic account of the defeat and retreat of the Serbian army for English readers is still John C. Adams, *Flight in Winter* [1]. It vividly recounts the difficulties encountered by the Serbs as they struggled to reach the Adriatic for evacuation. This retreat was accompanied by suffering aggravated by severe weather and rugged terrain. This drama is also reflected in accounts by Charles Fryer [62] and Monica Krippner [99]. There are several articles based on the reports of French military and diplomatic representatives that give new details about the evacuation of the Serbian forces to Corfu, where they were reorganized [220, 240]. General Piarron de Mondésir, who headed a French military mission to assist the reconstruction of the Serbian army, has left his account of this process [153]. This is also the theme of Ripert d'Alauzier's *Une drame historique. La résurrection d'armée serbe. Albanie-Corfou 1915–1916* [176].

Internal developments in Serbia during the war are the subject of a series of year-by-year volumes, each containing essays on a wide variety of subjects [131–134]. There are also monographs devoted to Serbian politics and diplomacy in 1916 and 1918 by the Russian Pisarev [156] and the Yugoslavs Bogumil Hrabak and Dragoslav Janković [75]. The enemy perspective on Serbia's occupation is covered in a volume by P. Kirch [94] and in a chapter in Hugo Kerchnawe's general history of Austro-Hungarian occupation forces during the war [90]. The Serbian historian Andrej Mitrović has written an important article based on research in Germany and Austria on the creation of the occupation zones [126].

Some of the reorganized Serb army eventually joined the Allied expeditionary force thathad opened a second Balkan theater of operations at Salonika late in 1915. Although this so-called Allied Army of the Orient [AAO] proved to be too little, too late to save Serbia, it built up a substantial force of British, French, Serbian, Italian, and even Russian troops that eventually exceeded 500,000 men. Inter-allied rivalry, inadequate support from France and England, logistical problems and the strong military positions of the opposing forces of the Central Powers prevented the AAO from undertaking significant offensive operations until late in 1918. The problems at Salonika are analyzed in Jan Tanenbaum's biography of General Maurice Sarrail, the French commander of the AAO [208]. He argues that Sarrail did more than could have been expected of him under the circumstances and does not deserve the bad press he has received. Alan Palmer gives us a very good, readable account in *The Gardeners of Salonika* [142], whose title comes from Clemenceau's derisive reference to the housekeeping duties of idle Allied soldiers encamped there. David Dutton is extremely critical of the Allied military involvement at Salonika, judging it doomed from the start while immobilizing men needed elsewhere. It illustrates, he maintains, the Allied conduct of the war at its worst. For the French it was motivated primarily by internal political needs, especially the attempt of parliament to reestablish control over the high command. For the English, who were never enthusiastic about it and continually dragged their feet, it was a concession to Paris deemed necessary to preserve the Anglo-French alliance [52]. A more positive evaluation of the AAO is given in the French official history [60] as well as in accounts by F. J. Deygas [41] and André Ducasse [51]. A recent article by Allain Bernède [10] explains in detail the logistical problems of the AAO. The Serbs have recorded their role in their official history [236] and Miladin Milošević's study details Serb relations with the Greeks while there [119]. The Italian official history has a volume on its troops in Greece [81]. There is also a recent article on the Italian presence from the Greek perspective [192]. It argues that, while not extremely important, Italian cooperation did aid in the transportation problem. Italy's participation, the author maintains, was motivated by her interest in Albania and concern about possible growth of Greek influence in the eastern Mediterranean. The Russian role at Salonika is well covered in a monograph on Russian expeditionary forces [25] and, more specifically, in an excellent article by Richard Spence [200]. Probably the most satisfactory single account of the Allied operations at Salonika is the two-volume British official history written by Cyril Falls [58]. For the perspective of the Central Powers there are the official histories [7, 21, 65]. These can be supplemented by Georg Strutz, *Herbstschlacht in Mazedonien* [205] and N. Nedev, *Les opérations en Macedoine: l'epopée de Dorian 1915–1918* [136].

The relative inactivity of the AAO during 1916–1917 has been blamed in part for the disastrous defeat of the Romanian army, which opened the third Balkan theater of operations by attacking Austria-Hungary on 27 August 1916. According to Romania's military convention with the Entente, the latter was obliged to launch an *offensive affirmée* from Salonika to prevent Bulgaria and her allies from attacking Romania's southern frontier. But a timely Macedonian offensive by the Central Powers themselves threw Sarrail's plans into disarray before he could attack. At the same time as Romania was sending the bulk of its army across the Carpathians into virtually undefended Transylvania, a strong German-Bulgarian-Turkish force led by General August von Mackensen, the conqueror of Serbia, penetrated Romania's southern defenses. Panicking, the Romanians called a halt to their promising success in the north and shifted their forces for an ill-fated offensive in the south. This gave German and Austro-Hungarian leaders time to assemble powerful forces in Transylvania, including a new Ninth German Army under General Erich von Falkenhayn, recently deposed head of the German High Command. The Romanian army was forced back into the Carpathians in October and in November Falkenhayn penetrated the Romanian heartland itself. At that very critical moment, von Mackensen launched a new attack across the Danube with a German-Austrian-Bulgarian-Turkish force. The Romanian army and government were forced to surrender two-thirds of their homeland and take refuge in a Moldavian enclave sheltered by the Russian army. In addition to the German [65], Austrian [7], and Bulgarian [21] official histories, the account of the 1916 campaign by Falkenhayn himself is essential [57]. Austrian [171], Bulgarian [216], and Turkish [55, 243] monographs add detail. The commander of a Russian expeditionary force that was sent into Dobrogea to aid the newest member of the Entente has an account in which he defends himself against the Romanian charge he left his ally in the lurch [238]. Of special interest is the personal account of Erwin Rommel [183], then a company grade officer in the Würtemberg Mountain Battalion. He chronicles both the ineptness of the inexperienced Romanian army in 1916 as well as its successful turnaround in 1917. It also demonstrates the driving leadership on the field of battle that made him one of the world's great military commanders.

    From the Romanian perspective, there are several very brief accounts in English, one by Costica Prodan [163] being the most recent. The very detailed and sober official Romanian military history [180] ends, unfortunately, in December 1916, its publication delayed by World War II and then suspended in the political upheaval that occurred in 1947. So, for the Romanian campaigns of 1916 and 1917, especially the latter in which a reconstructed Romanian army fought the Central Powers to a standstill, one must turn to the general histories already mentioned [95, 178, 179], and most importantly to the analytical four-volume work by Gheorghe Dabija [36], who was a member of the team that produced the Romanian official history. Although Dabija is outspokenly partisan on some controversial issues, his account is as yet unmatched. The renaissance of the Romanian army in 1917 was materially assisted by the Allies, especially by a French military mission under General Henri Berthelot. Insight into the Romanian front as well as Allied policy toward Romania and intervention in South Russia can be gained from accounts by or about Berthelot, including his memoirs and correspondence [12], a biography [212], two symposia [64, 104], and a doctoral thesis [66].

The successful defense of Moldavia by the Romanian army in 1917 in the face of a determined Austro-German offensive appeared to be for naught when the Bolsheviks came to power in Russia and forced the Romanian government to follow Moscow into an armistice (December 1917). The impact of revolutionary elements of the Russian army in Romania before and after the armistice is discussed in a monograph by Glenn Torrey [215]. Romanian-Russian relations during the war in a broader sense, including the Romanian annexation of Bessarabia, which followed in 1918, occupy most of Ion Oprea's recent monograph [139]. It sets forth a Romanian viewpoint that had to be ignored or soft-pedaled after World War II. For the separate peace into which the defection of Russia forced the Romanians (March 1918), see Elke Bornemann's *Der Frieden von Bukarest 1918* [19]. Despite its orientation toward the policy of the Central Powers, it is far and away the best account of the Romanian peace now available. Basing her research on exhaustive use of German and Austrian archives, she describes in detail the imposition of onerous peace terms in spite of anguished Romanian resistance. German dominance of the negotiations left her allies dissatisfied. After this "Peace of Bucharest," Wallachia remained under enemy occupation while a government in Moldavia, headed by Alexandru Marghiloman, functioned under vassalage to the Central Powers. Marghiloman's bilingual journal is essential for understanding this period of Romanian history [117]. The occupation regime in Wallachia is described by the Habsburg officers Hugo Kerchnawe [90] and Alexander Kontz de Körpenyes [97] and in the Romanian monographs of Grigore Antipa [5] and Emil Racila [164].

After the capitulation of Romania, military operations in the Balkans were quiescent until the autumn of 1918 when the AAO, now under the energetic leadership of General Franchet d'Esperey, mounted an offensive in Macedonia. During 1917, the Allies (led by the French) had forced Greek King Constantine, the neutralist brother-in-law of Emperor William II, out of office and installed Eleutherios Venizelos, an avid pro-Entente interventionist, as head of a new government. These machinations and the subsequent entry of Greece into the war are covered in a number of books. In addition to those on Constantine and Venizelos already mentioned [222] [239], there are studies by Alex Mitrakos [120], Yannis Mouréles [128], and N. Petsales-Diomedes [151]. Articles in a 1989 Greek-French symposium are also helpful [101]. But the best guide to events in Greece during this period is the most recent book by George Leon, *The Intervention of Greece in the First World War 1917–1918* [107]. It is based on extensive research in Greek, French, British, and American archival sources. The later chapters in Dutton [52] are also relevant to these events.

A successful offensive northward by the AAO in September 1918 knocked Bulgaria out of the war and liberated Serbia. In addition to the French [60], German [65], Austrian [7], Bulgarian [21], Italian [81], Serbian [236], and British [58] official histories already mentioned, this campaign is the subject of a volume of the Greek general staff [69] whose army now joined with the AAO. An older, shorter account of the Greek participation is available in French [20]. There are also monographs on the Salonika offensive by the Bulgarian Bozhan Deliiski [40], the Frenchmen Louis Cordier [28] and Roger Cros [33], the Yugoslavs Milivoje Alimpic [2] and Peter Opačic [138], and the German Alfred Dieterich [42]. Jean Bernachot has authored a multivolume account of the operations of the AAO, beginning with the surrender of Bulgaria on 29 September [9]. A recent article by Bruno Hamard gives an updated summary of these operations from September to November [71].

The collapse of Bulgaria and the imminence of an armistice in the West motivated the Romanians to remobilize their army and reenter the war to validate their claim to the promises of Austro-Hungarian territory contained in the Treaty of August 1916, which had been thrown into doubt by the Treaty of Bucharest. The collapse of German resistance in the West inclined Mackensen to evacuate Romania peacefully. This, coupled with the disintegration of the Austro-Hungarian Empire, allowed the Romanian army to reoccupy its prewar territory and then advance progressively into Transylvania despite Hungarian protests and Allied disapprobation. The story of Romanian remobilization, reentry, and advance into Hungary, which eventually reached Budapest, is amply recounted in Dumitru Preda et al., *La Roumanie et sa guerre pour l'unité nationale* [161]. The shifting and sometimes contradictory policy of the Allies in the face of this situation is analyzed very competently and in great detail by Maria Ormos in her monograph, *From Padua to the Trianon* [140].

Meanwhile, at the Paris Peace Conference, the Allied Powers found that achieving a generally acceptable settlement for the Balkans was one of their most vexing tasks. In an atmosphere poisoned by nationalist passions newly inflamed by the war, they had difficulty reconciling ethnic and historical claims with their own national interests and especially with their wartime commitments. The story of the evolution of these commitments can be followed in monographs by Kenneth J. Calder [24], Wilfried Fest [59], and Leo Valiani [223]. Several publications relating to the career of R. W. Seton-Watson, the indefatigable critic of Hungarian nationality policy, are essential, including a biography by his sons [191] and publication of his correspondence and writings regarding Yugoslavia [187] and Romania [186], both in bilingual editions. For the American attitude toward the Balkans during the war there is the older work by Victor Mamatey [116] as well as monographs by Ion Stanciu on American-Romanian relations [201] and Petko Petkov on American-Bulgarian relations [148]. Pietro Pastorelli has a monograph on Italian policy toward Albania [144].

There are monographs in English on Balkan countries as their cases were considered at Paris: Sherman Spector (Romania) [199], Ivo J. Lederer (Yugoslavia) [106], N. Petsales-Diomedes (Greece) [150]. There are theses on the Bulgarian [47] and Albanian [233] settlements at Paris. The Yugoslav settlement and its evolution during the war has provoked the most controversy and the most literature. A good starting point is the American symposium edited by Dimitrije Djordjević [43]. There are several Yugoslav general accounts of the question including a study by Andrej Mitrović [123]. Dragoslav Janković has written a monograph on the Corfu Declaration [82]. The prolific Mitrović also considers the Yugoslav-Romanian territorial settlement [125]. Dragovan Sepič [189] and Dragoljub Zivojinović [241] have monographs examining the attitudes of the Allies toward the Yugoslav movement. The Bulgarian Hristo Andonov-Poljanski has a study of the British attitude toward the Macedonian question [3]. The settlement that eventually emerged from Paris in 1919 became the touchstone for the domestic and foreign policies of the Balkan states in the interwar era and continues to remain the focus of lively debate.

FURTHER RESEARCH

Although we can rejoice in the important advances that have been made during the past generation in documenting the history of World War I in the Balkans, much remains to be done. First, despite the obvious interconnectedness of the region, there is as yet no satisfactory general survey devoted to the war period and its place in the overall history of the Balkans. The same can be said for an authoritative history of military operations. It is frustrating to read chapters in textbooks on World War I reflecting outdated clichés that could have been avoided if their authors had access to a reliable military history based on the monographic studies now available. Such a survey would be very helpful, not only in understanding the fighting in the Balkans but also in placing it in the context of the larger dimensions of the world war. For example, did the operations on the Salonika and Romanian fronts relieve pressure on the Western Front 1916–1917 or did they simply divert and dilute Entente forces from the main battle areas? The same question could be asked of the efforts of the Central Powers in the region. Also in need of more attention are the economic and social aspects of the war period in the Balkans. The Carnegie series is dated. Post–World War II Marxist studies, while not without value, are in need of revision. More complete information as well as more sophisticated methods of analysis are now available. New areas of research involving the attitudes and experiences of the mass of the population, which have characterized recent scholarship on wartime Western Europe, need to be undertaken.

Additional progress needs to be made toward consensus on a number of controversial issues. Enforced "brotherhood" in the "socialist camp" after World War II temporarily muted some of the most strident rivalries among Balkan nationalist historians. Unfortunately, developments since 1989 have revived certain controversies. One might mention, among others, differing interpretations between Croats and Serbs over the creation of Yugoslavia, between Romanians and Russians (including Moldavians) over the annexation of Bessarabia, and between Romanians and Hungarians over the status of Transylvania, as well as Bulgarian-Romanian and Yugoslav-Romanian territorial disputes. On the other hand, progress toward democracy and interest in European union will, it is hoped, impede the spread of extreme nationalist interpretations. Freer access to archives and international symposia should have the same effect. But it is equally important for Western scholars to play a larger role in improving our understanding of World War I in the Balkans. Not only can they provide a more detached perspective, which will give more credibility to Balkans studies, but by writing in Western languages their research will be available to a wider audience. Such insight into Balkan history during World War I is important not only for recapturing the past but for understanding present and future developments.

BIBLIOGRAPHY

1. Adams, John Clinton. *Flight in Winter.* Princeton: Princeton University Press, 1942.

2. Alimpic, Milivoje. *Solunski front (The Salonika Front].* Belgrade: Vojnoizdavacki zavod, 1967.

3. Andonov-Poljanski, Hristo. *Velika Britanija i makedonskoto prasanje na Pariskata mirovna konferencija vo 1919 godina. So izbor od dokumentacijata [Great Britain and the Macedonian Question at the Paris Peace Conference 1919. With a Selection of Documents].* Skopje: Arhiv na Makedonija, 1973.

4. Andreades, Andreas Michael. *Les effets économiques et sociaux de la guerre en Grèce [The Economic and Social Effects of the War in Greece].* New Haven: Yale University Press, 1928.

5. Antipa, Grigore. *L'occupation ennemie de la Roumanie et ses conséquences économiques et sociales [The Enemy Occupation of Romania and its Economic and Social Consequences].* New Haven: Yale University Press, 1929.

6. Atanasiu, Victor. *România în anii 1914–1916: atitudina şi rolul militar [Romania in the Years 1914–1916: Military Posture and Role].* Bucharest: Editura academiei de inalte studii militare, 1997.

7. Austria. Bundesministerium fur Landesverteidigung. *Österreich-Ungarns Letzter Krieg 1914–1918 [Austria-Hungary's Last War 1914–1918],* 7 vols. Vienna: Verlag der Militärwissenschaftlichen Mitteilungen, 1930–1938.

8. *Balkan Studies.* Thessalonika: The Institute of Balkan Studies, 1960.

9. Bernachot, Jean. *Les Armées françaises en Orient après l'armistice de 1918 [The French Armies in the East after the Armistice of 1918].* Paris: Imprimerie nationale, 1970.

10. Bernède, Allain. "'The Gardeners of Salonika': The Lines of Communication and the Logistics of the French Army of the East, October 1915–November 1918." *War and Society* (1998) 16(1): 43–60.

11. Berov, Ljuben. "The Bulgarian Economy During World War I" in Bela Király, ed., *East Central European Society in World War I.* Boulder, CO/New New York: Columbia University Press, 1985, 170–83.

12. Berthelot, Henri Mathias. *General Henri Berthelot and Romania: mémoires et correspondance, 1916–1919,* ed. with a biographical introduction, by Glenn E. Torrey. Boulder, CO/New New York: Columbia University Press, 1987.

13. *Bibliografia istorică a României [Historical Bibliography of Romania].* Bucharest: Editura academiei Republicii Socialiste România, 1970.

14. *Bibliografia militară românească 1831–1983 [Romanian Military Bibliography 1831–1983],* 4 vols. Bucharest: Editura Militara, 1975–1984.

15. *Bibliographie d'études balkaniques [Bibliography of Balkan Studies].* Sofia: Academie bulgare des sciences, 1966.

16. *Bibliographie Rumänien 1971–1988 [Romanian Bibliography 1971–1988].* Munich: Oldenbourg, 1992.

17. *Biographisches Lexikon zur Geschichte Südosteuropas [Biographical Lexicon for the History of Southeast Europe].* Munich: Oldenbourg, 1974–1981.

18. Boeckh, Katrin. *Von den Balkankriegen zum Ersten Weltkrieg: Kleinstaatenpolitik und ethnische Selbstbestimmung auf dem Balkan* [*From the Balkan Wars to the First World War: Small State Politics and Ethnic Selfdetermination in the Balkans*]. Munich: Oldenbourg, 1996.

19. Bornemann, Elke. *Der Frieden von Bukarest 1918* [*The Peace of Bucharest 1918*]. Frankfurt am Main: Lang, 1978.

20. Bujac, Jean Leopold Emile. *Les Campagnes de l'armée hellenique 1918–1922* [*The Campaigns of the Greek Army 1918–1922*]. Paris: Charles-Lavauzelle, 1930.

21. *Bulgarskata armiia v Svietovnata voina, 1915–1918 g.* [*The Bulgarian Army in the World War, 1915–1918*], 9 vols. Sofia: Durzh. pechatnitsa, 1939.

22. *Bulgarian Historical Review.* Sofia: Publishing House of the Bulgarian Academy of Sciences, 1993.

23. Burgwyn, H. James. "Italy's Balkan Policy 1915–1917, Albania, Greece, and the Epirus Question." *Storia delle relazioni internazionale* (1986) 2(1): 3–61.

24. Calder, Kenneth J. *Britain and the Origins of the New Europe, 1914–1918.* New York: Cambridge University Press, 1976.

25. Chiniakov, M. K. *Russkie voiska vo Frantsii i Makedonii (Salonikakh): 1916–1918* [*Russian Forces in France and Macedonia* [*Salonika*]: *1916–1918*]. Moscow: Reitar, 1997.

26. Clogg, Richard. *A Short History of Modern Greece.* New York: Cambridge University Press, 1986.

27. Constant, Stephen. *Foxy Ferdinand, Tsar of Bulgaria.* New York: Franklin Watts, 1980.

28. Cordier, Louis. *Victoire éclair en Orient, 15–29 Septembre 1918* [*Lightning Victory in the East, 15–29 September 1918*]. Aurillac: Ed. USHA, 1969.

29. Cornwall, Mark. "Serbia," in Keith Wilson, *Decisions for War, 1914.* London: UCL Press, 1995, 55–96.

30. Crampton, R. J. *Bulgaria.* Santa Barbara, CA: Clio Press, 1989.

31. Crampton, R. J. *Bulgaria, 1878–1918: A History.* Boulder, CO/New York: Columbia University Press, 1983.

32. Crampton, R. J. *The Hollow Detente: Anglo-Germans Relations in the Balkans, 1911–1914.* London: George Prior, 1980.

33. Cros, Roger. *La victoire des armées alliées en Orient, 1918* [*The Victory of the Allied Armies in the East, 1918*]. Montpellier: Causse et Cie, 1968.

34. Čubrilović, Vasa, ed. *Velike sile i Srbija pred prvi svetski rat* [*The Great Powers and Serbia on the Eve of the First World War*]. Belgrade: Srpska akademija nauka i umetnosti, 1976.

35. Curtright, Lynn H. *Muddle, Indecision, and Setback: British Policy and the Balkan States, August 1914 to the Inception of the Dardanelles Campaign.* Thessalonika: The Institute for Balkan Studies, 1986.

36. Dabija, Gheorge. *Armata română în războiul mondial (1916–1918)* [*The Romanian Army in the World War (1916–1918)*], 4 vols. Bucharest: Hertz, 1936.

37. Dallin, Alexander, ed. *Russian Diplomacy and Eastern Europe, 1914–1917.* New York: King's Crown Press, 1963.

38. Danailov, Georgi T. *Les effets de la guerre en Bulgarie* [*The Effects of the War in Bulgaria*]. New Haven: Yale University Press, 1932.

39. Dedijer, Vladimir. *The Road to Sarajevo.* New York: Simon and Schuster, 1966. Expanded Serbo-Croat edition: *Sarajevo 1914,* 2 vols. Belgrade: Prosveta, 1978.

40. Deliiski, Bozhan. *Doiranskata epopeia: zabravena i nezabravima* [*The Dorian Epic: Forgotten and Not Forgotten*]. Sofia: [s.n.], 1993.

41. Deygas, F.-J. *L'Armée d'Orient dans la guerre mondiale (1915–1919)* [*The Army of the East in the World War (1915–1919)*]. Paris: Payot, 1932.

42. Dieterich, Alfred. *Weltkriegsende an der mazedonischen Front* [*The End of the World War on the Macedonian Front*]. Oldenburg: G. Stalling, 1925.

43. Djordjević, Dimitrije, ed. *The Creation of Yugoslavia, 1914–1918.* Santa Barbara, CA: Clio Books, 1980.

44. Djordjević, Dimitrije. "Vojvoda Putnik, the Serbian High Command and Strategy in 1914" in Béla Király, ed., *East Central European Society in World War I*. Boulder, CO/New York: Columbia University Press, 1985, 569–92.

45. Djordjević, Dimitrije. "Vojvoda Radomir Putnk" in Bela Király, ed., *East Central European War Leaders: Civilian and Military*. Boulder, CO/New York: Columbia University Press, 1988, 223–48.

46. Djurišic, Mitar. *Bitka na Drini 1914 [Battle of Drina]*. Belgrade: Vojnoistorijski institute, 1969.

47. Drake, Edson James. *Bulgaria at the Paris Peace Conference; a Diplomatic History of the Treaty at Neuilly-sur-Seine*. Thesis, Georgetown University, 1967.

48. Drašković, Aleksandar. *Mojkovacka bitka: ratovanje crnogorske sandzacke vojske 1915–1916 [The Battle of Mojkovacka: Fighting of Montenegrin Sanjak Forces 1915–1916]*. Belgrade: Strucna knjiga, 1991.

49. Driault, Edouard. *Histoire diplomatique de la Grèce de 1821 à nos jours [Diplomatic History of Greece from 1821 to Our Times]*, vol. 5. Paris: Les Presses universitaires de France, 1926.

50. Duca, I. G. *Amintiri politice [Political Memoirs]*, 3 vols. Munich, 1981.

51. Ducasse, André. *Balkans 14–18*. Paris: Lafont, 1964.

52. Dutton, David. *The Politics of Diplomacy: Britain and France in the Balkans in the First World War*. New York: St. Martin's Press, 1998.

53. *East European Quarterly*. Boulder: University of Colorado, 1967.

54. Ekmečić, Milorad. *Ratni ciljevi Srbije 1914–1918 [The War Aims of Servia 1914–1918]*. Belgrade: Politika, 1992.

55. Ertem, Sefik. *Birinci Dünya savasinda Avrupa'da yüzbin Türk askeri [Turkish Troops in Europe during the First World War]*. Cagaloglu-Istanbul: Kastas Yayinlari A.S., 1992.

56. *Études balkaniques [Balkan Studies]*. Sofia: Édition de lAcadémie bulgare des sciences, 1964.

57. Falkenhayn, Erich von. *Der Feldzug der 9. Armee gegen die Rumänen und Russen, 1916/17 [The Campaign of the 9th Army Against the Romanians and Russians, 1916/1917]*. Berlin: E. S. Mittler & Sohn, 1921.

58. Falls, Cyril. *Military Operations, Macdeonia*, 2 vols. London: His Majesty's Stationery Office, 1933–35.

59. Fest, Wilfried. *Peace or Partition: The Habsburg Monarchy and British Policy, 1914–1918*. London: George Prior, 1978.

60. France. État-major de l'armée. *Les Armées françaises dans la grande guerre [The French Armies in the Great War]*. Paris: Imprimerie nationale, 1922.

61. Friedrich, Wolfgang-Uwe. *Bulgarien und die Mächte 1913–1915 [Bulgaria and the Powers 1913–1915]*. Stuttgart: F. Steiner, 1985.

62. Fryer, Charles. *The Destruction of Serbia in 1915*. Boulder, CO/New York: Columbia University Press, 1997.

63. Fryer, Charles. *The Royal Navy on the Danube*. Boulder, CO/New York: Columbia University Press, 1988.

64. *General H. M. Berthelot: 80 ans après la mission française en Roumanie [General H. M. Berthelot: 80 Years after the French Mission in Romania]*. Bucharest, Editura Universității din București, 1997.

65. Germany. Reichsarchiv. *Der Weltkrieg 1914–1918 [The World War 1914–1918]*, 14 vols. Berlin: Mittler, 1925–1956.

66. Grandhomme, Jean-Noel. *Le général Berthelot et l'action de France en Roumanie et en Russie Méridionale, 1916–1918 ["General Berthelot and French Action in Romania and South Russia, 1916–1918"]*. Thesis, University of Paris, 1998.

67. Great Britain. War Office. *Daily Review of the Foreign Press*. London: His Majesty's Stationery Office, 1914–1919.

68. *Greece and Great Britain during World War I: first symposium* (*December 15–17, 1983*). Thessalonika: The Institute for Balkan Studies, 1985.

69. Greece. Stratos. Genikon Epiteleion. Dieuthynsis Historias Stratou. *Ho Hellenikos Stratos kata ton Proton Pankosmion Polemon 1914–1918* [*The Greek Army during the First World War 1914–1918*], 2 vols. Athens: Ekdosis Dieuthynseos Historias Stratou, 1958, 1961.

70. Hall, Richard C. *Bulgaria's Road to the First World War.* Boulder, CO/New York: Columbia University Press, 1996.

71. Hamard, Bruno. "Quand la victoire s'est gagnée dans la Balkans septembre à novembre 1918" ["When Victory Was Earned in the Balkans September to November 1918"]. *Guerres mondiales et conflits contemporains* (1996) 46(184): 29–42.

72. Helmreich, Ernst Christian. *The Diplomacy of the Balkan Wars, 1912–1913.* Cambridge: Harvard University Press, 1938.

73. Hitchins, Keith. *Rumania, 1866–1947.* New York: Oxford University Press, 1994.

74. Horton, John J. *Yugoslavia.* Santa Barbara, CA: Clio Press, 1990.

75. Hrabak, Bogumil, and Janković, Dragoslav. *Srbija 1918* [*Serbia 1918*]. Belgrade: Sedma sila, 1968.

76. Ilchev, Ivan. *Bulgariia i antantata prez purvata svetovna voina* [*Bulgaria and the Entente during the First World War*]. Sofia: Nauka i izkustvo, 1990.

77. Ionescu-Sisești, Gheorghe. *L'agriculture de la Roumanie pendant la guerre* [*Romanian Agriculture during the War*]. New Haven: Yale University Press, 1929.

78. Iordache, Anastasie. *Ion I.C. Brătianu.* Bucharest: Editura Albatros, 1994.

79. *Istoriia na Bulgariia* [*History of Bulgaria*]. Sofia, Izd-vo Bulgarska Akademi na naukite, 1979.

80. *Istorija srpskog naroda* [*History of the Serbian People*]. Belgrade: Srpska knjizevna zadruga, 1981.

81. Italy. Esercito. Corpo di stato maggiore. Ufficio storico. *L'Esercito italiano nella grande guerra, 1915–1918* [*The Italian Army in the Great War, 1915–1918*], 7 vols. Rome: Provveditorato generale dello Stato, Liberia, 1927–1983.

82. Janković, Dragoslav. *Jugoslovensko pitanje i Krfska deklaracija 1917. godine* [*The Yugoslav Question and the Corfu Declaration 1917*]. Belgrade: Savremena administracija, 1967.

83. Jelavich, Barbara. *History of the Balkans,* 2 vols. New York: Cambridge University Press, 1983.

84. Jelavich, Charles and Barbara. *The Establishment of the Balkan National States, 1804–1920.* Seattle: University of Washington Press, 1977.

85. Jerábek, Rudolf. *Potiorek: General im Schatten von Sarajevo* [*Potiorek: General in the Shadow of Sarajevo*]. Graz: Verlag Styria, 1991.

86. Jessup, John E. *Balkan Military History: A Bibliography.* New York: Garland, 1986.

87. Kamburov, Gencho. *Fatalnata iliuziia: voennopoliticheski protivorechiia i konflikti mezhdu Bulgariia i TSentralnite sili v purvata svetovna voina 1914–1918* [*Fatal Illusion: Military-Political Contradictions and Conflicts between Bulgaria and the Central Powers in the First World War 1914–1918*]. Sofia: IK "Khristo Botev," 1999.

88. Karastoianova, Lubimka, ed. *Bulgarskata armiia, 1877–1944: Bibliografia* [*The Bulgarian Army, 1877–1944: Bibliography*]. Sofia: Voen. izd-vo, 1989.

89. Kazimirović, Vasa. *Nikola Pašić i njegovo doba, 1845–1926* [*Nikola Pasic and His Epoch, 1845–1926*], 2 vols. Belgrade: Nova Evropa, 1990.

90. Kerchnawe, Hugo. *Die Militärverwaltung in den von den österreichisch-ungarischen Truppen besetzten Gebieten* [*The Military Administration in the Areas Occupied by Austro-Hungarian Troops*]. New Haven: Yale University Press, 1928.

91. Király, Béla K., and Dimitrije Djordjević, eds. *East Central European Society and the Balkan Wars.* Boulder, CO/New York: Columbia University Press, 1987.

92. Király, Béla K., and Nándor F. Dreisziger, eds. *East Central European Society in World War I.* Boulder, CO/New York: Columbia University Press, 1985.

93. Király, Béla K., and Albert A. Nofi, eds. *East Central European War Leaders: Civilian and Military.* Boulder CO/New York: Columbia University Press, 1988.

94. Kirch, Paul. *Krieg und Verwaltung in Serbien und Mazedonien 1916–1918* [*War and Administration in Serbia and Macedonia 1916–1918*]. Stuttgart: W. Kohlhammer, 1928.

95. Kiriţescu, Constantin. *Istoria războiului pentru întregirea României 1916–1919* [*History of the War for the Integration of Romania 1916–1919*], 3 vols. Bucharest: Editurea Casei Şcoalelor, 1922.

96. Kiriţescu, Constantin. *La Roumanie dans la guerre mondiale 1916–1919* [*Romania in the World War 1916–1919*]. Paris: Payot, 1934.

97. Kontz de Körpényes, Alexander. *Österreichisch-Ungarisher Tätigkeitsbericht des Wirtschaftsstabes der Militärverwaltung in Rumänien* [*Austro-Hungarian Activity Report of the Economic Staff of the Military Administration in Romania*]. Vienna: Staatsdruckerei, 1918.

98. Korsun, Nikolai. *Balkanskii front mirovoi voiny, 1914–1918 gg* [*The Balkan Front in the World War, 1914–1918*]. Moscow: Gos. voen. izd-vo Narkomata oborony Souiuza SSR, 1939.

99. Krippner, Monica. *The Quality of Mercy: Women at War, Serbia, 1915–18.* Newton Abbot [Eng.]: David & Charles, 1980.

100. *La France et la Grèce dans la grande guerre: actes du colloque tenu en novembre 1989 à Thessalonique* [*France and Greece in the Great War: Proceedings of the Colloquium Held in November 1989 at Thessolonica*]. Thessalonika: Université de Thessalonique, Département d'histoire et d'archéologie; Paris: Institut d'histoire des conflits contemporains, 1992.

101. Lalkov, Milcho. *Balkanskata politika na Avstro-Ungariia, 1914–1917 g.* [*The Balkan Policy of Austria-Hungary, 1914–1917*]. Sofia: Nauka i izkustvo, 1983.

102. Lampe, John R., and Marvin R. Jackson. *Balkan Economic History, 1550–1950: From Imperial Borderlands to Developing Nations.* Bloomington: Indiana University Press, 1982.

103. Lampe, John R. *The Bulgarian Economy in the Twentieth Century.* London: Croom Helm, 1986.

104. *La Présence française en Roumanie pendant la grande guerre (1914–1918)* [*The French Presence in Romania during the Great War (1914–1918)*]. Cluj: Presa Universitară Clujeană, 1997.

105. Larcher, Maurice. *La Grande guerre dans les Balkans* [*The Great War in the Balkans*], 2 vols. Paris: Payot, 1929.

106. Lederer, Ivo J. *Yugoslavia at the Paris Peace Conference: A Study in Frontiermaking.* New Haven: Yale University Press, 1963.

107. Leon, George B. *Greece and the First World War: From Neutrality to Intervention, 1917–1918.* Boulder, CO/New York: Columbia University Press, 1990.

108. Leon, George. *Greece and the Great Powers, 1914–1917.* Thessolonnika: The Institute for Balkan Studies, 1973.

109. Loulos, Konstantin. *Die Deutsche Griechenlandspolitik von der Jahrhundertwende bis zum Ausbruch des Ersten Weltkrieges* [*German Policy Toward Greece from the Turn of the Century until the Outbreak of the First World War*]. Frankfurt am Main: Lang, 1986.

110. Lyon, James B. " 'A Peasant Mob': The Serbian Army on the Eve of the Great War." *The Journal of Military History* (1997) 61(3): 481–502.

111. Lyon James B. *Serbia and the Balkan Front 1914.* Thesis, University of California at Los Angeles, 1995.

112. MacKenzie, David. *Apis, the Congenial Conspirator: The Life of Colonel Dragutin T. Dimitrijević.* Boulder, CO/New York: Columbia University Press, 1989.

113. MacKenzie, David. *The "Black Hand" on Trial, Salonika, 1917.* Boulder, CO/New York: Columbia University Press, 1995.

114. MacKenzie, David. *The Exoneration of the "Black Hand," 1917–1953.* Boulder, CO/New York: Columbia University Press, 1998.

115. Madol, Hans Roger. *Ferdinand of Bulgaria; the Dream of Byzantium.* London: Hurst & Blackett, Ltd., 1933.

116. Mamatey, Victor S. *The United States and East Central Europe, 1914–1918*. Princeton: Princeton University Press, 1957.

117. Marghiloman, Alexandru. *Note politice [Political Notes]*, 5 vols. Bucharest: Eminescu, 1927.

118. Markov, Georgi. *Goliamata voina i bulgarskiiat kliuch za evropeiskiia pogreb, 1914–1916 [The Great War and the Bulgarian Key to the European Powderkeg 1914–1916]*. Sofia: Akademichno izd-vo "Prof. Marin Drinov", 1995.

119. Milošević, Miladin. *Srbija i Grcka 1914–1918. Iz istorije diplomatchik odnosa [Serbia and Greece 1914–1918. From the History of Diplomatic Relations]*. Belgrade: Zajecar, 1997.

120. Mitrakos, Alexander S. *France in Greece during World War I: A Study in the Politics of Power.* Boulder, CO/New York: Columbia University Press, 1982.

121. Mitrany, David. *The Effect of the War in Southeastern Europe.* New Haven: Yale University Press, 1936.

122. Mitrany, David. *The Land and the Peasant in Rumania: the War and Agrarian Reform (1917–21)*. New Haven: Yale University Press, 1930.

123. Mitrović, Andrej. *Jugoslavija na konferenciji mira 1919–1920 [Yugoslavia at the Peace Conference 1919–1920]*. Belgrade: Zavod za izdavanje udzbenika Socijalisticke Republike Srbije, 1969.

124. Mitrović, Andrej. *Prodor na Balkan: Srbija u planovima Austro-Ugarske i Nemacke, 1908–1918 [Penetration into the Balkans: Serbia in Austro-Hungarian and German Plans, 1908–1918]*. Belgrade: Nolit, 1981.

125. Mitrović, Andrej. *Razgranicenje Jugoslavije sa Madarskom i Rumunijom 1919–1920 [The Deliniation of Yugoslavia from Hungary and Romania 1919–1920]*. Novi Sad: Institut za izucavanje istorije Vojvodine, 1975.

126. Mitrović, Andrej. "Stvaranje nemače okupacione zone i austro-ungarske okupacione uprave u Srbiji (jesen 1915-proleče 1916) ["The Creation of the German Occupation Zone and the Austro-Hungarian Occupation Administration in Serbia (Autumn 1915–Spring 1916)"]. *Istorijski glasnik* (1977) (1–2): 7–38.

127. *Mojkovacka operacija, 1915–1916 [The Mojkovacka Operation, 1915–1916]*. Belgrade: Institut za savremenu istoriju, 1997.

128. Mourélos, Yannis G. *L'intervention de la Grèce dans la grande guerre: 1916–1917 [The Intervention of Greece in the Great War: 1916–1917]*. Athens: Institut français d'Athènes, 1983.

129. Mühlmann, Carl. *Oberste Heeresleitung und Balkan im Weltkrieg 1914–1918 [The Supreme Army Command and the Balkans in the World War 1914–1918]*. Berlin: Limpert, 1942.

130. Nastovici, Ema. *România şi puterile centrale în anii 1914–1916 [Romania and the Central Powers in the Years 1914–1918]*. Bucharest: Editura Politikă, 1979.

131. *Naucni skup Srbija 1915. godine [Scientific Colloquium. Serbia 1915]*. Belgrade: Istorijski institut, 1986.

132. *Naucni skup Srbija 1916. godine [Scientific Colloquium. Serbia 1916]*. Belgrade: Istorijski institut, 1987.

133. *Naunci skup Srbija 1917. godine [Scientific Colloquium. Serbia 1917]*. Belgrade: Istorijski institut, 1988.

134. *Naunci skup Srbija 1918. godine [Scientific Colloquium. Serbia 1918]*. Belgrade: Istorijski institut, 1989.

135. Nedev, N. *Bulgaria v svietovnata voina (1915–1918) [Bulgaria in the World War [1915–1918]*. Sofia, 1927.

136. Nedev, Nediu. *Les opérations en Macedoine l'epopée de Dorian, 1915–1918 [Operations in Macedonia. The Epic of Dorian 1915–1918]*. Sofia: Imprimerie Armeyski voenoisdatelski fond, 1927.

137. Nuţu, Constantin. *Româniă în anii neutralităţii 1914–1916 [Romania in the Years of Neutrality 1914–1916]*. Bucharest: Editura Stiintifica, 1972.

138. Opačić, Petar. *Srbija i Solunski front [Serbia and the Salonika Front]*. Belgrade: Knjizevene novine, 1984.

139. Oprea, Ion M. *România şi imperiul rus 1900–1924* [*Romania and the Russian Empire 1900–1924*], vol. 1 Bucharest: Albatros, 1998.

140. Ormos, Mária. *From Padua to the Trianon, 1918–1920.* Budapest: Akadémiai Kiadó, 1990.

141. *Österreich-Ungarn in der Weltpolitik 1900–1918* [*Austria-Hungary in World Politics 1900–1918*]. Berlin: Akademie Verlag, 1965.

142. Palmer, Alan Warwick. *The Gardeners of Salonika.* New York: Simon and Schuster, 1965.

143. Pastor, Peter, ed. *Revolutions and Interventions in Hungary and Its Neighbor States, 1918–1919.* Boulder, CO/New York: Columbia University Press, 1988.

144. Pastorelli, Pietro. *L'Albania nella politica estera italiana, 1914–1920* [*Albania in Italian Foreign Policy, 1914–1920*]. Naples: Jovene, 1970.

145. Pavlović, Zivko. *Bitka na Jadru avgusta 1914 god* [*Battle of Jadru August 1914*]. Belgrade: Graficki zavod makarije, 1924.

146. Pavlović, Zivko G. *Bitka na Kolubari* [*Battle of Kolubara*], 2 vols. Belgrade: Srpska kraljevska akademija, 1928–1930.

147. Pavlović, Zivko G. *Rat Srbije sa Austro-Ugarskom, Nemackom i bugarskom 1915. godine* [*The War of Serbia with Austria-Hungary, Germany and Bulgaria 1915*]. Belgrade: Naucno delo, 1968.

148. Petkov, Petko. *The United States and Bulgaria in World War I.* Boulder, CO/New York: Columbia University Press, 1991.

149. Petrovich, Michael Boro. *A History of Modern Serbia, 1804–1918,* 2 vols. New York: Harcourt Brace Jovanovich, 1976.

150. Petsales-Diomedes, N. *Greece at the Paris Peace Conference (1919).* Thessalonika: The Institute for Balkan Studies, 1978.

151. Petsales-Diomedes, N. *He Hellada ton dyo kyverneseon, 1916–17* [*The Greece of the Two Governments, 1916–1917*]. Athens: Ekdoseis Philippote, 1988.

152. Phrangoules [Frangulis], A.F. *La Grèce et la crise mondiale* [*Greece and the World Crisis*], 2 vols. Paris: F. Alcan, 1926.

153. Piarron de Mondésir, Lucien. *Souvenirs et pages de guerre* [*Recollections and Pages of War*]. Paris: Berger-Levrault, 1933.

154. Pisarev, IU. A. *Serbiia i Chernogoriia v pervoi mirovoi voine* [*Serbia and Montenegro in the First World War*]. Moscow: Nauka, 1968.

155. Pisarev, IU. A. *Serbiia na Golgofe i politika velikikh derzhav 1916 g.* [*Serbia on Golgotha and the Policy of the Great Powers 1916*]. Moscow: Nauka, 1993.

156. Pisarev, IU. A. *Tainy pervoi mirovoi voiny: Rossiia i Serbiia v 1914–1915 gg* [*Secrets of the First World War: Russia and Serbia in 1914–1915*]. Moscow: Nauka, 1990.

157. Pisarev, IU. A. *Velikie derzhavy i Balkany nakanune pervoi mirovoi voiny* [*The Great Powers and the Balkans Before the First World War*]. Moscow: Nauka, 1985.

158. Popović, Nikola. *Odnosi Srbije i Rusije u prvom svetskom ratu* [*Serbian-Russian Relations in the First World War*]. Belgrade: ISI-Narodna knjiga, 1977.

159. Popović, Nikola. *Srbija i carska Rusija* [*Serbia and Trarist Russia*]. Belgrade: Sluzbeni list SRJ, 1994.

160. Pournaras, Demetres. *Historia ton neoteron Hellenon: Eleutherios Venizelos* [*History of Modern Greece: Eleutherios Venizelos*], 4 vols. Athens: Ekdoseis-Vivlia "Eleutheros," 1957, 1959.

161. Preda, Dumitru, et al. *La Roumanie et sa guerre pour l'unité nationale: campagne de 1918–1919* [*Romania and Her War for National Unification: Campaign of 1918–1919*]. Bucharest: Éditions encyclopédiques, 1995.

162. *Proceedings of the Fifth Greek-Serbian Symposium 9–12 October 1987.* Thessalonika: The Institute for Balkan Studies, 1991.

163. Prodan, Costica. *The Romanian Army During the First World War.* Bucharest: Univers Enciclopedic, 1998.

164. Răcila, Emil. *Contribuţii privind lupta românilor pentru apărărea patriei, în primul război mondial: situaţia administrativă, economică, politicira şi socială a teritoriului românesc vremel-*

nic ocupat, 1916–1918 [*Contributions Relating to the Romanian Struggle for the Defense of the Fatherland, in the First World War: The Administrative, Economic, Political and Social Situation in Enemy-Occupied Romanian Territory 1916–1918*]. Bucharest: Editura Ştiinţifică si Enciclopedică, 1981.

165. Radoslavov, Vasil. *Bulgarien und die Weltkrise* [*Bulgaria and the World Crisis*]. Berlin: Ullstein, 1923.

166. Radoslavov, Vasil. *Dnevni belezhki, 1914–1916* [*Daily Notes*]. Sofia: Univ. izd-vo "Sv. Kliment Okhridski," 1993.

167. Rădulescu-Zoner, Şerban. *România şi Tripla Alianţá la începutul secoluliu al XX-lea 1900–1914* [*Romania and the Triple Alliance at the Beginning of the 20th Century 1900–1914*]. Bucharest: Editura Litera, 1977.

168. Rakočević, Novica. *Crna Gora i Austro-Ugarska 1903–1914* [*Montenegro and Austria Hungary 1903–1914*]. Cetinge: Istorijski institut, 1983.

169. Rakočević, Novica. *Crna gora u prvom svjetskom ratu 1914–1918* [*Montenegro in the First World War 1914–1918*]. Cetinge: Istorijski institut: 1969.

170. Rakočević, Novica. *Politicki odnosi Crne Gore i Srbije, 1903–1918* [*Montenegro and Serbia. Political Relations 1903–1918*]. Cetinge: Istorijski institut, 1981.

171. Regele, Oskar. *Kampf um die Donau, 1916. Betrachtung der Flüssubergänge bei Flămândă und Sistow* [*Battle Over the Danube, 1916. Consideration of the River Crossings at Flamanda and Sistov*]. Potsdam: L. Voggenreiter, 1940.

172. Remak, Joachim. *Sarajevo, The Story of a Political Murder.* New York: Criterion Books, 1959.

173. *Revista română de istorie militară* [*Romanian Review of Military History*]. Bucharest: Comisiei Române de Istorie Militară, 1984.

174. *Revue internationale d'histoire militaire* [*International Review of Military History*]. Paris: Commission Internationale D'histoire Militaire, 1939.

175. *Revue roumaine d'histoire* [*Romanian Review of History*]. Bucharest: Editura academiei, 1962.

176. Ripert d'Alauzier, Louis Marie Joseph de. *Un drame historique; la résurrection de l'armée serbe, Albanie-Corfou, 1915–1916* [*An Historical Drama: the Resurrection of the Serbian Army, Albania-Corfu, 1915–1916*]. Paris: Payot, 1923.

177. *România în anii primului război mondial* [*Romania in the Years of the First World War*], 2 vols. Bucharest: Editura militara, 1987.

178. *România în primul război mondial* [*Romania in the First World War*]. Bucharest: Editura militara, 1979.

179. *România în primul război mondial: contribuţii bibliografice* [*Romania in the First World War: Bibliographic Contributions*]. Bucharest: Editura militara, 1975.

180. *România în războiul mondial 1916–1919* [*Romania in the World War 1916–1919*], 4 vols. Bucharest: Imprimarea nationala, 1934–1946.

181. *Romanian Civilization.* Iaşi: Center for Romania Studies, 1992–.

182. *Romanian Military Bibliography.* Bucharest: Military Publishing House, 1985.

183. Rommel, Erwin. *Infantry Attacks.* Vienna, VA: Athena Press, 1979.

184. Rossos, Andrew. *Russia and the Balkans: Inter-Balkan Rivalry and Russian Foreign Policy, 1908–1914.* Toronto: University of Toronto Press, 1981.

185. Rothenberg, Gunther E. "The Austro-Hungarian Campaign Against Serbia in 1914." *The Journal of Military History* (1989), 53: 127–46.

186. *R. W. Seton-Watson and the Romanians,* 2 vols. Cornelia Bodea and Hugh Seton-Watson, eds. Bucharest: Editura Ştiinţifică şi Enciclopedică, 1988.

187. *R. W. Seton-Watson and the Yugoslavs: Correspondence 1906–1941.* London/Zagreb: British Academy/University of Zagreb, Institute of Croatian History, 1976.

188. Semov, Mincho. *Obrecheni pobedi. Bulgariia v purvata svetovna voina* [*Promised Victories. Bulgaria in the First World War*]. Sofia: Universitetsko izd-vo "Sv. Kliment Okhridski," 1998.

189. Sepič, Dragovan. *Italija, saveznici i jugoslavensko pitanjė 1914–1918* [*Italy, the Allies and the Yugoslav Question 1914–1918*]. Zagreb: "Skolska knjiga," 1970.

190. *Serbian Studies.* Chicago: North American Society for Serbian Studies, 1980.

191. Seton-Watson, Hugh and Christopher. *The Making of a New Europe: R. W. Seton-Watson and the Last Years of Austria-Hungary.* Seattle: University of Washington Press, 1981.

192. Sfika-Theodosiou, Angeliki. "The Italian Presence in the Balkan Front 1915–1916." *Balkan Studies,* (1995) 36(1): 69–82.

193. Siani-Davies, Peter. *Romania.* Santa Barbara, CA: Clio Press, 1998.

194. Silberstein, Gerard E. *The Troubled Alliance: German-Austrian Relations, 1914–1917.* Lexington: University Press of Kentucky, 1970.

195. Skoko, Savo. *Vojvoda Radomir Putnik,* 2 vols. Belgrade: Beogradski izdavacko-graficki zavod, 1984.

196. Smith, Jay, Jr. *The Russian Struggle for Power, 1914–1917; A Study of Russian Foreign Policy During the First World War.* New York: Philosophical Society, 1956.

197. *Southeastern Europe. L'Europe du Sud-Est.* Tempe, AZ: Arizona State University, 1974.

198. Spašić, Krunoslav. "Boravak srpskih trupa u Albaniji i Njihov transport na KRF (Decembar 1915–Januar 1916)" ["The Sojourn of Serbian Troops in Albania and Their Transport to Corfu (December 1915–January 1916)"]. *Vojnoistorijski glasnik* (1988) 39(1): 361–395, 39(2): 287–303; 39(3): 429–452.

199. Spector, Sherman David. *Rumania at the Paris Peace Conference; A Study of the Diplomacy of Ioan I.C. Brătianu.* New York: Bookman Associates, 1962; reprinted, Ia_i: Center for Romanian Studies, 1995.

200. Spence, Richard B. "Lost to the Revolution: The Russian Expeditionary Force in Macedonia 1916–1918." *East European Quarterly* (1986) 19: 417–37.

201. Stanciu, Ion. *Aliaţi fără alianţa: România şi S.U.A., 1914–1920* [*Allies Without Alliance: Romania and the U.S.A., 1914–1920*]. Bucharest: Albatros, 1992.

202. Stanković, Dorde D. *Nikola Pašić i jugoslovensko pitanje* [*Nikola Pasic and the Yugoslav Question*]. Belgrade: Beogradsk izdavacko-graficki zavod, 1985.

203. Stavrianos, Leften Stavros. *The Balkans Since 1453.* New York: Rinehart, 1958.

204. Stone, Norman. *The Eastern Front, 1914–1917.* London: Hodder and Stoughton, 1975.

205. Strutz, Georg. *Herbstschlacht in Mazedonien—Cernabogen 1916 . . .* [*Auturm Battle in Macedonia—Cernabogen 1916 . . .*]. Oldenbourg: G. Stalling, 1921.

206. *Südosteuropa-Bibliographie 1945–1970* [*Southeastern Europe Bibliography 1945–1970*], 5 vols. Munich: Oldenbourg, 1956–1976.

207. *Südost Forschungen* [*Southeast Research*]. Leipzig: S. Hirzel, 1940.

208. Tanenbaum, Jan Karl. *General Maurice Sarrail, 1856–1929: the French Army and Left-wing Politics.* Chapel Hill: University of North Carolina Press, 1974.

209. Thaden, Edward C. *Russia and the Balkan Alliance of 1912.* University Park: Pennsylvania State University Press, 1965.

210. Theodoulou, Christos. *Greece and the Entente August 1, 1914–September 25, 1916.* Thessalonika: The Institute for Balkan Studies, 1971.

211. *The Times History of the War,* 22 vols. London, *The Times,* 1914–21.

212. Torrey, Glenn E. *Henri Mathias Berthelot 1861–1931: Soldier of France/Defender of Romania.* Iaşi: Center for Romanian Studies, 2000.

213. Torrey, Glenn E. *Romania and World War I: A Collection of Studies.* Iaşi: Center for Romanian Studies, 1998.

214. Torrey, Glenn E. *Romania in the First World War, 1914–1919: An Annotated Bibliography.* Emporia, KS: Emporia State University, 1981.

215. Torrey, Glenn E. *The Revolutionary Russian Army and Romania, 1917.* Pittsburgh: University of Pittsburgh, 1995.

216. Toshev, Stefan. *Dieistviiata na III armiia v Dobrudzha priez 1916 godina* [*Activity of the III Army in Dobrogea During 1916*]. Sofia: Pechatnitsa S.M. Staikov, 1921.

217. *Transylvanian Review.* Cluj: Romanian Cultural Foundation, 1992.

218. Treadway, John David. *The Falcon and the Eagle: Montenegro and Austria-Hungary 1908–1914.* West Lafayette, IN: Purdue University Press, 1983.

219. Treptow, Kurt, ed. *Romania during the World War I Era.* Iaşi: Center for Romanian Studies, 1999.

220. Tripkovic, Djoko. "Francuska i evakuacija Srpske vojske iz Albanije 1916 godine" ["France and the Evacuation of the Serbian Forces from Albania 1916"]. *Vojno-istoriski glasnik* (1981) 32(3): 203–25.

221. Tunstall, Graydon A. *Planning for War Against Russia and Serbia: Austro-Hungarian and German Military Strategies, 1871–1914.* Boulder, CO/New York: Columbia University Press, 1993.

222. Vakas, Demetrios. *Venizelos, Ho polemikos egetes* [*Venizelos: War Leader*]. Athens: Oikos M. Salisverous a.e., 1950.

223. Valiani, Leo. *The End of Austria-Hungary.* London: Secker and Warburg, 1973.

224. Ventiris, Georgios. *He Hellas tou 1910–1920* [*Greece From 1910–1920*], 2 vols., 2nd ed. Athens, Ikaros, 1970.

225. Veremes, Thanos. *Greece.* Santa Barbara, CA: Clio Press, 1998.

226. Vesa, Vasile. *Les relations politiques roumano-françaises au début du XXe siècle, 1900–1916* [*Romanian-French Political Relations at the Beginning of the 20th Century, 1900–1916*]. Bucharest: Editura academiei Republicii Socialiste Româniă, 1986.

227. Vickers, Miranda. *The Albanians: A Modern History.* New York: I. B. Tauris, 1995.

228. Vinogradov, V. N. *Rumynii y gody pervoi mirovoi voiny* [*Romania in the Years of the First World War*]. Moscow: Nauka, 1969.

229. *Voenno-istoricheski sbornik* [*Military History Journal*]. Sofiia: Voenno-istoricheska komisiia pri Shtaba na armiiata, 1927-.

230. *Vojno-istoriski glasnik* [*Military History Herald*]. Belgrade: Vojno-istoriski institut, 1950.

231. Williamson, Samuel R., Jr., and Peter Pastor, eds. *Essays on World War I: Origins and Prisoners of War.* New York: Brooklyn College Press/Columbia University Press, 1983.

232. Wilson, Keith. ed. *Decisions for War, 1914.* New York: St. Martin's Press, 1995.

233. Woodall, Robert Larry. *The Albanian Problem During the Peacemaking, 1919–1920.* Thesis, Memphis State University, 1978.

234. Wulff, Olaf. *Die Österreichisch-Ungarische Donauflottille im Weltkriege 1914–1918* [*The Austro-Hungarian Danube Flotilla in the World War 1914–1918*]. Vienna: Braumüller, 1934.

235. Yovanović, Dragoljub. *Les effets économiques et sociaux de la guerre en Serbie* [*The Economic and Social Effects of the War in Serbia*]. New Haven: Yale University Press, 1930.

236. Yugoslavia. Ministarstvo voiske i mornarice. Glavni generalstab. *Veliki rat Srbije za oslobodenje i ujedinjenje Srba, Hrvata i Slovenaca* [*The Great War of Serbia for the Liberation and Unification of Serbia, Croatia and Slovenia*]. Belgrade: Stamparija "Ujedinjenje," 1924.

237. Yugoslavia. Voino-istoriski institut. *Operacije crnogorske vojske u prvom svetskom ratu* [*Operations of Montenegrin Forces in the First World War*]. Belgrade: Vojno delo, 1954.

238. Zaionchkovski, Andrei. "Dobrudza avgusta-oktiabr '1916 goda' " ["Dobrogea August-October 1916"]. *Krasnyi arkhiv,* vol. 58 Moscow-Leningrad: Gospolitizdat, 1933.

239. Zavitzianos, Konstaninos G. *Anamneseis tou ek tes historikes diaphonias Vasileos Konstantinou kai Eleutherios Venizelou* [*Recollections Concerning the Historic Dispute of King Constantine and Eleutherios Venizelos*], 2 vols. Athens: A. G. Rode, 1946, 1947.

240. Zivanović, Milan. "O evakuaciji srpske vojske iz Albanije i njenoj reorganizaciji na Krfu (1915–1916) prema francuskim documentima," ["About the Evacuation of the Serbian Army and its Reorganization on Corfu [1915–1916] According to French Documents"]. *Istorijski casopis* (1965), 14–15: 231–301.

241. Zivojinović, Dragoljub. *America, Italy, and the Birth of Yugoslavia (1917–1919).* Boulder, CO/New York: Columbia University Press, 1972.

242. Greece. Army History Directorate. *A Concise History of the Balkan Wars, 1912–1913.* Athens: Hellenic Army General Staff, 1998.

243. Turkey. Askeri Tarih ve Stratejik Etut Baskanligi yayiniari. *Birinci Dunva Harbi'nde Turk Harbi: Avrupa Cepheleri* [*The Turkish War in the First World War European Theater*]. Ankara: T. C. Genelkurmay Baskanligi, 1996.

10

Canada

Bill Rawling

Historians who have seen fit to study the subject have tended to agree that the First World War was a watershed in Canada's history, one that significantly affected the nation's international relations, industrial organization, relations between English- and French-speaking communities, female suffrage, and the union movement; and though the country's military experience is the main focus of the present work, one must keep in mind that these other themes are of equal importance. Even given such a caveat, the reader should be warned that the author found it necessary to narrow his horizons even further, so that theses, dissertations, and articles that were eventually modified into books will not be mentioned, except rarely, while most works appearing in this bibliographical essay date from the past few decades, with only passing mention of the literature of the 1920s through 1950s. Apart from such harsh methodology, the choice of works included in this study may appear somewhat idiosyncratic—and so it is—but it is hoped that even the reflections of one historian's personal journey through the historiography of Canada's military experience in the First World War may be helpful to others.

GENERAL BIBLIOGRAPHY

For a near-complete listing of the wide variety of books and printed sources dealing with Canada's military development in the First World War, an excellent start would be Owen A. Cooke, *The Canadian Military Experience* [2], the sections dealing with the period 1914–1918, which contain over a thousand entries; or C. E. Dornbusch, *The Canadian Army 1855–1965* [3]. Owen Cooke's

"Canada's Historiography and the First World War" [1] provides a brief study of those works dealing with the Canadian experience in its entirety, including developments on the home front. For an intimate look into how official histories were sometimes written, the reader is advised to consult Tim Travers, "Currie and 1st Canadian Division at Second Ypres, April 1915: Controversy, Criticism and Official History" [162].

PRIMARY SOURCES

Military institutions and individuals have left us a wealth of material, most notably at the National Archives of Canada, where the main bulk of information for military affairs can be found in Record Group 9, documents pertaining to the Canadian Militia and including the First World War. War diaries, prepared by individual formations and units down to battalion and battery level, are reasonably complete from the time they arrived in France in 1915 and 1916 to the occupation of Germany in 1919, and offer an opportunity to examine daily events, including training while the unit was in reserve, and artillery duels, patrols, and similar activities when the troops were in the trenches. They are, however, far less useful in studying the course of different battles for, prepared in haste, they offer only an outline of events and do not provide much detail on how operations evolved. Of far greater utility in describing the activities of soldiers in combat are the after-action reports and narratives prepared by battalion headquarters, often by companies; using field messages, oral reports, testimony from other units and similar sources of information, these documents piece together the events of each day, and some go so far as to give a minute-by-minute account of parts of a battle.

The files in Record Group 9 also include documents discussing the technical qualities, usefulness, and difficulties surrounding different pieces of equipment, including multitudinous files on the Ross rifle, bombs, trench mortars, rifle-grenades, signaling equipment, and other tools of trench warfare, while periodic revisions of doctrine sent to the Canadian Corps from the British Army help to trace tactical developments. Record Group 24, containing files pertaining to the Department of National Defence, founded only in 1923, contains valuable First World War material, though in much less volume.

For personal accounts of wartime experiences, transcripts are available in Record Group 41, the records of the Canadian Broadcasting Corporation, consisting of interviews the CBC carried out with veterans in the early to mid-1960s for a radio series entitled *Flanders Fields,* The Canadian Archives Branch (formerly the Manuscript Division) of the National Archives of Canada also has much to offer in this area, especially individual narratives and reminiscences which can be found in the personal papers of Canadians deposited in MG 30, especially section E. Also available in that branch are the papers of many who were responsible for the political direction of the war, including Sir Robert Borden (in MG 26), Canada's prime minister during this period, as well as many of his cabinet ministers and advisers. The leader of the opposition was Sir Wilfrid Laurier, whose official correspondence and files can also be found in MG 26.

Lest the reader be misled into believing that all documents of note have been left in the care of the National Archives of Canada, it should be pointed out here that many other institutions hold materials of equal value. The Public Archives of Nova Scotia, to give just one example, are an excellent depository of First World War material, as is the Canadian War Museum in Ottawa and various university archives across the country, mainly McGill, Queen's, the University of Toronto, and the Royal Military College of Canada. Certain private archives, such as those of *La Presse* newspaper, also hold useful research tools, many of them so far untapped by researchers. To conclude this all-too-short discussion of primary sources, the Directorate of History and Heritage at National Defence Headquarters in Ottawa has in its collection training pamphlets that help trace how doctrine was inculcated in the common soldier.

GENERAL WORKS

Desmond Morton and J. L. Granatstein, in *Marching to Armageddon* [77], discuss Canada's war experience as a whole—the trials, tribulations, and successes of the Canadian Expeditionary Force being one of their major themes, while Robert Craig Brown and Ramsay Cook, in *Canada, 1896–1921* [33], cover such issues as industrialization, labor, agriculture, and imperialism, devoting about a quarter of their study to the First World War. Also comprehensive in approach is Roch Legault and Jean Lamarre's *La première guerre mondiale et le Canada* [98], with articles on conscription, popular culture, censorship, medicine, the war of movement, and military society, among others. Providing an excellent background to the country's political economy at the time are two biographies: Robert Craig Brown's *Robert Laird Borden* [35] and Michael Bliss' *A Canadian Millionaire* [27], the latter a biography of the Canadian head of the Imperial Munitions Board, Sir Joseph Flavelle. For an *histoire des mentalités* approach, see Jonathan Vance's *Death So Noble: Memory, Meaning, and the First World War* [165], while Daphne Read relies on the techniques of oral history for *The Great War and Canadian Society: An Oral History* [140]. An interesting look at one episode of the war at home is provided by Robert E. Bartholomew in "Phantom German Air Raids on Canada: War Hysteria in Quebec and Ontario during the Great War" [21].

GENERAL MILITARY WORKS

Two official histories of the Canadian Expeditionary Force were prepared in the years after the war, the first being Fortesque Duguid's *Official History of the Canadian Forces in the Great War, 1914–1919* [65], but its title is misleading; only the first volume, ranging from August 1914 to September 1915, was ever published, the project being interrupted by Canada's declaration of war in 1939.

The second official history of the Canadian Corps is G. W. L. Nicholson's *Canadian Expeditionary Force 1914–1919* [128], which, published in 1962, makes an effective use of primary and secondary sources, Colonel Nicholson having put together a chronological history of the corps that concentrates on the battles it fought and the periods of organization and reorganization that punctuated its life.

Other works dealing with the activities of the Canadian Corps include John F. Meek's *Over the Top!* [112], which provides a pictorial and statistical history of the Canadians overseas, and Larry Worthington's *Amid the Enemy Guns Below* [178], a complimentary narrative of the Canadian Expeditionary Force's operations in France and Belgium. John Swettenham's *To Seize the Victory* [159] is a combination of biography and military narrative that follows the victories and vicissitudes of Corps Commander Arthur Currie and his troops as they adjust to new styles of warfare, giving some insight into the nature of innovation within the Canadian Corps and so helping to explain changes in tactics that took place under Byng and Currie. Desmond Morton's *When Your Number's Up* [124], capping decades of his research and writing on the subject, is perhaps the most comprehensive study of the CEF's experience, from life in the trenches to tactical developments to the treatment of Canadian prisoners of war in Germany. (The reader should note that the latter topic is covered in much greater detail in Morton's *Silent Battle* [122].)

Stephen J. Harris' seminal *Canadian Brass* [89], based on his dissertation for Duke University, devotes a large section to the First World War and its impact on Canadian military professionalism, while several theses and dissertations also deal with such developments, including M. V. Bezeau, "The Role and Organization of Canadian Military Staffs 1904–1945" [6], and Kenneth Eyre, "Staff and Command in the Canadian Corps." [9] How commanders, staff officers, and the rank and file applied their knowledge to solving the problems of the battlefield is related in a short thesis to come out of the University of New Brunswick, W. F. Stewart's "Attack Doctrine in the Canadian Corps, 1916–1918" [16], an in-depth study of the evolution of doctrine, including detailed discussion of the role of artillery in breaking the deadlock in some battles on the Western Front. Bill Rawling's work, later published as *Surviving Trench Warfare* [139] is in a similar vein, attempting to trace developments in training, tactics, and technology and their impact on operations—including casualty rates. Also studying tactics, but providing an excellent analysis of the operational art as well, is Shane Schreiber's *Shock Army of the British Army* [147], while Ian McCulloch, in "The Fighting Seventh: The Evolution and Devolution of Tactical Command and Control in a Canadian Brigade of the Great War" [14], provides a case study of how a small formation went about its task.

Canada's naval contribution was small compared to that of its land forces, but its story is well-told in Michael Hadley's and Roger Sarty's *Tin-pots and Pirate Ships* [87] and less entertainingly (and in far less detail) in G. N. Tucker's *The Naval Service of Canada: Volume I* [163]. A smaller but enlightening study, by Brian Tennyson and Roger Sarty, is "Sydney, Nova Scotia and the U-Boat War,

1918" [160]. For information concerning Canada and the air war, one can turn to S. F. Wise, *Canadian Airmen and the First World War* [175], which discusses in great detail the relationship between air power and the land battle, while also recounting the experiences of many individual Canadians.

BIOGRAPHIES AND PERSONAL ACCOUNTS

Sir Arthur Currie, who commanded the Canadian Corps in 1917 and 1918, has been the focus of several works, one of the first being Hugh M. Urquhart's *Arthur Currie* [164], which is laudatory to say the least, but which provides a reasonably detailed portrayal of the man who helped the Canadian Corps adopt more innovative techniques. A. M. J. Hyatt's Ph.D. dissertation, "The Military Career of Sir Arthur Currie" [12], concentrates, as its title implies, on the war years of Currie's life, examining the general's attempts to break the tactical deadlock on the Western Front—it was later published as a short book, *General Sir Arthur Currie* [94]. Daniel G. Dancocks' detailed study, *Sir Arthur Currie* [60], which appeared at about the same time as Hyatt's, covers the general's entire life but devotes the bulk of his narrative to the period 1914–1920. Biographies of other actors of that war include Jeffrey Williams' look at the Canadian Corps' second and highly influential commander, *Byng of Vimy* [169], Ronald Haycock's look at Minister of Militia *Sam Hughes* [92], and John Swettenham's *McNaughton* [158], the latter's first of three volumes studying an important innovator in the realm of artillery, especially in counter-battery work.

Other such works include E. L. M. Burns' autobiography, *General Mud* [38], which provides much that is useful concerning the world of communications, especially the application of new organizations and technology, while *Ghosts Have Warm Hands* [25], Will R. Bird's autobiographical account of the war, contains much detail about life in and out of battle. Similarly, one can turn to the work of a junior officer of the 4th Battalion, James H. Pedley, in *Only This: A War Retrospect, 1917–1918* [133]. There exist several studies of the life of John McCrae, the author of the poem "In Flanders' Fields"; Bev Dietrich takes a brief look at the medical officer's life in "Colonel John McCrae: From Guelph, Ontario to Flanders Fields," [64] John F. Prescott takes the title of McCrae's most famous work for his book *In Flanders Fields* [135], while Dianne Graves provides a more lengthy account of the poet-soldier's life and society in *A Crown of Life: The World of John McCrae* [79]. Less spiritual in tone—and hence more traditional in its approach to biography—is Jeffery Williams' *First in the Field: Gault of the Patricias* [170], which retraces the life of the man who formed Princess Patricia's Canadian Light Infantry in the early days of the war. Many short studies using biography as a means of understanding the First World War have been published in the journal *Canadian Military History,* including Desmond Morton's "A Canadian Soldier in the Great War: The Experiences of Frank Maheux" [118], Hal A. Skarrup's "Whiz Bangs and Whooly Bears: Walter Estabrooks and the Great War" [150], Ron Sorobey's "Filip Konowal, VC: The Rebirth of a Canadian Hero" [153], Thomas P. Leppard's " 'The Dashing

Subaltern' '': Sir Richard Turner in Retrospect" [99], Ian McCulloch's " 'Batty Mac': Portrait of a Brigade Commander of the Great War, 1915–1917" [109], and Andrew Coppolino's " 'While the Shells Crashed We Were Strong': The Life of War Poet 'Toronto' Prewett" [49].

For a close look at personal experiences in the air war, a good source is Brereton Greenhous' *A Rattle of Pebbles* [83], the edited diaries of two pilots (of quite differing personalities) that run from 1915 to 1916 and 1916 to 1918 respectively. Other airmen who were the subjects of book-length biographies include Billy Bishop, whose treatment at the hands of historians has varied from hero-worship, such as William Arthur Bishop's *The Courage of the Early Morning* [26], to denunciation, most evident in Brereton Greenhous' "The Sad Case of Billy Bishop, VC," [84] an article in the *Canadian Historical Review.* (Greenhous provides a lengthier critical analysis in *The Making of Billy Bishop.* [82] Wayne Ralph's treatment of William Barker represents perhaps the most analytical and balanced account of one man's war in the air [137].

In the decades following the Armistice the *Canadian Defence Quarterly* presented a series of accounts of battles written by veterans, while several organizations have published collections of letters, reminiscences, and similar documents, many of them soon after the war ended. For example, in 1920 the Canadian Bank of Commerce collected letters written to branch offices by employees who were serving overseas and published them as *Letters from the Front* [70]. Other collections were compiled long after the Armistice, such as the substantial, at over 360 pages, *Letters of Agar Adamson, 1914 to 1919: Lieutenant-Colonel, Princess Patricia's Canadian Light Infantry* [17], published in 1997. Still others have relied on the memories of their subjects to provide insight into how the war was fought. Gordon Reid's *Poor Bloody Murder* [141], a British work that contains much Canadian material, was published in 1980, when most of his subjects were in their seventies and eighties, and the bulk of their reminiscences deal with, to them, the more important issues of leave, food, and mud. William D. Mathieson's *My Grandfather's War* [108] is similar—Canadian veterans recounting their experiences—and some excerpts were taken from Gordon Reid's work. A different and more sophisticated approach can be seen in Reginald Roy's *The Journal of Private Fraser, 1914–1918* [143], in which the editor limited himself to correcting dates and names, in the process reproducing one of the great rarities of military narrative, the complete diary of a private soldier. A sadder subject, all the individuals being studied having died, is Andrew Godefroy's prosopographical *For Freedom and Honour? The Story of the 25 Canadian Volunteers Executed in the First World War* [74], while just as informative on the soldier experience is Mike Wert's "From Enlistment to the Grave: The Impact of the First World War on 52 Canadian Soldiers" [166].

TECHNICAL SERVICES AND SUPPORTING ARMS

The activities and technologies of ancillary units are important in modern war, and the operations of doctors, nursing sisters, gunners, signalers, and engineers can shed some light on the Canadian military experience as a whole. Sir Andrew McPhail's *The Medical Services* [106] accompanies Duguid's official history, and though it is somewhat idiosyncratic, it is still useful in its discussions not only of developments in wound treatment, but also of the medical profession's reaction to health problems, hygiene, and psychological casualties. Meanwhile, A. E Snell's *The CAMC with the Canadian Corps during the Last Hundred Days* [151] is, as its title implies, limited to the last campaigns of the war. *Canada's Nursing Sisters* [127] traces developments of that branch of the medical service throughout its history, but it has much to say about experiences in the First World War, while Geneviève Allard's M.A. thesis on nursing sisters [4] focuses exclusively on that conflict and provides a far more in-depth analysis. One aspect of medical technique to be discussed in detail is the treatment of shock, as described in the autobiographical *Transfusion: A Canadian Surgeon's Story in War and Peace,* by Norman Miles Guiou [86]; another, psychological injury, is analyzed in Tom Brown's "Shell Shock in the Canadian Expeditionary Force, 1914–1918" [37].

G. W. L. Nicholson's *The Gunners of Canada* [130], published in 1967, describes the development of Canadian Artillery from earliest times, devoting half of its first volume to the First World War. John Moir's *History of the Royal Canadian Corps of Signals* [115], which became available in 1962, provides one long chapter dealing with that conflict, while Bill Rawling's "Communications in the Canadian Corps, 1915–1918: Wartime Technological Progress Revisited," [138] focuses on the basic practices signalers relied upon in that conflict. *The History of the Corps of Royal Canadian Engineers* [96], prepared by A. J. Kerry and W. A. McDill, like all the corps histories listed here, presents a narrative of the events through which its subjects passed over a long period, and like *Gunners of Canada* and *Signals* it details changes in organization throughout the war. E. Hahn, meanwhile, looks at the information gathering sections at various levels from corps down to battalion in *The Intelligence Service within the Canadian Corps* [88]. Danny Jenkins, however, provides a far more scholarly and interesting study of the subject in his Ph.D. dissertation, "Winning Trench Warfare." [13] After years of historians' shying away from the subject, Tim Cook has provided an analytical and narrative account of the Canadian Corps and gas warfare in *No Place to Run: The Canadian Corps and Gas Warfare in the First World War* [46]. Various aspects of logistics and administration are examined in some detail in such articles as S.F. Wise, "The Garderners of Vimy: Canadian Corps' Farming Operations during the German Offensives of 1918" [176], Tim Cook, "More a Medicine than a Beverage: 'Demon Rum' and the Canadian Trench Soldier of the First World War" [45], and F. R. Phelan, "Army Supplies in the Forward Area and the Tumpline System: A First World War Canadian Logistical Innovation" [134].

As for regimental histories, one could compile a list by turning to Cooke [2] or Dornbusch [3] referred to above, though for a somewhat different approach to such studies, see Leslie Frost's *Fighting Men* [72], which traces the experiences of the townspeople of Orillia, those who remained behind as well as those who served overseas. Jackson's study of the 127th Battalion [95] is also worthy of note, as it is one of the few such histories to follow the experiences of an infantry unit converted to other work—in this case railway construction. Meanwhile, Jean-Pierre Gagnon, in his groundbreaking work, *Le 22e Battalion (canadien-français) 1914–1919* [73], is concerned with the background and experiences of all those involved with Canada's only francophone unit to fight as such on the Western Front, and provides an excellent example of the social military history which has begun to interest Canadian practitioners in the past few years. Another approach to regimental history can be found in Daniel G. Dancocks' *Gallant Canadians: The Story of the Tenth Canadian Infantry Battalion, 1914–1919* [58], which is a simple narrative that nevertheless tells us much about one unit's experiences.

OPERATIONS

The CEF's formative period can be said to have begun when it arrived at the front in February 1915 and ended with the battle of the Somme in November 1916. Daniel G. Dancocks' *Welcome to Flanders Fields* [62] is a straightforward narrative of Canadian Corps operations at Second Ypres, where it fought its first major battle, losing a third of its soldiers in the process. Shorter but also useful is N. M. Christie's *Gas Attack: The Canadians at Ypres, 1915* [55], while his book, *Futility and Sacrifice: The Canadians on the Somme, 1916* [54], though at 35 pages very short, is perhaps the only monograph to focus exclusively on the Canadian Corps' experiences in that campaign. In between Second Ypres and the Somme the formation fought at St Eloi, an engagement Tim Cook analyzes in "The Blind Leading the Blind: The Battle of St Eloi Craters" [44].

Many historians and enthusiasts have turned their attention to the battle of Vimy Ridge of Easter 1917, long considered to be a victory of sufficient proportions to contribute to the creation of a Canadian national identity—at least for the English-speaking community. Brereton Greenhous and Steve Harris' *Canada and the Battle of Vimy Ridge* [85], Herbert F. Wood's *Vimy!* [171], D. E. Macintyre's *Canada at Vimy* [103], D. J. Goodspeed's *The Road Past Vimy* [76], N. M. Christie's *Winning the Ridge* [57], and Pierre Berton's *Vimy* [23] all discuss the events leading up to what was perhaps the most famous battle the Canadian Corps was to fight in the war, and all provide reminiscences of some of the men who were there, while Macintyre's book is essentially autobiographical.

Vimy Ridge was not the Canadian Corps' only major battle of 1917, it being followed by such actions as Hill 70 and Passchendaele, the latter covered in N. M. Christie's provocatively titled *Slaughter in the Mud: The Canadians at Passchendaele, 1917* [56]. Daniel G. Dancocks' *Legacy of Valour* [59] and *Spearhead to Victory* [61] cover the experiences of the CEF at Passchendaele and in the 1918 offensives (called the Hundred Days) in a highly readable narrative, while a critical appraisal of the CEF's operations in the last offensives of the war can be found in the *Report of the Ministry, 1918* [39], which discusses a wide variety of activities, including those of ancillary units such as the Canadian

Railway Troops and the Canadian Forestry Corps. It is an excellent source for anyone interested in the administration and logistics of the Canadian Expeditionary Force in its final year. Dean Chappelle's "The Most Brilliant of Successes" [8] focuses on the August 1918 Battle of Amiens and is an excellent study of the preparations and operations that opened the last major offensive against Germany. A series of short studies by N. M. Christie, *The Canadians at Amiens* [51], *The Canadians at Arras and the Drocourt-Quéant Line* [52], and *The Canadians at Cambrai and the Canal du Nord* [53], all of which are subtitled "A Social History and Battlefield Tour," focus on specific battles of the Hundred Days campaign. As short (or shorter) but more analytical are Brereton Greenhous' *The Battle of Amiens, 8–11 August 1918* [80], Dean Chappelle's "The Canadian Attack at Amiens, 8–11 August 1918" [43], and John Swettenham's *Breaking the Hindenberg Line* [156]. A recent addition to the literature that does an excellent job of placing the Canadian Corps' contribution within a wider context is Syd Wise's "The Black Day of the German Army: Australians and Canadians at Amiens, August 1918" [174].

For smaller-scale operations or those not fitting the combat arms mold, one needs to look to article-length works, many of which have been published in *Canadian Military History* over the years. They include Michael Boire's "The Underground War: Military Mining Operations in Support of the Attack on Vimy Ridge, 9 April 1917" [29], Tim Cook's " 'A Proper Slaughter': The March 1917 Gas Raid at Vimy" [47], and Andrew Godefroy's "A Lesson in Success: The Calonne Trench Raid, 17 January 1917" [75].

That the field of First World War history is alive and well is evidenced by the number of works-in-progress, including a general history of the Battle of Amiens studying the Australian, British, and French experience as well as the Canadian. Still, much remains to be done. For example, readers still await a scholarly study of Canadian generalship in the First World War; the generals themselves, aside from Currie, have not been closely scrutinized as individuals, nor have the staff officers that dealt with planning, personnel, and other such issues. We know very little of the Canadian sailors who served with the Royal Navy, or of the development of Canadian tank battalions, to give just two other examples. Thus, so far, though historians have done much more than scratch the surface, they still have not completed the study of Canada's First World War military experience in all its myriad facets.

BIBLIOGRAPHY

Bibliographical Works

1. Cooke, Owen A. "Canada's Historiography and the First World War," *Neue Forschungen zum Ersten Weltkrieg.* Koblenz, 1985.

2. Cooke, Owen A. *The Canadian Military Experience 1867–1995: A Bibliography.* Ottawa, Department of National Defence, 1997

3. Dornbusch, C. E. *The Canadian Army, 1955–1965: Regimental Histories and a Guide to the Regiments.* Cornwallville, Hope Farm Press, 1966

Theses and Dissertations

4. Allard, Geneviève. "Les infirmières militaires canadiennes pendant la Première Guerre mondiale." Thèse de 2e Cycle, Université Laval, 1997.

5. Beahen, William. "A Citizen's Army: The Growth and Development of the Canadian Militia, 1904 to 1914." Ph.D., University of Ottawa, 1979.

6. Bezeau, M. V. "The Role and Organization of Canadian Military Staffs 1904–1945." M.A., Royal Military College, 1978.

7. Brown, Ian Malcolm. "Lieutenant-general Sir Arthur Currie and the Canadian Corps, 1917–1918." M.A., University of Calgary, 1991.

8. Chappelle, Dean. "The Most Brilliant of Successes: The Planning and Implementation of the Battle of Amiens, 8–11 August, 1918." M.A., University of New Brunswick, 1990.

9. Eyre, Kenneth Charles. "Staff and Command in the Canadian Corps: The Canadian Militia 1896–1914 as a Source of Senior Officers." M.A., Duke University, 1967.

10. Harris, Stephen J. "Canadian Brass: The Growth of the Canadian Military Profession, 1860–1919." Ph.D., Duke University, 1979.

11. Haycock, Ronald G. "Sir Sam Hughes: His Public Career, 1892–1916." Ph.D., University of Western Ontario, 1976.

12. Hyatt, A. M. J. "The Military Career of Sir Arthur Currie." Ph.D., Duke University, 1964.

13. Jenkins, Danny. "Winning Trench Warfare: Battlefield Intelligence in the Canadian Corps, 1914–1918." Ph.D., Carleton University, 1999.

14. McCulloch, Ian. "The Fighting Seventh: The Evolution and Devolution of Tactical Command and Control in a Canadian Infantry Brigade of the Great War. M.A., Royal Military College of Canada, 1997.

15. Rider, Peter E. "The Imperial Munitions Board and its Relationship to Government, Business and Labour, 1914–1920." Ph.D., University of Toronto, 1974.

16. Stewart, William F. "Attack Doctrine in the Canadian Corps, 1916–1918." M.A., University of New Brunswick, 1982.

Secondary and Published Sources

17. Adamson, Agar. *Letters of Agar Adamson, 1914 to 1919: Lieutenant-Colonel, Princess Patricia's Canadian Light Infantry.* Nepean, CEF Books, 1997.

18. Aitken, Sir Max. *Canada in Flanders.* New York, G. H. Doran Co., 1915.

19. Armstrong, Elizabeth H. *The Crisis of Quebec, 1914–1918.* New York, AMS Press, 1937.

20. Armstrong, John Griffith. *The Halifax Explosion and the Royal Canadian Navy: Inquiry and Intrigue.* Vancouver, UBC Press, 2002.

21. Bartholomew, Robert E. "Phantom German Air Raids on Canada: War Hysteria in Quebec and Ontario During the Great War." *Canadian Military History,* Autumn 1998.

22. Bashow, David L. *Knights of the Air: Canadian Fighter Pilots in the First World War.* Toronto, McArthur, 2000.

23. Berton, Pierre, *Vimy.* Toronto, McClelland and Stewart, 1986.

24. Bindon, Kathryn M. *More than Patriotism.* Don Mills, Personal Library Publishers, 1979.

25. Bird, Will R. *Ghosts Have Warm Hands: A Memoir of the Great War.* Nepean, CEF Books, 1997.

26. Bishop, William Arthur. *The Courage of the Early Morning: A Son's Biography of a Famous Father: The Story of Billy Bishop.* Toronto, McClelland and Stewart, 1985.

27. Bliss, Michael. *A Canadian Millionaire: The Life and Business Times of Joseph Flavelle, Bart, 1858–1939.* Toronto, Macmillan of Canada, 1978.

28. Bliss, Michael. "War Business as Usual: Canadian Munitions Production, 1914–1918," in N. F. Dreisziger, ed. *Mobilization for Total War: The Canadian, American and British Experience, 1914–1918, 1939–1945.*

29. Boire, Michael. "The Underground War: Military Mining Operations in Support of the Attack on Vimy Ridge, 9 April 1917." *Canadian Military History,* Autumn 1992.

30. Borden, Robert Laird. *Robert Laird Borden: His Memoirs.* Toronto, 1938.

31. Bray, Robert Matthew. "Fighting as an Ally: The English-Canadian Patriotic Response to the Great War." *Canadian Historical Review.* June, 1980.

32. Brown, Ian. "Not Glamorous, But Effective: The Canadian Corps and the Set-piece Attack, 1917–1918." *Journal of Military History,* July 1994.

33. Brown, Robert Craig, and Ramsay Cook. *Canada, 1896–1921, A Nation Transformed.* Toronto, McClelland and Stewart, 1974.

34. Brown, Robert Craig, and Desmond Morton. "The Embarrassing Apotheosis of a 'Great Canadian': Sir Arthur Currie's Personal Crisis in 1917." *Canadian Historical Review,* March 1979.

35. Brown, Robert Craig. *Robert Laird Borden, a Biography.* Toronto, Macmillan of Canada, 1980.

36. Brown, Robert Craig, and Donald Loveridge. "Unrequited Faith: Recruiting the CEF 1914–1918." *Revue internationale d'histoire militaire.* No 51, 1982.

37. Brown, Tom. "Shell Shock in the Canadian Expeditionary Force, 1914–1918: Canadian Psychiatry in the Great War." Roland, Charles, ed. *Health, Disease and Medicine: Essays in Canadian History.* Toronto, 1983.

38. Burns, E. L. M. *General Mud: Memoirs of Two World Wars.* Toronto, Clarke, Irwin, 1970.

39. Canada. *Report of the Ministry, Overseas Military Forces of Canada, 1918.* London, Ministry, Overseas Military Forces of Canada, 1918.

40. Canada. *Thirty Canadian VCs: 23rd April 1915 to 30th March 1918.* London, Skeffington, 1918.

41. Carter, David J. *Behind Canadian Barbed Wire: Alien, Refugee and Prisoner of War Camps in Canada, 1914–1946.* Calgary, Tumbleweed Press, 1980.

42. Chajkowsky, William E. *Royal Flying Corps: Borden to Texas to Beamsville.* Cheltenham, Boston Mills Press, 1979.

43. Chappelle, Dean. "The Canadian Attack at Amiens, 8–11 August 1918." *Canadian Military History,* Autumn 1993.

44. Cook, Tim. "The Blind Leading the Blind: The Battle of the St Eloi Craters." *Canadian Military History,* Autumn 1996.

45. Cook, Tim, " 'More a Medicine than a Beverage': 'Demon Rum' and the Canadian Trench Soldier of the First World War." *Canadian Military History,* Winter 2000.

46. Cook, Tim. *No Place to Run: The Canadian Corps and Gas Warfare in the First World War.* Vancouver, UBC Press, 1999.

47. Cook, Tim. " 'A Proper Slaughter': The March 1917 Gas Raid at Vimy." *Canadian Military History,* Spring 1999.

48. Collishaw, Raymond, and R. V. Dodds. *Air Command: A Fighter Pilot's Story.* London, W. Kimber, 1973.

49. Coppolino, Andrew. " 'While the Shells Crashed We Were Strong': The Life of War Poet 'Toronto' Prewett." *Canadian Military History,* Winter 1999.

50. Craig, Grace Morris. *But This Is Our War.* Toronto, University of Toronto Press, 1981.

51. Christie, N. M. *The Canadians at Amiens, August 8th to 16th, 1918: A Social History and Battlefield Tour.* Nepean, CEF Books, 1999.

52. Christie, N. M. *The Canadians at Arras and the Drocourt-Quéant Line, August–September, 1918: A Social History and Battlefield Tour.* Nepean, CEF Books, 1997.

53. Christie, N. M. *The Canadians at Cambrai and the Canal du Nord, September–October, 1918: A Social History and Battlefield Tour.* Nepean, CEF Books, 1999.

54. Christie, N. M. *Futility and Sacrifice: The Canadians on the Somme, 1916.* Nepean, CEF Books, 1998.

55. Christie, N. M. *Gas Attack: The Canadians at Ypres, 1915.* Nepean, CEF Books, 1998.

56. Christie, N. M. *Slaughter in the Mud: The Canadians at Passchendaele, 1917.* Nepean, CEF Books, 1998.

57. Christie, N. M. *Winning the Ridge: The Canadians at Vimy Ridge, 1917.* Nepean, CEF Books, 1998.

58. Dancocks, Daniel G. *Gallant Canadians: The Story of the Tenth Canadian Infantry Battalion, 1914–1919.* Calgary, Calgary Highlanders Regimental Funds Foundation, 1994.

59. Dancocks, Daniel G. *Legacy of Valour: The Canadians at Passchendaele.* Edmonton, Hurtig, 1986.

60. Dancocks, Daniel G. *Sir Arthur Currie: A Biography.* Toronto, Methuen, 1985

61. Dancocks, Daniel G. *Spearhead to Victory: Canada and the Great War.* Edmonton, Hurtig, 1987.

62. Dancocks, Daniel G. *Welcome to Flanders Fields: The First Canadian Battle of the Great War: Ypres, 1915.* Toronto, McClelland and Stewart, 1988.

63. Dodds, R. V. *The Brave Young Wings.* Stittsville, Canada's Wings, 1980.

64. Dietrich, Bev. "Colonel John McCrae: From Guelph, Ontario to Flanders Fields." *Canadian Military History,* Autumn 1996.

65. Duguid, Archer Fortescue. *Official History of the Canadian Forces in the Great War, 1914–1919.* Ottawa, King's Printer, 1938.

66. England, Robert. "A Victoria Real Estate Man: The Enigma of Sir Arthur Currie." *Queen's Quarterly,* Summer, 1958.

67. Fetherstonhaugh, R. C. *The Royal Montreal Regiment, 14th Battalion, CEF, 1914–1925.* Montreal, Gazette Print Co., 1927.

68. Fetherstonhaugh, R. C. *The 13th Battalion Royal Highlanders of Canada, 1914–1919.* Montreal, 13th Battalion Royal Highlanders of Canada, 1925.

69. Filteau, Gérard. *Le Québec, le Canada et la guerre, 1914–1918.* Montréal, Éditions de l'Aurore, 1977.

70. Foster, Charles Lyon and William S. Duthie, eds. *Letters from the Front: Being a Partial Record of the Part Played by Officers of the Bank in the Great European War.* Toronto, Canadian Bank of Commerce, 1920.

71. Fraser, W. B. *Always a Stracona.* Calgary, Comprint Pub Co., 1976.

72. Frost, Leslie M. *Fighting Men.* Toronto, Clarke, Irwin, 1967.

73. Gagnon, Jean-Pierre. *Le 22e Bataillon (canadien-français) 1914–1919, étude sociomilitaire.* Québec, Presses de l'Université de Laval, 1986.

74. Godefroy, Andrew. *For Freedom and Honour? The Story of the 25 Canadian Volunteers Executed in the First World War.* Nepean, CEF Books, 1998.

75. Godefroy, Andrew B. "A Lesson in Success: The Calonne Trench Raid, 17 January 1917." *Canadian Military History,* Spring 1999.

76. Goodspeed, D. J. *The Road Past Vimy: The Canadian Corps, 1914–1918.* Toronto, Macmillan of Canada, 1969.

77. Granatstein, J. L., and Desmond Morton. *Marching to Armageddon: Canadians and the Great War, 1914–1919.* Toronto, Lester and Orpen Dennys, 1989.

78. Granatstein, J. L., and J. M. Hitsman. *Broken Promises: A History of Conscription in Canada.* Toronto, Oxford University Press, 1977.

79. Graves, Dianne. *A Crown of Life: The World of John McCrae.* St Catharines, Vanwell Pub, 1997.

80. Greenhous, Brereton. *The Battle of Amiens, 8–11 August 1918.* Ottawa, Canadian War Museum, 1995.

81. Greenhous, Brereton. *Dragoon: the Centennial History of The Royal Canadian Dragoons, 1883–1983.* Belleville, Guild of the Royal Canadian Dragoons, 1983.

82. Greenhous, Brereton. *The Making of Billy Bishop.* Toronto, Dundurn Press, 2002

83. Greenhous, Brereton. *A Rattle of Pebbles: The First World War Diaries of Two Canadian Airmen.* Ottawa, Department of National Defence, 1987.

84. Greenhous, Brereton. "The Sad Case of Billy Bishop, VC." *Canadian Historical Review,* June 1989.

85. Greenhous, Brereton, and Steve Harris. *Canada and the Battle of Vimy Ridge.* Montreal, Department of National Defence, 1992.

86. Guiou, Norman Miles. *Transfusion: A Canadian Surgeon's Story in War and Peace.* Yarmouth Nova Scotia, Stoneycroft Pub., 1985.

87. Hadley, Michael H., and Roger Sarty. *Tin-Pots and Pirate Ships.* Montreal, McGill-Queen's University Press, 1991.

88. Hahn, E. *The Intelligence Service within the Canadian Corps, 1914–1918.* Toronto, Macmillan Co. of Canada, 1930.

89. Harris, Stephen. *Canadian Brass: The Making of a Professional Army, 1860–1939.* Toronto, University of Toronto Press, 1988.

90. Harris, Stephen. "From Subordinate to Ally: The Canadian Corps and National Autonomy, 1914–1918." *Revue internationale d'histoire militaire.* No. 51, 1982.

91. Hartney, Harold E. *Up and at 'Em.* Harrisburg, Stackpole, 1971

92. Haycock, Ronald G. *Sam Hughes: The Public Career of a Controversial Canadian, 1885–1916.* Waterloo, Wilfrid Laurier University Press, 1986.

93. Hodder-Williams, Ralph. *Princess Patricia's Canadian Light Infantry 1914–1919.* London, Hodder and Staughton, 1978.

94. Hyatt, Albert M. J. *General Sir Arthur Currie: A Military Biography.* Toronto, University of Toronto Press, 1987.

95. Jackson, H. M. *The 127th Battalion, CEF; 2nd Battalion, Canadian Railway Troops.* Ottawa, no pub, 1957

96. Kerry, A. J., and W. A. McDill. *The History of the Corps of Royal Canadian Engineers.* Ottawa, Military Engineers Association of Canada, 1962.

97. Laflamme, Jean. *Les camps de détention au Québec durant la Première Guerre Mondiale.* Montréal, Jean Laflamme, 1973.

98. Legault, Roch, and Jean Lamarre, eds., *La première guerre mondiale et le Canada.* Montréal, Méridien, 1999.

99. Leppard, Thomas P. " 'The Dashing Subaltern': Sir Richard Turner in Retrospect." *Canadian Military History,* Autumn 1997.

100. Luciuk, Lubomyr Y. *Internment Operations: The Role of Old Fort Henry in World War I.* Kingston, Delta Educational Consultants, 1980.

101. Lynch, Alex. *Dad, the Motors and the Fifth Army Show.* Westport, A. Lynch, 1978.

102. Lynch, John William. *Princess Patricia's Canadian Light Infantry, 1917–1919.* Hicksville, Exposition Press, 1976.

103. Macintyre, D. E. *Canada at Vimy.* Toronto, P. Martin Associates, 1967.

104. Macksey, Kenneth. *The Shadow of Vimy Ridge.* London, W. Kimber, 1965.

105. MacLaren, Roy. *Canadians in Russia, 1918–1919.* Toronto, Macmillan of Canada, 1976.

106. Macphail, Andrew. *The Medical Services.* Ottawa, Minister of National Defence, 1925.

107. Mann, Susan, ed. *The War Diary of Claire Gass, 1915–1918.* Montreal, McGill Queen's, 2000.

108. Mathieson, William D. *My Grandfather's War: Canadians Remember the First World War, 1914–1918.* Toronto, Macmillan of Canada, 1981.

109. McCulloch, Ian. " 'Batty Mac': Portrait of a Brigade Commander of the Great War, 1915–1917." *Canadian Military History,* Autumn 1998.

110. McKee, Alexander. *Vimy Ridge.* London, Souvenir Press, 1966.

111. McWilliams, James L., and James R. Steele. *The Suicide Battalion.* Edmonton, Hurtig, 1978.

112. Meek, John F. *Over the Top! The Canadian Infantry in the First World War.* Orangeville, no pub, 1971.

113. Metson, Graham. *The Halifax Explosion, December 6, 1917.* Toronto, McGraw-Hill Ryerson, 1978.

114. Mitchell, G. D. *RCHA—The Right of the Line.* Ottawa, RCHA History Committee, 1986.

115. Moir, John S., ed. *History of the Royal Canadian Corps of Signals 1903–1961.* Ottawa, Royal Canadian Corps of Signals, 1962.

116. Monaghan, Hugh B. *The Big Bombers of World War I: A Canadian's Journal.* Burlington, R. Gentle Communications, n.d.

117. Morton, Desmond. *The Canadian General, Sir William Otter.* Toronto, Hakkert, 1974.

118. Morton, Desmond. "A Canadian Soldier in the Great War: The Experiences of Frank Maheux." *Canadian Military History,* Autumn 1992.

119. Morton, Desmond. "Junior but Sovereign Allies: the Transformation of the Canadian Expeditionary Force, 1914–1918." *Journal of Imperial and Commonwealth History.* v. VIII, 1979.

120. Morton, Desmond. "Military Medicine during and after the First World War—Precursor of Universal Public health Care in Canada." *Canadian Defence Quarterly,* Summer, 1988.

121. Morton, Desmond. *A Peculiar Kind of Politics: Canada's Overseas Ministry in the First World War.* Toronto, University of Toronto Press, 1982.

122. Morton, Desmond. *Silent Battle: Canadian Prisoners of War in Germany, 1914–1919.* Toronto, Lester Pub, 1992.

123. Morton, Desmond. "The Supreme Penalty: Canadian Deaths by Firing Squad in the First World War." *Queen's Quarterly,* Autumn, 1972.

124. Morton, Desmond. *When Your Number's Up.* Toronto, Random House of Canada, 1993.

125. Munro, Iain R. *Canada and the World Wars.* Toronto, Wiley Publishers of Canada, 1979.

126. Murray, William W. *The History of the 2nd Canadian Battalion in the Great War 1914–1919.* Ottawa, Historical Committee 2nd Canadian Battalion, 1947.

127. Nicholson, G. W. L. *Canada's Nursing Sisters.* Toronto, A.M. Hakkert, 1975.

128. Nicholson, G. W. L. *Canadian Expeditionary Force, 1914–1919.* Ottawa, Queen's Printer, 1962.

129. Nicholson, G. W. L. *The Fighting Newfoundler: A History of the Royal Newfoundland Regiment.* St. John's, Govt of Newfoundland, 1964.

130. Nicholson, G. W. L. *The Gunners of Canada.* Toronto, McClelland and Stewart, 1967.

131. Nicholson, G. W. L. *Seventy Years of Service: A History of the Royal Canadian Army Medical Corps.* Ottawa, Borealis Press, 1977.

132. Ogilvie, William C. *Umpty-Iddy-Umpty: The Story of a Canadian Signaller in the First World War.* Erin, Boston Mills Press, 1982.

133. Pedley, James H. *Only This: A War Retrospect, 1917–1918.* Nepean, CEF Books, 1999.

134. Phelan, F. R. "Army Supplies in the Forward Area and the Tumpline System: A First World War Canadian Logistical Innovation." *Canadian Military History,* Winter 2000.

135. Prescott, John F. *In Flanders Fields: The Story of John McCrae.* Erin Ontario, Boston Mills Press, 1985.

136. Provencher, Jean. *Québec sous la loi des mesures de guerre, 1918.* Montréal, Éditions du Boréal Express, 1971.

137. Ralph, Wayne. *Barker VC.* Toronto, Doubleday Canada, 1997.

138. Rawling, Bill. "Communications in the Canadian Corps, 1915–1918: Wartime Technological Progress Revisited." *Canadian Military History,* Autumn 1994.

139. Rawling, Bill. *Surviving Trench Warfare: Technology and the Canadian Corps, 1914–1918.* Toronto, University of Toronto Press, 1992.

140. Read, Daphne, ed. *The Great War and Canadian Society: An Oral History.* Toronto, New Hogtown Press, 1978.

141. Reid, Gordon, ed. *Poor Bloody Murder: Personal Memoirs of the First World War.* Oakville, Mosaic Press, 1980.

142. Roy, Reginald H. *For Most Conspicuous Bravery: A Biography of Major-General George R. Pearkes, VC, through Two World Wars.* Vancouver, University of British Columbia Press, 1977.

143. Roy, Reginald H., ed. *The Journal of Private Fraser, 1914–1918, Canadian Expeditionary Force.* Victoria, Sono Nis Press, 1985.

144. Russenholt, E. S. *Six Thousand Canadian Men: Being the History of the 44th Battalion Canadian Infantry.* Winnipeg, 44th Battalion Association, 1932.

145. Santor, Donald M. *Canadians at War, 1914–1918.* Scarborough, Prentice-Hall of Canada, 1978.

146. Sarty, Roger. "Hard Luck Flotilla: The RCN's Atlantic Coast Patrol, 1914–1918." Douglas, W. A. B, ed. *The RCN in Transition, 1910–1985.* Vancouver, 1988.

147. Schreiber, Shane B. *Shock Army of the British Army: The Canadian Corps in the last 100 Days of the Great War.* Westport, Praeger, 1997.

148. Sharpe, C. A. "Enlistment in the Canadian Expeditionary Force 1914–1918: A Regional Analysis." *Journal of Canadian Studies,* Winter 1983/84.

149. Shrive, Frank J. *The Diary of a PBO. Poor Bloody Observer.* Erin, Boston Mills Press, 1981.

150. Skaarup, Hal A. "Whiz Bangs and Whooly Bears: Walter Estabrooks and the Great War, compiled from his diary and letters." *Canadian Military History,* Autumn 1995.

151. Snell, A. E. *The CAMC with the Canadian Corps during the Last Hundred Days of the Great War.* Ottawa, F. A. Acland, 1924.

152. Socknat, Thomas Paul. "Canada's Liberal Pacifists and the Great War." *Journal of Canadian Studies,* Winter 1983/84.

153. Sorobey, Ron. "Filip Konowal, VC: The Rebirth of a Canadian Hero." *Canadian Military History,* Autumn 1996.

154. Speaight, Robert. *Vanier: Diplomat and Governor General.* Toronto, Collins, 1970.

155. Swettenham, John. *Allied Intervention in Russia, 1918–1919: And the Part Played by Canada.* Toronto, Ryerson, 1967.

156. Swettenham, John. *Breaking the Hindenberg Line.* Ottawa, Canadian War Museum, 1986.

157. Swettenham, John. *Canada and the First World War.* Toronto, Ryerson Press, 1969.

158. Swettenham, John. *McNaughton.* Toronto, Ryerson Press, 1968–1969.

159. Swettenham, John. *To Seize the Victory: The Canadian Corps in World War I.* Toronto: Ryerson Press, 1965.

160. Tennyson, Brian, and Roger Sarty. "Sydney, Nova Scotia and the U-Boat War, 1918." *Canadian Military History,* Winter 1998.

161. Thompson, John Herd. *The Harvests of War: The Prairie West, 1914–1918.* Toronto, McClelland and Stewart, 1978.

162. Travers, Tim. "Currie and 1st Canadian Division at Second Ypres, April 1915: Controversy, Criticism and Official History." *Canadian Military History,* Autumn 1996.

163. Tucker, Gilbert Norman. *The Naval Service of Canada: Its Official History. Volume I: Origins and Early Years.* Ottawa, King's Printer, 1952.

164. Urquhart, Hugh M. *Arthur Currie: The Biography of a Great Canadian.* Toronto, J. M. Dents and Sons, 1950.

165. Vance, Jonathan. *Death So Noble: Memory, Meaning, and the First World War.* Vancouver, UBC Press, 1997.

166. Wert, Mike. "From Enlistment to the Grave: The Impact of the First World War on 52 Canadian Soldiers." *Canadian Military History,* Spring 2000.

167. *Veterans' Review: A Collection of War Stories.* Toronto, Veterans' Review, 1983.

168. Wheeler, Victor W. *The 50th Battalion in No Man's Land.* Nepean, CEF Books, 2000

169. Williams, Jeffrey. *Byng of Vimy: General and Governor-General.* London, L. Cooper, 1983.

170. Williams, Jeffrey. *First in the Field: Gault of the Patricias.* St. Catharines, Vanwell Pub, 1995.

171. Wilson, Barbara M., ed. *Ontario and the First World War, 1914–1918, a Collection of Documents.* Toronto, Champlain Society, 1977.

172. Wilson-Simmie, Katherine M. *Lights Out: a Canadian Nursing Sister's Tale.* Belleville, Mika, 1981.

173. Winter, Charles F. *Lieutenant-General the Hon. Sir Sam Hughes KCB, MP: Canada's War Minister 1911–1916, Recollections of Service as Military Secretary at Headquarters, Canadian Militia, Prior to and During the Early Stages of the Great War.* Toronto, Macmillan of Canada, 1931.

174. Wise, S. F. "The Black Day of the German Army: Australians and Canadians at Amiens, August 1918." Dennis, Peter, and Jeffrey Grey, eds. *1918: Defining Victory.* Canberra, 1999.

175. Wise, S. F. *Canadian Airmen and the First World War.* Ottawa, University of Toronto Press, 1980.

176. Wise, S. F. "The Gardeners of Vimy: Canadian Corps' Farming Operations during the German Offensives of 1918." *Canadian Military History,* Summer 1999.

177. Wood, Herbert F. *Vimy!* London, Macdonald and Co, 1967.

178. Worthington, Larry, *Amid the Enemy Guns Below: The Story of the Canadian Corps, 1914–1919.* Toronto, McClelland and Stewart, 1965.

11

United States

David J. Fitzpatrick

To many Americans, the U.S. experience in the Great War seems a rather brief and unimportant event in the broad expanse of the nation's history. This is especially true where the reading public is concerned. Though some historians of the conflict, most notably Paul Fussell [73] and John Keegan [106], have succeeded in reaching a broader audience, the war, for the most part, is not an important part of the nation's historical memory—World War II, due to its proximity in time, and the Civil War, for perhaps obvious reasons, resonate with Americans today far more than does the Great War.

This is not to say that academic historians have ignored the conflict. Indeed, scholarship over the past twenty years regarding the American experience in the war has been unusually rich. This essay will attempt to highlight the most important of this recent scholarship as well as less recent works that remain important in the field.

GENERAL REFERENCES

Keegan's *The First World War* [106] is an idiosyncratic volume that all but ignores the American contribution to the Allied war effort. Of more value are much earlier volumes that, though somewhat dated and themselves unique in their interpretations, provide a more well-rounded view of the conflict. These include works by J. E. Edmonds [59], Cyril Falls [61], B. H. Liddell Hart [121], and James Stokesbury [201].

Edward Coffman's *The War to End All Wars* [39] remains the best single-volume treatment of the U.S. military effort in the conflict, though Byron Farwell's

Over There [62] is an important recent work due to its efforts to go beyond the traditional limitations of military history, especially in its treatment of the experience of blacks and of Indians, as well as due to its effort to detail the AEF's war against venereal disease. Significant general works on the American experience in the Great War include Russell F. Weigley's *History of the United States Army* [206], Allan R. Millett and Peter Maslowski's *For the Common Defense* [149], and Weigley's *The American Way of War* [225].

Geoffrey Perret's somewhat disappointing *A Country Made by War* [165] is a recent popular effort to address the nation's wartime experiences as a whole. Though little regarding its treatment of World War I is new, it is worth consideration due to its point of view, which is expressed in its title. Of more interest and importance are numerous works by Arthur S. Link, [124, 125, 127, 128], Robert H. Ferrell's, *Woodrow Wilson and World War I, 1917–1921* [63], and David Kennedy's *Over Here* [108]. More recently, Meirion and Susan Harries have provided an account of the American home front in *The Last Days of Innocence* [87], which, though quite well written, breaks little new ground. Those seeking an encyclopedic approach would be well served by looking at Anne Cipriano Venzon's *The United States in the First World War: An Encyclopedia* [222] and Holger H. Herwig and Neil Heyman's *Biographical Dictionary of World War I* [92]. Numerous topic-specific essays in John E. Jessup and Louise B. Ketz's *Encyclopedia of the American Military* [103] are worthy of note. Bibliographic references include the World War I chapter in *A Guide to the Sources of United States Military History* [1] and Ronald Schaffer's *The United States in World War I* [184].

ENTRY INTO THE CONFLICT

Few issues in American historiography have been more contentious than that of American entry into the Great War, and fewer still have had the impact on current events than those historians who, in the 1930s, wrote accounts critical of Woodrow Wilson's decision to enter the conflict. Of these, Walter Millis's *Road to War* [150] stands out as a thoughtful and thought-provoking piece, arguing forcefully that entry into the war had been a mistake. Other revisionist accounts include those by Charles Tansill [204] and Charles A. Beard [12]. Daniel Smith's brief *The Great Departure* [193] and his biography of Secretary of State Robert Lansing [194] contend that Germany's violations of international law, vague perceptions of national interest, and Wilson's desire to influence the peace led to the president's decision to ask for a declaration of war. Numerous of Arthur Link's volumes [124–128] argue that Wilson's policies were based upon a "higher realism" that would achieve a just and lasting peace. Edward H. Buehrig, in *Woodrow Wilson and the Balance of Power* [23], asserts that the president entered the conflict to preserve the balance of power, not to destroy it. Ernest R. May's *The World War and American Isolationism, 1914–1917* [139] contends that America's international influence would have been severely undermined had Wilson backed down from the German submarine challenge. More recent works by Julius W. Pratt [173], John Coogan [43], and Patrick Devlin [57] have accepted some of the realists' findings while, at the same time, suggesting that American intervention was not in the nation's best interests. In *Power and Principle* [25] and in *Uses of Force and Wilsonian Foreign Policy* [26], Frederick Calhoun provides a sympathetic view of Wilson's employment of military force, not only in Europe but in Mexico, Central America, and the Caribbean as well. Barbara Tuchman's *The Zimmerman Telegram* [212] should also be consulted.

MOBILIZATION FOR WAR

The mobilization of the nation's resources is a subject rich in scholarship and debate. General treatments of the subject include Marvin A. Kriedberg and Merton G. Henry's *History of Military Mobilization in the United States Army, 1775–1945* [115], Paul Koistinen's *Mobilizing for Modern War: The Political Economy of American Warfare, 1865–1919* [114], and Koistinen's "The 'Industrial-Military Complex' in Historical Perspective" [113], as well as previously cited works by Weigley [226] and by Millett and Maslowski [149]. Koistinen's work is particularly valuable in its description of President Wilson's and Secretary of War Newton Baker's efforts to create a wartime economy controlled by neither the military nor by big business. John P. Finnegan's *Against the Specter of a Dragon* [66] is a valuable account of the 1914–1917 preparedness debate, and several of Arthur Link's volumes provide important insights and details [124, 125, 127, 128] regarding preparedness and mobilization.

The role played by the War Industry Board remains an important if less-than-controversial topic. Bernard Baruch's *American Industry in the War* [218] provides a firsthand account of the WIB's successes and failures, while Robert D. Cuff's *The War Industries Board* [54] remains the best scholarly work on the subject. The WIB's relationship with the Navy is addressed in John K. Ohl's "The Navy, the War Industries Board, and the Industrial Mobilization for War, 1917–1918" [161]. William J. Breen's *Labor Market Politics and the Great War* [19] is a not altogether successful effort to look at the U.S. Employment Service's failed efforts to exert central control over the labor market. The nation's railroad system proved to be one of the larger problems encountered in the mobilization process. Cuff's "United States Mobilization and Railroad Transportation" [53] and Daniel M. Vrooman's *Daniel Willard and Progressive Management on the B&O Railroad* [223] address this important topic. Organized labor played a key role in the nation's industrial mobilization. Frank L. Grubbs's *Samuel Gompers and the Great War* [79] and Valerie J. Conner's *The National War Labor Board* [42] are the most important scholarship in the field. William J. Breen looks at the political ramifications of mobilization in *Uncle Sam at Home* [20].

Various works by William J. Williams have addressed the Navy in crisis. *The Wilson Administration and the Shipbuilding Crisis of 1917* [231] is his most recent book-length work in this area, and it focuses its attention on the battle between William Denman and General George W. Goethals for control of the program. A subsequent journal article assesses the role of Secretary of the Navy Josephus Daniels [230]. Other articles by Williams include "Accommodating American Shipyard Workers, 1917–1918" [228] and "The American Concrete Shipbuilding Program of World War I" [229]. Daniel R. Beaver has done similar work regarding the Army's mobilization: *Newton D. Baker and the American War Effort* [14], "The Problem of American Military Supply, 1890–1920" [15], and "George W. Goethals and the Problems of Military Supply" [13]. More recently, Phyllis Zimmerman's *The Neck of the Bottle* [234] builds on Beaver's works, portraying effectively the battles between, on the one hand, Goethals, Baker, and Peyton March, and, on the other, the bureau chiefs. It concludes that Goethals, often for reasons beyond his control, failed in his efforts to systematize effectively the War Department's mobilization efforts.

The subject of manpower mobilization has produced a voluminous literature. John K. Ohl's "Hugh S. Johnson and the Draft, 1917–1918" [160] deals with that important figure's role in the Selective Service, while John W. Chambers II, in *To Raise an Army* [30], provides a much more comprehensive account of the service. Chambers' briefer account "Conscripting for Colossus" [29] is also worthy of note. The Plattsburg Movement is addressed in John Garry Clifford's *The Citizen Soldiers* [35]. Among the many works that argue the case for the National Guard, Jim Dan Hill's *The Minute Man in Peace and War* [95] is the earliest scholarly effort. John K. Mahon's *History of the Militia and the National Guard* [134] is probably the best single-volume history of those organizations. Recently Jerry Cooper has done groundbreaking work on the subject. His *Citizens as Soldiers* [50] looks at the experience of the North Dakota National Guard and concludes internal difficulties combined with War Department neglect to cause great problems during both the Mexican incursion and during its service with the AEF. Cooper's *The Rise of the National Guard* [49] looks at the Guard in broader terms, both chronologically and geographically, and strikes a similar note, arguing convincingly that lack of funding prior to the Great War severely hindered the Guard's value as a reserve force, and the subsequent implementation of conscription "fundamentally altered the character of the National Guard." Biographies of W. E. B. DuBois by David Lewis [120] Elliott Rudwick [182] and William Tuttle [215] address to varying degrees DuBois' efforts to generate black support for the conflict. Several works look at efforts to socialize and to assimilate the men who entered the service. Nancy K. Bristow's *Making Men Moral* [21] recounts the efforts of the Commission on Training Camp Activities to prevent the spread of venereal disease and to improve the soldiers' moral well-being. Steven W. Pope's "An Army of Athletes" [172] argues that athletics was injected into military training as a means of imbuing men with "soldierly values" while, at the same time, reducing class and ethnic tensions within the military. Its long-term impact, he concludes, was on the nature of sport itself.

Numerous works address the mobilization of public opinion during the war. Stephen Vaughn's *Holding Fast the Inner Lines* [221] is the best scholarly account of the Committee on Public Information. Other important works on the subject include Walton Rawls's *Wake Up, America!* [177], George T. Blakey's *Historians on the Homefront* [17], and John Thompson's *Reformers and War* [205]. George Creel's account of the CPI's activities [52] is a valuable firsthand account. *American Women in World War I,* by Lettie Gavin [74], provides a compelling narrative (though it contains little analysis) of those women who supported the war effort, while Maurine W. Greenwald's *Women, War, and Work* [75] looks at the role women played in the nation's economic effort.

TROUBLED HOME FRONT

The earliest important effort to assess the nation's antiwar movement is Horace C. Peterson and Gilbert C. Fite's *Opponents of the War* [167]. Recent scholarship has focused on the very important role women played in the peace movement. In *The Women and the Warriors* [70], Carrie Foster looks at the early history of the Women's International League for Peace and Freedom and finds that its experience during the Great War greatly shaped its view of the world and the strategies it pursued during the interwar period. Francis H. Early's *A World without War* [58] recounts the history of the Bureau of Legal Advice, an organization that provided legal assistance to opponents of the war and to political radicals, and whose leadership consisted primarily of women.

The Wilson administration's repression of dissent has given rise to a large volume of literature. Paul L. Murphy's *World War I and the Origins of Civil Liberties* [154], William Preston Jr.'s *Aliens and Dissenters* [174], and Harry N. Scheiber's *The Wilson Administration and Civil Liberties* [186] are among the best volumes on the subject. John Higham's *Strangers in the Land* [94] and Frederick Leubke's *Bonds of Loyalty* [118] address the impact of the Wilson administration's efforts on ethnic Americans. Donald Johnson's *The Challenge to American Freedoms* [104] recounts the wartime origins of the American Civil Liberties Union, while Samuel Walker's *In Defense of American Liberties* [224] is a more general history of that organization.

Despite the Wilson administration's efforts to solidify public opinion behind the war effort, few periods in American history were as turmoil-ridden as that of the Great War and the immediate postwar period. Carole Marks's *Farewell— We're Good and Gone* [135], and Florette Henri's *Black Migration* [91] are superior accounts of the northward black migration and its consequences, while James R. Grossman's *Land of Hope* [78] looks specifically at the migration's consequences in Chicago. Books by Elliott Rudwick [181] and by William Tuttle [215] address the East St. Louis and Chicago race riots, the most infamous of the numerous riots that broke out in 1919. Thomas Lee Philpott's *The Slum and the Ghetto* [168], though concerned with a much broader period than that of the Great War, provides compelling accounts of the circumstances that led to the Chicago riot and in its aftermath. Both Tuttle [216] and Rudwick [182] also have produced important biographies of W. E. B. DuBois, as has David Lewis [120].

Labor radicalism reached unprecedented proportions during and after the war. The Seattle general strike is addressed in Dana Frank's *Purchasing Power* [71], the Boston police strike in Francis Russell's *A City in Terror* [183], and the steel strike of 1919 by David Brody's *Labor in Crisis* [22]. Important works on the Red Scare include Stanley Coben's biography of Attorney General A. Mitchell Palmer [36], Robert K. Murray's, *Red Scare* [155], and Richard Polenberg's *Fighting Faiths* [171].

OTHER INTERVENTIONS

Woodrow Wilson's interventions in Mexico and in Siberia remain controversial subjects. The best recent works on the president's response to the Mexican Revolution are John S. D. Eisenhower's *Intervention* [60] and Joseph Allen Stout's *Border Conflict* [203]. Other important works include P. Edward Haley's *Revolution and Intervention* [80], Kenneth J. Grieb's *The United States and Huerta* [76], Linda Hall and Dan M. Coerver's *Revolution on the Border* [81], Robert Freeman Smith's *The United States and Revolutionary Nationalism in Mexico* [196], and Friedrich Katz's *The Secret War in Mexico* [105]. The military aspects of the intervention are addressed by Herbert Mason's *The Great Pursuit* [137], by Clarence Clendenen's *Blood on the Border* [34], and in biographies of John J. Pershing by Frank Vandiver [219], Gene Smith [195], and Donald Smythe [197].

Numerous authors have attempted to discern the motivations behind Woodrow Wilson's response to the Russian Revolution. George Kennan's *Soviet-American Relations, 1917–1920* [107] argues that Wilson intervened at Vladivostok in an effort to save the Czech army that was fleeing across Siberia. In *Woodrow Wilson: Revolution, War and Peace* (129], Arthur Link echoes Kennan's findings but adds to them, contending that Wilson's belief that the Russian people had the right of self-determination led him to refuse to participate in a French proposal for a broad intervention in Russia. The limited American support of the Allied force that landed at Archangel, according to Link, was due to a concern that supplies at northern Russian ports might fall into German hands. The title of Georg Schild's *Between Ideology and Realpolitik* [187] suggests it argument—that Wilson's decision to intervene was driven both by realistic political considerations and by his deep-rooted liberal democratic philosophy. N. Gordon Levin's *Woodrow Wilson and World Politics* [119] and Lloyd C. Gardner, *Safe for Democracy* [73], offer more critical assessments of Wilson's motives, as do David W. McFadden's more recent *Alternative Paths* [141] and David Foglesong's *America's Secret War Against Bolshevism* [69]. Victor Fic's recently published *The Collapse of American Policy in Russia and Siberia* [65] criticizes Wilson's *failure* to become more deeply involved in Russia, blaming the president for the Red victory and, thereby, for much that happened subsequently. Benjamin D. Rhodes's *The Anglo-American Winter War with Russia* [179] provides a solid account of the military aspects of the Archangel expedition, as does E. M. Halliday's *The Ignorant Armies* [84], while Donald Carey's *Fighting the Bolsheviks* [28] is a soldier's memoirs of his experiences there.

STRATEGIC DIRECTION AND COALITION WARFARE

Over the past two decades scholars of the American military effort in the Great War have focused much of their effort on assessing the nation's place in the Allied coalition and on looking at the formulation of strategy. Timothy K. Nenninger's *The Leavenworth Schools and the Old Army* [159] and Carol Reardon's *Soldiers and Scholars* [178] provide important detail regarding the professional milieu in which Army officers operated, and they argue convincingly that the Army's school system, both in its strengths and weaknesses, shaped in important ways the formulation of strategy and the conduct of the war. Margaret and Harold Sprout's *The Rise of American Naval Power* [199], though dated, remains unsurpassed in addressing the development of naval strategy in the two decades prior to the conflict. The first two chapters of Paul Y. Hammond's *Organizing for Defense* [86] provides a sound narrative history of military and naval reforms and the developments of both services' strategic thought prior to World War I. Weigley [226], Millett and Maslowski [149], Timothy K. Nenninger's "The Army Enters the Twentieth Century" [158], and Richard W. Turk's "Defending the New Empire" [213] also provide insight into the importance of prewar planning, education, and thought in the military's approach to the conflict.

Accounts that address the formulation of American strategy during the war include portions of Edward Coffman's *The War to End All Wars* [40] and Russell Weigley's *The American Way of War* [225], as well as an essay by Coffman entitled "American Command and Commanders in World War I" [37]. David Trask's *The United States in the Supreme War Council* [210], Trask is a penetrating assessment of the nation's role in the body's deliberations and decisions. Trask's *The AEF and Coalition Warmaking* [207] is a highly critical account of the fighting abilities of that organization as well of its commander, John Pershing. Ferdinand Foch, not Pershing, is the hero in this chronicle of the last year of the conflict. David R. Woodward's *Trial by Friendship* [233] is more forgiving of Pershing and of Wilson's desire to maintain an independent army in Europe. Still, it provides a detailed picture of the strains that plagued the Allied coalition, particularly those caused by the seemingly (to the British and French) slow American mobilization. Allan R. Millett's "Over Where? The AEF and the American Strategy for Victory" [147] is another account more sympathetic to the problems Pershing faced.

WAR AT SEA

Compared to its British counterpart, the U.S. Navy played a rather limited role in the Great War. That is not to say, however, that the navy's wartime experiences were not important to the service. Though U.S. naval operations necessarily play a small role in Paul G. Halpern's *A Naval History of World War I* [85], the book's comprehensive nature makes it very valuable. A. B. Feuer's *The United States*

Navy in World War I [64] provides a fuller, if idiosyncratic, account of the Navy's activities. The classic works by Harold and Margaret Sprout [199, 200] provide a broad overview of the formulation of American naval policy during this period. Brief but concise chronicles of the conflict's naval operations can be found in Steven Howarth's *To Shining Sea* [98] and in George Baer's *One Hundred Years of Sea Power* [8]. Baer is a highly critical of the Navy, charging that the experience of war did not alter significantly the Navy's Mahanian paradigm despite ample evidence that it should have. Dean C. Allard's "Anglo-American Differences during World War I" [3] and David Trask's *Captains and Cabinets* [209] discuss the critical issues that divided the Royal Navy and the U.S. Navy during the conflict. Prewar naval policy, construction, education, and strategic thought are addressed in B. Franklin Cooling III's *Grey Steel and Blue Water Navy* [48].

Important early works on the development of naval aviation include Archibald D. Turnbull and Clifford L. Lord's *History of United States Naval Aviation* [214] and Adrien O. Van Wyen's *Naval Aviation in World War I* [220]. (Despite its magazine-like appearance, Van Wyen combines a first-class narrative with some wonderful pictures.) The recently published diary and letters of Irving Edward Sheely [188] and of Kenneth MacLeish [132], the brother of Archibald MacLeish, have added great depth to our understanding of the naval aviators' trials and tribulations, while William F. Trimble's biography of Admiral William A. Moffett [211] explains how Moffett, while commander of the battleship *Mississippi* during the war, came to see the importance of aviation to the Navy's future. Biographies of other significant naval figures include Elting E. Morison's of William Sims [152], Paolo Coletta's work on Bradley Fiske [41], and Mary Klachko and David Trask's biography of William Shepard Benson [111]. A brief essay by Dean Allard [2] concerns itself with Admiral Sims's role in the formulation of American naval policy, while Sims's memoir [192], along with Secretary of the Navy Josephus Daniels's account of the conflict [55], provide important insights into the Navy's conduct of the war.

WAR IN THE AIR

The subject of the employment and importance of air power to the conduct of the Great War remains a vibrant areas of scholarship. Lee Kennett's *The First Air War, 1914–1918* [109] and John H. Morrow Jr.'s *The Great War in the Air* [153] provide well-written, broad, yet detailed accounts of the development of air power before and during the war. Morrow's comparative approach (he looks at all of the war's major participants) is particularly valuable. Kennett's *A History of Strategic Bombing* [110] is a broad overview of its subject, with its first three chapters addressing the pre–World War I roots of the concept of strategic bombing, its practice during the war, and the conflict's impact on postwar thought. Stephen McFarland, in *America's Pursuit of Precision Bombing* [142], finds that, despite an inadequate doctrine and lacking appropriate equipment (especially an accurate bombsight), the experience of the Great War convinced air power advocates of the utility of precision bombing. The official history of the U.S. Air Service during the war [138], James J. Cooke's *The U.S. Air Service in the Great War* [47], I. B. Holley Jr.'s *Ideas and Weapons* [97], and James J. Hudson's *Hostile Skies* [99] address in substantial detail the service's organization and operations, as do two volumes published recently by the U.S. Air Force, *Training to Fly* [27] and *The United States Army Air Arm, April 1861 to April 1917* [90]. Also see *The U.S. Air Service in World War I* [235]. Philip Flammer's *The Vivid Air* [67] is an important history of the Lafayette Escadrille. Though mostly narrative in nature, Lee Arbon's *They Also Flew* [5], provides a worthwhile portrait of the many men who served as enlisted pilots during the conflict. Alfred Hurley's biography of Billy Mitchell [100] remains the best work on that important figure, and Mitchell's memoir [151], along with that of Eddie Rickenbacker [180], and *The Great War at Home and Abroad—the World War I Dairies of W. Stull Holt* [236], provide valuable firsthand accounts of the American Air Service. See also the chapters on aviation in [1].

GROUND COMBAT

The conduct of American ground operations during the Great War has produced a voluminous literature. The U.S. Army's official documentary history [217] of the conflict remains an indispensable work (one that now is available on CD-ROM), as does the recently republished *American Armies and Battlefields in Europe* [4]. The subject of command and commanders is addressed in numerous works. Two previously cited volumes by David Trask [207, 210] look at the AEF's role in the coalition. *Pershing and His Generals,* by James J. Cooke [45], provides a more sympathetic view of Pershing than does Trask. Edward Coffman's "The American Military Generation Gap in World War I" [38] highlights the divisions within the AEF between those officers who had and had not attended the School of the Line and the Staff College at Fort Leavenworth. Previously cited biographies of General John J. Pershing by Vandiver [219], Smythe [197], and Smith [195] are important sources of detailed information about the strategy, operations, and decision-making within the AEF headquarters.

The tactical experience of the Great War is best addressed in Paddy Griffith's *Battle Tactics of the Western Front* [77] and by Tony Ashworth's *Trench Warfare, 1914–1918* [6], though the American experience is of little concern to either author. James W. Rainey's "Ambivalent Warfare" [175] takes a critical look at American tactical doctrine and preparation for the war, as does his "The Questionable Training of the AEF in World War I" [176]. Several recent works have looked at the machines that emerged due to the unique demands of the conflict and at the tactics they employed. Dale Wilson's *Treat 'em Rough* [232] is a well-written narrative of the development of American armor doctrine, while Robert M. Citino's *Armored Forces* [32] takes a broader view, both chronologically and nationally. His chapter on World War I provides a solid overview of the subject, and the book also contains an excellent bibliographic essay. Boyd Dastrup's *King of Battle* [56] provides a narrative history of the U.S. Field Artillery in the twentieth century, while articles by Scott R. McMeen [143] and Robert W. Madden [133] relate the development of field artillery doctrine. Charles Heller's *Chemical Warfare in World War I* [89] addresses that controversial weapon and its employment by the United States.

General accounts that place the American combat experience in the broader context of the 1918 campaign can be found in John Toland's *No Man's Land* [206], Rod Paschall's *The Defeat of Imperial Germany* [163], James H. Hallas' *Doughboy War* [82], and Barrie Pitt's *1918* [169]. Previously cited works by Coffman [40], Weigley [225, 226], and Millett and Maslowski [149] also provide sound overviews of the AEF's European combat experience. Accounts of specific battles include Robert B. Asprey's *At Belleau Wood* [7], Donald Smythe's account of St. Mihiel [198], Allan Millett's of the Battle of Cantigny [145], James H. Hallas's *Squandered Victory* [83], which concludes that the American tactical victory at St. Mihiel could have led to the "most-decisive [*sic*] strategic success of the war," and Paul F. Braim's *The Test of Battle* [18], a chronicle of the Meuse-Argonne campaign. Allan Millett's revised edition of *Semper Fidelis* [148] contains an excellent general account of the Marine combat experience on the Western Front. Works that provide more detailed descriptions of Marines in combat include George B. Clark's *Devil Dogs* [33] and Edwin H. Simmons articles on Soissons and the Meuse-Argonne [189–191]. James J. Cooke's works on the 82nd and Rainbow Divisions, *The All-Americans at War* [44] and *The Rainbow Division in the Great War* [46], are well researched and written, and they provide valuable insights into those units' experiences.

Perhaps influenced by recent trends in military history, many authors have attempted to come to grips with the war's impact on the individual soldier. Henry Berry's *Make the Kaiser Dance* [16], Samuel Hynes's *The Soldiers' Tale* [101], and Mark Meigs' *Optimism at Armageddon* [144] deal with the thorny questions of soldiers' motivations, experiences, and memory. Meigs also looks at the Army's treatment of its black soldiers and of those soldiers' reactions. More detailed works on the black experience include Garna L. Christian's *Black Soldiers in Jim Crow Texas* [31], Arthur E. Barbeau and Florette Henri's *The Unknown Soldier* [10], Robert V. Haynes's *A Night of Violence* [88], and Marvin E. Fletcher's *The Black Soldier and Officer in the United States Army* [68], while Bernard Nalty's *Strength for the Fight* [156] provides a fine general account of the African-American experience in the U.S. military. Two pieces that defy easy categorization but deserve mention are Alfred E. Cornebise's *Soldier-Scholars* [51], which details the establishment of the American Expeditionary Forces' University in Beaune, France, and Clayton D. Laurie's "The Chanting of Crusaders" [116], a chronicle of the AEF's propaganda efforts.

Many biographies and memoirs of both important and obscure figures round out the portrait of the U.S. Army and of the American experience in Europe. Important biographies include those of Pershing mentioned above [195, 197, 219], Daniel R. Beaver's of Newton Baker [14], Allan R. Millett's on Robert L. Bullard [146], Edward M. Coffman's on Peyton March [39], Forrest C. Pogue's on George C. Marshall [170], Merrill L. Bartlett's biography of John Lejeune

[11] and I. B. Holley's work on John MacAuley Palmer (which is part memoir, part biography) [96]. As always, Douglas MacArthur remains a controversial figure, and he continues to inspire much scholarship. Recent efforts by Geoffrey Perret [165] and Michael Schaller [185] have their strengths and weaknesses, but D. Clayton James's *The Years of MacArthur* [102] remains the best-researched work on the subject. Valuable memoirs include those of Pershing [166], Bullard [24], Lejeune [117], Marshall [136] and Hunter Liggett [122]. Memoirs of white officers who led black soldiers can be found in Arthur W. Little's *From Harlem to the Rhine* [123] and in Chester D. Heywood's *Negro Combat Troops in the World War* [93]. Elton Mackin's *Suddenly We Didn't Want to Die* [31] recounts a Marine's experiences during the war.

VERSAILLES

The outcome of the Paris Peace Conference and Wilson's role in it have provoked considerable controversy. Arthur Link's *Wilson the Diplomatist* [126] defends Wilson's actions in Paris and blames the Senate for its failure to ratify the treaty. Early critics of Wilsonian diplomacy in Paris include Thomas A. Bailey [9] and Robert Osgood [162]. Bailey's *Woodrow Wilson and the Lost Peace* contends Wilson compromised his principles in Paris while mishandling the Senate when he returned. Osgood's *Ideals and Self-Interest in America's Foreign Relations,* on the other hand, criticizes Wilson for failing to explain adequately to the American public how the treaty served American interests. Arno Mayer's *Politics and Diplomacy of Peacemaking* [140] and N. Gordon Levin's *Woodrow Wilson and World Politics* [119] argue that Wilson's major objective at Versailles was to contain the spread of Bolshevism, and they contend that the League of Nations and a conciliatory peace with Germany would have been the primary means of accomplishing this goal. Numerous authors have taken a closer look at the senators who opposed Wilson on the League and have concluded some had justifiable concerns about that treaty and their opposition was not motivated by purely political considerations. The most important of these studies include Ralph A. Stone's *The Irreconcilables* [202] and William C. Widenor's *Henry Cabot Lodge and the Search for an American Foreign Policy* [227]. Thomas J. Knock's *To End All Wars* [112], published in 1992, is a postrevisionist account of Versailles, arguing that Wilson's actions, rather than a response to the Bolshevik Revolution, are best understood as a pursuit of "progressive internationalism." Knock nevertheless is highly critical of Wilson in numerous ways. Keith Nelson's *Victor's Divided* [157] should be consulted regarding the Allied occupation of the Rhineland.

That the war altered American life in fundamental ways is beyond doubt. Its diplomatic implications can be seen in the retreat from internationalism in the 1920s, in the postwar period's various disarmament conferences, and in the strange circumstances surrounding the drafting and ratification of the Kellogg-Briand Pact. Its impact on culture and thought can be seen in the works of Hemingway, King Vidor, and Lewis Milestone. Warren G. Harding's oft-misquoted

254 RESEARCHING WORLD WAR I

desire for a return to "normalty" (whatever that might be) suggests the conflict's political and social repercussions. It is unfortunate today that the Great War's importance is so poorly comprehended, a fact certainly not due to the efforts of many authors, both those cited here as well as many others, whose works have made significant contributions to our understanding of this vital period.

SUGGESTIONS FOR FURTHER RESEARCH

Little has been written, and none of it is recent, regarding American military participation in the expeditions into the Soviet Union in 1918 and 1919. Also, most of the monographs that address organized labor, labor radicalism, and the Red Scare are dated. There is a real need for a comprehensive volume that addresses the United States during the Great War in all of its aspects—military, diplomatic, economic, political, and social—and that reflects recent scholarship in those fields. Finally, John Keegan's recent effort (106) notwithstanding, there is a great necessity for a broad military history of the war that, too, is reflective of recent work in the field.

BIBLIOGRAPHY

1. *A Guide to the Sources of United States Military History.* 6 vols. Eds. Robin Higham and Donald J. Mrozek. North Haven, CT: Archon Books, 1975–98.

2. Allard, Dean C. "Admiral William S. Sims and United States Naval Policy in World War I." *American Neptune,* 35, April 1975, 97–110.

3. Allard, Dean C. "Anglo-American Differences during World War I." *Military Affairs,* 44, April 1980, 75–81.

4. American Battle Monuments Commission. *American Armies and Battlefields in Europe: A History, Guide, and Reference Book.* Washington, DC: Center for Military History, 1992 (originally published 1938).

5. Arbon, Lee. *They Also Flew: The Enlisted Pilot Legacy, 1912–1942.* Washington, DC: Smithsonian Institution Press, 1992.

6. Ashworth, Tony. *Trench Warfare, 1914–1918: The Live and Let Live System.* New York: Holmes & Meier, 1980.

7. Asprey, Robert B. *At Belleau Wood.* New York: Putnam, 1965.

8. Baer, George. *One Hundred Years of Sea Power: The U.S. Navy, 1890–1990.* Stanford: Stanford University Press, 1994.

9. Bailey, Thomas A. *Woodrow Wilson and the Lost Peace.* New York: Macmillan, 1944

10. Barbeau, Arthur E., and Florette Henri. *The Unknown Soldier: Black American Troops in World War I.* Philadelphia: Temple University Press, 1974.

11. Bartlett, Merrill L. *Lejeune: A Marine's Life, 1867–1942.* Columbia: University of South Carolina Press, 1991.

12. Beard, Charles A. *The Devil Theory of War: An Inquiry into the Nature of History and the Possibility of Keeping out of War.* New York: Vanguard Press, 1936.

13. Beaver, Daniel R. "George W. Goethals and the Problems of American Military Supply." In Daniel R. Beaver, ed., *Some Pathways in Twentieth Century History.* Detroit: Wayne State University Press, 1969, 95–109.

14. Beaver, Daniel R. *Newton D. Baker and the American War Effort, 1917–1919.* Lincoln: University of Nebraska Press, 1966.

15. Beaver, Daniel R. "The Problem of American Military Supply, 1890–1920." In Benjamin Franklin Cooling, ed., *War, Business, and American Society.* Port Washington, NY: Kennikat Press, 1977, 73–92.

16. Berry, Henry. *Make the Kaiser Dance.* New York: Doubleday, 1978.

17. Blakey, George T. *Historians on the Homefront: American Propagandists for the Great War.* Lexington: University Press of Kentucky, 1970.

18. Braim, Paul F. *The Test of Battle: The American Expeditionary Forces in the Meuse-Argonne Campaign.* Newark: University of Delaware Press, 1987.

19. Breen, William J. *Labor Market Politics and the Great War: The Department of Labor, the States, and the First U.S. Employment Service, 1907–1933.* Kent, OH: Kent State University Press, 1997.

20. Breen, William J. *Uncle Sam at Home: Civilian Mobilization, Wartime Federalism, and the Council of National Defense.* Westport, CT: Greenwood Press, 1984.

21. Bristow, Nancy K. *Making Men Moral: Social Engineering During the Great War.* New York: New York University Press, 1996.

22. Brody, David. *Labor in Crisis: The Steel Strike of 1919.* Philadelphia: Lippincott, 1965.

23. Buehrig, Edward H. *Woodrow Wilson and the Balance of Power.* Bloomington: Indiana University Press, 1955.

24. Bullard, Robert L. *Personalities and Reminiscences of the War.* Garden City, NY: Doubleday, 1925.

25. Calhoun, Frederick S. *Power and Principle: Armed Intervention in Wilsonian Foreign Policy.* Kent, OH: Kent State University Press, 1986.

26. Calhoun, Frederick S. *Uses of Force and Wilsonian Foreign Policy.* Kent, OH: Kent State University Press, 1993.

27. Cameron, Rebecca Hancock. *Training to Fly: Military Flight Training, 1907–1945.* Washington, DC: Air Force History and Museums Program, 1999.

28. Carey, Donald E. *Fighting the Bolsheviks: The Russian War Memoirs of Private First Class Donald E. Carey, U.S. Army, 1918–1919.* ed. Neil G. Carey. Novato, CA: Presidio Press, 1997.

29. Chambers, John W., II. "Conscripting for Colossus: The Progressive Era and the Origins of the Modern Military Draft in the United States in World War I." In Peter Karsten, ed., *The Military in Modern America: From the Colonial Era to the Present.* New York: The Free Press, 1980.

30. Chambers, John W., II. *To Raise an Army: The Draft Comes to Modern America.* New York: The Free Press, 1987.

31. Christian, Garna L. *Black Soldiers in Jim Crow Texas, 1899–1917.* College Station: Texas A&M University Press, 1995.

32. Citino, Robert M. *Armored Forces: History and Sourcebook.* Westport, CT: Greenwood Press, 1994.

33. Clark, George B. *Devil Dogs: Fighting Marines of World War I.* Novato, CA: Presidio Press, 1999.

34. Clendenen, Clarence C[lemens]. *Blood on the Border: The United States Army and the Mexican Irregulars.* New York: Macmillan, 1969.

35. Clifford, John Garry. *The Citizen Soldiers: The Plattsburg Training Camp Movement, 1913–1920.* Lexington: University Press of Kentucky, 1972.

36. Coben, Stanley. *A. Mitchell Palmer: Politician.* New York: Columbia University Press, 1963.

37. Coffman, Edward M. "American Command and Commanders in World War I." In Russell F. Weigley, ed., *New Dimensions in Military History.* Novato, CA: Presidio Press, 1976, 17–34.

38. Coffman, Edward M. "The American Military Generation Gap in World War I: The Leavenworth Clique in the AEF." In Lt. Col. William Geffen, USAF, ed., *Command and Commanders in Modern Warfare: Proceedings of the Second Military History Symposium, U.S. Air Force Academy.* Colorado Springs: U.S. Air Force Academy, 1969.

39. Coffman, Edward M. *The Hilt of the Sword: The Career of Peyton C. March.* Lexington: University of Kentucky Press, 1966.

40. Coffman, Edward M. *The War to End All Wars: The American Military Experience in World War I.* New York: Oxford, 1968. [The University Press of Kentucky published a new edition in 1998 to which Dr. Coffman added an updated preface, though the base work remains the same.]

41. Coletta, Paolo E. *Admiral Bradley E. Fiske and the American Navy.* Lawrence: Regents Press of Kansas, 1979.

42. Conner, Valerie J. *The National War Labor Board : Stability, Social Justice, and the Voluntary State in World War I.* Chapel Hill: University of North Carolina Press, 1983.

43. Coogan, John W. *The End of Neutrality: The United States, Britain, and Maritime Rights, 1899–1915.* Ithaca: Cornell University Press, 1981.

44. Cooke, James J. *The All-Americans at War: The 82nd Division in the Great War.* Westport, CT: Praeger, 1999.

45. Cooke, James J. *Pershing and His Generals: Command and Staff in the AEF.* Westport, CT: Praeger, 1997.

46. Cooke, James J. *The Rainbow Division in the Great War, 1917–1919.* Westport, CT: Praeger, 1994.

47. Cooke, James J. *The U.S. Air Service in the Great War, 1917–1919.* Westport, CT: Praeger, 1996.

48. Cooling, B. Franklin, III. *Grey Steel and Blue Water Navy: The Formative Years of America's Military Industrial Complex, 1881–1917.* Hamden, CT: Archon Books, 1979.

49. Cooper, Jerry. *The Rise of the National Guard: The Evolution of the American Militia, 1865–1920.* Lincoln: University of Nebraska Press, 1997.

50. Cooper, Jerry, with Glenn Smith. *Citizens as Soldiers: A History of the North Dakota National Guard.* Fargo: North Dakota Institute for Regional Studies, 1986.

51. Cornebise, Alfred E. *Soldier-Scholars: Higher Education in the AEF, 1917–1919.* Philadelphia: American Philosophical Society, 1997.

52. Creel, George. *How We Advertised America.* New York: Harper and Brothers, 1920.

53. Cuff, Robert D. "United States Mobilization and Railroad Transportation: Lessons in Coordination and Control, 1917–1945." *The Journal of Military History,* 53, January 1989, 33–50.

54. Cuff, Robert D. *The War Industries Board.* Baltimore: Johns Hopkins University Press, 1973.

55. Daniels, Josephus. *Our Navy at War.* New York: G. H. Doran, 1922.

56. Dastrup, Boyd. *King of Battle: A Branch History of the U.S. Army's Field Artillery.* Fort Monroe, VA : Office of the Command Historian, U.S. Army Training and Doctrine Command, 1992

57. Devlin, Patrick. *Too Proud to Fight: Woodrow Wilson's Neutrality.* New York: Oxford University Press, 1974.

58. Early, Francis H. *A World Without War: How U.S. Feminists and Pacifists Resisted World War I.* Syracuse: Syracuse University Press, 1997.

59. Edmonds, J. E. *A Short History of World War I.* New York: Oxford, 1951.

60. Eisenhower, John S. D. *Intervention! The United States and the Mexican Revolution, 1913–1917.* New York: Norton, 1993.

61. Falls, Cyril. *The First World War.* London: Longmans, 1960.

62. Farwell, Byron. *Over There: The United States in the Great War, 1917–1918.* New York: Norton, 1999.

63. Ferrell, Robert H. *Woodrow Wilson and World War I, 1917–1921.* New York: Harper & Row, 1985.

64. Feuer, A. B. *The United States Navy in World War I: Combat at Sea and in the Air.* Westport, CT: Praeger, 1999.

65. Fic, Victor M. *The Collapse of American Policy in Russia and Siberia, 1918: Wilson's Decision not to Intervene.* Boulder, CO: East European Monographs, 1995.

66. Finnegan, John P. *Against the Specter of a Dragon: The Campaign for American Military Preparedness, 1914–1917.* Westport, CT: Greenwood Press, 1974.

67. Flammer, Philip M. *The Vivid Air: The Lafayette Escadrille.* Athens: University of Georgia Press, 1981.

68. Fletcher, Marvin. *The Black Soldier and Officer in the United States Army, 1891–1917.* Columbia: University of Missouri Press, 1974.

69. Foglesong, David S. *America's Secret War Against Bolshevism: U.S. Intervention in the Russian Civil War, 1917–1920.* Chapel Hill: University of North Carolina Press, 1995.

70. Foster, Carrie A. *The Women and the Warriors: The U.S. Section of the Women's International League for Peace and Freedom, 1915–1946.* Syracuse: Syracuse University Press, 1995.

71. Frank, Dana. *Purchasing Power: Consumer Organizing, Gender, and the Seattle Labor Movement, 1919–1929.* New York: Cambridge University Press, 1994.

72. Fussell, Paul. *The Great War in Modern Memory.* New York: Oxford University Press, 1975.

73. Gardner, Lloyd C. *Safe for Democracy: Anglo-American Response to Revolution, 1913–1923.* New York: Oxford University Press, 1984.

74. Gavin, Lettie. *American Women in World War I: They Also Served.* Niwot: University Press of Colorado, 1997.

75. Greenwald, Maurine. *Women, War, and Work: The Impact of World War I on Women Workers in the United States.* Westport, CT: Greenwood Press, 1980.

76. Grieb, Kenneth J. *The United States and Huerta.* Lincoln: University of Nebraska Press, 1969.

77. Griffith, Paddy. *Battle Tactics of the Western Front: The British Army's Art of Attack, 1916–18.* New Haven: Yale University Press, 1994.

78. Grossman, James R. *Land of Hope: Chicago, Black Southerners, and the Great Migration.* Chicago: University of Chicago Press, 1989.

79. Grubbs, Frank L. *Samuel Gompers and the Great War: Protecting Labor's Standards.* Wake Forest, NC: Meridional Publications, 1982.

80. Haley, P. Edward. *Revolution and Intervention: The Diplomacy of Taft and Wilson with Mexico, 1910–1917.* Cambridge: MIT Press, 1970.

81. Hall, Linda, and Dan M. Coerver. *Revolution on the Border: The United States and Mexico, 1910–1920.* Albuquerque: University of New Mexico Press, 1988.

82. Hallas, James H. *Doughboy War: The American Expeditionary Force [sic] in World War I.* Boulder, CO: Lynne Rienner Publishers, 2000.

83. Hallas, James H. *Squandered Victory: The American First Army at St. Mihiel.* Westport, CT: Praeger, 1995.

84. Halliday, E. M. *The Ignorant Armies.* New York: Harper and Brothers, 1958.

85. Halpern, Paul G. *A Naval History of World War I.* Annapolis: Naval Institute Press, 1994.

86. Hammond, Paul Y. *Organizing for Defense: The American Military Establishment in the Twentieth Century.* Princeton: Princeton University Press, 1961.

87. Harries, Meirion, and Susie Harries. *The Last Days of Innocence: America at War, 1917–1918.* New York: Random House, 1997.

88. Haynes, Robert V. *A Night of Violence: The Houston Riot of 1917.* Baton Rouge: Louisiana State University Press, 1976.

89. Heller, Charles E. *Chemical Warfare in World War I: The American Experience, 1917–1918.* Fort Leavenworth: Combat Studies Institute, 1985.

90. Hennessy, Juliette A. *United States Army Air Arm, April 1861 to April 1917.* Washington, DC: Office of Air Force History, U.S. Air Force, 1985.

91. Henri, Florette. *Black Migration: Movement North, 1900–1920.* Garden City, NY: Anchor Press, 1975.

92. Herwig, Holger H., and Neil Heyman, comps. *Biographical Dictionary of World War I.* Westport, CT: Greenwood Press, 1982.

93. Heywood, Chester. *Negro Combat Troops in the World War: The Story of the 371st Infantry.* New York: Negro Universities Press, 1969.

94. Higham John. *Strangers in the Land: Patterns of American Nativism, 1860–1925.* New Brunswick: Rutgers University Press, 1955.

95. Hill, Jim Dan. *The Minute Man in Peace and War: A History of the National Guard.* Harrisburg, PA: Stackpole, 1964.

96. Holley, I. B. *General John M. Palmer, Citizen Soldiers, and the Army of a Democracy.* Westport, CT: Greenwood Press, 1982.

97. Holley, I. B. *Ideas and Weapons: Exploitation of the Aerial Weapon by the United States During World War I.* Washington, DC: Office of Air Force History, 1983.

98. Howarth, Stephen. *To Shining Sea: A History of the United States Navy, 1775–1991.* New York: Random House, 1991.

99. Hudson, James J. *The Hostile Skies: A Combat History of the American Air Service in World War I.* Syracuse: Syracuse University Press, 1968.

100. Hurley, Alfred F. *Billy Mitchell, Crusader for Air Power.* Bloomington: Indiana University Press, 1975.

101. Hynes, Samuel. *The Soldiers' Tale: Bearing Witness to Modern War.* New York: Allen Lane, 1997.

102. James, D. Clayton. *The Years of MacArthur.* 3 vols. Boston: Houghton-Mifflin, 1970–1985.

103. Jessup, John E. and Louise B. Ketz, eds. *Encyclopedia of the American Military: Studies of the History, Traditions, Policies, Institutions, and Roles of the Armed Forces in War and Peace.* 3 vols. New York: Scribner's, 1994.

104. Johnson, Donald. *The Challenge to American Freedoms: World War I and the Rise of the American Civil Liberties Union.* Lexington: University of Kentucky Press, 1963.

105. Katz, Friedrich. *The Secret War in Mexico: Europe, the United States, and the Mexican Revolution.* Chicago: University of Chicago Press, 1981.

106. Keegan, John. *The First World War.* New York: Alfred A. Knopf, 1999.

107. Kennan, George. *Soviet-American Relations, 1917–1920.* 2 vols. Princeton: Princeton University Press, 1956.

108. Kennedy, David M. *Over Here: The First World War and American Society.* New York: Oxford University Press, 1980.

109. Kennett, Lee B. *The First Air War, 1914–1918.* New York: Free Press, 1991.

110. Kennett, Lee B. *A History of Strategic Bombing.* New York: Charles Scribner's Sons, 1982.

111. Klachko, Mary, and David F. Trask. *Admiral William Shepherd Benson: First Chief of Naval Operations.* Annapolis: U.S. Naval Institute Press, 1987.

112. Knock, Thomas J. *To End All Wars: Woodrow Wilson and the Quest for a New World Order.* New York: Oxford University Press, 1992.

113. Koistinen, Paul A. C. "The Industrial-Military Complex" in Historical Perspective." *Business History Review,* 41, Winter 1967, 378–403.

114. Koistinen, Paul A. C. *Mobilizing for Modern War: The Political Economy of American Warfare, 1865–1919.* Lawrence: University Press of Kansas, 1997.

115. Kreidberg, Marvin A., and Merton G. Henry. *History of Military Mobilization in the United States Army, 1775–1945.* Washington, DC: Department of the Army, 1955.

116. Laurie, Clayton D. " 'The Chanting of Crusaders': Captain Heber Blankenhorn and AEF Combat Propaganda in World War I." *The Journal of Military History,* 59, July 1995, 457–82.

117. Lejeune, John. *The Reminiscences of a Marine.* Philadelphia: Dorrance, 1930.

118. Leubke, Frederick. *Bonds of Loyalty: German-Americans and World War I.* DeKalb: Northern Illinois University Press, 1974.

119. Levin, N. Gordon, Jr. *Woodrow Wilson and World Politics: America's Response to War and Revolution.* New York: Oxford University Press, 1968.

120. Lewis, David. *W. E. B. Du Bois: Biography of a Race, 1868–1919.* New York: Henry Holt, 1993.

121. Liddell Hart, B. H. *The Real War, 1914–1918.* Boston: Little, Brown, 1963.

122. Liggett, Hunter. *Commanding an American Army: Recollections of the World War.* Boston: Houghton Mifflin, 1925.

123. Little, Arthur W. *From Harlem to the Rhine: The Story of New York's Colored Volunteers.* New York: Covici, Friede, 1936.

124. Link, Arthur S. *Wilson: Campaigns for Progressivism and Peace, 1916–1917.* Princeton: Princeton University Press, 1965.

125. Link, Arthur S. *Wilson: Confusions and Crises, 1915–1916.* Princeton: Princeton University Press, 1964.

126. Link, Arthur S. *Wilson the Diplomatist: A Look at His Major Foreign Policies.* Baltimore: Johns Hopkins University Press, 1957.

127. Link, Arthur S. *Wilson: The Struggle for Neutrality, 1914–1915.* Princeton: Princeton University Press, 1960.

128. Link, Arthur S. *Woodrow Wilson and the Progressive Era, 1910–1917.* New York: Harper, 1954.

129. Link, Arthur S. *Woodrow Wilson: Revolution, War and Peace.* Arlington Heights, IL: Harlan Davidson, 1979.

130. Little, Arthur W. *From Harlem to the Rhine: The Story of New York's Colored Volunteers.* New York: Covici, Friede, 1936.

131. Mackin, Elton. *Suddenly We Didn't Want to Die: Memoirs of a World War I Marine.* Ed. George B. Clark. Novato, CA: Presidio Press, 1993.

132. MacLeish, Kenneth. *The Price of Honor: The World War One Letters of Naval Aviator Kenneth MacLeish.* Annapolis: Naval Institute Press, 1992.

133. Madden, Robert W. "The Myth of Destruction: Artillery in the Great War." *Field Artillery,* August 1994, 44–47.

134. Mahon, John K. *History of the Militia and the National Guard.* New York: Macmillan, 1983.

135. Marks, Carole. *Farewell—We're Good and Gone: The Great Black Migration.* Bloomington: Indiana University Press, 1989.

136. Marshall, George C. *Memoirs of My Services in the World War, 1917–1918.* Ed. James L. Collins. Boston: Houghton Mifflin, 1976.

137. Mason, Herbert Molloy. *The Great Pursuit.* New York, Random House, 1970.

138. Maurer, Maurer. *The U.S. Air Service in World War I.* 4 vols. Washington, DC: The Office of Air Force History, Headquarters USAF, 1978.

139. May, Ernest R. *The World War and American Isolation, 1914–1917.* Cambridge: Harvard University Press, 1959.

140. Mayer, Arno. *Politics and Diplomacy of Peacemaking: Containment and Counterrevolution at Versailles, 1918–1919.* New York: Knopf, 1967.

141. McFadden, David W. *Alternative Paths: Soviets and Americans, 1917–1920.* New York: Oxford University Press, 1993.

142. McFarland, Stephen L. *America's Pursuit of Precision Bombing, 1910–1945.* Washington, DC: Smithsonian Institution Press, 1995.

143. McMeen, Scott R. "Testing the Principles of Fire Support: The Meuse-Argonne Offensive of 1918." *Field Artillery,* August 1994, 18–21.

144. Meigs, Mark. *Optimism at Armageddon: Voices of American Participants in the First World War.* New York: New York University Press, 1997.

145. Millett, Allan R. "Cantigny, 28–31 May 1918." In Charles E. Heller and William A. Stofft, eds., *America's First Battles, 1776–1965.* Lawrence: University Press of Kansas, 1986, 149–85.

146. Millett, Allan R. *The General: Robert L. Bullard and Officership in the United States Army, 1881–1925.* Westport, CT: Greenwood Press, 1975.

147. Millett, Allan R. "Over Where? The AEF and the American Strategy for Victory, 1917–1918." In Kenneth J. Hagan and William R. Roberts, ed., *Against All Enemies: Interpretations of American Military History from Colonial Times to the Present.* Westport, CT: Greenwood Press, 1986, 235–56.

148. Millett, Allan R. *Semper Fidelis: The History of the United States Marine Corps.* Rev. and expanded ed. New York: Free Press, 1991.

149. Millett, Allan R., and Peter Maslowski. *For the Common Defense: A Military History of the United States.* 2nd ed. New York: The Free Press, 1994.

150. Millis, Walter. *The Road to War: America, 1914–1917.* Boston: Houghton Mifflin, 1935.

151. Mitchell, William. *Memories of World War I: "From Start to Finish Our Greatest War."* New York: Random House, 1960.

152. Morison, Elting. *Admiral Sims and the Modern American Navy.* Boston: Houghton Mifflin, 1942.

153. Morrow, John H., Jr. *The Great War in the Air: Military Aviation from 1909–1921.* Washington, DC: Smithsonian Institution Press, 1993.

154. Murphy, Paul L. *World War I and the Origin of Civil Liberties in the United States.* New York: Norton, 1979.

155. Murray, Robert K. *Red Scare: A Study in National Hysteria, 1919–1920.* New York: McGraw-Hill, 1964.

156. Nalty, Bernard. *Strength for the Fight: A History of Black Americans in the Military.* New York: The Free Press, 1986.

157. Nelson, Keith L. *Victors Divided: America and the Allies in Germany, 1918–1923.* Berkeley: University of California Press, 1975.

158. Nenninger, Timothy K. "The Army Enters the Twentieth Century, 1904–1917." In Kenneth J. Hagan and William R. Roberts, ed., *Against All Enemies: Interpretations of American Military History from Colonial Times to the Present.* Westport, CT: Greenwood Press, 1986, 219–34.

159. Nenninger, Timothy K. *The Leavenworth Schools and the Old Army: Education, Professionalism, and the Officer Corps of the United States Army, 1881–1918.* Westport, CT: Greenwood Press, 1978.

160. Ohl, John K. "Hugh S. Johnson and the Draft, 1917–18." *Prologue,* 8, Summer 1976, 85–96.

161. Ohl, John K. "The Navy, the War Industries Board, and the Industrial Mobilization for War." *Military Affairs,* 40, February 1976, 17–22.

162. Osgood, Robert. *Ideals and Self-Interest in America's Foreign Relations: The Great Transformation of the Twentieth Century.* Chicago: University of Chicago Press, 1953

163. Paschall, Rod. *The Defeat of Imperial Germany, 1917–1918.* Chapel Hill, NC: Algonquin Books of Chapel Hill, 1989.

164. Perret, Geoffrey. *A Country Made by War: From Revolution to Vietnam—The Story of America's Rise to Power.* New York: Random House, 1989.

165. Perret, Geoffrey. *Old Soldiers Never Die: The Life of Douglas MacArthur.* New York: Random House, 1996.

166. Pershing, John J. *My Experiences in the World War.* 2 vols. New York: Frederick A. Stokes Company, 1931.

167. Peterson, Horace C., and Gilbert C. Fite. *Opponents of the War, 1917–1918.* Madison: University of Wisconsin Press, 1957.

168. Philpott, Thomas Lee. *The Slum and the Ghetto: Immigrants, Blacks, and Reformers in Chicago, 1880–1930.* New York: Oxford University Press, 1978.

169. Pitt, Barrie. *1918: The Last Act.* New York: W. W. Norton, 1962.

170. Pogue, Forrest C. *George C. Marshall: Education of a General, 1880–1939.* New York: Viking Press, 1963.

171. Polenberg, Richard. *Fighting Faiths: The Abrams Case, the Supreme Court, and Free Speech.* New York: Viking, 1987.

172. Pope, Stephen W. "An Army of Athletes: Playing Fields, Battlefields, and the American Military Sporting Experience, 1890–1920." *The Journal of Military History,* 59, July 1995, 435–56.

173. Pratt, Julius. *Challenge and Rejection: The United States and World Leadership, 1900–1921.* New York: Macmillan, 1967.

174. Preston, William, Jr. *Aliens and Dissenters: Federal Suppression of Radicals, 1903–1933.* Cambridge: Harvard University Press, 1963

175. Rainey, James W. "Ambivalent Warfare: The Tactical Doctrine of the AEF in World War I." *Parameters,* 13, September 1983, 34–46.

176. Rainey, James W. "The Questionable Training of the AEF in World War I." *Parameters,* 22, Winter 1992–93, 89–103.

177. Rawls, Walton. *Wake Up, America! World War I and the American Poster.* New York: Abbeville Press, 1988.

178. Reardon, Carol. *Soldiers and Scholars: The U.S. Army and the Uses of Military History, 1865–1920.* Lawrence: University Press of Kansas, 1990.

179. Rhodes, Benjamin D. *The Anglo-American Winter War with Russia, 1918–1919: A Diplomatic and Military Tragicomedy.* Westport, CT: Greenwood Press, 1988.

180. Rickenbacker, Edward V. *Fighting the Flying Circus.* Folkestone: Bailey and Swinfen, 1973 (reprint).

181. Rudwick, Elliott M. *Race Riot at East St. Louis, July 2, 1917.* Carbondale: Southern Illinois University Press, 1964.

182. Rudwick, Elliott M. *W. E. B. Du Bois: Propagandist of the Negro Protest.* 2nd ed. Philadelphia: University of Pennsylvania Press, 1968.

183. Russell, Francis. *A City in Terror: 1919, The Boston Police Strike.* New York: Viking Press, 1975.

184. Schaffer, Ronald. *The United States in World War I.* Santa Barbara, CA: Clio Books, 1978.

185. Schaller, Michael. *Douglas MacArthur: The Far Eastern General.* New York: Oxford University Press, 1989.

186. Scheiber, Harry N. *The Wilson Administration and Civil Liberties, 1917–1921.* Ithaca: Cornell University Press, 1960.

187. Schild, Georg. *Between Ideology and Realpolitik: Woodrow Wilson and the Russian Revolution, 1917–1921.* Westport, CT: Greenwood, 1995.

188. Sheely, Irving Edward. *Sailor of the Air: The 1917–1919 Letters and Diary of CMM/A Irving Edward Sheely,* ed. Lawrence D. Sheely. Tuscaloosa: University of Alabama Press, 1993.

189. Simmons, Edwin H. "Marines in the Meuse-Argonne, Part I: Reaching the Meuse." *Fortitudine,* 23, Winter 1993–94, 3–10.

190. Simmons, Edwin H. "Marines in the Meuse-Argonne, Part II: The Meuse." *Fortitudine,* 23, Spring 1994, 3–8.

191. Simmons, Edwin H. "The Second Day at Soissons." *Fortitudine,* 23, Fall 1993, 3–10.

192. Sims, William S. *The Victory at Sea.* London: J. Murray, 1920.

193. Smith, Daniel. *The Great Departure.* New York: J. Wiley, 1965.

194. Smith, Daniel. *Robert Lansing and American Neutrality, 1914–1917.* Berkeley: University of California Press, 1958.

195. Smith, Gene. *Until the Last Trumpet Sounds: The Life of General of the Armies John J. Pershing.* New York: Wiley, 1998.

196. Smith, Robert Freeman. *The United States and Revolutionary Nationalism in Mexico, 1916–1932.* Chicago: University of Chicago Press, 1972.

197. Smythe, Donald. *Pershing: General of the Armies.* Bloomington: Indiana University Press, 1986.

198. Smythe, Donald. "St. Mihiel: The Birth of an American Army." *Parameters,* 12, March 1983, 47–57.

199. Sprout, Harold, and Margaret Sprout. *The Rise of American Naval Power, 1776–1918.* Princeton: Princeton University Press, 1942.

200. Sprout, Harold and Margaret Sprout. *Toward a New Order of Sea Power: American Naval Policy and the World Scene, 1918–1922.* Princeton: Princeton University Press, 1942.

201. Stokesbury, James. *A Short History of World War I.* New York: Morrow, 1981.

202. Stone, Ralph A. *The Irreconcilables: The Fight Against the League of Nations.* Lexington: University Press of Kentucky, 1970.

203. Stout, Joseph A. *Border Conflict: Villistas, Carrancistas, and the Punitive Expedition, 1915–1920.* Fort Worth: Texas Christian University Press, 1999.

204. Tansill, Charles. *America Goes to War*. Boston: Little, Brown, 1938.

205. Thompson, John A. *Reformers and War: Progressive Publicists and the First World War*. New York: Cambridge University Press, 1987.

206. Toland, John. *No Man's Land: 1918, the Last Year of the Great War*. New York: Doubleday, 1980.

207. Trask, David F. *The AEF and Coalition Warmaking, 1917–1918*. Lawrence: University Press of Kansas, 1993.

208. Trask, David F. "The American Navy in a World at War, 1914–1919." In Kenneth J. Hagan, ed., *In Peace and War: Interpretations of American Naval History, 1775–1984*. Westport, CT: Greenwood Press, 1984, 205–20.

209. Trask, David F. *Captains and Cabinets: Anglo-American Naval Relations, 1917–1921*. Columbia: University of Missouri Press, 1972.

210. Trask, David F. *The United States in the Supreme War Council: American War Aims and Inter-Allied Strategy, 1917–1918*. Middletown, CT: Wesleyan University Press, 1961.

211. Trimble, William F. *Admiral William A. Moffett: Architect of Naval Aviation*. Washington, DC: Smithsonian Institution Press, 1994.

212. Tuchman, Barbara. *The Zimmerman Telegram*. New York: Viking, 1958.

213. Turk, Richard W. "Defending the New Empire, 1900–1914." In Kenneth J. Hagan, ed., *In Peace and War: Interpretations of American Naval History, 1775–1984*. Westport, CT: Greenwood Press, 1984, 186–204.

214. Turnbull, Archibald D., and Clifford L. Lord. *History of United States Naval Aviation*. New Haven: Yale University Press, 1949

215. Tuttle, William M. *Race Riot: Chicago in the Red Summer of 1919*. New York: Atheneum, 1974.

216. Tuttle, William M. *W. E. B. DuBois*. Englewood Cliffs, NJ: Prentice Hall, 1973.

217. U.S. Department of the Army. *United States Army in the World War, 1917–1919*. 17 vols. Washington, DC: U.S. Government Printing Office, 1948.

218. U.S. War Industries Board [Bernard Baruch]. *American Industry in the War*. New York: Prentice-Hall, 1941.

219. Vandiver, Frank E. *Black Jack: The Life and Times of John J. Pershing*. 2 vols. College Station: Texas A&M University Press, 1977.

220. Van Wyen, Adrien O. *Naval Aviation in World War I*. Washington, DC: Chief of Naval Operations, 1969.

221. Vaughn, Stephen. *Holding Fast the Inner Lines: Democracy, Nationalism, and the Committee on Public Information*. Chapel Hill: University of North Carolina Press, 1980.

222. Venzon, Anne Cipriano. *The United States in the First World War: An Encyclopedia*. New York: Garland, 1995.

223. Vrooman, Daniel M. *Daniel Willard and Progressive Management on the B&O Railroad*. Columbus: The Ohio State University Press, 1991.

224. Walker, Samuel. *In Defense of American Liberties: A History of the ACLU*. New York: Oxford University Press, 1990.

225. Weigley, Russell F. *The American Way of War: A History of United States Military Strategy and Policy*. New York: Macmillan, 1973.

226. Weigley, Russell F. *History of the United States Army*. New York: Macmillan, 1967.

227. Widenor, William C. *Henry Cabot Lodge and the Search for an American Foreign Policy*. Berkeley: University of California Press, 1980.

228. Williams, William J. "Accommodating American Shipyard Workers, 1917–1918: The Pacific Coast and the Federal Government's First Public Housing and Transit Programs." *Pacific Northwest Quarterly*, 84, April 1993, 51–59.

229. Williams, William J. "The American Concrete Shipbuilding Program of World War I." *American Neptune*, 52, Winter 1992, 5–15.

230. Williams, William J. "Josephus Daniels and the U.S. Navy's Shipbuilding Program During World War I." *Journal of Military History*, 60, January 1996, 7–38.

231. Williams, William J. *The Wilson Administration and the Shipbuilding Crisis of 1917.* Lewiston, N.Y.: Edwin Mellen Press, 1992.

232. Wilson, Dale E. *Treat 'em Rough: The Birth of American Armor, 1917–1920.* Novato, CA: Presidio Press, 1989.

233. Woodward, David R. *Trial by Friendship: Anglo-American Relations, 1917–1918.* Lexington: University Press of Kentucky, 1993.

234. Zimmerman, Phyllis A. *The Neck of the Bottle: George W. Goethals and the Reorganization of the U.S. Army Supply System, 1917–1918.* College Station: Texas A&M University Press, 1992.

235. *The U.S. Air Service in World War I,* 5 vols. Washington: USAF Office of Air Force History, 1978.

236. *The Great War at Home and Abroad—The World War I Dairies of W. Stull Holt,* edited by Maclyn P. Berg and Thomas J. Pressly. Manhattan, KS: Sunflower University Press, 2000.

12

Australia and New Zealand

Jeffrey Grey, Peter Dennis,
and Ian McGibbon

The Great War is one of the defining events in modern Australian and New Zealand history, perhaps second only to the acts of settlement and dispossession of the indigenous populations as a formative influence on the kinds of societies that have grown up there. Whilst there are certain superficial similarities between the two nations' experience of that conflict, and while in the popular mind they are linked inextricably through the network of ANZAC, there are in fact fundamental differences between them, and this is reflected equally in the manner in which historians in each country have dealt with the First World War.

The study of Australian and New Zealand military history has only recently come to enjoy anything like academic respectability, and this is reflected in the nature of what has been produced since 1919. It is only relatively recently (in practical terms, only since the Second World War) that each country's history has been seen as a thing apart, deserving in itself rather than as an appendage of British or Empire and Commonwealth history. Involvement in the Vietnam War and the considerable level of dissent from that commitment, especially in the universities, helped to ensure that until the 1970s the treatment of the First World War, and indeed of military history generally, would remain the province essentially of the participant and the amateur enthusiast, only occasionally of the university-trained scholar (and almost never of the ambitious graduate student). In the twenty years since the end of the Vietnam War, this has changed markedly, but the pattern of published work strongly reflects the earlier circumstance.

In Australia the study of the First World War is dominated, and indeed for many years was largely represented, by the massive official history of C. E. W.

Bean [8]. Published in fifteen volumes across a space of more than twenty years, in style and approach it marked a decided departure from the tradition of "general staff" histories published by belligerents and observers after the Franco-Prussian or Russo-Japanese Wars, for example, and which characterized most of the other major official histories of the Great War, especially the British. Bean was a journalist by trade and a lawyer by training; he had no military experience before the war and no obvious connections with the tiny Australian military establishment of 1914. His history largely eschewed grand strategy, in which Australia played no part in any case, and while he did not neglect the higher command questions (being highly critical of aspects of British command and policy at the Dardanelles or in France in 1917), he took as his focus the extraordinary experiences of ordinary men: the frontline soldiers, of whom 6,550 are mentioned by name with biographical footnotes attached. The principal theme of the history was the war's impact on the national character and the sense of national identity which derived from this experience, a subject that had begun to interest Bean well before the war when he wrote a series of articles (and subsequently two books) on life and work in rural Australia. The method of focusing on individual soldiers (and the plethora of small-scale sketch maps in the margins of the text used to illustrate individual experience and small unit actions) he probably derived from H. T. Siborne's *Waterloo Letters* (London, 1891), with which he was certainly familiar.

Bean went to the war with the first contingent in November 1914 as the official correspondent, selected by ballot among his peers and narrowly beating Keith Murdoch (father of Rupert) for the post. The commission to write the history, and the appointment as official historian that went with it, came much later in the war, and indeed was not formalized until 1 July 1919. Little attempt was made to collect historical and documentary material systematically until after the Australian Imperial Force went to France, and the Australian War Records Section, copied from its Canadian equivalent and charged with this responsibility, was not set up until 16 May 1917. While unit and formation records certainly exist from the Gallipoli campaign and 1916, the Australians' first year in France, Bean was thus more reliant than usual upon his own copious notebooks and diaries when writing the early volumes of the history. The diaries for Gallipoli at least have been published in annotated form, revealing both that Bean was a keen observer of his surroundings, roving about the rear areas and up in the front line virtually every day, and that his contemporary observations and reflections differed at times from the gloss he later chose to place on events when writing in the 1920s and 1930s [25]. By contrast, the New Zealand official war correspondent, Malcolm Ross, who accompanied Bean to many battlefields, was excluded from the subsequent writing of the New Zealand official history and wrote only one book about 1914–1918, *Light and Shade in War* [66].

The official history was dogged initially by publication difficulties (a problem experienced by Edmonds in Britain as well), and Bean was also greatly preoccupied with the establishment of the Australian War Memorial in the interwar years (conceived as a shrine to the "great hearted men" of the AIF) [49]. The problem of sales was solved by an innovative subscription scheme that enabled the books to be purchased by installment, while Bean's phenomenal industry ensured that the volumes appeared regularly throughout the 1920s and 1930s, eight volumes alone by 1931. Their influence with the war generation is difficult to judge, however; while sales figures were very healthy after the early 1930s, with the starting volumes going into ten or twelve reprints by 1941, the suspicion is that many sat on the shelf, referred to perhaps but rarely read. One wag even suggested that Bean included the large number of personal references in his history to stimulate sales!

What cannot be doubted is the influence of the history on subsequent generations, although again it remains the case that Bean's great work is more frequently cited than actually read in any depth. There can be no doubt that its monumental size is off-putting, while the exhaustive nature of the treatment for long probably precluded emulation, much less emendation. Of greater importance here, however, was the highly restrictive nature of federal archival legislation, which until 1974 operated on the basis of a "fifty year rule" that denied public access to government records for that length of time, coupled with a proprietarial attitude (and a gross lack of resources) at the Australian War Memorial that discouraged researchers from exploring the riches of the collections held there. When to this is added the lack of interest in military history displayed in the small pre-1960s university sector, the general absence of significant work on the Great War in Australia is not difficult to understand [22].

Such other work as did appear between the world wars was generally parochial in nature. This is not to underrate its usefulness to historians now. A large number of unit associations, especially among the infantry and light horse, produced battalion and regimental histories; these range from the amateurish to the exceedingly useful, but all contain material not available from other sources at this remove in time [26]. Of equal value were the publications of the Returned Soldiers, Sailors [and later Airmens] Imperial League of Australia (the RSSAILA, later shortened to RSL), especially the NSW branch journal, *Reveille,* replete in the interwar years with numerous articles on important actions and leading personalities, and once again written from a base of personal knowledge of the subject since lost. The journal of the Australian Capital Territory RSL branch, *Stand-To,* is also a useful source. A number of key, or merely prominent, individuals likewise burst in to print with their versions of events and lived experience: Monash gave the public a largely accurate but self-regarding account of the final six months of the Australians' war in France [51], while one of Bean's collaborators on the official history, F. M. Cutlack, author of the volume on the Australian Flying Corps, edited a collection of Monash's letters home [20]. His prodigious labors on the official history completed, Bean published a valuable and revealing account of Gallipoli more or less from the Turkish vantage point [9], and a dual biography of the first commanding general of the AIF, William Throsby Bridges, and its long-serving chief of staff and Bean's idol, C. B. B. White [10]. (Although published well after 1945, they are both very much interwar books in their style and perspective, and *Gallipoli Mission* was based closely on Bean's notes taken during his revisit to the peninsula in 1919 on his way home to Australia.) There were occasional reminiscences of other, lesser figures, of which that by Lieutenant Joe Maxwell, VC, MC, DCM, irreverent and mildly scatological in tracing the passage of innocent Australian youth through the trials of war and the peculiarities of foreigners, is representative [44].

The New Zealand government chose not to commission an official history series, largely one suspects for financial reasons. Instead, five volumes of popular campaign history were written by a number of relatively senior New Zealand army officers, given access to official documentation but working in their own time [76]. The results rarely strayed from objective battlefield narrative. There was the usual flow of unit histories, mostly published in the 1920s before economic downturn made it financially ruinous to do so, the memoirs of the Imperial officer who commanded the NZEF throughout the war, General Sir Alexander Godley, and which, revealingly titled, said at least as much about its author's passion for field sports as about the war and New Zealand's efforts in it [31], and a disturbing personal account of conscientious objection to conscription (adopted in New Zealand in 1916 but never in Australia despite two referendums), which is regarded deservedly as a classic in the literature [15].

While Anzac Day exercised a powerful cultural and mythic hold on the two societies (although more so in Australia), and the sons of the Great War generation who went to fight in 1939 consciously measured themselves against their fathers' achievements (again, probably more so in the Australians' case), analysis of the First World War or even reflection upon it was lacking in large part until the 1960s and 1970s. The reasons behind the resurgence in interest are worth noting, since it has given rise to a sizeable body of good quality historical literature in the field. One was the growth in Australian (and to a lesser extent, New Zealand) history in the universities following on in part from the rapid growth in the university sector in the 1960s and early 1970s. In keeping with resurgent national feeling, especially in the early 1970s and manifest in the renaissance of a local film industry and the assertiveness of a newly elected Labor government, a concern with Australian history for its own sake had a follow-on effect even in unfashionable fields such as military history. Finally, and perhaps paradoxically, opposition to Australian involvement in the Vietnam War spurred some academics to examine the links between their own antiwar activism and the earlier anticonscription movements of 1916 and 1917. From there it was a relatively short leap to a concern with involvement in the Great War more generally, although among university historians at least an interest in social history issues tended to predominate.

Modern work on the Great War can be broken down into three broad areas: biography, the home front (principally conscription), and the Anzac legend. There has been virtually no operational history and little examination of higher diplomatic/strategic/governmental policy. An exception is John Coates, *An Atlas of Australia's Wars,* which combines lavish maps with a thoughtful commentary, placing Australian operations in the First World War in a broader Allied context

[15]. The workings of the fledgling Department of Defence during the war, a hitherto almost totally neglected subject, is covered in Eric Andrews, *The Department of Defence* [1]. The neglect of broader strategic questions reflects the small part that the Pacific Dominions played in these matters; unlike the Canadians, neither Australia nor New Zealand based a Cabinet-level representative in London during the war to look out for their interests, and the role played by Dominion representatives in the Imperial War Cabinet of 1917–1918 was orchestrated carefully by Lloyd George. The exceptions relate entirely to the Pacific and the twin, and sometimes related, issues of the disposal of former German colonial territories [43], and the maintenance of the Anglo-Japanese alliance [27]. The lack of operational analyses is a consequence both of the dead hand of Bean and the general lack of interest and expertise in such matters among academic historians. In New Zealand, where writing in the field is much less advanced, there has been some interest in traditional operational questions, not least because of the inadequacy of the semi-official volumes published in the 1920s, but again home front issues tend to dominate.

The first of the modern wave of military biography was a study by A. J. Hill of Australia's other highly successful corps commander, General Sir Harry Chauvel [36]. Chauvel saw service in the Boer War and as a pre-1914 regular before commanding a light horse brigade on Gallipoli, a division in Sinai, and the Desert Mounted Corps from 1917 until the end of the war in Palestine. Hill's meticulous, scholarly and deeply informed biography nonetheless attracted a certain amount of hostility on its appearance, not least because he had had the temerity to suggest that it was generals, and not the other ranks, who had a decisive hand in war's outcome. The popularized antipathy toward officers that was allegedly a characteristic of the Australian soldier thus found an academic echo among historians and well illustrated the negative aspect of the official historian's elevation of the private soldier in his work, one emulated fully by what has become the most widely read and popular account of Australians in the First World War, Bill Gammage's *The Broken Years* [29]. Drawn from the extraordinary collection of private and personal papers held by the Australian War Memorial, Gammage's book helped popularize interest in the war among a new generation of Australians, but his analysis of the war experience presented no advance on Bean's forty years previously. The popular feature film, *Gallipoli* (Peter Weir dir., 1981), on which Gammage acted as historical adviser, showed where this tendency might lead; the depiction of the strategic reasoning behind the ill-fated charge of the light horse at the Nek was inverted completely once again to blame the British for Australian failures, while the Australian staff officer responsible for persisting with the charge was portrayed with an educated ("English") accent and depicted as a callous incompetent. The message for contemporary audiences was plain, the film's value as historical reconstruction decidedly more problematic.

Hill's lead was followed by a number of others, most of them former students of his at the Royal Military College, Duntroon. Modern studies of Bridges [18], Legge [19], and Monash [55] as commanders were matched in Monash's case by a massive and prize-winning biography of Australia's most notable soldier written by one of Australia's most distinguished academic historians [69]. Apart from a single, and not altogether satisfactory, chapter in a collection of essays [74], Brudenell White awaits his student, as do the majority of Australian commanders of brigadier-general rank and above. Roger Lee has written a preliminary study of the Staff Corps in a collection of conference papers dealing with Australian and Allied perspectives on the events of 1918 [41], and a major biography of General Sir Thomas Blamey, Australia's Commander-in-Chief in the Second World War, deals with his experiences in 1914–1918 as a senior staff officer [37]. There is no serious study of Birdwood, the Anglo-Indian Army officer whose wartime career was given considerable luster through the deeds of the Dominion troops he commanded, and in New Zealand there is nothing at all on Godley or on Major-General Andrew Russell, who commanded the 1st New Zealand Division throughout its time on the Western Front. The prime minister for most of the war, the highly controversial William Morris Hughes, has had both his life [28] and his diplomatic maneuverings analyzed [71], and there is a good if somewhat uncritical biography of the Minister for Defence, George Foster Pearce (a more important figure than is sometimes credited) [35], but there is generally little attempt made to understand the workings and wellsprings of government policy between 1914 and 1918, as opposed to domestic opposition to it. Several lesser figures have attracted monographic studies, the first Australian Victoria Cross winner of the war [33], and John Simpson Kirkpatrick, a medical orderly on Gallipoli whose image in wartime propaganda and postwar usage came to stand for one significant dimension of the Australian self-image [17], but after a promising beginning Australian military biography of the Great War generation entered a sparse period until a new series of biographies, together with more general studies of military history subjects, commissioned by the Army History Unit and published by Oxford University Press, began to appear in the late 1990s [67, 73], while in New Zealand it has yet to manifest anything at all. Volumes 7–12 of *The Australian Dictionary of Biography* contains entries on many major (and some minor) Australian participants in the war [3].

Proposals for conscription to maintain the strength of the expeditionary forces in France were a source of enormous controversy in all the Dominions; only in Australia were such measures defeated, in that case by two popular referenda in 1916 and 1917. As in Canada, the question of conscription proved enormously divisive in both Australia and New Zealand, despite the differing outcomes in each. Conscription and its impact in New Zealand are the subject of an excellent scholarly monograph that notes along the way the manner in which early twentieth-century New Zealand had become a different society from early twentieth-century Australia [5]. One of the important manifestations of this lay in differing attitudes to the indigenous population: dispossessed, disenfranchised, and forbidden to enlist in Australia (although a few managed to do so); originally recruited into the New Zealand Expeditionary Force in a noncombatant role although after the move to France in 1916 concentrated into a Pioneer Battalion, having been given a combat role at Gallipoli, which generated some controversy in New Zealand [62]. (The domestic situation of the Maori in New Zealand was scarcely a happy one, but the differences here speak volumes about perceptions of the process of settlement in the nineteenth century.)

Interest in conscription in Australia was driven in part by perceived parallels with the 1960s and Vietnam [65]. (This was much less of a factor in New Zealand, where the commitment of troops was much smaller and only regulars were sent.) With one or two exceptions, however, most of the work that resulted remained confined to the journal literature, a reflection perhaps of the fact that much of it was undertaken by younger historians not yet fully established in the profession, and of the smallness and conservatism of Australian publishing, at that stage heavily dominated by large overseas houses. In the Australian case the referendum campaigns degenerated quickly into loyalty tests, with extraneous issues such as the British suppression of the Easter rebellion in Ireland and extreme left-wing agitation by the tiny Australian chapter of the International Workers of the World diverting attention from the issues actually at hand [70]. But there were also regional and class dimensions to the conflict on the home front, and some of these continued to play themselves out in the war's immediate aftermath [24]. In general, work on the home front during the war has been highly selective in its focus, although Michael McKernan has provided a valuable overview and a more specifically focused study on the role of the churches in wartime [50], while Joan Beaumont and a group of younger historians from Deakin University have looked at some of the existing issues from a fresh perspective, and have also directed attention to neglected areas such as the wartime performance of the Australian economy [11].

Within Australian writing there has been a growing concern with the Anzac legend, and with its creation and propagation through the writings of C. E. W. Bean, a trend that has no parallel in New Zealand. For an historian allegedly so influential Bean has attracted remarkably little scrutiny, serious or otherwise. His biographer denied having presented a "warts and all" study on the grounds that Bean had no warts [28], and in any case the volume essentially ends with Bean's appointment as official historian. The notable Australian historian, Ken Inglis, presented a significant short appraisal of Bean the historian in 1970 [38], but for nearly twenty years no one else it seems thought his lead worth following. This has begun to change [2], but it remains the case that Bean is still too much deferred to and too little scrutinized. His history is an awesome achievement, and it has many of the virtues of Bean the journalist with its thick description of men and places and events, but its weaknesses are also those of the journalist who had too little understanding of, and apparently little interest in, the mechanics and technicalities of modern war.

That the war, returned soldiers, and what George Mosse has termed "the myth of the war experience" had a considerable impact on Australian society there has been little doubt; just what form that influence took and how it made itself felt is another matter altogether, and one still improperly understood. Inglis has shown himself one of the most perceptive students of this subject, one to which he has returned periodically during his career [39], and a few have seen fit to follow [40], but much of the work concerned treats its subject on its own terms. In particular, it lacks the comparative dimension which would help to contextualize the social and cultural phenomenon under discussion, and would enable historians to place some cherished national assumptions under close scrutiny, in most cases for the first time. Mosse's work suggests some possibilities, while the comparisons to be drawn with Canada or the cult of sacrifice on the Somme fostered assiduously in Ulster since 1916 would prove illuminating. Inglis has pioneered the way with a multi–prize-winning study of the ubiquitous war memorials in Australia [40], and several other historians have produced studies of the varied domestic reactions to and impacts of the war [21, 30]. The important question of the treatment of "veterans" (the American term was not adopted until after the Vietnam War, "returned" servicemen being the usual appellation) has been the subject of a major study of "repatriation" (the original name of what is now the federal Department of Veterans' Affairs) [42].

That new questions can be asked of old material has been demonstrated in four important books, two each on Australian and New Zealand experience and two concerned with the well-worked subject of the Gallipoli campaign. Chris Pugsley's book, the first examination of New Zealand's role in the Dardanelles in sixty years, not only revived interest in the subject in New Zealand but also corrected much of the established record while effectively differentiating the New Zealand experience of Anzac from that of their Australian comrades [60]. His subsequent work on the issue of discipline and punishment in the New Zealand Expeditionary Force not only broke new ground on a contentious subject (especially over the question of capital courts martial, which the New Zealand government sanctioned while the Australian government did not, although many senior Australian officers favored it), but also rounded out significantly our understanding of the New Zealanders' war, especially in France [61]. Glen Wahlert has examined the role of the Military Police in maintaining discipline in the Australian Imperial Force [75], but the broader question of discipline in the AIF has yet to be analyzed in detail. John Robertson likewise returned to the Gallipoli story; in a methodologically conservative but highly scholarly and deeply researched book he took issue with the revisionists who claimed that the Anzac legend was the product of postwar writings and demonstrated that whatever Bean and others had done with it subsequently, the received image of Australian courage, ingenuity, and stoicism was grounded solidly in fact [64]. Approaching the Australian soldiers' image from the other end, Suzanne Brugger analyzed their impact upon Egypt and the Egyptians, not least as enforcers of Empire in 1919 when they were used extensively to put down the Egyptian revolt [14]. A model scholarly monograph, it suggests fruitful lines of enquiry in other theatres and other wars. Similarly, Roger Noble's work on Australians taken prisoner on the Western Front, by examining the AIF on other than the terms of its own reputation, gives some indication of what can be done when the Australian military experience is matched against that of other combatants [53].

Although since 1984 scholarly attention to the First World War in New Zealand has been limited, a trickle of work has shed light on several aspects of

New Zealand's involvement in the conflict. The strategy that lay behind New Zealand's approach to the war, and its rapid contribution of an expeditionary force to the Imperial effort, is explored in Ian McGibbon, The *Path to Gallipoli: Defending New Zealand* [47], who shows that the decision was consistent with the stance adopted by New Zealand in the decades leading up to the war. The sustenance of the New Zealand Expeditionary Force (NZEF), which served initially in the Mediterranean but later went, in large part, to the Western Front, proved difficult after the waning of early enthusiasm for the war, and conscription was eventually introduced in 1916. The issues are discussed in an excellent work already mentioned [15].

Campaign studies have been conspicuous by their absence, with only Glyn Harper's *Massacre at Passchendaele: The New Zealand Story* [34] the first to appear since Christopher Pugsley's 1983 study of the Gallipoli campaign [60]. Harper's short account is marred, however, by an exaggeration of the casualties suffered during the "massacre." Pugsley has also published short accounts of the "Native Contingent" [62] and of the New Zealand Tunnelling Company's activities at Arras on the Western Front [63]. As well as Pugley's analysis of discipline [61], there is a much less satisfactory study in Nicholas Boyack, *Behind the Lines: The Lives of New Zealand Soldiers in the First World War* [12].

A range of participants' personal experiences, as told in their diaries and letters, has been published in *The Great Adventure: New Zealand Soldiers Describe the First World War* [57]. Oral testimony of New Zealand soldiers is to be found in Nicholas Boyack and Jane Tolerton (eds.), *In the Shadow of War: New Zealand Soldiers Talk about World War One and Their Lives* [13]. Jock Phillips's *A Man's Country: The Image of the Pakeha Male, A History,* addresses attitudes of the soldiers and questions of identity [56]. The latter question is also addressed in Phillips's articles, "Was the Great War New Zealand's War?" [59] and "The Great War and New Zealand Nationalism: The Evidence of War Memorials" [58].

The home front in New Zealand is an area that awaits substantial treatment. One chapter of Peter Cooke's two-volume *Defending New Zealand: Ramparts on the Sea 1840–1950s* [16] outlines in great detail the steps taken for local defense during the First World War. It also includes useful lists of New Zealand merchant ships lost to enemy action and of the ships carrying drafts of the NZEF. Some aspects relating to Germany, including anti-German hysteria and the activities of prisoner of war Count Felix von Luckner, are covered in essays in James Bade (ed.), *Out of the Shadow of War: The German Connection with New Zealand in the Twentieth Century* [4]. An aspect of postwar rehabilitation policy is studied in Ashley Gould, "Soldier Settlement in New Zealand after World War I: A Reappraisal." [32]

Biography remains conspicuous by its absence, with the exception of Jane Tolerton's *Ettie: A Life of Ettie Rout* [72]. This study of a notable anti-VD crusader won the New Zealand Book Award for nonfiction in 1993. Numerous New Zealanders who contributed to the war effort, both at home and abroad, are featured in *The Dictionary of New Zealand Biography, Volume III: 1901–1920* [52].

SUGGESTIONS FOR FURTHER RESEARCH

The field is still open for significant work on the war experience of the two Pacific Dominions, and with the recent greater relative acceptance of military history within the academic discipline there is some sign that this will eventuate. To give but one example, nothing has been written on either the Royal Australian Navy or the Australian Flying Corps since the official volumes published in the early 1920s; the Royal New Zealand Navy in the Great War is a subject that has hardly been treated at all [46]. What is badly needed, however, is a willingness on the part of Australian historians to rise above what one critic has termed the "parochial short-sightedness" characterizing so much Australian history generally, and an appreciation that comparative work, especially with the other Dominions, will not only provide a valuable context for their studies, but that the perspectives that emerge as a result will reveal the history of their own country in new, and perhaps unexpected, light.

In the meantime, those who want to engage with the Australian and New Zealand experience in the First World War should not overlook two important reference works: Peter Dennis, Jeffrey Grey, Ewan Morris and Robin Prior, *The Oxford Companion to Australian Military History* [23], and Ian McGibbon (ed.), *The Oxford Companion to New Zealand Military History* [48]. The advent of the World Wide Web has also made accessible further valuable resources: much of the vast photographic collection of the Australian War Memorial, together with an Australian Nominal Roll and Roll of Honour (the latter detailing all members of the Australian Imperial Force who died in the war), is now available on the Web at http://www.awm.gov.au. Also on the Web is a detailed organizational study of the AIF: http://www.adfa.edu.au/~rmallett/index.html.

BIBLIOGRAPHY

1. Andrews, Eric. *The Department of Defence.* Melbourne: Oxford University Press, 2001. This forms part of the seven-volume "Australian Centenary History of Defence" series, edited by Peter Dennis and John Coates and published in 2001 to commemorate the role of Defence in the first century of the Commonwealth of Australia, 1901–2001. The other volumes in the series, each of which (Horner's excepted) deals in part with the First World War, are: Jeffrey Grey, *The Australian Army;* Alan Stephens, *The Royal Australian Air Force;* David Stevens, *The Royal Australian Navy;* Joan Beaumont, *Australian Defence: Sources and Statistics;* John Coates, *An Atlas of Australia's Wars;* and David Horner, *Making the ADF* [Australian Defence Force].

2. Andrews, Eric. *The Anzac Illusion: Anglo-Australian Relations during World War I.* Melbourne: Cambridge University Press, 1993.

3. *The Australian Dictionary of Biography, Vols. 7–12, 1891–1939.* Melbourne: Melbourne University Press, 1979–1990.

4. Bade, James (ed.). *Out of the Shadow of War: The German Connection with New Zealand in the Twentieth Century.* Auckland: Oxford University Press, 1998.

5. Baker, Paul. *King and Country Call: New Zealanders, Conscription and the Great War.* Auckland: Auckland University Press, 1988.

6. Barrett, John, "No Straw Man: C. E. W. Bean and Some Critics," *Historical Studies* 23: 90 (April 1988), 102–14; Alistair Thompson, " 'Steadfast unto Death' ": C. E. W. Bean and the Representation of Australian Military Manhood," *Historical Studies* 24: 93 (October 1989), 462–78; E. M. Andrews, "Bean and Bullecourt: Weaknesses and Strengths of the Official History of Aus-

tralia in the First World War," in Peter Dennis and Jeffrey Grey (eds.), *Revue Internationale d'Histoire Militaire* 72 (edition Australienne, Canberra, 1990), and "The Media and the Military: Australian War Correspondents and the Appointment of a Corps Commander, 1918-A Case Study," *War & Society* 8: 2 (October 1990), 83–103.

7. Baxter, Archibald. *We Will Not Cease.* London: Victor Gollancz, 1939.

8. Bean, C. E. W. *Official History of Australia in the War of 1914–18,* 15 vols. Sydney: Angus & Robertson, 1921–1943: C. E. W. Bean, *The Story of Anzac: From the Outbreak of the War to the End of the First Phase of the Gallipoli Landing, May 4, 1915* (1921); *The Story of Anzac: From May 4, 1915 to the Evacuation of the Gallipoli Peninsula* (1924); *The AIF in France 1916* (1929); *The AIF in France 1917* (1933); *The AIF in France during the Main German Offensive 1918* (1937); *The AIF in France during the Allied Offensive 1918* (1942); H. S. Gullett, *The AIF in Sinai and Palestine 1914–1918* (1923); F. M. Cutlack, *The Australian Flying Corps in the Western and Eastern Theatres of War 1914–1918* (1923); A. W. Jose, *The Royal Australian Navy 1914–1918* (1928); S. S. Mackenzie, *The Australians at Rabaul: The Capture and Administration of the German Possessions in the Southern Pacific* (1927); Ernest Scott, *Australia During the War* (1936); and C. E. W. Bean and H. S. Gullett, *Photographic Record of the War: Reproductions of Pictures Taken by Australian Official Photographers . . . and Others* (1923). The medical series is by Butler, A. G., *Official History of the Australian Army Medical Services 1914–18.* Canberra: Australian War Memorial, 1930–43: *I. The Gallipoli Campaign, the Campaign in Sinai and Palestine, The Occupation of German New Guinea; II. The Western Front* (1940); *III. Special Problems and Services* (1943). Reprinted by the University of Queensland Press, 10 vols., 1981–1987.

9. Bean, C. E. W. *Gallipoli Mission.* Canberra: Australian War Memorial, 1948; repr. Sydney: ABC Books, 1990.

10. Bean, C. E. W. *Two Men I Knew: William Bridges and Brudenell White, Founders of the AIF.* Sydney: Angus & Robertson, 1957.

11. Beaumont, Joan (ed.). *Australia's War, 1914–1918.* Sydney: Allen & Unwin, 1995.

12. Boyack, Nicholas. *Behind the Lines: The Lives of New Zealand Soldiers in the First World War.* Wellington: Allen & Unwin/Port Nicholson Press, 1989.

13. Boyack, Nicholas, and Tolerton, Jane (eds.). *In the Shadow of War: New Zealand Soldiers Talk about World War One and Their Lives.* Auckland: Penguin, 1990.

14. Brugger, Suzanne. *Australians and Egypt 1914–1919.* Melbourne: Melbourne University Press, 1980.

15. John Coates, *An Atlas of Australia's Wars.* Melbourne: Oxford University Press, 2001. (See Note 1.)

16. Cooke, Peter. *Defending New Zealand: Ramparts on the Sea, 1840–1950s.* Wellington: Defence of New Zealand Study Group, 2000.

17. Cochrane, Peter. *Simpson and the Donkey: The Making of a Legend.* Melbourne: Melbourne University Press, 1992.

18. Coulthard-Clark, Chris. *A Heritage of Spirit: A Biography of Major-General Sir William Throsby Bridges.* Melbourne: Melbourne University Press, 1979.

19. Coulthard-Clark, Chris. *No Australian Need Apply: The Troubled Career of Lieutenant-General James Gordon Legge.* Sydney: Allen & Unwin, 1987.

20. Cutlack, F. M. (ed.). *War Letters of General Monash.* Sydney: Angus & Robertson, 1934.

21. Damousi, Joy. *Labour of Loss: Mourning, Memory, and Wartime Bereavement in Australia.* Melbourne: Cambridge University Press, 1999.

22. Dennis, Peter. "Military history in Australia," in P. H. Kamphuis (ed.). *Military History Around the World.* 's-Gravenhage: Sectie Militaire Geschiedenis, 1991.

23. Peter Dennis, Jeffrey Grey, Ewan Morris, Robin Prior, *The Oxford Companion to Australian Military History.* Melbourne: Oxford University Press, 1995.

24. Evans, Raymond. *The Red Flag Riots.* St Lucia: University of Queensland Press, 1988.

25. Fewster, Kevin (ed.). *Gallipoli Correspondent: The Frontline Diary of C. E. W. Bean.* Sydney: George Allen & Unwin, 1983.

26. Fielding, Jean, and O'Neill, Robert (eds.). *A Select Bibliography of Australian Military History 1891–1939*. Canberra: Australian National University Press, 1978, 221–36.

27. Fitzhardinge, L. F. "Australia, Japan and Great Britain, 1914–1918: A Study in Triangular Diplomacy," *Historical Studies* 14: 54 (April 1970), 250–59; Robert Thornton, "Invaluable Ally or Imminent Aggressor? Australia and Japanese Naval Assistance, 1914–1918," *Journal of Australian Studies* 12 (June 1983), 5–20.

28. Fitzhardinge, L. F. *The Little Digger, 1914–1952: William Morris Hughes. A Political Biography*. Sydney: Angus & Robertson, 1979.

29. Gammage, Bill. *The Broken Years: Australian Soldiers in the Great War*. Canberra: Australian National University Press, 1974, and numerous subsequent editions.

30. Garton, Stephen. *The Cost of War: Australians Return*. Melbourne: Oxford University Press, 1996.

31. Godley, General Sir Alexander. *Life of an Irish Soldier: Reminiscences*. London: John Murray, 1939.

32. Gould, Ashley. "Soldier Settlement in New Zealand after World War I: A Reappraisal," in Smart, Judith, and Wood, Tony (eds.). *An Anzac Muster: War and Society in Australia and New Zealand 1914–18 and 1939–45, Selected Papers*. Clayton: Monash Publications in History, 1992.

33. Grant, Ian. *Jacka, VC: Australia's Finest Fighting Soldier*. Melbourne: Macmillan, 1989.

34. Harper, Glyn. *Massacre at Passchendaele: The New Zealand Story*. Auckland: HarperCollins, 2000.

35. Heydon, Peter. *Quiet Decision: A Study of George Foster Pearce*. Melbourne: Melbourne University Press, 1965.

36. Hill, Alec. *Chauvel of the Light Horse: A Biography of General Sir Harry Chauvel*. Melbourne: Melbourne University Press, 1978.

37. Horner, David. *Blamey: The Commander-in-Chief*. Sydney: Allen & Unwin, 1998.

38. Inglis, K. S., *C. E. W. Bean: Australian Historian*. St Lucia: University of Queensland Press, 1970.

39. Inglis, K. S. "The Anzac Tradition," *Meanjin Quarterly* 24:1 (March 1965), 25–44, and "Anzac and the Australian Military Tradition," in Dennis and Grey (eds.), *Revue Internationale d'Histoire Militaire* 72; K. S. Inglis and Jock Phillips, "War Memorials in Australia and New Zealand: A Comparative Survey," *Australian Historical Studies* 24:96 (April 1991), 179–91.

40. Inglis, K. S. *Sacred Places: War Memorials in the Australian Landscape*. Melbourne: Miegunyah Press at Melbourne University Press, 1998.

41. Lee, Roger. "The Australian Staff: The Forgotten Men of the First AIF," in Dennis, Peter & Grey, Jeffrey (eds.). *1918: Defining Victory. The Chief of Army's History Conference, 1998*. Canberra: School of History, Australian Defence Force Academy, 1999.

42. Lloyd, Clem, and Rees, Jacqui. *The Last Shilling: A History of Repatriation in Australia*. Melbourne: Melbourne University Press, 1994.

43. Louis, Wm. Roger. "Australia and German Colonies in the Pacific, 1914–1919," *Journal of Modern History* 38: 4 (December 1966), 407–21; and *Great Britain and Germany's Lost Colonies 1914–1919*. Oxford: Clarendon Press, 1967.

44. Maxwell, J. *Hell's Bells and Mademoiselles*. Sydney: Angus & Robertson, 1932.

45. McCarthy, Dudley. *Gallipoli to the Somme: The Story of C. E. W. Bean*. Sydney: John Ferguson, 1983.

46. McGibbon, I. C. *Blue-Water Rationale: The Naval Defence of New Zealand 1914–1942*. Wellington: Government Printer, 1981.

47. McGibbon, I. C. *The Path to Gallipoli: Defending New Zealand 1840–1915*. Wellington: GP Books, 1991.

48. McGibbon, I. C. (ed.) *The Oxford Companion to New Zealand Military History*. Auckland: Oxford University Press, 2000.

49. McKernan, Michael. *Here Is Their Spirit: A History of the Australian War Memorial 1917–1990*. St Lucia: University of Queensland Press, 1991.

50. McKernan, Michael. *The Australian People and the Great War.* Melbourne: Nelson, 1980; *Australian Churches at War: Attitudes and Activities of the Major Churches 1914–1918.* Canberra: Australian War Memorial, 1980.

51. Monash, John, *The Australian Victories in France in 1918.* London: Hutchinson, 1920.

52. *The Dictionary of New Zealand Biography, Volume III: 1901–1920.* Auckland/Wellington: Auckland University Press/Department of Internal Affairs, 1996.

53. Noble, Roger. "Raising the White Flag: The Surrender of Australian Soldiers on the Western Front," in Dennis and Grey (eds.). *Revue Internationale d'Histoire Militaire* 72.

54. O'Connor, P. S. "The Recruitment of Maori Soldiers, 1914–1918," *Political Studies* [New Zealand] 19:2 (1967), 48–83.

55. Pedersen, Peter. *Monash as Military Commander.* Melbourne: Melbourne University Press, 1985.

56. Phillips, Jock. *A Man's Country: The Image of the Pakeha Male, A History.* Auckland: Penguin, 1987.

57. Phillips, Jock, Boyack, Nicholas, and Malone, E. P. *The Great Adventure: New Zealand Soldiers Describe the First World War.* Wellington: Allen & Unwin/Port Nicholson Press, 1988.

58. Phillips, Jock. "The Great War and New Zealand Nationalism: The Evidence of War Memorials," in Smart, Judith, and Wood, Tony (eds.). *An Anzac Muster: War and Society in Australia and New Zealand 1914–18 and 1939–45, Selected Papers.* Clayton: Monash Publications in History, 1992.

59. Phillips, Jock. "Was the Great War New Zealand's War?" in Craig Wilcox (ed.), *The Great War, Gains and Losses—Anzac and Empire.* Canberra: Australian War Memorial/Australian National University, 1995.

60. Pugsley, Christopher. *Gallipoli: The New Zealand Story.* Auckland: Hodder & Stoughton, 1984.

61. Pugsley, Christopher. *On the Fringe of Hell: New Zealanders and Military Discipline in the First World War.* Auckland: Hodder & Stoughton, 1991.

62. Pugsley, Christopher. *Te Hokowhitu a Tu: The Maori Battalion in the First World War.* Auckland: Reed, 1995.

63. Pugsley, Christopher. "The New Zealand Tunnellers at Arras, 1916–1918," in Alain Jacques (ed.), *La Bataille d'Arras, Avril–Mai 1917.* Arras: Le Cercle Archäologique Arrageois, 1997.

64. Robertson, John. *Anzac and Empire: The Tragedy and Glory of Gallipoli.* Melbourne: Hamlyn Australia, 1990.

65. Robson, L. L. *The First AIF: A Study of its Recruitment 1914–1918.* Melbourne: Melbourne University Press, 1970; Dawes, J. N. I., and Robson, L. L. *Citizen to Soldier: Australia before the Great War: Recollections of Members of the First AIF.* Melbourne: Melbourne University Press, 1977

66. Ross, Malcolm. *Light and Shade in War.* London: Arnold, 1916.

67. Sadler, Peter. *The Paladin: A Life of Major-General Sir John Gellibrand.* Melbourne: Oxford University Press, 2000.

68. Serle, Geoffrey. "The Digger Tradition and Australian Nationalism," *Meanjin Quarterly* 24:2 (June 1965), 149–58; Roe, Michael. "Comment on the Digger Tradition," *Meanjin Quarterly* 24:3 (September 1965), 357–58; McLachlan, Noel. "Nationalism and the Divisive Digger: three comments," *Meanjin Quarterly* 27:3 (September 1968), 302–8; Ross, Jane. *The Myth of the Digger: The Australian Soldier in Two World Wars.* Sydney: Hale and Iremonger, 1985; Gerster, Robin. *Big-Noting: The Heroic Theme in Australian War Writing.* Melbourne: Melbourne University Press, 1987; Welborn, Suzanne. *Lords of Death: A People, a Place, a Legend.* Fremantle: Fremantle Arts Centre Press, 1982; Robson, Lloyd. "The Australian Soldier: Formation of a Stereotype," in McKernan, M. and Browne, M. (eds.). Australia: *Two Centuries of War and Peace.* Canberra: Australian War Memorial, 1988.

69. Serle, Geoffrey. *John Monash: A Biography.* Melbourne: Melbourne University Press, 1982.

70. Smith, F. B. *The Conscription Plebiscites in Australia, 1916–1917.* Melbourne: Melbourne University Press, 1966; Gilbert, Alan D. "The Conscription Referenda, 1916–17: The Impact of the Irish Crisis," *Historical Studies* 14:53 (October 1969), 54–72, and "Protestants, Catholics and Loyalty: an aspect of the conscription controversies 1916–17," *Politics* [Sydney] 6:1 (May 1971), 15–25; McKernan, Michael. "Catholics, Conscription and Archbishop Mannix," *Historical Studies* 17:68 (April 1977), 299–314; Murphy, D. J. "Religion, Race and Conscription in World War I," *Australian Journal of Politics and History* 20:2 (1974), 155–63; Robertson, J. R. "The Conscription Issue and the National Movement in Western Australia: June 1916–December 1917," *University Studies in Politics and History* 3 (1959); Pearson, A. R. "Western Australia and the Conscription Plebiscites of 1916 and 1917," *RMC Historical Journal* 3 (1974); Gibson, P. M. "The Conscription Issue in South Australia, 1916–1917," *University Studies in Politics and History* 4 (1963–1964); Evans, P. M. *Loyalty and Disloyalty: Social Conflict on the Queensland Home Front 1914–1918.* St. Lucia: University of Queensland Press, 1987; Lake, Marilyn. *A Divided Society: Tasmania during World War I.* Melbourne: Melbourne University Press: Melbourne, 1975.

71. Spartalis, Peter. *The Diplomatic Battles of Billy Hughes.* Sydney: Hale and Iremonger, 1983.

72. Tolerton, Jane. *Ettie: A Life of Ettie Rout.* Auckland: Penguin, 1992.

73. Tyquin, Michael. *Neville Howse: Australia's First V.C. Winner.* Melbourne: Oxford University Press, 1999.

74. Verney, Guy. "General Sir Brudenell White: The Staff Officer as Commander," in Horner, D. M. (ed.). *The Commanders: Australian Military Leadership in the Twentieth Century.* Sydney: Allen & Unwin, 1984.

75. Wahlert, Glen. *The Other Enemy? Australian Soldiers and the Military Police.* Melbourne: Oxford University Press, 1999.

76. Waite, Major F. *The New Zealanders at Gallipoli.* Auckland: Whitcombe and Tombs Ltd., 1919; Stewart, Colonel H. *The New Zealanders in France 1916–1918.* Auckland: Whitcombe and Tombs Ltd., 1921; Powles, Lieutenant Colonel C. G. *The New Zealanders in Sinai and Palestine.* Auckland: Whitcombe and Tombs Ltd., 1922; Drew, Lieutenant H. T. B. *The War Effort of New Zealand.* Auckland: Whitcombe and Tombs Ltd., 1923; Studholme, Lieutenant Colonel J. (comp.). *Some Records of the New Zealand Expeditionary Force, Unofficial but Compiled from Official Records.* Auckland: Whitcombe and Tombs Ltd., 1928.

13

Africa

Michelle Moyd

World War I in Africa, perhaps more than other regions involved in the war, has received relatively little serious scholarly attention within the field of military history, although it has provided the inspiration for a number of popular films and fictional accounts, and has captured the imaginations of many.

Particularly in the 1980s and 1990s, scholarly treatments of this portion of the war have dwindled. Without question, this comparative dearth of historical materials on the war in Africa relates in part to its status as a "sideshow" to the war in Europe. Yet the East African campaign was, measured against all others, the longest of the war. As at least one scholar notes, "The War was very much a reality for Africa, a period of immense and significant change of which we have only just scratched the surface" [47].

Primary sources on the war in Africa are widely available in English as published memoirs, unit histories, and official histories. In addition, original documents from the war in Africa are accessible in various archives there and in Europe. A number of secondary sources, written mainly in the 1960s and 1970s, provide helpful syntheses of large quantities of disparate operational data. These works are the most readable narrative histories available. Although more recent works exist, they mainly consist of essays within edited collections or in journals. German and French scholarship on the subject in the form of dissertations, articles and book chapters can also be found with minimal effort.

An emergent genre of the 1990s, initiated by social historians of Africa, has been the close study of African colonial military forces. Troops and porters from all over the continent saw direct action, both in Africa itself and in Europe. This relatively new addition to African and military historiography attempts to assess the impact of the war on African peoples and communities. Works such as these make an essential contribution to a more thorough scholarship of the war, which is based on the perspective of those who fought in it. Moreover, these histories complement the operational and campaign histories mentioned above by adding a necessary human dimension to the technically detailed military accounts.

Sources and scholarship in this field reflect the immensely complex colonial backdrop against which the war in Africa was set. For example, in the East Africa campaign from 1914 to 1918, forces from British East Africa, German East Africa, South Africa, Rhodesia, Nigeria, the Gold Coast, and India fought under German or British command. Similarly, the campaigns in Cameroon and Togo involved still other African colonial subjects under French or German command. In short, those interested in studying World War I in Africa must be willing to use colonial-era histories from all participants' regions as well as the derivative secondary sources which have been written on the subject.

Not surprisingly, relatively few general texts exist that are devoted strictly to the African theater in World War I. Fortunately though, those that are available provide quite useful comprehensive summaries and bibliographies from which to start more specific inquiries into this historical field. As an introduction to the Great War in Africa, Byron Farwell's book of the same name is thus far unmatched in its rich detail, readability, logical presentation, and use of secondary sources [16]. Farwell's work is also the most recent general book-length treatment of this subject. Melvin E. Page's outstanding edited volume of scholarly essays, headed up by his own highly informative introduction, introduces the reader to some of the most important issues in this field from the perspectives of historians of Africa [43]. The essays touch on all African regions involved in the war. This volume includes several excellent essays on the issue of labor recruitment, particularly of porters, during the war. The significance of the carriers' role in the war in Africa cannot be underestimated, for in the absence of modern logistical support (i.e. railways), they were the only means available for transport of supplies. Moreover, many of the recruited laborers were sent to Europe as supply workers [43]. Thus anyone seeking to understand World War I in Africa must also understand the role of the porters. This topic is also addressed in an issue of *The Journal of African History* specifically devoted to the study of World War I and Africa [25, 44, 51, 55]. Finally, Hew Strachan's general history of World War I includes a fine chapter on the war in Africa by colonial military expert David Killingray [29].

Since the majority of the war in Africa was fought in German East Africa, an identification of the key texts for that campaign will nicely supplement the general texts mentioned above. Brian Gardner's [19] and Charles Miller's [37] books on the East Africa campaign are both logically written narrative histories of the campaign. Miller's work employs a wider variety of sources, including German ones, than does Gardner's, but he also confesses in his acknowledgments to have "[drawn] heavily on literary license and educated guesswork." Used with caution however, and as a gateway to more scholarly work, Miller's book is useful. A key work used by all scholars interested in this field (including

Gardner, Miller, and Farwell) is General Paul von Lettow-Vorbeck's *My Reminiscences of East Africa* [32]. Lettow-Vorbeck was the commanding general of the German forces, and he has been widely celebrated for his pioneering guerrilla-style tactics in the East Africa campaign. His memoir is detailed and thorough, and is thus indispensable in researching this period. Similarly requisite for serious scholars, Charles Hordern's official *History of the Great War: Military Operations, East Africa* [26] provides the most reliable statistics available on troop strength at the beginning of the war, as well as the minutiae of the units involved in the campaign up to September 1916 [38, 40]. While there are a number of other worthwhile sources that the researcher should eventually take up, those listed here will certainly provide a solid foundation for further inquiry.

Most of the works listed thus far also have excellent bibliographies that can assist those interested in further reading. Although quite dated, an excellent bibliographical essay by Hartmut Pogge von Strandmann and Alison Smith concludes Gifford and Louis' *Britain and Germany in Africa: Imperial Rivalry and Colonial Rule* [46]. Helmuth Stoecker's *German Imperialism in Africa* adds to this list by virtue of his inclusion of German-language sources on the Africa campaigns [54]. Woodruff D. Smith's general study of the German colonial empire also has an excellent categorized bibliography that makes extensive use of German sources [52]. Smith also has an updated article in Chickering's *Imperial Germany: A Historiographical Companion* [8]. Joe Lunn's [34] and Myron Echenberg's [13] bibliographies will lead the reader to appropriate French-language sources. Heggoy's bibliographical reference for French military history will also prove helpful [21]. For those interested in the Belgian role as Britain's ally in the African war, William Roger Louis' *Ruanda-Urundi 1884–1919* highlights the best related sources, many of which are also in French [33]. For the history of the campaign in East Africa, Ofcansky and Yeager's *Historical Dictionary of Tanzania* includes extensive bibliographical references specific to the region [42]. These bibliographies, taken together, define the scope of readily available general literature on World War I in Africa.

The political and diplomatic background to the war in Africa is best approached from the perspective of the primary colonial powers involved. That is to say, if one understands the political and diplomatic motives of Britain, Germany, Belgium, and France in 1914 with regard to their empires, one will also be able to grasp the basic dynamics that drove the war effort in Africa. References for historical works focused narrowly on political and diplomatic history generated within the colonies themselves do not seem to exist, although these may yet emerge as scholars continue to exploit the papers of colonial administrators. It seems clear, however, that colonial administrators had very little influence in the development of policy affecting decisions to go to war, although an argument can perhaps be made that colonial military leadership exerted a somewhat stronger influence on policy [32, 59].

For explanations of the political and diplomatic background to the war in Africa, readers should begin with classic works of political history for World War I. For example, David Stevenson's *The First World War and International*

Politics [53] or Fritz Fischer's *Germany's Aims in the First World War* [17] both situate the outbreak of war in Africa within the context of the specific goals of each of the colonial powers at the beginning of the war. Joll's *The Origins of the First World War* is also helpful on this score [28]. Prosser and Gifford's classic *Britain and Germany in Africa* [46] contains a number of excellent articles that elucidate the various colonial relationships between European nations and how these affected policy decisions. Although Germany had hoped to keep its colonies out of the war based on previously established neutrality claims, Britain, France, and Belgium viewed the colonies as prizes to be taken for the postwar future. This desire for acquisition of German colonial territories conflicted directly with the German notion of *Mittelafrika,* which called for the creation of "a large Central African colony . . . that would tie together the existing German colonies (except for Togo)" [52]. On the other hand, a German *Mittelafrika* could be attained only at the expense of Belgium or Portugal, since its formation would necessitate alteration of their colonial boundaries. These political considerations were, of course, at once superseded by warfare in 1914, when British and French forces quickly seized the German territory of Togoland. They followed with the more difficult, but nonetheless successful, conquest of Cameroon. South African forces then defeated the German *Schutztruppe* in Southwest Africa, and finally, a multinational and polyglot Allied force led by the British attacked the Germans under the command of General von Lettow-Vorbeck in East Africa. In so doing, they initiated a long and devastating four-year campaign that ended on 25 November 1918 in Abercorn, Portuguese East Africa, two weeks after the European armistice. Farwell's previously mentioned book [16] concisely summarizes the political dimensions of the early phase of the war in Africa, as do Louis' *Ruanda-Urundi 1884–1919* [33] and Stoecker's *German Imperialism in Africa* [54]. As mentioned above though, one would need to use archival collections to find further details of colonial decision-making within the colonies themselves.

An interesting indicator of the type of work that can be done in this area through a social history approach is Allen F. Roberts' article "Wartime Politics along the South-western Shore of Lake Tanganyika" [48]. He bases his study on a thorough examination of Belgian missionary and military documents for this region during the war years. He argues, "As people from distinct worlds were thrust together with great precipitance, so were politics—international, national (metropolitan and colonial) and local-level or village—collapsed in a manner never before experienced." His analysis hints at the possibilities available to future scholars to deepen the current historical understanding of the war years in Africa by delving into the local politics of diverse regions [41].

The 1914–1918 war in Africa caused economic disruption and devastation, particularly in East Africa, where the longest campaign occurred. Yet it was at least in part increasingly due to economic motives that the European colonial powers willingly fought to maintain their colonies, and perhaps even to extend their territorial holdings after the war. Indeed, Rathbone [47] argues that World War I "accelerated the process of political and economic change in colonial

Africa" inasmuch as it signaled the beginning of more centralized colonial processes. A number of studies present economic data on the colonies during the prewar period [27, 30]. The most interesting and important economic aspect of World War I, however, is that the European colonial powers, as they led their African troops through the countryside on campaign, increasingly were forced to live off the land. Very few supplies from Europe arrived after 1914, as the British and German navies and merchant fleets were otherwise occupied. Furthermore, the colonies were not a priority for resupply. Thus to a large extent the Europeans relied on their troops and carriers to guide them through unfamiliar terrain and to assist them in securing supplies from local inhabitants. As early as 1915, however, parts of German East Africa were experiencing famine caused by "requisitioning and drought" [14, 27]. In addition, because so many men were being conscripted as porters, few remained behind to assist women with cultivation, thus limiting crop yields. The impact of the war on local communities and their economies all over Africa was substantial, an assertion that is borne out by the conclusions of various authors in Page's collection of essays [43] and in the *Journal of African History* articles already mentioned [1, 25, 51, 55]. In short, the Great War in Africa was not a war between superior technologies. Rather, it was a war of attrition, albeit a different sort of attrition from what took place on the Western Front. General Lettow-Vorbeck's strategy, from the onset of war in East Africa in 1914, was to divert Allied resources from the war in Europe by forcing them to fight a highly mobile guerrilla war in East Africa. He was largely successful in that goal, but at a terrible expense to the Africans who were forced to endure food and manpower shortages, and their larger economic consequences, to suit his whims [32].

The social history of World War I in Africa is an area that needs substantial development. Very few complete social histories of Africa during the war exist, but those that do are excellent, and they bode well for the future of historiography in this field. Lunn [34] focuses on the impact of the war on the people of francophone West Africa as well as the experiences of African soldiers sent to fight on the Western Front. Echenberg's book [13] treats this subject more narrowly in his broader study of the *Tiraiileurs Sénégalais*. Similarly, Parsons [45] touches briefly on World War I in his history of the King's African Rifles. For the African soldiers under German authority, the *Schutztruppe*, the only study currently available is a Master's thesis by Michael von Herff [57]. While this study does not encompass World War I, it nonetheless provides important insights into the recruitment and organization of the troops, and touches on their living conditions in the *askaridorf*, or *askari* villages. Moreover, its analysis of the relationship between the German officers and their African troops fills a void in the current historiography. These authors have contributed greatly to an understanding of the lives of the African troops, porters, and families who fought the war for the Europeans. In addition, several of the regional general histories mentioned above elucidate the impact of the war on various communities of Africans [3, 14, 27, 41]. Military archival resources of the former colonial powers in France, Great Britain, Germany, and Portugal, as well as national archives of

Tanzania, Kenya, and South Africa, will have much more to add to these images once they are mined by historians engaged in the writing of social history. The locations of the specific archives can be found in works such as those edited by Higham, or in advanced scholarly works based on primary source research, such as Iliffe's general history of Tanzania [27].

Meanwhile, there are other ways to get at the social history of Africa during the World War. Some of the best tools available for this endeavor are the memoirs and biographies of participants or inhabitants of the regions affected by the war in Africa. Isak Dinesen's *Out of Africa* [11, 56] recalls how World War I affected the productivity of her coffee plantation in British East Africa as well as the immediate effects on the people around her, and of course, herself. General von Lettow-Vorbeck makes a number of key observations in his memoir [32], both on the military operations as they occurred and on the African troops with whom he spent most of his time during the campaign. A British perspective on the war is offered by Colonel R. Meinertzhagen in his *Army Diary 1899–1926* [36]. His colorful remembrances of his wartime experiences speak volumes on the complex relationship between the British and their troops, who came from far and wide to fight the Germans. F. Brett Young does the same in his memoir of the efforts of the 2nd Rhodesia Regiment fighting under General Smuts of South Africa [58]. We are fortunate to also have available several unit histories for troops who fought in both West and East Africa [9, 12, 26, 31, 38]. While these are more useful for reconstruction of the actual fighting in East Africa, they also sometimes yield brief glimpses into the lives of the troops. Rounding out the available sources on social history, but also pertaining to manpower estimates, are the various article-length works on the porters who served along with the troops as logistical support. The articles by Killingray [29], Page [44], and Hodges [25] in the *Journal of African History* all deal with this subject from varying regional perspectives. An earlier article by Savage and Munro [51] focuses specifically on Carrier Corps recruitment in British East Africa during the war. While recreating the social history of World War I is by no means an easy task, requiring diligence and willingness to use many different sources, it is a rewarding one. Without it, the African campaigns seem devoid of humanity, which of course makes their history an empty interpretation of what happened on the continent during the war.

The literature available on mobilization and preparation for war is relatively broad, although it focuses mainly on prewar recruitment efforts [32, 44, 51, 55, 57] . While many of the Europeans in the colonies perceived that a war of significant proportions might be imminent, they did not necessarily anticipate that they too would become involved, and the Germans in particular had hoped for neutral colonies if a war were to break out. They were thus ill-prepared for a major mobilization of forces. Statistical summaries of these forces are available in Hordern [26], Moyse-Bartlett [40], Lettow-Vorbeck [32], Iliffe [27], and Farwell [16], as well as Ludwig Boell's *Die Operationen in Ost-Afrika: Weltkrieg 1914–1918* [4]. It is fair to say though, in general, that each of the colonial powers possessed very small protective forces led by an even smaller contingent of

European officers and NCOs. For the Germans, the problem was especially acute. They had no allies with which to supplement their forces, and the seizure of their colonies in Togo, Cameroon, and Southwest Africa further weakened them militarily since unlike the British, they could not draw on troops from other parts of their empire. Nor could they count on reinforcements to come from Europe. Lettow-Vorbeck certainly took this into account in constructing his war plan of forcing the Allies to chase his small force out of German East Africa—a process that lasted for over four years. Both the British and the Germans required huge numbers of porters as well, and as the war dragged on, hardships and mortality rates for soldiers and porters increased dramatically, thus compounding the economic problems mentioned above, but more importantly, causing many Africans to resist recruitment efforts [25, 43, 44, 45, 55]. News of the horrible circumstances with which conscripts had to contend—disease, inadequate clothing, heavy loads, poor nutrition—spread rapidly throughout East Africa, and not surprisingly, many Africans tried to avoid being pressed into service [27]. French recruitment efforts in West Africa also met with considerable resistance, as demonstrated by both Echenberg [13] and Lunn [34] in their social histories.

The British mobilization of distant colonial troops from their expansive empire for war in Africa, as well as the French mobilization of troops to fight on the Western Front, should also be taken into consideration in any analysis of the effects of the war on Africa. On this issue Downes [12], Clifford [9], Farwell's *Armies of the Raj* [15], and Lawford & Catto [31] give details of how British colonial forces from the Gold Coast, Nigeria, and India deployed to East Africa. Brief summaries of the French deployment of West African troops appear in the previously mentioned *Journal of African History* article by Andrew and Kanya-Forstner [1], as well as in Killingray's chapter [29] in the Strachan general history of World War I. Most interesting and moving in this realm, however, is Lunn's short section on the West African recruits' overseas voyage to France, which is based on the oral histories of troops who took part in the deployment [34]. The dimensions of Africa's mobilization for war are quite striking once one begins to examine the sources closely. Hardly any region was ultimately left untouched.

As should be evident by this point, a reader interested in understanding how the war in Africa was actually fought will need to use a variety of sources, both secondary and primary. Fortunately, the preponderance of literature on World War I in Africa focuses on precisely this aspect. Most of the key sources have already been mentioned elsewhere in this chapter. Farwell's *The Great War in Africa* [16] does an good job of summarizing chronologically the major battles and confrontations in the war, beginning with Togo and Cameroon, moving to Southwest Africa, and then East Africa. He takes considerable effort to explain the minimal, but nonetheless fascinating, naval and air operations of the war. For example, he devotes an entire chapter to the saga of the *Königsberg,* a German cruiser deployed to support the East Africa campaign. After escaping from the coast into the Rufiji River delta, the *Königsberg* was blockaded by British warships, then pursued by the British monitors *Severn* and *Mersey* into the interior. The German cruiser was finally destroyed in July 1915. Other naval battles occurring between the Germans and British on Lake Tanganyika, also discussed at length in Farwell's work, inspired the novel and film versions of *The African Queen.*

Air power was also employed in the East Africa campaign, both by the Germans and the British. For detailed discussion of German attempts to use zeppelins to resupply General Lettow-Vorbeck, see Douglas H. Robinson's book-length study entitled *The Zeppelin in Combat: A History of the German Naval Airship Division, 1912–1918* [48]. Farwell [16] also covers the zeppelins as well as the British employment of aircraft for reconnaissance, particularly in locating the *Königsberg.* For those more interested in the technical details of troop movements and campaigns, Hordern [26], Moberley [38], and Moyse-Bartlett [40] make the best starting points. From there, the unit histories on individual regiments mentioned above add specificity. Lettow-Vorbeck [32] and Meinertzhagen [36] are both essential to understanding the mundane details of daily life on the march. Because Lettow-Vorbeck's style of guerrilla warfare is considered both pioneering and a work of genius among military historians, it is worth spending some time with his memoir. In addition to these book-length accounts of the fighting in Africa, several important articles may be helpful to understanding the key battles [6, 35, 50]. Unfortunately though, the nature of the war did not lend itself to traditional set battles, a fact that the available literature clearly reflects. Once these types of sources have been exhausted, one must turn to archival sources, which are quite rich with detail on the various campaigns, if one has the wherewithal to put them to use. These sources, located in various archives in Europe and Africa, include war diaries, official and unofficial correspondence, field reports, campaign maps, and similar items. The best way to begin locating such sources is by perusing the bibliographies of works mentioned in this article, and by using research handbooks such as the *Official Military Historical Offices and Sources,* edited by Robin Higham [24]. See also his *Official Histories,* published in 1970 [23].

Tropical diseases and the myriad challenges of fighting in a tropical environment, which Farwell collectively labels "The True Enemy," played a major role in how the war was fought. His chapter on this subject in *The Great War in Africa* [16] describes how the overwhelmingly debilitating disease environment of East Africa posed a serious impediment to military operations for both sides. Since European medical supplies or facilities were not readily accessible, particularly after Lettow-Vorbeck began his retreat out of German East Africa and the war became increasingly mobile, troops had to make do with whatever supplies they could scrounge from defeated enemy forces or from local communities. The disease problem was exacerbated by the lack of adequate nutrition, especially for African troops and porters. While disease was, of course, a factor in the European theater of World War I, its centrality in the conduct of the war in Africa makes it an important aspect to consider in studying this subject [14, 16, 27].

South Africa's position in this conflict also bears special importance in understanding the war in Africa, as well as the future development of South African politics. South African forces invaded Southwest Africa in September 1914 [16]. Before they could embark on the total conquest of German territory, however, they had to put down Afrikaner-led rebellions in the Boer republics of Orange Free State and Transvaal, which began in October 1914. These revolts grew out of virulent Afrikaner opposition to the British expectation that South Africa would fight against the Germans, with whom many Afrikaners sympathized. The resistance was finally put down in December 1914, and the South Africans turned their attention again to German Southwest Africa. German Southwest Africa fell to the Union of South Africa forces in July 1915, allowing these forces to now move to East Africa, under General Smuts' command, to supplement the Allied forces against Lettow-Vorbeck. Many of the South African troops employed in the campaign against Lettow-Vorbeck were blacks, as opposed to in Southwest Africa, where they were mainly white. Here again, Farwell's book provides the best starting point for those interested in the South African role in the war in Africa, and his bibliography lists several works that explore the theme more deeply [16]. Killingray's bibliography in Strachan also lists readings relevant to understanding South Africa's role [29]. Albert Grundlingh also explores the impact of the war on South African blacks in an article in Page's edited volume [43], although he devotes his attention to labor, political, and economic effects and does not discuss combatants.

The demobilization of forces in Africa has received very little attention, even in comparison to the overall state of scholarship in the field. This lacuna is a shame, because without an understanding of the demobilization period, it is very difficult to argue conclusively that the experience of the war in Africa made an impact on politics, economics, and social interactions of the interwar period in Africa. The relevant references are generally scattered and not very detailed, and even the otherwise useful writings by such authors as Lettow-Vorbeck [32], Farwell [16], and Hordern [26] do not help much with this topic. This field, therefore, will be wide open to researchers interested in studying it. Here it is only possible to recommend a few historians who include discussions of demobilization in their larger works. First, John Iliffe [27] broadly examines the consequences of the First World War in Tanganyika, touching on religious, economic, and political issues generated by the experience of war. His approach is a fine example of how such history can be reconstructed through use of diverse archival sources as well as more unconventional evidence. For example, he draws on Terence Ranger's research into "dance societies" of eastern Africa, arguing that "Those who returned [from the war] found an outlet for the frustrations of defeat in *beni* dance societies" [27]. His discussion of the transition to British mandatory control of the colony is also useful in explaining who most benefited politically and economically from the change in colonial leadership. As for the Senegalese troops deployed by France, Lunn's book [34] again provides interesting insights into their perceptions and expectations, as well as their growing political consciousness, as reflected in the formation of the Veterans'

Association. This organization would have "profound repercussions" on Sene-galese politics in the interwar period. For British colonial troops, Moyse-Bartlett's unit history [40] has a short relevant section, as does Clifford's [9]. Parsons' social history considers how King's Army Rifles veterans' expectations of greater political freedom and economic prosperity clashed with the reality of postwar government plans [45]. Additionally, although his coverage of the issue is also cursory, the conclusion of Leonard Mosley's book *Duel for Kilimanjaro* [39] is a vivid readable narrative of Lettow-Vorbeck's surrender and of the days following, in which the *Schutztruppe* were disbanded and the Germans returned home. Finally, Melvin Page's introduction to *Africa and the First World War* [43] poses thoughtful conclusions about what the war in Africa means in the context of world history. These few sources must suffice until further primary research is done on the interwar period in Africa.

FURTHER RESEARCH

Although this chapter has hinted at some of the areas needing further research, it remains now to present those in further detail. First, while there are a number of comprehensive historical studies of the German colonial era in Africa, almost all of these end in 1914 with the onset of the war. Furthermore, while works such as those mentioned in this chapter present clear pictures of the war from the European perspective, they do not do the same justice to African perspectives (nor did these authors have this as an objective). Consequently, the most important potential additions to this field would be social histories of World War I in East Africa that account for the lives and experiences of the thousands of Africans who fought the war, or who inhabited the regions involved in the fighting. Although Hermann Hiery [22] has done this type of research and analysis for Germany's Pacific colonies, nothing like his book has been done for its African colonies. Archival sources suited to researching this topic are available in at least Germany, England, and Tanzania, and perhaps in other countries as well, to support such a project. A related subject that would benefit from a book-length treatment is the history of the *Schutztruppe* of the German colonies similar to those by Echenberg [13] and Parsons [45]. The focus of such a work should be to uncover the lives of the troops who fought for the Germans not only in the war, but in the prewar period as well. What motivated them to enlist? What types of relationships did they form with their German leaders, and with their fellow soldiers [20]? What kinds of ideas about war-fighting and survival in the tropics were exchanged between the various groups involved in the fighting? How did they fit back into society after the war ended? We know so little about these troops in comparison to those who fought in Europe, yet their wartime experiences were certainly no less dramatic. These are some of the questions that need to be answered if we are to more completely comprehend the effects of the war in Africa.

Comparative studies of the various experiences of European, African, and Asian troops in World War I would also enhance this historiography tremendously. Such studies would make it possible for scholars to speak more authoritatively on how World War I in Africa may have affected later military decisions on how to manage colonial forces in peace and war. Even potentially more significant would be the contribution of such studies to wider questions about warfare in world history. Did World War I in Africa contribute anything special to the conduct of future warfare? Did it change how Africans, Europeans, and Asians regarded one another within the colonial context? The more we know about the people who fought the war, the more we can attempt to answer these questions.

A third area where fruitful research could be done is in unearthing the role of women in the African war. Although oblique references to women as camp followers and petty traders appear in Lettow-Vorbeck's memoirs [32] and in Iliffe's general history of Tanzania [27], and Parsons devotes a chapter of his book to "Army Women and Military Families" [45], a comprehensive study of women in the war has yet to be accomplished. Such a project will require serious archival research, which may, in the end, yield only minimal information on their roles. However, information does exist, and it should be exploited. Not only black African women have been ignored, though. Women of European descent in southern Africa and settler women in the colonies have also not received much scholarly attention [7]. Given the proliferation of works concerning the roles of women in Europe and the United States during the war, a scholarly portrait of African women and how they lived the war would be a welcome addition to the field.

In the area of political and diplomatic history, further study needs to be done on the level of communication between colonial representatives, military leaders, and European foreign or colonial offices in the months leading to the outbreak of war [59]. It would also be noteworthy to discover to what extent Africans in the colonies knew about the European crisis, how they interpreted it in their local settings, and whether or not they anticipated the tremendous impact it would have on their lives. Did they have particular aspirations for the postwar period, and if so, what were they?

More systematic study of the medical and disease history of the war in Africa could also provide substantive material to improve on current understanding of the regional peculiarities of the different theaters of war. Philip Curtin's *Disease and Empire: The Health of European Troops in the Conquest of Africa* [10], like so many important studies of the colonial period, ends in 1914. A similar study covering the war years and the aftermath would assist scholars in relating disease to the conduct of the war in Africa, particularly since Western militaries often pioneered in tropical medicine. Furthermore, since the 1918–1919 influenza epidemic affected Africa along with other parts of the world, such a study could enhance current assessments of how the epidemic changed postwar Africa. The researcher might begin searching for this type of historical information in indexes to medical journals.

Accomplishment of the suggested research on the war in Africa will take years, but it is a rich field that is certainly worth exploring for the potential contributions it can make in broadening the historiography. Because study of the war in Africa can be approached from so many different perspectives, and because it provides such a ready contrast to the war in Europe, there is little justification for its current status as an understudied field. For scholars who wish to conduct further study on a wide range of topics within the larger heading of the war in Africa, there is, without question, plenty of room.

BIBLIOGRAPHY

1. Andrew, C. M., and A. S. Kanya-Forstner, "France, Africa, and the First World War," *Journal of African History,* XIX, I (1978), 11–23.

2. Austen, Ralph A., *Northwest Tanzania Under German and British Rule: Colonial Policy and Tribal Politics, 1889–1939.* New Haven: Yale University Press, 1968.

3. Boahen, A. Adu, ed., *UNESCO General History of Africa Volume VII: Africa Under Colonial Domination 1880–1935.* Berkeley, CA: James Currey, 1990, 132–42.

4. Boell, Ludwig, *Die Operationen in Ostafrika, Weltkrieg 1914–18.* Hamburg: Walter Dachert, 1952.

5. Callwell, C. E., *Small Wars: Their Principles and Practice.* Wakefield, UK: EP Publishing, 1976.

6. Charlewood, Commander C. J., "Naval Actions on the Tanganyika Coast, 1914–1917," *Tanganyika Notes and Records* 54 (March 1960) and 55 (September 1960).

7. Chaudhuri, Nupur, and Margaret Strobel, eds., *Western Women and Imperialism.* Bloomington: Indiana University Press, 1992.

8. Chickering, Roger, *Imperial Germany: A Historiographical Companion.* Westport, CT: Greenwood, 1996.

9. Clifford, Sir Hugh, *The Gold Coast Regiment in the East African Campaign.* Nashville, TN: Battery Press, 1995.

10. Curtin, Philip, *Disease and Empire: The Health of European Troops in the Conquest of Africa.* Cambridge: Cambridge University Press, 1998.

11. Dinesen, Isak, *Out of Africa and Shadows on the Grass.* New York: Vintage International Books, 1989, 255–62.

12. Downes, Captain W. D., *With the Nigerians in German East Africa.* London: Methuen & Co, 1919.

13. Echenberg, Myron, *Colonial Conscripts: The Tirailleurs Sénégalais in French West Africa, 1857–1960.* Portsmouth, NH: Heinemann, 1991.

14. Ellison, James G., " 'A Fierce Hunger': Tracing the Impacts of the 1918–1919 Influenza Pandemic in Southwest Tanzania," in *The Spanish Flu Pandemic of 1918: New Perspectives,* Howard Phillips and David Killingray, eds. London: Routledge, 2001.

15. Farwell, Byron, *Armies of the Raj: From the Great Indian Mutiny to Independence: 1858–1947.* New York: W. W. Norton, 1989.

16. Farwell, Byron, *The Great War in Africa 1914–1918.* New York: W. W. Norton, 1986.

17. Fischer, Fritz, *Germany's Aims in the First World War.* New York: W. W. Norton, 1961.

18. Gann, L. H., and Peter Duignan, *The Rulers of German Africa 1884–1914.* Stanford: Stanford University Press, 1977.

19. Gardner, Brian, *German East: The Story of the First World War in East Africa.* London: Cassell, 1963.

20. Geary, Christaud M., "Political Dress: German-Style Military Attire and Colonial Politics in Bamum," in *African Crossroads: Intersections Between History and Anthropology in Cameroon,* eds. Ian Fowler and David Zeitlyn. Providence, RI: Berghahn, 1996, 165–92.

21. Heggoy, Alf Andrew, and John M. Haar, *The Military in Imperial History: The French Connection.* New York: Garland, 1984.

22. Hiery, Hermann Joseph, *The Neglected War: The German South Pacific and the Influence of World War I.* Honolulu: University of Hawai'i Press, 1995.

23. Higham, Robin, ed., *Official Histories: Essays and Bibliographies from Around the World.* Manhattan, KS: Kansas State University, 1970.

24. Higham, Robin, ed., *Official Military Historical Offices and Sources Volume I: Europe, Africa, the Middle East, and India.* Westport, CT: Greenwood, 2000.

25. Hodges, G. W. T., "African Manpower Statistics for the British Forces in East Africa, 1914–1918," *Journal of African History,* XIX, I (1978): 101–16.

26. Hordern, Lieutenant Colonel Charles, *History of the Great War: Military Operations, East Africa.* London: His Majesty's Stationery Office, 1941.

27. Iliffe, John, *A Modern History of Tanganyika.* Cambridge: Cambridge University Press, 1979.

28. Joll, James, *The Origins of the First World War,* 2nd ed. London: Longman, 1992.

29. Killingray, David, "The War in Africa," in *World War I: A History.* Oxford: Oxford University Press, 1998.

30. Koponen, Juhani, *Development for Exploitation: German Colonial Policies in Mainland Tanzania, 1884–1914.* Hamburg: Lit Verlag, 1994.

31. Lawford, Lieutenant Colonel J. P. and Major W. E. Catto, eds., *Solah Punjab: The History of the 16th Punjab Regiment.* Aldershot: Gale & Polden, 1967.

32. Lettow-Vorbeck, General Paul von, *My Reminiscences of East Africa.* London: Hurst & Blackett, 1920.

33. Louis, William Roger, *Ruanda-Urundi 1884–1919.* Oxford: Clarendon Press, 1963.

34. Lunn, Joe, *Memoirs of the Maelstrom: A Senegalese Oral History of the First World War.* Portsmouth, NH: Heinemann, 1999.

35. Magee, Frank J., "Transporting a Navy Through the Jungles of Africa in Wartime," *National Geographic,* October 1922.

36. Meinertzhagen, Colonel R. *Army Diary, 1899–1926.* Edinburgh: Oliver & Boyd, 1960.

37. Miller, Charles, *Battle for the Bundu: The First World War in East Africa.* New York: Macmillan, 1974.

38. Moberly, Frederick James, *Official History of the Great War: Military Operations, Togoland and the Camerouns, 1914–1916.* London: His Majesty's Stationery Office, 1931.

39. Mosley, Leonard, *Duel for Kilimanjaro.* New York: Ballantine, 1963.

40. Moyse-Bartlett, Lieutenant Colonel H., *The King's African Rifles: A Study in the Military History of East and Central Africa, 1890–1945.* Aldershot: Gale and Polden, 1956.

41. Njeuma, Martin, ed., *Introduction to the History of Cameroon in the Nineteenth and Twentieth Centuries.* New York: St. Martin's, 1989.

42. Ofcansky, Thomas P., and Rodger Yeager, *Historical Dictionary of Tanzania,* 2d ed., Lanham, MD: Scarecrow, 1997.

43. Page, Melvin E., ed., *Africa and the First World War.* New York: St. Martin's, 1987.

44. Page, Melvin E., ed., "The War of Thangata: Nyasaland and the East African Campaign, 1914–1918," *Journal of African History,* XIX, I (1978): 87–100.

45. Parsons, Timothy H., *The African Rank-and-File: Social Implications of Colonial Military Service in the King's African Rifles, 1902–1964.* Portsmouth, NH: 1999.

46. Pogge von Strandmann, Hartmut, and Alison Smith, "The German Empire in Africa and British Perspectives: A Historiographical Essay," in Prosser Gifford and William Roger Louis, eds., *Britain and Germany in Africa.* New Haven: Yale University Press, 1967.

47. Rathbone, Richard, "World War I and Africa: Introduction," in *Journal of African History,* XIX, I (1979).

48. Roberts, Allen F., "Insidious Conquests"" Wartime Politics Along the South-western Shore of Lake Tanganyika," in Melvin E. Page, ed., *Africa and the First World War.* New York: St. Martin's Press, 1987, 186–213.

49. Robinson, Douglas H. *The Zeppelin in Combat: A History of the German Naval Airship Division, 1912–1918.* London: G. T. Foulis, 1966.

50. Russell, Major A., "The Landing at Tanga, 1914," *Tanganyika Notes and Records,* 1962.

51. Savage, Donald C., and J. Forbes Munro, "Carrier Corps Recruitment in the British East Africa Protectorate 1914–1918," *Journal of African History,* VII, 2 (1966): 313–42.

52. Smith Woodruff D., *The German Colonial Empire.* Chapel Hill, NC: University of North Carolina press, 1978.

53. Stevenson, David, *The First World War and International Politics.* Oxford: Oxford University Press, 1988.

54. Stoecker, Helmuth, *German Imperialism in Africa.* London: C. Hurst & Co, 1986.

55. Summers, Anne, and R. W. Johnson, "World War I Conscription and Social Change in Guinea," *Journal of African History* XIX, I (1978): 25–38.

56. Thurman, Judith, *Isak Dinesen: The Life of a Storyteller.* New York: St. Martin's, 1982.

57. Von Herff, Michael, " 'They Walk through the Fire like the Blondest German.' African Soldiers Serving the Kaiser in German East Africa (1888–1914)." M.A. thesis, University of Montreal, 1991.

58. Young, F. Brett, *Marching on Tanga: With General Smuts in East Africa.* London: William Collins Sons, 1919.

59. Zirkel, Kirsten, "Military Power in German Colonial Policy" in *Guardians of Empire: The Armed Forces of the Colonial Powers c. 1700–1964.* Manchester: Manchester University Press, 1999.

14

Japan

Thomas W. Burkman

On August 23, 1914, Japan formally declared war on Imperial Germany. Four days later, the declaration was extended to Austria-Hungary. Japan's military role in the Great War was limited to modest and nearly bloodless campaigns in Asia and to convoy escort in the Mediterranean. Nonetheless, Japan was invited to serve in the Supreme War Council, and through its belligerency positioned itself to act as one of the Big Five at the Paris Peace Conference. Historians of the First World War generally focus on the European and African theaters and give scant reference to Japan and China; while those historians—both Western and Japanese—who treat Japanese military and diplomatic history of the twentieth century are naturally drawn to the pathos of the 1930s and the Pacific War. But in the broad framework of modern international history, Japan's activity in World War I is a chapter too significant to overlook.

THE PLACE OF WORLD WAR I IN JAPAN'S MODERN HISTORY

By the turn of the century, Japan had established itself as a modern nation-state of which the powers of the world took serious notice. Since the Meiji

The author acknowledges the assistance of several scholars in the preparation of this chapter: Frederick Dickinson of the University of Pennsylvania, Paul Guinn of the University at Buffalo, Hirama Yoichi of the Japanese Defense Academy, Nakanishi Hiroshi of Kyoto University, the late David Evans of the University of Richmond, and editor Robin Higham. Financial assistance was provided by Hamilton College. In this chapter, Japanese and Chinese personal names are written with family name preceding given name.

Restoration Japan had undergone a remarkable metamorphosis from a posture of minimum intercourse with the outside world to a position of regional power. Having withstood the threat of overt colonization and surmounted the obstacle of unequal commercial treaties, Japan allied itself in 1902 with Great Britain, the world's leading naval power. The Anglo-Japanese Alliance would remain the anchor of Japanese diplomacy until it was dismantled at the Washington Conference in 1922. Victory in 1905 over Russia accorded Japan titular recognition as a power, eighth among the "eight great powers." The years since the Russo-Japanese War had witnessed further advances in Japanese material power. Whereas in 1905 Japan had depended on European dockyards for first-class battleships, by 1919 Japan was building oil-fired dreadnoughts superior to those of every country except the United States. The circumstances of the European war provided Japan with an excellent opportunity to act out its status as a power, secure and extend its political and economic interests on the Asian continent, and assert diplomatic influence beyond the regional confines of East Asia.

In the war Japan followed the precepts of traditional imperialism. With the outbreak of the conflict, European imperial powers found their very existence at stake and themselves incapable of defending their far-flung territorial bases and supplying their Asian markets. Japan astutely avoided involvement in the European theater and stepped in to fill the military and economic vacuum in Asia. She had learned hard lessons in the Triple Intervention at the close of the Sino-Japanese War of 1894–1895, when a postwar power play by a coalition of European imperialists had forced Japan to retrocede territory it had seized on the battlefield. Hence during the World War Japan prepared for the postwar settlement by physically occupying and holding the territory it claimed and buttressing its demands by a web of wartime secret treaties. She was not averse to carrying out secret wartime negotiations with the Central Powers. At the same time Japan took pains to secure the Entente powers' acquiescence in its military operations by acting under the rubric of the Anglo-Japanese Alliance and joint Allied ventures. Japan consistently denied motives of outright territorial conquest, and paid appropriate lip service to the liberal internationalist pronouncements by Western statesmen concerning war aims and a new postwar order.

The war accelerated structural changes in the world's economy that benefited Japan at the expense of Europe. With commercial relations between Europe and the Orient suddenly eclipsed, Japanese enterprise stepped in to supply manufactured goods and investment capital for China and new markets like India and Southeast Asia. The war hastened a long-term shift in the composition of Japan's exports from textiles to heavy industrial goods. Shipbuilding rose rapidly to become Japan's fourth largest export item by 1917, and Japan became the major foreign supplier of arms and munitions to Imperial Russia. In China's Shandong (Shantung) province, Japanese entrepreneurs lost no time taking over existing German ventures and establishing new investments in salt production, rice and flour milling, canning, and spinning. Japan's share of the total Chinese import market rose from 20.4 to 36.3 percent between 1913 and 1919, while that of Britain fell from 16.5 to 9.5 percent, never to regain its prewar standing. Trans-

Pacific trade also prospered, with Japanese exports to the United States multiplying threefold and imports fivefold during the war years. The wartime industrial boom fostered a nouveau riche class and a fledgling labor union movement. Business interests, acting through the centrist political parties, made their influence felt in domestic politics and foreign policy. Just before the 1918 Armistice, Japan's first genuine party cabinet took office.

Although Japanese leaders sought to keep the nation's expansionist activities within the bounds of "respectable imperialism," bold action in the cases of the Twenty-one Demands (1915) and the Siberian Intervention (1918–1922) led to Allied suspicions and accusations of Japanese opportunism and adventurism. A new spirit of modern nationalism was spreading in China, which was neither understood nor tolerated by Japan. As the war upset the balance of external forces in China, this nationalism grew increasingly anti-Japanese in its expression. At the end of the war the Chinese took to the streets in defense of their national self-determination. Among foreign diplomats in China, the Americans were particularly bitter in their condemnation of Japan. Japan's overzealous troop commitment in Siberia and unwillingness to withdraw at the end of the war fed the store of suspicion toward Tokyo in the mind of the diplomatic community, some members of which believed that Japanese real sympathies lay with the Central Powers. Entente leaders were aware of secret Japanese-German talks in Beijing, Stockholm, and Tianjin (Tientsin) concerning a separate peace. During the war the American press charged that Japan was colluding with Germany in Mexico. By 1918 enough evidence of infidelity in deed and spirit had accumulated to evoke widespread allegations among the Entente that Japan, while a co-belligerent, was an ally in name only. The resulting diplomatic isolation would hobble Japanese initiatives at the Paris Peace Conference. The relatively internationalist policies Japan pursued in the decade following the Washington Conference in part obscured the Kaiser-like image Japan acquired during the war. But the smoldering embers of deep distrust that had been ignited in the World War I era would break into open conflagration in China during the grave decade of the 1930s.

JAPAN'S MILITARY ACTIVITY IN THE WAR

Japan declared war on Germany on 23 August 1914 on the basis of the Anglo-Japanese Alliance. The letter of the Alliance did not obligate Japan to enter a war that threatened Britain in Europe. Nonetheless, the cabinet and Anglophile Foreign Minister Kato Takaaki reasoned that the relationship with the British Empire and the opportunities that war among the European imperialists presented made it advisable to join the fray in the spirit of the pact. Japan's attention immediately focused on German naval facilities and economic enterprises in China's Shandong Peninsula, where Germany had leased the port of Qingdao (Tsingtao or Tsingtau) and the surrounding Jiaozhou (Kiaochow) Bay since 1898. During Germany's sixteen-year occupation, German investors had established banks, mining operations, industries, and a rail line to Jinan (Tsinan). The

German presence in the peninsula was the major foreign impediment to Japanese leadership in trade and investment in North China.

Governor Alfred Meyer-Waldeck was ordered by Berlin to defend Qingdao "to the bitter end," so he ignored a Japanese ultimatum to surrender. Japanese troops, aided in token by one British battalion and an Indian half-battalion, commenced a full-scale invasion on the north shore of the peninsula on 2 September. After two months of a quite leisurely overland trek and siege of Qingdao, 60,000 invaders overwhelmed 4,000 stubborn German defenders. Japanese naval losses in the attack on Jiaozhou Bay included an old cruiser, the *Takachiko,* a destroyer, a torpedo boat, and three trawlers. Japanese casualties on land and sea numbered 1,700.

Meanwhile, Japanese, British, and Australian warships routed remnants of the Kaiser's Asiatic fleet from the German Pacific islands. Some German vessels met their end at the hands of the British in the Falkland Islands as they attempted to sail home. In accordance with an agreement reached between the Japanese and British navies in October, Japan occupied the Marshalls, Marianas, Carolines, and Palaus—those archipelagoes north of the equator. By December 1914 the war against Germany was effectively over in East Asia and the Pacific. The Qingdao and Pacific episodes permanently stripped Germany of colonial holdings in East Asia and the western Pacific. For Japan it was a clear case of minimum expenditure and maximum gain.

The Empire then took the diplomatic offensive to secure the land and rights it had taken. Among the notorious Twenty-one Demands that Japan forced on a fragmented China in 1915 was a Chinese commitment to support Japan's claim to Shandong in the postwar settlement. Japan's aggressive diplomacy in the Demands was not out of character for a power seeking to enlarge its sphere of influence in China in the early twentieth century. However, the wartime inability of the European powers to counterbalance Japanese initiatives made the Europeans fearful for their own stake in China, and the Chinese government adroitly capitalized on European and American apprehensions. The Demands turned out to be an international public relations fiasco for Japan. A 20-million-yen loan to the warlord regime of Duan Qirui (Tuan Ch'i-jui) in September 1918 produced another Chinese pledge to back the Japanese acquisition of German leases in Shandong. In early 1917 Japan received secret assurances from Britain, France, Russia, and Italy that they would support Tokyo's position on the disposition of Shandong and the Pacific Islands, in exchange for Japanese convoying of Allied shipping in the Indian Ocean and the Mediterranean—a service that the Imperial Navy provided. Japan consistently pressured China not to declare war on Germany and thereby secure a voice at the postwar conference. However, China did join the Allies on American insistence in 1917.

Before the war ended Japan embarked upon one final military adventure, the Siberian Intervention. The power vacuum created in Russian Siberia by the fall of the Czarist and Provisional governments presented Japan with a golden opportunity to detach the eastern provinces from Muscovite control, create a new sphere of Japanese influence, and displace the Russian presence in northern

Manchuria. Moreover, Japanese shared with Britons and Americans the widespread misperception of the victorious Bolsheviks as disguised German agents. Secret Sino-Japanese military and naval agreements were signed in May 1918 for joint defense against "the gradual extension of enemy influence toward the east." These accords gave the Japanese army freedom to operate in any Chinese territory adjacent to Siberia, and helped pave the way for the Siberian expedition to begin in August. Japanese moderates succeeded in requiring that the expedition be an Allied venture. But Japan's overzealous troop commitment (70,000) for the rescue of isolated Czech army units increased the store of suspicion toward Tokyo in the minds of Western diplomats. Well after troops of the United States, Britain, and France were withdrawn at the time of the Armistice, the Japanese army remained in control of the Trans-Siberian corridor as far west as Lake Baikal. Eventually, Bolshevik massacres of Japanese soldiers combined with a postwar economic recession in Japan led to public disillusionment with the Intervention. The last personnel of this fruitless venture returned to Japan in 1922; northern Sakhalin was not evacuated until 1925.

IMPACT OF THE WAR ON JAPANESE MILITARY, NAVAL, AND DIPLOMATIC THEORY AND OPERATIONS

The most significant factors influencing Japanese military thinking were the temporary demise of Russian power and the global assertiveness of the United States. The Imperial Defense Plan of 1907, which posited Russia as Japan's major threat, was displaced in 1918 by a Plan that identified the United States as the most likely future enemy. While Wilsonian defense of Chinese territorial and political integrity was part of the picture, Japan reacted more concretely to the prewar and wartime growth of the U.S. Navy. The Japanese government in 1918 adopted an expansion program of eight battleships and eight battle cruisers.

Another factor was the rapid technological changes which were implemented on the battlefields of Europe. During the war, Japanese active infantry divisions increased by two to twenty-one. But Japan's arms and military training procedures remained pre-1914 vintage. Military attachés in Europe warned that the Empire lagged behind Britain in armed air development and Germany in submarine technology—innovations that could give an enemy the deciding edge over Japan's warships and island defenses. Tanaka Giichi, who became War Minister in September 1918, pressed successfully to implement new technologies. Ugaki Kazushige continued this emphasis in the following decade.

Japanese naval building had undergone abrupt change just after the Russo-Japanese War, when the first capital ships were laid down in Japanese dockyards and dreadnought size and design became the rule of the day. When the 27,000-ton battleship *Kongo* was launched in 1912 in Britain with eight 14-inch guns, she was the most formidable and superbly designed capital ship in the world when completed. This was the last Japanese capital ship ordered from a foreign yard. Japan had constructed 30,000-ton dreadnoughts at home during the Great War, in a building duel with the United States that did not subside until 1922.

This new era of capital ship construction was marked by a shift from coal to oil fuel. This development was particularly unsettling to Japan. The nation had adequate domestic supplies of steaming coal, but was almost totally dependent on foreign sources for oil. The acquisition of a new leasehold on the Asian mainland and control of Pacific archipelagoes—coupled with the continuing expedition in Siberia—also made the defense of extended sea lanes a vital concern.

During the First World War Japan suffered diplomatic isolation from the powers as a consequence of strong-arm tactics in China, secret negotiations with Germany, and an independent agenda in Siberia. Japanese expansionist ambitions were all too evident in a world tired of aggression and war and in shock from the horrors of the trenches in France. Japan's Kaiser-like image offset the careful territorial and treaty advantages Japan had constructed during the conflict in preparation for the postwar peace conference. Getting in line with the New World Order of the Western democracies would not be easy for Japan

THE PARIS PEACE CONFERENCE AND AFTER

Still wedded to the Old Diplomacy, Japan posited the displacement of German power in East Asia as the major objective for the postwar settlement. This aim was to be accomplished through the annexation of former German Pacific islands and the acquisition of Germany's Jiaozhou leasehold and economic rights in Shantung Province. For the Western delegations, the establishment of the League of Nations led the conference agenda. Japan exhibited indifference and inadequate preparation on the League question, a posture that served her well in unintended ways. At Paris President Woodrow Wilson had to accommodate Japanese demands to secure Japan's participation in the League. In response to Japanese public sentiment, an international statement disavowing racial discrimination was later added to Japan's conference goals.

Japan had partial success on the Pacific island issue by being assigned the mandatory power for the islands north of the Equator, though not in full sovereignty as she had hoped. Despite two efforts to moderate the wording of the demand on race, Japan was overwhelmed in this foray by the British dominions and the United States, despite a majority vote in the League of Nations Commission in Japan's favor. Stung in the equality bid, Japan was prepared to bolt the conference if it did not gain satisfaction on Shandong. The wartime secret treaties concerning the disposition of the former German leasehold in the end carried more weight than impassioned Chinese pleas for immediate restoration to China. In sum, Japan suffered setbacks on the equality and Pacific island issues, and secured its aims regarding Shandong only with excruciating difficulty. Japan signed the Treaty at Versailles—China did not—and Japan became a charter member of the League of Nations and a permanent member of the League Council.

During the months in Paris, the Japanese delegation became poignantly aware that its training, preparation, linguistic ability, and logistical support were not up to form for a major power. The mission lacked experts on critical economic and labor issues. It had hardly enough staff to attend the myriad commission meetings, let alone carry out research, drafting, private negotiations, communication, and public relations functions. Younger diplomats at Paris began the Kakushin Doshikai [Reform Fraternity] demanding the recruitment and promotion of men of talent, adequate provision of diplomats' expenses, and strengthening of the Foreign Ministry's departmental structure. A number of postconference alterations resulted from this inside pressure. A revised entrance examination system admitted as many new recruits (121) in the four years after World War I as had entered in the preceding quarter century. An Information Bureau was created, and separate Asia and Europe-America Bureaus replaced the Political Affairs Bureau. New departments were established to handle the implementation of the Versailles Treaty and relations with the League of Nations. Japan created diplomatic machinery commensurate with the increased international stature the Great War brought to the nation.

In the aftermath of the Peace Conference, the Foreign Ministry and the ruling Seiyukai Party in Tokyo reasoned that in the postwar era the Empire had no choice but to avoid conflict with the world program of the major powers. As a result, Japan threw its lot in with the new League of Nations and began disarmament preparations in anticipation of the Washington Naval Conference of 1921–1922. The army throughout the decade until 1927 pursued the moderate policies of modernization, reduction of personnel, cooperation with the political parties, and avoiding a challenge to the framework of Anglo-American cooperation.

BIBLIOGRAPHIES

The search for Western-language writings on Japan's role in World War I begins in bibliographies of diplomatic history dealing with East Asia and Japan. The Beers and Dingman chapters in Ernest R. May and James C. Thomson Jr., ed., *American-East Asian Relations* (1972) [88] cover the beginning of the war through the Washington Conference. In James W. Morley, ed., *Japan's Foreign Policy, 1868–1941* (1974) [92], a chapter on military foreign policies by James B. Crowley has a section on the Great War. Doctoral dissertations can be located through Frank Joseph Shulman's exhaustive annotated bibliographies of Western-language doctoral dissertations on Japan—*Japan and Korea: An Annotated Bibliography of Doctoral Dissertations in Western Languages, 1877–1969* (1970) [115] and *Doctoral Dissertations on Japan and Korea, 1969–1979* (1982) [114]—and the sixteen volumes of his bibliographical journal *Doctoral Dissertations on Asia* (1975–1996) [113] that update coverage through 1992/93.

The A. G. S. Enser bibliography (1979) [37] is of little usefulness except in that it lists several contemporary, wartime writings under its subject categories of Japan, China, Siberia, and Shantung. These works were typically published in London and display an anti-Japanese bias.

The Japanese-language literature can be identified through the Morley volume (above) and in the very thorough and authoritatively annotated chapter by

Ikei, Inouye, and Asada in Sadao Asada, ed., *Japan and the World, 1853–1952: A Bibliographic Guide to Japanese Scholarship in Foreign Relations* (1989) [4]. Shinji Kondo, *Japanese Military History: A Guide to the Literature* (1984) [74] has a short segment covering Japan-language writings on the Taisho Period (1912–1926). Researchers also have available bibliographies in monographs, such as Frederick Dickinson's *War and National Reinvention* (1999) [32], based primarily on Japanese-language materials.

GENERAL SURVEYS

Few of the general works on the Great War venture beyond the European theater. There are partial exceptions. Luigi Albertini's *The Origins of the War of 1914* (1952) [2] includes in the third volume extensive quotations of treaties involving Japan and Anglo-Japanese diplomatic correspondence, but little analysis. David Stevenson in his *The First World War and International Politics* (1988) [117] includes a short and intelligent discussion of Japanese war aims and diplomatic strategies in entering the war, in the Twenty-one Demands, and in the Siberian Intervention. He weaves Japan into the global picture of shifting politics during the war. The emphasis is diplomatic, and not military. *Germany's Aims in the First World War* (1967) by Fritz Fischer [41] devotes a section to the secret negotiations between Germany and Japan for a separate peace. Germany dangled before Japan the cession of Qingdao and the Pacific islands and a free hand in China, in exchange for Japanese and Russian withdrawal from the war. Nothing came of these talks. Cruttwell, in *A History of the Great War, 1914–1918* (1934) [28], is attendant to the exploits and fate of Asia-based, German cruisers like the *Emden* and the *Scharnhorst,* but says almost nothing about Japanese activities.

William Roger Louis's *Great Britain and Germany's Lost Colonies, 1914–1919* (1967) [80] stands out among the general works for its extensive treatment of the Shandong and Pacific island issues. Based primarily on British documentary sources, the book provides historical background on the nineteenth-century German acquisition of the territories, addresses the military action of 1914, and includes the diplomatic disposition of the holdings in 1919.

Surveys of Japanese international history do devote coverage to the First World War in Asia. Chapter 7 in Richard Storry's *Japan and the Decline of the West in Asia, 1894–1943* (1979) [118] is the best short treatment of the subject in its military and diplomatic aspects. Japan made significant material and diplomatic gains, but its failure to come to grips with new currents of Chinese nationalism and Wilsonian and Leninist ideology prevented Japan from capitalizing on its advances. Ian Nish, arguably the most distinguished Japanologist in Europe, looks at the diplomatic issues of the war through the views and actions of the diplomatists of the period, principally Kato Takaaki and Ishii Kikujiro. Nish's *Japanese Foreign Policy, 1869–1942* (1977) [98] is based solidly on research in Japanese and British documents, as is his *Alliance in Decline* (1972) [95], which treats in detail the impact of the war on the crucial Anglo-Japanese relationship.

Kajima Morinosuke, a diplomat-turned-historian, treats World War I extensively in the third volume of his *The Diplomacy of Japan, 1894–1922* (1976)
[63]. He provides historical narrative interspersed with useful documents translated from the original Japanese. Kajima's unique contributions are his treatments of the question of sending Japanese army and navy forces to Europe and
the issue of the Russo-Japanese secret alliance of 1917. In his *A Brief Diplomatic History of Modern Japan* (1965) [62], Kajima includes a short narrative
chapter on the war.

Two still-useful, English-language works written by Japanese scholars in the
1930s are Roy Hidemichi Akagi's *Japan's Foreign Relations, 1542–1936* (1972,
1936) [1] and Takeuchi Tatsuji's *War and Diplomacy in the Japanese Empire*
(1935) [119]. Akagi tends to be a Japanese apologist, picturing Japanese
wartime policies toward China and Siberia as benign but resulting in undeserved
friction with the United States and China. Takeuchi's five chapters on the war
and accompanying diplomacy represent the best prewar scholarship on the subject, based on Japanese published resources.

JAPAN'S ENTRY INTO THE WAR AND THE SHANDONG CAMPAIGN

The standard work is Charles B. Burdick, *The Japanese Siege of Tsingtau:
World War I in Asia* (1976) [13]. Based primarily on European sources, the book
includes a detailed bibliography which cites German and Austrian documents.
Despite the book's comprehensive subtitle, it does not deal with the Twenty-one
Demands nor the Siberian Intervention. It supersedes Jefferson Jones, *The Fall
of Tsingtau* (1971, 1915) [61], a wartime publication that is strongly anti-
Japanese in tone. Jones sees Japan's actions during the war placing China
"under the virtual domination of Japan." Peter Lowe, in *Great Britain and
Japan, 1911–1915* (1969) [81], treats the episode from a British perspective,
while Ian Nish is equally attentive to the Japanese perspective and documentary
record in *Alliance in Decline* (1972) [95]. Relevant articles are Ernest R. May,
"American Policy and Japan's Entrance into World War I" (1953) [89]; Charles
Spinks, "Japan's Entrance into the World War" (1936) [116]; Saito Seiji, "Nichi-
doku Chinto senso no kaisen gaiko" (1998) [104]; and Frederick R. Dickinson,
"Japan: Declaring War for the Anglo-Japanese Alliance" (2002) [31]. A readable, popular-level account, without documentation, is provided by British
author Edwin P. Hoyt: *The Fall of Tsingtao* (1975) [54]. Naval aspects of the
1914 campaign are covered in chapter 12 of Stephen Howarth, *The Fighting
Ships of the Rising Sun* (1983) [53]. Howarth notes that the combined force of
Japanese, British, and French vessels that participated in the landing at Qingdao
was the first ever international naval group under Japanese command. The Chinese perspective is addressed in two significant writings: Tsing Yuan, "The Japanese Intervention in Shantung during World War I" (1978) [131], and the
dissertation of Sinologist Craig Canning, "The Japanese Occupation of Shantung during World War One" (1975) [20]. The first chapter of Thomas La Far-

gue's *China and the World War* (1937) [75] treats the circumstances of the Japanese ultimatum to Germany and the military campaign across the Shandong Peninsula from the north. It is based primarily on U.S. diplomatic correspondence from Beijing.

Diplomatic aspects of the Shandong seizure and the postwar disposal of the leasehold are treated in Russell Fifield, *Woodrow Wilson and the Far East* (1952) [40]; Roy Watson Curry, *Woodrow Wilson and Far Eastern Policy, 1913–1921* (1957) [29]; and a dissertation by Harry L. Harvin, "The Far East in the Peace Conference of 1919" (1956) [45]. All are based primarily on Western language sources. Many of Curry's sources are older works of questionable veracity. It was Fifield's research that originally established that the Japanese were not bluffing in their threat to bolt the Peace Conference if their demand to retain Shandong was not met. His detailed account of the Paris negotiations is unsurpassed in its thoroughness. He ably sets the Shandong issue within the complex context of the world strategic struggle. The best writing on Japan's secret treaty activity to secure its retention of Shandong is the dissertation by Peter Berton, "The Secret Russo-Japanese Alliance of 1916" (1957) [9].

PACIFIC ISLANDS AND NAVAL OPERATIONS

The Japanese displacement of German authority in the Carolines, Palaus, Marshalls, and Marianas is described in the second chapter of Mark R. Peattie's *Nanyo: The Rise and Fall of the Japanese in Micronesia, 1885–1945* (1988) [100]. Peattie, a military historian, is firmly grounded in Japanese documentary and secondary sources supplemented by field research in the islands themselves. See also Hermann Hiery, *The Neglected War* (1995) [49]; William Roger Louis (1967) [80]; a dissertation: David Purcell, "Japanese Expansion in the South Pacific, 1895–1935" (1967) [103]; and journal articles by J. Charles Schencking [105, 106]. Hiery's work is based on archival sources in Australia, New Zealand, Micronesia, and Germany. On the peace conference decisions concerning the islands, see the dissertation by William S. Martin, Jr., "The Colonial Mandate Question at the Paris Peace Conference of 1919" (1982) [86]. Subsequent international status of the islands is treated in E. T. Williams, "Japan's Mandate in the Pacific" (1933) [126] and the classic legal treatise, Quincy Wright, *Mandates under the League of Nations* (1930) [129].

The five-volume British official naval history, Henry Newbolt, *History of the Great War: Naval Operations* (1920–1931) [27], includes material on the German navy in the Pacific. See vol. I (by Sir Julian S. Corbett), chapter 10, for detail on the positions and strength of the German Pacific Squadron in China waters and the South Seas in August 1914. Chapter 21 describes German and Japanese ship movements to mid-September, and chapter 26 provides a detailed account of the destruction of the German cruiser *Emden* by HMS *Sydney* in the Coco Islands. Vol. IV, by Newbolt, addresses in chapter 6 the Japanese escort services in the Indian Ocean, and chapter 8 describes the anti-submarine service of eight Japanese destroyers in the Mediterranean from February 1917 and their help in rescuing passengers from torpedoed British ships.

Howarth, *The Fighting Ships of the Rising Sun* (1983) [53] also provides an account of Japanese naval escort assistance in the Indian Ocean and the Mediterranean. For a popular account of the fate of the *Emden,* see Edwin P. Hoyt, *The Last Cruise of the Emden* (1966) [55].

SIBERIAN INTERVENTION

There is no work in English focusing on the military aspects of the Intervention. As is often the case, the historical literature treats the political and diplomatic aspects of the episode. The standard treatment of the Japanese domestic political aspects of the enigmatic Intervention is James W. Morley, *Japan's Thrust into Siberia, 1918* (1957) [93]. Essentially a work in political science, Morley's work deals exclusively with the decision-making process in Tokyo that led to the Intervention. He details the differing motives and tactics of the diplomats, the cabinet, and military expansionists; and the compromises made by all in the policy-making process. Similarly, the standard Japanese language account by Hosoya Chihiro, *Shiberia shuppei no shiteki kenkyu* (1955) [52] is focused on Tokyo.

Writings by American diplomatic historians generally take the view that the United States suspected Japan of economic and territorial expansionist goals in Siberia, and entered upon the expedition to chaperone the Japanese. Among these authors are John A. White (*The Siberian Intervention,* 1950) [125] who is highly critical of Japan; and Betty Unterberger (*America's Siberian Expedition,* 1956) [123]. In their references to the expedition, authors Fifield (*Woodrow Wilson and the Far East,* 1952 [40]), Curry (*Woodrow Wilson and Far Eastern Policy,* 1957) [29], Beers (*Vain Endeavor,* 1962 [8]), and Iriye (*Across the Pacific,* 1967) [60] also emphasize the United States' goal of restraining the Japanese. George F. Kennan (*The Decision to Intervene,* 1958) [70] and Asada Sadao ("Japan and the United States," 1963) [3], on the other hand, see fear of Japanese expansionism as secondary to the intent to rescue the isolated Czech soldiers. Restraining Japan, they argue, became a primary motive only after the joint Intervention was under way and Japanese activity surpassed Allied presuppositions. New Left historians, exemplified by William Appleman Williams ("American Intervention in Russia," 1963–1964) [127], attribute American policy to anti-Bolshevism.

JAPANESE DIPLOMACY DURING AND AFTER THE WAR

In the vacuum of European power in East Asia caused by the war against Germany, Japan moved to expand its political and economic position in China, acquire markets formerly supplied by European manufacturers, and tighten its grip on territories taken since the turn of the century. On the infamous Twenty-one Demands, a solid account based on Western sources is a chapter in Arthur S. Link, *Woodrow Wilson: The Struggle for Neutrality, 1914–1915* (1960) [78]. Noriko Kawamura, in *Turbulence in the Pacific: Japanese-U.S. Relations during World War I* (2000) [69], uses Japanese documents as well in her study of the Japanese-American and Sino-Japanese antagonism that surrounded the Demands. Her book goes on to treat the Lansing-Ishii Agreement, the Siberian Intervention, and the fate of Japanese claims at the postwar peace conference. La Fargue's *China and the World War* (1937) [75] devotes two chapters to the Demands. Burton F. Beers, in his *Vain Endeavor* [8], focuses on Secretary of State Lansing rather than President Wilson as a distinct and significant source of attitudes and actions regarding Japan. Lansing, Beers contends, sought not so much to meet Japan head-on, but to mend Japanese-American relations and thereby acquire leverage to exert a moderating influence. See also Curry, *Woodrow Wilson and Far Eastern Policy* (1957) [29]. Madeleine Chi's respected monograph, *China Diplomacy, 1914–1918* (1970) [22] treats China's actions to thwart the Demands. The book is based on Chinese, Japanese, and Western diplomatic documents. See also Tien-yi Li, *Woodrow Wilson's China Policy, 1913–1917* (1952). For translated documents, a useful collection is Carnegie Endowment for International Peace, *The Sino-Japanese Negotiations of 1915: Japanese and Chinese Documents and Chinese Official Statements* (1921) [21].

Most writers assess Japanese diplomatic pressure on China during the war as bullying and an outright threat to Chinese sovereignty, rightly opposed by the Western powers with interests in China. Payson Treat (*Japan and the United States, 1853–1921,* 1928) [120] is a rare exception among older works. He defends Japan as a conscientious backer of the Open Door principle, and finds Japanese attitudes, policies, and actions to be no less reprehensible than those of other powers at the time. A noteworthy recent work by a Japanese diplomatic historian, Frederick Dickinson (*War and National Reinvention: Japan and the Great War, 1914–1919,* 1999) [32], also evaluates Japan's China diplomacy by the standard of the prevailing imperialist mores. He asserts that the Twenty-one Demands were not a dramatic departure from established diplomatic practice in China, nor were they machinations of extremist elements in Japan. Drawing on his own primary research and that of Kitaoka Shinichi (*Nihon rikugun to tairiku seisaku,* 1978) [72], Dickinson also treats the diplomacy of intrigue carried out in China during the war by Japanese army elements.

Japanese secret wartime treaties and negotiations with the enemy are treated in the Berton dissertation, "The Secret Russo-Japanese Alliance of 1916" (1957) [9], and Frank W. Ikle, "Japanese-German Peace Negotiations during World War I" (1965) [59]. Miyake Masaki's work ("Dai ichiji sekai taisen ni okeru Nichi-Doku kankei to Nichi-Ro kankei," 1967) [91] is the best in its use of both Japanese and German documentary evidence. In *Power in the Pacific* (1976) [34], Roger Dingman provides a trinational study of American, British, and Japanese political and diplomatic stances toward disarmament beginning in 1914. In formulating his argument that domestic political considerations drove the disarmament agenda, Dingman skillfully probes the Japanese political scene during the war years on the question of naval expansion [33, 34].

For Japanese diplomacy at the Paris Peace Conference, the best published source is Russell Fifield's *Woodrow Wilson and the Far East: The Diplomacy of the Shantung Question* (1952) [40]. The issue of Japan's demand for a League Covenant statement of racial nondiscrimination is studied thoroughly in Naoko Shimazu, *Japan, Race and Equality: The Racial Equality Proposal of 1919* (1998) [110]. Careful scholars like Shimazu and Dickinson note that Japan's actual demand was not to establish racial equality per se, but to abolish racial discrimination. Shimazu's is the first monograph on the subject published outside of Japan, and the only one to incorporate in-depth treatment of the Japanese, British, Australian, and American positions on the question. She does not condemn Wilson's arbitrary ruling that a unanimous vote was required in the League of Nations Commission, noting that it was his prerogative as chair and that Cecil had warned the Japanese that unanimity was necessary. Hermann Hiery treats the Conference's disposal of the former German Pacific islands in his *The Neglected War* (1995) [49]. For Japan's planning and negotiation at Paris regarding the League of Nations, the Covenant, and the International Labor Convention, see the dissertation by Thomas Burkman, "Japan, the League of Nations, and the New World Order, 1918–1920" (1975) [19].

JAPANESE POLITICS DURING THE WAR

A number of works clarify the connection between Japanese domestic politics and the external policies Japan pursued during the Great War. Most noteworthy is Frederick Dickinson, *War and National Reinvention: Japan in the Great War* (1999) [32]. Dickinson probes the maneuverings that went on in Tokyo surrounding the major war epochs of Shandong, the Twenty-one Demands, Siberia, and Japanese demands at the Paris Peace Conference. He depicts a power struggle between the Anglo-oriented, Foreign Ministry-based faction of Kato Takaaki on the one hand, and the army-centered, Germanophile Yamagata Aritomo clique on the other in the quest for a new conceptualization of Japan in the post-Meiji era.

Shifts in army leadership during the World War I period are described in Leonard A. Humphreys, *The Way of the Heavenly Sword: The Japanese Army in the 1920's* (1995) [56]. Internal army politics and their outflow in China intrigue is the subject of Kitaoka Shinichi's *Nihon rikugun to tairiku seisaku, 1906–1918* [72]. The collapse of the Imperial regime in China in 1912 led to a debate within the army, which extended through the World War I years, over how to advance Japanese interests in a context of Chinese political instability. Changing power relations between the Army Ministry and the General Staff and between the Choshu faction and the anti-Choshu faction influenced these debates. After 1915, the army got involved in continental adventurism, supporting at times revolutionary elements in South China and at other times loans to the Duan regime in Beijing. Activist continental schemes were suppressed after Hara Takashi, a party politician, became prime minister in 1918 and promoted collaboration with the Western powers. The rise of the parties and the role of Hara are depicted in Peter Duus, *Party Rivalry and Political Change in Taisho Japan* (1968) [36] and Kawada Minoru, *Hara Takashi, tenkanki no koso* (1995) [67]. Political aspects of Japanese naval history of the period are treated by J. Charles Schencking of the University of Melbourne in his doctoral dissertation, "The Political Emergence of the Imperial Japanese Navy in Late Meiji and Early Taisho Japan" (1998) [107].

A NOTE ON JAPANESE DOCUMENTARY SOURCES

Unpublished documentary collections in military history of both army and navy are housed in the Boei Kenkyujo (National Institute for Defense Studies) [10] in Tokyo. The library, with extensive military and naval collections, is essentially closed to the public, but access may be gained on an introduction basis. The Military History Department of the Institute has produced the 102-volume, *Senshi sosho* [Military history series], completed in 1980 and published by Asagumo shinbunsha. Thirty-three volumes of the set deal with naval matters. Peattie and Evans give an informative description of the field of Japanese naval history and its archival repositories in their chapter in a 1994 volume, *Ubi Sumus?* in the Naval War College Historical Monograph Series [101].

Diplomatic materials are preserved and readily accessible at the Gaiko Shiryokan (Diplomatic Records Office). The papers of leading political figures are most commonly housed at the Kensei Shiryoshitsu (Archive of Constitutional Government) in the National Diet Library. The primary scholarly journal for military history is *Gunji shigaku* [Journal of military history] published by the Gunjishi Gakkai (Military History Society of Japan). The Kokusai Seiji Gakkai (Japan Association of International Relations) [73] publishes *Kokusai seiji* [International relations], with frequent articles of a diplomatic historical nature. The historical field in Japan since the Pacific War has focused more on diplomatic studies than military studies, due to pacifist sentiments. Annual volumes of diplomatic correspondence, including extensive materials on the World War I years, are published by the Foreign Ministry in the *Nihon gaiko bunsho* [Documents on Japanese foreign policy] series. Two useful published volumes of diplomatic documents covering World War I and the Paris Peace Conference are included in the *Nihon gaikoshi* [Japanese diplomatic history] series edited by Kajima Morinosuke [65, 66].

FURTHER RESEARCH

Due to its cataclysmic nature, the Pacific War has held the attention of historians both in Japan and in the West. Studies of Japan's experience in First World War have lagged in both quality and detail, particularly on the military side. Since Japan's military involvement in the war was minuscule compared to that of the other powers, and since the international political ramifications of Japanese action seem obvious, the diplomatic aspects of the war years have received the greatest scholarly attention.

Western scholars of Japan need to bring their insights to the study of Japanese army and naval affairs in the years of the Great War. There are available to Western readers no monographic studies of the military features and soldier experience of the Shandong, Pacific islands, and Siberian campaigns based on Japanese documentary sources. The Evans and Peattie, *Kaigun* [38] study significantly advances overall understanding of the development of Japanese naval armament and doctrine—including the World War I period—but a companion study for the army is needed. Army attaches made important observations in Europe during the conflict and at the Paris Peace Conference. Their reports and the army's handling of such intelligence would make an informative study.

Most of the diplomatic historical work for the period was done in the 1960s and 1970s and earlier. After twenty years of relative silence, new and creative conceptualizations of standard diplomatic issues have begun to appear, and Dickinson's work on national reinvention is exemplary. Let us hope that the new approaches of critical theory will stimulate other new interpretations in the international history of early twentieth century Japan. The international political impact of Wilsonianism on Japan has been covered quite well, but historians need to be more imaginative in exploring the myriad intellectual, social, and cultural challenges that both the New World Order and Leninism represented. Moreover, the economic impact of the Great War on Japan, while widely noted as important, has received insufficient research and interpretation. Kitaoka's work has brought to light the workings of army bureaucratism and factionalism in China relations. A similar study in naval politics is needed, and J. Charles Schencking's recent work is promising in this regard [105, 106]. More of Kitaoka's work needs to be introduced to Western readers. Just as Kitaoka has effectively joined military, political, and diplomatic history for the period, other new bridges need to be crossed and new coalitions formed among the subfields of history. The connections between the war and urban development, lifestyles, and popular culture could be fruitfully explored.

Japanese scholars today are better able to communicate their work in the West. The linguistic ability of a new generation of Western Japanologists surpasses that of their predecessors. New theoretical approaches will germinate revised interpretations. While substantial studies are now available, the best years for the World War I history for Japan may lie ahead.

BIBLIOGRAPHY

1. Akagi, Roy Hidemichi. *Japan's Foreign Relations, 1542–1936: A Short History.* Washington, DC: University Publications of America, 1979 (1936).

2. Albertini, Luigi. *The Origins of the War of 1914.* 3 vols. London: Oxford University Press, 1952.

3. Asada, Sadao. "Japan and the United States, 1915–1925." Ph.D. dissertation, Yale University, 1963.

4. Asada, Sadao, ed. *Japan and the World, 1853–1952: A Bibliographic Guide to Japanese Scholarship in Foreign Relations.* New York: Columbia University Press, 1989.

5. Ayusawa, Iwao F. *A History of Labor in Modern Japan.* Honolulu: University of Hawaii Press, 1966.

6. Ballendorf, Dirk Anthony. "Secrets without Substance: U.S. Intelligence in the Japanese Mandates, 1915–1935." *Journal of Pacific History.* 19 (1984), 83–99.

7. Beasley, W. G. *Japanese Imperialism, 1894–1945.* Oxford: Clarendon Press, 1987.

8. Beers, Burton F. *Vain Endeavor: Robert Lansing's Attempts to End the Japanese-American Rivalry.* Durham, NC: Duke University Press, 1962.

9. Berton, Peter. "The Secret Russo-Japanese Alliance of 1916." Ph.D. dissertation, Columbia University, 1957.

10. Boei kenkyujo, comp. *Senshi sosho* [Military history series]. 102 vols. Tokyo: Asagumo shinbunsha, 1966–1980.

11. Braisted, William Reynolds. *The United States Navy in the Pacific, 1909–1922.* Austin: University of Texas Press, 1971.

12. Burdick, Charles, and Ursula Moessner. *The German Prisoners-of-War in Japan, 1914–20.* Landham, MD: University Press of America, 1984.

13. Burdick, Charles B., *The Japanese Siege of Tsingtau: World War I in Asia.* Hamden, CT: Archon Books, 1976.

14. Burkman, Thomas W. " 'Sairento Patona' Hatsugen Su—Kokusai Renmei Kiyaku, Kokusai Rodo Kiyaku" [The 'Silent Partners' Speak Out: The Case of the League of Nations Covenant and the International Labor Convention]. *Kokusai Seiji.* 56 (1976), 102–16.

15. Burkman, Thomas W. "Internationalism on Trial in Taisho Japan: The Makino-Ito Debate." *Occasional Papers of the Virginia Consortium for Asian Studies.* 2 (Spring 1985), 22–37.

16. Burkman, Thomas W. "Japan, the League of Nations, and the New World Order, 1918–1920." Ph.D. dissertation, University of Michigan, 1975.

17. Burkman, Thomas W. "Japanese Christians and the Wilsonian World Order." *Japan Christian Quarterly.* 49:1(Winter 1983), 38–46.

18. Burkman, Thomas W. "The Geneva Spirit." John F. Howes, ed. *Nitobe Inazo: Japan's Bridge across the Pacific.* Boulder CO: Westview Press, 1995, 177–214.

19. Burkman, Thomas W. "Japan and the League of Nations: An Asian Power Confronts the 'European Club.' " *World Affairs.* 158:1(Summer 1995), 45–57.

20. Canning, Craig N. "The Japanese Occupation of Shantung during World War One." Ph.D. dissertation, Stanford University, 1975.

21. Carnegie Endowment for International Peace. *The Sino-Japanese Negotiations of 1915: Japanese and Chinese Documents and Chinese Official Statements.* Washington, DC: Carnegie Endowment for International Peace, 1921.

22. Chi, Madeleine. *China Diplomacy, 1914–1918.* Cambridge: Harvard University Press, 1970.

23. Chi, Madeleine. "Tsao Ju-lin (1876–1966): His Japanese Connections," in Akira Iriye, ed. *The Chinese and the Japanese: Essays in Political and Cultural Interactions.* Princeton: Princeton University Press, 1980, 140–60.

24. Clinard, Outten J. *Japan's Influence on American Naval Power, 1897–1917.* Berkeley: University of California Press, 1947.

25. Connors, Leslie. "Saionji Kinmochi and the Paris Peace Conference." *Proceedings of the British Association for Japanese Studies.* I, 2(1976), 28–35.

26. Connors, Leslie. *The Emperor's Adviser: Saionji Kinmochi and Pre-war Japanese Politics.* Beckenham, Kent, UK: Croom Helm, 1987.

27. Corbett, Sir Julian S., and Henry Newbolt. *History of the Great War: Naval Operations.* 5 vols. London: Longmans Green, 1920–1931.

28. Cruttwell, C. R. M. F. *A History of the Great War, 1914–1918.* Oxford: Clarendon, 1934.

29. Curry, Roy Watson. *Woodrow Wilson and Far Eastern Policy, 1913–1921.* New York: Bookman Associates, 1957.

30. Dickinson, Frederick R. "Japan's Asia in the Politics of a New World Order, 1914–19," in Harald Fuess, ed. *The Japanese Empire in East Asia and Its Postwar Legacy.* Munich: Iudicium-Verl, 1998, 27–48.

31. Dickinson, Frederick R. "Japan: Declaring War for the Anglo-Japanese Alliance," in Richard Hamilton and Holger Herwig, eds. *World War I: The Origins.* 2002.

32. Dickinson, Frederick R. *War and National Reinvention: Japan in the Great War, 1914–1919.* Cambridge: Harvard University Press, 1999.

33. Dingman, Roger. "Nihon to Uirusonteki chitsujo [The Wilsonian world order and Japan]." Sato Seizaburo and Roger Dingman, eds. *Kindai Nihon no taigai taido* [The attitude of modern Japan toward the external world]. Tokyo: Tokyo daigaku shuppankai, 1974, 93–122.

34. Dingman, Roger. *Power in the Pacific: The Origins of Naval Arms Limitation, 1914–1922.* Chicago: University of Chicago Press, 1976.

35. Dull, Paul S. "Count Kato Komei and the Twenty-One Demands." *Pacific Historical Review.* 19:2(May 1950), 151–61.

36. Duus, Peter. *Party Rivalry and Political Change in Taisho Japan.* Cambridge: Harvard University Press, 1968.

37. Enser, A. G. S. ed. *A Subject Bibliography of the First World War: Books in English, 1914–1978.* London: A. Deutsch, 1979.

38. Evans, David C., and Mark R. Peattie. *Kaigun: Strategy, Tactics, and Technology in the Imperial Japanese Navy, 1887–1941.* Annapolis: Naval Institute Press, 1997.

39. Falk, Edwin Albert. *From Perry to Pearl Harbor: The Struggle for Supremacy in the Pacific.* Garden City, NY: Doubleday, Doran, 1943.

40. Fifield, Russell H. *Woodrow Wilson and the Far East: The Diplomacy of the Shantung Question.* Hamden, CT: Archon Books, 1952.

41. Fischer, Fritz. *Germany's Aims in the First World War.* New York: W. W. Norton, 1967.

42. Gaimusho [Japanese Ministry of Foreign Affairs], ed. *Nihon gaiko bunsho* [Documents of Japanese foreign policy]. Annual volumes. Tokyo: Japanese Ministry of Foreign Affairs.

43. Griswold, A. Whitney. *The Far Eastern Policy of the United States.* New York: Harcourt, Brace, 1938.

44. Hara Keiichiro, ed. *Hara Takashi nikki* [The diary of Hara Takashi]. 6 vols. Tokyo: Fukumura shuppan, 1981 (1950–1952).

45. Harvin, Harry L. "The Far East in the Peace Conference of 1919." Ph.D. dissertation, Duke University, 1956.

46. Hatano Masaru. *Kindai higashi Ajia no seiji hendo to Nihon no gaiko* [Political upheaval in modern East Asia and Japanese diplomacy]. Tokyo: Keio gijuku daigaku, 1995.

47. Heinrichs, Waldo. "The Middle Years, 1900–1945, and the Question of a Large U.S. Policy for East Asia," in Warren I. Cohen, ed. *New Frontiers in American-East Asian Relations: Essays Presented to Dorothy Borg.* New York: Columbia University Press, 1983, 77–106.

48. Hicks, Charles. *Japan's Entry into the War, 1914.* Reno: University of Nevada Press, 1944.

49. Hiery, Hermann. *The Neglected War: The German South Pacific and the Influence of World War I.* Honolulu: University of Hawaii Press, 1995.

50. Hirama Yoichi. *Dai Ichiji sekai taisen to Nihon kaigun* [The First World War and the Japanese navy]. Tokyo: Keio gikuji daigaku, 1998.

51. Hosoya Chihiro. *Roshia kakumei to Nihon* [The Russian Revolution and Japan]. Tokyo: Hara shobo, 1972.

52. Hosoya Chihiro. *Shiberia shuppei no shiteki kenkyu* [Historical analysis of the Siberian expedition]. Tokyo: Yuhikaku, 1955.

53. Howarth, Stephen. *The Fighting Ships of the Rising Sun: The Drama of the Imperial Japanese Navy.* New York: Atheneum, 1983.

54. Hoyt, Edwin P. *The Fall of Tsingtao.* London: Arthur Baker, 1975.

55. Hoyt, Edwin P. *The Last Cruise of the Emden.* New York: Macmillan, 1966.

56. Humphreys, Leonard A. *The Way of the Heavenly Sword: The Japanese Army in the 1920s.* Stanford: Stanford University Press, 1995.

57. Ikei Masaru. "Pari kowa kaigi to jinshu sabetsu teppai mondai" [The Paris Peace Conference and the problem of the abolition of racial discrimination] Kokusai seiji gakkai, ed. *Nihon gaikoshi kenkyu: Dai ichiji sekai taisen* [Studies in the diplomatic history of Japan: The First World War]. Tokyo: Yuhikaku, 1962, 44–58.

58. Ikei Masaru. "Ugaki Kazushige's View of China and his China Policy, 1915–1930," in Akira Iriye, ed. *The Chinese and the Japanese.* Princeton: Princeton University Press, 1980, 199–219.

59. Ikle, Frank. "Japanese-German Peace Negotiations during World War I." *American Historical Review.* 71 (October 1965), 62–76.

60. Iriye, Akira. *Across the Pacific: An Inner History of American-East Asian Relations.* New York: Harcourt, Brace and World, 1967.

61. Jones, Jefferson. *The Fall of Tsingtau: With a Study of Japan's Ambitions in China.* Wilmington, DE: Scholarly Resources, 1971 (1915).

62. Kajima Morinosuke. *A Brief Diplomatic History of Modern Japan.* Rutland, VT: C. E. Tuttle, 1965.

63. Kajima Morinosuke. *The Diplomacy of Japan, 1894–1922.* Tokyo: Kajima Institute of International Peace, 1976.

64. Kajima Morinosuke. *The Emergence of Japan as a World Power, 1895–1925.* Rutland, VT: C. E. Tuttle, 1967.

65. Kajima Morinosuke, ed. *Dai ichiji sekai taisen sanka oyobi kyoryoku mondai* [Japanese participation in the First World War and the problem of cooperation]. Tokyo: Kajima kenkyusho shuppankai, 1971.

66. Kajima Morinosuke, ed. *Pari kowa kaigi* [The Paris Peace Conference]. Tokyo: Kajima kenkyusho shuppankai, 1971.

67. Kawada Minoru. *Hara Takashi, tenkanki no koso: Kokusai shakai to Nihon* [Hara Takashi's conception at the watershed: Japan and the international community]. Tokyo: Miraisha, 1995.

68. Kawakami Kiyoshi. *Japan and World Peace.* New York: Macmillan, 1919.

69. Kawamura, Noriko. *Turbulence in the Pacific: Japanese-U.S. Relations during World War I.* Westport, CT: Praeger, 2000.

70. Kennan, George F. *The Decision to Intervene: The Prelude to Allied Intervention in the Bolshevik Revolution.* Princeton: Princeton University Press, 1958.

71. Kennedy, Malcolm D. *The Estrangement of Great Britain and Japan, 1917–1935.* Berkeley: University of California Press, 1969.

72. Kitaoka Shinichi. *Nihon rikugun to tairiku seisaku, 1906–1918* [The Japanese army and continental policy, 1906–1918]. Tokyo: Tokyo daigaku shuppankai, 1978.

73. Kokusai seiji gakkai, ed. *Nihon gaikoshi kenkyu: Dai ichiji sekai taisen* [Studies in the diplomatic history of Japan: The First World War]. Tokyo: Yuhikaku, 1962.

74. Kondo, Shinji, ed. *Japanese Military History : A Guide to the Literature.* New York: Garland, 1984.

75. LaFargue, Thomas E. *China and the World War.* Stanford: Stanford University Press, 1937.

76. Langdon, Frank C. "Japan's Failure to Establish Friendly Relations with China in 1917–1918." *Pacific Historical Review.* 26:3 (August 1957), 245–79.

77. Li Tien-yi. *Woodrow Wilson's China Policy, 1913–1917.* Kansas City, MO: University of Kansas Press, 1952.

78. Link, Arthur S. *Woodrow Wilson: The Struggle for Neutrality, 1914–1915.* Princeton: Princeton University Press, 1960.

79. Lockwood, William W. *The Economic Development of Japan: Growth and Structural Change, 1868–1938.* Princeton: Princeton University Press, 1954.

80. Louis, William Roger. *Great Britain and Germany's Lost Colonies, 1914–1919.* Oxford: Clarendon, 1967.

81. Lowe, Peter. *Great Britain and Japan, 1911–1915: A Study of British Far Eastern Policy.* London: Macmillan, 1969.

82. Lyon, Jessie C. "Diplomatic Relations between the United States, Mexico, and Japan, 1913–1917." Ph.D. dissertation, Claremont Graduate School, 1975.

83. Maga, Timothy P. *Defending Paradise: The United States, Guam, and Pacific Expansion, 1898–1950.* New York: Garland, 1988.

84. Maga, Timothy P. "Prelude to War? The United States, Japan, and the Yap Crisis, 1918–22." *Diplomatic History.* 9:3 (1985), 215–31.

85. Makino Nobuaki. *Kaikoroku* [Kaiko memoirs]. 2 vols. Tokyo: Chuo koronsha, 1977 (1949).

86. Martin, William S., Jr. "The Colonial Mandate Question at the Paris Peace Conference of 1919: The U.S. and the Disposition of German Colonies in Africa and the Pacific." Ph.D. dissertation, University of Southern Mississippi, 1982.

87. Matsushita Masatoshi. *Japan in the League of Nations.* New York: Columbia University Press, 1929.

88. May, Ernest R., and James C. Thomson, Jr., eds. *American-East Asian Relations: A Survey.* Cambridge: Harvard University Press, 1972.

89. May, Ernest R., "American Policy and Japan's Entrance into World War I." *Mississippi Valley Historical Review.* 40:2 (1953), 279–90.

90. Miwa Kimitada. "Japanese Opinions on Woodrow Wilson in War and Peace." *Monumenta Nipponica* 22:3–4 (1967), 368–89.

91. Miyake Masaki. "Dai ichiji sekai taisen ni okeru Nichi-Doku kankei to Nichi-Ro kankei: Nichi-Doku Sutokuhorumu kosho to tai Ro buki kyoyo mondai [German-Japanese peace negotiations in Stockholm and Russo-Japanese negotiations for lend-lease and alliance during World War I]. Nihon kokusai seiji gakkai, ed. *Heiwa to senso no kenkyu,* II [Studies on peace and war, II]. Tokyo: Yuhikaku, 1967, 105–33.

92. Morley, James W., ed. *Japan's Foreign Policy, 1868–1941: A Research Guide.* New York: Columbia University Press, 1974.

93. Morley, James W. *Japan's Thrust into Siberia, 1918.* New York: Columbia University Press, 1957.

94. Nagaoka Shinjiro. "Oshu Taisen sanka mondai" [The issue of Japanese entry into World War I]. *Kokusai seiji.* 6 (1958).

95. Nish, Ian H. *Alliance in Decline: A Study in Anglo-Japanese Relations, 1908–1923.* London: Athlone Press, 1972.

96. Nish, Ian H. "Japan," in Keith Wilson, ed. *Decisions for War, 1914.* London: St. Martin's Press, 1995, 209–28.

97. Nish, Ian H. "Japan, 1914–18," in Allan Millett and Williamson Murray, eds. *Military Effectiveness, vol. 1: First World War.* Boston: Allen and Unwin, 1988, 229–48.

98. Nish, Ian H. *Japanese Foreign Policy, 1869–1922: Kasumigaseki to Miyakezaka.* London: Routledge and Kegan Paul, 1977.

99. Okamoto, Shumpei, "Ishibashi Tanzan and the Twenty-one Demands," in Akira Iriye, ed. *The Chinese and the Japanese: Essays in Political and Cultural Interactions.* Princeton: Princeton University Press, 1980, 184–98.

100. Peattie, Mark R. *Nanyo: The Rise and Fall of the Japanese in Micronesia, 1885–1945.* Honolulu: University of Hawaii Press, 1988.

101. Peattie, Mark R., and David C. Evans. "Japan," in John B. Hattendorf, ed. *Ubi Sumus? The State of Naval and Maritime History.* Newport, RI: Naval War College Press, 1994, 213–22.

102. Price, Ernest B. *The Russo-Japanese Treaties of 1907–1916 Concerning Manchuria and Mongolia.* Baltimore: The Johns Hopkins University, 1933.

103. Purcell, David. "Japanese Expansion in the South Pacific, 1895–1935." Ph.D. dissertation, University of Pennsylvania, 1967.

104. Saito Seiji. "Nichi-doku Chinto senso no kaisen gaiko" [Diplomacy surrounding the outbreak of the Japanese-German Qindao war]. *Kokusai seiji.* 119(October 1998), 192–208.

105. Schencking, J. Charles. "Bureaucratic Politics, Military Budgets, and Japan's Southern Advance: The Imperial Navy's Seizure of German Micronesia in World War I." *War in History.* 5:3 (July 1998), 308–26.

106. Schencking, J. Charles. "The Imperial Japanese Navy and the Constructed Consciousness of a South Seas Destiny, 1872–1921." *Modern Asian Studies.* 33:4 (November 1999), 769–96.

107. Schencking, J. Charles. "The Political Emergence of the Imperial Japanese Navy in Late Meiji and Early Taisho Japan." Ph.D. dissertation, Cambridge University, 1998.

108. Seguin, Paul B. "The Deteriorating Strategic Position of Japan, 1853–1945: A Study of the Revolution of Intercontinental Warfare." Ph.D. dissertation, University of Minnesota, 1972.

109. Shao, His-ping. "From the Twenty-one Demands to the Sino-Japanese Military Agreement, 1915–1918: Ambivalent Relations," in Alvin Coox and Hilary Conroy, eds. *China and Japan.* Santa Barbara: ABC Clio Press, 1978, 37–57.

110. Shimazu, Naoko. *Japan, Race and Equality: The Racial Equality Proposal of 1919.* London: Routledge, 1998.

111. Shotwell, James T. *At the Paris Peace Conference.* New York: Macmillan, 1937.

112. Shotwell, James T. *The Origins of the International Labor Organization.* 2 vols. New York: Columbia University Press, 1934.

113. Shulman, Frank Joseph, ed. *Doctoral Dissertations on Asia* (bibliographical journal of 16 vols., covering through 1992/93). Ann Arbor: Association for Asian Studies, 1975–1996.

114. Shulman, Frank Joseph, ed. *Doctoral Dissertations on Japan and on Korea, 1969–1979: An Annotated Bibliography of Studies in Western Languages.* Seattle: University of Washington Press, 1982.

115. Shulman, Frank Joseph, ed. *Japan and Korea: An Annotated Bibliography of Doctoral Dissertations in Western Languages, 1877–1969.* Chicago: American Library Association, 1970.

116. Spinks, Charles Nelson. "Japan's Entrance into the World War." *Pacific Historical Review.* 5 (1936), 297–311.

117. Stevenson, David. *The First World War and International Politics.* New York: Oxford University Press, 1988.

118. Storry, Richard. *Japan and the Decline of the West in Asia, 1894–1943.* New York: St. Martin's Press, 1979.

119. Takeuchi Tatsuji. *War and Diplomacy in the Japanese Empire.* New York: Doubleday, Doran, 1935.

120. Treat, Payson. *Japan and the United States, 1853–1921.* Revised ed. Stanford: Stanford University Press, 1928.

121. Tsunoda Jun, ed. *Ugaki Kazushige nikki* [The diary of Ugaki Kazushige]. 3 vols. Tokyo: Misuzu shobo, 1968.

122. Unno Yoshiro. *Kokusai Renmei to Nihon* [The League of Nations and Japan]. Tokyo: Hara shobo, 1972.

123. Unterberger, Betty M. *America's Siberian Expedition, 1918–1920: A Study of National Policy.* Durham, NC: Duke University Press, 1956.

124. Usui Katsumi. *Nihon to Chugoku: Taisho jidai* [Japan and China: The Taisho era]. Tokyo: Hara shobo, 1972.

125. White, John A. *The Siberian Intervention.* Princeton: Princeton University Press, 1950.

126. Williams, E. T. "Japan's Mandate in the Pacific." *American Journal of International Law.* 27 (July 1933), 428–39.

127. Williams, William Appleman. "American Intervention in Russia, 1917–1920." *Studies on the Left.* 3:4 (1963), 24–28; 4:1(1964), 39–57.

128. Williams, William Appleman. *The Tragedy of American Diplomacy.* Cleveland: World Publishing Co., 1957.

129. Wright, Quincy. *Mandates under the League of Nations.* Chicago: University of Chicago Press, 1930.

130. Young, A. Morgan. *Japan under Taisho Tenno, 1912–1926.* London: George Allen and Unwin, 1928.

131. Yuan, Tsing. "The Japanese Intervention in Shantung during World War I," in Alvin Coox and Hilary Conroy, eds. *China and Japan.* Santa Barbara: ABC Clio Press, 1978, 21–33.

15

The War at Sea

Eugene L. Rasor

INTRODUCTION

The important historical literature and conflicts of interpretation among historians of the war at sea before and during World War I will be reviewed.

For the first time in history naval warfare in three dimensions, surface, sub-
surface, and aerial, was demonstrated on a major scale. The submarine, mines,
torpedoes, and the aircraft, with versions of lighter- and heavier-than-air, were
introduced in an already unprecedented pace of technological change in surface
naval warfare. This precipitated changes in the concepts of sea power, naval
strategy and tactics. There had been relative peace during the long nineteenth
century while extraordinary advances in science, industry, and technology had
progressed unabated. Other innovations included the development of a system
of alliances based on a series of stated contingencies, restructuring of military
and naval organizations based on elaborate war planning and readiness for
mobilization; on strategic and tactical reorientations, such as how a blockade
was conducted; and on an unprecedented international arms race, especially
involving new super-battleships, the *Dreadnought,* and a cheaper, faster, but
more vulnerable, battle cruiser. Invasion scares, naval panics, and accusations of
encirclement resulted as inevitable consequences. For some, war came as a
relief. Despite warning signs, such as were evident from the American Civil War
and the Sino-Japanese and Russo-Japanese Wars of the late nineteenth and early
twentieth centuries, the predictions were that a future war would be short and
much glory would be attained.

When war finally came, at sea, participants, in order of importance and
appearance, were Great Britain, Germany, France, Russia, Italy, Austria-

Hungary, Turkey, Japan, and the United States. During the two decades of the prewar period, personal leadership in the naval realm became so prominent that historians have named those periods after British Admiral of the Fleet Lord John Fisher, First Baron of Kilverstone, and German Admiral Alfred von Tirpitz, respectively the Fisher era and the Tirpitz era. During the war, naval operations occurred worldwide but most were concentrated in the English Channel and the North Sea and in the Mediterranean and Baltic Seas. Germany and her ally, Austria-Hungary, were, in fact, encircled by the Allied, that is, Britain, France, and, later, the United States, naval blockade.

Historians have interpreted and described other episodes of the war at sea: the escape of the German warships *Goeben* and *Breslau* in the Mediterranean Sea to Turkey; Anglo-German confrontations such as Coronel, the Falklands, and the Channel encounters; a military stalemate leading to a major amphibious operation, the Dardanelles campaign, on-again, off-again, and on-again unrestricted submarine warfare initiated by Germany; the related sinking of the luxury liner *Lusitania;* the rush to develop anti-submarine techniques and construct massive underwater barriers blocking U-boat exit routes; the much-anticipated but indecisive battle of Jutland; the American and Japanese entries with naval forces deployed to European waters; final operations including the ineffective Zeebrugge landings, the Armistice, and the sensational scuttling of the entire German battle fleet at Scapa Flow. The peace settlement placed serious limitations on future German naval forces. The Allies agreed to their own limitations at a conference in Washington, 1921–1922. Naval blockade operations were much expanded by the Allies and were deemed decisive by many.

GENERAL TEXTS

Two general surveys are of interest. First is an extraordinary history of the war, *The World Crisis,* six volumes, by the participant-historian, Winston Churchill [52], First Lord of the Admiralty, 1911–1915, with flagrant inclusion of his apologetics, especially about the Dardanelles campaign and an anti-Jellicoe critique of the Battle of Jutland. Second is a recent anthology of over sixty essays by prominent authorities, *Facing Armageddon,* papers from a conference commemorating the eightieth anniversary to review the state of knowledge about "the Great War," including pertinent articles on the blockade, the Dardanelles campaign, and merchant seamen, all edited by Hugh Cecil [47]. *The World Crisis: A Criticism* was a response to Churchill, the lead author being Admiral Reginald Bacon [7]. It was a point-by-point refutation.

Two official naval histories of the war, *Naval Operations* [65] and *Der krieg zur see* [91], respectively, British and German, require notice. The famous strategic theorist-historian, Julian Corbett, an adviser to Admiral John Fisher, was the designated official British naval historian, later assisted by Henry Newbolt. Publication, five volumes, was delayed due to objections about coverage of the Dardanelles campaign by Winston Churchill and internal disagreements within the Admiralty over, among other things, interpretations of events of the

Battle of Jutland, and the pro-Jellicoe and pro-Beatty antagonisms, to be reviewed below. Corbett died in 1922 and publication of volume III, on Jutland, proceeded only after an Admiralty disclaimer about "the tendency to minimize the importance of seeking battle" was added. Otto Groos and Walter Gladisch wrote the German naval history [91], seven volumes, including insistence that the Battle of Jutland was a German victory and praise for the tactical achievements of John Jellicoe.

General naval histories of World War I are numerous. The best was *Naval History of World War I,* by Paul Halpern [96], covering all geographical areas including the Mediterranean, Baltic, Black, and Adriatic seas and the Danube river, and incorporating all the latest research and scholarly interpretations. The older three-volume history, *The Naval History of the World War* by Thomas Frothingham [78], featured the American perspective and used traditional narrative approaches. Another older book was *Naval Episodes of the Great War* by John Buchan [35]. The naval history of the war by Richard Hough [126], dedicated to Arthur Marder, was typically overly popularized and error-prone, a disappointment. More recently, Hough published *Naval Battles of the Twentieth Century* [127]. The effort by A. A. Hoehling and Mary Hoehling, *The Great War at Sea* [119], was somewhat better. For the *British Battles Series,* Geoffrey Bennett [21] summarized events of the naval battles of the war.

A general survey by John Southworth, *War at Sea* [235], three volumes in four books, covered all of history and included naval operations of World War I in superficial fashion. Allan Millett and Williamson Murray edited *Military Effectiveness* [171], a three-volume evaluation, a volume each for World War I, the interwar period, and World War II. It incorporated 21 case studies with assessments of politics, operations, strategy, and tactics. For example, for World War I, the Royal Navy was deficient in staff planning, intelligence, and communication. For Germany, Alfred Tirpitz insisted on maintaining one operational strategy even after drastic changes occurred in the basis for that strategy. In 1997, Holger Herwig [110] reviewed overall relationships between the Central Powers, Germany and Austria-Hungary, throughout the war.

Naval histories of the participating nations provided background. For the British navy, the best place to start would be Paul Kennedy, *The Rise and Fall of British Naval Mastery* [142], an excellent one-volume survey. In *A Naval History of the War,* Henry Newbolt [174], the official British naval historian, completed a separate naval history before his official status, in which he perceived the transformation in the nature of warfare from limited to unlimited. Another general survey was by Richard Humble, *Before the* Dreadnought*: The Royal Navy from Nelson to Fisher* [129]. *The British Navy in Battle* by Arthur H. Pollen [195], journalist and engineer, was of interest because the author was the designer of a controversial fire control system. N. A. M. Rodger [215] has begun a multivolume naval history of Britain, the first since 1900. The first volume is out and the second, covering up to 1815, is planned to be forthcoming. The third volume will be much anticipated. For Germany, go to Holger Herwig, *"Luxury Fleet"* [114] and, in German, *Der Seekrieg* by Lothar Persius [189]. The distinguished military historian Theodore Ropp best described the formative years of the French navy in *The Development of a Modern Navy* [216]. For Russia, go to René Greger, *The Russian Fleet* [90]. For the U.S. Navy, different interpretations can be seen in the histories of Robert Love, *History of the U.S. Navy* [158], and Kenneth Hagan, *The People's Navy* [94].

BIBLIOGRAPHIES

Robin Higham and Jacob W. Kipp have edited an important series of military history bibliographies for Garland Publishers. Two with extensive historiographical essays and coverage of the war at sea are pertinent: Keith Bird, *German Naval History: A Guide to the Literature* [28], with 4,178 entries, and Eugene Rasor, *British Naval History Since 1815: A Guide to the Literature* [200], with 3,125 entries.

Rasor has completed several that are more specific: *The Battle of Jutland: A Bibliography* [201], 538 entries, *Arthur James Balfour, 1848–1930: Historiography and Annotated Bibliography* [202], 425 entries, and *Winston S. Churchill, 1874–1965: A Comprehensive Historiography and Annotated Bibliography* [203], 3,099 entries. Both Churchill and Balfour were First Lords of the Admiralty during the war. Three other bibliographies should be consulted: Fred van Hartesveldt, *The Dardanelles Campaign, 1915: Historiography and Annotated Bibliography* [101], 765 entries, and two by Myron J. Smith, Jr., *The American Navy: A Bibliography* [233] and *Battleships and Battlecruisers, 1884–1984: A Bibliography and Chronology* [234], 5,500 entries.

ARCHIVES

Researchers, historians, and students of these events may conduct primary research in appropriate archives, especially the Public Record Office at Kew and the British Library, both in London, the recently relocated *Militargeschichtliches Forschungsamt* at Potsdam, and the new Archives II of the U.S. National Archives at the University of Maryland at College Park.

POLITICAL AND DIPLOMATIC BACKGROUND

The last great war had ended in 1815 followed by a hundred years of comparative peace, the long nineteenth century. However, tensions and antagonisms increased beginning about 1870 with the Franco-Prussian War. Europe divided. France and Russia on one side and Germany, Austria-Hungary, and Italy on the other, concluding two sets of opposing military alliances, Britain ostensibly remaining aloof. That, however, was illusory. Britain secretly made military and naval commitments to France, as described by John Coogan in an article, "The British Cabinet and Anglo-French Staff Talks" [62]. Previous areas of tension were also eliminated when Britain signed colonial understandings with France and separately with Russia, 1904 and 1907. Britain signed no formal military or naval alliances.

The formal alliances were based on a series of specified contingencies and incorporated rigid, elaborate mobilization plans. Associated arms races were inevitable. Italy changed sides after the war began, and Japan and the United States eventually joined the Allies against the Central Powers.

Looking at these issues from the present perspective, the most volatile and enduring antagonisms were those between Britain and Germany. The older, classic study of these matters, especially competition over naval arms, was by E. L. Woodward, *Great Britain and the German Navy* [275]. That now has been superseded by Yale University professor Paul Kennedy, *The Rise of Anglo-German Antagonism* [141]. It was an extraordinary *tour de force,* a broad-based, revisionist, structuralist study, incorporating traditional and several recent trends in historiography: analyses of political, economic, imperial, social, religious, dynastic, nationalist, militarist, and navalist trends. Included was the role of the official mind, and, perhaps, most influential in this case, the naval arms race. A similar structuralist-functionalist interpretation of German history of the time was incorporated in two works by Volker Berghahn, *Germany in the Age of Total War* [25] and *Germany and the Approach of War* [26]. These took up where Eckart Kehr [138, 139], an unknown German historian of the late 1920s, left off. Kehr stressed that domestic politics were primary. International, external crises were created by domestic politicians so as to distract from serious domestic tensions and transitions unfavorable to their continued domination, exemplified in the second title, *Primat der Innenpolitik.* Berghahn stressed such factors as colonial and imperial competition, the compulsive drive of Kaiser William II for "a place in the sun," the naval arms race, and fear of being "Copenhagened," a reference to a British surprise attack against Denmark a hundred years previously. As Jonathan Steinberg described it in an article, "The Copenhagen Complex" [236], fatalism and a "syndrome of inevitability" of war prevailed in Germany.

One title was deceptive. A reader might think *Dreadnought,* a best-selling, thousand-page tome by Robert Massie [168], would describe the revolutionary battleship design. But Massie was oblivious to revisionist and structuralist approaches. Instead, we find a potpourri of topics, presumably a summary of factors about the origins of World War I, for example, the Battle of Trafalgar, consanguinity in royal marriages, family life of Queen Victoria and Kaiser William II, the Boxer Rebellion, the Boer War, Admirals John Fisher and Alfred Tirpitz, and Winston Churchill and Arthur Balfour.

ECONOMIC AND INDUSTRIAL MATTERS

Economic and industrial, broadly defined, included economic, industrial, scientific, ship design, ship types, metallurgy, ordnance, intelligence, communication, logistics, and an especially prominent contemporaneous sensation, invasion scares. All concerned the war at sea.

An overall introduction to these matters would be the fascinating philosophical analysis of a thousand years of the military-industrial complex, *The Pursuit
of Power* [161] by the provocative historian, William McNeill, in which one case
study was the naval arms race and propaganda techniques identified with Admiral John Fisher.

Dramatic advances occurring in the nineteenth century resulted in innovations in metallurgy, ordnance, ship types, design, and construction. Peter Rippon, *Evolution of Engineering in the Royal Navy* [210], has contributed a
two-volume study of a wide variety of naval engineering developments, including propulsion, ordnance, armor protection, submarines, aviation, dockyards,
and electricity. A solid summary was provided by an anthology edited by Bryan
Ranft, *Technical Change and British Naval Policy* [199], which contains seven
scholarly essays on technical changes, research, and development during the
nineteenth and twentieth centuries. *The War of Invention* by Guy Hartcup [100]
described scientific advances throughout the war, focusing upon an institution-
alized approach involving cooperation of scientists and professional military
leaders. Case studies included developments in anti-submarine warfare and the
controversial Pollen naval gunnery fire-control system.

In the days of sailing ship warfare, a critical factor was the supply of wood;
during the nineteenth century, it was coal. Beginning with the twentieth century,
it became access to oil. Daniel Yergin was awarded the Pulitzer Prize of 1992 for
The Prize [278], a brilliant history of the "epic quest for oil." He opened the
book with the account of when, how, and what prompted Winston Churchill to
take "the fateful plunge" in 1912 to convert the Royal Navy from coal to oil.
Strategic implications were momentous.

Also in the run-up to the war, innovative and original ship types were introduced such as the submarine, the submarine destroyer, and the battlecruiser.
Existing types were enhanced such as the *Dreadnought* battleship. All were
described in detail in the noted reference publication, *Conway's All the World's
Fighting Ships* [61]. The Royal Navy gathered an official guide to all German
warships of World War I, originally confidential, recently published and edited
by Robert Gardiner [80].

David K. Brown was most noted for his trilogy [31, 32, 33], *The Eclipse of the
Big Gun Warship, The Grand Fleet,* and *Nelson to Vanguard,* describing developments in British naval construction and warship design before, during, and
after the war. And, as noted above, for the first time in World War I, major warfare was in three dimensions. The historian of naval aviation during World War
I was R. D. Layman [154]; supporting original documentation was supplied in a
volume sponsored by the Navy Records Society and edited by Stephen Roskill,
Documents Related to the Naval Air Service [221]. The Germans relied more on
lighter-than-air craft as described by Douglas Robinson, *The Zeppelin in Combat* [214]. In an article, Roskill [219] recounted an incident late in the war in
which a British Sopwith Camel aircraft took off from a towed launching plat-
form at sea and shot down German Zeppelin L.53, a taste of things to come. See
also Owen Thatford, *British Naval Aircraft Since 1912* [252].

No doubt, the submarine exerted more influence during World War I, aviation more influence in World War II. Nicholas Lambert has a dissertation, "A Revolution in Naval Strategy" [150], and a book, *The Submarine Service* [151], the latter a publication of the Navy Records Society, on the influence and impact of the submarine. Richard Compton-Hall [58, 59] and Sir William Jameson [135] presented its history before and during the war. Jameson called it *The Most Formidable Thing.* The British perspective was summarized in a book entitled *A Damned Un-English Weapon* by Edwyn Gray [89]. In a kind of memoir, Admiral John Jellicoe [136] called it "the greatest peril which ever threatened this country." He referred specifically to the German U-boat campaign launched first, then limited, then revived as unlimited submarine warfare. That was recounted in detail by Richard Gibson, *The German Submarine War* [81], and Edwyn Gray, *The Killing Time* [88].

German success precipitated a desperate search for countermeasures by the Allies. A major feature of the scientific and invention initiatives of the British and Americans was anti-submarine warfare. That massive effort, ultimately achieving increasing success, incorporated a variety of approaches, trial and error: hydrophones, depth charges, mines, minesweeping, nets, and formulation of convoy tactics. A recent synthesis of these matters was Dwight Messimer, *Find and Destroy* [169]. Other efforts were Willem Hackmann, *Seek and Strike* [93], Robert Grant, *U-Boats Destroyed* [86], and M. B. Wignall, "Collaboration in Anti-Submarine Warfare" [266].

Individual and regional submarine operations were presented by Michael Wilson. He described British submarine operations in the Mediterranean Sea [269], the Dardanelles [268], and in Russian waters [270]. Larger perspectives were presented by John Terraine, *Business in Great Waters* [249].

The submarine led to the creation of the submarine destroyer. Cruisers were for protection of commerce and reconnaissance for the battle fleet. The historian of British cruisers and destroyers of World War I was Ray Burt [39, 40].

Popular, professional, and naval interest during the first decades of the twentieth century was focused on the capital ships of that day, the battleship and battlecruiser. The literature has been expansive. The old standard survey was *Battleships in Action,* two volumes, by H. W. Wilson [267]. More reflective, more critical, and more irreverent was *Sacred Vessels* by the American military analyst Robert O'Connell [177]. The allusion to religion in the title was continued with title phrases: "prophet," "grail," "the evil below," and "requiem." It was "a cautionary tale." O'Connell concluded that the battleship was never an effective weapon, yet the authorities persisted in building these expensive behemoths, which proved to be worthless. *Conway's All the World's Battleships* [60] was an introductory reference guide. Then go to Antony Preston, *Battleships of World War I* [196]. There were four different accounts of British battleships, three by Ray Burt [36–38] and one by Oscar Parkes [183]. Burt also wrote about French battleships [41]. David Woodward [274] has compiled accounts of how 130 great battleships were lost, for example, those at the Battle of Jutland plus others such as the *Maine,* the *Hood,* and the *Bismarck.*

Two types of capital ships were credited to the initiatives of John Fisher, the battlecruiser and *Dreadnought*. Recent interpretation is that Fisher reluctantly accepted *Dreadnought* to appease critics. This extraordinary super-battleship featured several innovations. A general description, including 180 illustrations, was written by Richard Hough [125]. More specific accounts of HMS *Dreadnought* were by John Roberts [212], John Wingate [271], and David K. Brown [30]. The last class completed before the war was the *Queen Elizabeth,* described by N. J. M. Campbell [46]. Interestingly, two books have been published about *HMS Warspite* of the *Queen Elizabeth* class, one by Stephen Roskill [222] and another V. E. Tarrant [248]. She was hit 29 times at Jutland and became famous for a "death ride" when her rudder jammed and she went in circles, making a perfect target.

Holger Herwig [113] has published studies about the German reaction to the *Dreadnought* revolution. Fisher envisioned performance of combined functions of the battleship and cruiser, the battlecruiser, fast and powerful, but not well protected—and cheap. The first of "those ill-fated ships" was the *Invincible* class. The most recent study was by John Roberts [211], others by N. J. M. Campbell [43], Ronald Bassett [11], for the *Invincible* class, John Roberts [213], and for *Invincible* herself, V. E. Tarrant [247]. *Invincible* was one of the three that blew up at Jutland.

The British gunnery expert in preparation for the war was Percy Scott, his biographer being Peter Padfield [181]. Most details about naval gunnery of the era can be found in an 18-part series of articles by N. J. M. Campbell [44], who also conducted the extensive and detailed study of all aspects of gunnery on both sides during the Battle of Jutland. Fire control became a matter of contention. Arthur Hungerford Pollen was a journalist-engineer who designed a complicated and computerized gun fire control system for capital ships. Although it was known to be superior, it was not adopted. Later, Pollen was awarded 30,000 pounds sterling by the British government as a settlement. The son of Pollen called it *The Great Gunnery Scandal* [194]. Jon Sumida has edited the Pollen papers [245]. Related matters of communication, optics, and electricity require further study.

Intelligence institutions came into their own during the prewar period. Historians credited the modern origins of military intelligence to admiralties, especially the famous Room 40 within Admiralty headquarters in London. Such historians included Patrick Beesly [13], Nicholas Hiley [118], Michael Occleshaw [175], and Robert Grant [87]. A manifestation of significance was how British intelligence operatives gained control of cable communications worldwide, severing enemy ones when war began. Failures of Room 40 during the Battle of Jutland will be considered below, but Room 40 was responsible for the exposé of the Zimmermann telegram, a factor in the entry of the United States into the war.

The premier historian of British economic mobilization and strategic war planning was David French, *British Economic and Strategic Planning* [75] and *British Strategy and War Aims* [76], describing the conscious chronological transformation of national policy from peace to war, consecutively, "business as usual" to "a nation in arms" to "total war." The prolific and controversial American naval historian Jon Sumida, in *In Defense of British Naval Supremacy* [242] and in a series of trenchant articles [239, 240, 246], brings many of these matters together using structural analysis: administration, finance, policy-making, technological innovation, and strategic defense. He stressed the initiatives of John Fisher to reduce costs and develop a "cheap" capital ship that could operate in the line of battle, be faster than potential opponents, and provide security for commerce worldwide. The Pollen fire control system, described above, figured prominently. Despite catastrophes and serious questions about vulnerability of the battlecruiser, Fisher never conceded; even in 1919 he was still calling for a fast capital ship with 20-inch guns. Jon Sumida [241] has also reviewed the complexities of logistical support of modern naval forces.

The matter of invasion of Britain as history was treated by the great naval strategist-professor Herbert Richmond [207]. More pertinent to invasion scares, an important phenomenon during the prewar period, were the works of Friedrich von Bernhardi [27] and Erskine Childers [50]. The best summary was by I. F. Clarke, *Voices Prophesying War* [54]. Most influential in launching the trend was *The Battle of Dorking* by George Chesney [49], written in 1871. A virtual genre of literature accumulated, especially from Britain and Germany.

SOCIAL HISTORY AND MANPOWER

Significant, diverse, innovative, and revisionist historical writing has appeared on the impact of World War I, for example, the experiences of war at the front, at home, and sociological, prosopographical, psychological, literary, even postmodern interpretations. The social naval historian Henry Baynham wrote *Men from the Dreadnoughts* [12], the last of a chronological series. Peter Liddle [155, 156] created a virtual industry demonstrating the experience of war, creating the renowned Liddle Collection of archival materials, oral histories, and memorabilia at the Sunderland Polytechnic Institute, since moved to the University of Leeds. Hugh Cecil and Liddle [47] edited a collection of essays for a 70th-year commemoration, *Facing Armageddon.*

Sociological and prosopographical analyses of groups and classes can be instructive. Such analyses have appeared about military and naval classes, more on officers than enlisted men. A case in point was that of Holger Herwig [112], who characterized the German naval officer corps as "feudalization of the bourgeoisie," that is, at a time of dramatic industrialization, a collective aspiration of naval officers to move up to an aristocratic status. That same officer class has been blamed for precipitating forcewide mutinies. Daniel Horn [121, 122] and David Woodward [273] documented the notorious series of mutinies within the High Seas Fleet during the closing months of the war, Horn proving conclusively that poor or nonexistent officer-enlisted relations, not communist ideology, were decisive.

The noted naval historian, Charles Lloyd, *The Nation and the Navy* [157], wrote on the social side. Herbert Blumberg [29] described the Royal Marines during the war. A number of individual naval memoirs are also enlightening; for example, Victor Hayward [107], among other experiences, observed the scuttling of the High Seas Fleet, and H. P. K. Oram [180], serving on a British destroyer, observed the three battlecruisers blowing up during the Battle of Jutland.

The matter of personalities and leadership will be treated below.

MILITARY PREPARATIONS AND MOBILIZATION

For the war at sea, all the advances during the long nineteenth century precipitated change. Fundamental concepts about the nature of sea power, national and naval strategy, and military organizational structures were debated and transformed. For example, primary reasons Winston Churchill was appointed First Lord in 1911 included creation of a naval staff and restoration of sanity to the war planning process. The debate has continued to the present; the best source for a general overview is the classic anthology edited by Peter Paret, *The Makers of Modern Strategy* [182], revised and updated from a work of the same title edited by E. M. Earle.

A formative step in the debate over sea power occurred in 1890 when an American naval officer, Alfred Thayer Mahan, published *The Influence of Sea Power upon History* [162]. He had studied naval history, specifically the naval history of Britain in the seventeenth and eighteenth centuries, leading to the formulation of his famous concepts of sea power. Naval history was the key, as elaborated by Barry Hunt [130] writing on the outstanding naval strategic writers of the century, and by the recently appointed Professor of Naval History at the University of London, Andrew Lambert, *The Foundations of Naval History* [146]. A group of interrelated British naval historians exerted influence upon Mahan, for example, John and Philip Colomb and John Knox Laughton. More about them, the role of history, and the development of strategic thought is incorporated in a brilliant study by Donald Schurman, *The Education of a Navy* [228].

The works of Mahan were acclaimed by naval and political leaders, especially in the United States; Britain, where he received honorary degrees; Germany, where copies were placed aboard most warships; and Japan. Alternatives were touted: Julian Corbett and Herbert Richmond. The theories of Mahan continue to be debated. Papers from two conferences of 1991 and 1992 sponsored by the U.S. Naval War College at Newport demonstrated this: *The Influence of History upon Mahan,* edited by John Hattendorf [104] and *Mahan Is Not Enough,* edited by James Goldrick [84].

A major aspect of the debate concerned critiques and questions about the theories of Mahan, especially those of a noted British naval historian and adviser to Fisher, Julian Corbett, later the official British naval historian of the war. Corbett contributed significantly to the debate, especially his *Some Principles of Naval Strategy* [66], his theories ultimately being proclaimed as preferable. Corbett wrote several naval histories [65] and conducted an extensive analysis of naval operations during the Russo-Japanese War of 1904–1905 [64]. Mahan advocated the decisiveness of large battle fleets, the "blue water school." As a deliberate counterpoint to Mahan, Corbett formulated concepts of limited and balanced warfare, "the British way of warfare," a combination of continental and maritime strategies incorporating mobilization of naval, military, economic, and diplomatic resources. Schurman was the biographer of Corbett [229].

Stephen Roskill [223], Liam Cleaver [55], Barry Hunt [131], and David MacGregor [159] have elaborated on the debate. Mahan and Corbett based their theories on British naval history, which Corbett had formulated into a more effective strategy. Those theories were actually put into practice, and, as a result, the Royal Navy was more effectively employed in the 1914 war. Relevant today, Corbett distinguished between limited and unlimited warfare. His protégé was Herbert Richmond, who interpreted from a postwar perspective, and who wrote Corbett's obituary, crediting him with raising the study of naval history to a new level and integrating naval operations into what John Hattendorf called "the Anglo-American Way in Maritime Strategy" in *Maritime Strategy and the Balance of Power* [105].

But is the debate over? Jon Sumida in *Inventing Grand Strategy* [244] carefully reread all of the works of Mahan; Sumida concluded that Mahan was more perceptive and sophisticated than some have claimed and that he consciously wrote at a variety of levels to suit different audiences.

German naval strategic theory for the prewar period was denounced, indeed, indicted, in a classic treatise and critique, *The Naval Strategy of the World War,* written in 1929 by Wolfgang Wegener [263], who said that "Risk theory," formulated by Admiral Tirpitz, and the quest for the big battle were hollow and without purpose. "We never really understood the sea. Not one of us."

Simultaneously, military-naval command organization was undergoing change. Initiatives originated in Prussia, later Germany, in the 1860s, the result being the general-staff structure. A series of successes in war planning, mobilization, and operations seemed to demonstrate the validity of these innovative structures and war planning. Other big powers adopted them. The equivalent for Britain was the Committee of Imperial Defence, created in 1902. A General Staff was urged upon the Royal Navy. These matters and their consequences were reviewed by Nicholas d'Ombrain, *War Machinery and High Policy* [68]. For Britain, the resulting naval force was the Grand Fleet, a concentration of capital ships to overawe the Germans. Its commander, John Jellicoe, wrote a memoir [137] and its historian was David K. Brown [32].

While these debates continued, naval developments of great import were unfolding separately in Great Britain and in Germany; Admirals John Fisher and Alfred von Tirpitz were men of enormous influence in their respective countries over the coming war at sea.

Fisher became First Sea Lord of the Admiralty on Trafalgar Day 1904, precipitating a new wave of naval reform, some calling it the "Fisher revolution," for example, Nicholas Lambert [152] and Charles Fairbanks [71]. An underlying mandate was to reduce costs, and naval estimates did decrease for a year or two. The reforms were pervasive and comprehensive, restructuring squadrons and fleets, calling home all capital ships, ruthless scrapping of obsolete ships, and reforms on the lower deck. As suggested, historians have focused on the impact on capital ship design, notably the battlecruiser and *Dreadnought.*

No era of naval history has been subjected to more historiographical disputes than the Fisher era, then and now. The most extensive survey of what he dubbed "the Fisher era," increasingly problematical and controversial, was the total of seven volumes by an American professor, Arthur Marder. The first volume, covering the period 1880–1905, was published in 1940 [164]. Best known was *From* Dreadnought *to Scapa Flow: The Royal Navy in the Fisher Era, 1904–1919* [167], five volumes being published between 1961 and 1970, with volume III on the Battle of Jutland revised in 1978. The seventh volume was a collection of essays, including an assessment of the Dardanelles campaign [166]. For more on Fisher, Marder, critics of both, and all other prominent personalities of the war at sea, see the end of this section.

Marder depicted a sleepy, inefficient, backward-looking service suddenly awakened by a dynamic new force. Rising opposition at the time within the navy split the service. The leaders were Admiral Lord Charles Beresford, articulating his concerns in *The Betrayal* and a memoir [22, 23], and other critics, described by Matthew Allen [3]. Supporters loyal to Fisher were called "the Fish Pond," and he dubbed the opposition "the Syndicate of Discontent" and "Adullamites." After Fisher left the Admiralty in 1910, he continued as adviser to Winston Churchill, for example, influencing features of the new *Queen Elizabeth* class of battleships, especially 15-inch guns and, perhaps, most importantly, oil fuel. In 1914, Churchill called Fisher back to the Admiralty. They fell out over the Dardanelles campaign, an incident that precipitated one of the most serious political crises in British history. A failed naval and amphibious operation covering all of 1915 was blamed on Churchill. Fisher "disappeared" at a crucial time and Churchill was replaced.

Equally interesting, decisive, and controversial were corresponding machinations within the German navy identified with Alfred von Tirpitz [253, 254, 255], who fancied himself as a disciple of Mahan. Kaiser William II selected Tirpitz to head the navy in the late 1890s with a mandate to expand the German battle fleet known as the High Seas Fleet. In 1898, encouraged by the ambitious Kaiser, Tirpitz launched a sustained campaign to build a German battle fleet. His memoirs were published [254], but Gary Weir, *Building the Kaiser's Navy* [264], has described "the Tirpitz era," 1890–1919. Brilliantly exploiting the peculiarities of the Kaiser Reich, creating the Imperial Naval Office controlled by himself and cooperating with the German military-industrial complex, and passing a series of "Naval Laws" in, for example, 1898, 1908, and 1912, that committed the Reichstag to automatic financing of the fleet were extraordinary achievements initiated and led by Tirpitz. Michael Epkenhans [69] documented a notorious Tirpitz-Krupp industry relationship with enormous political, economic, financial, and military-naval consequences. Curiously, the German navy officialdom played a minor role. Later, when war was anticipated, it stepped in and Tirpitz was shunted aside, exerting little or no influence on strategy, tactics, and operations. Effectively, the navy had been the personal fiefdom of Tirpitz. He rationalized its existence and place in the scheme of things with his "Risk-Fleet theory," that the German fleet would be of sufficient size that the British would not risk a confrontation. Tirpitz was wrong, but by that time, he no longer had a say. A broader and more consequential interpretation of all of these naval matters was subject to brilliant and prescient analyses by a contemporaneous young German historian, Eckert Kehr [138, 139], as noted above.

Excellent surveys of these matters were by Jonathan Steinberg, *Yesterday's Deterrent: Tirpitz and the Birth of the German Battle Fleet* [238], and an article, two general surveys and *Der Tirpitz-Plan* by Volcker Berghahn [24], by Ivo Lambi [153], by Raffael Scheck [225], by Michael Epkenhans [70], by Holger Herwig [108], and by Walter Hubatsch [128]. Herwig [115] reviewed the effect of these and later naval matters on the eventual entry of the United States both into World War I and World War II.

A case has been made that Fisher and Tirpitz were important influences on the war at sea. They and a number of other "personalities" require elaboration: memoirs, published papers and letters, autobiographies, biographies, and biographical studies.

A large literature has been devoted to "Jackie" Fisher, that dynamic, zealous, ruthless, innovative, and charismatic leader, if not the creator, of the modern Royal Navy. Fisher published his memoirs [73]. In addition to the seven volumes mentioned above, Marder edited *Fear God and Dread Nought* [165], three volumes of correspondence and papers plus two more volumes edited by Peter Kemp [140]. Reginald Bacon of the "Fish Pond" wrote the official biography [6]. The best recent portrait was by Ruddock Mackay [160] who, among other things, stressed the successful exploitation of propaganda by Fisher through close relations with powerful press lords. The ubiquitous Richard Hough [123] produced an "authorized" biography, hagiographical and hyperbolic. Truly bizarre was *Fisher's Face: Or Getting to Know the Admiral* by Jan (formerly James) Morris [173]. She was fascinated by a portrait of this "half-caste," "half-Asiatic" person, and parts of her work were engaging. William Jameson wrote *The Fleet That Jack Built* [134], about Fisher and other naval innovators. The contemporaneous nemesis of Fisher was Admiral Lord Charles Beresford, who wrote a memoir and an attack on Fisher [22, 23]. Geoffrey Bennett wrote a biography of "Charlie B" Beresford [17]. Peter Padfield [181] wrote a life of Percy Scott, the great gunnery expert.

Grand Fleet commanders included John Jellicoe and David Beatty, themselves antagonists. Jellicoe articulated his own apologetics [136, 137]. Reginald Bacon [5] has done the official biography of Jellicoe; John Winton [272], an unofficial one, while Temple Patterson [186, 187] wrote a life and edited the papers. Stephen Roskill wrote a piece about Jellicoe's dismissal [220]. Roskill [217] and Geoffrey Rawson [204] described Beatty, and Bryan Ranft [197] edited his papers. Francis Hunter [132] wrote about both Jellicoe and Beatty.

Other British naval figures were Winston Churchill, subject of the largest bio-graphical project of modern times, by Randolph Churchill and Martin Gilbert [51]. Eugene Rasor completed a recent historiographical-bibliographical survey on Winston Churchill [203], which includes over 3,000 annotated entries.

Informative were the memoirs of Roger Keyes [145], a participant in the Dar-danelles campaign and other events. Paul Halpern edited the Keyes papers [97].

Works by and about Alfred Tirpitz were reviewed above. Other German naval commanders included Reinhard Scheer and Franz von Hipper. Scheer left a memoir [226]. And there are lives of von Hipper by Tobias R. Philbin [190] and Hugo von Waldeyer-Hartz [261].

The historian of the Fisher era was Arthur Marder, who was glorified and lion-ized as the ultimate authority for decades. Some continue to defend him. How-ever, increasingly, in the 1970s, 1980s, and 1990s there have arisen critiques of the depth of his research and awareness of details and technicalities, for exam-ple, about naval technology, naval administration, and governmental finance. Some have called it "Marder-bashing." The most public and sensational conflict has been between Marder and Stephen Roskill, author of *Churchill and the Admirals* [218]. The conflict was ostensibly over how each interpreted relations between Winston Churchill and the admirals. Bryan Ranft chided both of them in an article, "Naval Historians at War" [198]. Most persistent, most telling, and prolific has been a series of studies by Jon Sumida [240, 242, 246]. There is a summary critique and articles by Nicholas Lambert [147, 148, 152], as well as by Charles Fairbanks [71] and Thomas Hone [120].

FIGHTING THE WAR

In the account above on the developments of naval strategy and strategic thinking, the naval blockade was stressed. Advances in the nineteenth century forced alterations. An early and continuous strategy of the Allies was the imple-mentation of the naval blockade of the Central Powers, something that did not end with the Armistice of November 1918 but was extended through the first half of 1919, ending with the signing of the Versailles Settlement in late June 1919. Though controversial then, it obviously proved to be effective, and it has continued to be disputed up to the present day. Germany formulated its own ver-sion of blockade with unrestricted submarine warfare, reviewed elsewhere.

Blockade has several features. It is a technical legal term used in international law, initiated by a declaration published by a belligerent power forbidding trade with a designated enemy power. In military terms it means obstructing move-ment of enemy naval forces from their bases. Close blockade, common in the days of sailing ship warfare, entailed continuous operations off enemy ports. Guns, mines, torpedoes, the submarine, and the airplane meant a change to "far" blockade and trade interception out at sea. After a review of the maneuvers of the Royal Navy in the late 1880s and subsequent debate, the conclusion was made that close blockade was out of the question. Nevertheless, Germany could be isolated by patrolling the narrow entrances to the Channel and North Sea.

The British, French, and, later, American, navies were responsible for implementing the blockade of the Central Powers. Motives were strategic and economic. Hundreds of merchant ships were intercepted, diverted, or seized. Citizens of the Central Powers suffered significantly and that suffering got worse with time, especially during the winter of 1918–1919, after the Armistice was concluded.

A. C. Bell [15] and Louis Guichard [92] wrote, respectively, the official British and French histories of the blockade. The British history was ready in 1937 but not published until 1961. Marion Siney [231] wrote a detailed description of British, French, and American naval operations establishing and enforcing the blockade and a historiographical essay. Early reports of the blockade were by G. A. Schreiner [227] and Maurice Parmelee [184]. The subject was controversial. A critical analysis, *The Politics of Hunger* by Paul Vincent [260], called it "political famine" and presented statistical details about the brutal outcome: malnutrition, psychological trauma, starvation, and death. An innovative and impressive study emphasizing implications and consequences was Avner Offer, *The First World War: An Agrarian Interpretation* [178], its themes being wheat, blockade, and economy. The impact on Germany has been underestimated. These latter works were critical of the blockade, especially the extension into 1919. The strategic questions and issues, for example, the shift from close- to far-blockade, the naval forces involved, and the technical mechanisms such as mines and reconnaissance devices were reviewed by M. S. Partridge [185]. Margaret Barnett [10] and Mancur Olson [179] dealt with the British logistical program for maintaining food supplies. Other accounts of the blockade and its consequences were by Edwin Clapp [53] and E. K. Chatterton [48].

As the blockade was being prepared and put in place, other naval operations commenced. The Grand Fleet took up its far-blockade position at Scapa Flow, a large anchorage north of Scotland in the Orkney Islands. An analysis of opening operations, *The King's Ships Were at Sea* by James Goldrick [83], described events of the first six months. Goldrick contended that this period represented the true beginning of modern naval warfare, the salient features being the submarine, aircraft, the mine, surface actions at long range and high speeds, and wireless communications. Alan Coles wrote of an early incident with serious implications, *Three before Breakfast* [57], when on 22 September 1914, three British cruisers were sunk in the North Sea within an hour by the German submarine *U-9,* 1,500 lives being lost. Precautions, redistributions, withdrawals, and recriminations followed.

The war at sea occurred all over the world but, increasingly, operations and confrontations narrowed down to those of the North Sea, English Channel, the Mediterranean, and the Baltic Seas. In the Mediterranean, another formative drama unfolded. The German battlecruiser *Goeben* and cruiser *Breslau* were in the Adriatic Sea in Austrian ports as the war opened. They were able to "escape" and become the most powerful naval units of Turkey, a German ally. British and French forces, potentially superior, had concentrated to eliminate them, but a series of lapses and confusion, some linked to Churchill, led to the escape. Dan

Van Der Vat recounted the episode, but the account and the title were exaggerated, *The Ship That Changed the World.* [259].

No history of naval operations has been so extensively and comprehensively covered as those in the Mediterranean Sea before and during the war by the American naval historian, Paul Halpern [95, 98, 99], in three works. Pertinent prewar diplomatic and strategic developments, the complexities of coalition warfare, the escape of *Goeben,* the Dardanelles campaign, submarine operations, and the Allied build-up at Salonika were all described in detail. Such analyses required research in archives in Britain, France, Italy, Austria, Russia, Turkey, and the United States. He concluded that more than any other factor, the fleet created by Tirpitz moved Britain from splendid isolation to continental commitment. An overall perspective of naval operations in the Mediterranean Sea, past, present, and future, was presented in an edition by John Hattendorf [106].

Early confrontations of capital ships in the North Sea such as Heligoland Bight and Dogger Bank were described by Reginald Bacon, *The Dover Patrol* [4].

On the international scene, British sea power was to dominate the world. This was confirmed after a short time. Dozens of individual actions, German surface raiders sinking British merchant ships, and two important naval battles, closely connected, occurred during the early months. The German Pacific Squadron was commanded by Admiral von Spee, who operated strictly under rules of international law, in contrast to German unrestricted submarine warfare. Churchill praised von Spee and predicted his demise: "a cut flower in a vase, fair to see, yet bound to die," as described by Keith Yates [277]. Operating off the western coast of South America in the Pacific, the German squadron annihilated a British rival. Fisher immediately ordered battlecruisers to the South Atlantic, where they caught the German squadron and annihilated it near the Falkland Islands in December 1914. These battles of Coronel and the Falklands were covered by Geoffrey Bennett [18], Barrie Pitt [191], John Irving [133], Neville Hilditch [116], and by Hans Pochhamer [193] in a rare account by a German survivor. Keith Middlemas [170] told of the far-reaching campaign all over the world to seek and destroy German surface raiders.

As indicated above, the Germans implemented unrestricted submarine warfare, had second thoughts and canceled it after the *Lusitania* was sunk, then, somewhat dramatically, resumed it in February 1917. The U.S. entered the war in April 1917.

On 7 May 1915, a sensational naval incident occurred with immediate and long-term consequences. The then largest and fastest passenger ship in the world, the Cunard liner *Lusitania,* en route from New York to Britain, was torpedoed eleven miles off the coast of Ireland, near Kinsale, by *U-20.* One thousand two hundred people, including 130 Americans, were lost, 61 percent of all aboard. Complications, controversies, and conspiracy theories arose then and later. The Germans had taken out an advertisement in *The New York Times* warning the public that *Lusitania* was subject to attack as she proceeded through a declared war zone. The literature on *Lusitania* was expansive.

In 1972, Colin Simpson [230], a journalist, published a sensational series of accusations—in sum: *Lusitania* was an armored merchant cruiser with 12 hidden, or "phantom," six-inch guns; was carrying munitions and weapons, the explosions of which must have accelerated her sinking; that a contingent of Canadian soldiers was aboard; that *Lusitania* was not zig-zagging and had actually reduced her speed; that the captain was violating four of five regulations; that the Admiralty purposely had not provided escorts; that only one torpedo was used but two major explosions ensued; that "neutral" America was providing war material to the British; for these reasons, the Germans were justified in attacking her, that *U-20* actually set out specifically to sink *Lusitania,* and that following the sinking, essential documents disappeared and a cover-up was executed. The Admiralty, and particularly Winston Churchill, purposely set up *Lusitania* to be sunk so as to create an incident sufficiently extreme to bring America into the war. On 10 May 1915, Churchill answered questions in the House of Commons about the incident. Fisher openly declared the captain incompetent.

Later, Thomas A. Bailey [8], doyen of American foreign policy historians, conducted a thorough investigation. Bailey disputed Simpson, point by point, and presented a balanced, sophisticated, scholarly study. Admittedly, there were 4,200 cases of rifle cartridges, but there were no guns, no soldiers, and no cargo of munitions, and the second explosion was the boilers. Within the last decade, a new element has been added to these stories of sinkings of famous ships. In 1993, Robert Ballard, the famous nautical archaeologist, searched for and found *Lusitania,* "the most mysterious liner of all time," and in his book subtitled *Probing the Mysteries of the Sinking That Changed History* [9], he concluded that the second explosion was neither munitions nor the boiler, but coal dust from the bunkers.

Odds and ends were covered as follows: British naval operations in the Baltic by Geoffrey Bennett [19], the naval situation on the Danube River, especially activities of a British naval mission, by Charles Fryer [79], the role of the Royal Navy in support of land operations on the Western Front by Andrew Weist [265], and a notorious incident involving a British Q-Ship sinking a U-Boat, an atrocity, and an alleged cover-up, by Alan Coles [56].

The most significant example of amphibious warfare during the war at sea was the Anglo-French expedition against the Dardanelles in the eastern Mediterranean, sometimes called the Gallipoli campaign. A strategic objective was to bypass the stalemate on the Western Front and assist the Russian ally. "By ships alone" was the initial plan. The Admiralty planners backed by the French proposed to breach the defenses of the Dardanelles Strait by bombardment from capital ships, proceed into the Sea of Marmora, overawe and capture Constantinople, breach the defenses of the Bosporus Strait, and proceed into the Black Sea to aid the Russians. By late February and early March 1915, the naval forces were ready. They began attacking the forts. The Turks mined the waters. Minesweepers were rushed in, but could not sweep because of both the forts and the current, so the bombarding ships could not silence the forts. There were several attempts and some capital ships were sunk. The army was called in and an invasion of the Gallipoli peninsula was mounted. Troops of Australia and New Zealand, "Anzacs," participated in large numbers and with many casualties. The Turks, supported with supplies and by a brilliant commander from Germany, Liman von Sanders, contained the bungled invasion. Hindsight and reconstruction have confirmed, and the Turks admitted later, that the naval effort almost succeeded and the invasion almost broke through, but it was not to be. The withdrawal, in December 1915, was a spectacular success with no casualties.

A general history of the campaign was by Robert Rhodes James [206], who used new sources and presented a solid, scholarly survey. Naval operations were reviewed by Jeffrey Wallin, *By Ships Alone* [262], and Thomas Frame [74], who covered operations of the Royal Navy and the Royal Australian Navy. In a recent assessment Geoffrey Penn [188] was an apologist for Fisher and highly critical of Churchill. Raymond Callahan [42] reviewed some of the literature: clearly, interservice cooperation and Anglo-French cooperation were rare, no joint planning occurred, and the failure frustrated amphibious operations for decades. The next such operation, Zeebrugge, late in the war, was a failure, as described by Roger Keyes [144] and Barrie Pitt [192].

On 31 May and 1 June 1916, what was hoped to be another Battle of Trafalgar for the British, *Der Tag* for the Germans, failed to happen in both cases, although the Germans immediately announced a great victory. In fact, the Battle of Jutland (or the Skagerrak) was a strategic victory for the British. In the North Sea to the west of the Jutland peninsula of Denmark, the British Grand Fleet and the German High Seas Fleet met in the late afternoon of 31 May. There were several confrontations, first of Battle Cruiser Squadrons, then two episodes involving the main battle fleets, the Germans turning away both times, and, during the night of 31 May–1 June, a mêlée of confused night fighting by destroyers. The Germans had deployed both submarines and aircraft, but they played no role in the battle. The Germans effectively escaped and returned to port. Nothing changed and, although the Germans did come out later, no other major battle occurred.

The pertinent commanders were Admirals John Jellicoe for the Grand Fleet, Reinhard Scheer for the High Seas Fleet, and David Beatty for the British and Franz von Hipper for the German Battle Cruiser Squadrons, the advanced guards. The line-up of sides (in parenthesis, the number of units sunk during the battle in each category): for the Grand Fleet, 28 battleships (0), 9 battlecruisers (3), 34 cruisers (3), and 80 destroyers (8); for the High Seas Fleet, 16 battleships (2), 6 pre-*Dreadnoughts* (0), 5 battlecruisers (0), 11 cruisers (4), 63 destroyers (5); total losses: tonnage, British, 111,980, German, 62,233; casualties, British, 6,094, German, 3,058.

The literature about the battle is expansive. The pertinent volume, Volume III, of the British official naval history of the war was by Julian Corbett [65]. Arthur Marder [167] devoted Volume III of his five-volume history of the Royal Navy during the Fisher era to Jutland. An American naval analyst, H. H. Frost [77], wrote an extensive and thoroughly researched study, faulting Beatty more than

Jellicoe. Geoffrey Bennett wrote a book and an article [16, 20]. Nicholas Lambert [149] presented the latest scholarly and scientific interpretations about the explosions aboard the battlecruisers. Three British ones had blown up. Most thorough and detailed was the analysis of every shot, its disposition, the damage done, if a hit, and measures taken subsequently, was by N. J. M. Campbell, *Jutland: An Analysis of the Fighting* [45]. Among his conclusions: the German hit rate was slightly better than the British, but still only between 2 percent and 4 percent hits. Georg von Hase presented the German perspective [102, 103]. Charles C. Gill [82] focused on the tactics. Consequences and "lessons" of this battle and other naval operations were reviewed by David MacGregor [159]. The latest study is by Keith Yates, *Flawed Victory* [276].

With emphasis on sociocultural factors, the brilliant naval historian Andrew Gordon recently introduced a fascinating juxtaposition in *The Rules of the Game: Jutland and British Naval Command* [85]. He recalled the tragic collision between HMS *Victoria* and *Camperdown* during fleet exercises in 1893, an incident described by Richard Hough, *Admirals in Collision* [124]. Over 300 died, including Admiral George Tryon, a leading naval tactician identified with the command-and-control school called "empiricist." The consequence of that tragedy was subsequent dominance of a competing school, "rationalist," calling for rigid rules and centralized control. Projecting ahead to Jutland, Jellicoe and Admiral Evan-Thomas of the Fifth Battle Squadron, were of the rationalist school, Beatty of the empiricist school. Thus, in the view of Gordon, Jutland was a tactical debacle.

The United States was, of course, neutral during the first years of the war. Richard Van Alstyne [257], John Coogan [63], and Edwin Clapp [53] described Anglo-American tensions related to neutral rights and commerce. After entry, an American naval fleet proceeded to European waters, the commander being Admiral William Sims. Sims was the subject of a book by Elting Morison [172]. Dean Allard [1, 2] wrote of Anglo-American relationships, noting Sims was Anglophile while his superiors were Anglophobe. Best on relationships, strategy, and cooperation was the scholarly study by David Trask, *Captains and Cabinets* [256]. Operations were described by A. B. Feuer, *The U.S. Navy in World War I* [72].

DEMOBILIZATION

The Armistice was signed on 11 November 1918 and the treaty went into effect on 28 June 1919. As noted above, the Allied blockade continued until the treaty was concluded. After the Armistice, the High Seas Fleet was interned, escorted to the British anchorage at Scapa Flow to await disposition. There, on 21 June 1919, a week before the treaty was signed, 52 of the total of 74 German major warships were sunk in what Dan Van Der Vat called "Grand Scuttle" [258]. The German commander, Ludwig von Reuter [205], and the future German naval commander, Friedrich Ruge [224], wrote accounts. Salvage operations for scrap continued into the 1930s.

FURTHER RESEARCH NEEDED

It should be clear that much of the story has been told and told well. However, further research is needed to fill some gaps in the literature.

With his extraordinary grasp for European languages, Paul Halpern has well described the naval war in the Mediterranean [95, 98, 99]. Some equivalent studies for English readers are required for the naval war in the Baltic and Russo-German naval operations. Even extensive British naval operations there, especially concerning submarines, need further study and clarification. So do the secret and complicated operations of the notorious Allied Intervention in Russia which began in 1918. That involved forces of Britain, France, the United States, Japan, and Italy. Another related blank needing further study is the naval war fought mostly in the Black Sea between Russia and Turkey. Also needing description and analysis is the story of the Japanese squadron that operated in European waters.

The battleship and other surface forces are covered well. The torpedo, mine, and submarine are adequately described. The story of that third dimension, naval aviation, is less clear. There were aircraft carriers and a fleet of lighter-than-air craft in the Royal Navy. If the Germans had such a capability, apart from Robinson [214], we know little about it, and thus need further research and publication.

Ship design, ship types, gunnery, and intelligence matters are covered well. But communications, a critical problem at Jutland, optics for reconnaissance and gunnery spotting, and the important innovation in electricity need more work.

Jon Sumida [240, 243] has filled other lacunae related to naval history concerning administration and finance, but he has lamented the universal neglect of studies of the decisive factor of operational logistics for naval forces.

Some personalities have been covered well, perhaps, too well in the cases of Churchill, Fisher, Jellicoe, Beatty, Kaiser William II, and Tirpitz. Some have been neglected, for example, Admiral Reinhard Scheer of the High Seas Fleet and the high command of the German submarine service.

The influence of naval officers has been demonstrated in the cases of John Fisher and Alfred Tirpitz. However, no systematic study of the naval officer corps with political implications has been conducted. A model would be to duplicate the formative study by Gordon Craig, *The Politics of the Prussian Army* [67]. Projects might be "the politics of the officer corps of the Royal Navy" or "the politics of the German naval officer corps."

Noted has been adequate coverage of science, engineering, and shipbuilding. Related matters of communication, optics, night fighting tactics, and electricity require further study. We also know less about ship navigation and cartography. For example, in reconstructing ship locations during the Battle of Jutland, differing navigational positions varied drastically. What was the status of knowledge about these matters and why were there such major deficiencies?

The approach of social history incorporates sociological and prosopographical studies. Some have been conducted of officers and enlisted men, for example for Germany and the United States. The largest weaknesses here are for British, French, Russian, and Italian naval forces.

BIBLIOGRAPHY

1. Allard, Dean C. "Admiral William S. Sims and United States Naval Policy in World War I." *American Neptune,* 35 (April 1975): 97–110.

2. Allard, Dean C. "Anglo-American Naval Differences during World War I." *Military Affairs,* 44 (April 1980): 75–81.

3. Allen, Matthew. "Rear Admiral Reginald Custance: Director of Naval Intelligence, 1899–1902." *Mariner's Mirror,* 78 (February 1992): 61–75.

4. Bacon, Reginald. *The Dover Patrol, 1915–1917.* 2 vols. London: Hutchinson, 1919.

5. Bacon, Reginald. *The Life of John Rushworth, Earl Jellicoe.* London: Cassell, 1936.

6. Bacon, Reginald. *The Life of Lord Fisher of Kilverstone: Admiral of the Fleet.* 2 vols. London: Hodder, 1929.

7. Bacon, Reginald, Maurice, Frederick, Sydenham, Lord George, Bird, W. D., and Oman, Charles. *"The World Crisis" by Winston Churchill: A Criticism.* London: Hutchinson, 1927, 1928.

8. Bailey, Thomas A., and Ryan, Paul B. *The Lusitania Disaster: An Episode in Modern Warfare and Diplomacy.* New York: Free Press, 1975.

9. Ballard, Robert D., and Dunmore, Spencer. *Exploring the* Lusitania: *Probing the Mysteries of the Sinking that Changed History.* New York: Warner, 1995.

10. Barnett, L. Margaret. *British Food Policy during the First World War.* Boston: Allen, 1985

11. Bassett, Ronald. *Battle-Cruisers: A History, 1908–1948.* London: Macmillan, 1981.

12. Baynham, Henry W. F. *Men from the* Dreadnoughts. London: Hutchinson, 1976.

13. Beesly, Patrick. *Room 40: British Naval Intelligence, 1914–1918.* London: Hamilton, 1982.

14. Bell, Archibald C. *Die Englische Hungerblockade im Weltkrieg, 1914–1915.* Essen: Essener, 1943.

15. Bell, Archibald C. *A History of the Blockade of Germany: And the Countries Associated with Her in the Great War, 1914–1918.* London: Her Majesty's Stationery Office, 1937, 1961.

16. Bennett, Geoffrey M. *The Battle of Jutland. British Battles* series. London: Batsford, 1964, 1972, 1999.

17. Bennett, Geoffrey M. *Charlie B: A Biography of Admiral Lord Beresford of Melemmeh and Curaghmore.* London: Dawnay, 1968.

18. Bennett, Geoffrey M. *Coronel and the Falklands. British Battles* series. London: Batsford, 1962.

19. Bennett, Geoffrey M. *Cowan's War: The Story of British Naval Operations in the Baltic, 1918–1920.* London: Collins, 1964.

20. Bennett, Geoffrey M. "The Harper Papers: Fresh Light on the Jutland Controversy." *Quarterly Review* (January 1965): 16–25.

21. Bennett, Geoffrey M. *Naval Battles of the First World War. British Battles* series. London: Batsford, 1968, 1969.

22. Beresford, Charles W. P. *The Betrayal: Being a Record of Facts Concerning Naval Policy and Administration from the Year 1902 to the Present Time.* London: King, 1912.

23. Beresford, Charles W. P. *The Memoirs of Admiral, Lord Charles Beresford: Written by Himself.* 2 vols. London: Methuen, 1914.

24. Berghahn, Volcker R. *Der Tirpitz-Plan: Genesis und Verfall einer innerpolitischen Krisenstratagie unter Wilhelm II.* Dusseldorf: Droste, 1971.

25. Berghahn, Volcker R. *Germany in the Age of Total War.* London: Helm, 1981.

26. Berghahn, Volcker R. *Germany and the Approach of War in 1914. Making of the Twentieth Century* series. London: Macmillan, 1973, 1994.

27. Bernhardi, Friedrich von. *Germany and the Next War.* London, 1912, 1914.

28. Bird, Keith W. *German Naval History: A Guide to the Literature. Military History Bibliographies* series #7. New York: Garland, 1985, 4,178 entries.

29. Blumberg, Herbert E. *Britain's Sea Soldiers: A Record of the Royal Marines during the War, 1914–1919.* Devonport: Swiss, 1927.

30. Brown, David K. "The Design and Construction of the Battleship *Dreadnought.*" *Warship,* 13 (1980): 39–52.

31. Brown, David K. *The Eclipse of the Big Gun Warship, 1906–1945.* London: Conway, 1992.

32. Brown, David K. *The Grand Fleet: Warship Design and Development, 1906–1922.* London: Chatham, 1999.

33. Brown, David K. *Nelson to Vanguard: Warship Design and Development, 1923–1945.* London: Chatham, 2000.

34. Brown, David K. *Warrior to Dreadnought: Warship Development, 1860–1905.* Annapolis: Naval Institute Press, 1997.

35. Buchan, John. *Naval Episodes of the Great War.* London: Nelson, 1938.

36. Burt, Ray A. and Trotter, Wilfrid P. *Battleships of the Grand Fleet: A Pictorial Review of British Battleships and Battlecruisers, 1906–1921.* Annapolis: Naval Institute Press, 1982.

37. Burt, Ray A. *British Battleships, 1889–1904.* Annapolis: Naval Institute Press, 1988.

38. Burt, Ray A. *British Battleships of the World War One.* Annapolis: Naval Institute Press, 1986.

39. Burt, Ray A. *British Cruisers in World War One.* New York: Sterling, 1987.

40. Burt, Ray A. *British Destroyers in World War One.* New York: Sterling, 1986.

41. Burt, Ray A. *French Battleships, 1876–1946.* London: A&A, 1991.

42. Callahan, Raymond A. "What about the Dardanelles: A Review Article." *American Historical Review,* 78 (July 1973): 641–48.

43. Campbell, N. J. M. *Battlecruisers: The Design and Development of British and German Battlecruisers of the First World War.* London: Conway, 1978.

44. Campbell, N. J. M. "British Naval Gunnery, 1880–1945." *Warship,* 17–38 (1981–1986), 18 parts.

45. Campbell, N. J. M. *Jutland: An Analysis of the Fighting.* London: Conway, 1986.

46. Campbell, N. J. M. *Queen Elizabeth Class.* London: Conway, 1972.

47. Cecil, Hugh P., and Liddle, Peter H., eds. *Facing Armageddon: The First World War Experienced.* London: Cooper, 1996.

48. Chatterton, Edward K. *The Big Blockade.* London: Hurst, 1932.

49. Chesney, George. "The Battle of Dorking." *Blackwood's Magazine,* May 1871.

50. Childers, Erskine. *The Riddle of the Sand: A Record of Secret Service Recently Achieved.* London: Nelson, 1903, 1913, 1927, 1970, 1977.

51. Churchill, Randolph S., and Gilbert, Martin. *Winston S. Churchill.* 8 vols. & 15 Companion vols. London: Heinemann; Boston: Houghton, 1966–1988.

52. Churchill, Winston S. *The World Crisis.* 6 vols. and 4, 2, and 1 vol. eds. I: *1911–1914.* II: *1915.* III: *1916–1918: Part I.* IV: *1916–1918: Part II.* V: *The Aftermath.* VI: *The Eastern Front.* London: Butterworth; New York: Scribner; London: Hutchinson; Sydney: Macmillan, 1923–1931, 1951, 1959, 1960, 1963, 1964, 1992, 1993.

53. Clapp, Edwin J. *Economic Aspects of the War: Neutral Rights, Belligerent Claims, and American Commerce in the Years, 1914–1915.* New Haven: Yale University Press, 1915.

54. Clarke, Ignatius F. *Voices Prophesying War, 1763–1984.* London: Oxford University Press, 1966, 1992.

55. Cleaver, Liam J. "The Pen and the Fleet: The Influence of Sir Julian Corbett on British Naval Development, 1898–1918." *Comparative Strategy,* 14 (January 1995): 45–57.

56. Coles, Alan. *Slaughter at Sea: The Truth behind a Naval War Crime.* London: Hale, 1986.

57. Coles, Alan. *Three before Breakfast: A True and Dramatic Account of How a German U-boat Sank Three Cruisers in One Desperate Hour.* Havant: Mason, 1979.

58. Compton-Hall, Richard. *Submarine Boats: The Beginnings of Underwater Warfare.* London: Conway, 1983.

59. Compton-Hall, Richard. *Submarines and the War at Sea, 1914–1918*. London: Macmillan, 1991.

60. *Conway's All the World's Battleships, 1906 to the Present*. London: Conway, 1987, 1988.

61. *Conway's All the World's Fighting Ships, 1906–1921*. London: Conway, 1984, 1985.

62. Coogan, John W. "The British Cabinet and the Anglo-French Staff Talks, 1905–1914: Who Knew What and When Did He Know It?" *Journal of British Studies*, 24 (January 1985): 110–31.

63. Coogan, John W. *The End of Neutrality: The United States, Britain, and Maritime Rights, 1899–1915*. Ithaca: Cornell University Press, 1981.

64. Corbett, Julian S. *Maritime Operations in the Russo-Japanese War, 1904–1905*. 2 vols. Rockville: Kramer, 1994.

65. Corbett, Julian S., and Newbolt, Henry. *Naval Operations. History of the Great War Based on Official Documents*. 5 vols. London: Longmans, 1920–1931, 1938, 1940.

66. Corbett, Julian S. *Some Principles of Maritime Strategy*. London: Conway; Annapolis: Naval Institute Press, 1911, 1972, 1987.

67. Craig, Gordon A. *The Politics of the Prussian Army, 1640–1945*. New York: Oxford University Press, 1955, 1964.

68. D'Ombrain, Nicholas J. *War Machinery and High Policy: Defence Administration in Peacetime Britain, 1902–1914*. London: Oxford University Press, 1973.

69. Epkenhans, Michael. "Krupp and the Imperial German Navy, 1898–1914: A Reassessment." *Journal of Military History*, 64 (April 2000): 335–70.

70. Epkenhans, Michael. *Die Wilhelminische Flottenrustung, 1908–1914: Weltmachtstreben industrieller Fortschritt, soziale Integration*. Munich: Oldenbourg, 1991.

71. Fairbanks, Charles. "The Origins of the *Dreadnought* Revolution: A Historiographical Essay." *International History Review*, 13 (May 1991): 246–72.

72. Feuer, A.B. *The U.S. Navy in World War I: Combat at Sea and in the Air*. Westport, CT: Praeger, 1999.

73. Fisher, John. *Memories and Records*. 2 vols. New York: Doran, 1919–1920.

74. Frame, Thomas R. *First In, Last Out: The Navy at Gallipoli*. New South Wales: Kangaroo, 1990.

75. French, David. *British Economic and Strategic Planning, 1905–1915*. London: Allen, 1982.

76. French, David. *British Strategy and War Aims, 1914–1916*. London: Allen, 1986.

77. Frost, Holloway H. *The Battle of Jutland*. Annapolis: Naval Institute Press, 1936, 1964.

78. Frothingham, Thomas G. *The Naval History of World War*. 3 vols. Cambridge: Harvard University Press, 1924–1925, 1971.

79. Fryer, Charles E. J. *The Royal Navy on the Danube*. New York: Columbia University Press, 1988.

80. Gardiner, Robert, ed. *German Warships of World War I: The Royal Navy's Official Guide*. Annapolis: Naval Institute Press, 1991, 1992.

81. Gibson, Richard H., and Prendergast, Maurice. *The German Submarine War, 1914–1918*. London: Smith, 1931, 1941.

82. Gill, Charles C. *What Happened at Jutland: The Tactics of the Battle*. New York: Doran, 1921.

83. Goldrick, James. *The King's Ships Were at Sea: The War in the North Sea, August 1914– February 1915*. Annapolis: Naval Institute Press, 1984.

84. Goldrick, James, and Hattendorf, John B., eds. *Mahan Is Not Enough: The Proceedings of a Conference on the Works of Sir Julian Corbett and Admiral Sir Herbert Richmond*. Newport: Naval War College Press, 1993.

85. Gordon, G. A. H. *The Rules of the Game: Jutland and British Naval Command*. London: Murray, 1996.

86. Grant, Robert M. *U-Boats Destroyed: The Effect of Anti-Submarine Warfare, 1914–1918*. London: Putnam, 1964.

87. Grant, Robert M. *U-Boat Intelligence, 1914–1918*. Hamden: Archon, 1969.

88. Gray, Edwyn. *The Killing Time: The U-Boat War, 1914–1918.* New York: Scribner, 1972.

89. Gray, Edwyn. *A Damned Un-English Weapon: Submarines, 1914–1918.* New York: Scribner, 1971.

90. Greger, Rene. *The Russian Fleet, 1914–1917.* London: Allen, 1972.

91. Groos, Otto, and Gladisch, Walter. *Der Krieg zur see, 1914–1918.* 7 vols. Berlin: Mittler, 1920–1937, 1965.

92. Guichard, Louis. *The Naval Blockade, 1914–1918.* London: Allan, 1929, 1930.

93. Hackmann, Willem D. *Seek and Strike: Sonar, Anti-Submarine Warfare and the Royal Navy, 1914–1954.* London: Her Majesty's Stationery Office, 1984.

94. Hagan, Kenneth J. *The People's Navy: The Making of American Sea Power.* New York: Free Press, 1990, 1992.

95. Halpern, Paul G. *The Mediterranean Naval Situation, 1908–1914. Harvard Historical Studies* #86. Cambridge: Harvard University Press, 1971.

96. Halpern, Paul G. *A Naval History of World War I.* Annapolis: Naval Institute Press, 1994, 1995.

97. Halpern, Paul G., ed. *The Keyes Papers: Selections from the Private and Official Correspondence of Admiral of the Fleet Baron Keyes of Zeebrugge.* 3 vols. *Publications of the Navy Records Society,* vols. 117, 121, 122. London: Navy Records Society, 1979–1981.

98. Halpern, Paul G. *The Naval War in the Mediterranean, 1914–1918.* Annapolis: Naval Institute Press, 1987.

99. Halpern, Paul G., ed. *The Royal Navy in the Mediterranean, 1915–1918. Publications of the Navy Records Society,* vol. 126. Aldershot: Gower, 1987.

100. Hartcup, Guy. *The War of Invention: Scientific Developments, 1914–1918.* London: Brassey, 1988.

101. Hartesveldt, Fred R. van. *The Dardanelles Campaign, 1915: Historiography and Annotated Bibliography. Bibliographies of Battles and Leaders* series, #21. Westport, CT: Greenwood, 1997, 765 entries.

102. Hase, Georg von. *Kiel and Jutland.* London: Skeffington, 1920, 1921, 1927, 1934.

103. Hase, Georg von. *Skagerrak: Die Grosste Seeschlacht der Weltgeschichte.* Leipzig: Koehler, 1920.

104. Hattendorf, John B., ed. *The Influence of History on Mahan: The Proceedings of a Conference Marking the Centenary of Alfred Thayer Mahan's "Influence of Sea Power upon History."* Newport: Naval War College Press, 1991.

105. Hattendorf, John B., and Jordon, Robert S., eds. *Maritime Strategy and the Balance of Power: Britain and America in the Twentieth Century.* New York: St. Martin, 1989.

106. Hattendorf, John B., ed. *Policy and Strategy in the Mediterranean Sea: Past, Present and Future.* London: Cass, 2000.

107. Hayward, Victor. *HMS Tiger as Bay: A Sailor's Memoir, 1914–1918.* London: Kimber, 1977.

108. Herwig, Holger H. "Admirals versus Generals: The War Aims of the Imperial German Navy, 1914–1918." *Central European History,* 5 (September 1972): 208–33.

109. Herwig, Holger H. "Feudalization of the Bourgeoisie: The Role of the Nobility in the German Naval Officer Corps, 1890–1918." *The Historian,* 38 (February 1976): 268–80.

110. Herwig, Holger H. *The First World War: Germany and Austria-Hungary, 1914–1918.* New York: St. Martin, 1997.

111. Herwig, Holger H. "Fisher, Tirpitz and the *Dreadnought*." *MHQ,* 4 (Autumn 1991): 96–104.

112. Herwig, Holger H. *The German Naval Officer Corps: A Social and Political History, 1890–1914.* London: Oxford University Press, 1973.

113. Herwig, Holger H. "The German Reaction to the *Dreadnought* Revolution." *International History Review,* 13 (May 1991): 273–83.

114. Herwig, Holger H. *"Luxury Fleet": The Imperial German Navy, 1888–1918.* London: Allen, 1980, 1987.

115. Herwig, Holger H. *Politics of Frustration: The United States in German Naval Planning, 1889–1941.* Boston: Little, Brown, 1976.

116. Hilditch, A. Neville. *Coronel and the Falkland Islands.* London: Oxford University Press, 1915.

117. Higham, Robin. *The British Rigid Airship: 1908–1931.* London: Foulis, 1981.

118. Hiley, Nicholas P. "The Strategic Origins of Room 40." *Intelligence and National Security,* 2 (April 1987): 245–73.

119. Hoehling, A. A., and Hoehling, Mary. *The Great War at Sea: A History Naval Action, 1914–1918.* New York: Crowell, 1965.

120. Hone, Thomas C. "Jackie Fisher's Revenge." *Proceedings of the Naval Institute,* 126 (February 2000): 82–85.

121. Horn, Daniel. *The German Naval Mutinies of World War I.* New Brunswick: Rutgers University Press, 1969.

122. Horn, Daniel. *War, Mutiny and Revolution in the German Navy: The World War I Diary of Seaman Richard Stumpf.* New Brunswick: Rutgers University Press, 1967.

123. Hough, Richard A. *Admiral of the Fleet: The Life of John Fisher.* Alt. title: *First Sea Lord: An Authorized Biography of Admiral Lord Fisher.* New York: Macmillan, 1969, 1970, 1977.

124. Hough, Richard A. *Admirals in Collision.* New York: Viking, 1959.

125. Hough, Richard A. Dreadnought: *A History of the Modern Battleship.* London: Allen, 1964, 1968, 1975, 1979.

126. Hough, Richard A. *The Great War at Sea, 1914–1918.* New York: Oxford University Press, 1983, 1986, 1987.

127. Hough, Richard A. *Naval Battles of the Twentieth Century.* London: Constable, 1999.

128. Hubatsch, Walter. *Die Ara Tirpitz: Studien zur deutschen Marinepolitik, 1890–1918.* Gottingen: Musterschmidt, 1955.

129. Humble, Richard. *Before the* Dreadnought: *The Royal Navy from Nelson to Fisher.* London: Macdonald, 1976.

130. Hunt, Barry D. "The Outstanding Naval Strategic Writers of the Century." *NWCR,* 37 (September 1984): 86–107.

131. Hunt, Barry D., and Preston, Adrian, eds. *War Aims and Strategic Policy in the Great War, 1914–1918.* London: Croom, 1977.

132. Hunter, Francis T. *Beatty, Jellicoe, Sims, and Rodman.* London: Curtis, 1919.

133. Irving, John J. C. *Coronel and the Falklands.* London: Philpot, 1927.

134. Jameson, William S. *The Fleet That Jack Built: Nine Men Who Made a Modern Navy.* London: Hart-Davis, 1962.

135. Jameson, William S. *The Most Formidable Thing: The Story of the Submarine from Its Earliest Days to the End of World War I.* London: Hart-Davis, 1965.

136. Jellicoe, John R. *The Crisis of the Naval War.* London: Cassell, 1920.

137. Jellicoe, John R. *The Grand Fleet, 1914–1916: Its Creation, Development, and Work.* London: Cassell, 1919.

138. Kehr, Echart. *Battleship Building and Party Politics in Germany, 1894–1901.* New York: Kraus, 1930, 1965, 1975.

139. Kehr, Echart. *Der Primat der Innenpolitik: Gesammelte Aufsatze zur preussisch-deutschen Sozialgeschichte im 19. und 20. Jahrhundert.* Berlin: de Gruyter, 1930, 1965, 1970.

140. Kemp, Peter K., ed. *The Papers of Admiral Sir John Fisher. Publication of the Navy Records Society* 2 vols. London: Navy Records Society, 1960–1965.

141. Kennedy, Paul M. *The Rise of the Anglo-German Antagonism, 1860–1914.* Boston: Allen, 1980, 1982, 1987.

142. Kennedy, Paul M. *The Rise and Fall of British Naval Mastery.* London: Allen, 1976, 1982, 1983, 1986, 1998.

143. Keyes, Roger. *Adventures Ashore and Afloat.* London: Harrap, 1939, 1940, 1973.

144. Keyes, Roger. *Amphibious Warfare and Combined Operations.* New York: Macmillan, 1943.

145. Keyes, Roger. *The Naval Memoirs of Admrial of the Fleet Sir Roger Keyes.* 2 vols. London: Butterworth, 1934–1935, 1941.

146. Lambert, Andrew D. *The Foundations of Naval History: Sir John Knox Laughton, the Royal Navy and the Historical Profession.* London: Chatham, 1998.

147. Lambert, Nicholas A. "Admiral Sir John Fisher and the Concept of Flotilla Defence, 1904–1909." *Journal of Military History,* 59 (October 1995): 639–60.

148. Lambert, Nicholas A. "British Naval Policy, 1913–1914: Financial Limitations and Strategic Revolution." *Journal of Modern History,* 67 (September 1995): 595–626.

149. Lambert, Nicholas A. " 'Our Bloody Ships' or 'Our Bloody System'? Jutland and the Loss of the Battle Cruisers, 1916." *Journal of Military History,* 62 (January 1998): 27–55.

150. Lambert, Nicholas A. "A Revolution in Naval Strategy: The Influence of the Submarine upon Maritime Thought, 1898–1914." Ph.D. diss., Oxford, 1992.

151. Lambert, Nicholas, ed. *The Submarine Service, 1990–1918. A Publications of the Navy Records Society, vol. 142.* Aldershot: Ashgate, 2001.

152. Lambert, Nicholas A. *Sir John Fisher's Naval Revolution.* Columbia: South Carolina University Press, 1999.

153. Lambi, Ivo N. *The Navy and German Power Politics, 1862–1914.* Boston: Allen, 1984.

154. Layman, R. D. *Naval Aviation in the First World War: Its Impact and Influence.* London: Chatham, 1996.

155. Liddle, Peter H., ed. *Home Fires and Foreign Fields: British Social and Military Experience in the First World War.* London: Brassey, 1985.

156. Liddle, Peter H. *The Sailor's War, 1914–1918.* Poole: Blandford, 1985.

157. Lloyd, Charles C. *The Nation and the Navy: A History of Naval Life and Policy.* New York: Macmillan, 1954, 1961, 1965.

158. Love, Robert W., Jr. *History of the U.S. Navy, 1795–1991.* 2 vols. Harrisburg: Stackpole, 1992.

159. MacGregor, David R. "The Use, Misuse, and Non-Use of History: The Royal Navy and the Operational Lessons of the First World War." *Journal Military History,* 56 (October 1992): 603–15.

160. Mackay, Ruddock F. *Fisher of Kilverstone.* New York: Oxford University Press, 1973, 1974.

161. McNeill, William H. *The Pursuit of Power: Technology, Armed Forces, and Society since 1000.* Chicago: Chicago University Press, 1982.

162. Mahan, Alfred Thayer. *The Influence of Sea Power upon History, 1660–1783.* Boston: Little, Brown, 1890, 1980, 1987.

163. Mahan, Alfred Thayer. *The Influence of Sea Power upon the French Revolution and Empire, 1793–1812.* 2 vols. Boston: Little, Brown, 1892.

164. Marder, Arthur J., 1910–1981. *The Anatomy of British Sea Power: A History of British Naval Power, 1880–1905.* New York: Knopf, 1940, 1972.

165. Marder, Arthur J. *Fear God and Dread Nought: The Correspondence of Admiral of the Fleet Lord Fisher of Kilverstone.* 3 vols. London: Cape, 1952–1959.

166. Marder, Arthur J., *From the Dardanelles to Oran: Studies of the Royal Navy in War and Peace, 1915–1940.* New York: Oxford University Press, 1974.

167. Marder, Arthur J., *From the* Dreadnought *to Scapa Flow: The Royal Navy in the Fisher Era, 1904–1919.* 5 vols. London: Oxford University Press, 1961–1970, 1978.

168. Massie, Robert K. Dreadnought*: Britain, Germany, and the Coming of the Great War.* London: Cape, 1991, 1992.

169. Messimer, Dwight R. *Find and Destroy: Antisubmarine Warfare in World War I.* Annapolis: Naval Institute Press, 2001.

170. Middlemas, R. Keith. *Command the Far Seas: A Naval Campaign of the First World War.* London: Hutchinson, 1961.

171. Millett, Allan R. and Murray, Williamson, eds. *Military Effectiveness.* 3 vols. Boston: Unwin, 1988.

172. Morison, Elting E. *Admiral Sims and the Modern American Navy.* New York: Russell, 1942, 1968.

173. Morris, Jan. *Fisher's Face: or, Getting to Know the Admiral.* New York: Random House, 1995.

174. Newbolt, Henry. *A Naval History of the War, 1914–1918.* London: Hodder, n.d.

175. Occleshaw, Michael E. *Armour against Fate: British Military Intelligence in the First World War.* Columbus: Ohio University Press, 1989.

176. O'Connell, Robert L. "Dreadnought? The Battleship, the U.S. and the World Naval Community." Ph.D. diss., Virginia, 1974.

177. O'Connell, Robert L. *Sacred Vessels: The Cult of the Battleship and the Rise of the U.S. Navy.* Boulder, CO: Westview, 1991, 1993.

178. Offer, Avner. *The First World War: An Agrarian Interpretation.* Oxford: Clarendon, 1989.

179. Olson, Mancur. *The Economics of Wartime Shortage: A History of British Food Supplies in the Napoleonic Wars and World Wars I and II.* Durham, NC: Duke University Press, 1963.

180. Oram, H. P. K. *Ready for Sea.* London: Seeley, 1974.

181. Padfield, Peter. *Aim Straight: A Biography of Admiral Sir Percy Scott.* London: Hodder, 1966, 1967.

182. Paret, Peter. *Makers of Modern Strategy: From Machiavelli to the Nuclear Age.* Princeton: Princeton University Press, 1986 (1942 title edited by E. M. Earle).

183. Parkes, Oscar. *British Battleships:* Warrior *1860 to* Vanguard *1950: A History of Design, Construction and Armament.* London: Seeley, 1957, 1958, 1972, 1990.

184. Parmelee, Maurice. *Blockade and Sea Power: The Blockade, 1914–1919, and Its Significance for a World State.* New York: Crown, 1924.

185. Partridge, M. S. "The Royal Navy and the End of the Close Blockade, 1885–1905." *Mariner's Mirror,* 75 (May 1989): 119–36.

186. Patterson, A. Temple. *Jellicoe: A Biography.* London: Macmillan, 1969.

187. Patterson, A. Temple, ed. *The Jellicoe Papers: Selections from Private and Official Correspondence.* 2 vols. *Publications of the Navy Records Society,* Vols. 108 and 111. London: Navy Records Society, 1966–1968.

188. Penn, Geoffrey. *Fisher, Churchill and the Dardanelles.* London: Cooper, 1999.

189. Persius, Lothar. *Der Seekrieg.* Charlottenburg: Weltbuhne, 1919.

190. Philbin, Tobias R. *Admiral von Hipper: The Inconvenient Hero.* New York: Humanities, 1982.

191. Pitt, Barrie. *Coronel and Falkland.* London: Cassell, 1960, 1964.

192. Pitt, Barrie. *Zeebrugge.* New York: Ballantine, 1958, 1966.

193. Pochhamer, Hans. *Before Jutland: Admiral von Spee's Last Voyage: Coronel and the Battle of the Falklands.* London: Jarrolds, 1931.

194. Pollen, Anthony. *The Great Gunnery Scandal: The Mystery of Jutland.* London: Collins, 1980.

195. Pollen, Arthur H. *The British Navy in Battle.* London: Chatto, 1919.

196. Preston, Antony. *Battleships of World War I: An Illustrated Encyclopedia of the Battleships of All Nations, 1914–1918.* Harrisburg, PA: Stackpole, 1972.

197. Ranft, Bryan M., ed., *The Beatty Papers: Selections from the Private and Official Correspondence of Admiral of the Fleet Earl Beatty. Publication of the Navy Records Society* #s 128 and 132. London: Scolar, 1989–1993.

198. Ranft, Bryan M. "Naval Historians at War." *Journal of the Royal United Services Institution,* 120 (March 1975): 79–80.

199. Ranft, Bryan M., ed. *Technical Change and British Naval Policy, 1860–1939.* London: Hodder, 1977.

200. Rasor, Eugene L. *British Naval History since 1815: A Guide to the Literature.* Vol. 13 of Garland's *Military History Bibliographies* series. New York: Garland, 1990, 3,125 entries.

201. Rasor, Eugene L. *The Battle of Jutland: A Bibliography.* Vol. 7 of *Bibliographies of Battles and Leaders* series. Westport, CT: Greenwood, 1991, 538 entries.

202. Rasor, Eugene L. *Arthur James Balfour, 1848–1930: Historiography and Annotated Bibliography.* Vol. 22 of *Bibliographies of British Statesmen* series. Westport: Greenwood, CT: 1998, 425 entries.

203. Rasor, Eugene L. *Winston S. Churchill, 1874–1965: Comprehensive Historiography and Annotated Bibliography. Bibliographies of World Leaders* series, vol. 6. Westport: Greenwood, 2000, 3,099 entries.

204. Rawson, Geoffrey. *Earl Beatty: Admiral of the Fleet.* London: Jarrolds, 1930.

205. Reuter, Ludwig von. *Scapa Flow: The Account of the Greatest Scuttling of All Time.* London: Hurst, 1940.

206. Rhodes James, Robert. *Gallipoli.* London: Batsford, 1965, 1989, 1999.

207. Richmond, Herbert W. *The Invasion of Britain: An Account of Plans, Attempts, and Countermeasures from 1586 to 1918.* London: Methuen, 1941.

208. Richmond, Herbert W. *National Policy and Naval Strength, and Other Essays.* London: Longman, 1928.

209. Richmond, Herbert W. *Statesman and Sea Power: The Navy as an Instrument of Power.* Oxford: Clarendon, 1946, 1953.

210. Rippon, Peter M. *Evolution of Engineering in the Royal Navy.* 2 vols. London: Spellmount, 1988–1994.

211. Roberts, John. *Battlecruisers.* Annapolis: Naval Institute Press, 1998.

212. Roberts, John A. *The Battleship* Dreadnought. Annapolis: Naval Institute Press, 1992.

213. Roberts, John A. Invincible *Class. Warship Monographs.* London: Conway, 1972, 51 pp.

214. Robinson, Douglas H. *The Zeppelin in Combat.* London: Foulis, 1962.

215. Rodger, N. A. M. *A Naval History of Britain.* Vol. 1: *The Safeguard of the Sea, 600–1649.* Vol. 2: *1649–1815.* London: Harper, 1997.

216. Ropp, Theodore. *The Development of a Modern Navy: French Naval Policy, 1871–1904.* Annapolis: Naval Institute Press, 1937, 1987.

217. Roskill, Stephen W. *Admiral of the Fleet Earl Beatty: The Last Naval Hero: An Intimate Biography.* London: Collins, 1980.

218. Roskill, Stephen W. *Churchill and the Admirals.* London: Collins, 1977.

219. Roskill, Stephen W. "The Destruction of Zeppelin L.53." *Proceedings of the Naval Institute,* 86 (August 1960): 70–78.

220. Roskill, Stephen W. "The Dismissal of Admiral Jellicoe." *Journal of Contemporary History,* 1 (October 1966): 69–93.

221. Roskill, Stephen W., ed. *Documents Related to the Naval Air Service. Publication of the Navy Records Society* #113. London: Navy Records Society, 1969.

222. Roskill, Stephen W. *HMS* Warspite*: The Story of a Famous Battleship.* London: Collins, 1957, 1997.

223. Roskill, Stephen W. *The Strategy of Sea Power: Development and Application.* London: Collins, 1962.

224. Ruge, Friedrich. *Scapa Flow, 1919: The End of the German Fleet.* London: Allan, 1969, 1973.

225. Scheck, Raffael. *Alfred von Tirpitz and German Right-Wing Politics, 1914–1930.* New York: Humanities, 1998.

226. Scheer, Reinhard. *Germany's High Sea Fleet in the World War.* London: Cassell, 1920.

227. Schreiner, George Abel. *The Iron Ration: The Economic and Social Effects of the Allied Blockade on Germany and the German People.* London: Murray, 1918.

228. Schurman, Donald M. *The Education of a Navy: The Development of British Naval Strategic Thought, 1867–1914.* Chicago: Chicago University Press, 1965, 1984.

229. Schurman, Donald M. *Julian S. Corbett, 1854–1922: Historian of British Maritime Policy from Drake to Jellicoe.* London: Royal Historical Society, 1981.

230. Simpson, Colin. *The* Lusitania. London: Longman, 1972, 1990.

231. Siney, Marion C. *The Allied Blockade of Germany, 1914–1916.* 1957, 1960, 1973.

232. Siney, Marion C. "British Official Histories of the Blockade of the Central Powers during the First World War." *American Historical Review,* 68 (January 1963): 392–401.

233. Smith, Myron J., Jr. *The American Navy: A Bibliography.* 5 vols. Metuchen: Scarecrow, 1972–1974.

234. Smith, Myron J., Jr. *Battleships and Battlecruisers, 1884–1984: A Bibliography and Chronology.* New York: Garland, 1985, 5,500 entries.

235. Southworth, John van Duyn. *War at Sea.* 3 vols. New York: Twayne, 1970.

236. Steinberg, Jonathan. "The Copenhagen Complex." *Journal of Contemporary History,* 1 (July 1966): 23–46.

237. Steinberg, Jonathan. "The Novelle of 1908: Necessities and Choices in the Anglo-German Naval Arms Race." *Transactions of the Royal Historical Society,* 5th ser., 21 (1971): 25–43.

238. Steinberg, Jonathan. *Yesterday's Deterrent: Tirpitz and the Birth of the German Battle Fleet.* New York: Macmillan, 1965.

239. Sumida, Jon T. "British Capital Ship Design and Fire Control in the *Dreadnought* Era: Sir John Fisher, Arthur Hungerford Pollen, and the Battle Cruiser." *Journal of Modern History,* 51 (June 1979): 205–30.

240. Sumida, Jon T. "British Naval Administration and Policy in the Age of Fisher." *Journal of Military History,* 54 (January 1990): 1–26.

241. Sumida, Jon T. "British Naval Operational Logistics, 1914–1918." *Journal of Military History,* 57 (July 1993): 447–80.

242. Sumida, Jon T. *In Defense of British Naval Supremacy: Finance, Technology and British Naval Policy, 1889–1914.* Boston: Hyman, 1989, 1993.

243. Sumida, Jon T. "Financial Limitations, Technological Innovation, and British Naval Policy, 1904–1910." Ph.D. diss., Chicago, 1982.

244. Sumida, Jon T. *Inventing Grand Strategy and Teaching Command: The Classic Works of Alfred Thayer Mahan Reconsidered.* Baltimore: Johns Hopkins University Press, 1997, 1998, 2000.

245. Sumida, Jon T. *The Pollen Papers: The Privately Circulated Works of Arthur Hungerford Pollen, 1901–1916. Publication of the Navy Records Society* #124. London: Allen, 1984.

246. Sumida, Jon T. "Sir John Fisher and the *Dreadnought:* The Sources of Naval Mythology." *Journal of Military History,* 59 (October 1995): 619–37.

247. Tarrant, V. E. *Battle Cruiser* Invincible*: The History of the First Battlecruiser, 1909–1916.* Annapolis: Naval Institute Press, 1986.

248. Tarrant, V.E. *Battleship* Warspite. Annapolis: Naval Institute Press, 1990.

249. Terraine, John. *Business in Great Waters: The U-Boat Wars, 1916–1945.* London: Cooper, 1989.

250. Terraine, John. *The First World War, 1914–1918.* London: Hutchinson, 1965.

251. Terraine, John. *To Win a War, 1918: The Year of Victory.* London: Sidgwick, 1978.

252. Thatford, Owen. *British Naval Aircraft since 1912.* London: Putnam, 1958.

253. Tirpitz, Alfred von. *Deutsche Ohnmachtspolitik im Weltkriege.* Hamburg: Hanseatische, 1926.

254. Tirpitz, Alfred von. *My Memoirs.* 2 vols. New York: AMS, 1919, 1970.

255. Tirpitz, Alfred von. *Politische Dokumente: Der Aufbau der deutschen Weltmacht.* 2 vols. Berlin: Cotta, 1924–1926.

256. Trask, David F. *Captains and Cabinets: Anglo-American Naval Relations, 1917–1918.* Columbia: University of Missouri Press, 1972.

257. Van Alstyne, Richard W. "The Policy of the U.S. Regarding the Declaration of London at the Outbreak of the Great War." *Journal of Modern History,* 7 (December 1935): 434–47.

258. Van Der Vat, Dan. *Grand Scuttle: The Sinking of the German Fleet at Scapa Flow in 1919.* London: Hodder, 1982, 1986.

259. Van Der Vat, Dan. *The Ship That Changed the World: The Escape of the* Goeben *to the Dardanelles in 1914.* London: Hodder, 1985.

260. Vincent, C. Paul. *The Politics of Hunger: The Allied Blockade of Germany, 1915–1919.* Athens: Ohio University Press, 1985.

261. Waldeyer-Hartz, Hugo von. *Admiral von Hipper.* London: Rich, 1933.

262. Wallin, Jeffrey D. *By Ships Alone: Churchill and the Dardanelles.* Durham, NC: Carolina Academic, 1981.

263. Wegener, Wolfgang. *The Naval Strategy of the World War. Classics of Sea Power.* Annapolis: Naval Institute Press, 1929, 1989.

264. Weir, Gary. *Building the Kaiser's Navy: The Imperial Navy Office and German Industry in the von Tirpitz Era, 1890–1919.* Annapolis: Naval Institute Press, 1992.

265. Weist, Andrew A. *Passchendaele and the Royal Navy.* Westport, CT: Greenwood, 1995.

266. Wignall, M. B. "Collaboration in Anti-submarine Warfare, 1914–1921." Ph.D. diss., London, 1987.

267. Wilson, Herbert W. *Battleships in Action.* 2 vols. Annapolis: Naval Institute Press, 1926, 1995.

268. Wilson, Michael. *Destination Dardanelles: The Story of HMS E-7.* Hamden: Shoe String, 1988.

269. Wilson, Michael and Kemp, Paul. *Mediterranean Submarine Warfare in the First World War.* London: Crecy, 1997.

270. Wilson, Michael. *Baltic Assignment: British Submariners in Russia, 1914–1919.* London: Cooper, 1985.

271. Wingate, John. *HMS* Dreadnought/*Battleship, 1906–1920.* Windsor: Profile, 1970.

272. Winton, John. *Jellicoe.* London: Michael Joseph, 1981.

273. Woodward, David. *The Collapse of Power: Mutiny in the High Seas Fleet.* London: Barker, 1973.

274. Woodward, David. *Sunk! How the Great Battleships Were Lost.* Boston: Allen, 1982.

275. Woodward, E. L. *Great Britain and the German Navy.* Oxford: Clarendon, 1935.

276. Yates, Keith. *Flawed Victory: Jutland, 1916.* Annapolis: Naval Institute Press, 2000.

277. Yates, Keith. *Graf Spee's Raiders Challenge to the Royal Navy, 1914–1915.* London: Cooper, 1995.

278. Yergin, Daniel. *The Prize: The Epic Quest for Oil, Money and Power.* London: Simon, 1991.

16

The War in the Air

John H. Morrow

THE ARCHIVES

The sources on the air war of 1914–1918 are numerous and significant, although naturally not of the extent of those on the much greater aerial conflict from 1939 to 1945, in which the bombing campaign destroyed many of the World War I German sources. Yet substantial documentation still exists.

In Britain the records of the Public Record Office, the Imperial War Museum, the Air Historical Branch of the Ministry of Defense, and the Royal Air Force Museum at Hendon are indispensable to the study of the British air effort. Particularly the Australian, New Zealand, and Canadian histories rely on sources held in those archives. In France the Service Historique de l'Armée de l'Air at Vincennes, the Musée de l'Air ar le Bourget, and the Archives Nationales all hold valuable documentation of the French experience.

For the German and Austro-Hungarian aerial efforts, the materials in the Bundesarchiv Koblenz, the Zentral Archiv in Potsdam (which has absorbed the documentation from the earlier Bundesarchiv-Militär Archiv in Freiburg), the Deutsches Museum and the Bayerisches Kriegsarchiv in Munich are plentiful and important. Researchers should also investigate the state archives that remain from the imperial era, such as the Wuerttemberg and Saxon archives in Stuttgart and Dresden respectively. The Osterreichisches Kriegsarchiv records in Vienna are invaluable, while in Italy government sources are supplemented by the Caproni Museum in Trento. In the former Soviet Union government archives heretofore closed to Western researchers until the 1990s should provide documentation on the imperial Russian air effort.

In the United States the documents of the National Archives and the National Air and Space Museum in Washington, the Air Force Historical Research Center at Maxwell Air Force Base in Alabama, and the Air Force Museum in Dayton, Ohio, are indispensable for the study of origins of American air power, which was not much in evidence in the First World War. Moreover, the extensive pictorial and archival accumulations of private collectors in the field, such as Peter Grosz of Princeton, New Jersey, are also invaluable.

SCHOLARSHIP

The scholarship on the air war continues to grow, as academic researchers have entered a realm that in the 1970s was considered often in scholarly circles to be "aviation buff" literature. Studies written between the wars ranged from official histories, such as the six-volume British study *The War in the Air* [93], the only official history completed in the interwar years, and now superseded by Wise's Canadian volume [94] to firsthand accounts of war by its participants [see memoirs], to semi-official histories often edited and compiled by experts in the field who were recording their knowledge of the war, such as *L'Aéronautique pendant la Guerre Mondiale* (Aviation during the War) [187] and the articles by Hans Arndt [252–254]. These accounts often make for fascinating reading, although particularly in the case of the official and semi-official histories, they are often sanitized and written to defend a particular position, to praise or occasionally to condemn the air effort of a particular country. This information, nevertheless, is often accurate and informative, and it provides as much a sense of the crucial issues in aviation current when it was written as it does of the first air war.

The great air aces of the war were certainly its major heroes, and accounts and recounts of their exploits will probably never cease to be popular items. Manfred von Richthofen, the Red Baron of Germany, undoubtedly leads in the number of works written on him as he reigned in the air war in numbers of official victories [266]. Fine studies of the other great aces such as the British, Albert Ball [96], Hawker [118], Mannock [140], the Frenchman Nungesser [208], and the Italian Baracca [301], as well as well-written and highly informative first-person accounts by wartime aviators [see memoirs], make for highly exciting reading. More technical works on the airplanes of the First World War abound, because the famous biplanes, triplanes, and monoplanes continue to fascinate the general public even in the space age.[1–6, 21, 27]

General studies of the air war by Lee Kennett [22] and John Morrow [29], Wise [94], and Robert Wohl's cultural history of aviation in the decade 1908–1918 [43] serve as more recent general texts on World War I aviation.

BIBLIOGRAPHIES

Two very serviceable bibliographies are Myron J. Smith's *World War I in the Air: A Bibliography and Chronology* [39] and Edward Homze's *German Military Aviation. A Guide to the Literature* [18]. Morrow's works on 1914–1918 contain extensive bibliographies [267–268]. In this day of the Internet, the use of a system like WorldCat makes available to the browser a variety of items that may well supersede the published bibliographies of the past.

1908–1914

Prewar Europe from 1908 to 1914 witnessed the militarization of flight, in the midst of spiraling international tensions with crises in Morocco and the Balkans from 1905 to 1914 and arms races on land and sea. In 1908 and 1909 such events as a twelve-hour Zeppelin epic, and the flights of Henri Farman, Wilbur Wright, and ultimately Louis Bleriot's crossing of the English Channel stimulated public enthusiasm for aviation. Military aviation leagues formed in France and Germany and then across Europe, as Wohl noted [43]. These extraparliamentary aviation pressure groups, which emulated the naval leagues that had preceded them, included prominent military, political, and industrial leaders; developed their own press organs; and encouraged parliamentary representatives to support military aviation. Highly placed patrons, such as Prince Heinrich of Prussia [236, 267], Grand Duke Alexander Mikhailovich of Russia [280], and First Lord of the Admiralty Winston Churchill in Britain [114] as Penrose [144], and for France, as Marie [179] and Etévé [171] demonstrated, sponsored military aviation. In the absence of substantial sport or commercial markets, and in an atmosphere of increasing nationalistic bellicosity, supporters of military aviation molded popular attitudes to benefit their cause. By the end of 1909 France and Germany were forming military air services, and the other powers would soon follow suit in the effort to keep pace with potential opponents and allies in the European armaments race.

Public perceptions and expectations of air power's future importance for aggression or defense fueled its growth and the development of small prewar aviation industries primarily dependent upon military contracts for their survival. Prewar literature, as Goldstein [8] and Ingold [17] noted, foretold nearly every role that aircraft would actually play in the First World War, including the bombing of civilians to destroy morale. From its very origins military aviation captured the rapt attention of civilians, who regarded the aeronautical achievements as measures of the greatness of nations at the beginning of the twentieth century, as Paris, *Winged Warfare* [141] shows. Although the airplanes of the day were too small and fragile to factor into prewar international politics, Germany's development of the giant dirigible, the Zeppelin, did prompt some German aviation magazines to threaten a preemptive air strike against Germany's enemies, thereby rendering the airship a diplomatic weapon and heightening prewar tensions, Fritzsche [259] showed.

AIRCRAFT INDUSTRY

By 1912 prewar aviation manufacturers were indissolubly tied to the military through contracts. Designers and manufacturers like the Farman [230] and

Voisin brothers [186], Louis Breguet [169], and Louis Bechereau of SPAD in France, on which see Chadeau's *L'Industrie Aéronautique en France* (Aeronautical Industry in France) [196]; Anthony Fokker [240], Robert Thelen, and Ernst Heinkel in Germany [241]; Geoffrey de Havilland's *Sky Fever* [59] and T.O.M. Sopwith in Britain. Engine firms like Rolls-Royce in Britain [133], Gnome et Rhône [211], Renault in France [200], and Daimler in Germany would form the nucleus of the wartime aviation industry, as Herschel Smith has shown [38]. The military, in its role as sole consumer, sought to control their production. By 1914 the French aviation industry, with 3,000 workers in nine firms, was larger than Germany's 2,500 workers, also in nine firms [268], and Britain's 1,000 workers in 12 firms [45]. The British would need French assistance, as would the tiny aviation industries in Russia and Italy, while the minuscule Austro-Hungarian industry relied on Germany. The United States, far from the bellicose European cockpit, had the smallest industry of all.

The aviation industry's reliance on a small pool of highly skilled craftsmen meant that future expansion, particularly in engine manufacture, would depend on a reservoir of trained talent. France could turn to its vaunted automobile industry [212], second only to that of the United States, while German automotive production, although third in rank, was in effect a Daimler monopoly [267]. Britain, despite its industrial potential, depended on France, as did Russia [272]. Fiat endowed Italy with the greatest potential of the lesser powers, while Austria, though the home of Ferdinand Porsche, lacked the industrial foundation to exploit such talent [267]. The United States, which came last to the war, with the world's greatest automobile industry, had virtually no aero engine makers, as Holley noted [328].

AVIATION'S IMAGE

In prewar Europe and America, aviation had displaced auto racing as the most popular and dangerous sport; some reporters observed that possibility of witnessing bloodshed attracted large crowds, and the aviation crashes the press described with gusto left their victims impaled on engines, grilled crisply in flaming wreckage, or crushed to a pulp. By comparison, auto racing was merely child's play. Aviators had become popular heroes, daredevil sportsmen, conquerors of speed, height, and distance, masters of the use of technology in the conquest of nature. In the small air services of all countries a different type of warrior arose, exemplified by the dashing and audacious hero of British doggerel "Lieutenant Daedalus Icarus Brown." See Villard [42], Penrose [144], Porret [227].

The new aviators, like the aviation manufacturers, usually came from the middle class, although military aviators might well be aristocrats. A certain material ease enabled the inventor-entrepreneur's pursuit of the fanciful goal of flight, while the early pilots often had themselves to pay for their initial flight instruction before they underwent military training in cross-country flight and observation. By August 1914 the larger air arms of France and Germany possessed only 250 to 300 airworthy craft ready for frontline service, and each service had some 250 active-duty field pilots; see Morrow [29]. In German two-seat observation planes, the observer was a commissioned officer and the aircraft commander, the pilot, a noncommissioned officer, according to Boelcke. [237]

MOBILIZATION AND WAR

When the European air services departed for mobilization and war, all expected the impending conflict to be short and sharp. The airplane would be used for artillery observation and reconnaissance over enemy lines, while the Zeppelin was expected to perform long-range bombing attacks and reconnaissance. The air services had practiced reconnaissance on military maneuvers since 1910 but had spent little or no time on bombing and in fact had no aerial bombs at the beginning of the war. Air-to-air combat, if envisaged by a few farsighted individuals, was a task for which they had neither planned nor practiced. All the air services had a variety of types of aircraft, some of which would prove ill suited for wartime conditions.

With mobilization, the French aviation director actually closed the aviation schools and ordered no more airplanes, as the anticipated shortness of the war would make new pilots and planes useless. Many pilots in rear echelon units actually departed for the front, even if as reserve pilots, to participate in the great adventure. As the units mobilized and advanced to war, if they found themselves short of aircraft, their commanders, as occurred in Germany, often returned to the factories to commandeer airplanes without regard for orderly supply or contracts. Commanders could occasionally be found at factories bickering with each other and the manufacturer over who was going to take available airplanes. Despite such incidents, the new air arms by and large moved as efficiently as could be expected to the front to assume their duties with the advancing armies. See Chadeau [197].

BECOMING A WEAPON

During the First World War aircraft evolved from an instrument of reconnaissance used singly in 1914 to a weapon for fighting, bombing, and strafing in 1918. Aviation played a significant role, first in rendering ground forces more effective through reconnaissance or by artillery observation. Later, its efficiency required its deployment en masse against the enemy. Air services that had begun the war with 200 frontline airplanes had 2,000 to 3,000 airplanes at the front in 1918. National aviation industries that had a few thousand workers to deliver a hundred planes a month in 1914 employed hundreds of thousands of workers to deliver thousands of planes and engines monthly in 1918.

French, German, and English wartime aircraft manufacture was 52,000, 48,000, and 43,000 respectively, but the French produced some 88,000 engines to English and German totals of 41,000 each. By 1918 the English were surpassing the French in monthly airframe production, occasionally exceeding

3,000 planes a month compared to the French maximum of 2,700, but French industry was delivering some 4,000 engines at peak production, more than double British manufacture. The Germans, reaching exhaustion in manpower and materials in 1918, topped out at 2,200 planes and 1,900 engines. [Aspects of this story are to be found in bibliographic entries 1 (Angelucci), 29 (Morrow); for Britain in 38 (Smith), 45 (Ministry of Munitions), 110 (Fearon), 144 (Penrose); for France in 161 (D'Aubigny), 171 (Etévé), 187 (Official Histories), 194 (Cantener), 195–196 (Chadeau), 203 (Hodeir), 212 (Laux), 216 (Marchis), 217 (Morgat), 232 (Vincent); for Germany in 241 (Heinkel), 242 (Lowenstern), 256 (von Bülow), 263 (Grey and Thetford), 269 (Robinson); for Russia in 278 (Hardesty) and for the U.S. in 307 (Biddle), and 329 (Hudson).]

In what by 1917 had become an aerial war of attrition above the one in the trenches, some generals and politicians now recognize the importance of mass. Gen. Henri Pétain, the French Commander-in-Chief [223], and Winston Churchill, English Minister of Munitions, both recognized the capital importance of aviation when deployed in mass, Churchill desiring to replace the attrition of men with a war of machines using "masses of guns, mountains of shells, clouds of aeroplanes." [102]

Aviation was the most advanced and innovative technological arm, the one that epitomized the new total warfare in its requirement of meshing the military, political, economic, technological, and industrial aspects of war—the front and the rear, the military and civilian. Military and political leaders had to make crucial decisions to expand the tiny air arms of 1914 and mobilize the embryonic supporting industries, for in airpower more than in any other realm of combat in the First World war, technological and industrial superiority essentially determined the outcome of the struggle. The race for aerial superiority had to be won first in design offices and then on factory floors, as the airplane evolved from an experimental vehicle into a weapon. Aircraft manufacturers like Albatross, SPAD, and Sopwith; engine manufacturers, as Herschel Smith noted [38], like Daimler, Hispano Suiza, and Rolls Royce [129 and 133]—their designers and skilled workers—were the essential backbone of their countries' aerial effort.

The airplane and its engine exemplified the harsh demands and enormous waste of modern industrial warfare, as the intensifying air war necessitated increased production to replace destroyed craft and to meet the front's incessant demands for more aircraft. They had to be sufficiently simple to lend themselves to serial production, yet of sufficient reliability and performance to be effective under rapidly changing frontline conditions despite their limited combat life. Planes and engines demanded much higher standards of precision and reliability than the automobile, and their rapid obsolescence in wartime rendered them unlike small arms or artillery, which were of standard types that changed infrequently and could be produced by state-run arsenals [45, 129]. The air war also emphasized salvage, repair and reconstruction.

In wartime Europe, public fascination with this new realm of warfare encouraged a mythologizing of the air war into a single image of individual combat, deadly but chivalrous. In the trenches mass slaughter on an unprecedented scale rendered individuals insignificant. Aerial heroes provided a much needed affirmation of the importance of the individual and youth in a slaughter of both. Fighter pilots, as Campbell points out [2], consequently became not only the symbols of aviation but also the ultimate heroes of World War I. Aerial combat—individual, chivalrous, and deadly—dominates the popular conception of aviation in the First World War [30 (Norman), 33 (Reynolds), and 199 (Facon)].

Airmen were *the* heroes of the great war of 1914–1918. Immortalized through their exploits, the air aces are probably far better remembered today than the political and military leaders of the time. It was natural for aviators to become the heroes of that conflict. Dreams of flight embodied in the myths of Daedalus and Icarus long antedated the actual achievement of powered flight, just as visions of aerial warfare preceded the formation of air arms. The great war fliers, particularly in France and Germany, were worshipped by the public. Oswald Boelcke, one of Germany's first and most famous aces [237], won Germany's highest award for valor, the pour le Mérite, early in 1916. Photographs of the handsome youth and jaunty verses about his victories flooded the press. When he visited Frankfurt in the spring, crowds stared at him in the streets. During intermission at the opera, the audience crowded around him, and at the finale, instead of singing an encore, the Heldentenor sang a verse in Boelcke's honor. The audience went mad, clapping, shouting, and tramping their feet. Boelcke, imperturbable in aerial combat, was so startled that he fled the theater. He crashed to his death in October 1916, the victim of a collision in combat after 40 victories. A German nation in mourning commemorated Boelcke in two elaborate funerals, sent condolences to the family, and composed eulogies to inspire German youth to protect the fatherland as their hero had.

Manfred von Richthofen, Boelcke's pupil and heir, elicited the same worship during 1917 and 1918. The first two editions of his wartime memoirs, *Der Rote Kampfflieger* (The Red Battleflier) [246], which appeared in 1918, sold a half million copies. His funeral service in Berlin in May 1918 was even more spectacular than Boelcke's, as the Hohenzollern royal family joined the Richthofens in the pew [247 (Schaefer) and 264 (Morrow)].

The legendary Georges Guynemer was France's greatest hero, and upon his death in the fall of 1917 after scoring 53 victories, teachers instructed schoolchildren that he had flown so high that he could not descend. In October the government enshrined "Capt. Guynemer, symbol of the aspirations and enthusiasm of the army of the nation," in France's memorial to its national heroes, the Panthéon, "whose cupola alone has sufficient span to shelter such wings." The frail youth embodied the victory of the spirit over the flesh, of France's will to endure despite her grave wounds [218, 219, 221, 226, 227].

In England the Royal Flying Corps characterized air combat as a sport, a notion that stemmed from the corps' composition early in the war—commissioned officers recruited mainly from the ranks of public-school sportsmen attracted to military aviation for the adventure. The image of the air war passed down to us in most of their memoirs and histories is one of a clean and glorious struggle, far above the mud and squalor of the Western Front below. In the most literary British memoirs, such as Cecil Lewis's *Sagittarius Rising* [71], the war assumed the characteristics of sport and medieval tournament, a joust between heroes who bore only the utmost respect for one another, as, bound together in the brotherhood of the air, they rose daily to do battle. They fought and lived by unwritten codes. In squadron at the end of the day, for example, they were never to dwell on their losses except in absolute privacy. Instead, maintenance of a "stiff upper lip" was mandatory; these young aviators consequently released nerves, rage, and fears together in "rags," or brawls, in the mess or in bruising football games [65 (Jones), 124 (Jones), 132 (Liddle), and 158 (Winter)]. Mess bills for broken furniture were common, and though no intrepid historian has yet studied the casualty rates for these "friendly" terrestrial struggles, at least one top British aviator, 40-victory ace Philip Fullard, suffered a seriously broken leg in 1917. Fullard, a tremendously gifted flier and shot, was scoring at such a rapid rate that he seemed destined to become Britain's greatest ace. Yet he never returned to combat, as his nerves gave way when he was finally scheduled to rejoin his squadron at the front after a long and difficult recovery, his sense of invincibility apparently as shattered as his limb. [132]

British aviation magazines such as *Flight* and *The Aeroplane* romanticized the RFC and the sporting, chivalric, heroic, and sacrificial images of the air war. From RFC headquarters Philip Gibbs' column "Daily Chronicle" depicted the RFC as "Knights-Errant of the Air," recalling the Black Prince in Flanders during the Hundred Year's War. In a war with precious little romance, he found it in the "daily tourneys" in the air, as fearless British fliers fought with the ardor of schoolboys flinging themselves into a football scrimmage. And why not? They were, in fact, like their counterparts in all countries, overwhelmingly youths in their late teens and early twenties, schoolboys transformed into warriors by the greatest war humankind had witnessed to that date, as detailed in Kennett [22] and Morrow [29].

The Aeroplane of 30 May carried a poem, "The Lament of the Broken Pilot," who bid farewell to France, "the land of adventure and knightly deeds, / where the pilot faces the foe / in single combat as was of yore— / giving him blow for blow." No longer among the "throng of chivalry, youth, and pride," where his comrades entered the "airy lists in the name of Freedom and Right," our broken pilot would now keep their "armour bright." Exclusive London stores like Moss Bros. advertised aviation clothing intended to dress the wealthy young sportsman-knight stylishly and appropriately for the airy lists.

The greatest of these warriors—Ball [96], Baracca [289 and 301], Boelcke [237], Bishop [53], Fonck, Guynemer, Mannock [77 and 124], and Richthofen [266]—were legendary, lionized by adoring publics; their exploits, the material of myth. Yet their lives were often terribly short. It is sobering to reflect that of those eight men, six died in 1916, 1917, and 1918, waging an aerial conflict that became a mass war of attrition just like the struggle on the ground, thereby seriously eroding any notions of chivalry or sport that still lurked in the breasts of aerial combatants. These aviators are the symbols of the first war in the air, its heroes and victims, and the focus of most studies of the subject [118 (Hawker), 140 (Mannock), 158 (Winter), 218, 221 (Mortane), 237 (Boelcke), and 247 (Schaefer)].

The sheer numbers of airplanes on the Western Front by 1918, more than 8,000 British, French, German, and American in sum, indicate that the air war in general, and aerial combat in particular, was no longer an individual affair but instead a mass struggle of attrition [in general see 4, 5, and 6]. As the war had expanded in scope, the basic tactical unit, the French escadrille of 6 planes, the German Flieger-Abteilung of 6, and the British squadron of 12 planes expanded in size to 12, 9, and 18 planes respectively. These units were subsumed under increasingly larger ones, like the German fighter circuses of 60 planes, as the attempt to achieve aerial superiority led to concentration of forces, as Hallion notes [10, 11]. The ultimate unit was the French aerial division of 1918, with more than 700 bombers and fighters intended for tactical air raids over German lines [225, 229, 231].

War flying was dangerous, as illustrated by the most accurate figures available of losses in aviation. Thirty-nine percent of France's more than 18,000 aircrew trained in the five years from 1914 to 1919 were lost. More than 50 percent of 22,000 British pilots trained became casualties. In the absence of figures for aircrew trained in Germany, one can assume that their percentage of casualties was at least as high as that of the French and perhaps higher than that of the British, since their force was proportionately smaller while their total number of casualties nearly equaled that of the British. While it is hard to compare these loss rates with those in the infantry, in the first six months of 1918, French infantry losses amounted to 51 percent of effectives, while the losses of pilots at the front reached 71 percent. This toll is ample proof that aviators paid no less a price in wartime sacrifice than infantry [29].

The Royal Air Force was sufficiently concerned about fragmentary evidence of casualties to trace the careers to 31 October 1918 of nearly 1,500 pilots sent to France from July to December 1917. The results: 18 percent had been killed; 26 percent had been injured or sick and admitted to hospital; 20 percent were missing over the lines; 25 percent had been transferred home; and 11 percent were still in France. Overall, then, 64 percent of those nearly 1,500 pilots were killed, wounded (or sick), or missing, and of the surviving 36 percent, about a quarter returned to England early in their tour. Only about a fourth of all pilots completed a tour of duty of nine months [29].

The circumstances of their deaths were grim. Take, for example, the case of the Red Baron, ace of aces. The debate over whether Richthofen fell to another airman or to groundfire has a certain symbolic significance. Those who view the air war romantically would prefer the former. The second befits the capricious nature of total war—the Baron, like the Irishman Mannock and the Italian Baracca, the leading aces of the Royal Air Force and Italian air service respectively, was brought down by a bullet from an anonymous machine gunner on the ground. The manner of death does violence to the mythology of the knights of the air in the same way that, centuries before, the firearm's ability to kill impersonally and at long range first occasioned the resentment and ultimately the demise of the knight.

A further examination of casualties also indicates why authors, especially those preoccupied with the heroic nature of the air war, shy away from them. Accidents, termed by an American medical officer "the most important medical problem of aviation," were the greatest source of fatalities. In the U.S. Air Service, of 681 fatalities among flight personnel, 25 percent fell in combat and 75 percent in accidents, most of which occurred in flight school. According to Maurer Maurer [305], as slightly more than 2,000 American flying personnel arrived at the front during the war, for every four who survived to fight, one had not, that one symbolized by the short-lived Gary Cooper character in the movie *Wings*. In 1918 five Italian aviators were killed in accidents for every one in combat. But these were relatively small forces.

Among the major combatants, just over 36 percent of French fliers dead, or missing and presumed dead, perished in accidents in the rear areas. Of German losses, more than half were not attributable to enemy action [29]. It is impossible to determine similar breakdowns of British losses, but training casualties were high. Admiral Mark Kerr, who commanded the southwest training area in England in 1918, lamented that nearly 300 pilots were killed in his region in three months [68].

Aviators in all countries were more likely to die in accidents than in combat. And the youthful volunteers knew that. Initially their irrepressibility and the callousness of wartime enabled them to cope with the situation. French aviation artist Marcel JeanJean remembered one exchange on the training school flight line while watching a crash: "Those poor fellows, they are going to kill themselves." "Too bad! That's war" [174]. A British pilot recalled that fatal crashes on Sopwith Camels in training were so frequent that they stopped bothering to look up when they heard a Camel go into a spin and took for granted that they had lost another pilot trainee [62, 78, 146, 150].

An American pilot who flew with the British, after surviving training in which three pilots practicing on Camels were killed in one day, commented that fighting Fokkers in Camels during the summer was exhausting and caused high losses. He concluded that it was "only a matter of time until we all get it." As another American explained, more humorously, "A Camel pilot had to shoot down every German plane in the sky to get home himself, as the Camel could neither outclimb nor outrun a Fokker" [11, 107, 308, 314].

And in most accounts there is a near total absence of blood and gore, giving death in the air a certain cleanliness. But hear the following account from Bernard Lafont's *Au Ciel de Verdun* [177]. Two aviators have fallen from their Farman when attacked:

The first of the two men is impaled on the iron gate. There is the pierced body, a bloody rag. The wounds are enormous. Purple streams flow onto the clothes; drops hang and then fall one by one in a large puddle on the ground below.

 The second fell on the roof of the house. I clearly heard the dull sound of the body when it was crushed in a heap. Flouc! The body was recovered from the roof, entirely broken, shattered, shapeless and without rigidity like a heap of slime. They filled a coffin with it.

Contrary to the myth of Guynemer's death, that he had flown so high he could not descend, Lafont's account graphically reminds us that all aviators returned to earth, one way or another.

This was no sport, no game. It was a deadly, ruthless, and capricious business, where a man's life depended not solely on his individual skills but on a combination of those skills, luck, and on machines that were very far from perfect. The widespread incidence of occupational hazards like nerves indicated the stress involved in war flying. Many men fell victim to flying fatigue, which caused sleeplessness, irritability, exhaustion, and shakiness after landing, and most dangerous, carelessness in combat. The great French ace Guynemer may have suffered from tuberculosis, which, exacerbated by his refusal to rest, meant that he was not only sick but increasingly nervous and irritable in the period before his death in combat in 1917. An American pilot complained that his nerves were shot; he knew that he would die sooner or later, but waiting for the moment was killing him. American Edwin Parsons attributed the consumption of liquor to the need for a sedative for strained nerves [312]. Opinions varied on the value of liquor, as German ace Max Immelmann, a physical fitness fanatic, believed that liquor led to overstrained nerves. If this was the case, the accounts of some Americans suggest that they must have suffered a surfeit of nerves [318], and one British author humorously conceded that if the British and Americans had drunk as much as some memoirs declared, they would not have lasted very long at the front [22 (Kennett), 29 (Morrow), 313 (Porter), and 319 (Winslow)].

Perhaps the most graphic account of one pilot's struggle with nerves is contained in the diary of Edward "Mick" Mannock, the Irishman who was Britain's highest scoring ace [77]. According to his biographer Frederick Oughton, Mannock had two temporary nervous breakdowns and was often sick before patrols, much of his tension occasioned by the constant failure of his airplane, or bus, as he called it [140]. His diary recounts constant engine failures, gun jams; once during target practice his right bottom wing fell off. By the summer of 1918 the nervous strain was so great that his hands shook and he would burst into tears. He knew that he would die, but he feared burning to death, a hell to which he had consigned many of the "Huns" that he passionately hated, so he carried a pistol to shoot himself. Shot down in flames from groundfire, Mannock's remains were never found, thus no one will ever know whether he had time to use the pistol. And he had no parachute.

Beneath the veneer of glamour and chivalry, aerial combat was undeniably exhilarating and intoxicating for many of its participants, but also nerve-racking and frightening as well. But aerial fighting was only one aspect of air warfare. Ground attack, reconnaissance, and bombing were significant roles that directly intruded on the course of the war on the ground.

One of the most difficult, and important tasks of aviation as the war continued was ground attack, for which the Germans evolved special units of battle or storm fliers equipped with light, maneuverable two-seaters. These infantry fliers became an effective offensive and defensive weapon in 1917, attacking enemy batteries, strong points, and infantry reserves with machine guns, grenades, and light fragmentation bombs. They suffered high losses in their dangerous work, as they ranged in squadron or group strength over the front at 600 meters altitude, buffeted by the drafts of passing shells, and then descended to strafe troops from 100 meters above the trenches in the dead zone between the artillery fire from both sides. In these German ground attack units, only the commander was a commissioned officer; the crews were almost entirely NCOs and soldiers. Their fighting spirit was high, as they protected their infantry brothers below by flying above the "rue de merde," or "shit street," as they called the front, on days when heavy rain and low cloud grounded other units. This was the air war at its grittiest, and at the battle of Messines in June 1917 and then at Cambrai in November and December, they effectively controlled British breakthroughs and led attacks with demoralizing battlefield strafes [11 (Hallion), 29 (Morrow), 116 (Greenhous), 239 (Eddelbütel)].

British counterparts to these storm fliers in 1918 flew Sopwith Camels, which had won praise as the war's preeminent dogfighter in 1917 but whose essential task in 1918 was ground attack in high-risk assault squadrons. V. M. Yeates, author of the novel *Winged Victory* and survivor of 248 hours and four crashes in Camels during 1918 before being discharged with tuberculosis in the summer, termed ground strafing "the last occupation on earth for longevity" and "the great casualty maker." Yeates considered it the most dangerous and valuable work that fighter pilots performed, though they received little credit for it [86]. From March to November, No. 80 (Assault) Squadron, with a strength of 22 officers, suffered 168 casualties from all causes, or about 75 percent monthly, with almost half killed.

The essential task of aviation throughout the war was reconnaissance, and in the French and German air arms these army-cooperation planes were the preponderant types. The crews of these two-seaters, who routinely carried out these missions, often flew in machines that left much to be desired. British Be2 biplanes, already obsolete in 1915, remained in service, cannon fodder for German fighters, into 1917, in part to complete production runs but also because many RFC pilots were not sufficiently well trained to fly higher performance planes. The "Quirks," as fighter pilots named these two-seater crews, flew straight to their target and back at low altitude. An awed fighter pilot presumed that they were so accustomed to being "ruthlessly archied," shot at by ground fire, at low altitude that they had become fatalistic, like infantrymen. It never occurred to him that inadequate training may also have limited their ability to perform intricate maneuvers. [70]

In French aviation many army corps crews similarly struggled in the AR biplane, which was intended only as a stopgap when it appeared in 1916 but which served into 1918 [196 (Facon)]. At least the Germans tended to equip their reconnaissance crews with better planes to husband their dwindling manpower. They sent expert crews alone and at high altitude in high-performance machines, using their skill and the planes' ability to evade the enemy. By the end of 1917 their Rumpler biplanes were capable of 20,000-foot ceilings on these missions with little loss of altitude, thanks to their high compression engines [247 (Schaefer)]. British aces had a healthy respect for these crews, some of whom were formidable [81 (Strange)]. In James McCudden's accounts of separate combats with four two-seaters at high altitude in December 1917, three of them escaped. Canadian ace Billy Bishop's patrol of six once jumped a lone German two-seater, which turned in a flash, attacked them head-on, hitting Bishop's plane and another member of his squadron, and escaped, earning Bishop's accolade "a very fine pilot and a very brave man" [53 (Bishop)]. Two-seat crews were usually the prey of fighter pilots, but occasionally the prey became the predator [64 (Insall), 79 (Noble), 138 (Mead)], 183 (Thébault), 199 (Facon), and 246 (Richthofen)].

A final task of wartime aviation was bombing [4 (Cross), 23 (Kennett), 193 (Bitchakdjian), and 293 (Bompiani)]. On the Italian front by 1917, waves of 30 to 40 Caproni trimotored biplane bombers supported infantry attacks by bombing Austro-Hungarian troops [296 (Lodi) and 297 (Ludovico)]. The Capronis also staged long-distance raids across the Adriatic to bomb targets, sometimes flying as low as twelve meters above the waves in their effort to strike by surprise and avoid anti-aircraft defenses [290 (D'Annunzio)].

Over the Western Front in 1918 General Duval's French air division, whose nucleus was the superlative Breguet 14, a fast, sturdy biplane carrying 24 10-kg bombs and defended by gunners armed with twin Lewis guns, aggressively raided across the lines in massed formations. Gen. Pétain, the French Commander-in-Chief, sought certain aerial superiority in 1918 and methodically attacked enemy lines of communication continually and in mass [223 (Pedroncini)]. The culmination of these massed tactical raids was the aerial support of the American Expeditionary Force's attack on St. Mihiel in September 1918. There Col. Billy Mitchell commanded nearly 1,500 airplanes, half American and half French, including the aerial division—the largest concentration of Allied air forces during the war. This armada gained aerial control as the fighters penetrated over German airfields and the bombers struck targets on the battlefield and in the rear [311 (Mitchell)].

Tactical bombardment of enemy forces was one thing; the strategic bombing of enemy cities and civilians in no way comports with ideals of sport, chivalry, and individual combat. The German government launched Zeppelins in 1915 and 1916 [263 (Robinson)], and then large bombers in 1917 and 1918 to bomb England and drive it from the war [264 (Haddow and Grosz)]. The attempt failed, but the campaign indicated a willingness to strike at civilian morale. The French had waged an unsuccessful strategic campaign against west German industrial towns in 1915 [224–225 (Pesquiès-Courbier)]. The British, unable to retaliate against German civilians until 1918, wanted to start, in the words of Secretary of State for Air Lord Weir, "a really big fire" in a German town, assuming that such attacks would undermine German morale [147 (Reader)]. The war ended with the British poised to begin bombing Berlin, and with the value of grand-strategic bombing unproven, but with the notion that the bombing of civilians could undermine their morale [23 (Kennett), 104 (Collier) 125 (Jones), 157 (Williams), and 159 (Wynn)].

As opposed to the concentration on knights of the air, the myth of the potency of the bombing of civilians was the less often acknowledged and darker side of the legacy of the air war. It reminds us that the air weapon of World War I was truly the child of the era of total war, which conflated civilian and military targets and deemed the bombing of civilians, women and children included, an acceptable means of winning a war. Both of these illusionary images—the romantic idealization of individual aerial combat rooted in the past and the brutal vision of massive civilian destruction foreshadowing the future—constituted the dual legacy for airpower in the twentieth century. They remain with us today, a final reminder that a single image of air warfare in World War I is inappropriate in a conflict that witnessed the origins of all facets of military aviation.

NAVAL AVIATION

The air war at sea was pioneered by the British Royal Naval Air Service (RNAS), from 1911 to 1918 independent of the Royal Flying Corps (RFC). From the development of seaplanes and blimps it progressed to aircraft carriers by 1918 and a seat, as Fifth Sea Lord, on the Board of Admiralty. It was opposed by the German Naval Air Service, whose Zeppelins led the air war at sea.

Though the air war at sea was minor compared to that over land, there is a substantial literature on it from documentary collections such as Roskill on the RNAS [46], through major narratives such as Arthur Marder's multivolume *From the Dreadnought to Scapa Flow* [136], and the various official histories that have appeared in the twentieth century for which see Higham's 1970 *Official Histories* [15] and his 2000 two-volume *Official Military Historical Offices and Sources* [16].

The Royal Naval Air Service was the premier air power at sea and an innovative one as Norman Friedman's work on aircraft carriers shows [113]. Details of its aircraft are to be found in J. M. Bruce's *British Aeroplanes 1914–1918* [99], and in Higham on airships [120, 121], Owen Thereford on naval aircraft [155], Snowden Gamble's station history [61], and Johnstone's *Naval Eight* [123]. Memoirs of senior officers who served in the RNAS are by Mark Kerr [68], Arthur Longmore [73], and Murray Sueter [82].

P. K. Kemp provides an overall view at the start of his *Fleet Air Arm* [128], as does Norman Macmillan [135]. The German naval air story is less well covered. Robinson on naval Zeppelins is a detailed study [269]. Gray and Thetford provide details on aircraft [263] and Morrow on the industry that produced them [267, 268]. An introduction to Russian naval aviation is provided in *Russian Aviation and Air Power* [280]. For the U.S. Naval Air Service a start can be made with Turnbull and Lord [332], Van Wyen [334], and Knott on flying boats [331], as well as on naval aircraft. Much neglected have been the Austro-Hungarian naval air services, which has only Schupita's work in German [288], while there are only some official histories of the Italian naval air effort [19 (Jane's)] and Macmillan's work on the British air arms in Italy [135] and Longmore's memoirs [73]. The French naval air service in the 1914–1918 War remains a cipher. There is much still to be done concerning aviation and the sea.

POSTWAR

The postwar demobilization in aviation was so rapid that air forces and aviation industries shrank within two or three years to mere shadows of their wartime selves. The losers of the war, such as Germany, were forced to disarm and forbidden to possess an air force, but even the victors confronting huge wartime debts, dismantled their air forces so fast that they did not give the industry sufficient time for transition into civil aviation and many aircraft firms disappeared. The French air service, for example, shrank from 90,000 officers and men in November 1918 to 39,055 in October 1920; its airplanes, from a total of 11,000 combat and training planes to under 4,000 in March 1920, most of which were in storage. British compression was even more dramatic, as the RAF's total strength of 295,000 officers and men in November 1918 diminished to 38,000 in October 1919. The air services and the aviation industry survived, if just barely, as overseas empire beckoned as a realm that offered opportunities for a new mode of communication, transport, and policing—by air [110 (Fearon)]. Tiny civil air transport firms sprang up, often using modified warplanes, to carry the mail and those few passengers sufficiently daring to risk travel by air to their destinations [111 (Fearon)]. And some companies, like the German Junkers firm [255 (Blunck)], had actually anticipated the opportunities looming in the realm of commercial aviation, and were soon ready to put wartime experience to good use, in Junkers' case the development of all-metal aircraft, carrying passengers faster than they had ever traveled before. As for military aviation, it would survive, if just, on a shoestring, the foundations laid in the war of 1914–1918 for a future war some twenty years later in which air forces and aviation industries would play prominent roles.

CONCLUSION

The Fall of the Berlin Wall and the Iron Curtain, the re-unification of Germany, and the collapse of the former Soviet Union have opened substantial documentary sources on military aviation in the First World War to researchers from the west, for whom access used to be limited, difficult, or impossible. Some researchers have already begun to exploit these sources. Important work remains to be done using these sources, as well as archival and museum sources in Italy, where the Caproni Museum was re-established in the 1990s. The Italian aerial effort in the 1914–1918 war certainly exceeded those of Russia, Austria-Hungary, and the United States and represented an exceptional achievement in the context of limited resources and finances. The histories of military aviation in Italy and Russia, on which few studies exist in any language, merit substantial historical studies, while a dearth of works in English on French aviation in general, and on such important topics as the French High Command's management of the air war in particular, is inexcusable for the country that staged the most extensive mobilization, by far, of aviation in the First World War. The realms of naval aviation, and of more technical subjects such as logistics and maintenance, deserve the attention of historians. These are fertile and important fields for historical research in the new millennium, beyond the reworking of studies of more extensively researched topics that will continue to attract scholars and the general public interested in the fascinating and important topic of military aviation during the First World War.

BIBLIOGRAPHY

The following bibliography is by no means exhaustive.

General Works

1. Angelucci, Enzo. *The Rand McNally Encyclopedia of Military Aircraft, 1914–1980.* New York: Military Press, 1981.

2. Campbell, Christopher. *Aces and Aircraft of World War I.* New York: Greenwich House, 1984 [1981].

3. *Color Profiles of World War I Combat Planes.* New York: Crescent Books, 1974.

4. Cross, Robin. *The Bombers. The Illustrated Story of Offensive Strategy and Tactics in the Twentieth Century.* New York: Macmillan, 1987.

5. Fitzsimons, Bernard. *Warplanes and Air Battles of World War I.* New York: Beekman House, 1973.

6. Franks, Norman. *Aircraft versus Aircraft. The Illustrated Story of Fighter Pilot Combat since 1914.* New York: Macmillan,1986.

7. Gibbs-Smith, Charles H. *The Aeroplane. An Historical Survey of its Origins and Development.* London: Her Majesty's Stationery Office, 1960.

8. Goldstein, Laurence. *The Flying Machine and Modern Literature.* London: Macmillan, 1986.

9. Groehler, Olaf. *Geschichte des Luftkriegs 1910 bis 1980* (*History of Aerial Warfare, 1900–80*). Berlin: Militärverlag der DDR, 1981.

10. Hallion, Richard P. *Rise of the Fighter Aircraft, 1914–1918.* Annapolis: Nautical and Aviation Publishing Co., 1984.

11. Hallion, Richard P. *Strike from the Sky. The History of Battlefield Air Attack, 1911–1945.* Washington: Smithsonian Institution Press, 1989.

12. Hartcup, Guy. *The War of Invention. Scientific Developments, 1914–18.* London: Brassey's, 1988.

13. Hezlett, Sir Arthur. *Aircraft and Sea Power.* New York: Stein and Day, 1970.

14. Higham, Robin. *Air Power. A Concise History.* New York: St. Martin's Press, 1972.

15. Higham, Robin. *Official Histories.* Manhattan, KS: Sunflower University Press, 1970.

16. Higham, Robin. *Official Military Historical Offices and Sources.* Westport, CT: Greenwood Press, 2000.

17. Ingold, Felix P. *Literatur und Aviatik. Europäische Flugdichtung 1909–1927* (*Literature and Aviation. European Aviation Writing, 1900–27*). Basel: Birkhäuser Verlag, 1978.

18. Homze, Edward. *German Military Aviation. A Guide to the Literature.* New York: Garland, 1984.

19. *Jane's Fighting Aircraft of World War I.* New York: Military Press, 1990 [1919].

20. Johnson, J. E. *Full Circle. The Tactics of Air Fighting, 1914–1964*. New York: Ballantine, 1964.

21. Kennett, Lee. *French Military Aviation: A Bibliographic Guide*. New York: Garland, 1989.

22. Kennett, Lee. *The First Air War, 1914–1918*. New York: Free Press, 1991.

23. Kennett, Lee. *A History of Strategic Bombing*. New York: Scribner's, 1982.

24. Kern, Stephen H. *The Culture of Time and Space, 1880–1918*. Cambridge, MA: Harvard University Press, 1983.

25. Lamberton, W. M., and E. F. Cheesman. *Reconnaissance and Bomber Aircraft of the 1914–1918 War*. Letchworth, Hertsfordshire: Harleyford, 1962.

26. Layman, R. D. *To Ascend from a Floating Base. Shipboard Aeronautics and Aviation, 1783–1914*. Teaneck, NJ: Fairleigh Dickinson University Press, 1979.

27. Loftin, Laurence K., Jr. *Quest for Performance. The Evolution of Modern Aircraft*. Washington: NASA, 1985.

28. Millett, Allan R., and Williamson Murray, eds. *Military Effectiveness*. Vol. 1 *The First World War*. Boston: Allen & Unwin, 1988.

29. Morrow, John H., Jr. *The Great War in the Air. Military Aviation from 1909 to 1921*. Washington: Smithsonian Institution Press, 1993.

30. Norman, Aaron. *The Great Air War*. New York: Macmillan, 1968.

31. Nowarra, Heniz J. *Marine Aircraft of the 1914–1918 War*. Letchworth, Hertsfordshire: Harleyford, 1966.

32. Quester, George H. *Deterrence before Hiroshima*. New York: Wiley, 1966.

33. Reynolds, Quentin. *They Fought for the Sky*. New York: Holt, Rinehart and Winston, 1957.

34. Robertson, Bruce, et al. *Air Aces of the 1914–1918 War*. Letchworth, Hertsfordshire: Harleyford, 1964.

35. Robinson, Douglas H. *The Dangerous Sky. A History of Aviation Medicine*. Seattle: University of Washington Press, 1973.

36. Robinson, Douglas H. *Giants in the Sky. A History of the Rigid Airship*. Seattle: University of Washington Press, 1973.

37. Schlaifer, Robert, and S. D. Heron. *Development of Aircraft Engines. Development of Aviation Fuels*. Boston: Harvard University Graduate School of Business Administration, 1950.

38. Smith, Herschel. *A History of Aircraft Piston Engines*. Manhattan, KS: Sunflower University Press, 1986 [1981].

39. Smith, Myron J. *World War I in the Air: A Bibliography and Chronology*. Metuchen: Scarecrow, 1977.

40. Stokesbury, James L. *A Short History of Air Power*. New York: William Morrow and Co., 1986.

41. Taylor, C. Fayette. *Aircraft Propulsion. A Review of the Evolution of Aircraft Piston Engines*. Smithsonian Annals of Flight, Vol. 1, no. 4, 1971.

42. Villard, Henry S. *Contact! The Story of the Early Birds*. Washington: Smithsonian Institution Press, 1987.

43. Wohl, Robert. *A Passion for Wings: Aviation and the Western Imagination*. New Haven: Yale University Press, 1994.

England and the Dominions

Published Documents

44. Air Ministry. "Synopsis of British Air Effort during the War." *Cmd. 100*. London: His Majesty's Stationery Office, April 1919.

45. Ministry of Munitions. *History of the Ministry of Munitions*. 8 Vols. London: His Majesty's Stationery Office, 1922.

46. Roskill, S. W., ed. *Documents Relating to the Naval Air Service*. Vol. 1. 1908–1918. Publications of the Navy Records Society, Vol. 113. 1969.

Memoirs

47. Addison, Christopher. *Politics from Within, 1911–1918.* Vol. 2. London: Jenkins, 1924.

48. Balfour, Harold. *An Airman Marches. Early Flying Adventures, 1914–1923.* London: Greenhill Aeolus, 1985 [1935].

49. Baring, Maurice. *Flying Corps Headquarters, 1914–1918.* Edinburgh: Blackwood, 1968 [1920].

50. Bartlett, C. P. O. *Bomber Pilot 1916–1918.* London: Allen, 1974.

51. [Aitken, Max]. Lord Beaverbrook. *Men and Power 1917–1918.* New York: Duell, Sloan and Pearce, 1956.

52. Bewsher, Paul. *Green Balls: The Adventures of a Night Bomber.* Greenhill, Hertsfordshire: Aeolus, 1986 [1919].

53. Bishop, William A. *Winged Warfare.* Garden City, NY: Doubleday, 1967.

54. Bott, Alan. *An Airman's Outings with the RFC, June–December 1916.* Elstree, Hertsfordshire: Greenhill, 1986 [1917].

55. Callender, Gordon W., Jr., and Gordon W. Callender Sr. *War in an Open Cockpit. The Wartime Letters of Captain Alvin Andrew Callender, R.A.F.* West Roxbury, MA: World War I Aero Publishers, 1978.

56. Cobby, A. H. *High Adventure.* Melbourne: Kookaburra, 1981.

57. Collishaw, Raymond, with R. V. Dodds. *Air Command. A Fighter Pilot's Story.* London: Kimber, 1973.

58. Davies, Richard B. *Sailor in the Air.* London: Davies, 1967.

59. de Havilland, Sir Geoffrey. *Sky Fever.* London: Hamilton, 1961.

60. Douglas, Sholto, with Robert Wright. *Combat and Command.* New York: Simon and Schuster, 1963.

61. Gamble, C. F. Snowden. *The Story of a North Sea Air Station.* London: Oxford University Press, 1928.

62. Grinnell-Milne, Duncan. *Wind in the Wires.* Garden City, NY: Doubleday, 1968.

63. Harvey, W. J. [Night-Hawk]. *Rovers of the Night Sky.* Greenhill, Hertsfordshire: Aeolus, 1984 [1919].

64. Insall, A. J. *Observer. Memoirs of the RFC, 1915–1918.* London: Kimber, 1970.

65. Jones, Ira. *Tiger Squadron. The Story of 74 Squadron, RAF, in Two World Wars.* London: W. H. Allen, 1954.

66. Jones, Ira. *An Air Fighter's Scrapbook.* London: Nicholson and Watson, 1938.

67. Joubert de la Ferte, Sir Philip. *The Fated Sky. An Autobiography.* London: Hutchinson, 1952.

68. Kerr, Mark. *Land, Sea, and Air. Reminiscences of Mark Kerr.* New York: Longmans, Green & Co., 1927.

69. Lee, Arthur Gould. *No Parachute. A Fighter Pilot in World War I.* New York: Harper and Row, 1968.

70. Lee, Arthur Gould. *Open Cockpit. A Pilot of the Royal Flying Corps.* London: Jarrolds, 1969.

71. Lewis, Cecil. *Sagittarius Rising.* New York: Harcourt, Brace and Company, 1936.

72. Long, S. H. *In the Blue.* London: John Lane, 1920.

73. Longmore, Arthur. *From Sea to Sky, 1910–1945.* London: Bles, 1946.

74. McCudden, James T. B. *Flying Fury.* London: Hamilton, 1930 [1918].

75. MacLanachan, W. [McScotch]. *Fighter Pilot.* London: Routledge, 1936.

76. Macmillan, Norman. *Into the Blue.* London: Jarrolds, 1969.

77. Mannock, Edward. *The Personal Diary of Maj. Edward "Mick" Mannock.* Introduced and annotated by Frederick Oughton. London: Spearman, 1966.

78. Moore, W. Geoffrey. *Early Bird.* London: Putnam, 1963.

79. Noble, Walter. *With a Bristol Fighter Squadron.* Portway, Bath: Chivers, 1977 [1920].

80. Slessor, John C. *The Central Blue. Recollections and Reflections.* London: Cassell, 1956.

81. Strange, Lewis A. *Recollections of an Airman.* London: John Hamilton Ltd., 1933.

82. Sueter, Murray F. *Airmen or Noahs.* London: Putnam, 1928.

83. Sykes, Frederick. *From Many Angles. An Autobiography.* London: Harrap, 1942.

84. [Voss, Vivian]. "Vee, Roger." *Flying Minnows.* London: Arms and Armour, 1977 [1935].

85. Worley, Rothesay S. *Letters from a Flying Officer.* Gloucester: Sutton, 1982 [1928].

86. Yeates, V. M. *Winged Victory.* London: Buchan and Wright, 1985 [1934]. A novel based on the author's wartime experiences.

Official and Squadron Histories

87. Burge, C. Gordon. *The Annals of 100 Squadron.* London: Reach, 1919.

88. Cole, Christopher. *Royal Air Force 1918.* London: Kimber, 1918.

89 Cole, Christopher. ed. *Royal Flying Corps 1915–1916.* London: Kimber, 1969.

90. Cutlack, F. M. *The Australian Flying Corps in the Western and Eastern Theatres of War 1914–1918.* Sydney: Angus and Robertson, 1933.

91. Jones, H. A. *Over the Balkans and South Russia, 1917–1919. Being the History of No. 47 Squadron Royal Air Force.* Elstree, Hertsfordshire: Greenhill, 1987 [1923].

92. Pattinson, Lawrence A. *History of 99 Squadron. Independent Force, Royal Air Force. March, 1918–November, 1918.* Cambridge: Heffer, 1920.

93. Raleigh, Walter, and H. A. Jones. *The War in the Air.* Vols. 1–6. Oxford: Clarendeon, 1922–1937.

94. Wise, S. F. *Canadian Airmen and the First World War. The Official History of the Royal Canadian Air Force.* Vol. 1. Toronto: University of Toronto Press, 1980.

Secondary Sources

95. Adkin, Fred. *From the Ground Up. A History of R.A.F. Ground Crew.* Shrewsbury: Airlife, 1983.

96. Bowyer, Chaz. *Albert Ball, VC.* London: Kimber, 1977.

97. Bowyer, Chaz. *For Valour. The Air VCs.* London: Kimber, 1978.

98. Bruce, J. M. *The Aeroplanes of the Royal Flying Corps (Military Wing).* London: Putnam, 1982.

99. Bruce, J. M. *British Aeroplanes 1914–1918.* London: Putnam, 1957.

100. Castle, H. G. *Fire over England. The German Air Raids in World War I.* London: Secker & Warburg, 1982.

101. *A Century of British Aeronautics. A Centenary Journal,* Journal of the Royal Historical Society, Vol. 70 (January 1966).

102. Churchill, Randolph S. *Winston S. Churchill.* Vols. 2–4. Boston: Houghton Mifflin, 1967, 1971, 1975.

103. Cole, Christopher, and E. F. Cheesman. *The Air Defense of Great Britain 1914–1918.* London: Putnam, 1984.

104. Collier, Basil. *Heavenly Adventurer. Sefton Brancker and the Dawn of British Aviation.* London: Secker & Warburg, 1959.

105. Collier, Basil. *Leader of the Few. The Authorized Biography of Air Chief Marshal the Lord Dowding of Bentley Priory.* London: Jarrolds, 1957.

106. Cooper, Malcolm. *The Birth of Independent Air Power. British Air Policy in the First World War.* London: Allen and Unwin, 1986.

107. Dean, Sir Maurice. *The Royal Air Force and Two World Wars.* London: Cassell, 1979.

108. Dixon, Ronald, ed. *Echoes in the Sky. An Anthology of Aviation Verse from Two World Wars.* Poole, Dorset: Blandford, 1982.

109. Divine, David. *The Broken Wing. A Study in the British Exercise of Air Power.* London: Hutchinson, 1966.

110. Fearon, Peter. "The Formative Years of the British Aircraft Industry, 1913–1924." *Business History Review,* 43 (1969): 476–95.

111. Fearon, Peter. "The Vicissitudes of a British Aircraft Company: Handley Page Ltd. between the Wars." *Business History,* 20, no. 1 (January 1978): 66–86.

112. Fredette, Raymond H. *The Sky on Fire. The First Battle of Britain 1917–1918.* New York: Harcourt Brace Jovanovich, 1966.

113. Friedman, Norman. *British Carrier Aviation: The Evolution of the Ships and Their Aircraft.* Annapolis, MD: Naval Institute Press, 1989.

114. Gollin, Alfred. *The Impact of Air Power on the British People and Their Government, 1909–1914.* Stanford: Stanford University Press, 1989.

115. Gollin, Alfred. *No Longer an Island. Britain and the Wright Brothers, 1902–1909.* Stanford: Stanford University Press, 1984.

116. Greenhous, Brereton. *The Making of Billy Bishop.* Toronto: Dundurn Press, 2002.

117. Greenhous, Brereton. "Close Support Aircraft in World War I. The Counter Anti-Tank Role." *Aerospace Historian,* (Summer, 1974): 87–93.

118. Hawker, Tyrrel M. *Hawker, VC.* London: Mitre, 1965.

119. Higham, Robin. "The Dangerously Neglected—The British Military Intellectuals, 1918–1939." *Military Affairs,* 29, No. 2 (summer 1965): 73–87.

120. Higham, Robin. *The British Rigid Airship, 1908–1931. A Study in Weapons Policy.* London: Foulis, 1961.

121. Higham, Robin. "The Peripheral Weapon in Wartime: A Case Study." *Air Power Historian,* 8, no. 2(April 1961): 67–78.

122. Hyde, H. Montgomery. *British Air Policy between the War, 1918–1939.* London: Heinemann, 1976.

123. Johnstone, E. G., ed. *Naval Eight.* London: Arms and Armour, 1972 [1931].

124. Jones, Ira. *King of the Air Fighters. Biography of Maj. "Mick" Mannock, VS, DSO, MC.* London: Nicholson and Watson Ltd., 1934.

125. Jones, Neville. *The Origins of Strategic Bombing. A Study of the Development of British Air Strategic Thought up to 1918.* London: Kimber, 1973.

126. Joubert de la Ferte, Sir Philip. *The Third Service. The Story behind the Royal Air Force.* London: Thames and Hudson, 1955.

127. Keaney, Thomas A. "Aircraft and Air Doctrinal Development in Great Britain, 1912–1914." Ph.D. Diss., University of Michigan, 1975.

128. Kemp, P. K. *The Fleet Air Arm.* London: Jenkins, 1954.

129. King, H. F. *Armament of British Aircraft, 1909–1939.* London: Putnam, 1971.

130. Kingston-McCloughry, E. J. *War in Three Dimensions. The Impact of Air Power upon the Classical Principles of War.* London: Jonathan Cape, 1949.

131. Laffin, John. *Swifter than Eagles. The Biography of Marshal of the RAF Sir John Maitland Salmond.* Edinburgh: Blackwood, 1964.

132. Liddle, Peter H. *The Airman's War 1914–18.* Poole, Dorset: Blandford, 1987.

133. Lloyd, Ian. *Rolls-Royce—The years of endeavour.* London: Macmillan, 1978.

134. Loraine, Winifred. *Robert Loraine. Soldier Actor Airman.* London: Collins, 1938.

135. Macmillan, Norman. *Offensive Patrol. The Story of the RNAS, RFC, and RAF in Italy 1917–1918.* London: Jarrolds, 1973.

136. Marder, Arthur. *From the Dreadnought to Scapa Flow.* 5 vols. London: Oxford University Press, 1961–1970.

137. Mason, R. A. "The British Dimension," pp. 22–35 in *USAFA Symposium on the History of Airpower.*

138. Mead, Peter. *The Eye in the Air. History of Air Observation and Reconnaissance for the Army 1785–1945.* London: Her Majesty's Stationery Office, 1983.

139. Norris, Geoffrey. *The Royal Flying Corps: A History.* London: Muller, 1965.

140. Oughton, Frederick, and Vernon Smyth. *Ace with One Eye. The Life and Combats of Maj. Edward Mannock.* London: Muller, 1963.

141. Paris, Michael. *Winged Warfare: The Literature of Aerial Warfare in Britain, 1859–1917.* Manchester: Manchester University Press, 1992.

142. Parker, Peter. *The Old Lie. The Great War and the Public School Ethos.* London: Constable, 1987.

143. Penrose, Harald. *British Aviation. The Great War and Armistice 1915–1919.* London: Putnam, 1969.

144. Penrose, Harald. *British Aviation. The Pioneer Years 1903–1914.* London: Putnam, 1967.

145. Powers, Barry D. *Strategy without Slide-Rule. British Air Strategy 1914–1939.* London: Croom Helm, 1976.

146. Rawlinson, A. *The Defense of London 1915–1918.* London: Melrose, 1924 [1923].

147. Reader, W. J. *Architect of Air Power. The Life of the First Viscount Weir of Eastwood 1877–1959.* London: Collins, 1968.

148. Revell, Alex. *High in the Empty Blue. The History of 56 Squadron RFC RAF, 1916–1919.* Mountain View: Flying Machines Press, 1995.

149. Richardson, Kenneth. *The British Motor Industry 1896–1939.* London: Macmillan, 1977.

150. Robertson, Bruce. *Sopwith—The Man and His Aircraft.* Letchworth, Hertsfordshire: Air Review Ltd., 1970.

151. Saundby, Sir Robert. *Air Bombardment. The Story of Its Development.* New York: Harper and Brothers, 1961.

152. Saunders, Hilary St. G. *Per Ardua. The Rise of British Air Power 1911–1939.* London: Oxford University Press, 1945.

153. Slessor, John C. *Air Power and Armies.* London: Oxford University Press, 1936.

154. Smith, Malcolm. *British Air Strategy between the Wars.* Oxford: Clarendon Press, 1984.

155. Thetford, Owen. *British Naval Aircraft Since 1912.* London: Putnam, 1958.

156. Tredrey, Frank D. *Pioneer Pilot. The Great Smith Barry Who Taught the World to Fly.* London: Davies, 1976.

157. Williams, George Kent. Dissertation. "Statistics and Strategic Bombardment: Operation and Records of the British Long-range Bombing Force during World War I and Their Implications for the Development of the Post-war Royal Air Force, 1917–1923." Dissertation, Oxford University, 1987.

158. Winter, Denis. *The First of the Few. Fighter Pilots of the First World War.* London: Penguin, 1983 [1982].

159. Wynn, Humphrey. *The Black Cat Squadron. Night Bombing in World War I.* Washington: Smithsonian Institution Press, 1990 [1989].

160. Young, Desmond. *Member for Mexico—A Biography of Weetman Pearson, First Lord Cowdray.* London: Cassell, 1966.

France

Published Primary Sources

161. D'Aubigny. "Rapport sur les Travaux de la Commission de l'Armée pendant la Guerre 1914–1918" ["Report on the Work of the Army Commission During the War, 1914–1918"], No. 6999. Chambre des Députés, 11e Législature, Session de 1919. Paris: Martinet, 1919.

162. Grand Quartier Général (GQG) des Armées du Nord et du Nord Est. Etat-Major. 3e Bureau et Aéronautique. "Instruction sur l'organisation et l'emploi de l'aéronautique aux armées" ["Instructions on the organization and employment of aviation with the Armies"]. Mars 1918. Titre II. "Aviation de Combat" ["II. Fighters"]. Titre III. "Aviation de Bombardement" ["III. Bombers"]. Paris: Charles Lavauzelle, 1918.

163. Ministère de la Guerre. "Instruction du 28 Décembre 1917 sur Liaison pour les Troupes de Toutes Armes" ["Instructions on Liaison with the Troops of all Armies"]. Paris: Charles Lavauzelle, 1920.

Memoirs

164. d'Arnoux, Jacques. *Paroles d'un Revenant* [*Measuring Words*]. Paris: Plon, 1925.

165. Barthelemy, Raymond. ed. *Le Temps des Hélices* [*Propeller Times*]. Paris: Editions France-Empire, 1972.

166. Boulenger, Jacques. *En Escadrille* [*A Squadron*]. Paris: La Renaissance du Livre, 1918.

167. Chambe, René. *Au Temps des Carabines* [*To the Times of Carbines*]. Paris: Flammarion, 1955.

168. Chaput, Jean. *Quelques lettres de Jean Chaput* [*Some Letters of Jean Chaput*]. Paris: Tolmer, 1920.

169. Dassault, Marcel. *The Talisman.* transl. Patricia High Painton. New Rochelle: Arlington House, 1971 [1969].

170. Duvau, Andre. *Br. 29. Souvenirs d'Escadrille* [*Memoirs of a Squadron*]. Vincennes: Service Historique de l'Armée de l'Air, 1976.

171. Etévé, Albert. *Avant les Cocardes. Les Débuts de l'Aéronautique militaire* [*Before the Uniforms—The Beginnings of Military Aviation*]. Paris: Lavauzelle, 1961.

172. Etévé, Albert. *La Victoire des Cocardes* [*Victory of the Uniforms*]. Paris: Lavauzelle, 1970.

173. *Forces Aériens Français* [*French Air Forces*]. Special Cinquantenaire de la victoire. *Revue Mensuelle de l'Armée de l'Air,* 23, no. 252 (November 1968).

174. JeanJean, Marcel. *Des Ronds dans l'Air* [*Circles in the Air*]. *Souvenirs Illustrés* [*Souvenir Illustrations*]. Aurillac: Imprimerie Moderne, 1967.

175. JeanJean, Marcel. *Sous les Cocardes. Scènes de l'aviation militaire* [*Under the Cockades: Military Aviation Scenes*]. Paris: SERMA, 1964 [1919].

176. Laffray, Jean. *Pilote de chasse aux Cicognes* [*Fighter Pilots of the Cicognes*]. Paris: Fayard, 1968.

177. Lafont, Bernard. *Au Ciel de Verdun. Notes d'un aviateur* [*The Skies Over Verdun—flier's notes*]. Paris: Berger-Levrault, 1918.

178. Marc, Lieutenant. [Jean Beraud Villars]. *Notes d'un pilote disparu* (1916–1917). Paris: Hachette, 1918. trans. by S. J. Pincetl and Ernest Marchand, *Notes of a Lost Pilot.* Hamden CT: Archon, 1975.

179. Marie, Félix. *Les Origines de l'Aéronautique militaire, Novembre 1909–Novembre 1910* [*The Origins of Military Aeronautics, 1909–1910*]. Paris: Lavauzelle, 1924.

180. Mirande, Henri and Louis Livier. *Sur la Bataille. Journal d'un Aviateur Francais à l'Armée Bulgare au Siège d'Andrinople* [*Over the Battle: Notes of a French pilot in the Bulgarian Army at the Siege of Adrianople*]. Paris: Ambert, 1913.

181. Nadaud, Marcel. *En plein vol. Souvenirs de Guerre aérienne* [*In Full Flight—Memories of the Air War*]. Paris: Hachette, 1916.

182. Odier, Antoine. *Souvenirs d'une vielle Tige* [*Memoirs of a old Stalk*]. Paris: Fayard, 1955.

183. Thébault, Louis. *L'Escadrille 210* [*210 Squadron*]. Paris: Jouve, 1925.

184. Thenault, Georges. *L'Escadrille Lafayette (Avril 1916–Janvier 1918)* [*Lafayette Escadrille (April 1916–January 1918)*]. Paris: Librairie Hachette, 1939.

185. Violan, Jean. *Dans l'Air et dans la Boue. Mes Missions de Guerre* [*In the Air and in the Mud—My War Missions*]. Paris: Librairie des Champs-Elysees, 1933.

186. Voisin, Gabriel. *Men, Women, and 10,000 Kites.* transl. Oliver Stewart. London: Putnam, 1963 [1961].

Official Histories

187. *L'Aéronautique pendant la Guerre Mondiale* [*Aviation during the War*]. Paris: Maurice de Brunoff, 1919.

Secondary Sources

188. "L'Aéronautique Militaire Française pendant la Guerre de 1914–1918." 2 Vols. "1914. 1915. 1916" and "1917. 1918" in *Icare, revue de l'aviation française.* Special Numbers, 1978.

189. Audigier, Francois. "Histoire de l'Aviation Militaire Française des Origines à 1939" ["History of French Aviation from the Beginnings to 1939"]. In-House Work, Service Historique de l'Armée de l'Air, 1971.

190. Barthelemy, Raymond. ed. *Le Temps des Hélices* [*Propeller Times*]. Paris: Editions France-Empire, 1972.

191. Benoist, Odile. "Le Recrutement des Aviateurs Français pendant la Guerre 1914–1918" ["The Recruitment of French Airmen . . . 1914–1918"]. Mémoire de Maitrise. Université de Paris I, 1974–75.

192. Bernard, Philippe. "A Propos de la Stratégie Aérienne pendant la Première Guerre Mondiale: Mythes et Réalités" ["On Aerial Strategy in the First World War—Myths and Realities"]. *Revue d'Histoire Moderne et Contemporaine.* 16 (1969): 350–75.

193. Bitchakdjian, J. "Les débuts des industries françaises d'aéronautique. La Société des moteurs Salmson 1913–1917" ["The Beginning of French Aeronautical Industry: Salmson Engines, 1913–1917"]. Mémoire de Maitrise, Université de Paris X—Nanterre.

194. Cantener, Henri. *Hommage aux Ailes Lorraines* [*Homage to the Wings of Lorraine*]. Nancy, 1968.

195. Chadeau, Emmanuel. "Etat, Entreprise et Développement Economique: L'Industrie Aéronautique en France (1900–1940)" ["State, Enterprise, and Economic Development"]. 2 Vols. Dissertation. Université de Paris X—Nanterre, 1986.

196. Chadeau, Emmanuel. *L'Industrie Aéronautique en France 1900–1950. De Blériot à Dassault* [*French Aeronautical Industry 1900–1950. From Bleriot to Dassault*]. Paris: Fayard, 1987.

197. Chadeau, Emmanuel. "L'industrie française d'aviation à la veille de la première guerre mondiale" ["French aeronautical industry to the eve of the First World War"]. *Revue Historique des Armées,* 1981, no. 2: 61–81; no. 3: 181–206.

198. Dournel, Jean-Pierre. "L'image de l'aviateur francais en 1914–1918" ["The Image of French Flyers 1914–1918"]. *Revue Historique des Armées,* 1975, no. 4: 58–83; 1976, no. 1: 95–123.

199. Facon, Patrick. "L'aviation française au 'Chemin des Dames' " ["French Aviation at the Chemin des Dames"]. *Aviation Magazine,* no. 805 (1 July 1981): 80–87.

200. Fridenson, Patrick. *Histoire des Usines Renault* [*History of the Renault Works*]. Vol. 1. *Naissance de la grande Entreprise 1898–1939.* Paris: Seuil, 1972.

201. le Goyet, P. "Evolution de la doctrine d'emploi de l'aviation française entre 1919 et 1939" ["Evolution of the doctrine for the employment of French Aviation 1919–1939"] in Numéro spécial sur l'aviation française (1919–1940), *Revue d'Histoire de la Deuxiéme Guerre Mondiale,* 19, no. 73 (January 1969): 3–41.

202. Hatry, Gilbert. *Renault, Usine de Guerre 1914–1918* [*Renault, Munitions Maker, 1914–1918*]. Paris: Lafourcade, 1975.

203. Hodeir, Marcellin. "L'Aviation militaire française de la première guerre mondiale (1917–1918). Etude du milieu social. Approche des mentalités" ["French Air Force in the First World War, 1917–1918—a study of the social milieu and mentality"]. Mémoire de Maitrise, Université de Paris IV, 1976–77.

204. Huisman, Georges. *Dans les Coulisses de l'Aviation 1914–1918. Pourquoi n'avons nous pas toujours garder la maitrise des airs?* [*In Aviation Affairs 1914–1918. Why didn't we always keep air superiority?*] Paris: Renaissance du Livre, 1921.

205. Icare. "1914–1918 L'Aeronautique militaire francaise" tome I. *Icare* No. 85 Automne 1978.

206. Jauneaud, Marcel. *L'Aviation militaire et la guerre aérienne* [*Military Aviation at the War in the Air*]. Paris: Flammarion, 1923.

207. Jullian, Marcel. *La Grande Bataille dans les Airs 1914–1918* [*Great Air Battles, 1914–1918*]. Paris: Presses de la Cité, 1967.

208. Jullian, Marcel. *Le Chevalier du Ciel* [*Knight of the Skies*]. *Charles Nungesser.* Paris: Amiot Dumont, 1953.

209. Kaspi, Andre. *Le Temps des Américains. Le Concours Américain à la France en 1917–1918* [*The American Time—the gathering of Americans in France 1917–1918*]. Paris: Publications de Sorbonne, 1976.

210. Kerisel, Jean. *Albert Caquot 1881–1976. Créateur et Précurseur.* Paris: Editions Eyrolles, 1978.

211. Laux, James. "Gnome et Rhône: une firme de moteurs d'avion durant la Grande Guerre" ["Gnome et Rhone—a French aero engine firm in the First World War"], in *1914–1918. L'Autre Front*. Cahiers du "Mouvement Social" no. 2. Paris: Les Editions Ouvrières, 1977.

212. Laux, James. *In First Gear. The French Automobile Industry to 1914*. Montreal: McGill Queens University Press, 1976.

213. Laux, James. "The Rise and Fall of Armand Deperdussin." *French Historical Studies,* 8, no. 1 (Spring 1973): 95–104.

214. Lissarrague, Pierre. *Mémento d'Histoire de l'Aéronautique militaire française [Memento of French military aeronautics]*. Vol. 2 *La Guerre 1914–1918.* Ecole militaire de l'air, 1978.

215. *Livre d'Or de la Société Française Hispano-Suiza [The Gold Book of the French Hispano-Suiza Company]*. Paris: Draeger Freres, 1924.

216. Marchis, Lucien. *Vingt-Cinq Ans d'Aéronautique française [Twenty-five years of French Aviation]*. 2 Vols. Paris: Chambre syndicale des Industries aéronautiques, 1934.

217. Morgat, Louis. "L'aviation en Berry avant la Grande Guerre" ["Aviation in Berry before the Great War"]. *Revue Historique des Armées,* 1980, no. 1: 158–216.

218. Mortane, Jacques. *Les As nous parlent [We talk to the Aces]*. Paris: Baudinière, 1937.

219. Mortane, Jacques. *Histoire Illustrée de la Guerre Aérienne (1914–1918) [Illustrated History of the Air War 1914–1918]*. Paris: L'Edition Française Illustrée, 1921.

220. Mortane, Jacques. *Les Vols Emouvants de la Guerre [Great Flights of the War]*. Paris: Hachette, 1917.

221. Mortane, Jacques et Jean Dacay. *La Guerre des Nues racontée par ses morts [The War in the Clouds as told by the Dead]*. Paris: L'Edition Française Illustrée, 1918.

222. Orthlieb, Commandant. *L'Aéronautique Hier—Demain [Flying Today and Tomorrow]*. Paris: Masson, 1920.

223. Pedroncini, Guy. *Pétain Général en Chef 1917–1918.* Paris: Presses Universitaires de France, 1974.

224. Pesquiès-Courbier, Simone. "'Le bassin ferrifère de Briey durant la guerre de 1914–1918" ["The Briey Iron Foundries during the War"]. *Revue Historique des Armées,* 1981, no. 2, 91–128.

225. Pesquiès-Courbier, Simone. "La politique de bombardement des usines sidérurgiques en Lorraine et au Luxembourg pendant la Première Guerre mondiale" ["The Politics of Bombing the steel works in Lorraine and in Luxemburg in the First World War"]. *Revue Historique des Armées,* 1981, no. 4, 127–59.

226. Petit, Edmond. *La Vie Quotidienne dans l'Aviation en France au Debut du XXe Siècle (1900–1935) [Daily Life in the French Air Force at the Beginning of the Twentieth Century]*. Paris: Hachette, 1977.

227. Porret, D. *Les 'As' français de la Grande Guerre [French Aces in the Great War]*. 2 Vols. Paris: Service Historique de l'Armée de l'Air, 1983.

228. Quellennec, Jacques. *Roland Garros. Mémoires*. Paris: Hachette, 1966.

229. Renaud, Paul. *L'Evolution de l'Aéronautique pendant la Guerre 1914–1918 [The Evolution of Aviation during the War]*. Paris: 1921.

230. Sahel, Jacques. *Henri Farman et l'aviation*. Paris: Grasset, 1936.

231. Truelle, J. "La Production aéronautique militaire française jusqu'en Juin 1940" ["French Military Aircraft Production to June 1940"], in Numéro special sur l'aviation française (1919–1940), *Revue d'Histoire de la Deuxième Guerre Mondiale,* 19, no. 73 (January 1969): 75–110.

232. Vincent, Daniel. *La Bataille de l'Air*. Paris: Berger-Levrault, 1918.

233. Voisin, André P. *La Doctrine de l'Aviation française de combat au cours de la guerre (1915–1918) [French Aviation Doctrine during the War]*. Paris: Berger-Levrault, 1932.

Germany

For additional sources on German aviation, see the bibliographies in the author's works cited below.

Official Histories

234. Kriegswissenschaftliche Abteilung der Luftwaffe (Air Force Military History Department). *Die Luftstreitkräfte in der Abwehrschlacht zwischen Somme und Oise vom 8. bis 12. August . . . (The Air Force in the Defensive Battle between the Somme and Oise Rivers 8–12 August 1918)*. Berlin: Mittler und Sohn, 1942.

235. Kriegswissenschaftliche Abteilung der Luftwaffe (Air Force Military History Department). *Die Militärluftfahrt bis zum Beginn des Weltkrieges 1914 (Military Aviation at the Beginning of the World War)*. 3 Vols. 2d rev. ed. Edited by Militärgeschichtliches Forschungsamt. Frankfurt a. Main: Mittler und Sohn, 1965–66.

236. Kriegswissenschaftliche Abteilung der Luftwaffe (Air Force Military History Department). *Mobilmachung, Aufmarsch, und erster Einsatz der Deutschen Luftstreitkräfte im August 1914 (Mobilization, Deployment, and First Use of the German Air Service)*. Berlin: Mittler und Sohn, 1939.

Memoirs

237. Boelcke, Oswald. *Hauptmann Boelckes Feldberichte (Captain Boelcke's Field Reports)*. Gotha: Perthas, 1917.

238. Bullinger. "Kriegserfahrungen in der Motorenabteilung der Fluzeugmeisterei." ("Wartime Experiences in the Aircraft Depot's Engine Department.") Reports in Peter Grosz Archive, Princeton, NJ.

239. Eddelbüttel, F. W. *Artillerie-Flieger (Artillery Flier)*. Dresden: Das Grössere Deutschland, 1939.

240. Fokker, A. H. G., and Bruce Gould. *Flying Dutchman: The Life of Anthony Fokker*. New York: Holt, Rinehart and Winston, 1931.

241. Heinkel, Ernst. *Stürmisches Leben (Stormy Life)*. Ed. Jürgen Thorwald. Stuttgart: Mundus-Verlag, 1953.

242. Loewenstern, Elard von. *Der Frontflieger aus Vorkriegs-, Kriegs und Nachkriegs-Fliegertagen (The Frontflier of Prewar, Wartime, and Postwar Days.)*. Berlin: Bernard und Graefe, 1937.

243. Marben, Rolf. *Zeppelin Adventures*. Greenhill, Herts.: Aeolus, 1986 [1931].

244. Neumann, Georg P., ed. *In Der Luft Unbesiegt (Unconquered in the Skies)*. Munich: Lehmanns, 1923.

245. Radenbach, F. W. *Weit im Rucken des Feindes. Kriegserlebnisse eines Fernaufklärers (Far in the Rear of the Enemy. Wartime Experiences of a Long-range Reconnaissance Flier)*. Berlin: Traditions-Verlag, 1938.

246. Richthofen, Manfred von. *Der rote Kampfflieger (The Red Battleflier)*. Berlin: Ullstein, 1917.

247. Schaefer, Leutnant. *Vom Jäger zum Flieger (From Hunter to Flier)*. Berlin: Scherl, 1918.

248. Schleustedt, Franz. *Vollgas. Ein Fliegerleben (Full Gas. A Flier's Life)*. Berlin: Steiniger, 1939.

249. Schroeder, Hans. *A German Airman Remembers*. Greenhill, Herts.: Aeolus, 1986 [1935].

250. Udet, Ernst. *Mein Fliegerleben (My Flying Life)*. Berlin: Ullstein, 1935.

251. Weltkoborsky, Norbert. *Vom Fliegen, Siegen und Sterben einer Feldflieger-Abteilung (Of Flying, Victories, and Death of a Field Flight Unit)*. Vol. 80 of series *Deutsche Tat im Weltkrieg 1914–1918 (German Deeds in the First World War)*. Berlin: Verlag Bernard & Graefe, 1939.

Secondary Sources

252. Arndt, Hans. "Die Fliegerwaffe." ("The Air Arm") In *Der Stellungkrieg 1914–1918* (in *The War of Position*). Ed. Friedrich Seeselberg, pp. 310–69. Berlin: Mittler und Sohn, 1926.

253. Arndt, Hans. "Die Fliegerwaffe im Weltkrieg." ("The Air Arm in the World War") In *Ehrendenkmal der deutschen Armee und Marine* (in *Memorial of the German Army and Navy*). Ed. Ernst von Eisenart-Rothe, pp. 281–95. Berlin: Deutscher National-Verlag AG, 1928.

254. Arndt, Hans. "Der Luftkrieg." ("The Air War") In *Der Weltkampf um Ehre und Recht* (in *The World Struggle for Honor and Justice*). Ed. Max Schwarte, 4: 529–651. Leizig: Finking, 1922.

255. Blunck, Richard. *Hugo Junkers: ein Leben für Technik und Luftfahrt* (*Hugo Junkers. A Life for Technology and Aviation*). Dusseldorf: Econ-Verlag, 1951.

256. Bülow, Hilmer von. *Geschichte der Luftwaffe* (*History of the Air Force*). Frankfurt am Main: Moritz Diensterweg, 1934.

257. Cuneo, John R. *Winged Mars.* 2 Vols. Harrisburg: Military Service Publishing Company, 1942, 1947.

258. Eichler, Jürgen. "Die Militärluftschiffahrt in Deutschland 1911–1914 und ihre Rolle in den Kriegsplänen des deutschen Imperialismum." ("Military Airships in Germany 1911–1914 and Their Role in the War Plans of German Imperialism") in *Zeitschrift für Militärgeschichte* (in *Journal of Military History*), 24, no. 4 (1985): 350–60; no. 5: 403–12.

259. Fritzsche, Peter. *A Nation of Fliers: German Aviation and the Popular Imagination.* Cambridge: Harvard University Press, 1992.

260. Gengler, Ludwig. *Rudolf Berthold.* Berlin: Schlieffen, 1934.

261. Gersdorff, Kyrill von, and Kurt Grassmann. *Flugmotoren und Strahltriebwerke* (*Aviation Engines and Jets*). Munich: Bernard & Graefe.

262. Gilles, J. A. *Flugmotoren 1910 bis 1918* (*Aviation Engines*). Frankfurt am Main: Mittler und Sohn, 1971.

263. Grey, Peter, and Owen Thetford. *German Aircraft of the First World War.* London: Putnam, 1962.

264. Haddow, G. W., and Peter M. Grosz. *The German Giants: The Story of the R-planes, 1914–1919.* London: Putnam, 1962.

265. Imrie, Alex. *Pictorial History of the German Army Air Service, 1914–1918.* Chicago: Henry Regnery Co., 1973.

266. Kilduff, Peter. *Richthofen. Beyond the Legend of the Red Baron.* New York: John Wiley & Sons, 1993.

267. Morrow, John H., Jr. *Building German Air Power, 1909–1914.* Knoxville: University of Tennessee Press, 1976.

268. Morrow, John H. *German Air Power in World War I.* Lincoln: University of Nebraska Press, 1982.

269. Robinson, Douglas H. *The Zeppelin in Combat; A History of the German naval Airship Division, 1912–1918.* London: Foulis, 1962.

270. Supf, Peter. *Das Buch der deutschen Fluggeschichte* (*The Book of German Aviation History*). 2nd ed. 2 Vols. Stuttgart: Drei Brunnen Verlag, 1956, 1958.

271. Zuerl, Walter, ed. *Pour Le Merite–Flieger* (*Blue Max Pilots*). Munich: Pechstein, 1938.

Russia

Official Histories

272. Kozlow, N. "A Study of the Military-Technical Supply of the Russian Army in the World War. Part I. From the Beginning of the War to the Middle of 1916." pp. 86–148 on "Army Aircraft Equipment." Translated by Charles Berman. Moscow: Government Military Publications Division, 1926.

Memoirs

273. Finne, K. N. *Igor Sikorsky. The Russian Years.* Eds. Carl Bobrow and Von Hardesty. Translated and adapted by Von Hardesty.

274. Riaboff, Alexander. *Gatchina Days. Reminiscences of a Russian Pilot.* Von Hardesty, ed. Washington: Smithsonian Institution Press, 1986.

275. Sikorsky, Igor. *The Story of the Winged S. An Autobiography.* New York: Dodd, Mead, 1938.

Secondary Sources

276. Durkota, Alan, Thomas Darcey, and Victor Kulikov. *The Imperial Russian Air Service. Famous Pilots and Aircraft of World War I.* Mountain View: Flying Machines Press, 1995.

277. Duz, Petr Dmitrievich. *History of Aeronautics and Aviation in the USSR. The First World War Period (1914–1918).* Moscow: Oborongiz, 1960 (NASM translation from the Russian).

278. Hardesty, Von. "Aeronautics Comes to Russia: The Early Years, 1908–1918," pp. 23–44, National Air and Space Museum Research Report 1985.

279. Higham, Robin, and Jacob W. Kipp. *Soviet Aviation and Air Power. A Historical View* Boulder: Westview, 1977. See especially introduction by Higham and essays by David R. Jones (pp. 15–33), Jacob W. Kipp (pp. 137–65), and Otto Chaney and John Greenwood (pp. 265–87).

280. Higham, Robin, John T. Greenwood, and Von Hardesty, eds. *Russian Aviation and Air Power.* London: Lars, 1998.

281. Kilmarx, Robert A. *A History of Soviet Air Power.* New York: Praeger, 1962.

282. Kilmarx, Robert A. "The Russian Imperial Air Forces of World War I," *Airpower Historian,* 10 (July 1963): 90–95.

283. Strizhevsky, S. *Nikolai Zhukovsky. Founder of Aeronautics.* Moscow: Foreign Languages Publishing House, 1957.

Austria-Hungary

Secondary Sources

284. Grosz, Peter M., George Haddow, Peter Schiemer. *Austro-Hungarian Army Aircraft of World War I.* Mountain View: Flying Machines Press, 1993.

285. O'Connor, Martin. *Air Aces of the Austro-Hungarian Empire, 1914–1918.* Mesa: Champlin Fighter Museum Press, 1986.

286. Peter, Ernst. *Die k.u.k. Luftschiffer- und Fliegertruppe Oesterreich-Hungarns, 1794–1919* (*Austro-Hungarian Airship and Aviation Troops*). Stuttgart: Motorbuch Verlag, 1981.

287. Peters, Klaus. "Zur Entwicklung der oesterreichisch-ungarischen Militaerluftfahrt von den Anfaengen bis 1915." ("On the Development of Austro-Hungarian Military Aviation from the Beginnings to 1915") Diss., University of Vienna, 1971.

288. Schupita, Peter. *Die k.u.k. Seeflieger. Chronik und Dokumentation der oesterreichisch-ungarischen Marineluftwaffe 1911–1918* (*Austro-Hungarian Naval Aviators: Chronology and Documents of Austro-Hungarian Naval Aviation*). Koblenz: Bernard und Graefe Verlag, 1983.

Italy

Memoirs

289. Baracca, Francesco. *Memorie di Guerra Aerea* (*Memoirs of the Air War*). Roma: Edizioni Ardita, 1934.

290. D'Annunzio, Gabriele. *Aviatore di Guerra. Documenti E Testimonianze* (*War Aviators: Documents and Testimonials*). Milan: Impresa editoriale Italiana, 1930.

Official Histories

291. Molfese, Manlio. *L'Aviazione da Ricognizione Italiana durante la Guerra Europea (Maggio 1915–Novembre 1918)* (*Italian Reconnaissance Aviation during the European War May 1915–November 1918*). Roma: Provveditorato Generale dello Stato Libreria, 1925.

Secondary Sources

292. Apostolo, Giorgio, and Rosario Abate. *Caproni nella Prima Guerra Mondiale* (*Caproni in the First World War*). Europress, 1970.

293. Bompiani, Giorgio, and Clemente Prepositi. *Le Ali della Guerra* (*Wings of War*). Milan: Mondadori, 1931.

294. Camurati, Gastone. "Aerei italiani 1914–1918." ("Italian Aviators") *Rivista Aeronautica*. Vols. 48 and 49.

295. Cappelluti, Frank J. "The Life and Thought of Giulio Douhet." Diss., Rutgers University, 1967.

296. Lodi, Angelo. *Storia delle Origini dell'Aeronautica Militare 1884–1915* (*History of the Origins of Military Aviation*). 2 Vols. Roma: Edizioni Bizzarri, .

297. Ludovico, Domenico. *Gli Aviatori Italiani del Bombardimento nella Guerra 1915–1918* (*Italian Bombers in the War*). Rome: Ufficio Storico Aeronautica Militare, 1980.

298. Mandel, Roberto. *La Guerra Aerea* (*The Air War*). 2nd ed. Milan: Scrittori, 1933.

299. Porro, Felice. *La Guerra nell'aria* (*War in the Air*). 5th ed. Milan: Corbaccio, 1940.

300. Prepositi, Clemente. *I Cavalieri dell'Aria nella Grande Guerra. Il primato Italiano nella Guerra aerea (1911–1912. 1915–1918)* (*Aerial Cavalry in the Great War. Italian Primacy in the Air War*). Bologna: Cappelli, 1933.

301. Prepositi, Clemente. *Francesco Baracca*. Milan: Zucchi, 1937.

302. Vergnano, Piero. *Origins of Aviation in Italy, 1783–1918*. Genoa: Intyprint, 1964.

United States

Official Histories

303. Thayer, Lucien H. *America's First Eagles. The Official History of the U.S. Air Service, A.E.F. (1917–1918)*. San Jose and Mesa: Bender Publishing and Champlin Fighter Aces Museum Press, 1983.

304. Maurer, Maurer. *Aviation in the U.S. Army, 1919–1939*. Washington: Office of Air Force History, 1987.

305. Maurer, Maurer. *The U.S. Air Service in World War I*. 4 Vols. Washington: Office of Air Force History, 1978–1979.

306. Mixter, G. W., and H. H. Emmons. *United States Army Aircraft Production Facts*. Washington: Government Printing Office, 1919.

Memoirs

307. Biddle, Charles J. *Fighting Airman: The Way of the Eagle*. Doubleday, 1968 [1919].

308. Channing, Grace E., ed. *War Letters of Edmond Genet*. New York: Charles Scribner's Sons, 1918.

309. Loening, Grover. *Our Wings Grow Faster*. Garden City, NY: Doubleday, Doran & Co., Inc., 1935.

310. McConnell, James R. *Flying for France*. Garden City NY: Doubleday, Page & Co., 1917.

311. Mitchell, William B. *Memoirs of World War I*. New York: Random House, 1956 [1928].

312. Parsons, Edwin C. *I Flew with the Lafayette Escadrille*. Indianapolis: Seale, 1963 [1937].

313. Porter, Harold E. *Aerial Observation*. New York: Harper and Brothers, 1921.

314. Rickenbacker, Eddie V. *Fighting the Flying Circus*. New York: Doubleday, 1965 [1919].

315. Rowe, Josiah P. *Letters from a World War I Aviator*. Boston: Sinclaire, 1986.

316. Rossano, Geoffrey L. *The Price of Honor. The World War One Letters of Naval Aviator Kenneth MacLeish*. Annapolis: Naval Institute Press, 1991.

317. Springs, Elliott White. *Nocturne Militaire*. New York: Doran, 1927.

318. Springs, Elliott. *War Birds. Diary of an Unkown Aviator.* New York: Doran, 1926.

319. Winslow, Carroll Dana. *With the French Flying Corps.* New York: Charles Scribner's Sons, 1917.

Secondary Sources

320. Bilstein, Roger E. *Flight in America, 1900–1983.* Baltimore: The Johns Hopkins Press, 1984.

321.Carisella, P. J. and James W. Ryan. *The Black Swallow of Death.* Boston: Marlborough House, 1972.

322. Cooke, David C. *Sky Battle: 1914–1918.* New York: Norton, 1970.

323. Davis, Burke. *War Birds. The Life and Times of Elliott White Springs.* Chapel Hill: The University of North Carolina Press, 1987.

324. Dickey, Philip S. *The Liberty Engine, 1918–1942.* Smithsonian Annals of Flight, Vol. 1, no. 3, 1968.

325. Flammer, Philip M. *The Vivid Air. The Lafayette Escadrille.* Athens: University of Georgia Press, 1981.

326. Freudenthal, Elsbeth. *The Aviation Business. From Kitty Hawk to Wall Street.* New York: Vanguard, 1940.

327. Futrell, Robert F. *Ideas, Concepts, Doctrine: A History of Basic Thinking in the United States Air Force, 1907–1964.* Vol. 1. Montgomery: Aerospace Studies Institute, Air University, 1971.

328. Holley, I. B., Jr. *Ideas and Weapons.* Washington: Office of Air Force History, 1983 [1953].

329. Hudson, James J. *Hostile Skies. A Combat History of the American Air Service in World War I.* Syracuse: Syracuse University Press, 1968.

330. Hudson, James J. *In Clouds of Glory. American Airmen Who Flew with the British during the Great War.* Fayetteville: University of Arkansas Press, 1990.

331. Knott, Richard. *The American Flying Boat. An Illustrated History.* Annapolis: Naval Institute Press, 1979.

332. Turnbull, Archibald D., and Clifford L. Lord. *History of United States Naval Aviation.* New Haven: Yale University Press,1949.

333. Vander Meulen, Jacob A. "The American Aircraft Industry to World War II." Draft Diss., University of Toronto, 1989.

334. Van Wyen, Adrian O. *Naval Aviation in World War I.* Washington: Chief of Naval Operations, 1969.

17

Industrial Mobilization and Military Technology

Daniel R. Beaver

INTRODUCTION

This chapter is an introduction to the vast literature on the industrial and technological impact of the Great War. It begins with a discussion of the better books that link the war with the political and organizational changes wrought by industrial modernization during the nineteenth and early twentieth centuries. It then turns to general works that in some way address wartime command and control of industry and technology or contain useful bibliographies on those issues. It surveys studies of industrial mobilization by nation and deals with technological developments topically. It includes volumes on inter-alliance cooperation and some representative works on wartime agriculture, transportation, communication, and labor relations. The essay concentrates on the Entente powers, the United States, and the Central powers. The satellite states of both the Entente and Central powers depended on their sponsors for arms and equipment and their problems are dealt with together at the end of the section on command and control. The Italians are included with the satellite powers because of the relative scarcity of Italian sources. The essay ends with a modest effort to integrate thematically some of the current scholarship on industrial mobilization and technology.

From the available material, including thousands of books and articles accumulated over more than eighty per year, I have listed just 459 sources. They consist of published documents, letters and papers, official histories, political and strategic studies and studies of class, gender, and interest group politics in wartime that can be obtained at any competently organized research library. All either give some attention to command, control, and execution of industrial and technical programs directly or contain useful bibliographies that give entrée to more specialized literature. The selections will not please every scholar. My inadequacy in German and especially in Russian and other Eastern European languages is bound to set some academic teeth on edge.

Great War studies have appeared in waves, usually as a result of the release of new sources, serious changes in the contemporary political climate, or a combination of both. The first wave, which began during the war itself and continued through the early depression, consisted of apologias, official histories, officially supported topical monographs, and the first "special studies," many sponsored by the Carnegie Foundation, which dealt with nonmilitary aspects of the contest. The second wave, which appeared during the 1930s and 1940s, included several rounds of revisionist rejoinders to the official conventional wisdom and included important reconsiderations of wartime leadership. The third wave, which began in the mid-1950s with the publication of Fritz Fischer's *Germany's Aims in the First World* [120], expanded with the approach of the fiftieth anniversary of the outbreak of the war and has not yet lost its momentum. The fourth wave, which emerged concurrently in the 1960s, returned to themes of class, gender, interest group politics, and state-building, which had received little attention since the 1920s and early 1930s. Since then practitioners of the "new military history" and the "new social history," drawing upon academically popular sociological, anthropological, and psychological theories, have constructed multidisciplinary, methodologically sophisticated studies of domestic questions that add further dimensions to the traditional ones covered by conventional diplomatic and military historians.

MODERNIZATION AND THE GREAT WAR—AN OVERVIEW

Three older general works, Quincy Wright's *A Study of War* [452], Lewis Mumford's *Technics and Civilization* [295] and John U. Nef's *War and Human Progress* [296] dealt very early with the idea of modernization and set the stage for the "war and society" approach, which some contemporary historians consider their own invention. The best recent books are Cyril E. Black's *The Dynamics of Modernization* [35], Paul Kennedy's *The Rise and Fall of the Great Powers* [218], and William H. McNeill's *The Pursuit of Power* [278]. Several significant economic histories also serve to put the war into a broader developmental context. David Landes' two volumes, *The Unbound Prometheus* [244] and *The Wealth and Poverty of Nations* [245], and Alfred D. Chandler's *The Visible Hand* [58] and *Scale and Scope* [57] are essential. Both Landes and Chandler address the implicit connections that developed during the war period. The Chandler volumes have organizational implications beyond the American scene. See also A. S. Milward and S. B. Saul, *The Economics of Continental Europe 1850–1914* [284], and Clive Trebilock, *The Industrialization of the Continental Powers 1890–1914* [407]. Norman Stone's *Europe Transformed 1878–1919* [386] is insightful and also contains an excellent bibliography. Raymond Aron in *The Century of Total War* [11] and *War and Industrial Society* [12] links modernization, culture, and politics in his usual brilliant fashion. His chapter on the opening of the Great War in *The Century of Total War* is among the most provocative explanations of the war's organizational trajectory in twentieth century political literature. Several articles in J. M. Winter, ed., *War and Economic Development* [448] apply particularly to the First World War.

All the general histories of the war allude to industrial mobilization and weapons development, but the majority emphasize politics, strategy, and tactics. Bernedotte E. Schmitt and Harold Vedeler, *The World in the Crucible* [357], is a distinguished exception that deals with the nonmilitary aspects of the struggle. The various official histories and the multivolume series, *Economic and Social History of the War,* sponsored during the 1920s and 1930s by the Carnegie Endowment for International Peace, were the first to deal systematically with industrial and technological issues involving all the major powers. Although almost three generations old, many remain the most reliable, often the only available scholarly studies on non–politico-military issues. Niall Ferguson's *The Pity of War* [115], despite its "counterfactual" declaration of the obvious—that the war was not inevitable and was a great mistake—includes provocative discussions of wartime industrial organization among the belligerents. Gerd Hardach's *The First World War* [171] offers the best recent one-volume comparative approach to state organization and economic mobilization during the war. Both the Ferguson and Hardach volumes contain excellent English and non-English language bibliographies. Marc Ferro's *The Great War 1914–1918* [117], which deals with military issues within a political and socio-economic context, is an excellent complement to the Hardach volume. Avner Offer's *The First World War: An Agrarian Interpretation* [301] is the first fresh interpretive approach to the war in years.

On the war itself, Winston S. Churchill's brilliant and deeply personal *The World Crisis* [64], Basil Liddel-Hart, *The Real War 1914–1918* [255], and Cyril Falls, *The Great War* [106] are the best of the older traditional histories in English. Sir James Edmonds, *History of World War I* [99] is the British official history. Martin Gilbert's recent *The First World War* [144] is not comparable to Liddel-Hart and Falls and is far from a complete history. The most recent traditional military history, *The First World War* [215] by John Keegan, is, as always, enlivened by the famous Keegan style and insight. Correlli Barnett's *The Sword Bearers* [19] is a comparative biography of the military and naval leaders of the major belligerent powers.

In recent years a substantial amount of the newer material on the Great War has been published in general anthologies. Paul Kennedy. ed., *The War Plans of the Great Powers.* [219] is an excellent set of essays on prewar plans and preparations and on the opening months of the war. Military Effectiveness: *The First World War* [282], the first volume of Allan Millett and Williamson Murray's well-edited trilogy, covers far more than doctrine and tactics. Two other important volumes have emerged from scholarly conferences. Hugh Cecil and Peter H. Liddle, eds., *Facing Armageddon* [54] was inspired by the international historical conference supported by the University of Leeds and held in that city in 1994, and John Horne, ed., *State, Society and Mobilization in Europe during the First World War* [198] contains a selection of the papers presented at the international conference on mobilization during the Great War held at Trinity College, Dublin, in 1993. J. M. Winter and Jean-Louis Robert have published important work on comparative wartime urban history in *Capital Cities at War* [445]. The Oxford Illustrated History of the First World War [388], a set of essays edited by Hew Strachen, *The Home Fronts: Britain, France and Germany 1914–1918* [440], edited by J. Williams, and *1914–1918: The Other Front* [131], edited by Patrick Fridenson, include essays by outstanding authors on industrial and logistical topics. The essays in *European Societies and the War 1914–1918* [27], edited by J. J. Becker and S. Audoin-Rouzeau, *War, Peace and Social Change in Twentieth Century Europe* [103], edited by Ian C. Emsley, Arthur Marwick and W. Simpson, and Marwick's own *War and Social Change in the Twentieth Century* [273] are all representative of the new military history and the new social history.

THE PROBLEM OF COMMAND AND CONTROL

The Great War was the first to require the careful prioritization, organization, and allocation of human and natural resources and the integration of industry and technology into complex command economies to support the belligerents' war efforts. There is a large literature on the political and strategic direction of the war and a smaller but useful one on the connections that developed between government, the military and industry. The British, operating within a parliamentary cabinet system, established an independent civilian ministry of munitions in 1915, but it was 1916 before it was integrated it with existing ministries of transportation, commerce, and agriculture and the military. The most important records and reports on British command and control are in the voluminous *Parliamentary Papers* [41] and in the twelve-volume *History of the Ministry of Munitions* [286]. The developing connections between the War Cabinet, the Imperial General Staff, the Admiralty and the Munitions Board can be traced through Maurice Hankey's *The Supreme Command* [170]. Sir William Robertson's *Soldiers and Statesmen* [344] shows how unimportant the members of the Imperial General Staff at first considered the links between industrial production and military effectiveness and how they grew to appreciate their importance. David Lloyd George's *War Memoirs* [261] should be used with discretion. Among secondary sources David French's three volumes, *British Economic and Strategic Planning 1905–1915* [129], *British Strategy and War Aims 1914–1916* [127], and *The Strategy of the Lloyd George Coalition 1916–1918* [128] comprise the best available study of British war government at the cabinet level. R. J. Q. Adams, *Arms and the Wizard* [1] deals skillfully with the early years of the British industrial war effort. Martin Gilbert's *Winston S. Churchill* [143], George H. Cassar, *Kitchener: Architect of Victory* [53], Randolph Churchill, *Lord Derby* [63], and, for the later years of the Lloyd George war government, Keith Grieves, *Sir Eric Geddes* [156] are all excellent sources.

The French parliamentary system functioned in a different manner. Although a ministry of munitions was established in 1915, the military was not as closely linked with industry as was the case with the British. The vast French official history published by the Ministry of War, *The French Armies in the Great War* [285] contains many critical documents on the command and control of the war effort. Georges Clemenceau, *The Grandeur and Misery of Victory* [67] and Marshal Ferdinand Foch's *Memoirs* [123] are useful for supply and logistical problems later in the war. Among the secondary sources P. Bruneau's older *The High Command and the Economy 1914–1918* [45] and Jere King's more recent *Generals and Politicians* [228] reveal the lack of connection between those who established military requirements in France and those who strove to meet them.

The Russian command and control system, hampered by the Czar's intervention and favoritism, confusion and jealousy among the members of the "Stavka" and the relatively undeveloped power of the Duma or parliament, never worked well. The war effort was uncoordinated, and connections between the home front and the battleline were tenuous and often ineffective. Primary sources that contain material on Russian command and control and give some attention to industrial mobilization are limited. They include the semi-official *Disintegration of the Army in 1917* [84] and memoirs and apologias, the best of which is Alexander F. Kerensky's *Russia and History's Turning Point* [221]. The older works, Winston Churchill's *The Unknown War* [65], Bernard Pares' *The Fall of the Russian Monarchy* [306], and Michael T. Florinsky's *The End of the Russian Empire* [122], are all critical of Czar Nicholas' direction of the war. Among the best recent secondary materials are Bruce Lincoln's *Passage Through Armageddon* [258] and Norman Stone's *The Eastern Front* [387], which are a bit less disparaging. Both of the latter works contain very useful bibliographies, including hard-to-find materials in Russian.

In the United States President Woodrow Wilson himself had all the formal, constitutional power of command and control vested by the British and French parliaments in their war cabinets. Arthur S. Link's *The Papers of Woodrow Wilson* [259], especially volumes 51 and 52, contain critical correspondence between the President and his war administrators on organizational matters. For the Army, the seventeen-volume *The United States Army in the First World War* [55] contains correspondence on everything from military command and control to tanks and airplanes. The multivolume *Annual Reports of the War Department* [415] for 1917–1919 contain the reports of the Secretary of War and the bureau chiefs as well as those of the commander of the American Expeditionary Forces [AEF]. There is no similar set of documents for the Navy but the *Annual Reports of the Navy Department* [417] are of some value. Franklin H. Martin's *Digest of the Minutes of the Council of National Defense* [CND] [413], an excellent source for the day-to-day business of war government, was published as part of the Nye Committee investigations during the mid-1930s. There is a substantial secondary literature on American command and control. For conditions before the war see John P. Finnegan, *Against the Spector of a Dragon* [119], which covers the preparedness period. The best general account of the American war effort is Robert H. Ferrell's, *Woodrow Wilson and World War I* [116]. Edward M. Coffman's *The War to End All War* [69] and Daniel R. Beaver's *Newton D. Baker* [22] cover the development of command and control mechanisms at the War Department level. Elting Morison's *Admiral Sims and the Modern American Navy* [289] is excellent on naval issues involving shipbuilding and command and control.

Both Germany and Austria-Hungary had traditional hierarchical imperial control systems, modified to a degree by elected parliaments. The best secondary account of the central powers at war is Holger Herwig's *The First World War 1914–1918* [186], which deals with command and control, industrial mobilization, and technology, as well as German and Austro-Hungarian battlefield performance. It also contains an excellent bibliography. The work of Fritz Fischer, *Germany's Aims in the First World War 1914–1918* [120] and Gerhard Ritter, *The Sword and the Septre: The Problem of German Militarism* [340] establish the dimensions of debate over command and control between the German and Austro-Hungarian leaders. There is a vast storehouse of published materials available for Germany. The Reichsarchiv made a considerable number of critical documents available in *The World War 1914–1918: War Armaments and War Economy* [139] and *The World War 1914–1918: Military Operations on Land* [140]. Field Marshal Erich Ludendorff published several books on his war experiences. The most representative of them available in English is *Ludendorff's Own Story* [264]. Conventional organizational historians divide Imperial German command and control of the war into three periods—the first or Molke period, the second or Falkenhyn period and the third or Luddendorf-Hindenburg period. The best books on command and control, especially for the later period are Martin Kitchen's *The Silent Dictatorship* [232] and Robert B. Asprey's *The German High Command at War* [14]. Michael Geyer argues in his article "German Strategy in the Age of Machine Warfare 1914–1945" [141] that Ludendorff defined war as something more metaphysical than mere doctrine and tactics when he wrote in his memoirs of a "Military-Machine Culture." For command and control issues in the German Navy and for the decision to go to unrestricted submarine warfare see Holger Herwig, *Luxury Fleet: The Imperial German Navy, 1888–1918* [185] and Maurice Prendergast, *The German Submarine War 1914–1918* [324].

The most easily accessible published documents on Habsburg command and control are in the substantial Austria-Hungary Kriegsarchiv-sponsored volumes edited by Edmund G. von Horstenau and Rudolph Kiszling, *Austria-Hungary during the War 1914–1918* [17]. Josef Redlich's diary, *Austria's Fateful Years 1908–1919: The Political Diary of Josef Redlich* [113], and his *Austrian War Government* [331], published in 1929, are also useful. Among memoirs and apologias the most revealing are Franz Conrad von Hotzendorf, *From My Time of Service* [72] and General Alfred Kraus, *The Causes of Our Defeat* [240]. The best secondary sources on Austro-Hungarian command and control include Gunther Rothenberg, *The Army of Franz Joseph* [348], Graydon Tunstall, *Planning for War against Russian and Serbia* [410], Christopher Fuhr, *The K.U.K.*

High Command and Austrian Domestic Politics 1914–1917 [135], and Manfried Rauchehsteiner, *The Death of the Two-Headed Eagle* [328]. For a broader look at imperial politics see the essays in Mark Cornwall, ed., *The Last Years of Austria-Hungary* [76] and Edmund G. von Horstenau's *The Collapse of the Austro-Hungarian Empire* [199]. Wilhelm Czermak's *The Austro-Hungarian Army As Few Knew It* [85] gives a different perspective. Hans Hugo Sokol, *Austria-Hungary's War at Sea 1914–1918* [377] and Lawrence Sondhaus, *The Naval Policy of Austria-Hungary 1867–1918* [378] are useful studies of naval command and control. They also contain important information on Habsburg warship production.

The bibliography for Italian war direction is limited. For the Italian military before the war see John Gooch's *Army, State, and Society in Italy 1870–1915* [150]. Most of the significant recent material is contained in anthologies. John Gooch, "Italy During the First World War" [151], Douglas J. Forsyth, *The Crisis of Liberal Italy 1914–1922* [125], V. Guiffrida Pietra, *Provital: Food Supply in Italy during the Great War 1914–1918* [316] and G. Rochat, *Italy in the First World War: Problems of Interpretation and Opportunities for Research* [345] are useful for general background. For certain other issues see Ferricio Botti and Mario Cermelli, eds., *Air War Theory in Italy from the Beginning to the Second World War* [37]. For the social impact of the war, L. Tomassini, "Industrial Mobilization and State Intervention in Italy in the First World War: Effects on Labor Unrest" [400] and the sections on Italy in John Horne, ed., *State, Society, and Mobilization in Europe during the First World War* [198] are all significant. There is no reliable history of either the Serbian Army or the Rumanian Army, but see Michael Boro Petrovich, *A History of Modern Serbia* [315] and for the Serbian command, Vladimir Belic, *Putnick* [31]. For both Serbia and Romania the best sources are in Bela Kiraly et al., eds., *East Central European Society in World War I* [229]. Apparently the only essay in English on the Bulgarian war effort is Stilyan Noykov's "The Bulgarian Army in World War I" [299]. For the Ottoman war effort see the official history, *Official History of the Turkish Army during the First World War* [30] and Ahmed Emin, *Turkey in the World War* [102]. See also Ulrich Trumpener, *Germany and the Ottoman Empire 1914–1918* [409], Frank G. Weber, *Eagles on the Crescent* [428] and M. Larcher, *The Turks in the Great War* [246]. References previously cited to the British, French, German, and Habsburg command and control systems also contain considerable material on Entente and Austro-German satellites.

INDUSTRIAL MOBILIZATION

For general background on industry, society, and the war see David Stevenson, *Armaments and the Coming of War: Europe 1904–1914* [385] and William McNeill, *The Pursuit of Power* [278]. Gerd Hardach's *The First World War* [171] deals with the industrial mobilization of all the belligerents. An older comparative study by the Bureau Internationale du Travail of the League of Nations is *Growth and Effectiveness of Trade Unions from 1910–1919* [48]. Many of the essays in John Horne's *State, Society and Mobilization in Europe during the First World War* [198], Patrick Fridenson's *1914–1918: The Other Front* [131] and H. A. Winkler's *Organized Capitalism* [444] discuss the indirect and unanticipated impact of the war. We do know that the blockade had some affect on the Central Powers; the best books on the subject are A. C. Bell's *A History of the Blockade of Germany, Austria-Hungary, Bulgaria and Turkey 1914–1918* [32], M. C. Sidney's, *The Allied Blockade of Germany 1914–1916* [367], and C. Paul Vincent's, *The Politics of Hunger: The Allied Blockade of Germany 1915–1919* [424].

There are several comparative studies of the Entente and American war efforts. N. F. Dreisziger, ed., *Mobilization for Total War: The Canadian, American and British Experience 1914–1918; 1939–1945* [96] includes Arthur Marwick's incisive "Problems and Consequences of Organizing Society for Total War." John Horne's, *Labour at War: France and Britain 1914–1918* [197] is comparative econosocial history with important insights into Entente industrial life. There are a number of primary sources on the British industrial war effort, many of them contained in the *Parliamentary Papers* [41] and *History of the Ministry of Munitions* [286]. John A. Fairlie's *British War Administration* [105], published in 1919, can be considered a primary source. R. A. S. Redmayne's *The British Coal Mining Industry during the War* [332] and J. Cunnison and W. R. Scott's *The Industries of the Clyde Valley during the War* [83] were published in the 1920s as well. Samuel Hurwitz's *State Intervention in Great Britain* [203], Hugh B. Peebles' *Warshipbuilding on the Clyde* [311], and Kathleen Burk's *War and the State* [51], which contains an excellent set of essays on the wartime expansion of the British government, are examples of recent scholarship on the industrial and organizational impact of the war. Peter Simpkins, *Kitchner's Army* [370], a groundbreaking piece of social history, and Desmond Chapman-Huston and Owen Rutter, *General Sir John Cowan: The Quartermaster General of the Great War* [59] include hard to get information on supply and equipment and excellent bibliographies. Clive A. Trebilcock's book *The Vickers Brothers* [406] and his article "War and the Failure of Industrial Mobilization, 1899 and 1914" [408] reveal the connections between public investment in arms technology, national growth, and economic modernization before the war began. Peter Dewey's "The New Warfare and Economic Mobilization" [91] is good for the war period, while John T. Sumida's article, "Forging the Trident: British Naval Industrial Logistics 1914–1918" [391], which analyses conflicts over priority between the British Army and the Navy during the war, is a unique study of military power and budget building. It also contains an excellent, very specific, bibliography on the Admiralty and industrial mobilization. Conversion was a critical issue during the war and Kenneth Richardson's *The British Motor Industry 1896–1939* [336] and Wayne Lewchuk's *American Technology and the British Motor Vehicle Industry* [252] deal with the introduction of assembly line practices among British automakers. For a general introduction to the indirect political and social impact of industrial mobilization see Arthur Marwick's *The Deluge: British Society and the First World War* [274]. Gerry Rubin's *Law and*

Labour: The Munitions Acts, State Regulation and the Unions 1915–1921 [350], H. Wolfe's *Labour Supply and Regulation* [449], published in the 1920s, and G. D. H. Cole's old but still valuable works, *Trade Unionism and Munitions* [70] and *Workshop Organization* [71] deal with the allocation of labor and labor-management relations. The newer *The First Shop Steward's Movement* [193] by James Hinton and *The Politics of Manpower* [155] by Keith Grieves reflect current attitudes toward wartime labor allocation and workplace relations. For gender issues see Marwick's *Women at War 1914–1918* [272] and Angela Woollacott's *On Her Their Lives Depend: Munitions Workers in the Great War* [451]. British agricultural policies were among the great successes of the war. For their development see William Beveridge's semi-official *British Food Control* [33], which was published in 1928. More analytical studies are Peter Dewey's *British Agriculture during the First World War* [92] and Margaret L. Barnett's *British Food Policy during the First World War* [18]. Transportation and logistical questions are dealt with in E. A. Pratt's official *British Railways and the Great War* [323], published in 1921.

The French official history, *The French Armies in the Great War* [285], contains substantial materials on industrial production. During the 1920s and 1930s a large official and semi-official literature on French industrial mobilization appeared. Pierre Renouvin's *The Forms of War Government in France* [334] is part of the series on the political and economic impact of the war sponsored by the Carnegie Endowment, while T. Kemp, *The French Economy 1913–1939* [216], C. Reboul, *Industrial Mobilization in France 1914–1918* [330], Arthur Fontaine, *French Industry during the War* [124], Robert Pinot, *The Organization of Steel in the Service of the Nation* [317], Raymond Guilhon, *Industrial Associations in France during the War* [159], and A. Aftalion, *The Textile Industry in France during the War* [4] are all either Carnegie studies or officially sponsored works that deal favorably with the achievements of wartime industry. B. W. Shaper's *Albert Thomas: Twenty Years of Social Reform* [364] is a biography of the first Director of Munitions in the French war government. Since 1960 there has been a massive reconsideration of the indirect impact of the French war effort. Jean-Jacques Becker's *The Great War and the French People* [26], Patrick Fridenson's *The French Home Front 1914–1918* [130], and Jean-Baptiste Duroselle's *France in the Great War 1914–1918* [98] are general overviews of French civilian life during the war. John F. Godfrey's *Capitalism at War: Industrial Policy and Bureaucracy in France 1914–1918* [146] and Gerd Hardach's two articles, "La mobilization industrielle en 1914–1918: Production, planification et ideologie" [172] and "Franzosiche Rustungspolitik 1914–1918" [173], are examples of the recent work being done on the organization of French industry during the war. The first volume of Patrick Fridenson's significant *History of the Renault Auto Company 1898–1939* [132] and Gilbert Hatry's *Renault: Automobiles at War 1914–1918* [174] deal with the mobilization of the French auto industry and its expansion into other branches of the war effort. See also J. P. Bradou et al. [James M. Laux, trans.], *The Automobile Revolution: The Impact of an Industry* [39] for the work of auto manufacturers besides Renault. Michel

Auge-Laribe's *Agriculture during the War* [16], another of the early monographs with a semi-official imprimatur, is favorable toward the French food program. A. M. Henniker, *Transportation on the Western Front 1914–1918* [184], written at the end of the 1930s, and James M. Laux's narrower "Trucks in the West during the First World War" [247] deal with transportation and logistics.

Despite almost a generation of industrialization, the Russian government lacked the transportation, communications and industrial capacity to support a large scale war of material. There is a scarcity of published material on Russian industrial mobilization. See Joseph Bradley, *Guns for the Tsar* [40] for background on Russian small arms development. A. A. Manikovski's massive *The Russian Army in the 1914–1918 War* [269], published in 1919, contains difficult-to-find information about the production of Russian munitions and gun plants and the numbers of workers involved in the munitions industry during the war. See also General Vasilii Gurko's *War and Revolution in Russia 1914–1918* [161], published the same year. A. A. Kersnovski's *History of the Russian Army* [223], published in Belgrade in the 1930s, is good on bureaucracy and logistical support. The Carnegie Foundation sponsored a series of monographs on the Czarist war effort during the 1920s and 1930s. They include Nicholas J. Astrov and Paul P. Gronsky's *The War and the Russian Government* [15], Alexis N. Antiferov and Eugen M. Kayden's *The Cooperative Movement in Russian during the War* [7], and S. O. Zagorsky's *State Control of Industry in Russia during the War* [456]. However, Nicholas N. Golovin's *The Russian Army in the World War* [148] is suspect and should be used with great care. A. L. Sidorov's *The Economic Position of Russia during the First World War* [368] and N. Kozlow's *A Study of the Military-Technical Supply of the Russian Army in the World War* [239] are two of the few Soviet publications translated into English. For more recent work see Hans Rogger's *Russia in the Age of Modernization and Revolution* [346] and Lewis H. Seigelbaum's *The Politics of Industrial Mobilization in Russia 1914–1917: A Study of the War Industries Committees* [361]. Norman Stone, *The Eastern Front* [387] with its excellent bibliography is one of the few English-language sources available on the Russian war effort. It contains an excellent general analysis of production and persuasive arguments that lack of munitions did not cause the breakup of the army and the beginning of the revolution. Stone admits, however, that the Russians depended on the British and French for complex equipment. Bruce Lincoln's, *Passage Through Armageddon* [258] also gives a generally positive account of Russian war production in 1916 and early 1917. Allan K. Wildman's two excellent volumes, *The End of the Russian Imperial Army: The Old Army and the Soldier's Revolt* [438] and *The End of the Russian Imperial Army: The Road to Soviet Power and Peace* [437], contain somewhat contradictory material on conditions at the front in 1917. A. N. Antiferov et al., *Russian Agriculture during the War* [8] is another of the Carnegie studies that really have not yet been supplanted by material in English on the collapse of Russian transportation during the war. Last, one should never neglect the insights in Michael T. Florinsky's *The End of the Russian Empire* [122].

There is an extensive literature on the American industrial effort. For a general introduction to the official sources see Waldo G. Leland and Newton D. Mereness, comp., *Introduction to the American Official Sources for the Economic and Social History of the World War* [251]. There is a large reservoir of published documents covering the American industrial war effort in *The United States Army in the First World War* [55]. The *Annual Reports of the War Department* [415] include everything from the reports of the Secretary of War and the bureau chiefs, with critical comments on war materials, to those of the commander of the American Expeditionary Forces. Benedict Crowell's *America's Munitions 1917–1918: The Report of the Director of Munitions* [79] contains much information on industrial production. The Nye Committee, *Hearings: Munitions Industry* [413], which is an gold mine of primary documents, contains over forty volumes of critical materials, including the *Minutes of the General Munitions Board* and *Minutes of the War Industries Board* [WIB]. Bernard Baruch, the Chairman of the WIB, published his account of events in 1921 in *American Industry in the War* [20]. Another group of books on the American industrial effort, which should be considered primary sources, were published in the first decade after the war ended. Assistant Secretary of War Crowell republished and expanded his annual report for 1919 in five volumes entitled *How America Went to War* [78], and Grovsenor Clarkson, a former head of the Council of National Defense and a colleague of Bernard Baruch, gave industry's side of the story in *Industrial America in the World War* [66]. A few years later Thomas Frothingham put the best light possible on War and Navy Department efforts in *The American Reinforcement* [133] and *The Naval History of the World War* [134]. There is a significant American literature written during the 1920s on wartime rail transportation and sea lift. Walker Hines, who was active in the war administration, wrote the *War History of American Railroads* [192], a defense of Director General of Railroads William G. McAdoo and the Railroad Administration. Edward N. Hurley, *The Bridge to France* [202] and Rear Admiral Albert Gleaves, *A History of the Transport Service* [145] wrote apologias for their records in shipping troops and cargo to France. A little over decade later, just before the United States entered the Second World War, William C. Mallendore in his *History of the United States Food Administration 1917–1919* [267] dealt with Herbert Hoover and the American food supply program. Among the best of the critical secondary literature on the war effort is Frederick Paxson's three-volume study, *American Democracy and the World War* [309], which contains information available in no other place. Among the best recent works on the American war effort at home are David Kennedy, *Over Here* [217] and Ellis Hawley's superb *The Great War and the Search for a Modern Order* [177]. Stephen Skowronek, *Building a New American State* [373] and James Weinstein, *The Corporate Ideal in the Liberal State 1900–1918* [433] take the currently popular corporatist and state building approach. Ronald Shaffer's *America in the Great War: The Rise of the War Welfare State* [362] is not as comprehensive as its title indicates. David A. Hounshell discusses American manufacturing during the war in *From the American System to Mass Production*

1800–1932 [201], while Merritt Roe Smith deals with government-owned factories in "Military Arsenals and Industry before World War I" [376]. Hugh G. J. Aitken discusses other aspects of the same issue in *Taylorism at Watertown Arsenal* [6]. A recent critical study of the railroads is Austin K. Kerr, *American Railroad Politics, 1914–1920* [222]. William J. Williams' *The Wilson Administration and the Shipbuilding Crisis of 1917* [442] is critical of the Wilson administration's maritime programs. For the so-called Military Industrial Complex and the Great War see Paul A. C. Koistinen, *Mobilizing For Modern War* [236] and Robert Cuff, *The War Industries Board* [82]. B. F. Cooling in *Grey Steel and Blue Water* [73] and Daniel R. Beaver in "George W. Goethals and the PS and T" [21] and "The Problem of Military Supply 1890–1920" [24] give a somewhat different historical perspective to the controversy.

Both German and Austro-Hungarian industrial mobilization organization were hierarchical and, in theory, controlled by the military. For primary material on the German industrial effort, the German Reichsarchiv, *The World War 1914–1918: War Armaments and War Economy* [139] and *The World War 1914–1918: Military Operations on Land* [140] have much material on production and supplies. Walther Rathenau's diary, *Diary 1907–1922* [327] covers wartime raw material organization and control, as does General Wilhelm Groener's *Memoirs: Youth, General Staff, World War* [157]. There are a number of good general books in the secondary literature. For the central powers and wartime industrial mobilization see Holger Herwig's *The First World War* [186] and Gerd Hardach's *The First World War* [171]. Wilhelm Deist's *The Army and Domestic Politics in the World War 1914–1918* [90] and "The German Army, the Authoritarian Nation-State and Total War" [89] are excellent introductions to German organization. L. Burchardt's *The Peacetime Economy and Preparations for War* [47] and Martin Kitchen's *The Political Economy of Germany 1815–1945* [231] are still good for the prewar years and general context. Ernst von Wrisberg's *Army and Homeland 1914–1918* [453], F. Zunkel's *Industry and State Socialism* [459], and Hans Herzfeld's two books, *The First World War* [188] and *German Armaments Policy before the World War* [189] cover the entire war period. See also A. Schroter's *War-State-Monopoly 1914–1918* [358]. Holger H. Herwig's "Industry, Empire and the First World War" [187] is a insightful essay on the broader meaning of German industrial participation in the Great War. O. Goebel's *Germany's Raw Materials Economy in the World War* [147] covers the distribution of raw material to German industry. Several good biographical studies, H. Haeussler's *General Wilhelm Groener and the Imperial German Army* [176], G. Hecker's *Walter Rathenau* [180], R. O. Henderson's "Walter Rathenau: A Pioneer of the Planned Economy" [183], Harmut Pogge von Strandmann's *Walther Rathenau: Industrialist, Banker, Intellectual and Politician* [389], and "Walter Rathenau and the 'Coming Economy' " [280] by W. Michalka cover many organizational aspects of the German war effort. For a biographical approach to the supreme command and industrial organization see H. Weber's *Ludendorff and Monopoly: German War Policy 1916–1918* [429]. Hans C. von Scherr-Thoss' *The German Automobile Industry* [355] is an excellent study of the conversion to war production in one industry. For the mechanization of coal mining during the war see Uwe Burghardt's *The Mechanization of Mining in the Rhur Land 1890–1930* [49]. Among the many fine new works on the indirect impact of the war on the German home front are J. Kocha's *Facing Total War: German Society 1914–1918* [235] and Robert B. Armseson's less ambitious *Total Warfare and Compulsory Labor: A Study of the Military-Industrial Complex in Germany during World War I* [9]. For food production see Joe Lee, "Administrators and Agriculture: Aspects of German Agricultural Policy in the First World War" [250], F. Aereboe, *The Influence of War on Agricultural Production in Germany* [3], and August Skalweit, *The German War Economy and Food Provision* [372]. For transportation problems see Adolph Sarter, *German Railroads in War* [354]. By far the most significant work on German industrial mobilization has been written by Gerald Feldman. His *Army, Industry and Labor in Germany 1914–1918* [111] and *The Great Disorder: Politics, Economics and Society in the German Inflation 1914–1924* [112] have created a standard of scholarship against which all other work on the era must be measured.

For Austria-Hungary, Edmund G. von Horstenau and Rudolph Kiszling's *Austria-Hungary during the War 1914–1918* [17] is widely available. Miklos Komjathy's *Protocols of the Joint Military Council of the Austro-Hungarian Monarchy 1914–1918* [238] is also useful. Fritz Fellner, *Austria's Fateful Years 1908–1919: The Political Diary of Josef Redlich* [113] and Redlich's own *Austrian War Government* [331] are essentially self-protective. Another apologia is August von Cramon's *Our Austro-Hungarian Ally in the World War* [77]. See also Wilhelm Czermak's *The Austro-Hungarian Army As Few Knew It* [85] which can be treated as a primary source. Conrad von Hotzendorf's *From My Time of Service* [72] and General Alfred Kraus' *The Causes of Our Defeat* [240] reveal Conrad's lack of interest in matters industrial and logistical. It should be added that among the biographies of Conrad, including August Urbanski's laudatory *Conrad von Hotzendorf* [418] and Oscar Regele's more critical *Feldmarschall Conrad: Mission and Accomplishment 1906–1918* [333], none is satisfactory. There is a respectable secondary literature on the Habsburg high command and industrial mobilization but much less for the actual operation of Austro-Hungarian industry. For the high command see Christopher Fuhr's *The K.U.K. High Command and Austrian Domestic Politics 1914–1917* [135]. The classic study is Arthur J. May's *The Passing of the Hapsburg Monarchy 1914–1918* [277], but see also Z. A. B. Zeman's *The Break-up of the Habsburg Empire 1914–1918* [457] and Rudolf Kiszling's *Austria-Hungary's Role in the First World War* [230]. Other significant studies of Habsburg war management are Edmund Glaise von Horstenau's *The Collapse of the Austro-Hungarian Empire* [199] and Manfried Rauchehsteiner's *The Death of the Two-Headed Eagle* [328]. J. Galantai's *Hungary in the First World War* [138] describes the insurmountable supply and logistical difficulties of the Dual Monarchy. Among the older works on Hapsburg industry is Richard Riedl's *The Industry of Austria-Hungary during the War* [338]. For some information on Habsburg steel mills and their expansion during the First World War see Rolf Niederhuemer's *Papers on the History of Technology* [298]. There are several essays in Robert A. Kahn, Bela Kiraly, and Paula Fichtner's *The Habsburg Empire in World War I* [213] and Kiraly's own *East Central European Society in World War I* [229], which deal with industrial mobilization. Robert J. Wegs, *Austrian Economic Mobilization during World War I with Particular Attention to Heavy Industry* [430] and *The Austrian War Economy 1914–1918* [431] are the most important comprehensive studies of Habsburg industrial mobilization and logistical support. His "Transportation: The Achilles Heel of the Habsburg War Effort" [432] is a badly needed addition to a very limited literature. For the apparently insurmountable food crisis that lasted from 1915 to the end of the war see Hans Loewenfeld-Russ' *The Regulation of Public Food Provisions in War* [262].

MILITARY TECHNOLOGY

A most controversial literature involves the introduction of new weapons and equipment during the war. For a general theoretical introduction to the idea of scientific and technological change see Thomas Kuhn's path breaking *The Structure of Scientific Revolutions* [242]. For a recent attempt to integrate technology and military history see Barton Hacker's two articles, "Engineering a New Order" [163] and "Military Institutions, Weapons and Social Change" [164]. Both include superior bibliographical surveys of the secondary literature and contain arguments for a more inclusive, multi-national and multi-cultural approach. Among the standard general references are Charles Singer et al., *A History of Technology* [371] and Trevor Williams, ed., *The Oxford Illustrated Encyclopedia of Invention and Technology* [441]. The most ambitious early attempt to integrate energy sources and weapons innovation into a "systems" approach is J. F. C. Fuller's *Armaments and History* [137]. Bernard and Fawn Brodie's *From Crossbow to H Bomb* [43] and Martin Van Creveld's *Technology and War* [422] contain more conventional discussions of the role of technology. Van Creveld's *Supplying War* [421] should also be consulted. Peter Young's *The Machinery of War* [454], although essentially a picture book, is still a good nuts and bolts introduction to modern weaponry. Daniel R. Headrick's *The Tools of Empire* [178], although it deals with nineteenth-century topics, remains one of the best contemporary arguments for "technological determinism" in international affairs, but see also Jay Wheldon's *Machine Age Armies* [436]. Guy Hatcup's *The War of Invention* [175] is a comparative history of Great War technology. John Ellis, *A Social History of the Machine Gun* [101], although quite eccentric, remains among the few attempts to carry the impact of technology on war beyond the conventional wisdom. A good place to begin the study of the current American literature is A. Hunter Dupree's *Science in the Federal Government* [97], followed by Merritt Roe Smith's introduction to *Military Enterprise and Technological Change* [375]. There is a masterful historiographical summary by Alex Roland, "Science and War" in Sally Gregory Kohlstedt and Margaret W. Rossiter, ed., *Historical Writing On American Science: Perspectives and Prospects* [237].

For an overview of the connections between technological development, production and battlefield performance see the first volume of Allan R. Millett and Williamson Murray's *Military Effectiveness* [282]. There was little difficulty securing small arms, mortars, and grenades. Peter Simkins, *Kitchner's Armies* [370] is a representative study of the development and production of trench warfare equipment. Prewar connections between small arms design, production, development. and deployment are explored by David Armstrong in *Bullets and Bureaucrats* [10] and George M. Chinn, *The Machine Gun* [60]. The late Edward C. Ezell describes small arms development issues in *The Great Rifle Controversy* [104]. For artillery see Ian Hogg's *The Guns 1914–1918* [195], and, with John Batchelor, *Artillery* [194]. Bruce Gundmunsson's more recent *On Artillery* [160] is also useful. Sheldon Bidwell and Dominick Graham, *Firepower* [34] is the only book available that deals with, among other important issues, the very difficult production problems involved with the development of super-sensitive artillery fuses. For representative new approaches to combined arms doctrine and technology see John Terraine, *White Heat* [397] and Tim Travers, *How the War Was Won* [405]. For German developments, David T. Zabecki's *Steel Wind* [455] and M. Schwarte's old but still useful volume of essays, *The Great War* [359], are essential. See also Hans Linnenkhol, *From Single Shot to Creeping Barrage* [260] and, for the Kaiser und Koenig Armee, J. Lucas' *Fighting Troops of the Austro-Hungarian Empire* [263]. References to armor and armor doctrine and production are liberally scattered through all the official histories. See *The Armies of France in the Great War* [285], the *History of the Ministry of Munitions* [286], and the documents in *The United States Army in the First World War* [55]. The best general history of tanks is Richard M. Ogorkiewicz, *Armoured Forces* [302]. For technical developments during the war and the emergence of early armored warfare doctrine see Basil Liddell-Hart, *The Tanks* [257] and J. F. C. Fuller, *Tanks in the Great War* [136]. Ralph E. Jones, George H. Rarey, and Robert J. Icks, *The Fighting Tanks Since 1916* [211] and Chris Ellis and Peter Chamberlain, *The Great Tanks* [100] are classically technocratic. David E. Johnson's *Fast Tanks and Heavy Bombers* [208] has two good chapters on the Great War, but they are limited to the American experience and give little attention to matters of wartime production. See Albert G. Stern's *Tanks: 1914–1918* [382] for the ambitious and technologically overly ambitious inter-allied tank project of 1918. L. F. Haber, *The Poisonous Cloud* [162] is a general overview of chemical warfare. For the British experience see Donald Richter, *Chemical Soldiers* [337]. For the American experience see Charles E. Heller, *Chemical Warfare in World War I* [182] and Edward M. Spier, *Chemical Warfare* [379]. For a German perspective on the broader aspects of science as well as on chemical warfare, Fritz Stern, "Fritz Haber: The Scientist in Power and in Exile" [383] and Jeffrey Allan Johnson, *The Kaiser's Chemists* [209] are more than useful. Daniel Headrick, *The Invisible Weapon* [179] is an important introduction to the subject of communications. Gordon Bussey, *Wireless: The Crucial Decade* [52] gives an essentially British perspective. David Pritchard's *The Radar Wars: Germany's Pioneer Achievement 1904–1945* [325] contains references to telephone, wireless and sound ranging experiments. Hugh G. J. Aitken, *The Continuous Wave* [5] gives an American view of wireless, voice radio, and telephone developments. Susan Douglas has an important essay on the Navy and wireless in Merritt Roe Smith's *Military Enterprise and Technological Change* [375]. All those sources have excellent bibliographies.

A large body of literature on technology and the Great War involves its impact on sea power. The best overview is in Arthur J. Marder's multivolume *The Anatomy of British Sea Power* [270]. Brian Ranft's *Technical Change and British Naval Policy 1860–1939* [326] also provides an overview. The best recent work on the British Navy and technology is John T. Sumida, *In Defense of Naval Supremacy* [393]. For British surface ships see Stanley Sandler's, *The Emergence of the Modern Capital Ship* [353], F. J. Dittmar and J. J. Colledge, *British Warships 1914–1919* [94], and Oscar Parkes, *British Battleships: Warrior to Vangard* [308]. The difficult problem of improving long-range sighting and fire control involved the coordination of technical systems rather than production. See Peter Padfield, *Aim Straight: A Biography of Admiral Sir Percy Scott* [303] and *Guns at Sea* [304] and John Sumida's edited volume, *The Pollen Papers* [392]. Pollen's son Anthony wrote a defense of his father in *The Great Gunnery Scandal: The Mystery of Jutland* [321]. There are no similar American general works, but Kenneth J. Hagan's *This People's Navy* [166] and Harold and Margaret Sprout's older *The Rise of American Sea Power 1776–1918* [380] are more than adequate. Hagan's book contains an excellent bibliography. Bernard Brodie, *Sea Power in the Machine Age* [42], Elting E. Morison, *Men, Machines and Modern Times* [290], and Taylor Peck, *Round Shot to Rockets* [310] provide effective introductions to naval technology and logistics. For the impact of the submarine see Maurice Prendergast, *The German Submarine War 1914–1918* [324] and Willem Hackmann, *Seek and Strike* [165]. See Edwyn A. Gray, *The Devil's Device* [149] for the development of the torpedo.

The development and production issues involving aircraft have received more attention that any other technological issue of the Great War. Robin Higham's *Air Power: A Concise History* [191], Lee Kennett's *The First Air War* [220], and John Morrow's *The Great War in the Air* [291] are good general introductions. The Kennett and Morrow books also include extensive bibliographies. Richard Hallion's two books, *Rise of the Fighter Aircraft 1914–1918* [168] and *Strike From The Sky* [169], are useful as is W. M. Lamberton's *Fighter Aircraft of the 1914–1918 War* [243], but for the characteristics and specifications of all the belligerent's aircraft *Janes Fighting Aircraft of World War I* [206] is the indispensable source. For an overview of British air policy see Malcolm Cooper, *The Birth of Independent Air Power* [75]. The official British history is H. A. Jones and Walter Raleigh, *The War in the Air* [210]. Harald Penrose's two volumes, *British Aviation: The Pioneer Years 1903–1914* [312] and *British Aviation: The Great War and Armistice 1915–1918* [313], cover the development of the industry. See also Peter Fearon's "The Formative Years of the British Aircraft Industry 1913–1924" [110]. For the technological development of British aircraft, John M. Bruce's *British Airplanes 1914–1918* [44] and Peter M. H. Lewis' two volumes, *The British Fighter since 1912* [253] and *The British Bomber since 1914* [254] are the most available sources. For French aviation developments the best studies are Maurice de Brunoff's very early and semi-official *Air Power during the Great War* [46] and General Charles Christienne's recent and massive *History of French Military Aviation* [English edition translated by Francis Kianka as *A History of French Military Aviation*] [61]. The same author's *The Golden Age of French Aviation 1890–1919* [62] approaches the definitive. See also Emmanuel Chadeau's *From Bleriot to Dassault* [56] and Jacques Sahel's *Henri Farman and Aviation* [351]. James M. Laux's two important pieces, "Gnome and Rhone" [248] and "The Rise and Fall of Armand Deperdussin" [249], also examine the development of French aviation. For the Italians see Pierto Vergnanao's *Origins of Aviation in Italy* [423]. For Russia, Robert A. Kilmarx's *A History of Soviet Airpower* [226] and his excellent article "The Russian Imperial Air Forces of World War I" [227] provide excellent overviews. Robin Higham and Jacob W. Kipp's *Soviet Aviation and Airpower* [190] deals with the efforts to build aircraft and engines during the war. K. N. Finne, *Igor Sikorsky: The Russian Years* [118], edited and translated by Carl J. Bobrow and Von Hardesty, tells the story of how the Russo-Baltic Wagon Company built the big Il'ya Murometsy aircraft. The most comprehensive works on American wartime air technology are Maurer Maurer, ed., *The U.S. Air Service in World War I* Vol. IV. *Postwar Review* [276] and Arthur Sweetser's *The American Air Service* [394]. However, Irving B. Holley's brilliant *Ideas and Weapons* [196] is the most extraordinary work on the subject in forty years and has applications far beyond airpower. Georg P. Neumann, ed., *The German Air Force in the World War* [297] is the classic study of the development of German wartime airpower, but John Morrow Jr.'s two volumes, *Building German Air Power 1909–1914* [293] and *German Airpower in World War I* [292], are far more analytical. See also Peter Kilduff's recent *Germany's First Air Force 1914–1918* [225] and Peter Gray and Owen Thetford's *German Aircraft of the First World War* [154]. For Austria-Hungary Gunther Rothenburg's "Military Aviation in Austria-Hungary 1893–1918" [349] and Peter Ernst, *The K.U.K. Aircraft and Flying Forces of Austria-Hungary 1794–1919* [314] are the best available sources. For Habsburg aircraft themselves, Peter Groz, George Haddow, and Peter Schiemer's *Austro-Hungarian Military Aircraft of World War I* [158] is a workmanlike job. For engine technology the best studies are Herschel Smith, *A History of Aircraft Piston Engines* [374] and Robert Schlaifer and S. D. Heron, *Development of Aircraft Engines* [356]. Philip S. Dickey's *The Liberty Engine 1918–1942* [93], a classic monograph on a very difficult subject, is also very useful.

For the broader impact of technological change on logistical support see G. C. Shaw, *Supply in Modern War* [365], Julian Thompson, *The Lifeblood of War* [399] and John Lynn's two edited volumes, *The Tools of War* [266] and *Feeding Mars* [265]. General histories of logistics in the U.S. Army include Marvin A. Kreidberg and Merton G. Henry, *History of Military Mobilization in the United States Army* [241], James A. Huston, *The Sinews of War* [204], and Erna Risch, *Quartermaster Support of the Army* [339]. For the development of soft transport see Daniel R. Beaver's "Deuce and a Half" [25] and Mark K. Blackburn's *A New Form of Transportation* [36].

INTERNATIONAL INDUSTRIAL AND TECHNOLOGICAL COOPERATION

The war required industrial and technological cooperation as well as political and strategic consultation. Prior to 1917 inter-allied consultation on industrial and military affairs was intermittent and formal cooperation was limited to annual conferences on strategy. After 1917 The Entente and the Americans developed systematic structures for cooperation that expanded throughout 1918. The Central Powers never achieved the kind of organization that the Entente and the United States secured in the creation of the Supreme War Council. During 1916 the Germans simply bulldozed their reluctant and often resentful Austro-Hungarian, Bulgarian, and Ottoman associates. There is a small but significant body of research on industrial and technological issues which arose among the Entente powers and between them and the Americans during the war. For primary sources on Entente relations in the early years of the war see *Parliamentary Papers* [41] and the *History of the Ministry of Munitions* [286]. For the Americans and the creation of the Supreme War Council in November 1917, *The Foreign Relations of the United States 1914–1918* and its *Supplements* [414] are essential. The latter contain much information on the work of the inter-allied economic councils formed during the last six months of the war. The Center of Military History series, *The United States Army in the First World War* [55] and the two-volume *Report of the Military Board of Inter-Allied Supply* [416] contain information on efforts to pool inter-allied resources during the spring and summer of 1918. For the AEF's procurement from European sources, see AEF General Purchasing Agent Charles G. Dawes, *A Journal of the Great War* [86] and William J. Wilgus, *Transporting the AEF in Western Europe* [439], both of which refer to American steel rails, shell steel, castings and forgings shipped in ballast in return for completed equipment for the AEF. Albert G. Stern's *Tanks: 1914–1918* [382] has much information on the possibly ill-conceived and certainly ill-fated inter-allied tank program. Marshal Foch in his *Memoirs* [123] refers occasionally to inter-allied industrial cooperation during the last year of the war and shows the importance of American raw materials for the French war effort. Former commerce minister Etienne Clementel's *France and the Interallied Political Economy* [68] is essentially an apologia. A. Salter's *Allied Shipping Control* [352] deals with the allocation of merchant tonnage in 1918. Gerd Hardach's *The First World War* [171] has two excellent chapters on inter-allied economic and industrial cooperation. For other secondary treatments see Kathleen Burk's *Great Britain, America and the Sinews of War* [50] and David Trask's *The United States at the Supreme War Council* [403]. Trask's *Captains and Cabinets* [401] includes a discussion of merchant shipping, warship construction, and interallied trade competition. Andre Kaspi's excellent *The Time of the Americans 1917–1918* [214] deals at length with Franco-American logistical cooperation. Clarkson's *Industrial America in the World War* [66] and Crowell and Wilson's *How America Went to War* [78] cover the inter-allied conferences that began during the summer of 1918. William C. Mallendore's *History of the Food Administration 1917–1919* [267] discusses the inter-allied food situation and the American cereal supply program, which saved the French from disaster. A unique short study is Marjorie M. Farrar, "Preclusive Purchases: Politics and Economic Warfare in France during the First World War" [107]. There is no equivalent body of literature on cooperation among the Central Powers. The sources on the forced creation of a unified command by the Germans have already been cited in Section II, Section III and Section IV. The best studies of Austro-German diplomatic connections during the war are Gary W. Shanafelt, *The Secret Enemy* [363] and Gerard E. Silberstein, *The Troubled Alliance* [369]. Other sources containing information on the transfer of arms and equipment between the Central Powers and their associates include Ulrich Trumpener, *Germany and the Ottoman Empire 1914–1918* [409] and Frank G. Weber, *Eagles on the Crescent* [428].

INDUSTRIAL MOBILIZATION AND MILITARY TECHNOLOGY DURING THE GREAT WAR—A WORK IN PROGRESS

Although conventional academic wisdom has always depicted the Great War as the first authentic *Materielschlachen* struggle, current scholarship also identifies it as instrumental in "modernization" and as a principal catalyst in the appearance of the twentieth-century corporate state. During the past forty years scholars have turned their attention from the battlefield and the conference table to comparative studies of the home front that link wartime industrial mobilization with broader historical themes. Currently, scholars describe those events as part of a two-phased process that brought renegotiation of the basic social contracts that had bound the peoples of the belligerent powers together and encouraged the emergence of "modern" societies with redefined individual, class, and interest group rights and obligations.

According to this "corporatist" or "organizational synthesis," which has been too often associated with only Marxists and other with scholars on the Left, support of the first phase of industrial mobilization [1914–1915] was based on the traditional ideals of the *Burgfrieden* or the *Union Sacree* and required little change in existing institutional connections. It was assumed that the war would be short and existing reserves of standard weapons, ammunition, and equipment would suffice. But in late 1914 the ammunition ran out, the guns broke down, the uniforms and boots wore out and the war did not end. In early 1915, so it is claimed, a second, or remobilization, phase began which brought notable modifications in government and, temporarily at least, in traditional class, gender and interest group relationships. In 1916 whole industries were converted to military production and new plant capacity was created, while questions of material and human resource allocation and production priority required extraordinary government control, enforced industrial cartelization and the emergence of command economies and authoritarian state bureaucracies.

Scholars have changed their views about the relative war making effectiveness of the belligerents. The British, the French and the Americans succeeded better at the task than the Italians, the Russians, the Germans and the Austro-Hungarians. In England a separate civilian ministry of munitions was organized to coordinate war production. In France industrial production was controlled through a directorate of munitions and great semi-autonomous production combines and syndicates were created. After April 1917, the Americans, with a strong tradition of antitrust and anti-monopoly politics before they entered the war, moved reluctantly toward corporatist solutions similar to those developed by the British and French. The Italians, who lacked political cohesion, suffered from raw material shortages and had insufficient capacity to carry on the war without outside assistance. The Russian government attempted to militarize industry but, despite some success in increasing production of standard military supplies and equipment, remained dependent on the Entente for sophisticated weapons. At first the Central Powers seemed to handle the critical issues more effectively. The Germans, already heavily cartelized, integrated and militarized control of industrial production while the Austro-Hungarians followed a similar path only to fall short in late 1915 and early 1916 and grow increasingly dependent on the Germans. The unindustrialized Ottoman Empire and Bulgaria relied on the Austro-Germans for all except the simplest supplies. But in the end, the leaders of the Central Powers proved inept and made critical mistakes in allocating agricultural and transportation resources which ultimately helped bring disaster at the front.

Considerable attention has also been devoted to industrial policies and the impact of technological innovation. At the center of the wartime crisis were rapidly expanding military and naval demands. When the Great War began armies were relatively unmechanized. Small arms and artillery technology were robust and well integrated, but aircraft, tanks, automobiles, trucks, wireless radio communication, and chemical warfare technologies were either fragile or volatile. Navies were technologically robust, driven by reliable coal- and oil-fired steam engines or turbines, and heavily dependent on sophisticated command, control and communications equipment. They also practiced advanced gunnery and their sighting and ranging devices were on the cutting edge of current technology. During the war, however, new or improved technologies transformed war on land and in the sky. Soldiers competed with sailors for production capacity. Problems in industrial mobilization became even more challenging as airmen, relatively insignificant as consumers before the war, began after 1916 to contend strenuously for manufacturing facilities.

There was a vast difference between the relatively well-established practices involved in securing coal and other raw materials, producing castings and forgings, meat and potatoes, clothing, boots, harness and animal fodder, and the not so well known practices involved in fabricating arms and producing munitions and new technologies. Although standardization of military equipment and serial production had been common practice for over a century, the ability to mass produce such equipment with interchangeable parts on an assembly line was another matter entirely. Even the Americans, who prided themselves on the "new American system" of scientifically organized assembly-line manufacturing, found interchangeability difficult to achieve. Traditionally, complex hardware had to be machined to close tolerances by highly skilled labor, but the widespread introduction of semi-automatic machine tools, the subcontracting of parts manufacturing and the concurrent creation of central assembly plants increased production and brought great numbers of unskilled and semiskilled workers, including women, into the factories. One of the unanticipated consequences of the industrial war effort was the improved bargaining power of those particular groups of working class people, which in turn created labor-management conflict, potentially dangerous to national war efforts. It is not only Marxist historians who assert that wartime technical and manufacturing problems catalyzed powerful political and social forces that threatened traditional power relationships. Other, less ideologically defined scholars have also demonstrated that the war not only expanded the influence of corporate business but also increased, at least temporarily, the power of the working classes.

Recent scholarship has shown that during the second or remobilization phase the war developed a dynamic rationality of its own. After 1915, issues of inter-coalition economic and industrial planning and cooperation grew increasingly significant. During late 1916 and early 1917 members of both the Entente and the Central Powers suffered from the strain. Russia and Austria-Hungary paid a heavy price for their unsuccessful attempts to remobilize their peoples. In March 1917 the Russians collapsed. During that spring the French Army mutinied. In the autumn of 1917 the Italians began to disintegrate, and for a time during the great German spring offensive of 1918 even the British trod a thin line between social cohesion and internal turmoil.

This has led many scholars to re-emphasize the significance of the American intervention. Although they reject Yankee triumphalism, they assert that the Central Powers might have prevailed in 1918 without the American food, raw materials, and unfinished and semi-finished forgings and castings that helped keep French and British factories going and helped restore sagging internal cohesion. Some even declare that the Americans should have minded their own business and that the world might have been a better place if a stalemate had occurred or if the Central Powers had succeeded.

But it was, in the end, still essentially a European war. The French and English, who managed to remobilize, renegotiate their social contracts and organize effective national command structures, managed to survive the spring battles and counter-attack. During the summer of 1918 the Austro-Hungarians began to collapse and that autumn Imperial Germany finally cracked. By 1920 old Central and Eastern Europe was gone. Although a few historians argue that the war had less effect than has been previously thought, most still associate the corporate totalitarianism of the next eighty years with its impact. They argue that by end of the war statesmen, military men, industrialists and labor leaders had created, ironically, through their own actions, the potential for political, social, and cultural violence unparalleled since 1789. They confronted, in the words of William McNeill, one of the few historians who has taken the impact of war on industrial life into account:

The irrationality of rational, professionalized planning [which] aptly symbolized the central dilemma of [the] age—the dissonance of the whole introduced, or enormously exacerbated, by a closer harmony and superior organization of its separate parts.[1]

SUGGESTIONS FOR FURTHER RESEARCH

Every aspect of the Great War is under renewed scrutiny. Even the military and diplomatic aspects of the war are being reconsidered. But it is the social impact of the struggle in its broader perspectives that needs the most attention. It is here that younger scholars could concentrate their efforts to the greatest effect. All aspects of the field are open to reinterpretation. The primary sources available for the belligerent powers, especially the Italians, the French, and the Austro-Hungarians, have not been systematically examined since the 1920s and, with the opening of the Russian archives, closed by the Communists for eighty years to most outside researchers, the way is open for really creative scholarship. The challenge is clear and the opportunities are there. The only thing that is required is hard and sustained scholarly work.

NOTE

1. William H. McNeill, *The Pursuit of Power: Technology, Armed Forces and Society since A.D. 1000,* p. 309.

BIBLIOGRAPHY

1. Adams, R. J. Q. *Arms and the Wizard: Lloyd George and the Ministry of Munitions 1915–1916.* College Station, TX: Texas A&M Press, 1978.

2. Addington, Larry H. *The Blitzkrieg Era and the German General Staff 1865–1941.* New Brunswick, NJ: Rutgers University Press, 1971.

3. Aereboe, F. *Einfluss des Kriegs auf die landwirtschaftliche Produktion in Deutschland [The Influence of War on Agricultural Production in Germany].* Berlin: Deutsche Verlag-Anstalt, 1927.

4. Aftalion, A. *L'industrie textile en France penant la guerre [The Textile Industry in France during the War].* Paris: University Presses of France, 1924.

5. Aitken, Hugh G. J. *The Continuous Wave: Technology and American Radio 1900–1932.* Princeton: Princeton University Press, 1985.

6. Aitken, Hugh G. J. *Taylorism at Watertown Arsenal: Scientific Management in Action.* Cambridge: Harvard University Press, 1960.

7. Antsiferov, Alexis N., and Eugene M. Kayden. *The Cooperative Movement in Russian during the War.* New Haven: Yale University Press, 1929.

8. Antsiferov, Alexis N., et al. *Russian Agriculture during the War.* New Haven: Yale University Press, 1930.

9. Armseson, Robert B. *Total Warfare and Compulsory Labor: A Study of the Military-Industrial Complex in Germany during World War I.* The Hague: Nijhoff, 1964.

10. Armstrong, David. *Bullets and Bureaucrats: The Machine Gun and the United States Army.* Westport, CT: Greenwood Press, 1982.

11. Aron, Raymond. *The Century of Total War.* New York: McMillan, 1954.

12. Aron, Raymond. *War and Industrial Society.* Oxford: Oxford University Press, 1958.

13. Arthur, Sir George. *Life of Lord Kitchner.* 3 vols., London: Cassell, 1928.

14. Asprey, Robert B. *The German High Command at War: Hindenburg and Ludendorff Conduct World War I.* New York: William Morrow and Co., 1991.

15. Astrov, Nicholas J., and Paul P. Gronsky. *The War and the Russian Government.* New Haven: Yale University Press, 1929.

16. Auge-Laribe, Michel. *L'agriculture pendant la guerre* [*Agriculture during the War*]. Paris: University Presses of France, 1925.

17. Austria-Hungary Kriegsarchiv: Edmund Glaise von Horstenau and Rudolph Kiszling. eds. *Österriech-Ungarns Letzter Krieg 1914–1918* [*Austria Hungary during the War 1914–1918*]. 7 vols., Vienna: Verlag der Militarwissenschaftlichen Mitteilungen, 1931–1938.

18. Barnett, L. Margaret. *British Food Policy during the First World War.* London: Allen and Unwin, 1985.

19. Barnett, Correlli. *The Sword Bearers: Supreme Command in the World War.* Bloomington: Indiana University Press, 1975.

20. Baruch, Bernard. *American Industry in the War: A Report of the War Industries Board.* Washington: Government Printing Office, 1921.

21. Beaver, Daniel R. "George W. Goethals and the PS and T" in Daniel R. Beaver. ed., *Some Pathways in Twentieth Century History.* Detroit: Wayne State University Press, 1969.

22. Beaver, Daniel R. *Newton D. Baker and the American War Effort 1917–1919.* Lincoln: University of Nebraska Press, 1966.

23. Beaver, Daniel R., ed. *Some Pathways in Twentieth Century History.* Detroit: Wayne State University Press, 1969.

24. Beaver, Daniel R. "The Problem of Military Supply 1890–1920," in B. Franklin Cooling. ed., *War, Business and American Society: Historical Perspectives on the Military-Industrial Complex.* Port Washington, New York: Kennikat Press, 1977.

25. Beaver, Daniel R. "Deuce and a Half": Selecting U.S. Army Trucks 1920–1945," in John A. Lynn, *Feeding Mars: Logisitics in Western Warfare from the Middle Ages to the Present.* Boulder, San Francisco, and Oxford: Westview Press, 1993.

26. Becker, Jean-Jacques. *The Great War and the French People.* Leamington Spa: Berg, 1985.

27. Becker, J. J., and S. Audoin-Rouzeau, eds. *Les Societies europeenes et la guerre 1914–1918* [*European Societies and the Great War 1914–1918*]. Paris: Centre d'Histoire de la France Contemporaine, University of Paris, 1990.

28. Beckett, Ian F. W., and Keith Simpson, eds. *A Nation In Arms: A Social History of the British Army in the First World War.* Manchester: Manchester University Press, 1985.

29. Beckett, Ian F. W., "Total War" in Emsley, C., Marwick A. and Simpson, W., eds. *War, Peace and Social Change in Twentieth Century Europe.*

30. Belen, Fahri. *Bircini Cihan Harbinde Turk Harbi* [*Official history of the Turkish Army during the First World War*]. Ankara: Belen, 1963–1967.

31. Belic, Vladimir. *Putnick.* Belgrade: Slovo, 1938.

32. Bell, A. C. *A History of the Blockade of Germany, Austria-Hungary, Bulgaria and Turkey 1914–1918.* London: His Majesty's Stationery Office, 1937.

33. Beveridge, William. *British Food Control.* New Haven: Yale University Press, 1928.

34. Bidwell, Sheldon Bidwell, and Dominick Graham. *Firepower: British Army Weapons and Theories of War 1904–1945.* London: Allen and Unwin, 1982.

35. Black, Cyril E. *The Dynamics of Modernization: A Study in Contemporary History.* New York: Harper and Row, 1966.

36. Blackburn, Mark Kelling. *A New Form of Transportation: the Quartermaster Corps and the Standardization of US Motor Trucks 1909–1939.* Westport, CT: Greenwood Press, 1996.

37. Botti, Ferrucio, and Mario Cermelli. eds. *La teoria della guerra aerea in Italia delle origini alla seconda querra mondiale* [*Air War Theory in Italy from the Beginning to the Second World War*]. Rome: SME, Ufficio Storico, 1989.

38. Bourne, John M. *Britain and the Great War 1914–1918.* London: Edward Arnold, 1989.

39. Bradau, J. P., et al., [James M. Laux, trans.]. *The Automobile Revolution: The Impact of an Industry.* Chapel Hill: University of North Carolina Press, 1982.

40. Bradley, Joseph. *Guns for the Tsar: American Technology and the Small Arms Industry in Nineteenth Century Russia.* DeKalb: Northern Illinois University Press, 1990.

41. British *Parliamentary Papers.* multiple volumes, 1914–1919, London: His Majesty's Stationery Office, 1914–1919.

42. Brodie, Bernard M. *Sea Power in the Machine Age.* Princeton: Princeton University Press, 1941.

43. Brodie, Bernard, and Fawn Brodie. *From Crossbow to H Bomb.* rev. ed. Bloomington: Indiana University Press, 1973.

44. Bruce, John M. *British Aeroplanes 1914–1918.* London: Putnam, 1957.

45. Bruneau, P. *Le rôle du Haut Commandement au point de vue economique de 1914–1918* [*The High Command and the Economy 1914–1918*]. Nancy/Paris/Strasbourg: Berger-Levrault, 1924.

46. Brunoff, Maurice de. *L'aeronautique penant la Guerre Mondiale* [*Air Power during the World War*]. Paris: Maurice de Brunoff, 1919.

47. Burchardt, L. *Friedenswirtschaft und Kriegsvorsorge. Deutchlands wirtschaftliche Rustungbestrebungen vor 1914* [*The Peacetime Economy and Preparations for War: Germany's Economic Efforts at Armaments Reduction before 1914*]. Boppard: Bolt, 1968.

48. Bureau Internationale du Travail. *L'accroissement del'effectiv des sydicats au course des annees 1910–1919* [*Growth and Effectiveness of Trade Unions from 1910–1919*]. Geneva: League of Nations, 1921.

49. Burghardt, Uwe. *Die Mechanisierung des Ruhrbergbaus, 1890–1930* [*The Mechanization of Mining in the Rhurland 1890–1930*]. Munich: C. H. Beck, 1995.

50. Burk, Kathleen. *Great Britain, America and the Sinews of War, 1914–1918.* London and Boston: Allen and Unwin, 1984.

51. Burk, Kathleen, ed. *War and the State: The Transformation of British Government 1914–1919.* London: Allen and Unwin, 1982.

52. Bussey, Gordon. *Wireless: The Crucial Decade: History of the British Wireless Industry.* London: Peregrinis, 1990.

53. Cassar, George H. *Kitchner: Architect of Victory.* London: Kimber, 1977.

54. Cecil, Hugh, and Peter H. Liddel, eds. *Facing Armageddon: The First World War Experienced.* London: Pen and Sword Books Ltd., 1996.

55. Center for Military History. *The United States Army in the First World War.* 17 vols., Washington: Center for Military History, original printing, 1948.

56. Chadeau, Emmanuel. *De Bleriot a Dassault: L'Industrie Aeronautique en France 1900–1950* [*From Bleriot to Dassault: The Aircraft Industry in France 1910–1950*]. Paris: Fayard, 1987.

57. Chandler, Alfred D. *Scale and Scope: The Dynamics of Industrial Capitalism.* Cambridge: Belnap, 1990.

58. Chandler, Alfred D. *The Visible Hand: The Managerial Revolution in American Business.* Cambridge: Harvard University Press, 1977.

59. Chapman-Huston, Desmond, and Owen Rutter. *General Sir John Cowan: The Quartermaster General of the Great War.* 2 vols., London: Hutchinson, 1924.

60. Chinn, George M. *The Machine Gun: History, Evolution, and Development of Manual, Automatic, and Airborne Repeating Weapons.* 3 Vols., Washington: Government Printing Office, 1951.

61. Christienne, Charles, and Pierre Lissarrague. *Histoire de L'aviation militaire Francaise.* Paris: Charles Lavauzelle, 1980. [English edition translated by Francis Kianka as *A History of French Military Aviation* Washington: Smithsonian Press, 1986].

62. Christienne, Charles. *L'aviation francaise 1890–1919: Un certain age d'or* [*The Golden Age of French Aviation 1890–1919*]. Paris: Charles Lavauzelle, 1988.

63. Churchill, Randolph. *Lord Derby.* London: Heinemann, 1960.

64. Churchill, Winston S. *The World Crisis.* 6 Vols., London: Thorton-Butterworth, 1923–1931.

65. Churchill, Winston S. *The Unknown War: The Eastern Front.* New York: Scribner's, 1931.

66. Clarkson, Grovsenor. *Industrial America in the World War: The Strategy behind the Lines 1917–1918.* Boston: Houghton-Mifflin, 1923.

67. Clemenceau, Georges. *The Grandeur and Misery of Victory.* New York: Harcourt Brace, 1930.

68. Clementel, Etienne. *La France et la Politique Economique Interalliee* [*France and the Interallied Political Economy*]. New Haven: Yale University Press, 1931.

69. Coffman, Edward M. *The War to End All Wars: The American Military Experience in World War I.* 2nd ed. Lexington: University of Kentucky Press, 1998.

70. Cole, G. D. H. *Trade Unionism and Munitions.* Oxford: Clarendon Press, 1923.

71. Cole, G. D. H. *Workshop Organization.* Oxford: Clarendon Press, 1923.

72. Conrad von Hotzendorf, Franz . *Aus meiner Dienstzeit* [*From My Time of Service*]. 5 vols., Vienna: Rikola Verlag, 1921–1925.

73. Cooling, B. F. *Grey Steel and Blue Water: The Formative Years of America's Military-Industrial Complex 1881–1917.* New York: Archon Books, 1979.

74. Cooling, B. F., ed. *War, Business and American Society: Historical Perspectives on the Military-Industrial Complex.* Port Washington, NY: Kennikat Press, 1977.

75. Cooper, Malcolm. *The Birth of Independent Air Power: British Air Policy in the First World War.* London: Allen and Unwin, 1986.

76. Cornwall, Mark, ed. *The Last Years of Austria-Hungary 1908–1918: Essays in Political and Military History.* Exeter: University of Exeter Press, 1990.

77. Cramon, August von. *Unser österreichische-ungarischer Bundesgenosse im Weltkriege* [*Our Austro-Hungarian Ally in the World War*]. Berlin: E. S. Mittler and Sohn, 1922.

78. Crowell, Benedict, and Robert F. Wilson. *How America Went to War.* 5 vols., New Haven: Yale University Press, 1921.

79. Crowell, Benedict. *America's Munitions 1917–1918: The Report of the Director of Munitions.* Washington: Government Printing Office, 1919.

80. Crozier, William. *Ordnance and the World War.* New York: Scribner's, 1920.

81. Cruttwell, C. R. M. F. *A History of the Great War 1914–1918.* 2nd ed. Oxford: Clarendon Press, 1936.

82. Cuff, Robert. *The War Industries Board: Business-Government Relations during World War I.* Baltimore: Johns Hopkins University Press, 1973.

83. Cunnison, J., and W. R. Scott. *The Industries of the Clyde Valley during the War.* Oxford: Clarendon Press, 1924.

84. Czarist Russian semi-official material. *Razlozhenie Armee v 1917* [*Disintegration of the Army in 1917*]. n.p., n.d.

85. Czermak, Wilhelm. *In Deinem Lager war Oesterreichisch-Ungarishe Armee, wie man sie nicht kennt* [*The Austro-Hungarian Army as Few Knew It*]. Breslau: W. G. Korn, 1938.

86. Dawes, Charles G. *A Journal of the Great War.* 2 vols., Boston: Houghton-Mifflin, 1921.

87. Davies, W. J. K. *Light Railways in the First World War.* Newton Abbot: David and Charles, 1967.

88. Dearle, N. B. *An Economic Chronicle of the Great War for Great Britain and Ireland 1914–1919.* London: Humphrey Milford, 1929.

89. Deist, Wilhelm. "The German Army, the authoritarian nation-state and total war," in John Horne, ed., *State, Society and Mobilization in Europe during the First World War.*

90. Deist, Wilhelm, ed. *Militar und Innenpolitik im Weltkrieg 1914–1918* [*The Army and Domestic Politics in the World War 1914–1918*]. 2 vols., Dusseldorf: Droste Verlag, 1970.

91. Dewey, Peter. "The New Warfare and Economic Mobilization" in Turner, John, ed., *Britain and the First World War.*

92. Dewey, Peter. *British Agriculture during the First World War.* London: Royal Historical Society, 1989.

93. Dickey, Philip S. *The Liberty Engine 1918–1942.* Washington: Smithsonian Annals of Flight, vol. 1, No. 3, 1968.

94. Dittmar, F. J., and J. J. Colledge. *British Warships 1914–1919.* London: Ian Allan, 1972.

95. Downs, Laura Lee. *Manufacturing Inequality: Gender Division in the French and British Metal-working Industries 1914–1939.* Ithaca: Cornell University Press, 1995.

96. Dreisziger, N. F., ed. *Mobilization for Total War: The Canadian, American and British Experience 1914–1918; 1939–1945.* Waterloo, Ontario: Wilfred Laurier University Press, 1981.

97. Dupree, A. Hunter. *Science in the Federal Government: A History of Policies and Activities.* Baltimore: Johns Hopkins University Press, 1986.

98. Duroselle, Jean-Baptiste. *Le Grande Guerre des Francais 1914–1918* [*France in the Great War 1914–1918*]. Paris: Perrin, 1998.

99. Edmonds, J. E. *History of the Great War: Military Operations France and Belgium.* 14 vols., London: His Majesty's Stationery Office, 1922–1948.

100. Ellis, Chris, and Peter Chamberlain. *The Great Tanks.* London: Hamlyn Publishing Group, 1975.

101. Ellis, John. *A Social History of the Machine Gun.* New York: Random House, 1975.

102. Emin, Ahmed. *Turkey in the World War.* New Haven: Yale University Press, 1930.

103. Emsley, C., A. Marwick, and W. Simpson, eds. *War, Peace and Social Change in Twentieth Century Europe.* Philadelphia: Open University Press, 1989.

104. Ezell, Edward C. *The Great Rifle Controversy: The Search for the Ultimate Infantry Weapon through Vietnam and Beyond.* Harrisburg: Stackpole, 1985.

105. Fairlie, John A. *British War Administration.* New York: Oxford University Press, 1919.

106. Falls, Cyril. *The Great War.* New York: G. P. Putnam, 1959)

107. Farrar, Majorie M. "Preclusive Purchases: Politics and Economic Warfare in France during the First World War," in *Economic History Review* ser. 2, 26 no. 1, 1973.

108. Fayle, C. Ernest. *Seaborne Trade.* 3 vols., New York: Longman's Green, 1924.

109. Fayle, C. Ernest. *The War and the Shipping Industry.* London: Humphrey Milford, 1927.

110. Fearon, Peter. "The Formative Years of the British Aircraft Industry 1913–1924," in *Business History* 43, 1969.

111. Feldman, Gerald. *Army, Industry and Labor in Germany 1914–1918.* Princeton: Princeton University Press, 1966.

112. Feldman, Gerald. *The Great Disorder. Politics, Economics and Society in the German Inflation 1914–1924.* New York: Oxford University Press, 1993.

113. Fellner, Fritz. ed. *Schicksalsjahre Osterreichs 1908–1919: Das politische Tagebuch Josef Redlichs* [*Austria's Fateful Years 1908–1919: The Political Diary of Josef Redlich*]. 2 vols., Graz: Verlag Hermann Bohlaus Nachf, 1954.

114. Ferguson, Niall. *Paper and Iron: Hamburg Business and German Politics in the Era of Inflation 1897–1927.* Cambridge: Cambridge University Press, 1995.

115. Ferguson, Niall. *The Pity of War: Explaining World War I.* London: Penguin Group, 1998.

116. Ferrell, Robert H. *Woodrow Wilson and World War I 1917–1921.* New York: Harper and Row, 1985.

117. Ferro, Mark. *The Great War 1914–1918.* London: Routledge, 1973.

118. Finne, K. N. *Igor Sikorsky: The Russian Years.* Edited and translated by Carl J. Bobrow and Von Hardesty. Washington: Smithsonian Press, 1987.

119. Finnegan, John P. *Against the Spector of A Dragon: The Campaign for American Military Preparedness 1914–1917.* Westport, CT: Greenwood Press, 1974.

120. Fischer, Fritz. *Germany's Aims in the First World War 1914–1918.* Published in German, Dusseldorf: Droste Verlag, 1961.

121. Fischer, Fritz. *War of Illusion: German Policies from 1911 to 1914.* New York: Oxford University Press, 1975.

122. Florinsky, Michael T. *The End of the Russian Empire.* New Haven: Yale University Press, 1931.

123. Foch, Ferdinand. *The Memoirs of Marshal Foch.* Translated by Col. T. Bentley Mott, New York: Doubleday, Doran, 1931.

124. Fontaine, Arthur. *French Industry during the War.* New Haven: Yale University Press, 1926.

125. Forsyth, Douglas J. *The Crisis of Liberal Italy 1914–1922.* Cambridge: Cambridge University Press, 1993.

126. Fraser, Peter. "The British "Shells Scandal" of 1915," in *Canadian Journal of History,* XVIII, 1, 1983.

127. French, David. *British Strategy and War Aims 1914–1916.* London: Allen and Unwin, 1986.

128. French, David. *The Strategy of the Lloyd George Coalition 1916–1918.* Oxford: Clarendon Press, 1995.

129. French, David. *British Economic and Strategic Planning 1905–1915.* London: Allen and Unwin, 1982.

130. Fridenson, Patrick. *The French Home Front 1914–1918.* Oxford: Oxford University Press, 1992.

131. Fridenson, Patrick. ed. 1914–1918: L'autre front [*1914–1918: The Other Front*]. Paris: Les Editions Ouvrieres, 1977.

132. Fridenson, Patrick. *Histoire des Usines Renault.* Vol 1, *Naissance de la Grande Entreprise, 1898–1939* [*History of the Renault Auto Company*]. Paris: Seuil, 1972.

133. Frothingham, Thomas. *The American Reinforcement.* New York: Doubleday Page, 1927.

134. Frothingham, Thomas. *The Naval History of the World War: The United States in the War 1917–1918.* 3 vols., Cambridge: Harvard University Press, 1924–1926.

135. Fuhr, Christopher. *Das K.U.K. Armeeoberkommando und die innerpolitik in Osterreich 1914–1917* [*The K.U.K. High Command and Austrian Domestic Politics*]. Graz, Vienna, and Cologne: Hermann Bohlaus Nachf., 1968.

136. Fuller, J. F. C. *Tanks in the Great War 1914–1918.* London: J. Murray, 1920.

137. Fuller, J. F. C. *Armaments and History.* New York: Charles Scribner's Sons, 1945.

138. Galantai, J. *Hungary in the First World War.* Budapest: Akademiai Kiado, 1989.

139. German Reichsarchiv. *Der Weltkrieg 1914–1918: Kriegsrustung und Kriegswirtschaft* [*The World War 1914–1918; War Armaments and War Economy*]. 2 vols., Berlin: E. S. Mittler und Sohn, 1930.

140. German Reichsarchiv. *Der Weltkrieg 1914–1918: Die Militarischen Operationen zu Landes* [*The World War 1914–1918: Military Operations on Land*]. 14 vols., Berlin: E. S. Mittler and Sohn, 1925–1944.

141. Geyer, Michael. "German Strategy in the Age of Machine Warfare 1914–1945" in Peter Paret, ed., *Makers of Modern Strategy.*

142. Geyer, Michael. *Deutsche Rustungpolitik 1860–1980* [*Germany's Armaments Policy 1860–1980*]. Frankfurt: Suhrkamp, 1984.

143. Gilbert, Martin. *Winston S. Churchill.* Vols. III–V, London: Heinemann, 1971.

144. Gilbert, Martin. *The First World War: A Complete History.* New York: Henry Holt and Co., 1994.

145. Gleaves, Albert. *A History of the Transport Service.* New York: Doran, 1921.

146. Godfrey, John. *Capitalism at War: Industrial Policy and Bureaucracy in France 1914–1918.* Leamington Spa: Berg, 1987.

147. Goebel, O. *Deutschlands Rohstoffwirtschaft im Weltkrieg* [*Germany's Raw Materials Economy in the First World War*]. Berlin: Deutsche Verlags-Anstalt, 1930.

148. Golovin, Nicholas N. *The Russian Army in the World War.*. New Haven: Yale University Press, 1931.

149. Gray, Edwyn A. *The Devil's Device: Robert Whitehead and the History of the Torpedo.* Annapolis: Naval Institute Press, 1991.

150. Gooch, John. *Army, State and Society in Italy 1870–1915.* New York: St. Martin's Press, 1989.

151. Gooch, J. "Italy during the First World War" In Allan Millett and Williamson Murray, eds., *Military Effectiveness.*

152. Good, D. F. *The Economic Rise of the Habsburg Empire 1750–1914.* Berkeley: University of California Press, 1984.

153. Graham, Dominick. "Sans Doctrine: British Army Tactics in the First World War" in Travers, Tim and Archer, C., eds., *Men at War.*

154. Gray, Peter, and Owen Thetford. *German Aircraft of the First World War.* London: Putnam, 1962.

155. Grieves, Keith. *The Politics of Manpower 1914–1918.* New York: St. Martin's Press, 1988.

156. Grieves, Keith. *Sir Eric Geddes: Business and Government in War and Peace.* Manchester and New York: Manchester University Press and St. Martin's Press, 1989.

157. Groener, Wilhelm. *Lebenserinnerungen, Jugend, Generalstab, Weltkrieg* [*Memoirs: Youth, General Staff, World War*]. Gottingen: Vandenrhoeck and Ruprecht, 1957.

158. Groz, Peter, George Haddow, and Peter Schiemer. *Austro-Hungarian Military Aircraft of World War I.* Mountainview, CA: Flying Machine Press, 1993.

159. Guilhon, Raymond. *Les consortiums en France pedant la guerre* [*Industrial Associations in France during the War*]. Paris: Librairie Generale, 1924.

160. Gundmunsson, Bruce. *On Artillery.* New York: Praeger Publishers, 1993.

161. Gurko, Vasilii. *War and Revolution in Russia 1914–1918.* New York: Macmillan, 1919.

162. Haber, L. F. *The Poisonous Cloud: Chemical Warfare in the First World War.* New York: Oxford University Press, 1986.

163. Hacker, Barton. "Engineering a New Order: Military Institutions, Technical Education and the Rise of the Industrial State," in *Technology and Culture,* vol. 34, no. 1, Jan. 1993.

164. Hacker, Barton. "Military Institutions, Weapons and Social Change: Toward a New History of Military Technology," in *Technology and Culture* vol. 35, no. 4, October 1994.

165. Hackmann, Willem. *Seek and Strike: Anti-Submarine Warfare and the Royal Navy 1914–1954.* London: Her Majesty's Printing Office, 1984.

166. Hagan, Kenneth J. *This People's Navy: The Making of American Sea Power.* New York: The Free Press, 1990.

167. Haimson, L., and G. Sapelli, eds. *Strikes, Social Conflict and the First World War: An International Perspective.* Milan: Annali Fondazione Giangiacomo Feltrinelli, 1991.

168. Hallion, Richard. *Rise of the Fighter Aircraft 1914–1918.* Annapolis: Nautical and Aviation Publishing Co., 1984.

169. Hallion, Richard. *Strike from the Sky: The History of Battlefield Air Attack 1911–1945.* Washington, DC: Smithsonian Institution Press, 1989.

170. Hankey, Lord Maurice. *The Supreme Command.* 2 vols., London: Allen and Unwin, 1960.

171. Hardach, Gerd. *The First World War 1914–1918.* Berkeley and Los Angeles: University of California Press, 1977.

172. Hardach, Gerd. "Franzosiche Rustungspolitik 1914–1918" in H. A. Winkler, ed., *Organizierter Kapitalismus* [Organized Capitalism].

173. Hardach, Gerd. "La mobilization industrielle en 1914–1918: Production, planification et ideologie." ["Industrial Mobilization during 1914–1918"] in Fridenson, Patrick, ed., *1914–1918: L'autre front.*

174. Hartry, Gilbert. *Renault: Usine de Guerre 1914–1918* [*Renault: Work during the War 1914–1918*]. Paris: Lafourcade, 1975.

175. Hatcup, Guy. *The War of Invention: Scientific Developments 1914–1918.* London: Brassey's, 1988.

176. Hauessler, H. *General Wilhelm Groener and the Imperial German Army.* Madison: University of Wisconsin Press, 1962.

177. Hawley, Ellis W. *The Great War and the Search for a Modern Order: A History of the American People and Their Institutions 1917–1933.* New York: St. Martin's Press, 1979.

178. Headrick, Daniel R. *The Tools of Empire: Technology and European Imperialism in the Nineteenth Century.* New York: Oxford University Press, 1981.

179. Headrick, Daniel R. *The Invisible Weapon: Telecommunications and International Politics 1851–1945.* New York: Oxford University Press, 1991.

180. Hecker, G. *Walther Rathenau und sein verhaltnis zu militar und krieg* [*Walther Rathenau and His Relation to the Military and the War*]. Boppard: Bolt, 1983.

181. Helfferich, K. *Der Welkrieg* [*The World War*]. 3 vols., Berlin: Ullstein, 1919.

182. Heller, Charles E. *Chemical Warfare in World War I: The American Experience.* Fort Leavenworth, KS: Government Printing Office, 1984.

183. Henderson, R. O. "Walter Rathenau: A Pioneer of the Planned Economy," in *Economic History Review*, 4, 1951/52.

184. Henniker, A. M. *Transportation of the Western Front 1914–1918.* London, Imperial War Museum: Battery Press, 1937.

185. Herwig, Holger. *Luxury Fleet: The Imperial German Navy, 1888–1918.* London and Atlantic Highlands, NJ: Ashland Press, 1980.

186. Herwig, Holger. *The First World War: Germany and Austria-Hungary 1914–1918.* London: Arnold, 1997.

187. Herwig, Holger H. "Industry, Empire and the First World War," in Martel, Gordon, ed., *Modern Germany Reconsidered 1870–1945.*

188. Herzfeld, Hans. *Der Erste Weltkrieg* [*The First World War*]. Munich: Deutscher Taschenbuch Verlag, 1968.

189. Herzfeld, Hans. *Die deutsche Rustungspolitik vor dem Weltkrieg* [*Germany's Armaments Policy before the World War*]. Bonn, Leipzig: Kurt Schroeder, 1923.

190. Higham, Robin and Jacob W. Kipp, eds. *Soviet Aviation and Airpower: A Historical View.* Boulder: Westview Press, 1977.

191. Higham, Robin. *Air Power: A Concise History.* New York: St. Martin's Press, 1972.

192. Hines, Walker. *War History of American Railroads.* New Haven: Yale University Press, 1928.

193. Hinton, James. *The First Shop Steward's Movement.* London: Allen and Unwin, 1973.

194. Hogg, Ian, and John Batchelor. *Artillery.* New York: Ballintine, 1972.

195. Hogg, Ian. *The Guns 1914–1918.* New York: Ballantine, 1971.

196. Holley, Irving B. *Ideas and Weapons: Exploitation of the Aerial Weapon by the United States during World War I: A Study in the Relationships of Technological Advance, Military Doctrine, and the Development of Weapons.* New Haven: Yale University Press, 1953.

197. Horne, John. *Labour at War: France and Britain 1914–1918.* Oxford: Clarendon, 1991.

198. Horne, John, ed. *State, Society and Mobilization in Europe during the First World War.* New York: Cambridge University Press, 1997.

199. Horstenau, Edmund Glaise von. *The Collapse of the Austro-Hungarian Empire.* London: Dent, 1930.

200. Hough, Richard. *The Great War At Sea 1914–1918.* New York: Oxford University Press, 1983.

201. Hounshell, David A. *From the American System to Mass Production 1800–1932: The Development of Manufacturing Technology in the United States.* Baltimore: Johns Hopkins University Press, 1984.

202. Hurley, Edward N. *The Bridge to France.* Philadelphia: J. B. Lippincott, 1927.

203. Hurwitz, Samuel. *State Intervention in Great Britain: A Study of Economic Control and Social Response 1914–1918.* New York: AMS Press, 1949.

204. Huston, James A. *The Sinews of War: Army Logistics 1775–1953.* Washington: OCMH, 1966.

205. Jacoby, Sanford M. *Employing Bureaucracy: Managers, Unions and the Transformation of Work in American Industry 1900–1945.* New York: Columbia University Press, 1985.

206. *Janes Fighting Aircraft of World War I.* Reprint: New York: Military Press, 1990.

207. Jelavich, Barbara. *Modern Austria: Empire and Republic.* Cambridge: Cambridge University Press, 1987.

208. Johnson, David E. *Fast Tanks and Heavy Bombers: Innovation in the US Army 1917–1945.* Ithaca and London: Cornell University Press, 1998.

209. Johnson, Jeffrey Allan. *The Kaiser's Chemists: Science and Modernization in Imperial Germany.* Chapel Hill: University of North Carolina Press, 1990.

210. Jones, H. A., and Walter Raleigh. *The War in the Air: Being the Story of the Part Played in the great War by the Royal Air Force.* 6 vols., Oxford: Clarendon Press, 1922–1937.

211. Jones, Ralph E., George H. Rarey, and Robert J. Icks. *The Fighting Tanks since 1916.* Washington: National Service Publishing Co., 1933.

212. Justrow, Karl. *Feldherr und Kriegstechnik [Commander in Chief and War Technology].* Oldenburg: G. Stalling, 1933.

213. Kann, Robert A., Bela Kiraly, and Paula Fichtner, eds. *The Habsburg Empire in World War I: Essays on the Intellectual, Military, Political and Economic Aspects of the Habsburg War Effort.* New York: Columbia University Press, 1977.

214. Kaspi, Andre. *Le temp des Américaines: Le concours américains à la France 1917–1918 [The Time of the Americans: American Assistance to France 1917–1918].* Paris: Publications de Sorbonne, 1976.

215. Keegan, John. *The First World War.* New York: Alfred Knopf, 1999.

216. Kemp, T. *The French Economy 1913–1939: The History of a Decline.* London: Longman, 1972.

217. Kennedy, David. *Over Here: The First World War and American Society.* New York: Oxford University Press, 1980.

218. Kennedy, Paul. *The Rise and Fall of the Great Powers: Economic Change and Military Conflict From 1450 to 2000.* New York: Random House, 1987.

219. Kennedy, Paul, ed. *The War Plans of the Great Powers 1880–1914.* London: Allen and Unwin, 1979.

220. Kennett, Lee. *The First Air War 1914–1918.* New York: Free Press, 1991.

221. Kerensky, Alexander. *Russia and History's Turning Point.* London: Cassell, 1965.

222. Kerr, Austin K. *American Railroad Politics, 1914–1920: Rates, Wages and Efficiency.* Pittsburgh: University of Pittsburgh Press, 1968.

223. Kersnovski, A. A. *Istoriia Russkoi Armii [History of the Russian Army].* 3 vols., Belgrade: Slovo, 1933–1938.

224. Kielmannsegg, Peter Graf. *Deutschland und der Erste Weltkrieg [Germany and the First World War].* Stuttgart: Klett-Cotta, 1980.

225. Kilduff, Peter. *Germany's First Air Force 1914–1918.* London: Arms and Armour Press, 1991.

226. Kilmarx, Robert A. *A History of Soviet Airpower.* New York: Praeger, 1962.

227. Kilmarx, Robert A. "The Russian Imperial Air Forces of World War I," in *Airpower Historian,* 10, July, 1963.

228. King, Jere Clements. *Generals and Politicians: Conflict Between France's High Command, Parliament and Government 1914–1918.* Berkeley: University of California Press, 1951.

229. Kiraly, Bela K., et al., eds. *East Central European Society in World War I.* New York: Columbia University Press, 1985.

230. Kiszling, Rudolf. *Oesterreich-Ungarns Anteil an Ersten Weltkrieg [Austria-Hungary's Role in the First World War].* Graz: Stiansny Verlag, 1958.

231. Kitchen, Martin. *The Political Economy of Germany 1815–1945.* London: Croom-Helm, 1978.

232. Kitchen, Martin. *The Silent Dictatorship: The Politics of the German High Command under Hindenburg and Ludendorff 1916–1918.* New York: Holmes and Meier, 1976.

233. Klein, Fritz, et al., eds. *Deutschland im Ersten Weltkrieg [Germany in the First World War].* 3 vols., Berlin: Akademie Verlag, 1968–1969.

234. Knox, Alfred. *With the Russian Army 1914–1918.* 2 vols., London: Hutchinson and Co., 1921.

235. Kocha, Jurgen. *Facing Total War: German Society 1914–1918.* Leamington, Spa: Berg, 1984.

236. Koistinen, Paul A. C. *Mobilizing for Modern War: The Political Economy of American Warfare 1865–1919.* Lawrence: University Press of Kansas, 1997.

237. Kohlstedt, Sally Gregory, and Margaret W. Rossiter, eds. *Historical Writing on American Science: Perspectives and Prospects.* Baltimore: Johns Hopkins University Press, 1985.

238. Komjathy, Miklos, ed. *Protokolle des Gemeinsamen Ministerrates der Oesterriechisch-Ungarischen Monarchie 1914–1918* [*Protocolsof the Joint Military Council of the Austro-Hungarian Monarchy 1914–1918*]. Budapest: Akademiai Kiado, 1966.

239. Kozlow, N. [translator, Charles Berman]. *A Study of the Military-Technical Supply of the Russian Army in the World War.* Moscow: Military Government Publications Division, 1926.

240. Kraus, Alfred [General]. *Die Ursachen unserer Niederlage* [*The Causes of Our Defeat*]. Munich: F. J. Lehmanns Verlag, 1921.

241. Kreidberg, Marvin A., and Merton G. Henry. *History of Military Mobilization in the United States Army 1775–1945.* Washington: Government Printing Office, 1955.

242. Kuhn, Thomas. *The Structure of Scientific Revolutions.* Chicago: University of Chicago Press, rev. ed., 1970.

243. Lamberton, W. M. *Fighter Aircraft of the 1914–1918 War.* Letchworth: Harleyford Pub., 1960.

244. Landes, David S. *The Unbound Prometheus: Technological Change and Industrial Development in Western Europe from 1750 to the Present.* London and New York: Cambridge University Press, 1969.

245. Landes, David. *The Wealth and Poverty of Nations: Why Some Are So Rich and Some So Poor.* New York: W. W. Norton, 1998.

246. Larcher, M. *La guerre turque dans la guerre mondiale* [*The Turks in the Great War*]. Paris: Ciron, Berger-Levrault, 1926.

247. Laux, James M. "Trucks in the West during the First World War," in *The Journal of Transport History,* vol. 6, no. 2, 1985.

248. Laux, James M. "Gnome et Rhone: Une firm des moteurs d'avion durnat la Grande Guerre." ["Gnome and Rhone: An Aircraft Engine Firm during the Great War"] in Patrick Fridenson, ed., *1914–1918: L'autre front.*

249. Laux, James M. "The Rise and Fall of Armand Deperdussin," in *French Historical Studies,* 8, no. 1, Spring, 1973.

250. Lee, Joe. "Administrators and Agriculture: Aspects of German Agricultural Policy in the First World War" in J. M. Winter, ed., *War and Economic Development.*

251. Leland Waldo D., and Newton D. Mereness., comp. *Introduction to the American Official Sources for the Economic and Social History of the World War.* New Haven: Yale University Press, 1926.

252. Lewchuk, Wayne. *American Technology and the British Motor Vehicle Industry.* New York: Cambridge University Press, 1987.

253. Lewis, Peter M. H. *The British Fighter Since 1912: Fifty Years of Design and Development.* London: Putnam, 1965.

254. Lewis, Peter M. H. *The British Bomber Since 1914: Fifty Years of Design and Development.* London: Putnam, 1967.

255. Liddell Hart, Basil. *The Real War 1914–1918.* Boston: Little Brown and Co., 1930.

256. Liddell Hart, Basil. *A History of the World War 1914–1918.* Boston: Little Brown, 1935.

257. Liddell Hart, Basil. *The Tanks: History of the Royal Tank Regiment and Its Predecessors.* 2 vols., London: Cassell, 1959.

258. Lincoln, W. Bruce. *Passage Through Armageddon: The Russians in War and Revolution 1914–1918.* New York: Simon and Schuster, 1986.

259. Link, Arthur S., ed. *The Papers of Woodrow Wilson.* Vols. 51 and 52, Princeton: Princeton University Press, 1985–86.

260. Linnenkhol, Hans. *Vom Einzelschuss zur Feuerwalze. Der Wettlauf Zwischen Technik und Taktik in Ersten Weltkrieg* [*From Single Shot to Creeping Barrage: The Competition Between Technology and Tactics in the First World War*]. Koblenz: Bernard und Graefe, 1990.

261. Lloyd George, David. *War Memoirs.* 6 vols., London: Nicholson and Watson, 1933–1936.

262. Loewenfeld-Russ, Hans. *Die Regelung der Volksernährung im Krieg* [*The Regulation of Public Food Provisions in War*]. Vienna: Holder-Pichler-Tempsky, 1926.

263. Lucas, James. *Fighting Troops of the Austro-Hungarian Empire.* New York: Hippocrene, 1987.

264. Ludendorff, Erich. *Ludendorff's Own Story: August 1914–November, 1918.* 2 vols., New York and London: Harper and Bros., 1919.

265. Lynn, John, ed. *Feeding Mars: Logistics in Western Warfare from the Middle Ages to the Present.* Boulder, San Francisco, and Oxford: Westview Press, 1993.

266. Lynn, John, ed. *The Tools of War: Ideas, Instruments and Institutions of Warfare 1445–1871.* Bloomington: Indiana University Press, 1990.

267. Mallendore, William C. *History of the United States Food Administration 1917–1919.* Stanford: Stanford University Press, 1941.

268. Manchester, William. *The Arms of Krupp 1587–1968.* Boston: Little, Brown, 1964.

269. Manikovski, A. A. *Boevye Snabzhenie Russkoi Armii v Voinu 1914–1918* [*The Russian Army in the 1914–1918 War*]. 4 vols., Moscow: Military University Press, 1920.

270. Marder, Arthur J. *The Anatomy of British Sea Power: From Dreadnought to Scapa Flow.* 5 vols., New York: Oxford University Press, 1961–1970.

271. Martel, Gordon, ed. *Modern Germany Reconsidered 1870–1945.* London and New York: Routledge, 1992.

272. Marwick, Arthur. *Women at War 1914–1918.* London: Fontana, 1977.

273. Marwick, Arthur. *War and Social Change in the Twentieth Century: A Comparative Study of Britain, France, Germany, Russia and the United States.* London: Macmillan, 1974.

274. Marwick, Arthur. *The Deluge: British Society and the First World War.* Boston: Little Brown, 1966.

275. Marwick, Arthur. "Problems and Consequences of Organizing Society for Total War" in N. F. Dreisziger, ed., *Mobilization for Total War: The Canadian, American and British Experience 1914–1918; 1939–1945.*

276. Maurer, Maurer, ed. *The U.S. Air Service in World War I.* 4 vols., Washington: Government Printing Office, 1978–1979; vol. IV. *Postwar Review.*

277. May, Arthur J. *The Passing of the Hapsburg Monarchy 1914–1918.* 2 vols., Philadelphea: University of Pennsylvania Press, 1966.

278. McNeill, William H. *The Pursuit of Power: Technology, Armed Force, and Society Since AD 1000.* Chicago: University of Chicago Press, 1982.

279. Meyer, Stephen. "Technology and the Workplace: Skilled and Production Labor at Allis-Chalmers, 1900–1941," in *Technology and Culture* vol. 29, no. 4, October, 1988.

280. Michalka, W. "Kriegsrohstoffbewirtschaftung. Walter Rathenau und die kommende Wirtschaft." ["The Management of Raw Materials in War: Walter Rathenau and the Coming Economy"] in Michalka, W., ed., *Der erste Weltkrieg.*

281. Michalka, W., ed. *Der erste Weltkrieg. Wirkung, Wahrnehmung, Analyse* [*The First World War: Operation, Management and Analysis*]. Munich: Piper, 1994.

282. Millett, Allan R., and Williamson Murray, eds. *Military Effectiveness.* 3 vols., Boston: Allen and Unwin, 1988; vol. I, *The First World War.*

283. Millett, Allan R., and Williamson Murray, eds. *Military Innovation in the Interwar Period.* Cambridge: Cambridge University Press, 1996.

284. Milward, A. S., and S. B. Saul. *The Economics of Continental Europe 1850–1914.* Cambridge: Harvard University Press, 1977.

285. Ministere de la Guerre. Etat-major de L'armeè, Service Historique. *Les Armeès Francaises dans la grande guerre* [*The Armies of France in the Great War*]. Paris: Imprimerie Nationale, 1922–1925.

286. Ministry of Munitions. *History of the Ministry of Munitions.* 12 vols., London: His Majesty's Stationery Office, 1922.

287. Montgomery, David. *The Fall of the House of Labor: The Workplace, the State, and American Labor Activism 1865–1925.* Cambridge: Cambridge University Press, 1987.

288. Montgomery, David. *Worker's Control in America: Studies in the History of Work, Technology and Labor Struggles.* New York: Cambridge University Press, 1979.

289. Morison, Elting E. *Admiral Sims and the Modern American Navy.* Boston: Houghton-Mifflin, 1942.

290. Morison, Elting E. *Men, Machines and Modern Times.* Cambridge: MIT Press, 1966.

291. Morrow, John T., Jr. *The Great War in the Air: Military Aviation from 1909 to 1921.* Washington and London: Smithsonian Institution Press, 1993.

292. Morrow, John T., Jr. *German Airpower in World War I.* Lincoln: University of Nebraska Press, 1982.

293. Morrow, John T., Jr. *Building German Air Power 1909–1914.* Knoxville: University of Tennessee Press, 1976.

294. Moyer, Laurence V. *Victory Must Be Ours: Germany in the Great War 1914–1918.* New York: Hippocrene Books, 1995.

295. Mumford, Lewis. *Technics and Civilization.* New York: Harcourt Brace, 1934.

296. Nef, John U. *War and Human Progress.* Cambridge: Harvard University Press, 1950.

297. Neumann, Georg Paul, ed. *Die Deutschen Luftstreikräfte im Weltkrieg* [*The German Air Force in the World War*]. Berlin: Mittler und Sohn, 1920.

298. Niederhuemer, Rolf, ed. *Blätter für Technikgeschichte* [*Papers on the History of Technology*]. Vienna: Springer-Verlag, 1985.

299. Noykov, Stilyan. "The Bulgarian Army in World War I," in Kiraly et al., *East Central European Society in World War I.*

300. Nuwer, Michael. "From Batch to Flow: Production Technology and Work-Force Skills in the Steel Industry 1880–1920," in *Technology and Culture,* vol. 29, no. 4, October 1988.

301. Offer, Avner. *The First World War: An Agrarian Interpretation.* New York: Oxford University Press, 1989.

302. Ogorkiewicz, Richard M. *Armoured Forces: A History of Armoured Forces and their Vehicles.* New York: ARCO Publishing Co., 1960.

303. Padfield, Peter. *Aim Straight: A Biography of Admiral Sir Percy Scott.* London: Hodder and Stoughton, 1966.

304. Padfield, Peter. *Guns at Sea.* New York: St. Martin's Press, 1974.

305. Pares, Bernard. *Day by Day with the Russian Army 1914–1915.* London: Constable and Co., 1915.

306. Pares, Bernard. *The Fall of the Russian Monarchy.* 2 vols., London: J. Cape, 1939.

307. Paret, Peter, ed. *Makers of Modern Strategy: From Machiavelli to the Nuclear Age.* Princeton: Princeton University Press, 1986.

308. Parkes, Oscar. *British Battleships: Warrior to Vanguard.* London: Seely Service, 1957.

309. Paxson, Frederick. *American Democracy and the World War.* 3 vols., Boston: Houghton-Mifflin, 1936–1948.

310. Peck, Taylor. *Round Shot to Rockets: A History of the Washington Navy Yard and the Naval Gun Factory.* Annapolis: Naval Institute Press, 1949.

311. Peebles, Hugh B. *Warshipbuilding on the Clyde: Naval Orders and the Prosperity of the Clyde Shipbuilding Industry 1889–1939.* Edinburgh: John Donald, 1987.

312. Penrose, Harald. *British Aviation: The Pioneer Years 1903–1914.* London: Putnam, 1967.

313. Penrose, Harald. *British Aviation: The Great War and Armistice 1915–1919.* London: Putnam, 1969.

314. Peter, Ernst. *Die K.U.K. Lufschiffer-und Fliegertruppe Osterreich-Hungarns, 1794–1919* [*The K.U.K. Aircraft and Flying Forces of Austria-Hungary 1794–1919*]. Stuttgart: Motorbuch Verlag, 1981.

315. Petrovich, Michael Boro. *A History of Modern Serbia.* New York: Harcourt Brace and Jovanovich, 1972.

316. Pietra, V. Guiffrida. *Provital. Approvvigionamenti alimentari d'Italia durante la grande guerra 1914–1918* [*Food Supply in Italy during the Great War 1914–1918*]. Padua: Cedam, 1936.

317. Pinot, Robert. *Le Comite des Forges en service de la nation* [*The Organization of Steel in the Service of the Nation*]. Paris: Colin, 1919.

318. Pitreich, Max von. *Der Osterriechische-ungarnische Bundesgenosse im Sperrfeur* [*Our Austro-Hungarian Ally in the Barrage-Fire*]. Klagenfurt: Arthur Killitsch, 1930.

319. Plaschka, Richard G., Horst Haselsteiner, and Arnold Suppan. *Innere Front: Militärassistenzen, Widerstand, und Umsurz in der Donaumonarchie 1918* [*The Home Front: Military Assistance, Resistance, and Subversion in the Danuban Monarchy in 1918*]. 2 vols., Vienna: Verlag fur Geschichte und Politik, 1974.

320. Playne, Caroline E. *Society at War 1914–1918.* Boston: Houghton Mifflin, 1931.

321. Pollen, Anthony. *The Great Gunnery Scandal: The Mystery of Jutland.* London: Collins, 1980.

322. Pragenau, Ottokar Landwehr von. *Hunger: Die Erschöpfungsjahre der Mittelmächte 1917–1918* [*Hunger: The Years of Exhaustion for the Central Powers 1917–1918*]. Zurich, Leipzig, and Vienna: Amalthea, 1931.

323. Pratt, E. A. *British Railways and the Great War: Organization, Efforts, Difficulties and Achievements.* 2 vols., London: Selwyn and Blount, 1921.

324. Prendergast, Maurice. *The German Submarine War 1914–1918.* London: Constable, 1931.

325. Pritchard, David. *The Radar Wars: Germany's Pioneer Achievement 1904–1945.* Wellingborough, UK: Patrick Stephens Ltd., 1989.

326. Ranft, Brian. ed. *Technical Change and British Naval Policy 1860–1939.* London: Hodder and Stoughton, 1977.

327. Rathenau, Walther. *Tagebuch 1907–1922* [*Diaries 1907–1922*]. Dusseldorf: Droste Verlag, 1967.

328. Rauchehsteiner, Manfried. *Der Tod des Doppeladlers: Osterreich-Ungarn und der Erste Weltkrieg* [*The Death of the Two Headed Eagle: Austria Hungary and the First World War*]. Graz: Verlag Styria, 1994.

329. Reader, W. J. *The Imperial Chemical Industries: A History;* vol. I, *The Forerunners 1870–1926.* New York: Oxford University Press, 1970.

330. Reboul, C. *Mobilisation industrielle: Les fabrications de guerre en France de 1914–1918* [*Industrial Mobilization: Production of War Materials in France 1914–1918*]. Nancy/Paris: Berger-Levrault, 1925.

331. Redlich, Josef. *Austrian War Government.* New Haven: Yale University Press, 1929.

332. Redmayne, R. A. S. *The British Coal Mining Industry during the War.* Oxford: Clarendon Press, 1923.

333. Regele, Oscar. *Feldmarschall Conrad: Auftrag und Erfüllung 1906–1918* [*Field Marshal Conrad: Mission and Accomplishments 1906–1918*]. Vienna and Munich: Verlag Herold, 1955.

334. Renouvin, Pierre. *The Forms of War Government in France.* New Haven: Yale University Press, 1931.

335. Revue Historique de L'Armeè. [Special Issue]. *L'Aviation Militaire Francaise 1909–1969* [*French Military Aviation 1909–1969*]. Vincennes: Revue Historique de L'Armeè, 1969.

336. Richardson, Kenneth. *The British Motor Industry 1896–1939.* London: Macmillan, 1977.

337. Richter, Donald. *Chemical Soldiers: British Gas Warfare in World War I.* Lawrence: University Press of Kansas, 1992.

338. Riedl, Richard. *Die Industrie Osterreichs während des Kriegs* [*Austro-Hungarian Industry during the War*]. Vienna: Holder-Pichler-Tempsky, 1932.

339. Risch, Erna. *Quartermaster Support of the Army: A History of the Corps 1775–1939.* Washington: Government Printing Office, 1962.

340. Ritter, Gerhard. *The Sword and the Septre: The Problem of German Militarism.* 4 vols., especially vol. 3, [English Translation] London: Allen Lane, 1972–1973.

341. Ritter, Gerhard. *The Schlieffen Plan.* New York: Praeger, 1958.

342. Robbins, Keith. *The First World War.* New York: Oxford University Press, 1983.

343. Robertson, Rodrigo Garcia y. "Failure of the Heavy Gun at Sea 1898–1922," in *Technology and Culture,* vol. 28, no. 3, July 1987.

344. Robertson, Sir William. *Soldiers and Statesmen.* 2 vols., London: Cassell, 1926.

345. Rochat, G. *L'Italia nella prima guerra mondiale: Problemi di interpretazione e prospecttive di ricera* [*Italy in the First World War: Problems of Interpretation and Opportunities for Research*]. Milan: Feltrinelli, 1976.

346. Rogger, Hans. *Russia in the Age of Modernization and Revolution 1881–1917.* London: Longman, 1983.

347. Roland, Alex. "Science and War." in Kohlstedt, Sally Gregory and Rossiter, Margaret W. (eds.) *Historical Writing on American Science: Perspectives and Prospects.*

348. Rothenberg, Gunther. *The Army of Franz Joseph.* West Lafayette, IN: Purdue University Press, 1976.

349. Rothenburg, Gunther E. "Military Aviation in Austria-Hungary 1893–1918," in *Aerospace Historian* 29, 1972.

350. Rubin, Gerry. *Law and Labour: The Munitions Acts, State Regulation and the Unions 1915–1921.* Oxford: Clarendon Press, 1987.

351. Sahel, Jacques. *Henri Farman et L'aviation* [*Henri Farman and the Aviation Industry*]. Paris: Grasset, 1936.

352. Salter, A. *Allied Shipping Control: An Experiment in International Administration.* Oxford: Clarendon Press, 1921.

353. Sandler, Stanley. *The Emergence of the Modern Capital Ship.* Newark, NJ: University of Delaware Press, 1979.

354. Sarter, Adolph. *Die deutschen Eisenbahnen in Krieg* [*The German Automobile Industry*]. Berlin: Deutsche-Verlags-Anstalt, 1930.

355. Scherr-Thoss. Hans C. von, *Die deutsche Automobileindustrie* [*The German Automobile Industry*]. Stuttgart: Deutsche Verlags-Anstalt, 1974.

356. Schlaifer, Robert, and S. D. Heron. *Development of Aircraft Engines: Development of Aviation Fuels.* Boston: Harvard Graduate School of Business Administration, 1950.

357. Schmitt, Bernedotte E., and Harold Vedeler. *The World in the Crucible.* New York: Harper and Row, 1984.

358. Schroter, A. *Krieg-Staat-Monopol 1914–1918: Die Zusammenhänge vom imperialisticher Kriegsswirtschaft, Militärisierung der Volkswirtschaft und staatmonopolistschen Kapitalismus in Deutschland während des ersten Weltkrieges* [*War and State Monopoly 1914–1918: The Relationship between the Imperialist War Economy, the Militarization of the National Economy and Monopoly Capitalism during the First World War*]. Berlin: Akademie-Verlag, 1965.

359. Schwarte, Max. ed. *Der Grosse Krieg.* Leipzig: Barth in Auslg., 1921.

360. Scott, J. D. *Vickers: A History.* London: Weidenfeld and Nicolson, 1962.

361. Seigelbaum, Lewis H. *The Politics of Industrial Mobilization in Russia 1914–1917: A Study of the War Industries Committees.* New York: St. Martin's Press, 1983.

362. Shaffer, Ronald. *America in the Great War: The Rise of the War Welfare State.* New York: Oxford University Press, 1991.

363. Shanafelt, Gary W. *The Secret Enemy: Austria-Hungary and the German Alliance 1914–1918.* New York: Columbia University Press, 1985.

364. Shaper, B. W. *Albert Thomas: Trente ans de reformisme sociale* [*Albert Thomas: Twenty Years of Social Reform*]. Assen: Van Gorcum, 1959.

365. Shaw, G. C. *Supply in Modern War.* London: Faber and Faber, 1938.

366. Showalter, Dennis. *Tannenburg: Clash of Empires.* Hamden, CT: Archon Books, 1991.

367. Sidney, M. C. *The Allied Blockade of Germany 1914–1916.* Ann Arbor: University of Michigan Press, 1957.

368. Sidorov, A. L. *The Economic Position of Russia during the First World War.* Moscow: Izd-vo-Akademii, nauk, USSR, 1973.

369. Silberstein, Gerald E. *The Troubled Alliance: German-Austrian Relations 1914 to 1917.* Lexington: University of Kentucky Press, 1970.

370. Simpkins, Peter. *Kitchner's Army: The Raising of the New Armies 1914–1916.* Manchester and New York: Manchester University Press by St. Martin's Press, 1988.

371. Singer, Charles, et al. *A History of Technology.* 5 vols., New York and London: Oxford University Press, 1954–1958.)

372. Skalweit, August. *Die deutsche Kriegsnahrungswirtschaft* [*The German War Economy and Food Supply*]. Berlin: Deutsche Verlags-Anstalt, 1927.

373. Skowronek, Stephen. *Building a New American State: The Expansion of National Administrative Capacity 1877–1920.* Cambridge: Cambridge University Press, 1982.

374. Smith, Herschel. *A History of Aircraft Piston Engines.* Manhattan, KS: Sunflower University Press, 1986.

375. Smith, Merritt Roe. ed. *Military Enterprise and Technological Change: Perspectives on the American Experience.* Cambridge: MIT Press, 1985.

376. Smith, Merritt Roe. "Military Arsenals and Industry Before World War I," in B. Franklin Cooling, ed., *War, Business and American Society.*

377. Sokol, Hans Hugo. *Osterriech-Ungarns Seekrieg 1914–1918* [*Austria-Hungary's War at Sea 1914–1918*]. Zurich, Leipzig, and Vienna: Almalthea-Verlag, 1933.

378. Sondhaus, Lawrence. *The Naval Policy of Austria-Hungary 1867–1918: Navalism, Industrial Development and the Politics of Dualism.* West Lafayette, IN: Purdue University Press, 1994.

379. Spier, Edward M. *Chemical Warfare.* Urbana and Chicago: University of Illinois Press, 1986.

380. Sprout, Harold and Margaret. *The Rise of American Sea Power 1776 1918.* Princeton: Princeton University Press, 1942.

381. Stegemann, Bernrd. *Die Deutsch Marinepolitik 1916–1918* [*German Naval Policy 1916–1918*]. Berlin: Dunckerand Humblot, 1970.

382. Stern, Albert G. *Tanks: 1914–1918: The Logbook of a Pioneer.* London: Hodder and Stoughton, 1919.

383. Stern, Fritz. "Fritz Haber: The Scientist in Power and in Exile" in Stern Fritz, ed., *Dreams and Delusions.*

384. Stern, Fritz, ed. *Dreams and Delusions: The Drama of German History.* New York: Knopf, 1987.

385. Stevenson, David. *Armaments and the Coming of War: Europe 1904–1914.* Oxford: Clarendon Press, 1996.

386. Stone, Norman. *Europe Transformed 1878–1919.* 2nd ed., Oxford: Blackwell, 1999.

387. Stone, Norman. *The Eastern Front.* London: Hodder and Stoughton, 1975.

388. Strachen, Hew, ed. *The Oxford Illustrated History of the First World War.* New York: Oxford University Press, 1998.

389. Strandmann, Harmut Pogge von, ed. *Walther Rathenau: Industrialist, Banker, Intellectual and Politician. Notes and Diaries1907–1922.* Oxford: Clarendon Press, 1985.

390. Strandmann, Hartmut Pogge von. "Widerspruche in Modernisierungsprozess Deutschlands" ["Contradictions in the Modernizing Process in Germany"] in Wendt, Bernd Jurgen et al., eds., *Industrielle Gesellschaft und politisches System.*

391. Sumida, John T. "Forging the Trident: British Naval Industrial Logisitics 1914–1918," in John Lynn, *Feeding Mars.*

392. Sumida, John T., ed. *The Pollen Papers: The Privately Circulated Printed Works of Arthur Hungerford Pollen 1901–1919.* London: Allen and Unwin, 1984.

393. Sumida. John T. *In Defense of Naval Supremacy: Finance, Technology and British Naval Policy 1889–1914.* New York: Routledge, 1993.

394. Sweetser, Arthur. *The American Air Service: A Record of Its Problems, Its Difficulties, Its Failures, and Its Final Achievments.* New York and London: D. Appleton, 1919.

395. Taylor, A. J. P. *The Hapsburg Monarchy.* New York: Harper and Row, 1965.

396. Taylor, A. J. P. *The First World War.* New York: Putnam, 1979.

397. Terraine, John. *White Heat: The New Warfare 1914–1918.* London: Sedgwick and Jackson, 1982.

398. Thayer, J. *Italy and the Great War: Politics and Culture 1870–1925.* Madison: University of Wisconsin Press, 1964.

399. Thompson, Julian. *The Lifeblood of War: Logisitics and Armed Conflict.* London: Brassey's, 1991.

400. Tomassini, L. "Industrial Mobilization and State Intervention in Italy in the First World War: Effects on Labor Unrest," in Haimson, L., and Sapelli, G., eds., *Strikes, Social Conflict and the First World War.*

401. Trask, David F. *Captains and Cabinets: Anglo-American Naval Relations 1917–1918.* Columbia: University of Missouri Press, 1972.

402. Trask, David F. *The AEF And Coalition Warmaking, 1917–1918.* Lawrence: University Press of Kansas, 1993.

403. Trask, David. *The United States in the Supreme War Council: American War Aims and Inter-Allied Strategy 1917–1918.* Middletown, CT: Wesleyan University Press, 1961.

404. Travers, Tim and C. Archer. eds. *Men at War: Politics, Technology and Innovation in the Twentieth Century.* Chicago: University of Chicago Press, 1982.

405. Travers, Tim. *How the War was Won: Command and Technology in the British Army on the Western Front 1917–1918.* London: Routledge, 1992.

406. Trebilcock, Clive A. *The Vickers Brothers: Armaments and Enterprise 1854–1914.* London: Europas, 1977.

407. Trebilcock, Clive A. *The Industrialization of the Continental Powers 1890–1914.* London: Longman, 1981.

408. Trebilcock, Clive A. "War and the Failure of Industrial Mobilization, 1899 and 1914" in J. M. Winter, ed., *War and Economic Development.*

409. Trumpener, Ulrich. *Germany and the Ottoman Empire 1914–1918.* Princeton: Princeton University Press, 1968.

410. Tunstall, Graydon A. Jr. *Planning for War Against Russian and Serbia: Austro-Hungarian and German Military Strategies 1871–1914.* New York: Columbia University Press, 1993.

411. Turner, John, ed. *Britain and the First World War.* London: Unwin Hyman, 1988.

412. Tweedale, Geoffrey. "Metallurgy and Technological Change: A Case Study of Sheffield Specialty Steel and America 1830–1930" in *Technology and Culture,* vol. 27, no. 2, April 1986.

413. United States Senate [The Nye Committee]. *Hearings: Munitions Industry.* Washington: Government Printing Office, 1934–1937.

414. United States Government. *Foreign Relations of the United States and Supplements 1917–1919.* Washington: Government Printing Office, 1926–1932.

415. United States Government. *Annual Reports of the War Department.* multivolumes, Washington: Government Printing Office, 1916–1920.

416. United States Government. *The Report of the Military Board of Allied Supply.* 2 vols., Washington: Government Printing Office, 1924–1925.

417. United States Government. *Annual Reports of the Navy Department.* multi-volumes, Washington: Government Printing Office, 1916–1920.

418. Urbanski, August von Ostrymiecz. *Conrad von Hotzendorf: Soldat und Mensch [Conrad Von Hotzendorf: Soldier and Man].* Graz-Leipzig-Vienna: Ulrich Mosers Verlag, 1938.

419. Urovsky, Melvin I. *Big Steel and the Wilson Administration: A Study in Business-Government Relations.* Columbus: Ohio State University Press, 1969.

420. Valiani, Leo. *The End of Austria-Hungary.* New York: Knopf, 1973.

421. Van Creveld, Martin. *Supplying War: Logistics from Wallenstein to Patton.* Cambridge: Cambridge University Press, 1977.

422. Van Creveld, Martin. *Technology and War from 2000 BC to the Present.* New York: Free Press, 1989.

423. Vergnanao, Pietro. *Origins of Aviation in Italy 1783–1918.* Genoa: Edizioni Intyprint, 1964.

424. Vincent, C. Paul. *The Politics of Hunger: The Allied Blockade of Germany 1915–1919.* Athens, Ohio: Ohio University Press, 1985.

425. Wagner, Anton. *Der Erste Weltkrieg [The First World War].* Wien: Ueberreuter, 1968.

426. Wall, Richard, and Jay Winter. eds. *The Upheaval of War: Family Work and Welfare in Europe 1914–1918.* Cambridge: Cambridge University Press, 1988.

427. Wartzbacker, Ludwig. "Die Versorgung des Herres mit Waffen und Munition" ["Provisioning the Army with Weapons and Munitions"] in Max Schwarte, ed., *Der Grosse Krieg.*

428. Weber, Frank G. *Eagles on the Crescent: Germany, Austria-Hungary and the Turkish Alliance 1914–1918.* Ithaca: Cornell University Press, 1970.

429. Weber, H. *Ludendorff und die Monopole, Deutsche Kriegspolitik 1916–1918.* Berlin: Akademie-Verlag, 1966.

430. Wegs, Robert J. *Austrian Economic Mobilization during World War I with Particular Attention to Heavy Industry.* Ph.d. Diss., University of Illinois, 1970.

431. Wegs, Robert J. *Die Osterreichische Kriegswirtschaft 1914–1918 [The Austrian War Economy 1914–1918].* Vienna: A. Schendl, 1979.

432. Wegs, Robert J. "Transportation: The Achilles Heel of the Habsburg War Effort," in Robert A. Kann, Bela Kiraly, and Paula Fichtner, eds. *The Habsburg Empire in World War I.*

433. Weinstein, James. *The Corporate Ideal in the Liberal State 1900–1918.* Boston: Beacon Press, 1968.

434. Wendt, Bernd Jurgen, et al., eds. *Industrielle Gesellschaft und politisches System [Industrial Society and the Political System].* Bonn: Verlag Neue Gesellschaft, 1978.

435. Westwood, John. *Railways at War.* San Diego, Calif: Howell-North Books, 1981.

436. Wheldon, John. *Machine Age Armies.* London: Abelard-Schuman, 1968.

437. Wildman, Alan K. *The End of the Russian Imperial Army: The Road to Soviet Power and Peace.* Princeton: Princeton University Press, 1987.

438. Wildman, Alan K. *The End of the Russian Imperial Army: The Old Army and the Soldier's Revolt.* Princeton: Princeton University Press, 1980.

439. Wilgus, William J. *Transporting the AEF in Western Europe.* New York: Columbia University Press, 1931.

440. Williams, J. *The Home Fronts: Britain, France and Germany 1914–1918.* London: Constable, 1972.

441. Williams, Trevor, ed. *The Oxford Illustrated Encyclopedia of Invention and Technology.* Oxford: Oxford University Press, 1992.

442. Williams, William J. *The Wilson Administration and the Shipbuilding Crisis of 1917: Steel Ships and Wooden Steamers.* Lampeter, UK: Edwin Mellen Press, 1992.

443. Wilson, Trevor. *The Myriad Faces of War: Britain and the Great War 1914–1918.* Oxford: Polity Press, 1986.

444. Winkler, H. W., ed. *Organisierter Kapitalismus: Voraussetzungen und Anfänge [Organized Capitalism: Perquisites and Beginnings].* Gottingen: Vandenhoeck and Ruprecht, 1973.

445. Winter, J. M., and Jean-Louis Robert, eds. *Capital Cities at War: Paris, London, Berlin 1914–1919.* Cambridge, Cambridge University Press, 1996.

446. Winter, J. M. *The Experience of World War I.* New York: Oxford University Press, 1989.

447. Winter, J. M. *The Great War and the British People.* London: Macmillan, 1985.

448. Winter, J. M., ed. *War and Economic Development.* Cambridge: Cambridge University Press, 1975.

449. Wolfe, Humbert. *Labour Supply and Regulation.* Oxford: Clarendon Press, 1923.

450. Woodward, David R. *Trial By Friendship: Anglo-American Relations 1917–1918.* Lexington: University of Kentucky Press, 1993.

451. Woollacott, Angela. *On Her Their Lives Depend: Munitions Workers in the Great War.* Berkeley: University of California Press, 1994.

452. Wright, Quincy, ed. *A Study of War.* 2nd ed., Chicago: University of Chicago Press, 1965.

453. Wrisberg, Enst von. *Heer und Heimat 1914–1918 [Army and Homeland 1914–1918].* Leipzig: K. F. Koehler, 1921.

454. Young, Peter. *The Machinery of War: An Illustrated History of Weapons.* London: Hart Davis, MacGibbon, 1973.

455. Zabecki, David T. *Steel Wind: Georg Bruchmiller and the Birth of Modern Artillery.* Westport, CT: Praeger, 1994.

456. Zagorsky, S. O. *State Control of Industry in Russia during the War.* New Haven: Yale University Press, 1928.

457. Zeman, Z. A. B. *The Break-Up of the Habsburg Empire 1914–1918: A Study in National and Social Revolution.* London: Oxford University Press, 1961.

458. Zimmerman, Phyllis A. *The Neck of the Bottle: George W. Goethals and the Reorganization of the U.S. Army Supply System, 1917–1918.* College Station, TX: Texas A & M Press, 1992.

459. Zunkel, F. *Industrie and Staatssozialismus: Der Kampf um die Wirtschaftsordnung im Deutschland 1914–1918.* Dusseldorf: Droste, 1974.

Index of Authors' Names

Index of Titles

Index of Subjects

About the Contributors

Daniel R. Beaver is Professor Emeritus of History at the University of Cincinnati. He is the author of several books and articles on American military organization and technology in the twentieth century, including a Phi Alpha Theta prize-winning biography of Newton D. Baker, American Secretary of War during the Great War (1966), and a Moncado Prize–winning article for the *Journal of Military History* on the development of American soft transport (1984). He has served as Harold K. Johnson Visiting Professor at the U.S. Army Military History Institute at Carlilse Barracks, Pennsylvania, and as Distinguished Visiting Scholar at the U.S. Army Center of Military History in Washington, D.C.

Ian F. W. Beckett is Professor of Modern History at the University of Luton, England. A Fellow of the Royal Historical Society, he was formerly Senior Lecturer in War Studies at the Royal Military Academy, Sandhurst, and, in 1992–93 was Visiting Professor of Strategy at the U.S. Naval War College. He has written extensively on the British army and British military policy between 1870 and 1918. His book, *The Great War,* was published by Longman in 2000.

David L. Bullock currently is a Department of Defense historian and an adjunct associate professor at Colorado Technical University. He earned his doctorate in European military history from Kansas State University. A former Air Force officer, Dr. Bullock has traveled in 47 countries. He has authored one book, *Allenby's War: The Palestine-Arabian Campaigns, 1916–1918,* and 60 articles, and has a contract for four military history books about the Russian Civil War.

Thomas W. Burkman is Associate Professor of Asian Studies and Director of the Center for Asian Studies at the State University of New York at Buffalo. Dr. Burkman received his Ph.D. in modern Japanese history from the University of Michigan. His research focuses on Japan's relationship to world order from World War I to the 1930s. He has published numerous scholarly articles on the subject of Japan and the League of Nations. He has also edited three volumes of scholarly papers on the Allied occupation of Japan. He has been a Fulbright scholar and a visiting research professor at the University of Tokyo. Before going to the University at Buffalo in 1994, he taught at Kwansei Gakuin University in Japan, Colby College, Old Dominion University, the University of California at Davis, and Hamilton College.

Gary Cox is Tenure Professor of History at Gordon College in Barnesville, Georgia. He has written *The Halt in the Mud: French Strategic Planning from Waterloo to Sedan,* and is working on a narrative history of the Seven Years' War. A military historian, he brings to this work a lifelong fascination with the Great War.

Peter Dennis is Professor of History at University College, The University of New South Wales, Australian Defence Force Academy, Canberra. He is a graduate of Duke University (Ph.D. 1970) and has held positions at The Royal Military College of Canada, The University of Western Ontario, and the National University of Singapore. As well as authoring three books on aspects of British defense and foreign policy, he is the joint editor and author of *The Oxford Companion to Australian Military History* (1995), joint author of *Emergency and Confrontation: Australian Military Operations in Malaya and Borneo 1950–1966* (a volume in the official history of Australian involvement in southeast Asian conflicts, 1948–72), and joint editor of the seven-volume *Australian Centenary History of Defence* (2001). He was joint founding editor of the journal *War & Society,* 1982–88, 1994–99.

David J. Fitzpatrick graduated from the U.S. Military Academy, West Point, in 1978. He earned his Ph.D. from the University of Michigan in 1996 with a dissertation on Emory Upton, and has since then been a tenured instructor in history at Washtenaw Community College, Ann Arbor, Michigan.

Jeffrey Grey is Associate Professor of History in the School of History, University College, Australian Defence Force Academy. He is the author or editor of 20 books, including *A Military History of Australia* (1990, 1999), *The Oxford Companion to Australian Military History* (1995, with others), and *The Australian Army* (2001), a volume in the *Australian Centenary History of Defence.* From 2000 to 2002, Dr. Grey held the Major General Matthew C. Horner Chair of Military Theory at the Marine Corps University, Quantico, Virginia.

Robin Higham was born in England in 1925, the son of a wounded infantry officer of World War I. Educated in Great Britain and the United States, he served as a pilot with the Royal Air Force, 1943–47. After stints as Editor of *Military Affairs* (1968–1988) and of *Aerospace Historian* (1970–1988), he remains Professor of Military History at Kansas State University, Manhattan.

David R. Jones was educated at Dalhousie, Duke, and Oxford universities. He has edited 12 volumes of *The Soviet Armed Forces Review Annual* (SAFA) and eight volumes of *The Military-Naval Encyclopedia of Russia and the Soviet Union*. He numerous articles include specialized studies of the Russian Army in World War I, and his most recent book (with Boris Raymond) is *The Russian Diaspora 1917–1941* (2000). He presently lives and works in Halifax, Nova Scotia, Canada.

Ian McGibbon is a senior historian in the History Group, Ministry for Culture and Heritage, Wellington, New Zealand. A graduate of Victoria University of Wellington, he has written or edited eight books on aspects of New Zealand's international relations or defense. These include the two-volume official history of New Zealand's involvement in the Korean War, and two books on defense policy in the period 1840–1942. He edited the *Oxford Companion to New Zealand Military History* (2000) and has recently published *New Zealand Battlefields and Memorials of the Western Front*. In 1997, he was appointed an Officer of the New Zealand Order of Merit for services to historical research.

Daniel Moran teaches international history and strategic theory in the Department of National Security Affairs at the Naval Postgraduate School in Monterey, California. He is also a Fellow of the Hoover Institution at Stanford University. His most recent publication is the volume on *Wars of National Liberation* in the Cassell History of Warfare series.

John H. Morrow (Ph.D. Pennsylvania) is Franklin Professor of History at the University of Georgia. His books include *Building German Air Power, 1909–1914* (1976), *German Air Power in World War I* (1982), and *The Great War in the Air, 1909–1921* (1993). He also authored the chapter on air power in the *Oxford Illustrated History of the First World War* (1998). Professor Morrow is completing a manuscript on the First World War for Routledge Press.

Michelle Moyd received her Bachelor of Arts in International Affairs from Princeton University in 1990 and her Master of Arts in African history from the University of Florida in 1996. She served for nearly 10 years in the U.S. Air Force, concluding her career as an instructor in the Department of History at the U.S. Air Force Academy. During her assignment there, she taught world history, military history, the history of women and war, and African history. She is currently a graduate student in African history at Cornell University in Ithaca, New York.

Eugene L. Rasor is Professor of History Emeritus at Emory & Henry College in Virginia. He has published a dozen historiographical-bibliographical surveys for Greenwood Press in the tradition of Robin Higham on British naval history and World War II subjects, such as the Spanish Armada, the Battle of Jutland, Winston Churchill, Douglas MacArthur, the Southwest Pacific Campaign, and the China-Burma-India Campaign. Forthcoming are *English/British Naval History to 1815, William Gladstone,* and *Benjamin Disraeli.*

Bill Rawling is the author of *Surviving Trench Warfare: Technology and the Canadian Corps, 1914–1918, Death Their Enemy: Canadian Medical Practitioners and War,* and *Technicians of Battle: Canadian Field Engineering from Pre-Confederation to the Post-Cold War Era.* He is a graduate of the University of Ottawa and the University of Toronto and is currently a research historian with Canada's Department of National Defence.

John R. Schindler is a writer and historian specializing in military and intelligence history, with particular emphasis on Central Europe and the Balkans. He is a researcher at the American Enterprise Institute for Public Policy Research in Washington, D.C., and he also teaches history at the University of Maryland, Baltimore County. He holds three degrees in history: a B.A. (Hons.) and an M.A. from the University of Massachusetts, and a Ph.D. from McMaster University. He is the author of numerous articles as well as *Isonzo: The Forgotten Sacrifice of the Great War* (2001) and the soon-to-be-published *Tito's Ghost: Inside the World's Most Dangerous Intelligence Agency.* He is at work on his third book, *Redl: Spy of the Century.*

Dennis Showalter is Professor of History at Colorado College and Past President of the Society for Military History. Among his publications on World War I are *Tannenberg: Clash of Empires* (1991) and *History in Dispute: The Great War* (forthcoming).

Brian R. Sullivan served as a Marine officer in Vietnam before receiving a Ph.D. in history from Columbia University. Thereafter, he taught military and Italian history at Yale University and strategy at the Naval War College. From 1991 to 1997, he was a senior research professor in the Institute for National Strategic Studies of National Defense University. Dr. Sullivan consults for the Defense Department while continuing research in Italian military history. Current projects include histories of Italian intelligence, Italian naval doctrine, and Italy's withdrawal from the Axis in 1942–43.

Glenn E. Torrey retired in 1996 as Professor of History from Emporia State University. He continues to write on Romanian diplomatic and military history during World War I, supported by research carried out in Romania and Western Europe over more than 30 years. His most recent book is on the career of General Henri Berthelot both in Romania and on the Western Front. He currently lives in Bellevue, Washington.